The International Economy

THE INTERNATIONAL ECONOMY

Third Edition

PETER B. KENEN

CAMBRIDGE
UNIVERSITY PRESS

Published by the Press Syndicate of the University of Cambridge
The Pitt Building, Trumpington Street, Cambridge CB2 1RP
40 West 20th Street, New York, NY 10011-4211, USA
10 Stamford Road, Oakleigh, Melbourne 3166, Australia

First published 1994

Printed in the United States of America

Library of Congress Cataloging-in-Publication Data

Kenen, Peter B., 1932–
    The International economy / Peter B. Kenen. —3rd ed.
        p.   cm.
    Includes index.
    ISBN 0-521-43026-7 (hard). — ISBN 0-521-43618-4 (pbk.)
    1. International economic relations.   2. International economic
relations—Mathematical models.   I. Title.
HF 1359.K46   1994
337—dc20   93-17334
                                                   CIP

A catalog record for this book is available from the British Library

ISBN 0-521-43026-7   hardback
ISBN 0-521-43618-4   Paperback

Contents

Preface

This book grew out of another. The earlier one, *International Economics*, was published in 1964 and widely used but was sometimes criticized; it was too difficult for elementary courses and too brief for intermediate courses. I began work on the first edition of this book expecting to fill gaps in the earlier one but to keep it shorter than most other textbooks. Each chapter turned into three, however, as I filled more gaps and carried the analysis further. I can only hope that quality has kept pace with quantity.

Like most texts on international economics, this book aims at showing students how international transactions affect the domestic economy and the conduct of national economic policies. Unlike many other texts, it tries to introduce quite rigorously the analytical tools that economists use to examine these matters, and it stresses the assumptions made when developing those tools. Furthermore, it integrates empirical work with pure theory. Finally, it reviews the history of the international economy to show how it has shaped the views of economists and governments and how it has affected the development of international economic institutions, such as the General Agreement on Tariffs and Trade and the International Monetary Fund.

The first edition of this book appeared in 1985. The second appeared in 1989, and differed greatly from the first. In the first edition, for example, two trade models featuring factor substitution appeared in a single chapter, and the analysis of trade and growth appeared in another chapter. In the next edition, each model appeared in a separate chapter, along with the analysis of trade and growth in the context of that model. Furthermore, I added a chapter on trade and trade policy under imperfect competition.

This third edition differs in five ways from the previous editions. Two relate to substance and three to presentation:

- The theory of trade policy is integrated with pure trade theory. The analysis of tariffs begins in Chapter 2, right after an analysis of the gains from trade.

The effects of tariffs are examined in the context of the various trade models presented in subsequent chapters. The results are then summarized in a single chapter on the instruments and uses of trade policies.

- The chapters on history and policy have been revised completely to focus heavily on new issues. Previous editions of this book devoted one chapter to the political economy of international trade and another chapter to the political economy of international money; this edition has two chapters on each subject, the first on the history of the subject and the second on current and emerging policy problems.

- The captions beneath the diagrams have been revised to provide detailed descriptions of the analytical processes involved. I have thus been able to eliminate some of this material from the text and to focus the text more concisely on the basic economic issues. The diagrams themselves have been drawn in two colors, not to make them prettier but to make them clearer.

- The algebraic notes that appeared previously in many chapters have been consolidated into two self-contained appendixes. Appendix A is concerned with trade theory. Appendix B is concerned with monetary theory.

- Each chapter is followed by questions and problems to help students test their understanding of the methods and issues in that chapter. Answers to the even-numbered questions and problems, including new diagrams, where appropriate, are outlined in Appendix C, at the end of the book.

Although this text is more rigorously than some others, it is designed mainly for undergraduates. Those who have taken intermediate courses in micro and macro theory (or are taking them concurrently) will not find it difficult. Those who have less preparation will have to work harder, but they will find that new concepts and tools are explained as they are introduced. Mathematical sophistication is not needed. There is very little algebra in the text. I rely mainly on diagrams. (Equations are used extensively in the presentation of national-income analysis, but it is the sort that students usually encounter in the principles course.) Some of the diagrams are complicated, because trade problems are complicated; they typically involve two countries and goods, and sometimes involve two factors of production. But I have tried to lead the reader through each diagram carefully, even a bit tediously, in the caption beneath it. I have also tried to follow the advice of my own students, who urged me not to introduce a new diagram unless I used it more than once.

The book is designed for full-year courses on international economics, but it can also be used in separate one-semester courses on international trade and on international monetary economics. Those who want to use the book in a one-semester survey course will have to omit some chapters, but I have made that rather easy by the way in which I have organized the presentation. It is possible to omit Chapters 6, 7, and 8, on the general Heckscher-Ohlin model, imperfect competition, and factor movements. Subsequent chapters do not use any of the diagrams developed. It is likewise possible to omit Chapters 16, 17, and 18, on expectations and capital movements, the monetary model, and the portfolio-balance model.

Some things have been left out of this book. I have not dealt thoroughly with North–South relations or with the problems of economic reform in Eastern Europe and the former Soviet Union. Furthermore, my account of current issues will, no doubt, be overtaken by events. My treatment of the Uruguay Round, for example, may prove to be too optimistic, and the foreign-exchange markets have already called into question the attention I give to the Maastricht Treaty. Most instructors will want to assign supplementary readings to bring these stories up to date.

I am grateful to students and colleagues at Princeton University who used the previous editions of this book and made many helpful suggestions. I am also grateful to colleagues who read parts of the manuscript in its initial and revised versions and helped me to improve it, especially to Polly Allen, Robert Baldwin, Richard Cooper, Alan Deardorff, Avinash Dixit, Gene Grossman, Anne Krueger, and Harvey Lapan. I thank Margaret Riccardi for editorial help, Myra Klockenbrink for producing the diagrams, my daughter, Stephanie Kenen, for help with the proofs, and Scott Parris of Cambridge University Press for strong support and sensible advice.

PART ONE

INTRODUCTION

1

The Nation as an Economic Unit

ORIGINS AND ISSUES

The study of international trade and finance is among the oldest specialties in economics. It was conceived in the sixteenth century, a child of Europe's passion for Spanish gold, and grew to maturity in the turbulent years that witnessed the emergence of modern nation states. It attracted the leading economists of the eighteenth and nineteenth centuries, including David Hume, Adam Smith, David Ricardo, and John Stuart Mill, whose work supplied a legacy of insights and concepts that continue to guide us today. In fact, their work on international economic problems produced some of the most important analytical tools used by modern economics. An early version of the quantity theory of money was developed by David Hume to show how foreign trade affects the level of domestic prices. The first full formulation of the law of supply and demand was developed by John Stuart Mill to explain how prices are determined in international markets. International problems have been studied by many recipients of the Nobel Prize in economics, including Paul Samuelson, Wassily Leontief, Bertil Ohlin, and James Meade.

International economics flourishes today because the analytical and policy issues that brought it into being continue to demand attention.

By participating in international trade, each national economy can use its resources most efficiently, concentrating on those activities it is best suited to conduct, and can reap significant economies of scale. In consequence, trade raises real income in each country. These are the same sorts of gains we reap as individuals by specializing in a single occupation rather than meeting all our needs by producing our own food, clothing, and so on. Trade is beneficial in other ways. Improvements in technology developed in one country are shared automatically with other countries. They are shared directly when they are embodied in new capital equipment that is sold on world markets. They are shared indirectly when they raise

1

efficiency or product quality in the export industries of the country in which they originate.

By participating in international capital markets, countries can grow faster. By borrowing on those markets, countries can supplement domestic savings and raise their rates of capital formation. The United States borrowed abroad in the nineteenth century, and many developing countries do so now. By lending on those markets, countries can put their savings to work more productively. International trade in claims and liabilities raises the efficiency with which an economy can allocate resources across time, just as trade in goods and services raises the efficiency with which it can allocate resources at each point in time.

International trade and finance pose hard problems as well as opportunities. They raise economic problems by affecting the internal behavior of each national economy. They raise political problems by affecting relations among governments.

By affecting the allocation of domestic resources, trade affects the distribution of domestic incomes. Changes in the level or composition of a country's trade can require large shifts in resource allocation and thus redistribute incomes. The astonishing growth of the Japanese economy forced the older industrial economies of the United States and Western Europe to make adaptations affecting major industries and whole regions. This process is far from complete. The rapid growth of manufacturing in Korea, Taiwan, and other developing countries has required additional adaptations, not only in the older industrial countries but in Japan as well.

Events in international markets can affect levels of domestic employment, growth rates, and inflation rates. The unprecedented increase in the world price of oil that began in 1973 was an important cause of *stagflation* in oil-importing countries—the painful combination of high unemployment, slow growth, and rapid inflation. Changes in the prices of other raw material affect the export earnings of developing countries, which determine their ability to import machinery and other capital goods. Therefore, those prices influence the pace of development.

Commercial and financial arrangements among countries affect the functioning of domestic policies. The effectiveness of monetary policy, for example, is influenced strongly by exchange-rate arrangements. A government that tries to peg its exchange rate—to fix the price of its currency in terms of some other currency—cannot pursue an independent monetary policy. Changes in its money supply will spill out through its balance of payments with the outside world, and this will happen rapidly when, as now, national financial markets are closely linked. A government that allows its exchange rate to float—to respond to changes in supply and demand in the foreign-exchange market—can pursue an independent monetary policy. It will discover, however, that a change in its monetary policy affects its exchange rate in ways that magnify and modify the domestic impact of the policy change.

THE GROWTH OF ECONOMIC INTERDEPENDENCE

Trade and other international transactions have been growing rapidly. Here are some broad indicators:

- In 1980, all countries' exports taken together totaled $1.9 trillion; ten years later, in 1990, they totaled $3.3 trillion, an increase of almost 75 percent.

- In 1980, the world's major banks had $1.8 trillion of claims on residents of foreign countries; in 1990, their claims exceeded $6.7 trillion, an increase of 270 percent.

- In 1980, foreigners held $90 billion of U.S. stocks and bonds; in 1990, they held more than $600 billion, an increase of 560 percent.

The rapid growth of international transactions has been reflected in an even faster growth of foreign-exchange trading. In 1980, daily trading in American currency markets averaged less than $18 billion; in 1986, it averaged almost $60 billion; and in 1992, it averaged more than $190 billion. Daily trading in London, the world's largest currency market, averaged $300 billion in 1992.

These rapidly growing international transactions have forged strong links between national economies. An increase in one country's income will raise its demand for imports, and the imports of one country are the exports of another. Therefore, the increase in one country's income will raise other countries' exports and thus raise their incomes. An increase in one country's interest rates will attract capital from other countries and thus tend to raise other countries' interest rates.

THE DIMENSIONS OF POLICY INTERDEPENDENCE

Interdependence between national economies leads to interdependence between national policies. When a government cuts taxes to stimulate domestic demand, it stimulates demand in other countries too, by raising its imports and thus raising their exports. Other governments must therefore modify their policies in order to stabilize their own economies.

The money flows that take place with pegged exchange rates offer another illustration. An increase in one country's money supply that spills out through its balance of payments tends to increase other countries' money supplies, and they must then modify their monetary policies to combat the "imported" inflationary pressure.

These money flows do not take place when exchange rates float, but policy interdependence crops up in another form. Exchange rates are *shared* variables. The price of the Deutsche mark in terms of the U.S. dollar defines the price of the dollar in terms of the mark. When one mark costs 60 cents, one dollar costs 1.67 marks. A change in one country's exchange rate translates automatically into changes in other countries' rates.

The domestic effects of a change in the exchange rate are less obvious in a large economy like that of the United States than in smaller, more open economies like those of Western Europe. Until recently, indeed, exchange-rate changes went almost unnoticed in the United States. When asked to rank three key prices in order of their influence on the domestic economy, an American would have put the wage rate first, the price of oil next, and the exchange rate last. A German would probably have put the exchange rate first, the price of oil next, and the wage rate last. (The German might have pointed out, moreover, that the price of oil in Germany depends on the exchange rate. Because world oil prices are quoted in dollars, the price expressed in Deutsche marks is determined in part by the price of the dollar in terms of the mark.)

In the 1970s, however, the trade of the United States grew faster than its gross domestic product, raising the ratio of trade to output, as shown in Table 1-1. The ratio remained much lower than those of many other countries, but the U.S. economy became more open in this and other ways, and the trend began to influence its policies. The United States is able to pursue an independent monetary policy because it allows its exchange rate to float, but it cannot exercise its independence without allowing for the impact of exchange-rate changes on its own economy, the economies of other countries, and the policies of other countries. The character of policy interdependence is affected by exchange-rate arrangements, but the fact of interdependence is inescapable.

No government can be totally indifferent to the economic policies of other governments, and increased openness has raised sensitivities. Governments pay close attention to each others' policies. They watch each others' agricultural policies, which can affect global food prices and supplies. They watch each other's energy policies, which can affect the world price of oil. They watch each others' subsidies to domestic industries, which can affect the fortunes of their own export industries. As in the past, however, they pay closest attention to the policies that have the most direct effects on trade flows and exchange rates. For this reason, changes in tariffs and other trade restrictions are regulated by a formal code of conduct, the General Agreement on Tariffs and Trade (GATT), and policies affecting exchange rates are subject to looser but regular review in the International Monetary Fund (IMF) and other international organizations.

Policy interdependence has an extra dimension in the case of the United States. Although it does not dominate the world economy as it did in the decades following World War II, it is still the largest national economy, and the U.S. dollar is still the world's most important currency. American monetary and fiscal policies have worldwide effects through their influence on economic activity in the United States and thus the American demand for imports, through their influence on world prices, and through their influence on interest rates, financial flows, and exchange rates. The tightening of U.S. monetary policy that brought on the deep recession of 1981–82 helped to trigger the international debt crisis that began in 1982; by raising world interest rates, it raised the debtor countries' interest payments, and by reducing the debtors' exports, it reduced their ability to make those payments. American trade, agricultural, and energy policies are no less important for the health of the world economy. As a consequence, the policies of the United States are subject to close scrutiny by other governments and to frequent criticism.

The criticism is not always justified. It is sometimes used to cloak the deficiencies of other countries' policies and frequently reflects dissatisfaction with the state of the world, not with U.S. policy. It can be exasperating. Some years ago, the United States was accused of following a lax monetary policy and "exporting" inflation to the rest of the world. The charge had some validity. But when the United States tightened its monetary policy to combat inflation, it was accused of raising world interest rates and depressing economic activity in other countries. One European economist, sympathetic to the plight of U.S. officials obliged to respond to incessant

Table 1-1. Trends in Economic Openness in the Seven Summit Countries: Averages of Exports and Imports of Goods and Services as Percentages of Gross Domestic Product

Country	1970	1980	1990
Canada	21.3	27.4	25.0
France	15.5	22.1	22.6
Germany	21.6	28.5	32.9
Italy	15.2	22.0	19.3
Japan	10.2	14.1	10.4
United Kingdom	21.9	25.9	25.6
United States	5.6	10.6	10.7

Source: International Monetary Fund, *International Financial Statistics.*

criticism, put the matter nicely. According to the critics, he said, "the American economy is unsafe at any speed."

Nevertheless, the United States must pay attention to its large role in the international economy and to the concerns of other countries. Controversies about economic policies migrate quickly into the political domain, affecting the quality of cooperation in diplomatic and strategic matters. Governments dissatisfied with U.S. economic policies soon start to express dissatisfaction with U.S. leadership in political affairs. The importance of economic issues is underscored by a practice adopted several years ago. The leaders of the seven main industrial countries, listed in Table 1-1, attend an annual economic summit to review economic problems and policies. (The countries are known as the Group of Seven, or simply the G-7.)

SOVEREIGNTY AND TRADE

Economists are fond of abstract formulations. We build elaborate models, with *n* countries, *m* goods, and so on. But the questions we study and the examples we choose to illustrate our findings are frequently inspired by practical concerns. In his famous demonstration of the gains from trade, David Ricardo dealt with two countries, England and Portugal, trading two goods, cloth and wine. He chose this example because it would be meaningful to his British audience. It evoked the oldest international agreement to reduce trade barriers, the Methuen Treaty of 1703, which cut British tariffs on Portuguese wines in exchange for the free entry of British textiles into Portugal.

The Mercantilist View

Early writers on international trade, the Mercantilists of the seventeenth century, were also concerned with a practical problem—establishing and consolidating royal authority at home and abroad. Royal authority was challenged at home by the old nobility, whose power derived from its feudal right to raise both revenues and armies from the countryside. The crown was challenged abroad by the rivalry for empire in the New World. To establish royal authority at home, the crown had to raise and pay armies. To compete for empire abroad, it had to build ships. Its power, then, depended on its ability to cultivate new sources of revenue—to foster and tax domestic and foreign commerce.

The most famous French Mercantilist, Jean Baptiste Colbert, minister to Louis XIV, dismantled internal trade barriers and subsidized new industries. In one decree, he offered bounties to companies that brought Flemish weavers to France and trained new craftsmen. It was also necessary, however, to acquire an adequate supply of money—gold and silver in those days. Money was required to carry out trade and to pay the taxes levied on that trade. The crown had also to accumulate money to pay for its armies and navies. Critics of the Mercantilists, including Adam Smith, accused them of confusing gold and silver with national wealth. Some of them did, but others were quite clear about their policy objectives. They stressed the gathering of gold and silver because they identified the nation with the crown and therefore identified the wealth of the nation with the gold and silver that the crown could accumulate—with the means of payment for military power.

Spain extracted gold and silver from the Aztecs and Incas. Britain, France, and other countries had then to extract gold and silver from Spain through their foreign trade. For the Mercantilists, gold and silver were the gains from trade, to be earned by encouraging exports and discouraging imports. These are the words of Thomas Mun, a British merchant, published in 1664:[1]

> The ordinary means... to increase our wealth and treasure is by *Forraign Trade*, wherein wee must ever observe this rule; to sell more to strangers yearly than wee consume of theirs in value. For suppose that when this Kingdom is plentifully served with the Cloth, Lead, Tinn, Iron, Fish and other native commodities, we doe yearly export the overplus to forraign Countries to the value of twenty two hundred thousand pounds; by which means were are enabled beyond the Seas to buy and bring in forraign wares for our use and Consumptions, to the value of twenty hundred thousand pounds; By this order duly kept in our trading, we may rest assured that the Kingdom shall be enriched yearly two hundred thousand pounds, which must be brought to us in so much Treasure; because that part of our stock which is not returned to us in wares must necessarily be brought home in treasure.

One can find many flaws in Mercantilist logic, the chief flaw being one that David Hume attacked. A country that increases its money supply by exporting more than it imports will find that its prices start to rise. This will undermine its competitive position in world markets. Its exports will fall, its imports will rise, and it will start to export money. It was, indeed, the main aim of the Classical economists, including David Hume and Adam Smith, to prove that the crown and its ministers cannot defy the "natural laws" that govern social processes—that intervention by the state is self-defeating in the long run and apt to reduce national prosperity.

---

[1] Thomas Mun, *Englands Treasure by Forraign Trade*, 1664, ch. ii.

The Classical View

The Mercantilists of the seventeenth century believed in a world of conflict, the world of Thomas Hobbes in which the state of nature was a state of war. They took for granted the need for regulation to maintain order in human affairs, including economic affairs. The Classical economists of the eighteenth century believed in a world of harmony, the world of John Locke in which the state of nature was a state of peace. They rejected regulation as unnecessary. When Hume explained that prices and trade flows would regulate the quantity of money automatically, and Smith explained that an "invisible hand" would cause competition in the market-place to serve society at large, both were expressing their belief in a benign natural to serve society at large, both were expressing their belief in a benign natural order.

Most important for our purposes, the Classical economists defined national prosperity quite differently than the Mercantilists. The Classical economists were concerned with the welfare of the crown's subjects, not of the crown itself. Therefore, they measured the gains from trade in different terms. Exports were the means of acquiring imports, rather than gold and silver, and thus using the nation's resources efficiently. Restrictions on imports were illogical. In 1776, slightly more than a century after Thomas Mun, Adam Smith wrote:[2]

> To give the monopoly of the home-market to the produce of domestic industry, in any particular art or manufacture, is in some measure to direct private people in what manner they ought to employ their capitals, and must, in almost all cases, be either a useless or a hurtful regulation. ... It is the maxim of every prudent master of a family, never to attempt to make at home what it will cost him more to make than to buy. The taylor does not attempt to make his own shoes, but buys them of the shoemaker. The shoemaker does not attempt to make his own clothes, but employs a taylor....
>
> What is prudence in the conduct of every private family, can scarce be folly in that of a great kingdom. If a foreign country can supply us with a commodity cheaper than we ourselves can make it, better buy it of them with some part of the produce of our own industry, employed in a way in which we have some advantage. The general industry of the country, being always in proportion to the capital which employs it, will not thereby be diminished, no more than that of the above-mentioned artificers; but only left to find out the way in which it can be employed to the greatest advantage. It is not employed to the greatest advantage when it is thus directed toward an object which it can buy cheaper than it can make.

Smith's reasoning is not rigorous. What is "prudence" for a family *can* be "folly" for a kingdom. Furthermore, "advantage" must be defined quite carefully. That task was left to David Ricardo. Nevertheless, Smith's argument illustrates effectively the approach adopted by the Classical economists.

As Smith and his successors believed that the role of government should be sharply limited, they did not pay much attention to the ways in which national sovereignty affects foreign trade and causes it to differ intrinsically from domestic

---

[2] Adam Smith, *The Wealth of Nations*, 1776, bk. iv, ch. ii.

trade. When we come to Ricardo's demonstration of the gains from trade, we will see that the countries in his model could be towns or regions instead of sovereign states. They are places with endowments of labor and capital that can move freely between economic activities but cannot move from place to place. In Classical trade theory and much modern theory, too, international trade is differentiated from domestic trade by the international mobility of goods and the *im*mobility of labor and capital.

We will use this same device to simplify the presentation of trade theory but should not be misled by it. At times, especially in the nineteenth century, international movements of labor have been larger than internal movements. Furthermore, distances within a country can be greater than distances between them, affecting the costs of moving goods and people. New York is farther from California than France is from Germany. In any case, trade theory is not interested primarily in flows of goods from place to place; it is interested in flows from country to country. Countries are distinguished from places or regions by the forms and functions of their governments. The separate study of international economics must take as its starting point the existence and variety of sovereign states.

How Governments Affect International Transactions

Trade and other international transactions are treated differently than domestic transactions. Most governments use taxes, subsidies, and direct controls to discriminate between residents and foreigners even when they undertake identical activities. But there are many other ways in which the exercise of national sovereignty can influence the conduct of international trade. All governments supply *public goods*, including the legal and monetary systems that furnish the framework for economic activity. They may not discriminate deliberately between domestic and foreign transactions when they discharge these basic functions. Each government, however, discharges them differently, which means that transactions between countries are affected differentially.

The various activities of governments have three effects on international transactions. First, they produce differences in the ways the residents of a single country perceive and respond to domestic and foreign opportunities. Second, they produce differences in the ways the residents of different countries perceive and respond to identical opportunities. Third, they add to the risks and costs of all transactions, but add more to those of foreign than domestic transactions, because changes in one country's national policies affect that country's residents without necessarily affecting other countries' residents.

Laws and customs are fairly uniform within individual countries. It is therefore quite easy to move goods, labor, and capital from place to place. The tax system is also homogeneous within a country, but tax systems differ markedly from country to country. True, the tax laws of the 50 U.S. states differ in important ways. But the federal tax system tends to neutralize differences among the states' tax systems, because state taxes are deductible from federal income taxes. Furthermore, federal grants and spending tend to diminish local differences in the quantity and quality of public services that might otherwise influence decisions about the location of economic activity.

Internal monetary differences are smallest of all. Nationwide markets connect financial institutions within the United States. Funds flow freely from region to region, and borrowers can raise funds where it is cheapest, whittling down regional differences in credit conditions. Finally, and most important, a single currency is used throughout the country. A five-dollar bill issued by the Federal Reserve Bank of Richmond circulates freely in the United States; it must be accepted everywhere. How much more complicated life would be if merchants refused to accept currency coming from another Federal Reserve district! You would have to look at every dollar bill, weed out those from other districts, and take them to a bank to swap them for local currency. You would have to trade one kind of dollar for another whenever you crossed state lines.

Goods flow freely among the 50 states. In fact, the U.S. Constitution expressly forbids local interference with interstate commerce. The authors of the Constitution believed that free trade among the states would help to cement a fragile political union. The countries of Western Europe created the Common Market for similar reasons, as a first step toward political confederation. They allow goods to move freely within Western Europe and impose a common tariff on goods from outside. But international trade is usually burdened by tariffs and is often limited by other devices—quotas that restrict quantities imported and controls on purchases of foreign currencies.

These trade barriers are doubly restrictive. First, they raise the domestic prices of foreign goods, which handicaps those goods in competition with domestic products. Second, they impose a costly workload on the would-be importer. Figure 1-1 reproduces a fragment from the U.S. tariff schedule. Use it to find the duty on a watch without a battery or self-winding mechanism, having 15 jewels and a $12 movement measuring less than 15 millimeters.

International transactions usually involve two or more currencies. An American wholesaler importing French champagne has first to determine its price in French francs, then the price of the franc in terms of the dollar, to calculate the price that must be charged in the United States. After ordering the champagne, the wholesaler must buy francs with dollars and pay them to the French supplier. There are thus extra costs and risks involved in the transaction. The costs are the commissions charged by the dealers in foreign currencies. The risks arise because exchange rates can change.

Under current international monetary arrangements, exchange rates for most major currencies float. They move up and down from day to day, responding to changes in supply and demand, and the fluctuations can be very large. In December 1984, the U.S. dollar bought 9.59 French francs, but two years later, it bought only 6.45 francs. In June 1991, the dollar bought 6.14 francs; one year later, it bought only 5.13 francs; and in January 1993, it bought 5.53 francs (see Figure 1-2). Similar risks existed, however, when exchange rates were pegged, as was the case for most currencies before 1973. Rates did not fluctuate significantly from day to day, but they could be altered abruptly and by large amounts. In 1957, the French government

Wrist watches, battery powered, whether or
not incorporating a stop watch facility:
  With mechanical display only:
    Having no jewels or only one jewel
    in the movement...................................51¢ each + 6.25% on the case and strap or
                                     or band or bracelet + 5.3% on the battery

    Other...87¢ each + 6.25% on the case...
                                     + 5.3% on the battery
  With opto-electronic display only:
    ......
    ......

Other wrist watches, whether or not
incorporating a stop watch facility:
  With automatic winding:
    Having over 17 jewels in the movement......$2.30 each + 6.25% on the case and strap,
                                     band or bracelet
  Other:
    Having no jewels or only one jewel in
    the movement...................................51¢ each + 6.25% on the case...
    Having over 1 jewel but not over 7
    jewels in the movement.........................87¢ each + 6.25% on the case...
    Having over 7 jewels but not over 17
    jewels in the movement:
      With movement valued not over $15 each:
        With movement measuring not
        over 15.2 mm.............................. $2.85 each + 6.25% on the case...
        With movement measuring
        over 15.2 mm.............................. $2.40 each + 6.25% on the case...
      With movement valued over $15 each... $1.27 each + 6.25% on the case...
    Having over 17 jewels in the movement......$2.30 each + 6.25% on the case...

FIGURE 1-1
A Fragment of the U.S. Tariff Schedule

devalued the franc from 4.20 to 4.90 per dollar; in 1969, there was another devaluation, to 5.55 per dollar.[3] Each change took place suddenly.

Changes in exchange rates can cut into traders' profits, and large changes can turn profits into losses. An American wholesaler importing French champagne could lose heavily if the price of the franc rose on the foreign-exchange market after the firm had signed its contract with its French supplier but before it had purchased its francs.[4]

---

[3] As indicated earlier, exchange rates can be quoted in another way. One can deal with the dollar price of the French franc. Using this approach, the franc fell from 23.8 cents to 20.4 cents in 1957 and to 18.0 cents in 1969. These computations make it easy to see why the changes are described as devaluations; they reduced the dollar value of the franc. Hereafter, exchange rates will be defined as the prices of foreign currency in units of domestic currency. From the French standpoint, then, the franc-dollar rate in Figure 1-2 was 5.53 francs per dollar on January 15, 1993; from the American standpoint, it was 18.09 cents per franc.

[4] Traders and investors can sometimes protect themselves against exchange-rate changes by buying or selling foreign currency on the *forward* market. There, they can arrange to swap dollars for French francs in 30, 60, or 90 days at a price (exchange rate) agreed on today. Forward rates for certain currencies are shown in Figure 1-2. They will be discussed again in Chapter 16.

FOREIGN EXCHANGE

FRIDAY, JANUARY 15, 1993

	Fgn. currency in dollars		Dollar in fgn. currency	
	Fri.	Thu.	Fri.	Thu.
f-Argent (Peso)	1.0100	1.0100	.9901	.9901
Australia (Dollar)	.6730	.6690	1.4948	1.4948
Austria (Schilling)	.0869	.0876	11.506	11.421
c-Belgium (Franc)	.0299	.0299	33.45	33.40
Brazil (Cruzeiro)	.00008	.00008	13184	13031
Britain (Pound)	1.5300	1.5368	.6536	.6507
30-day fwd	1.5247	1.5316	.6559	.6529
60-day fwd	1.5205	1.5274	.6577	.6547
90-day fwd	1.5162	1.5230	.6595	.6566
Canada (Dollar)	.7802	.7826	1.2818	1.2778
30-day fwd	.7778	.7802	1.2857	1.2818
60-day fwd	.7757	.7783	1.2891	1.2849
90-day fwd	.7737	.7763	1.2925	1.2881
y-Chile (Peso)	.002688	.002684	372.09	372.56
China (Yuan)	.1743	.1743	5.7374	5.7374
Colombia (Peso)	.001693	.001693	590.75	590.75
c-Czechosl (Koruna)	.0351	.0351	28.51	28.46
Denmark (Krone)	.1593	.1592	6.2790	6.2795
z Ecudr (Sucre)	.000552	.000552	1812.02	1812.02
ECU	1.20775	1.20770	.8280	.8280
d-Egypt (Pound)	.3008	.3008	3.3245	3.3245
Finland (Mark)	.1842	.1848	5.4277	5.4100
France (Franc)	.1809	.1814	5.5265	5.5135
Germany (Mark)	.6116	.6165	1.6350	1.6220
30-day fwd	.6088	.6136	1.6427	1.6297
60-day fwd	.6064	.6112	1.6490	1.6360
90-day fwd	.6040	.6088	1.6556	1.6425
Greece (Drachma)	.004574	.004609	218.65	216.95
Hong Kong (Dollar)	.1292	.1292	7.7375	7.7375
Hungary (Forint)	.0121	.0121	82.69	82.75
y-India (Rupee)	.0346	.0346	28.820	28.820
Indnsia (Rupiah)	.000485	.000485	2060.03	2060.03
Ireland (Punt)	1.6142	1.6240	.6195	.6158
Israel (Shekel)	.3662	.3657	2.7309	2.7344
Italy (Lira)	.000667	.000671	1499.00	1490.75
Japan (Yen)	.007932	.007946	126.07	125.85
30-day fwd	.007926	.007942	126.17	125.91
60-day fwd	.007925	.007940	126.18	125.95
90-day fwd	.007925	.007939	126.18	125.96
Jordan (Dinar)	1.4810	1.4810	.67522	.67522
Lebanon (Pound)	.000547	.000547	1828.00	1828.00
Malaysia (Ringgit)	.3858	.3846	2.5920	2.6000
z-Mexico (N. Peso)	.32154	.32154	3.1100	3.1100
Nethrlnds (Guilder)	.5475	.5482	1.8265	1.8240
N Zealand (Dollar)	.5138	.5118	1.9463	1.9539
Norway (Krone)	.1854	.1453	5.3950	6.8820
Pakistan (Rupee)	.0388	.0388	25.75	25.75
v-Peru (New Sol)	.6173	.6211	1.620	1.610
z-Philpins (Peso)	.0398	.0398	25.12	25.15
Poland (Zloty)	.000066	.000066	15255	15255
Portugal (Escudo)	.006807	.006878	146.90	145.40
a-Russia (Ruble)	.002262	.002262	442.00	442.00
Saudi Arab (Riyal)	.2667	.2667	3.7500	3.7495
Singapore (Dollar)	.6033	.6037	1.6575	1.6565
c-So.Africa (Rand)	.3250	.3258	3.0765	3.0690
f-So.Africa (Rand)	.2080	.2080	4.8076	4.8076
So. Korea (Won)	.001262	.001262	792.60	792.40
Spain (Peseta)	.008669	.008684	115.35	115.15
Sweden (Krona)	.1384	.1379	7.2270	7.2525
Switzerlnd (Franc)	.6680	.6743	1.4970	1.4830
30-day fwd	.6666	.6729	1.5002	1.4861
60-day fwd	.6653	.6717	1.5030	1.4888
90-day fwd	.6641	.6703	1.5059	1.4918
Taiwan (NT $)	.0393	.0393	25.44	25.44
Thailand (Baht)	.03914	.03914	25.55	25.55
Turkey (Lira)	.000116	.000116	8611.00	8611.00
U.A.E. (Dirham)	.2723	.2723	3.6727	3.6727
f-Uruguay (Peso)	.000277	.000277	3604.01	3604.01
z-Venzuel (Bolivar)	.0124	.0124	80.5000	80.4500
Yugoslv (NewDinar)	.00133	.00133	750.00	750.00

ECU: European Currency Unit, a basket of European currencies. The Federal Reserve Board's index of the value of the dollar against 10 other currencies weighted on the basis of trade was 93.13 Friday, up 0.45 points or 0.48 percent from Thursday's 92.68. A year ago the index was 88.00.

a-auction result, Moscow Foreign Currency Exchange. c-commercial rate, d-free market rate, f-financial rate, y-official rate, z-floating rate.

Prices as of 3.00 p.m. Eastern Time from Telerate Systems and other sources.

FIGURE 1-2
Exchange Rates
The prices of currencies are quoted in dollars per unit of foreign currency and in units of foreign currency per dollar. The French franc, for example, was quoted on January 15, 1993, at $0.1809 per franc (i.e., at 18.09 cents). It was therefore quoted at 5.5265 francs per dollar. For most currencies, rates are quoted for spot (immediate) delivery. For some important currencies, rates are also quoted for forward (future) delivery in 30, 60, or 90 days. Copyright © 1993 by *The New York Times Company;* reprinted by permission.

PERSPECTIVES AND CRITERIA

International economists view the world as a community of separate states, each with its own constellation of natural resources, capital, labor, and knowledge, its own social and economic institutions, and its own economic policies. We usually assume that transport costs are negligible and that world markets are perfectly competitive, though recent theoretical work has studied other market structures, and we will do so too. We frequently adopt the Classical assumption that capital and labor are perfectly mobile within a country but not free to move from one country to another.

Using these assumptions, we seek to explain international flows of goods, services, and assets; appraise their impact on domestic economic welfare; and forecast their responses to changes in policies. We concentrate on policies designed expressly to regulate trade and payments—those involving tariffs, exchange rates, and the tax treatment of foreign-source income. But we also look at general economic policies, especially at fiscal and monetary policies, and at labor laws and environmental standards, because they define the economic climate in which international transactions take place.

We have two ways of viewing policies, and we can use a number of criteria to judge them.

Two Perspectives

When appraising policies and other events that influence trade and payments, we sometimes adopt a *national* perspective, asking how those policies and other events affect the situation of a single country. For many purposes, however, we find it useful to adopt a *cosmopolitan* perspective, asking how policies and other events affect the situations of all countries jointly.

When taking the national perspective, we often begin by pretending that a country has been isolated from the outside world, then starts to trade with other countries. When taking the cosmopolitan perspective, we sometimes begin by pretending that there have been no differences in economic policies and no barriers to trade between regions; we then turn those regions into nations, each with its own policies and institutions, to see how trade and payments change. We will find, for example, that free trade is the best regime from the global perspective but not necessarily from the national perspective. A large country can sometimes increase its gains from trade by imposing certain tariffs. In the process, however, it reduces the global gains from trade. Conflicts of this sort arise frequently between cosmopolitan and national objectives.

Many rules and arrangements have been adopted by the international community to prevent individual governments from pursuing national objectives at the expense of cosmopolitan objectives. The General Agreement on Tariffs and Trade, mentioned earlier, was adopted to prevent them from using tariffs to increase their gains from trade or for other narrowly national purposes. The International Monetary Fund was designed to prevent them from engaging in competitive devaluations or using inappropriate domestic policies to deal with temporary payments problems. Similar purposes are served by frequent policy consultations in the Organization for Economic Co-operation and Development (OECD) and other international gatherings, including the annual economic summits. These aim at encouraging the governments of major industrial countries to adopt *cooperative* solutions to their problems, especially in macroeconomic matters. Such solutions are frequently superior to those resulting from decentralized national decisions but are not always seen that way by individual governments. Cooperative approaches are also required to deal with a number of global problems that cannot be handled effectively by individual governments. Some of these problems are global in nature, such as oceanic and atmospheric pollution. Other problems have become global in scope because they pertain to the activities of large transnational actors, such as multinational firms and banks, and thus lie beyond the reach of any single government.

Transnational factors have many significant effects on the functioning of the international economy and on relations among national governments. They tend to enhance the efficiency of the world economy and to reduce cross-country differences in national policies. Nevertheless, their activities pose major challenges, producing disputes between governments but also encouraging them to devise common rules or standards, most notably in matters relating to the supervision of international financial institutions and markets. Critics of international cooperation frequently charge that it threatens national sovereignty. That misses the point. The case for cooperation starts when sovereignty has been impaired by economic interdependence and governments acting individually can no longer perform their functions effectively.

International cooperation is cumbersome and costly, and it should not be undertaken unless it is necessary. National governments can still perform many tasks effectively. But the globalization of economic activity has strengthened the case for collective action in many areas that used to belong to individual governments.

Four Criteria

Although international economists treat nation states as actors on the global stage, we are concerned primarily with individuals. We therefore appraise economic policies by the same criteria used in other branches of economics. We treat a policy change as being good potentially if the individuals who benefit from it can compensate the individuals who lose.[5] Furthermore, we use the same tests of economic performance that guide economists in other fields.

First, we are concerned with efficiency: How do international trade and payments affect the allocation of resources within a country? How do they redistribute economic tasks among the participating countries?

---

[5] We do not agree among ourselves, however, on the need to carry out this compensation. Some of us believe that we have done our work when we have shown that compensation is possible—that the gains of those who come out ahead are large enough to offset the losses of those who fall behind. Others say that compensation must actually be made before we can endorse a policy change. Some take an intermediate position, saying that compensation should be undertaken if the losers have smaller incomes than the gainers, a view that embodies a personal judgment about inequality. These issues will crop up again in Chapter 9.

Second, we are concerned with equity: How does trade redistribute income and wealth within a country? How does it redistribute them among countries?

Third, we are concerned with stability: How do trade and payments affect an economy's responses to disturbances, its vulnerability to unemployment and inflation, and the uses of monetary and fiscal policies to achieve stability?

Fourth, we are concerned with growth: How does trade affect a country's growth rate? How does growth affect its trade? Should the developing countries gear their economies to international markets or should they protect their infant industries from international competition?

Efficiency, equity, and growth will be the main issues in Part Two of this book, where standard tools of microeconomic analysis are used to show how trade affects domestic resource allocation and the distribution of the national income. Stability will be the chief concern in Part Three, where standard tools of macroeconomic analysis are used to show how trade and other international transactions affect the levels of economic activity, unemployment, and inflation, and the conduct of monetary and fiscal policies.

SUMMARY

The earliest writers on international economics, the Mercantilists of the seventeenth century, gave great weight to the role of the state. They measured the gains from trade by the "treasure" that a country could accumulate through trade, and they urged the state to maximize this sort of gain by encouraging exports and discouraging imports. The Classical economists of the eighteenth century took a different view. They measured the gains from trade by the increase in efficiency that could be achieved by concentrating on those activities in which an economy had a competitive advantage, and they urged the state to abstain completely from regulating foreign trade.

Modern economists measure the gains from trade in much the same way as the Classical economists, but they pay more attention to the role of government. Trade and other international transactions are influenced by many economic policies, including those adopted for domestic reasons. Conversely, a country's international transactions impinge on the conduct of domestic policies. The exchange-rate regime can influence heavily the effectiveness of monetary policy. Furthermore, the tasks of domestic policies are complicated by international disturbances—by changes in incomes, prices, and interest rates in other countries.

The problems of economic interdependence have long been familiar to policy-makers in most countries; their national economies are very open compared to the U.S. economy. But the problems are becoming familiar to Americans, too. The American economy has become more open. Furthermore, U.S. economic policies affect the health of the world economy, and controversies about economic policies tend to migrate into the political arena, affecting the quality of international cooperation in diplomatic and strategic matters.

RECOMMENDED READINGS

Many topics covered briefly in this chapter will be studied thoroughly in later chapters, and longer lists of readings are appended to those chapters. Here are three references that do not fit in elsewhere:

On the contributions of the Mercantilists and Classical economists, see Joseph Schumpeter, *History of Economic Analysis* (New York: Oxford University Press, 1954), pt. II, chs. 3, 7.

The opening of the U.S. economy and its implications are examined in Richard N. Cooper, "The United States as an Open Economy," in R. W. Hafer, ed., *How Open Is the U.S. Economy?* (Lexington, Mass: Lexington Books, D.C., Heath, 1986), ch. 1.

On trends in openness and related issues, see Sven Grassman, "Long-Term Trends in Openness of National Economies," *Oxford Economic Papers*, 32 (March 1980).

PART TWO

INTERNATIONAL TRADE THEORY AND POLICY

2

Comparative Advantage and the Gains from Trade

THE ISSUES

This chapter introduces the main methods of trade theory and uses them to study three basic issues:

- Why countries trade and how they gain from trade.
- How trade affects the allocation of domestic resources in each trading country.
- How tariffs and other trade barriers affect the gains from trade and modify the allocation of resources.

The chapter begins by using demand and supply curves to analyze the principal effects of trade, then introduces more powerful techniques.

PRICES AND TRADE PATTERNS

Differences in prices from country to country are the basic cause of trade. They reflect differences in costs of production. Trade serves in turn to minimize the real resource costs of worldwide production, which is the same as saying that trade serves to maximize the real value of production from worldwide resources. It does so by permitting and encouraging producers in each country to specialize in those economic activities that make the best uses of their country's physical and human resources.

Why should costs differ from country to country? How can Japan produce cars, cameras, and calculators more cheaply than the United States? Many people would reply that Japan has lower costs because it has lower wage rates, and wages are important costs. This explanation sounds plausible enough and is based in fact. But it is inadequate. If wage rates were decisive for cost differences and trade, Japan would undersell the United States in every product line and market. Yet Japan imports many products from the United States, from aircraft to grain, and other countries with much lower wage rates than Japan import American products in great variety and quantity. Differences in wage rates by themselves cannot explain trade patterns. We must look further for the basis of trade.

An enduring two-way flow of goods must reflect systematic international differences in *structures* of costs and prices. Some things must be cheaper to produce at home and will be exported to other countries. Other things must be cheaper to produce abroad and will be imported from other countries. This generalization is known as the *law of comparative advantage* and can be put this way:

> **In a world of competitive markets, trade will occur and be beneficial whenever there are international differences in relative costs of production.**

Japan can export cars and cameras because its endowment of land, labor, capital, and technology allow it to increase its output of those goods with the smallest sacrifice in output of other goods. The United States can export aircraft and grain because it can expand its output of those goods with the smallest sacrifice in output of other goods. Cars may be less costly than aircraft in both countries, grain less costly than cameras, but the cost differences vary across countries, and the variation in those differences leads to beneficial trade.

This chapter will prove the law of comparative advantage. Reasons for differences in relative costs are explored in Chapters 3 and 4.

PRODUCTION, CONSUMPTION, AND TRADE IN A SINGLE COMMODITY

The effects of differences in relative costs cannot be examined by looking at one market at a time. It is necessary to look at an entire national economy and compare it with other national economies. Therefore, international trade theory cannot make much use of partial-equilibrium price theory—of ordinary demand and supply curves. It must use general-equilibrium theory most of the time. Nevertheless, supply and demand curves can be used to show how trade in a single commodity affects production and consumption in the domestic market and to quantify the gains from trade.

Equilibrium Before Trade Is Opened

In Figure 2-1, the domestic demand curve for cameras is D_H, and the domestic supply curve is S_H. When there is no international trade in cameras, equilibrium will be established at E. The domestic price of a camera will be OP, production will be OA, and production will necessarily equal consumption. The diagram, however, says much more.

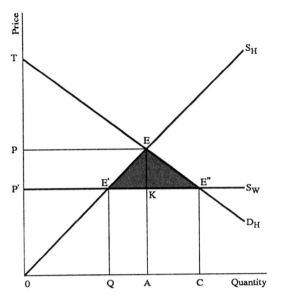

FIGURE 2-1
Trade in a Single Good
The domestic demand curve is D_H, the domestic supply curve is S_H, and the domestic price is OP before trade is opened; the quantity OA is produced to meet domestic demand. When trade is opened at the world price OP', domestic production falls to OQ, consumption rises to OC, and QC is imported to close the gap. Before trade, producer surplus was OEP, and consumer surplus was PET. After trade, producer surplus is $OE'P'$, and consumer surplus is $P'E''T$. Hence, producer surplus falls by $P'E'EP$, but consumer surplus rises by $P'E''EP$, which is $E'E''E$ larger than the fall in producer surplus. This is the welfare gain from opening trade. The production effect of opening trade is QA, and it contributes $E'KE$. This is the welfare gain resulting from the substitution of low-cost foreign output for high-cost domestic output. The consumption effect is AC, and it contributes $KE''E$. This is the welfare gain resulting from the increase in consumption caused by the reduction in the price of a camera.

When domestic markets are perfectly competitive, the supply curve is the sum of the marginal cost curves of domestic firms. Accordingly, the area under the supply curve measures the total cost of camera production. (Strictly speaking, it measures the total variable cost, but fixed cost plays no role in this analysis.) If OA cameras are produced, total cost is given by the area of the triangle OAE. But total payments to producers (revenues) are given by the area of the rectangle $OAEP$. Therefore, the area of the triangle OEP measures profit or *producer surplus*.

The area under the demand curve is meaningful, too. Under somewhat restrictive assumptions that need not detain us here, it measures the cash equivalent of the utility that consumers derive from their purchases of cameras.[1] If OA cameras are consumed, that cash equivalent is the area $OAET$. But consumers pay $OAEP$ for

---

[1]There are three such assumptions: (1) Utility can be measured in *cardinal* numbers, allowing us to know the *size* of the increase in utility conferred by an increase in consumption, not merely that there is an increase. (2) The utilities of individuals are measured in comparable units, allowing us to give them *common* cash equivalents. (3) The marginal utility of income is constant, allowing us to use an income or cash measure that does not grow or shrink when price changes alter incomes.

their cameras. Therefore, the area of the triangle *PET* measures the net benefit or *consumer surplus*.

Equilibrium After Trade Is Opened

Now suppose that trade in cameras is opened and that the world's supply curve is S_W. The world price of cameras is *OP'*, below the old domestic price, *OP*, and this is the price that must come to prevail in the domestic market if there are no transport costs or tariffs. How will this happen? As imported cameras are less expensive than domestic cameras, consumers will cease to buy domestic cameras at the old domestic price, and they will raise their total purchases as well. They will move along their demand curve from *E* to *E''*, increasing consumption by *AC* to *OC*. As consumers start to buy foreign cameras, however, domestic producers will reduce their prices in order to stay in business, but they cannot do that without cutting production. They will move along their supply curve from *E* to *E'*, decreasing production by *AQ* to *OQ*. The gap between domestic demand and domestic supply, *QC*, will be filled by imports.

What are the effects on economic welfare? Domestic consumers will gain from the opening of trade, and domestic producers will lose. But the gain to consumers will be larger than the loss to producers, allowing consumers to compensate producers and still come out ahead. Accordingly, there will be a welfare gain from trade for the nation as a whole. The text attached to Figure 2-1 shows that consumer surplus will rise by *P'E''EP*, that producer surplus will fall by *P'E'EP*, and that the difference between them is *E'E''E*. This measures the welfare gain from trade. Note 2-1 proves that the size of this gain depends on the size of the change in the domestic price and of the resulting change in import volume. (In this case, the price change is *PP'*, and the volume change is *QC*, the whole quantity of imports made available by trade.)

This simple diagram is deficient in many ways. It relies on rather restrictive assumptions to measure consumer surplus. It does not describe the economic costs and benefits of exporting other goods to pay for imported cameras. It says nothing about the reasons for the price difference that leads to trade—why the world price of cameras is lower than the pretrade domestic price. To investigate these matters, we must use general-equilibrium models. Before turning to them, however, let us ask how a tariff on imported cameras would affect the gains from trade.

Effects of an Import Tariff

Consumers do not voluntarily compensate producers when consumers gain and producers lose. Hence, producers often seek protection from import competition. Many methods can be used to provide protection, and we will compare them in Chapter 9. Here, we examine the most common method. What will happen if domestic producers of cameras persuade their government to impose a tariff on each imported camera?

The principal effects of an import tariff are shown in Figure 2-2, which reproduces the demand and supply curves used in Figure 2-1 and the equilibrium at the world price *OP'*. Domestic producers supply *OQ* cameras, domestic consumers demand

---

NOTE 2-1
Measuring the Welfare Effects of Trade and Tariffs

The area of a triangle is $\frac{1}{2} \times$ Base $\times$ Height. Hence, the area of $E'E''E$ in Figure 2-1 is $\frac{1}{2} \times E'E'' \times KE$. But $E'E'' = QC$, the increase in import volume (the whole import volume here), and $KE = PP'$, the change in the domestic price caused by shifting from the pretrade domestic price to the lower world price. Therefore, the increase in welfare is

$$\Delta W = \tfrac{1}{2} \times QC \times PP' = \tfrac{1}{2} \times \Delta M \times \Delta p.$$

where Δ denotes a change, M is the quantity of imports, and p is the initial domestic price.

Similarly, the area of $E'F'H'$ *plus* $FE''H$ in Figure 2-2 is $\frac{1}{2} \times (E'F' \times F'H'$ *plus* $FE'' \times FH)$. But $E'F' = QQ'$, $FE'' = C'C$, and $F'H' = FH = P'P''$. Therefore, the decrease in welfare is

$$\Delta W = -\tfrac{1}{2} \times (QQ' + C'C) \times P'P''.$$

But $QQ' + C'C$ is the change in imports, and $P'P''$ is the change in price, which can be written in this case as $p_w \times t$, where p_w is the world price and t is the *ad valorem* (percentage) tariff rate. Accordingly,

$$\Delta W = -\tfrac{1}{2} \times \Delta M \times p_w \times t,$$

where $\Delta M \times p_w$ can be interpreted as the change in imports valued at their world price.

OC, and imports are QC. An import tariff will raise the domestic prices of imported cameras, and consumers will stop buying them. As they switch to domestic cameras, however, they will bid up their prices until they are equal to the prices of imported cameras. If the tariff is $P'P''$ per camera, the domestic price will rise to OP''. Domestic consumers will reduce their purchases to OC', domestic producers will raise their sales to OQ', and imports will fall from QC to $Q'C'$.

To measure the welfare effects of the tariff, we must know what the government does with the tariff revenue. It collects $P'P''$ on each imported camera and thus collects $F'FHH'$ in total tariff revenue. Let us assume that it cuts some other tax and thus returns the revenue to consumers. The text attached to Figure 2-2 shows that producer surplus will rise by $P'E'H'P''$ and that consumer surplus will fall by $P'E''HP''$. Hence, the consumers' loss will exceed the producers' gain, even when consumers get back the tariff revenue. The difference between the consumers' loss and the producers' gain is $E'F'H'$ *plus* $FE''H$, which measures the welfare loss resulting from the tariff. Note 2-1 proves that the size of the loss depends on the tariff rate and on the size of the resulting change in import volume.

PRODUCTION AND CONSUMPTION
IN GENERAL EQUILIBRIUM

Much of international trade theory can be developed using a very simple general-equilibrium model. It contains two countries that produce two goods

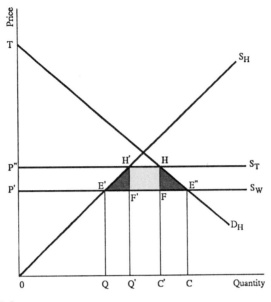

FIGURE 2-2
A Tariff on a Single Good
The demand and supply curves, D_H, S_H, and S_W, are reproduced from Figure 2-1. Domestic production is OQ initially, domestic consumption is OC, and imports are QC. A tariff that adds $P'P''$ to the import price raises the domestic price to OP''. Therefore, it raises domestic production to OQ' and reduces domestic consumption to OC'. Imports fall to $Q'C'$. Producer surplus was $OE'P'$ initially and is $OH'P''$ with the tariff. Consumer surplus was $P'E''T$ initially and is $P''HT$ with the tariff. Hence, producer surplus rises by $P'E'H'P''$, and consumer surplus falls by $P'E''HP''$, which is $E'E''HH'$ larger than the rise in producer surplus. But the government collects $P'P''$ of tariff revenue on each imported unit, or $F'FHH'$ in total tariff revenue, and remits it to consumers by cutting some other tax. Therefore, the net welfare loss is $E'E''HH'$ *less* $F'F''HH'$, or $E'FH'$ *plus* $FE''H$. The production effect, QQ', also called the protective effect, contributes $E'FH'$, which reflects the substitution of high-cost domestic output for low-cost foreign output. The consumption effect, CC', contributes $FE''H$, which reflects the reduction in consumption caused by the increase in the price of a camera.

requiring two factors of production. The model cannot yield testable hypotheses about the commodity composition of trade; a more complicated model with many countries and goods is needed for that purpose. Nevertheless, the simple model can be used to illustrate the law of comparative advantage and the nature of the gains from trade. It also furnishes testable hypotheses about the general character of trade.

The model is developed in three steps. First, we will show how production, consumption, and prices are determined when there is no trade. Second, we will show how trade affects a single country. Third, we will look at two countries together to show how world prices are determined and how the gains from trade are distributed.

Supply Conditions

Supply conditions in a country producing two goods can be described by a *production transformation curve* (sometimes called a production possibilities curve). It shows the combinations of goods that the country can produce, given its resources,

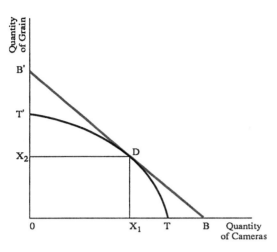

FIGURE 2-3
The Production Transformation Curve
The position and shape of the curve TT' depend on the country's supplies of the factors of production and its technology. When the relative price of a camera is given by the slope of the line BB', the country will produce at D. Its camera output will be OX_1, and its grain output will be OX_2. As the slope of BB' is (OB'/OB), which equals (X_2B'/X_2D), and X_2D equals OX_1, the relative price of a camera can be written as (X_2B'/OX_1). Hence, the national product measured in grain will be OX_2 plus $OX_1 \times (X_2B'/OX_1)$ or OX_2 plus X_2B', which equals OB'. Similarly, the national product measured in cameras will be OB.

technology, and economic organization. The curve TT' in Figure 2-3 is the transformation curve for a country producing cameras and grain. If the country were to devote all its resources to the production of cameras, output would be OT cameras. If it were to devote all its resources to the production of grain, output would be OT' grain. If it were to divide its resources between the two activities, it would arrive at a point such as D, where camera output is OX_1 and grain output is OX_2.

The position and shape of the transformation curve depend on the quantities of land, labor, and other resources with which the country is endowed and on its technology. If it had more land, it could produce more grain; the distance OT' would be longer, and the whole transformation curve would be steeper. If it had a better way of making cameras, it could produce more cameras; the distance OT would be longer, and the whole transformation curve would be flatter. These possibilities are explored in Chapters 3 and 4, which deal with sources of comparative advantage.

Note that the curve TT' gets steeper as camera output rises. The country must sacrifice increasingly large quantities of grain output to raise camera output. This property has many names—convexity, increasing opportunity cost, and so on. It can have many causes. There may be decreasing returns to scale in one or both sectors. There may be a fixed factor of production in each sector, which means that the other (variable) factors will have diminishing marginal products. (If the number of camera factories is fixed, for example, the hiring of additional workers will raise camera output by smaller and smaller amounts.) The same result will obtain, however, when all factors of production are freely transferable from one sector to the other but must be combined differently in each sector. Whatever the cause, the property appears to be pervasive.

Prices, Outputs, and National Product

When domestic markets are perfectly competitive and firms maximize profits, the economy will maximize its national product measured in real terms, and production will be determined uniquely by relative prices.[2] To prove these statements, let us choose a set of prices arbitrarily and show how it determines the output of each good.

Let the relative price of a camera be equal to the *slope* of the line BB' in Figure 2-3 and thus equal to the slope of the curve TT' at D. A competitive economy will produce at D and will thereby maximize its national product. An algebraic demonstration is given in Section 1 of Appendix A. A geometric demonstration can be furnished by showing that (1) the distances OB and OB' measure the national product in real terms, and (2) production at D maximizes the distances OB and OB' and thus maximizes the national product.

To show that OB and OB' measure the national product in real terms, let us write out the definitions of the national product. It is the sum of the values of the country's outputs measured at their market prices:

Value of national product

$= $ grain output $\times$ price of grain

$+$ camera output $\times$ price of a camera.

Dividing both sides by the price of grain,

$$\frac{\text{Value of national product}}{\text{Price of grain}}$$

$$= \text{grain output} + \text{camera output} \times \frac{\text{price of a camera}}{\text{price of grain}},$$

or

National product measured in grain

$= $ grain output $+$ camera output $\times$ relative price of a camera.

The relative price of a camera is its price expressed in grain. It measures the amount of grain that must be given up to purchase a camera. Let that price be equal to the slope of the line BB':

$$\text{Relative camera price} = \left(\frac{OB'}{OB}\right).$$

---

[2]This list of conditions is not complete. Two others receive attention in advanced trade theory: (1) There can be no tax or subsidy on the output of one good or use of one factor; taxes and subsidies must be uniform. (2) Uncertainty about future prices must not affect producers' and consumers' responses to current prices.

But the text attached to Figure 2-3 shows that (OB'/OB) is equal to (X_2B'/OX_1). When production is at D, moreover, grain output is OX_2, and camera output is OX_1. Therefore,

National product measured in grain

$$= OX_2 + OX_1 \times \left(\frac{X_2B'}{OX_1}\right) = OX_2 + X_2B' = OB'.$$

National product measured in grain is actual grain output *plus* the grain equivalent at market prices of actual camera output. National product measured in cameras can be obtained in a similar way or more directly. Divide the national product measured in grain by the relative price of a camera:[3]

National product measured in cameras

$$= \frac{\text{national product measured in grain}}{\text{relative price of a camera}}$$

$$= OB' \div \left(\frac{OB'}{OB}\right) = OB' \times \left(\frac{OB}{OB'}\right) = OB.$$

It is actual camera output *plus* the camera equivalent at market prices of actual grain output.

To show that production at D maximizes real national product, whether we measure it in cameras or grain, let us perform an experiment using Figure 2-4. As before, the transformation curve is TT', and the relative price of a camera is given by the slope of the line BB'. But suppose that production starts at H, not D, and draw the line AA' passing through H and parallel to BB'. This line marks off the distances OA and OA', which measure real national product in cameras and grain, respectively, when H is the output point. Clearly, these are smaller than OB and OB', which measure real national product when D is the output point.

Competitive firms will not stay at H. They will produce more cameras and less grain, moving the economy along the transformation curve in the direction of D. They will do this because it will increase their profits. (The line AA' is steeper than the transformation curve at H. Therefore, the value of an increase in camera output will exceed the value of the corresponding decrease in grain output.) By moving in this direction, moreover, firms raise real national product, and they maximize it when they arrive at D. The gaps AB and $A'B'$ disappear. If firms were to go beyond D, they would reduce real national product. If they were to move to H', for example, it would fall again to OA and OA'. But profits would fall, too.

---

[3]This equation follows from the fact that

National product measured in cameras × price of a camera
$$= \text{national product measured in grain} \times \text{price of grain},$$

so that

National product measured in cameras
$$= \text{national product measured in grain} \times \frac{\text{Price of grain}}{\text{price of a camera}}$$

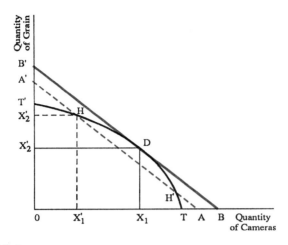

FIGURE 2-4
Efficiency in Domestic Production
When the relative price of a camera is given by the slope of the line *BB'*, production at *D* is efficient and production at *H* is not. Both points lie on the same transformation curve but do not provide the same levels of real national product. When the economy produces at *D*, camera output is OX_1, grain output is OX_2, and real national product is *OB* in terms of cameras. When the economy produces at *H*, camera output is OX_1', grain output is OX_2', and real national product is only *OB'* in terms of cameras. But profit-maximizing firms will move the economy from *H* to *D*, maximizing real national product.

In brief, a competitive economy will arrive and stay at *D*, where the relative price of a camera is equal to the slope of the transformation curve, also known as the *marginal rate of transformation*.

Demand Conditions

Demand conditions in a country consuming two goods can be described by a *community indifference map*. It is built from individuals' indifference maps, which show how those individuals rank various collections of goods.[4]

An indifference map is made up of *indifference curves*. Two are shown in Figure 2-5. The point *P* defines a collection of goods, OC_1 cameras and OC_2 grain. The indifference curve U_1 divides all such collections into three groups. Those that lie below U_1 are inferior to the collection at *P*; they furnish lower levels of utility (satisfaction). Those that lie above it are superior to the collection at *P*; they furnish higher levels of utility. And those that lie right on U_1 are equivalent to the collection

---

[4]To build a community indifference map from individual indifference maps, one must make a number of assumptions, but these are less restrictive than those one must make to measure consumer surplus. It is not necessary to adopt a cardinal measure of utility, to measure the utilities of individuals in comparable units, or to keep the marginal utility of income constant. It is sufficient to assume that all individuals have the same indifference maps and that income elasticities of demand are unity (that a 1 percent increase in real income causes a 1 percent increase in the demand for each good). Alternatively, it is sufficient to assume that all individuals have the same sources of income.

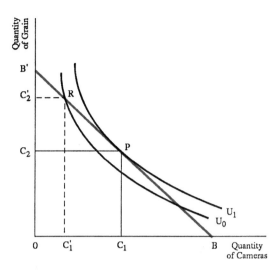

FIGURE 2-5
The Indifference Map
All collections of goods that lie on one indifference curve yield the same level of utility (satisfaction), but any collection on U_1 is superior to any collection on U_0. When income is *OB* measured in cameras, and the relative price of a camera is given by the slope of the line *BB'*, consumers will choose the collection given at *P*, purchasing OC_1 cameras and OC_2 grain. That collection is superior to any other on or below *BB'*, such as the one at *R*.

at *P*; they furnish the same level of utility, which is why the consumer is said to be indifferent when asked to choose among them.

Note that the indifference curves get flatter as cameras replace grain in the collection of goods. This property can be derived from a fundamental axiom in the theory of consumer behavior—the law of diminishing marginal utility. It says that each increase in the consumption of one good furnishes a smaller addition to utility. The larger the consumption of cameras, the smaller the increase in utility obtained by adding one more camera. By implication, a consumer will require larger and larger increases in camera consumption to offset successive decreases in grain consumption.

To show how indifference curves describe demand conditions, suppose that consumers have *OB* of real income measured in cameras and that the relative price of a camera is given by the slope of the line *BB'*. Consumers can buy any combination of cameras and grain lying on *BB'*. They can have OC_1' cameras and OC_2' grain and will then wind up at *R* on the indifference curve U_0. They can also have OC_1 cameras and OC_2 grain and will then wind up at *P* on the indifference curve U_1. Consumers will choose *P*, of course, and they can do no better. It lies on the highest indifference curve attainable when consumers are constrained by the line *BB'*.

Because of the role that it plays in Figure 2-4, the line *BB'* is often called a *budget line*. It depicts the two constraints that confront consumers: the incomes they can spend and the prices at which they can spend them. Therefore, the outcome shown at *P* can be described by saying that the composition of demand is given by the point on the budget line at which its slope is equal to the slope of an indifference curve, also known as the *marginal rate of substitution.*

Equilibrium in the Closed Economy

When we looked for equilibrium in a single market and there was no trade, we sought the price at which the domestic market cleared—at which domestic demand was equal to domestic supply. It was given by the point E in Figure 2-1. When we look for equilibrium in two markets together, we must seek the point at which both markets clear. It is the point E in Figure 2-6. Let us see what happens at that point.

When production takes place at E, the supply of cameras is OQ_1 and the supply of grain is OQ_2. In a competitive economy, however, production will remain at E only when the relative price of a camera is equal to the slope of the transformation curve at E and thus equal to the slope of the line BB'. When this condition is satisfied, moreover, the national product measured in cameras is OB, and it must equal the national income in this simple economy (where there are no adjustments for depreciation, indirect taxes, etc.). The values of the goods produced at E must equal the wages, rents, and profits paid to the factors of production. Therefore, the line BB' must be the budget line, and consumers will wind up at E, because U_1 is the highest indifference curve they can reach when they face that budget line. The demand for cameras will be OQ_1 and will equal the supply. The demand for grain will be OQ_2, and it will also equal the supply.

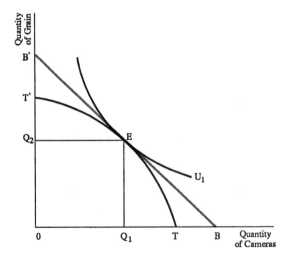

FIGURE 2-6
Equilibrium in the Closed Economy
Under competitive conditions, equilibrium will be established at E. Camera output will be OQ_1 and will equal the demand for cameras. Grain output will be OQ_2 and will equal the demand for grain. The relative price of a camera will equal the slope of the line BB', and real national product will be OB measured in cameras.

Two features of this equilibrium deserve special attention:

(1) We can locate E without knowing the relative price of a camera. When firms maximize profits and consumers maximize utility, equilibrium in a closed economy is established at the *tangency* between the transformation curve and an indifference curve, just as equilibrium in a single market is established at the intersection between the supply and demand curves. The marginal rate of transformation is equated to the marginal rate of substitution, and each of them must equal the relative price of a camera. Hence, we can infer that price from the slopes of the two curves at their tangency; we can draw BB' after we have found E.

(2) When one market clears, the other must clear, too. When we have found the relative price that clears the camera market, we have found the one that clears the grain market too. In other words, there is only one independent market in a two-good model. This important point is proved algebraically in Section 1 of Appendix A.

What would happen if, by chance, the relative price of a camera were different from the equilibrium price? Suppose that the price were lower than the one given by the slopes of the curves at E. Firms would move to the northwest along the transformation curve, reducing the supply of cameras below OQ_1. Consumers would move to the southeast through the indifference map, raising the demand for cameras above OQ_1. There would be an *excess demand* for cameras, which would raise the relative price of a camera, moving the economy back to E. Hence, E is the only equilibrium point for the closed economy.

TRADE IN GENERAL EQUILIBRIUM

When analyzing trade in a single good, using Figure 2-1, we asked what would happen if the world price of a camera was lower than the domestic price prevailing before trade. Let us address the same question to the two-good economy. How does trade affect production, consumption, and economic welfare when the relative price of a camera is lower in the world market than in the domestic market before trade was opened?

Equilibrium in the Open Economy

The effects of trade are shown in Figure 2-7. Before the opening of trade, the economy is in equilibrium at E (just as it was in Figure 2-6). The relative price of a camera is given by the slopes of the transformation curve TT' and the indifference curve U_1. The budget line BB' is omitted from this and later diagrams, because it would clutter the diagram unnecessarily.

Suppose that the relative price of a camera is lower in the outside world. Represent it by the slope of the line FF'. When trade is opened (and there are no transport costs or tariffs), the world price replaces the earlier domestic price. Guided by the world price, profit-maximizing firms will move the output point to D, where the slope of the transformation curve is equal to the slope of FF'. The national product

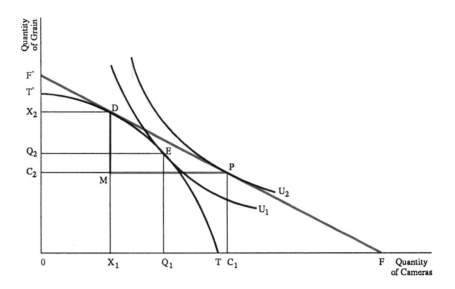

FIGURE 2-7
Equilibrium in the Open Economy
Before trade is opened, production and consumption take place at E, and the relative price of a camera is given by the slope of the transformation curve at E. When trade is opened at a lower world price, given by the slope of the line FF', production moves to D and consumption moves to P. Camera output falls to OX_1, consumption rises to OC_1, and X_1C_1 of camera imports fill the gap. Grain production rises to OX_2, consumption falls to OC_2, and C_2X_2 of grain exports remove the surplus. Consumers gain by moving from E on the indifference curve U_1 to P on the higher indifference curve U_2. Production and consumption effects are readily identified. Looking first at camera imports, the production effect is the decrease in domestic supply, Q_1X_1, and the consumption effect is the increase in domestic demand, Q_1C_1. Together, they define total imports, X_1C_1 or MP. Looking next at grain exports, the production effect is the increase in domestic supply, Q_2X_2, and the consumption effect is the decrease in domestic demand, Q_2C_2. Together, they define total exports, C_2X_2 or MD.

measured in cameras will be OF, it will equal the national income, and FF' will be the budget line. Accordingly, consumers will maximize utility by moving to the point P, where the slope of the budget line is equal to the slope of the indifference curve U_2.

If the economy were closed, there would be an excess demand for cameras (equal to X_1C_1) and an excess supply of grain (equal to C_2X_2). The new situation would not be sustainable. When the economy can trade with the outside world, however, it can satisfy its excess demand for cameras by importing X_1C_1 and sell off its excess supply of grain by exporting C_2X_2. Production at D can be reconciled with consumption at P, because domestic markets can be cleared by trading grain for cameras. Trade is beneficial, moreover, because consumers can choose any collection of goods lying on the budget line FF' and thus reach the indifference curve U_2. They are not compelled to choose the particular collection given at E by the tangency of the transformation curve with the lower indifference curve U_1.[5]

The grain exports shown in Figure 2-7 are just large enough to pay for the camera imports. This is proved algebraically in Section 1 of Appendix A, and it can be illustrated geometrically by looking at two triangles, OFF' and MPD. The legs of

OFF' measure the relative price of a camera in the world market:

$$\text{Relative camera price} = \frac{\text{price of a camera}}{\text{price of grain}} = \left(\frac{OF'}{OF}\right).$$

But OFF' is similar to MPD, identified hereafter as the *trade triangle*. Therefore, (OF'/OF) equals (MD/MP). Furthermore, MD equals C_2X_2, the quantity of grain exports, and MP equals X_1C_1, the quantity of camera imports. Therefore,

$$\frac{\text{Price of a camera}}{\text{Price of grain}} = \left(\frac{MD}{MP}\right) = \frac{\text{quantity of grain exports}}{\text{quantity of camera imports}},$$

and

Quantity of camera imports $\times$ price of a camera

$=$ quantity of grain exports $\times$ price of grain.

The country's foreign trade is balanced.

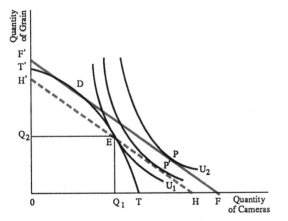

FIGURE 2-8
Decomposing the Gains from Trade
The gain from international exchange is measured by holding the output point at E and drawing the line HH' through E. As HH' is parallel to FF', its slope measures the relative price of a camera in the world market, and the distance OH measures real national product in cameras; it is pretrade camera output, OQ_1, *plus* the camera equivalent of pretrade grain output, OQ_2. As OH also measures real income, HH' is the budget line when E is the output point, and consumers move to P', which lies on an indifference curve higher than U_1 but lower than U_2. The gain from international specialization is defined by allowing the output point to shift from E to D. This permits the additional shift of consumption from P to P', which lies on the indifference curve U_2.

---

[5]Note that the gains from trade can be illustrated easily without drawing indifference curves. As the budget line FF' lies to the northeast of the old equilibrium point E, it includes collections of goods containing more cameras and more grain. Unless consumers' demands can be *satiated* by finite quantitiEs of goods, these collections are necessarily superior to the collection defined by E. (Consumers may prefer the collection defined by P, containing more cameras and less grain, but could have a collection containing more of *both* goods.)

Decomposing the Gains from Trade

The text attached to Figure 2-7 breaks down the effects of trade into production and consumption effects, but there is a better way to decompose the effects of trade in a general-equilibrium model. Figure 2-8 replicates the trading equilibrium derived in Figure 2-7 and shows that the increase in economic welfare can be divided into two parts.

The first part can be measured by supposing momentarily that the output point remains at E even after trade is opened. Draw the line HH' through E and parallel to FF', so that the slope of HH' measures the relative price of a camera in the world market. As the distance OH measures real income in cameras, consumers will move to P' and reach an indifference curve higher than U_1 but lower than U_2. The movement of consumption from E to P' is the *gain from international exchange*.

The second part of the increase in welfare can be measured by relaxing the assumption that production is fixed at E, and allowing the output point to move from E to D. National product and national income rise from OH to OF. Consumers move from P' to P and reach the higher indifference curve U_2. The movement of consumption from P' to P is the *gain from international specialization*, made possible by the shift in the composition of production.[6]

DETERMINATION OF INTERNATIONAL PRICES

We have completed two of the three steps required to prove the law of comparative advantage. We have shown how supply and demand conditions determine domestic prices in a closed economy producing two goods. We have shown how that economy responds when confronted by world prices different from domestic prices, a process summarized by the appearance of the trade triangle defining the demand for imports and supply of exports. We are now ready to take the final step: to show how world prices are determined and that they reflect international differences in cost and price structures.

The trade triangle was MPD in Figure 2-7. When the relative price of a camera was equal to the slope of FF', the quantity of grain exports was MD, and the quantity of camera imports was MP. Furthermore, trade was balanced. Grain exports were just large enough to pay for camera imports when they were exchanged at world prices.

When an economy is very small, its trade does not affect world prices. Like an individual producer or consumer in a competitive domestic market, it can exchange any quantity of grain for the corresponding quantity of cameras without affecting relative prices in the world market. When an economy is not that small, however, its attempt to sell MD of grain and buy MP of cameras will affect world prices. When

---

[6]The term *specialization* is often used in trade theory to describe a limiting case in which a country devotes all its resources to the production of the export good and does not produce any of the import-competing good. We will encounter such a case in the next chapter. In this book, specialization is used more broadly to describe the movement of production away from the pretrade point. The limiting case will be described as *complete* specialization.

this happens, the shape of the trade triangle is altered, changing the supply of grain exports and the demand for camera imports.

When can we be sure that a trade triangle depicts an international equilibrium? The conditions can be identified easily by looking at a simple two-country world. (World markets can be competitive even when there are only two countries. The number of countries does not matter if each country's markets are competitive and governments do not monopolize their countries' foreign trade. Trade unites the countries' competitive markets, and the sums of competitive markets are also competitive.)

Equilibrium with Trade Between Two Countries

The two countries are described by Figure 2-9. The domestic transformation curve is TT'. The foreign transformation curve is $T_fT'_f$. As OT' is larger than OT'_f and OT is smaller than OT_f, there is an obvious sense in which the domestic

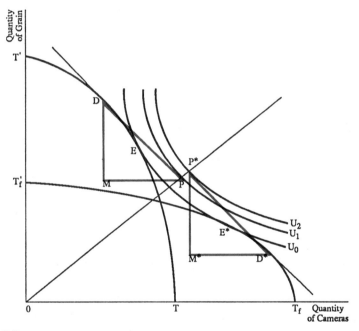

FIGURE 2-9
Equilibrium in a Two-Country World
Before trade is opened, domestic production and consumption take place at E on the domestic transformation curve TT'; foreign production and consumption take place at E^* on the foreign transformation curve $T_fT'_f$. Consumers in both countries reach the indifference curve U_0. The relative price of a camera is higher at E than at E^*. Trade establishes a common price equal to the slopes of the (parallel) lines PD and P^*D^*. Domestic production moves to D, domestic consumption moves to P, and domestic consumers reach the higher indifference curve U_1. Foreign production moves to D^*, foreign consumption moves to P^*, and foreign consumers reach the higher indifference curve U_2. The common price must be one at which the trade triangles are equal. Domestic grain exports, DM, must equal foreign grain imports, P^*M^*. Domestic camera imports, PM, must equal foreign camera exports, D^*M^*.

economy is better suited to produce grain than cameras, compared to the foreign economy.

To emphasize the influence of cost conditions on international trade, the two countries are assumed to have identical demand conditions, represented by the common indifference curves U_0, U_1, and U_2.

Look first at the internal equilibria before trade is opened. In the domestic economy, production and consumption take place at E, where the transformation curve TT' is tangent to the indifference curve U_0. In the foreign economy, they take place at E^*, where the transformation curve $T_f T_f'$ is tangent to that same indifference curve.[7] Clearly, the relative price of a camera is higher in the domestic economy than in the foreign economy, which is what we would expect, because the domestic economy is better suited to producing grain than cameras.

Look next at the effects of opening trade. When the two countries' markets are unified, common prices must prevail, and they must clear the unified markets. There are two ways to state this last condition: (1) Global camera output, defined as the sum of the two countries' outputs, must equal the global demand for cameras, and global grain output must equal the global demand for grain. (2) The quantity of camera imports demanded by one country must equal the quantity of camera exports supplied by the other, and the same equality must hold for trade in grain.[8] Geometrically, the two countries must have identical (congruent) trade triangles. These conditions can be fulfilled only when the relative price of a camera on the world camera market lies between the prices that prevailed internally before trade was opened.

This common price is represented by the slopes of the parallel lines PD and P^*D^* in Figure 2-9. They are flatter than the slope of the indifference curve U_0 at E (the world price is lower than the old internal price in the domestic economy). They are steeper than the slope of that indifference curve at E^* (the world price is higher than the old internal price in the foreign economy). The common price is the equilibrium price, because the unified market clears.

As the opening of trade reduces the relative price of a camera in the domestic economy, production moves to D and consumption moves to P, just as they did in Figure 2-7. The trade triangle is MPD. The domestic economy demands MP of camera imports in exchange for MD of grain exports. As the opening of trade raises the relative price of a camera in the foreign economy, production moves to D^*, and consumption moves to P^*. The trade triangle is $M^*D^*P^*$. The foreign economy demands M^*P^* of grain imports in exchange for M^*D^* of camera exports.

Furthermore, the common price is the one at which the two trade triangles are identical. Therefore, the domestic demand for camera imports is equal to the foreign supply of camera exports (MP equals M^*D^*), and the foreign demand for grain

---

[7]The two countries do not have to start on the same indifference curve. This special case is chosen to simplify the diagram, and the conclusions drawn from it are quite general. But the common *set* of indifference curves has a special property that could be important if the countries started on different curves. The income elasticities of demand are unity. Geometrically, points of common slope such as P and P^* lie on a straight line from the origin. In technical terms, the indifference curves are *homothetic*. This property prevents country size from influencing demand conditions and relative prices.

[8]The equivalence of these two conditions is demonstrated in Section 1 of Appendix A.

imports equals the domestic supply of grain exports ($M*P*$ equals MD). When one of these conditions is satisfied, moreover, the other must also be satisfied. This follows from the fact that both world markets have to clear whenever one of them clears. It follows also from the fact that each country's trade is balanced: its demand for imports is equal in value to its supply of exports.

To prove that the relative price of a camera has to lie between the old internal prices, suppose momentarily that this were not so. Let the common price be equal to the old internal price in the foreign economy (i.e., to the slope of U_0 at $E*$). Outputs and consumption would not change in the foreign economy, and it would not offer exports or demand imports. But outputs and consumption would change significantly in the domestic economy. The change in output, indeed, would be larger than the change shown in Figure 2-9, because the relative price of a camera would fall farther. Therefore, the domestic economy would demand camera imports and offer grain exports, and world markets would not clear. There would be an excess demand for cameras and an excess supply of grain, and these would raise the relative price of a camera until it came to lie between the old internal prices in the two national economies.

The Terms of Trade and Gains from Trade

The common price given by the lines PD and $P*D*$ defines the *terms of trade* between the two economies. These are the terms on which each economy can acquire imports from the other. A reduction in the relative price of its import improves a country's terms of trade. In this particular illustration, a reduction in the relative price of a camera, making PD and $P*D*$ flatter, would improve the terms of trade of the domestic economy and worsen the terms of trade of the foreign economy. The terms of trade determine the distribution of the gains from trade. If PD and $P*D*$ were flatter, domestic consumers could reach an indifference curve higher than U_1 but foreign consumers could not even reach U_2. Consumers in both countries would still gain from trade, but domestic consumers would gain more and foreign consumers would gain less.

Comparative Advantage Once Again

Figure 2-9 has several uses. It shows how world prices are established. They must clear the unified national markets of the trading countries by equating one country's demand for imports to the other's supply of exports. It shows that each country gains from trade and the distribution of the gains. Domestic consumers move from E to P and thus to the higher indifference curve U_1. Foreign consumers move from $E*$ to $P*$ and thus to the higher indifference curve U_2. Finally, it illustrates the law of comparative advantage.

If the two countries shown in Figure 2-9 had identical transformation curves, there could be no trade between them. The points E and $E*$ would coincide, and the two countries' prices would be the same before trade. The unification of national markets would be without consequence, because it would not alter relative prices. Each country's firms would stay at E, and each country's consumers would stay there, too. Internal supplies would satisfy internal demands in each country separately. There would be no gain from international specialization and no gain from international exchange.

When the countries' transformation curves are different, the unification of national markets changes relative prices, affecting production and consumption in each country. Both countries gain from specialization and exchange. Note in particular the nature of the gain from international specialization. The domestic economy is better suited to produce grain than cameras, compared to the foreign economy. With the opening of trade, it exploits its comparative advantage. Reacting to the fall in the relative price of a camera, domestic firms produce more grain and fewer cameras, and the economy thus tends to specialize in grain production. The foreign economy has a comparative advantage in camera production—the mirror image of the domestic economy's advantage in grain production—and also exploits its advantage. Reacting to the rise in the relative price of a camera, foreign firms produce more cameras and less grain, and the economy thus tends to specialize in camera production.

Looking at these same reactions from another standpoint, we can say that trade offsets the difference in relative scarcities. Before trade is opened, cameras are relatively scarce in the domestic economy, because it is not well suited to produce them. Trade diminishes that scarcity. Similarly, grain is relatively scarce in the foreign economy, but trade diminishes that scarcity.

When demand conditions are identical, as in Figure 2-9, a difference in relative scarcities is necessarily due to a difference in supply conditions. It could be due, however, to a difference in demand conditions. If two countries have identical transformation curves but different indifference maps, their relative prices will differ before trade, but the opening of trade will equalize their prices and be beneficial to consumers.

To take account of this last possibility, the law of comparative advantage can be restated in terms of price differences rather than cost differences:

In a world of competitive markets, trade will occur and be beneficial whenever countries' relative prices would be different without trade.

The difference in pretrade prices can be due to a difference in supply (cost) conditions, a difference in demand conditions, or a combination of the two.

OFFER CURVES AND INTERNATIONAL EQUILIBRIUM

How do market processes establish the sort of equilibrium described by Figure 2-9, involving trade between two countries? This question can be answered most easily by deriving an *offer curve* to summarize the relevant conditions in each country and then putting the two countries' offer curves together.

Deriving an Offer Curve

An offer curve for the domestic economy is shown in the upper part of Figure 2-10. The horizontal axis records its trade in cameras. The vertical axis

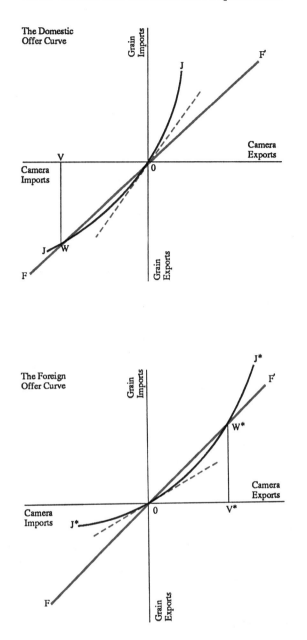

FIGURE 2-10
Offer Curves
The curve JOJ is the domestic offer curve. It shows export supply and import demand at each set of prices. When the relative price of a camera is equal to the slope of the line FF', the domestic economy will supply VW of grain exports and demand OV of camera imports. The trade triangle OVW corresponds to the trade triangle MPD in Figure 2-9. The slope of the curve at its origin, shown by the dashed line, corresponds to the slope of the indifference curve U_0 at E in Figure 2-9; the domestic economy will not offer or demand either good when world and domestic prices are the same. The curve J*OJ* is the foreign offer curve. When the relative price of a camera is equal to the slope of FF', the foreign economy will supply OV* of camera exports and demand V*W* of grain imports. The trade triangle OV*W* corresponds to the trade triangle M*D*P* in Figure 2-9.

records its trade in grain. The offer curve JOJ uses information about relative prices to connect the two trade flows. When the relative price of a camera is equal to the slope of the line FF', the domestic economy demands OV of camera imports and supplies VW of grain exports.

The offer curve is derived from the transformation curve and the indifference map. Look back at Figure 2-9. When the relative price of a camera is equal to the slope of U_0 at E, the domestic economy does not make any export offer. This point corresponds to the origin of the offer curve in Figure 2-10. The slope of the offer curve at its origin, given by the dashed line tangent to it, corresponds to the slope of U_0 at E. When the relative price of a camera is lower than the price at E in Figure 2-9, the economy offers grain exports for camera imports. When the price is equal to the slope of PD, for instance, it offers MD of grain exports and demands MP of camera imports. These quantities are reproduced in Figure 2-10. The line FF' has the same slope as PD in Figure 2-9. The offer of grain exports is VW, the demand for camera imports is OV, and the trade triangle OVW is identical to the trade triangle MPD in Figure 2-9.

Each point on the offer curve JOJ produces one such triangle. Those in the southwest quadrant of Figure 2-10 are generated when the relative price of a camera is lower than the one given by the slope of the dashed line. The economy offers grain exports in exchange for camera imports. Those in the northeast quadrant are generated when the relative price of a camera is higher than the one given by the slope of the dashed line. The economy offers camera exports in exchange for grain imports.[9]

Each point on the offer curve corresponds uniquely to a production point on the transformation curve and a consumption point on an indifference curve. Offer curves, said one economist, resemble the hands of a clock. They convey much information in a simple fashion but are driven by a complex mechanism hidden behind them.

The offer curve for the foreign economy is shown in the lower part of Figure 2-10. It is flatter at its origin than the domestic offer curve, because U_0 is flatter at E^* than at E in Figure 2-9. Furthermore, the line FF' intersects the foreign offer curve in the northeast quadrant. The foreign economy supplies OV^* of camera exports and demands V^*W^* of grain imports, and the trade triangle OV^*W^* is identical to the trade triangle $M^*D^*P^*$ in Figure 2-9.

Combining Offer Curves

Figure 2-10 could be used to locate equilibrium. We could rotate the line FF' through each origin until we generated the matching pair of trade triangles OVW and OV^*W^*. By putting the two offer curves in one diagram, however, we can locate equilibrium more easily.

This is done in Figure 2-11. The foreign offer curve J^*OJ^* is drawn as before. The domestic offer curve JOJ has been flipped over. The part appearing in the northeast

---

[9]The offer curve cannot pass through the northwest quadrant when trade is balanced; the economy cannot demand camera and grain imports simultaneously. The curve cannot pass through the southwest quadrant either; the economy cannot offer camera and grain exports simultaneously.

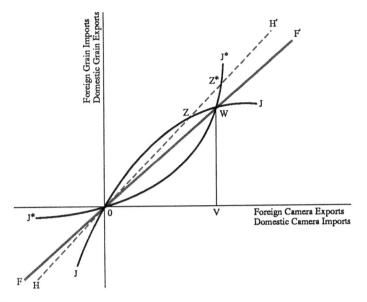

FIGURE 2-11
Locating Equilibrium with Offer Curves
The foreign offer curve, *J*OJ**, is drawn as in Figure 2-10. The domestic offer curve, *JOJ*, is redrawn with axes reversed. The intersection of the curves at *W* defines the trading equilibrium. The relative price of a camera in the world market is given by the slope of *FF'*, drawn from the origin through the point *W*. Domestic grain exports are equal to foreign grain imports, and domestic camera imports are equal to foreign camera exports. If the relative price of a camera was equal to the slope of *HH'*, the domestic economy would be at *Z* and the foreign economy would be at *Z**. The domestic economy would demand fewer cameras than the foreign economy would offer, and the relative price of a camera would fall until it was equal to the slope of *FF'*.

quadrant now shows the domestic demand for camera imports and the domestic supply of grain exports. This is done so that the horizontal axis of the diagram can measure the domestic demand for camera imports along with the foreign supply and the vertical axis can measure the domestic supply of grain exports along with the foreign demand.

If the two offer curves had the same slopes at the origin, they would be tangent to each other and would not intersect elsewhere in Figure 2-11. This repeats a statement made before. When two countries' internal prices are identical before trade is opened, they will not engage in trade when markets are unified. If the curves have different slopes, however, they will always intersect at some other point. This repeats the law of comparative advantage. When two countries' prices differ before trade is opened, they will engage in trade when markets are unified.

In Figure 2-11, the domestic offer curve is steeper at the origin than the foreign offer curve, so the two curves intersect at *W* in the northeast quadrant. World prices (the terms of trade) are given by the slope of the line drawn from the origin through the intersection. It is labeled *FF'* as usual. The domestic economy demands *OV* of camera imports, and the foreign economy supplies them. The foreign economy demands *VW* of grain imports, and the domestic economy supplies them.

Finally, Figure 2-11 repeats an exercise presented earlier. It shows how world prices are established. Suppose that the world price of a camera were higher than the one given by the slope of FF'. The foreign economy would supply more camera exports, the domestic economy would demand fewer camera imports, and there would be an excess supply of cameras on the world market. This would drive down the relative price of a camera, reducing export supply, raising import demand, and thus reducing the excess supply. The process would end when the relative price of a camera was equal to the slope of FF'.

Offer Curves and the Effects of an Import Tariff

Offer curves are used in subsequent chapters to show how demand conditions, economic growth, and other phenomena affect the distribution of the gains from trade. They are also used to analyze the effects of tariffs.

When we used demand and supply curves to study the effects of an import tariff, we simplified the problem by fixing the price of a camera on the world market. (It was OP' in Figure 2-2.) We can do that here by fixing the relative price of a camera on the world market. It is the slope of the line OJ^* in Figure 2-12. The initial equilibrium occurs at W, where OJ^* intersects OJ, the domestic offer curve, and the domestic price of a camera is equal to the world price. A tariff on imported cameras will raise their domestic price. Let that price be given by the slope of the line OJ_T. Note 2-2 proves that the tariff rate can be measured by $W'Z'/Z'V'$. The demand for

---

Note 2-2
Measuring the Level of a Tariff

Let the world price of a camera be p_1^* and the world price of grain be p_2^*. If the tariff rate on an imported camera is t, the domestic price of a camera is

$$p_1 = (1 + t)p_1^*.$$

As there is no tariff on grain, its domestic price is equal to its world price. Dividing both sides of the previous equation by p_1^*,

$$p = p_1/p_2 = (1 + t)(p_1^*/p_2^*) = (1 + t)p^*,$$

where p is the relative price of a camera in the domestic market and p^* is its relative price in the world market.

In Figure 2-12, domestic consumers pay $W'V'$ grain for OV' imported cameras, so p is $W'V'/OV'$. Foreign suppliers receive $Z'V'$ grain for OV' cameras, so p^* is $Z'V'/OV'$. Accordingly,

$$(W'V'/OV') = (1 + t)(Z'V'/OV'),$$

and

$$(W'V'/Z'V') = 1 + t.$$

But $W'V' = W'Z' + Z'V'$, so $(W'V'/Z'V') = 1 + (W'Z'/Z'V')$, and

$$t = W'Z'/Z'V'.$$

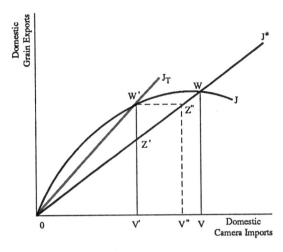

FIGURE 2-12
A Tariff in a Two-Good World
When an economy is too small to affect world prices, the foreign offer curve becomes the straight line OJ*, and the slope of OJ* measures the relative price of a camera on the world market. Equilibrium occurs at W initially, where OJ* intersects OJ, the domestic offer curve. The economy imports OV cameras and exports VW grain, and the domestic price of a camera is equal to its world price. A tariff on camera imports raises the domestic price of a camera above the world price. Let that new domestic price be given by the slope of OJ_T. The demand for camera imports will fall to OV', the supply of grain exports will fall to V'W', and the government will collect tariff revenue equivalent to Z'W' grain. The new equilibrium must lie on OJ*, but the location of that point will depend on the way that the government behaves. If it spends the tariff revenue on grain, the new equilibrium will occur at Z', where consumers will import OV' cameras and pay for then with V'Z' grain (the amount of grain remaining after the government has bought Z'W'). If the government spends the tariff revenue on cameras, the new equilibrium will occur at Z", where consumers will import OV' cameras and pay for them with V'Z' grain, and the government will import V'V" cameras and pay for them with Z'W' grain. As V'Z' and Z'W' add up to V'W', and V'W' equals V"Z", total grain exports will be just large enough to pay for total camera imports.

camera imports will fall from OV to OV', the supply of grain exports will fall from VW to $V'W'$, and the government will collect tariff revenue equivalent in value to $Z'W'$ grain.

The new equilibrium must lie on $OJ*$, the foreign offer curve. To locate it precisely, however, we must know how the government spends its tariff revenue. If it spends the revenue on grain, the new equilibrium will occur at Z'. The supply of grain exports will be reduced by $Z'W'$ and thus fall to $V'Z'$, but this is just enough to pay for OV' of camera imports. If it spends the revenue on cameras, the new equilibrium will occur at $Z"$. The supply of grain exports will remain at $V'W'$, which equals $Z"V"$, and this is just enough to pay for $OV"$ of camera imports. (Consumers will buy OV', as before, and the government will buy $W'Z"$, the number it can buy with $Z'W'$ of grain, raising the demand to $OV"$.)

When supply and demand curves were used in Figure 2-2 to illustrate the impact of a tariff, we could see how it affected consumption and production. That cannot be done in Figure 2-12, which does not show what happens to production or consumption. But offer curves are helpful in another way. By showing what happens to relative prices, they tell us how the tariff affects trade in grain, as well as trade in cameras. Camera imports fall to OV' or OV'' (depending on the way in which the revenue is spent). Grain exports fall to $V'Z'$ or $V''Z''$. We will return to these matters in Chapter 9, where we look more thoroughly at the effects of tariffs.

SUMMARY

Trade arises and is mutually beneficial whenever there are international differences in relative costs of production. This is the *law of comparative advantage* and the fundamental proposition of trade theory. Trade restrictions, such as tariffs, tend to reduce the gains from trade.

Ordinary supply and demand curves can be used to illustrate the main effects of trade. When the world price of a commodity is lower than its domestic price, trade raises the quantity demanded by domestic consumers and reduces the quantity supplied by domestic producers. The resulting increase in consumer surplus exceeds the decrease in producer surplus, and the difference measures the welfare gain from trade. Supply and demand curves can also be used to illustrate the main effects of a tariff, which reduces the quantity demanded by domestic consumers and raises the quantity supplied by domestic consumers. The resulting decrease in consumer surplus exceeds the increase in producer surplus, and the difference measures the welfare cost of the tariff.

But trade involves a two-way flow of goods and can be analyzed completely only by using general-equilibrium models. The simplest model of this sort contains two goods. Supply conditions are represented by a transformation curve. Demand conditions are represented by an indifference map.

In a closed economy, the markets for the two goods can clear when production and consumption take place at a common point. In an open economy, they can clear when production and consumption take place at different points defining a trade triangle. The gains from trade are represented by the movement to a higher indifference curve. They can be decomposed into gains from international exchange and gains from international specialization.

A two-country model is required to show how the terms of trade are established. The quantity of exports offered by one country must equal the quantity of imports demanded by the other. (The two countries' trade triangles must be identical.) The terms of trade determime how the gains from trade are distributed. Offers curves can be used to illustrate the determination of the terms of trade in a two-good model and the effects of tariffs on the terms of trade.

RECOMMENDED READINGS

On transformation curves, indifference curves, and trade patterns, see Wassily W. Leontief, "The Use of Indifference Curves in the Analysis of Foreign Trade," *Quarterly Journal of Economics*, 24 (May 1933); reprinted in American Economic Association, *Readings in the*

Theory of International Trade (Philadelphia: Blakiston, 1949), ch. 10. For another derivation of the offer curve and extensive applications, see James E. Meade, *A Geometry of International Trade* (London: Allen & Unwin, 1952), chs. i–v.

For a way to illustrate the gains from trade without using community indifference curves, see Peter B. Kenen, "On the Geometry of Welfare Economics," *Quarterly Journal of Economics*, 71 (August 1957); reprinted in P. B. Kenen, *Essays in International Economics* (Princeton, N.J.: Princeton University Press, 1980).

The most general restatement of the gains from trade, going beyond the two-good model, is given by Paul A. Samuelson, "The Gains from International Trade Once Again," *Economic Journal*, 72 (December 1962); reprinted in J. N. Bhagwati, ed., *International Trade: Selected Readings* (Cambridge, Mass.: MIT Press, 1981), ch. 10.

QUESTIONS AND PROBLEMS*

(1) Adapt Figure 2-1 to show that a country will export a product when the world price is higher than the pretrade domestic price. Identify the quantity of exports, the changes in domestic production and consumption, the changes in producer and consumer surplus, and the net change in welfare.

(2) Adapt Figure 2-1 to show how a fall in the world price of a camera affects an economy importing cameras. Identify the effects on the quantities produced, consumed, and imported, the changes in producer and consumer surplus, and the change in welfare.

(3) Use your answer to (2) to show that an import tariff can be used to prevent domestic production from changing in response to the fall in the world price of a camera. Identify the tariff rate and tariff revenue, the effects on quantities consumed and imported, and the effects on welfare, compared to conditions prevailing before and after the fall in price. Would you favor or oppose this policy? Explain.

(4) Adapt Figure 2-7 to show how an increase in the relative price of a camera affects an economy exporting cameras. Identify the effects on the quantities of cameras and grain produced and consumed, on the quantities exported and imported, and on welfare.

(5) Adapt Figure 2-9 to prove the statement in the text that countries with identical transformation curves can gain from trade if they have different indifference maps. Identify the quantities produced and consumed before and after the opening of trade, the quantities traded, and the effects on welfare in each country. Explain how your diagram illustrates the restatement of the law of comparative advantage, which says that beneficial trade will occur whenever two countries' relative prices would be different without trade.

(6) Figure 2-12 was said to represent the effects of a tariff on imported cameras, and Note 2-2 showed that the tariff rate is equal to $W'Z'/Z'V'$. Show that Figure 2-12 can be said to represent the effects of a tariff on exported grain equal to $V''V'/OV'$ and that this export tariff rate is equal to the import tariff rate.

(7) When describing the effects of an increase in the relative price of a camera, the text said that firms will produce more cameras and less grain. But firms that grow grain do not normally make cameras. Hence, it would be more accurate to say that firms growing grain will contract as their profits fall and firms making cameras will expand as their profits rise. To complete this story, explain how the behavior of investors could force firms producing grain to contract and allow firms making cameras to expand.

---

*See Appendix C for outlines of answers to the even-numbered questions.

3

Economic Efficiency and Comparative Advantage

THE ISSUES

Opportunities for international trade arise because supply and demand conditions differ from country to country. That was the main point made in Chapter 2. In that chapter, however, we focused on supply conditions, and we will continue to do so in this chapter and the next. These chapters study three issues:

- Why supply conditions differ from country to country, leading to price differences between countries.

- How they are reflected in the pattern of trade.

- How the trade pattern and terms of trade affect internal conditions in each country.

The model presented in this chapter concentrates on differences in technology as sources of differences in supply conditions. It is based on the example that David Ricardo used to prove the law of comparative advantage. The model developed in the next chapter concentrates on differences in factor supplies. It is an outgrowth of the model used by Eli Heckscher and Bertil Ohlin, two Swedish economists, to demonstrate the influence of factor endowments on international specialization.

SOURCES OF COMPARATIVE ADVANTAGE

The shape and position of a country's transformation curve depend on its factor supplies and the efficiency with which it uses them. In other words, they depend on its endowment of land, labor, and capital and on its technology.

Differences between endowments and technologies lead to predictable differences between transformation curves.

There are large differences in national endowments, reflecting the gifts of nature and the fruits of human effort. The gifts of nature are not distributed evenly. Some countries are rich in petroleum, coal, and iron ore. Some have huge waterfalls that can generate cheap power. Some have fertile plains that can grow great grain crops. Some have the rainfall needed to grow rice or cotton. Others have too much or next to none. Most important, some countries have the *combinations* of resources required for certain activities. One may have the plains *and* rainfall needed to grow grain. Another may have a rich deposit or iron ore close to a river that can carry it to coal. Finally, some countries have supplies of labor adequate to operate large factories, but others have too little to work their land efficiently.

In one sense, a country's labor force is a natural resource. In another, it reflects human ingenuity. Mere numbers are the gift of nature, but the skills and attitudes of workers reflect schooling and training, and they have large effects on comparative advantage. A country rich in people but poor in skills may be well suited to certain activities but not to producing manufactured goods. It is also important to distinguish among types of skills. Some countries have large numbers of factory workers adept at assembling cars, cameras, and calculators. Others have abundant supplies of scientists and engineers, and they can specialize in new, research-laden products. It has been argued, for example, that the United States enjoys a comparative advantage in research and innovation but loses out to other countries as each new product ages, the market for it grows, and the knowledge needed to produce it spreads to other countries. The *product cycle*, it is said, forces the United States to race ahead in research and innovation merely to stand still in world markets.

One part of a country's capital stock is embodied in its labor force. Scientific, industrial, and other skills represent investments in human capital. Another part of the capital stock is embodied in physical equipment: roads, harbors, and dams; trucks, aircraft, and ships; factories and office buildings; tractors, lathes, and computers. These represent the portion of past output that was saved and invested, rather than being consumed.

Natural resources and knowledge can interact powerfully. Bauxite was not valued as a natural resource until the development of the electrolytic process for extracting aluminum and of the cheap power required by that process. Aluminum itself was not very valuable until the metal-working industries found ways to use it instead of steel. Pitchblende was a geological curiosity until human ingenuity and malevolence found a use for uranium and ways to separate its isotopes.

Population and technology interact, too. Modern mass-production methods need large markets and are apt to take root first in regions of dense settlement that can consume large quantities of standardized products. As a consequence, such regions are likely to enjoy a comparative advantage in mass-produced goods and may be able to retain its vis-à-vis regions that start later or start on a smaller scale. Note that comparative advantage has a time dimension. It depends on the state of technology at a given moment and on the subsequent diffusion of technology. It also depends on the history of capital accumulation and the composition of the capital stock resulting from it.

For these same reasons, moreover, comparative advantage has a policy dimension, because governments influence levels of investment in human and physical capital. They make investments of their own in education, innovation, and transportation. They use the tax system and other policies to influence the volume and direction of investment by the private sector.

The models presented in this chapter and the next cannot capture all these important phenomena. In fact, they make drastic simplifications. The quantity of labor is assumed to be uniform within each country. Workers can move from industry to industry without retraining. Capital can be transferred, too, without the need to extract it from one embodiment and lodge it in another—without running down the stock of tractors and building up the stock of computers. In this initial presentation, moreover, labor and capital requirements are assumed to be fixed in each industry and country, although they differ between industries and may also differ between countries. These last assumptions are not relaxed until Chapter 5.

PRODUCTION AND TRADE IN THE RICARDIAN MODEL

Consider two countries, Britain and Portugal, producing two goods, cloth and wine. Each country has a fixed supply of labor. Each industry requires a fixed number of workers to produce one unit of output.[1] These requirements describe the state of technology in each country, and they are not the same in Britain and Portugal.

The British Economy

Britain has 180 workers. Three are needed to produce 1 yard of cloth per day. Six are needed to produce 1 gallon of wine. This is all we need to know to derive the British transformation curve. If all of Britain's workers were employed in cloth production, the country could produce 60 yards per day; this quantity is represented by the distance OB in Figure 3-1. If all those workers were employed in wine production, Britain could produce 30 gallons per day; this quantity is represented by the distance OB'. The line BB' is Britain's transformation curve.

Unlike the transformation curves in Chapter 2, this curve is a straight line. Its slope is given by the ratio of labor requirements in the cloth and wine industries, and labor requirements are constant. They do not depend on output. The relative price of cloth is given by the slope of the transformation curve and is thus equal to

---

[1]The Ricardian model is thus based on a labor theory of value, but Ricardo and other Classical economists used that theory only as an analytical convenience. It was not the centerpiece for Classical economics in the way that it was for Marxian economics. There is a role for capital in Classical economics, but it is complementary to the role of labor. Capital is used to hire labor (and buy raw materials) during the "period of production" before output emerges and can be sold. It constitutes a "wages fund" rather than a stock of machinery. When wage rates are the same in each industry, however, the wages fund is proportional to employment in each industry. Therefore, total costs, including the costs of capital, are proportional to labor costs. When working with the Ricardian model, then, we can focus exclusively on labor requirements. When working with the factor-endowments model, where capital plays a separate role in production, we have to take account of capital requirements as well.

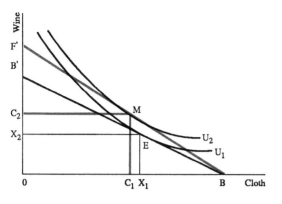

FIGURE 3-1
The British Economy
With a fixed supply of labor and fixed labor requirements in each sector, Britain's transformation curve is BB'. Before trade is opened, the relative price of cloth is given by the slope of the transformation curve, and equilibrium is established at E, where the indifference curve U_1 is tangent to the transformation curve. Britain produces and consumes OX_1 cloth and OX_2 wine. When trade is opened and the relative price of cloth is given by the slope of the line BF', Britain specializes completely in cloth production, producing OB. Consumers move to M on the higher indifference curve U_2, demanding OC_1 cloth and OC_2 wine. The trade triangle is C_1BM.

the ratio of labor requirements. When Britain produces both goods, then, the relative price of cloth is fixed. It does not depend on demand conditions. An algebraic demonstration of these propositions is supplied in Section 2 of Appendix A.

Here is a numerical illustration of the relationship between the relative price of cloth and the ratio of labor requirements. Under competitive conditions, prices equal total unit costs in long-run equilibrium. When labor is the only input, moreover, total unit costs must equal unit labor costs. Therefore,

$$\text{Price} = \text{wage rate} \times \text{labor required per unit of output,}$$

and

$$\frac{\text{Price of cloth}}{\text{Price of wine}} = \frac{\text{labor required per yard of cloth}}{\text{labor required per gallon of wine}}$$

$$= \frac{3}{6} = \frac{1}{2},$$

which corresponds to the slope of BB' in Figure 3-1, where OB' is half as long as OB.

Although demand conditions do not affect the relative price of cloth, they do affect the output mix. In the absence of foreign trade, equilibrium will be established at E, where an indifference curve is tangent to the British transformation curve. Cloth output will be OX_1 and will equal cloth consumption. Wine output will be OX_2 and will equal wine consumption.

Trade and the Offer Curve

If Britain confronts foreign prices different from domestic prices, it will specialize completely in one good and import the other. Let the slope of the line BF' be the relative price of cloth in the world market. Britain will abandon the production of wine, and all of Britain's workers will be hired to make cloth. Cloth output will rise to OB. When cloth is the only output, moreover, OB also measures real income in terms of cloth, and BF' is the budget line. British consumers will move to M, where BF' is tangent to a higher indifference curve. They will demand OC_1 cloth and OC_2 wine. Therefore, Britain's export offer will be BC_1 cloth (domestic output *less* domestic demand), and Britain's import demand will be OC_2 wine.

The same outcome is depicted in Figure 3-2, which shows the British offer curve. The linear segment AA' corresponds to the transformation curve BB' in Figure 3-1, having the same length and slope. The distance OA' is equal to the distance EB in Figure 3-1. It shows that British firms will increase cloth output from OX_1 to OB when the relative price of cloth exceeds by the slightest amount the slope of the transformation curve. The extension $A'J'$ reflects the behavior of British consumers as the relative price of cloth rises farther. Similarly, the distance OA is equal to the distance EB' in Figure 3-1, showing that British firms will increase wine output from OX_2 to OB' when the relative price of cloth falls below the slope of the transform-

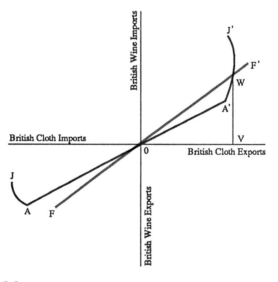

FIGURE 3-2
The British Offer Curve
The offer curve $JAOA'J'$ is derived from the transformation curve and indifference map shown in Figure 3-1. The segment AA' corresponds to the transformation curve BB'. The distance OA' equals EB in Figure 3-1, and the distance OA equals EB'. When the relative price of cloth is higher than that given by the slope of the segment AA', Britain will offer cloth exports and demand wine imports. When it equals the slope of FF' (the slope of BF' in Figure 3-1), Britain will offer OV cloth exports (equal to C_1B in Figure 3-1) in exchange for VW wine imports (equal to C_1M in Figure 3-1). The trade triangle OVW is thus identical to the trade triangle C_1BM in Figure 3-1.

ation curve. The extension AJ reflects the behavior of British consumers as the relative price of cloth continues to fall. When the relative price of cloth is equal to the slope of FF', Britain's export offer is OV cloth and its import demand is VW wine.

The Portuguese Economy

Portugal is smaller than Britain. It has only 120 workers. But Portuguese technology is more advanced. Two workers are required to produce 1 yard of cloth, compared with three in Britain. Three workers are required to produce 1 gallon of wine, compared with six in Britain. If Portugal employs all its workers in cloth production, its output will be 60 yards per day; this is the distance OP in Figure 3-3. If it employs all of them in wine production, its output will be 40 gallons per day; this is the distance OP'. The Portuguese transformation curve is PP' and is steeper than the British curve. Portugal has an *absolute* advantage in both wine and cloth production, because it has smaller labor requirements in both industries. It has a *comparative* advantage in wine production, however, because its absolute advantage is bigger in that industry.

In the absence of foreign trade, the Portuguese economy will be at E^*, producing OX_1^* of cloth and OX_2^* of wine. If trade is opened with the outside world and the relative price of cloth is given by the slope of FP' (equal to that of BF' in Figure 3-1), Portugal will specialize completely in wine, producing OP' gallons. Its export offer will be C_2^*P' wine, and its import demand will be OC_1^* cloth.[2] The linear segment of Portugal's offer curve will be steeper than that of Britain's offer curve, because its transformation curve is steeper.

Equilibrium in International Trade

In Chapter 1, you read a famous passage in which Adam Smith argued for free trade, but were warned that Smith's argument was not precise enough. Recall one sentence:

> If a foreign country can supply us with a commodity cheaper than we ourselves can make it, better buy it of them with some part of the produce of our own industry, employed in a way in which we have some advantage.

If the words "cheaper" and "advantage" are not qualified carefully, this sentence cannot forecast trade between Britain and Portugal. Wine is "cheaper" in Portugal than in Britain, because labor requirements are lower, but cloth is cheaper, too.

---

[2]Figures 3-1 and 3-3 have been drawn to illustrate two possibilities. In Figure 3-1, OC_1 is smaller than OX_1. The opening of trade reduces British cloth consumption. Accordingly, the British export offer, C_1B, is larger than the increase in cloth production, X_1B. In Figure 3-3, OC_2^* is larger than OX_2^*. The opening of trade raises Portuguese wine consumption, and the Portuguese export offer, C_2^*P', is smaller than the increase in wine production, X_2^*P'. British consumers demand more wine and less cloth as wine becomes cheaper in Britain, but Portuguese consumers demand more wine and more cloth as cloth becomes cheaper in Portugal. In both countries, however, consumers gain from trade by moving to higher indifference curves.

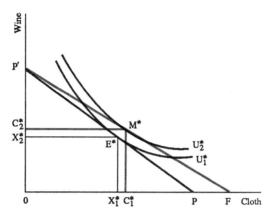

FIGURE 3-3
The Portuguese Economy
Portugal's transformation curve is PP'. Before trade is opened, the relative price of cloth is given by the slope of the transformation curve, and equilibrium is established at E^*. Portugal produces and consumes OX_1^* cloth and OX_2^* wine. When trade is opened and the relative price of cloth is given by the slope of the line FP' (equal to the slope of BF' in Figure 3-1), Portugal specializes completely in wine, producing OP'. Consumers move to M^*, demanding OC_1^* cloth and OC_2^* wine. The trade triangle is $C_2^* M^* P'$.

Britain does not have an outright "advantage" in wine or cloth production. If "cheaper" is used in the relative sense however, and "advantage" in the comparative sense, the passage tells us what we need to know. As wine is relatively cheap in Portugal and cloth relatively cheap in Britain, there can be gainful trade. Portugal can export wine, and Britain can export cloth.

In the Ricardian model, demand conditions do not affect internal prices before trade is opened. Prices are determined by labor requirements. Therefore, demand conditions cannot affect the trade pattern. But they do affect the terms of trade and thus the distribution of the gains from trade.

The British offer curve is flatter at its origin than the Portuguese offer curve. In consequence, the two curves must intersect in the northeast quadrant when they are put together in a single diagram. That quadrant is shown in Figure 3-4. The relevant portion of the British offer curve is OJ, and the relevant portion of the Portuguese offer curve is OJ^*.[3] Equilibrium in trade between Britain and Portugal is established at W. Britain exports OV cloth and imports VW wine. Portugal exports VW wine and imports OV cloth. The terms of trade are given by the slope of OF. Because each country lies on the curved portion of its offer curve, both countries gain from trade. Consumers reach indifference curves higher than those tangent to their countries' transformation curves.

There are two instances, however, in which one country's consumers can appropriate all the gains from trade.

---

[3]The portion OJ of the British curve is the portion shown as $OA'J'$ in Figure 3-2. The portion OJ^* of the Portuguese curve is the one that would lie in the southwest quandrant when drawn by itself, but it has been flipped over, as in Chapter 2, to measure matching trade flows on the same axes.

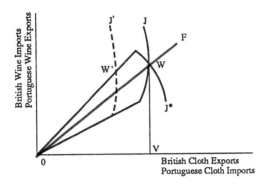

FIGURE 3-4
Trade Between Britain and Portugal
The curve *OJ* is the relevant portion of the British offer curve, taken from Figure 3-2.
The curve *OJ** is the relevant portion of the Portuguese offer curve, derived from
Figure 3-3 but flipped over to measure the same trade flows on the same axes.
Equilibrium is established at *W*, and the terms of trade are given by the slope of *OF*.
Britain exports *OV* cloth to Portugal in exchange for *VW* wine. If British tastes are
strongly biased toward cloth or Britain is much smaller than Portugal, the British offer
curve will be *OJ'*, and equilibrium will be established at *W'*.

(1) If British tastes are biased strongly in favor of cloth consumption, *E* will be
closer to *B* in Figure 3-1, and the segment *EB* will be shorter. Therefore, the linear
segment of the British offer curve will be shorter, too, causing the curve to look like
OJ' in Figure 3-4. Equilibrium in trade between Britain and Portugal will be
established at *W'*, and the terms of trade will be given by the slope of the Portugese
offer curve. Portugal will export wine and import cloth but will not specialize
completely in wine production; it will continue to produce some cloth because
Britain cannot produce enough to meet the entire Portugese demand as well as its
own large domestic demand. More important, trade will not reduce the relative price
of cloth in Portugal, and Portuguese consumers will remain on the same indifference
curve they reached before trade was opened. Market forces will still cause trade, but
Portuguese consumers will not gain or lose. British consumers will appropriate all
the gains from trade.

(2) If the British economy is much smaller than the Portuguese economy, Britain's
transformation curve will be shorter, and its offer curve will have a shorter linear
segment, just as it did in the previous case. Britain will specialize completely in
cloth production, but it will not produce enough to satisfy British and Portuguese
demands. Portugal will produce some cloth, and the relative price of cloth in the
world market will be what is was in Portugal before trade was opened. Once again,
British consumers will appropriate all the gains from trade.

This last result may puzzle you. A small country, you may say, will be relatively
weak. Why should its consumers be able to appropriate all the gains from trade? The
puzzlement derives from a common mistake—associating economic size with market
power. No one is exercising market power in this illustration. Both countries'
markets are perfectly competitive, and so are the sums of those markets. Govern-

ments do not attempt to influence quantities or prices. Therefore, a small country can appropriate large gains from trade. The merging of its markets with those of another country will not have much effect on the other country's prices, and it will have no effect at all if the small country is very small indeed.

Output Patterns in the Ricardian Model

Supply and demand conditions can generate three sets of outcomes in this simple Ricardian model. They are summarized by Figure 3-5, using a *global* transformation curve, PQB', built up from the national transformation curves. (The British curve is shown here as $P'QB'$. The Portuguese curve is shown as BPQ.) These are the three outcomes:

(1) When the terms of trade are given by the slope of FF' and thus lie between the prices that prevailed in Britain and Portugal before trade was opened, equilibrium will lie at Q. Britain will specialize completely in cloth, producing OB, and Portugal will specialize completely in wine, producing OP'. This outcome will prevail when

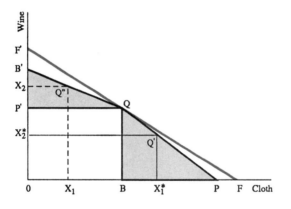

FIGURE 3-5
Demand Conditions and Specialization
When the terms of trade are given by the slope of *FF'*, which is steeper than the British transformation curve but flatter than the Portuguese, global output will be *Q*. Britain will specialize completely in cloth, producing *OB*, and Portugal will specialize completely in wine, producing *OP'*. When the terms of trade are given by the slope of *PQ*, which is equal to the slope of the Portuguese transformation curve, global output will be at some point such as *Q'*. Britain will specialize completely in cloth, producing *OB*, and Portugal will specialize partially in wine, producing OX_2^* wine and BX_1^* cloth. This will be the equilibrium point if the two countries' consumers demand OX_1^* cloth (equal to *OB* produced by Britain *plus* BX_1^* produced by Portugal) and demand OX_2^* wine (equal to the amount produced by Portugal). When the terms of trade are given by the slope of *QB'*, which is equal to the slope of the British transformation curve, global output will be at some point such as *Q''*. Britain will specialize partially in cloth, producing OX_1 cloth and $P'X_2$ wine, and Portugal will specialize completely in wine, producing *OP'*. This will be the equilibrium point if the two countries' consumers demand OX_1 cloth (equal to the amount produced by Britain), and OX_2 wine (equal to *OP'* produced by Portugal and $P'X_2$ produced by Britain).

the two countries' consumers demand OB cloth and OP' wine at the relative price of cloth given by the slope of FF'. Both countries' consumers will gain from trade.

(2) When the terms of trade are given by the slope of PQ, which is equal to the relative price of cloth that prevailed in Portugal before trade was opened, equilibrium will lie at some such point as Q'. Britain will specialize completely in cloth, producing OB, but Portugal will specialize partially, producing only OX_2^* wine in order to produce BX_1^* cloth. This outcome will prevail when the two countries' consumers demand OX_1^* cloth and OX_2^* wine at the relative price of cloth given by the slope of PQ. British consumers will appropriate all the gains from trade. Portuguese consumers will not gain or lose.

(3) When the terms of trade are given by the slope of QB', which is equal to the relative price of cloth that prevailed in Britain before trade was opened, equilibrium will lie at some such point as Q''. Britain will specialize partially, producing only OX_1 cloth in order to produce $P'X_2$ wine, and Portugal will special completely in wine, producing OP'. This outcome will prevail when the two countries' consumers demand OX_1 cloth and OX_2 wine at the relative price of cloth given by the slope of QB'. Portuguese consumers will appropriate all the gains from trade. British consumers will not gain or lose.

In all three cases, of course, Britain will export cloth and Portugal will export wine. The pattern of trade is determined completely by comparative costs, represented by the slopes of the countries' transformation curves. The pattern of production, however, is determined by demand and supply conditions jointly, because they determine the terms of trade. The distribution of the gains from trade is likewise affected by demand conditions, because of their influence on the terms of trade.

WAGES, PRICES, AND COMPARATIVE ADVANTAGE

British consumers do not examine comparative costs when deciding whether to buy British or Portuguese cloth. They look at the prices charged for the two countries' products. It is therefore important to show how market forces translate comparative costs into market prices. This is done algebraically in Section 2 of Appendix A and illustrated here by a numerical example.

Recall the statement made before, that prices have to equal unit labor costs in the Ricardian model. Therefore, we know each country's prices when we know its wage rate and its labor requirements per unit of output. Exchange rates must be used, however, to compare two countries' prices.

Suppose that the British wage rate is £1.50 per day and that the exchange rate between the pound and dollar is $2.00 per pound. The British wage rate works out at $3.00 per day. As three workers are required to produce 1 yard of cloth in Britain and six are required to produce 1 gallon of wine, these will be the dollar prices of British goods:

Price of British cloth	$ 9.00 per yard
Price of British wine	18.00 per gallon

Suppose that the Portuguese wage rate is E 150 per day and that the exchange rate between the escudo and dollar is $0.02 per escudo. The Portuguese wage rate also works out at $3.00 per day. As two workers are required to produce 1 yard of cloth in Portugal and three are required to produce 1 gallon of wine, these will be the dollar prices of Portuguese goods:

Price of Portuguese cloth	$6.00 per yard
Price of Portuguese wine	9.00 per gallon

If trade were opened at these wage rates and exchange rates, both products would be cheaper in Portugal than in Britain. Portugal's absolute advantage in cloth and wine would mask Britain's comparative advantage in cloth.

Under these circumstances, however, both counties' consumers would try to buy both cloth and wine in Portugal, increasing the demand for labor in Portugal and decreasing the demand for labor in Britain. The wage rate would rise in Portugal and fall in Britain. Suppose that the Portuguese wage rate were to rise to $3.75 per day when expressed in dollars while the British wage rate fell to $2.25 per day. The price of cloth in Portugal would rise to $7.50 per yard, the price in Britain would fall to $6.75, and both countries' consumers would start to buy British cloth. The price of wine in Portugal would rise to $11.25 per gallon, the price in Britain would fall to $13.50, and both countries' consumers would continue to buy Portuguese wine. The changes in the two countries' wage rates would allow market prices to reflect Britain's comparative advantage in cloth. They would offset Portugal's absolute advantage by charging a higher wage for more efficient Portuguese labor.

Changes in exchange rates can substitute for changes in wage rates. Suppose that wage rates are rigid in Britain and Portugal but that exchange rates fluctuate freely in response to changes in supply and demand. With the opening of trade at the initial exchange rates, the increase in demand for Portuguese goods will raise the demand for escudos, which are needed to pay for Portuguese goods. This will raise the dollar price of the escudo, which will raise the dollar value of the Portuguese wage. If the escudo rises to $0.025 per escudo, for example, the value of the Portuguese wage will rise to $3.75 per day, just as it did in the previous example. Furthermore, the decrease in demand for British goods will reduce the demand for pounds, which will reduce the dollar price of the pound and the dollar value of the British wage. If the pound falls to $1.50 per day, for example, the value of the British wage will fall to $2.25, just as it did before.[4]

We cannot know where wage rates will settle, however, without more information. The terms of trade between Britain and Portugal are determined by supply and demand conditions, and we need to know the terms of trade before we can know where wage rates will come to rest. When Britain produces cloth and Portugal

---

[4]This result has an important implication. Any judgment one might make about comparative wage rates is an implicit judgment about the exchange rates used to express the wage rates in a common currency. Judgments about exchange rates, however, should be made in a broad macroeconomic framework, which is therefore the *only* legitimate framework for making broad judgments about comparative wage rates.

produces wine, the terms of trade, wage rates, and labor requirements must satisfy this equation:

$$\frac{\text{Price of British cloth}}{\text{Price of Portuguese wine}} = \frac{\text{British labor requirement per yard}}{\text{Portuguese labor requirement per gallon}}$$
$$\times \frac{\text{British wage rate}}{\text{Portuguese wage rate}}.$$

We cannot know the wage-rate ratio without knowing the terms of trade and labor requirements per unit of output.

One general conclusion can be drawn without knowing more, and it is one of the most important points made by trade theory. Differences in wage rates usually reflect differences in productivity. Countries with low wage rates do not necessarily have an "unfair" advantage over their competitors. Low wage rates compensate for low productivity and are needed to translate comparative advantage into market prices. This point will crop up again when we look at a famous statistical test of the Ricardian model and at the "cheap foreign labor" argument for tariffs.

One other point deserves attention. The Ricardian model provides a neat relationship between the consumers' gains from trade and the real wage rate expressed in terms of the imported good. Consider the relationship from the British standpoint. When prices equal unit labor costs,

Price of cloth = British wage rate × labor requirement per yard in Britain.

Therefore, the real wage expressed in cloth is given by

$$\frac{\text{British wage rate}}{\text{Price of cloth}} = \frac{1}{\text{labor requirement per yard in Britain}}.$$

Hence, this real wage is one-third of a yard of cloth per day. Furthermore, it is not affected by the opening of trade, because cloth production continues in Britain, and labor requirements do not change. But the real wage expressed in wine is given by

$$\frac{\text{British wage rate}}{\text{Price of wine}} = \frac{\text{British wage rate}}{\text{price of cloth}} \times \frac{\text{price of cloth}}{\text{price of wine}}.$$

Therefore, this real wage will rise whenever the opening of trade raises the relative price of cloth in Britain, permitting British consumers to gain from trade. Looking at matters from the Portuguese standpoint, the opening of trade will not change the real wage expressed in wine but will raise the real wage in terms of cloth whenever it raises the relative price of wine in Portugal, permitting Portuguese consumers to gain from trade. (Coming at these propositions from the opposite direction, the opening of trade will not change the real wage in terms of *either* good if the country concerned does not specialize completely, so that its consumers do not gain or lose from trade.)

Tariffs and Real Wages

These relationships between the terms of trade and real wages tell us how a tariff will affect real wages. Suppose that Britain imposes a tariff on imported wine. The tariff will not affect the British real wage in terms of cloth, because it is given by the fixed amount of labor required to produce a yard of cloth. We have already seen, however, that a tariff tends to raise the relative price of the imported good. Therefore, it will reduce the British real wage in terms of wine by raising the relative price of wine in Britain. In Chapter 9, moreover, we will show that a British tariff on imported wine tends to raise the relative price of cloth in Portugal. (This is because it raises the relative price of wine in Britain, causing British consumers to substitute cloth for wine, and thus reduces the supply of cloth available for export from Britain to Portugal.) Therefore, the British tariff will reduce the Portuguese real wage in terms of cloth. By implication, a tariff on one country's import can reduce *both* countries' gains from trade.[5]

EXTENDING THE RICARDIAN MODEL

The Ricardian model is easily extended to cover many countries and goods if it is extended in one direction at a time.

Trade with Many Countries

Figure 3-6 extends the model to cover four countries producing wine and cloth. The four countries' transformation curves are identified by Roman numerals and are used to build a global transformation curve much like the one in Figure 3-5.

Suppose that the terms of trade are equal to the slope of FF'. Global output will be at Q, and all four countries will specialize completely. Countries I and II will specialize in cloth, and they will export cloth in exchange for wine. Countries III and IV will specialize in wine, and they will export wine in exchange for cloth. World markets will be in equilibrium if the four countries' consumers, taken together, demand OX_1 cloth and OX_2 wine. All four countries' consumers will gain from trade. The situation is perfectly analogous to the one at Q in Figure 3-5.

Suppose that the terms of trade are equal instead to the slope of country II's transformation curve. Global output will be at a point such as Q', and three countries will specialize completely. Country I will specialize in cloth and will therefore export cloth in exchange for wine. Countries III and IV will specialize in wine and will export wine in exchange for cloth. Country II, however, will produce both cloth and wine, and we cannot say anything about the direction of its trade. World markets will be in equilibrium if the four countries' consumers demand OX_1' cloth and OX_2' wine. Consumers in countries I, III, and IV will gain from trade, but

---

[5]In Chapter 9, however, we will show that a tariff can raise one country's gains from trade at the expense of the other's gains from trade.

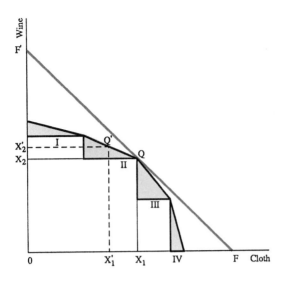

FIGURE 3-6
Trade with Two Goods and Several Countries
When the relative price of cloth is equal to the slope of FF', countries I and II specialize completely in cloth, and countries III and IV specialize completely in wine. Total cloth output is OX_1, and total wine output is OX_2. When the relative price of cloth is equal to the slope of country II's transformation curve, country I specializes completely in cloth, country II produces some cloth and some wine, and countries III and IV specialize completely in wine. Total cloth output is OX'_1, and total wine output is OX'_2.

those in country II will not gain or lose. The situation is closely analogous to the one at Q' in Figure 3-5, apart from the uncertainty about country II's trade.

Why is there uncertainty in one case and not the other? In the two-country case, one country had to export wine when the other imported it. As Britain had to import wine, because it specialized completely in cloth, we could be sure that Portugal exported wine, even when it did not specialize completely. In the four-country case, some country has to export wine when others import it, but this does not tell us what country II will do. Country I must import wine, and countries III and IV must export wine. Hence, there are three possibilities at Q' in Figure 3-6: (1) Supplies of wine from countries III and IV are equal to country I's demand, and country II does not trade at all. (2) Supplies from countries III and IV are smaller than country I's demand, so country II exports wine. (3) Supplies from countries III and IV are larger than country I's demand, so country II imports wine. Supply and demand conditions in the world as a whole, including those in country II, dictate the outcome for country II.

Trade with Many Goods

Figure 3-7 extends the Ricardian model to cover four goods produced by two countries, Britain and Portugal. It uses information about labor requirements

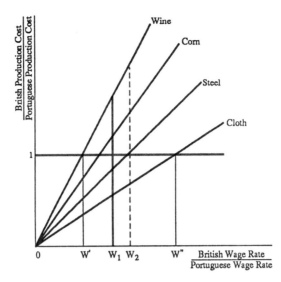

FIGURE 3-7
Trade with Two Countries and Several Goods
In equilibrium, the wage ratio can be no lower than *OW'* and no higher than *OW"*. If it were lower than *OW'*, the costs of producing all four goods would be lower in Britain than in Portugal; if it were higher than *OW"*, the costs of producing all four goods would be higher in Britain than in Portugal. When the wage ratio is OW_1, Britain produces cloth and steel, and Portugal produces corn and wine. When the ratio is OW_2, Britain produces cloth, Portugal produces corn and wine, and both countries produce steel.

to show how the costs of producing each good depend on relative wage rates. When labor is the only input, this statement must be true:

$$\frac{\text{British production cost}}{\text{Portuguese production cost}} = \frac{\text{labor requirement in Britain}}{\text{labor requirement in Portugal}} \times \frac{\text{British wage rate}}{\text{Portuguese wage rate}}.$$

Therefore, the ratio of production costs rises with the ratio of wage rates, but the amount by which it rises depends on the ratio of labor requirements.

To illustrate, assume that three workers are needed to produce 1 yard of cloth in Britain while two are needed to produce 1 yard in Portugal. The slope of the cloth line in Figure 3-7 is thus (3/2). It shows the amount by which an increase in the wage ratio raises the cost ratio. By making it the flattest line in Figure 3-7, we assume that the ratio of British to Portuguese labor requirements is lower in cloth production than in steel, corn, or wine production.

If the cost of producing a good is higher in Britain than in Portugal, Britain will not produce that good. Therefore, the horizontal line in Figure 3-7, denoting cost ratios equal to 1, plays a crucial role. Its intersections with the four goods lines define the pattern of production at each wage ratio.

Suppose that the wage ratio is equal to *OW'*. The costs of producing wine are equal in Britain and Portugal, but the costs of producing corn, steel, and cloth are lower in Britain. Therefore, Britain will produce all four goods, and Portugal will specialize completely in wine. By implication, Portugal must export wine in exchange for corn, steel, and cloth, and Britain must import wine, although it produces some wine of its own.

Going to the opposite extreme, suppose that the wage ratio is equal to OW''. The costs of producing cloth are equal in Britain and Portugal, but the costs of producing steel, corn, and wine are higher in Britain. Therefore, Britain will specialize completely in cloth, and Portugal will produce all four goods. By implication, Britain must export cloth in exchange for steel, corn, and wine, and Portugal must import cloth although it produces some cloth of its own.

When equilibrium occurs at one of these extremes, there are no ambiguities. The pattern of production is clear. So is the trade pattern. Outcomes are equally clear at certain other points. If the wage ratio equals OW_1, the costs of producing cloth and steel are lower in Britain than in Portugal, and those of producing corn and wine are lower in Portugal. Therefore, Britain will specialize completely in cloth and steel, and Portugal will specialize completely in corn and wine. Britain will export cloth and steel in exchange for corn and wine.

At certain other points, however, the trade pattern is ambiguous. If the wage ratio equals OW_2, the cost of producing cloth is lower in Britain, the costs of producing corn and wine are lower in Portugal, and the costs of producing steel are the same in the two countries. The pattern of production is clear. Britain will produce cloth and steel; Portugal will produce steel, corn, and wine. Some trade flows are equally clear. Britain will export cloth; Portugal will export corn and wine. But we cannot know which country will export steel. If Britain is large compared to Portugal, it may be able to satisfy both countries' demand for cloth and its own demand for steel, yet have enough labor to export steel to Portugal. If Portugal is large compared to Britain, it may be able to satisfy both countries' demands for wine and cloth and its own demand for steel, yet have enough labor to export steel to Britain.

When there are more goods than countries, there can be uncertainty about the trade pattern, even when the pattern of production is clear. The problem is similar to that encountered when there are more countries than goods. When output is at Q' in Figure 3-6, we do not know which product country II will export. When the wage ratio is OW_2 in Figure 3-7, we do not know which country will export steel. When there are many countries or goods, it is possible to forecast some trade flows, but comprehensive information on supply and demand conditions is required to forecast others.

AN EMPIRICAL TEST OF THE RICARDIAN MODEL

Economic models can never be completely realistic. If they were not simpler than the real world, they could not help us to cut through complexities and organize our thinking. The Ricardian model is far too simple to describe precisely the causes and effects of international trade. The main statements made by the model, however, highlight important relationships, and some of them are verifiable. They can be used to forecast actual trade flows, despite the existence of tariffs and other trade barriers.

Table 3-1. Output per Worker and Comparative Export Performance, Great Britain and the United States, 1950

Difference in Output per Worker	Number of Industries		
	Total	U.S. Exports Smaller than British	U.S. Exports Larger than British
U.S. output per worker less than 3.4 times British	26	22	4
U.S. output per worker at least 3.4 times British	13	3	10
Total	39	25	14

Source: Adapted from Robert M. Stern, "British and American Productivity and Comparative Costs in International Trade," *Oxford Economic Papers,* 14 (October 1962).

One test of the Ricardian model was conducted by Robert M. Stern, and his work is summarized in Table 3-1. The table looks at the exports of Great Britain and the United States in 1950, a year for which we have detailed data on productivity (labor requirements) in both countries' industries. It concentrates on British and American exports to third countries, to avoid distortions introduced by differences in British and American trade barriers.[6]

In 1950, output per worker was much higher in the United States than in Great Britain. In other words, labor requirements were much lower. This was true in almost every industry, conferring an absolute advantage on the United States. But wage rates in the United States were about 3.4 times as high as those in Great Britain, washing out that absolute advantage and allowing each country to exploit its comparative advantage.

To show that this was true, we can use the wage differences between the two countries to classify the 39 industries included in Stern's study. In 26 industries, output per worker in the United States was less than 3.4 times as high as in Great Britain. In light of what we have just learned from Figure 3-7, we should expect Great Britain to have its comparative advantage in those industries. In 13 other industries, output per worker in the United States was at least 3.4 times as high as in Great Britain, and we should expect the United States to have its comparative advantage in them. These predictions are borne out in Table 3-1. In 22 of the first 26 cases, British exports were larger than American exports. In 10 of the other 13 cases, American exports were larger.

---

[6]British exports to the United States are affected by American trade barriers, and American exports to Britain are affected by British barriers. Therefore, the two countries' *bilateral* trade is distorted by the differences between their trade barriers. British and American exports to France are both affected by French trade barriers, but the effects on the two countries' exports are more or less uniform. This was not completely true in 1950, when European countries discriminated against goods from the United States to conserve scarce dollars, and members of the British Commonwealth gave preferential treatment to British exports. It would not be true today, because Britain and France are members of the European Community, whose members accept each others' exports freely.

These uniformities are striking. The number of exceptions, seven in all, is smaller than one might anticipate, knowing that tariffs and other trade barriers distort trade flows, that each of the 39 industries contains many firms producing distinct commodities, and that differences in productivity are not the only cause of trade.

SUMMARY

In the Ricardian trade model, cross-country differences in relative prices are due to differences in labor requirements. One country may use less labor in all its industries. Its *absolute advantage* in efficiency, however, does not prevent it from trading beneficially with other, less efficient countries. It will have a *comparative advantage* in those activities where its absolute advantage is largest.

As labor requirements are constant in the Ricardian model, labor costs are constant, too. Therefore, demand conditions do not determine the trade pattern in the two-country, two-good case. They do help to determine the terms of trade, however, and thus influence the distribution of the gains from trade. If one country's tastes are strongly biased toward the other's export good (or if one country is much larger than the other), it will not specialize completely, and the other country will appropriate all the gains from trade.

When there are many countries or commodities, moreover, demand and supply conditions work jointly to determine the pattern of production in each country and, therefore, the commodity composition of each country's trade.

Money wage rates are determined in the process of transforming absolute into comparative advantage. A country with low labor requirements in all its industries will have a higher money wage than a country with high labor requirements, given the exchange rate between their currencies. Therefore, a country with low wages need not enjoy an "unfair" advantage in trade; low wages usually reflect low productivity. Empirical work on the Ricardian model confirms the model's predictions concerning the effects of cross-country differences in productivity and wage rates on the composition of trade.

Real wage rates are determined by the pattern of production and the terms of trade. When two countries specialize completely, trade does not affect each country's real wage in terms of its own export good, but it raises the real wage in terms of the country's import good. Accordingly, a tariff tends to reduce the gains from trade by raising the price of the import good and thus lowering the real wage expressed in terms of the import good.

RECOMMENDED READINGS

The model developed in this chapter is based on the example in David Ricardo, *On the Principal of Political Economy and Taxation*, 1821, ch. vii; the definitive version is in P. Sraffa, ed., *The Works and Correspondence of David Ricardo* (New York: Cambridge University Press, 1953), Vol. I. The contributions of Ricardo and other Classical economists are reviewed in Jacob Viner, *Studies in the Theory of International Trade* (New York: Harper & Row, 1937), ch. viii.

For an early attempt to extend the Ricardian model to many countries and goods, see Frank D. Graham, "The Theory of International Values Re-examined," *Quarterly Journal of Economics*, 28 (November 1928); reprinted in American Economic Association, *Readings in the Theory of International Trade* (Philadelphia: Blakiston, 1949), ch. 14. Another way of extending the model to many goods is given in Rudiger Dornbusch, Stanley Fischer, and Paul A. Samuelson, "Comparative Advantage, Trade, and Payments in a Ricardian Model with a Continuum of Goods," *American Economic Review*, 67 (December 1977).

For empirical work on the Ricardian model, see Robert M. Stern, "British and American Productivity and Comparative Costs in International Trade," *Oxford Economic Papers*, 14 (October 1962). Also G. D. A. MacDougall, "British and American Exports: A Study Suggested by the Theory of Comparative Costs," *Economic Journal*, 61 (December 1951); reprinted in American Economic Association, *Readings in International Economics* (Homewood, Ill.: Richard D. Irwin, 1968), ch. 32.

QUESTIONS AND PROBLEMS

(1) "As the government can affect comparative advantage by subsidizing firms to invest in raising productivity, the gains from trade are artificial. Hence, no one should object when the government uses tariffs instead to protect those firms from foreign competition." Comment.

(2) "In the Ricardian model, the opening of trade raises the real wage in terms of the import good without reducing it in terms of the export good, so workers should favor trade. But workers facing import competition usually oppose trade, so something is wrong with the model." Comment.

(3) Using the following numbers for France and Germany and for grain and steel, develop a world transformation curve for those two countries:

		Workers Needed to Produce		
Country	Number of Workers	Bushel of Grain	Ton of Steel	Pair of Shoes
France	100	2	5	4
Germany	160	4	10	6
Italy	60	5	20	1

Which country will export steel? Let the wage rate be $10 in both France and Germany before trade is opened and suppose that the German wage is fixed. What must happen to the French wage for both countries to specialize completely after trade is opened?

(4) Using the numbers in (3) for Germany and Italy and for steel and shoes, calculate the relative price of steel in each country before trade is opened and each country's real wage in terms of steel and in terms of shoes. Let the relative price of steel be 4 pairs of shoes per ton of steel after trade is opened. What will happen to each country's real wage in terms of steel and in terms of shoes?

(5) Using the numbers in (3) for France, Germany, and Italy and for grain and shoes,

draw a world transformation curve for the three countries. Then list all of the possible trade patterns and the relative prices of grain at which they will prevail.

(6) Using the numbers in (3) for Germany and Italy and for grain, steel, and shoes, identify the lowest and highest wage ratios (German wage divided by Italian wage) at which trade can occur. What will each country produce at those ratios? If the wage ratio is 1.25, what will each country produce? What can you say about the trade pattern at each wage ratio?

4

Factor Endowments and Comparative Advantage

THE ISSUES

The Ricardian model presented in Chapter 3 served several important purposes. It provided an explanation for international differences in supply conditions, traced the roles of supply and demand conditions in determining trade patterns and distributing the gains from trade, and focused on the wage-price adjustments needed to achieve equilibrium in international markets. But it shed less light on other important issues, and we need another model to study them:

- How differences in factor endowments contribute to differences in supply conditions.
- How these differences are reflected in factor and product prices.
- How trade affects factor prices and the income distribution.

The model presented in this chapter was developed by Eli Heckscher and Bertil Ohlin in the 1920s and was refined by many economists, including Paul Samuelson. To focus on the influence of factor supplies, it assumes that all countries have the same technologies, suppressing the differences in labor requirements that were the main cause of trade in the Ricardian model. It rules out some other causes, too. The version we will study, for example, rules out the influence of country size by assuming that there are no economies of scale, and it rules out the influence of demand conditions by assuming that consumers have identical tastes.

THE HECKSCHER-OHLIN THEOREM

The Heckscher–Ohlin approach to trade theory, also known as the factor-endowments approach, is based on two suppositions:

1.   Goods differ in their factor requirements. Cars require more capital per worker than, say, furniture or cloth, and aircraft require more than cars. In other words, goods can be ranked by *factor intensity*.

2.   Countries differ in their factor endowments. Some have much capital per worker and some have very little. In other words, countries can be ranked by *factor abundance*.

These two suppositions lead to the fundamental theorem of the Heckscher–Ohlin model. A capital-abundant country will tend to specialize in capital-intensive goods and will therefore export those goods in exchange for labor-intensive goods. This will relieve its relative scarcity of labor. Putting the theorem in general terms:

Trade is based on differences in factor abundance and reduces the principal effects of those differences.

There are two ways to prove the Heckscher–Ohlin theorem. We can show that differences in factor endowments lead to differences in transformation curves. This first strategy produces the *factor-proportions version* of the Heckscher–Ohlin theorem. Alternatively, we can show that differences in factor prices lead to differences in goods prices. This second strategy produces the *relative-price version* of the theorem. Under certain strong assumptions, moreover, it leads to another proposition: Trade eliminates differences in factor prices. Both strategies are illustrated in this chapter.

There are several variants of the Heckscher–Ohlin model. The version studied in this chapter borrows an assumption used by the Ricardian model. It works with fixed factor requirements per unit of output. The version to be studied in Chapter 6 relaxes that assumption. Factor requirements will depend on factor prices.

FACTOR ENDOWMENTS, PRODUCTION, AND TRADE IN THE HECKSCHER–OHLIN MODEL

In the Ricardian model, the shape of the transformation curve depended on labor requirements and on the supply of labor. In the Heckscher–Ohlin model, its shape depends on labor and capital requirements, taken together, and on the supplies of labor and capital.

Factor Endowments and the Transformation Curve

If a country had an unlimited supply of capital, its outputs would depend on labor requirements and on the supply of labor, just as in the Ricardian model. The country would operate on its *labor constraint*, represented by the line LL' in Figure 4-1, which looks like a Ricardian transformation curve. By using all its labor to grow corn, the country could produce OL bushels. By using all its labor to make steel, it could produce OL' tons. By dividing its labor between the two activities, it could produce combinations of corn and steel lying on LL'. At each

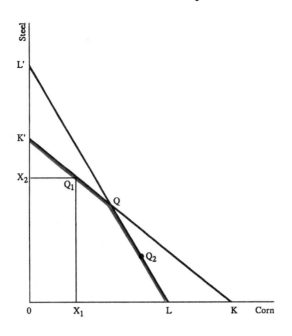

FIGURE 4-1
Factor Supplies, Factor Requirements, and Output
The supply of labor and labor requirements locate the labor constraint *LL'*. The supply of capital and capital requirements locate the capital constraint *KK'*. The two constraints define the transformation curve *LQK'*, and the full-employment output point is *Q*. If the country produces at Q_1, the relative price of corn will be given by the slope of *KK'*, and some labor will be unemployed. If it produces at Q_2, the relative price of corn is given by the slope of *LL'*, and some capital will be unemployed.

point on *LL'*, moreover, the relative price of corn would be given by the slope of the labor constraint, which equals the ratio of labor requirements in the two activities.

If the country had an unlimited supply of labor, its outputs would depend on capital requirements and on the supply of capital. It would operate on the line *KK'*, the country's *capital constraint*. By using all its capital to grow corn, it could produce *OK* bushels. By using all its capital to make steel, it could produce *OK'* tons. By dividing its capital between the two activities, it could produce combinations of corn and steel lying on *KK'*. At each point on *KK'*, the relative price of corn would be given by the slope of the capital constraint, which equals the ratio of capital requirements.

When the supplies of labor and capital are both limited, the labor and capital constraints operate together to define a country's transformation curve. It is *L QK'* in Figure 4-1 which is obtained by asking what the country can produce with limited supplies of labor and capital. Suppose that it produces OX_1 bushels of corn. Because its supply of capital is limited, its steel output is limited to OX_2 tons.

Three output points are shown in Figure 4-1. At the one just mentioned, Q_1, outputs are determined by the capital constraint, and the relative price of corn is given by the slope of that constraint. The economy is using all its capital, but some of its labor is unemployed. At Q_2, by contrast, outputs are determined by the labor constraint, and the relative price of corn is given by the slope of that constraint. The country is using all its labor, but some of its capital is unemployed. Finally, there is Q, where LL' and KK' intersect, and outputs are determined by both constraints together. The country is using all its labor and all its capital, and Q can therefore be described as the *full-employment output point*. The relative price of corn at Q is given by demand conditions. When the country produces and consumes at that point, an indifference curve passes through it, and the relative price of corn is equal to the slope of that indifference curve.

Note that the labor constraint is steeper than the capital constraint. This says that steel is the capital-intensive good and corn the labor-intensive good. Proof is provided in Section 3 of Appendix A, but a simple experiment can make the point clearly. Let the country start at Q, where both factors of production are fully employed. Suppose that it raises its corn output. It will move to some such point as Q_2, lying on the labor constraint, where labor is fully employed, but capital is not. The increase in corn output has absorbed the labor released by the decrease in steel output, but it has not absorbed all the capital released. By implication, steel uses more capital per worker than corn, and steel is the capital-intensive good.

The Rybczynski Theorem

What happens with an increase in the supply of capital? The answer is given by Figure 4-2. The capital constraint shifts outward from KK' to $K^*K^{*'}$, and the transformation curve becomes $LQ^*K^{*'}$. The full-employment output point moves from Q to Q^*, so steel output rises and corn output falls.

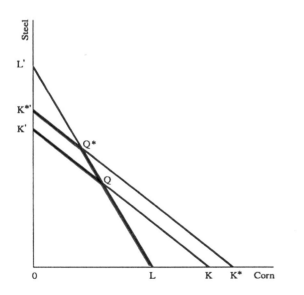

FIGURE 4-2
The Rybczynski Theorem
An increase in the supply of capital shifts the transformation curve from LQK' to $LQ^*K^{*'}$ and shifts the full-employment point from Q to Q^*. As steel is more capital intensive than corn, the full-employment output of steel rises and the full-employment output of corn falls.

The outcome is known as the Rybczynski theorem, after the economist who discovered it, and can be stated this way:

> **When factor supplies are fully employed and factor requirements are given, an increase in the supply of one factor of production raises the output of the good uses that factor intensively and reduces the output of the other good.**

This theorem is basic to the functioning of the Heckscher–Ohlin model. We will use it shortly to show how international differences in factor endowments determine the trade pattern. We will use it again in Chapter 6 to show how changes in factor endowments affect the terms of trade.

A formal proof of the Rybczynski theorem is given in Section 3 of Appendix A. Another illustration is given in Figure 4-3, which shows explicitly how factor supplies and factor requirements determine the location of the full-employment output point. The slope of the line OC measures the *capital-labor ratio* in corn production, and distances along the line measure corn output. The slope of the line OS measures the capital-labor ratio in steel production, and distances along the line measure steel output. As steel is the capital-intensive good, OS is steeper than OC.

Suppose that the country has $O\bar{L}$ labor and $O\bar{K}$ capital. Its factor endowment is defined by the point N. If it produces nothing but corn, the labor-intensive good, it can grow OC_1 bushels; it uses all its labor and $\bar{L}C_1$ of its capital, so C_1N of its

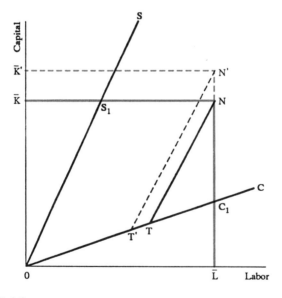

FIGURE 4-3
Factor Supplies, Factor Requirements, and the Output Mix
Distances along OC measure corn output, and its slope measures the capital-labor ratio in corn production. Distances along OS measure steel output, and its slope measures the capital-labor ratio in steel production. A country with $O\bar{L}$ labor and $O\bar{K}$ capital can produce as much as OC_1 corn, but C_1N of its capital will be idle. It can produce as much as OS_1 steel, but S_1N of its labor will be idle. It can produce combinations of corn and steel, however, and one such combination employs both factors fully. It is OT corn and NT steel. An increase in the supply of capital to $O\bar{K}'$ raises the full-employment output of steel to $N'T'$ and reduces the full-employment output of corn to OT'.

capital is idle. If it produces nothing but steel, the capital-intensive good, it can make OS_1 tons. It uses all its capital and $\bar{K}S_1$ of its labor, so S_1N of its labor is idle. There is just one way that it can use its factor endowment fully. Draw a line NT parallel to OS until it intersects OC at T. This line can be used to measure steel output, along with the quantities of labor and capital used in making steel. At T, then, the country produces NT steel and OT corn. These are the amounts that were shown at Q, the full-employment output point in Figures 4-1 and 4-2.

Increase the supply of capital to $O\bar{K}'$, holding the supply of labor constant. The new factor endowment is given by N', and the full-employment outputs of steel and corn are given by T'. The country can produce $N'T'$ steel, which is more than NT, and can produce OT' corn, which is less than OT. Therefore, the increase in the supply of capital raises the full-employment output of steel, the capital-intensive good, and reduces the full-employment output of corn, the labor-intensive good.

The Factor-Proportions Version of the Heckscher–Ohlin Theorem

To see how a difference in factor endowments leads to international trade, consider two countries, Manymen and Fewmen, described by Figure 4-4. The two countries have identical demand conditions, represented by the set of indifference curves. They have the same technologies, which means that the slopes of the labor and capital constraints will be the same in the two countries. They differ only in their factor endowments. Manymen has a large labor force and small stock of capital. Fewmen has a small labor force and large stock of capital.

The Rybczynski theorem tells us how their transformation curves will differ. The curve for Manymen is LQK. The curve for Fewmen is $L^*Q^*K^*$. When labor and capital are fully employed in each country, at Q and Q^*, Manymen produces more corn than Fewmen, because corn is the labor-intensive good, and Fewmen produces more steel than Manymen, because steel is the capital-intensive good.[1]

Before trade is opened between the two countries, Manymen produces at its full-employment point Q, putting its consumers on U_0, the highest indifference curve they can reach. Fewmen produces at E^*, on its labor constraint, putting its consumers on that same indifference curve.[2] The relative price of corn in each country is given by the slope of the indifference curve at the country's output point. But U_0 is flatter at Q than at E^*, so the relative price of corn, the labor-intensive good, is lower in Manymen, the labor-abundant country. This creates the opportunity for trade.

After trade is opened, the relative price of corn must be the same in Manymen

---

[1] The two countries' transformation curves can be derived by supposing that they start with the same factor supplies, then increasing the supply of labor in Manymen and the supply of capital in Fewmen. Suppose that they start with factor supplies that give them the transformation curve L^*ZK. An increase in the supply of labor shifts the labor constraint from L^*Z to LQ, giving the transformation curve for Manymen. An increase in the supply of capital shifts the capital constraint from KZ to K^*Q^*, giving the transformation curve for Fewmen.

[2] It is possible to draw U_0 in a way that would put Fewmen at its full-employment point and is likewise possible to draw it in a way that would put Manymen on its capital constraint. The case shown in Figure 4-4 was chosen to cover two possibilities at once. (The two countries need not start on the same indifference curve; this solution was chosen for convenience, as in Chapter 2.)

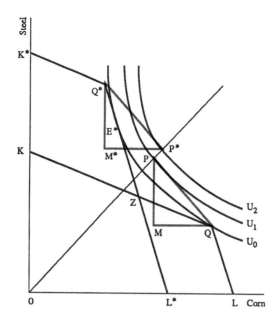

FIGURE 4-4

Trade Between Manymen and Fewmen

Before trade is opened, Manymen is at the full-employment point Q on its transformation curve LQK. The relative price of corn is given by the slope of the indifference
curve U_0 where it intersects Q. Fewmen is at the labor-constrained point E^* on its
transformation curve $L^*Q^*K^*$. The relative price of corn is given by the slope of the
indifference curve U_0 where it intersects E^*. As U_0 is flatter at Q than at E^*, the relative
price of corn is lower in Manymen than Fewmen. When trade is opened, the relative
price of corn is given by the slopes of the parallel lines QP and P^*Q^*. In Manymen,
producers stay at Q, and consumers move to P on the indifference curve U_1.
Manymen's trade triangle is MQP. In Fewmen, producers move to the full-employment point Q^*, increasing steel output and reducing corn output, and consumers
move to P^* on the indifference curve U_2. Fewmen's trade triangle is $M^*P^*Q^*$.

and Fewmen. It is given by the slopes of the (parallel) lines QP and P^*Q^* connecting
the countries' production and consumption points and forming their trade triangles.
The relative price of corn must rise in Manymen and fall in Fewmen. In Manymen,
production remains at Q, but consumers move to P on the higher indifference curve
U_1. In Fewmen, production moves to Q^*, and consumers move to P^* on the higher
indifference curve U_2. Manymen exports MQ corn, the labor-intensive good.
Fewmen exports M^*Q^* steel, the capital-intensive good.

Note that both countries wind up at their full-employment output points. This
diagram, then, illustrates two possibilities. Outputs do not change in Manymen,
which started and remains at Q. In other words, its gains from trade are gains from
international exchange. But outputs change in Fewmen as it moves from E^* to Q^*,
increasing its steel production and decreasing its corn production. Its gains from
trade include gains from international specialization.

We have thus proved the factor-proportions version of the Heckscher–Ohlin
theorem, linking the trade pattern to factor endowments. The labor-abundant
country always exports the labor-intensive good, and increases its production of that
good if it did not start at its full-employment point. The capital-abundant country

always exports the capital-intensive good, and increases its production of that good if it did start at its full-employment point. (In the more general version of the model presented in Chapter 6, the labor-abundant country will always increase its production of the labor-intensive good, and the capital-abundant country will always increase its production of the capital-intensive good.)

FACTOR PRICES, GOODS PRICES, AND TRADE IN THE HECKSCHER–OHLIN MODEL

There is a strong relationship between goods prices and factor prices in the Heckscher–Ohlin model. An increase in the relative price of the labor-intensive good raises the relative price of labor, defined as the wage of labor divided by the return to capital.

Factor Use and Factor Prices

Look back at Figure 4-1, where labor and capital constraints were used to derive the transformation curve. At a point such as Q_1 on the capital constraint, some of the country's labor is unemployed. In the absence of institutional arrangements that keep wage rates from falling (union contracts, for example, or minimum-wage laws), the wage rate must be zero. Therefore, the relative price of labor must be zero. At a point such as Q_2 on the labor constraint, some of the country's capital is unemployed, and the return to capital must be zero. Therefore, the relative price of labor must be infinite. At the point Q, however, both factors are fully employed, the wage rate and return to capital are both positive, and the relative price of labor must be positive, too.

At points such as Q_1, moreover, the relative price of corn is given by the slope of the capital constraint, and it is not lower at any other point on the transformation curve. At points such as Q_2, the price is given by the slope of the labor constraint, and it is not higher at any other point. At Q, of course, the relative price of corn must lie between the two extremes.

These results are summarized in Figure 4-5. The horizontal axis shows the relative price of corn, and the vertical axis shows the relative price of labor. The distance OP' is the relative price of corn when Q_1 is the output point in Figure 4-1 and that price can go no lower. The curve in the diagram says that the relative price of labor is zero at that point, because some of the country's labor is unemployed and the wage rate must be zero. The distance OP'' is the relative price of corn when Q_2 is the output point in Figure 4-1 and that price can go no higher. The curve says that the relative price of labor tends to infinity at that point, because some of the country's capital is unemployed and the return to capital must be zero. The curve itself makes an additional statement. The relative price of labor rises with the relative price of corn, because corn is the labor-intensive good.

An algebraic proof of this proposition is given in Section 3 of Appendix A, which also shows that the relationship in Figure 4-5 holds in both countries when Manymen and Fewmen have the same technologies. They have different transformation curves, because they have different factor endowments. But both of them will

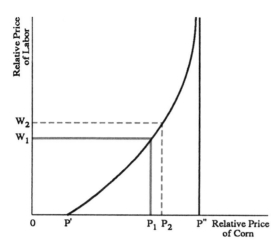

FIGURE 4-5
Factor Prices and Goods Prices
When the relative price of corn is given by the slope of the capital constraint, shown here by the distance *OP'*, some labor is unemployed, the wage rate is zero, and the relative price of labor is zero. When the relative price of corn is given by the slope of the labor constraint, shown here by the distance *OP"*, some capital is unemployed, the return to capital is zero, and the relative price of labor is infinite. When the relative price of corn lies between these extremes, the relative price of labor is positive and rises with the relative price of corn. When the relative price of corn rises from *OP_1* to *OP_2*, the relative price of labor rises from *OW_1* to *OW_2*.

have idle workers (wage rates will be zero) when the relative price of corn is equal to the slope of the capital constraint, and both of them will have idle capital (the return to capital will be zero) when the relative price of corn is equal to the slope of the labor constraint. Furthermore, the curves connecting those two outcomes will be the same in both countries, because they have the same factor requirements.

Figure 4-5 has three uses. It can be used to prove the relative-price version of the Heckscher–Ohlin theorem, to show how trade affects the income distribution in each country, and to show when trade will equalize the two countries' factor prices.

The Relative-Price Version of the Heckscher–Ohlin Theorem

Before the opening of trade, the relative price of corn must be lower in Manymen than in Fewmen. That was true in Figure 4-4, where Manymen began at Q and Fewmen began at E^*. It is also true when both countries start at their full-employment points. Therefore, the curve in Figure 4-5 tells us that the relative price of labor had to be lower in Manymen before trade was opened, which leads us directly to the relative-price version of the Heckscher–Ohlin theorem. If the relative price of labor is lower in one country before trade is opened, the relative price of the labor-intensive good must likewise be lower, and the country will export the labor-intensive good.

The Stolper–Samuelson Theorem

The effects of trade on factor prices and the income distribution are described by the Stolper–Samuelson theorem, named after the two economists who proved it. It can be put this way:

The opening of trade raises the relative price of labor in the labor-abundant country and reduces it in the capital-abundant country.

By implication, trade will raise the *share* of labor in the national income of the labor-abundant country and reduce the share of capital. It will have the opposite effect on the income distribution in the capital-abundant country.

The proof of the theorem is simple. We have already seen that trade raises the relative price of corn in the labor-abundant country. But an increase in the relative price of corn raises the relative price of labor, the factor used intensively in growing corn. Therefore, trade raises the relative price of labor in the labor-abundant country.

The basic economics behind the theorem are equally simple. An increase in the relative price of corn encourages corn production and discourages steel production. But corn is labor intensive, so the resulting increase of corn production raises the demand for labor by more than the decrease of steel production reduces it. This drives up the wage rate. At the same time, the decrease of steel production reduces the demand for capital by more than the increase of corn production raises it. This drives down the return to capital.

The Stolper–Samuelson theorem can be put in stronger form. The increase in the relative price of corn that occurs in the labor-abundant country raises the *real* wage of labor and reduces the *real* return to capital. The decrease that occurs in the capital-abundant country reduces the *real* wage and raises the *real* return to capital. These assertions hold, moreover, for both definitions of the real wage, in terms of corn or steel, and of the real return to capital. This strong form of the theorem is proved in Section 3 of Appendix A.

The Stolper–Samuelson theorem can be rephrased to focus on the basic role of trade in the factor-endowments model. The opening of trade reduces the effects of differences in factor endowments. Labor is abundant in Manymen and scarce in Fewmen, a fact reflected by the countries' factor prices before trade is opened. The relative price of labor is lower in Manymen than Fewmen. By raising the relative price of labor in Manymen and reducing it in Fewmen, trade compensates for the effects of the difference between the two countries' factor endowments. It relieves the relative shortage of labor in Fewmen and relieves the relative shortage of capital in Manymen.

The Stolper–Samuelson theorem can be used to deal with two special cases—the effects of perfectly free trade and the effects of a tariff.

The Factor-Price-Equalization Theorem

The factor-price-equalization theorem carries the Stolper–Samuelson theorem to its logical limit. If there were no trade barriers or transport costs, trade would *equalize* the trading countries' factor prices, not merely reduce the difference between them. It would therefore compensate completely for the effects of the difference in factor endowments.

If there were no trade barriers or transport costs, trade would equalize completely the relative prices of corn in Manymen and Fewmen. That is what it did in Figure 4-4. When the countries have the same technologies, moreover, they will share the relationship described by Figure 4-5, connecting the relative prices of corn and labor. Therefore, trade will equalize completely the relative prices of labor in Manymen and Fewmen. If the relative prices of corn were equalized at OP_1 in Figure 4-5, the relative prices of labor would be equalized at OW_1.

The factor-price-equalization can be extended in the same way as the Stolper–Samuelson theorem. By equalizing the relative prices of labor in Manymen and Fewmen, perfectly free trade will also equalize the two countries' real wage rates and their real returns to capital. This strong form of the theorem is proved in Section 3 of Appendix A and is taken up again in Chapter 6.

Tariffs and Factor Prices

By starting from the case of perfectly free trade, it is easy to show how a tariff affects factor prices in the factor-endowments model. Suppose that Fewmen imposes a tariff on corn imports. We have already said that an import tariff will tend to raise the domestic price of the imported good in the importing country and to reduce it in the exporting country. Starting at the free-trade point in Figure 4-5, then, the relative price of corn will rise from OP_1 to OP_2 in Fewmen, raising the relative wage of labor from OW_1 to OW_2. It will therefore raise the real wage and reduce the real return to capital. It will have the opposite effects in Manymen.

A tariff can thus influence the income distribution, but it does so by interfering with the fundamental role of trade in the factor-endowments model. Because it drives a wedge between the two countries' product prices, a tariff likewise drives a wedge between their factor prices, and trade can no longer compensate completely for the effects of the difference in their factor endowments.

EXTENDING THE HECKSCHER–OHLIN MODEL

The Heckscher–Ohlin model can be extended by adding more countries, more goods, and more factors of production. When we move in one direction at a time, however, we run into difficulties.

Adding Countries

When we add a third country by itself, the pattern of trade becomes ambiguous, much as it did when we extended the Ricardian model. The country with the largest stock of capital per worker will export the capital-intensive good, and the country with the smallest stock per worker will export the labor-intensive good. But we cannot predict the trade of the third country without detailed information about supply and demand conditions. All three countries will produce at their full-employment points; the pattern of production is unambiguous. The third country's trade, however, can go either way.

Adding Goods

When we add a third good by itself, the pattern of production becomes ambiguous. Consider again a country that has $O\bar{L}$ labor and $O\bar{K}$ capital. When there are two goods, corn and steel, the country can employ its factors fully by producing at T in Figure 4-6, where it grows OT corn and makes NT steel. When it can manufacture blankets, too, and the capital intensity of that activity is given by the slope of the line OB, it has other ways to use its factors fully. It can produce at T', where it manufactures OT' blankets and makes NT' steel. It can also produce more complicated combinations. Draw a line HH' parallel to OB. The country can produce OH corn, HH' blankets, and NH' steel. When the number of goods exceeds the number of factors, we cannot predict production in each country. And when we do not know the pattern of production, we cannot predict the pattern of trade.

It is still possible, however, to make useful statements about the factor content of a country's trade. It can be shown, for example, that Manymen's exports are more labor intensive *on average* than Fewmen's exports. It can likewise be shown that trade has the usual effects on factor prices. The relative price of labor rises in Manymen and falls in Fewmen, and free trade can still equalize the two countries' factor prices.

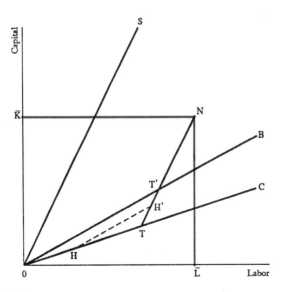

FIGURE 4-6
Factor Supplies, Factor Requirements, and the Output Mix When Goods Outnumber Factors
A country with $O\bar{L}$ labor and $O\bar{K}$ capital can employ both factors fully by producing OT corn and NT steel. It can also do so by producing OT' blankets and NT' steel. And it can do so by producing OH corn, HH' blankets, and NH' steel.

Adding Factors

When we add a third factor by itself, the Heckscher–Ohlin model tends to break down. The number of goods is too small to determine the prices of the factors of production. It is therefore impossible to identify an abundant factor in each country, to forecast the trade pattern, or to forecast the effects of trade on factor prices and the income distribution.

Another Approach

The Heckscher–Ohlin model can be extended neatly to more complicated cases by adding countries, goods, and factors of production at the same time, but only in a way that satisfies a special condition. The number of countries must equal the number of goods, which must equal the number of factors. (The two-country, two-good, two-factor model is, of course, the smallest model that can satisfy this condition.) In models that are "even" in this sense, each country will have a full-employment point at which it produces a collection of goods uniquely linked to its factor endowment. Factors prices will differ from country to country before trade is opened, and trade will have predictable effects on factor prices.

But it is hard to make simple statements about these large models. When there are many factors of production, it is hard to say that one factor is "the" abundant factor in a particular country. It is also hard to say that a particular good is intensive in one factor. The detailed study of these models may be more interesting to mathematicians than to economists.

EMPIRICAL WORK ON THE HECKSCHER–OHLIN MODEL

The first and most famous quantitative study of the Heckscher–Ohlin model was conducted by Wassily Leontief, using trade data and factor requirements for the United States. Some of his results are shown in Table 4-1, along with results obtained by Robert Baldwin, who worked with later data.

The Leontief Paradox

Leontief computed the amounts of capital and labor required to produce $1 million of U.S. exports in 1951 and those required to produce $1 million of import-competing goods. Believing that the United States is a capital-abundant country and invoking the Heckscher–Ohlin theorem, Leontief expected to show that U.S. export production is more capital intensive than U.S. import-competing production. That is not what he found. The capital-labor ratio was about $13,000 per worker year in export production and about $13,700 per worker year in import-competing production. His numbers therefore say that a $1 million increase in U.S. exports balanced by an increase in U.S. imports (and, therefore, a cutback in import-competing production) would reduce the demand for capital by about

Table 4-1. Capital and Labor Requirements of Export and Import-Competing Production in the United States, 1951 and 1962

Computation	Requirements Per Million Dollars of Production		Capital per Worker ($ thousands)
	Capital ($ thousands)	Labor (worker years)	
Trade in 1951 and input requirements for 1947 (Leontief):			
Export production	2,257	174	12.97
Import-competing production	2,303	168	13.71
Effect on factor use of			
balanced increase in trade	−46	+6	—
Trade in 1962 and input requirements for 1958 (Baldwin):			
Export production	1,876	131	14.32
Import-competing production	2,132	119	17.92
Effect on factor use of			
balanced increase in trade	−256	+12	—

Sources: Adapted from Wassily W. Leontief, "Factor Proportions and the Structure of American Trade: Further Theoretical and Empirical Analysis," *Review of Economics and Statistics*, 38 (November 1956), and Robert E. Baldwin, "Determinants of the Commodity Structure of U.S. Trade," *American Economic Review*, 61 (March 1971).

$46,000 and raise the demand for labor by about 6 worker years. Baldwin's calculations lead to similar results.[3]

Many efforts have been made to resolve this paradox, and they have helped us to understand the strengths and weaknesses of the Heckscher–Ohlin model. Some concentrated on the underlying logic of the model, with particular attention to the possibility of *demand reversals* and *factor reversals* that can upset the principal predictions of the model. Others concentrated on the limitations of the two-factor framework, and they sought ways of introducing additional factors of production into empirical and theoretical work.

Demand Reversal and Factor Reversals

What is a demand reversal and how might it explain the Leontief paradox? Suppose that the United States had more capital per worker than its trading partners, the supposition with which Leontief began, but that tastes in the United

---

[3]Using data for 1972, however, another study comes up with rather different findings. The capital-labor ratio is higher in export production, and a balanced increase in U.S. trade raises the demands for capital *and* labor. See Robert M. Stern and Keith E. Maskus, "Determinants of the Structure of U.S. Foreign Trade, 1958–76," *Journal of International Economics*, 11 (May 1981).

States were more strongly biased in favor of capital-intensive goods. In the absence of international trade, the relative price of labor might be lower, not higher, than in other countries, and the United States would then export labor-intensive goods with the opening of trade. It was this possibility that led economists to distinguish carefully between definitions of factor abundance in terms of factor supplies and in terms of relative factor prices, the distinction that produced the two versions of the Heckscher–Ohlin theorem. (Those versions coincided in the case of Manymen and Fewmen, because they had identical demand conditions.)

Demand reversals, however, are not likely to explain the Leontief paradox. Evidence about demand conditions suggests that they are similar in the major industrial countries, which account for the largest part of world trade. If there were important differences, moreover, they would probably reflect differences in income levels, which cannot explain the paradox. Consumers with high incomes tend to demand large quantities of services, and services tend to be labor intensive. We would therefore expect demand conditions in the United States, a high-income country, to raise the relative price of labor rather than reduce it.

A factor reversal is a difference between countries' rankings of goods according to factor requirements. There would be a factor reversal if steel were more capital intensive than corn in the United States, but corn were more capital intensive than steel in other countries. If the United States exported corn and other countries exported steel, and we looked at the factor requirements of U.S. foreign trade, we would find that its export production was less capital intensive than its import-competing production. When we looked at the factor requirements of other countries' trade, however, we would find that their export production was also less capital intensive than their import-competing production. These findings would not resolve the Leontief paradox, but they would warn us against drawing general conclusions from calculations based on one country's data, which is what Leontief tried to do.

Factor reversals do occur, although their frequency is subject to dispute, and they need not be due to differences in technology. In Chapter 6, we will examine the general version of the Heckscher–Ohlin model, where requirements depend on factor prices, and we will see that factor reversals can occur even when countries have access to the same technologies. As a practical matter, however, factor reversals do not appear to account for the Leontief paradox. In fact, the one reversal that has been well documented makes the paradox even more paradoxical. The United States does export corn, along with other agricultural commodities, but agriculture is capital intensive in the United States and labor intensive in other countries.[4] By removing agricultural commodities from the trade calculations, then, we would reduce even further the capital intensity of U.S. export production.

Natural Resources, Skills, and Human Capital

Soon after the publication of Leontief's work, two economists suggested explanations of his paradox that have one theme in common. The two-factor form of the Heckscher–Ohlin model, using only capital and labor, is not sufficiently realistic.

---

[4]Seiji Naya, "Natural Resources, Factor Mix, and Factor Reversal in International Trade," *American Economic Review*, 57 (May 1967).

Jaroslav Vanek called attention to the role of nonagricultural land, represented by the roles of raw materials in U.S. foreign trade.[5] As minerals bulk large on the import side, import-competing production may be regarded as being more intensive in *non*agricultural land than is export production. Vanek went on to argue that capital and land are *complementary* in the production of raw materials, especially in the United States, so that the apparent capital intensity of import-competing production shown by Leontief's calculations may actually reflect the land intensity of that production.

Donald Keesing showed that it may be misleading to treat labor as a single factor of production. When we subdivide the U.S. labor force by skill, we find that export production is more skill intensive in the United States than import-competing production.[5] It may therefore be best to think of the United States as a skill-abundant country. Alternatively, we may treat skills as investments in human capital, estimate the amounts of human capital employed in export production and import-competing production, and add these estimates of human capital to Leontief's estimates of physical capital. This procedure reverses the paradox. Export production in the United States turns out to be more capital intensive than import-competing production.[7]

Both points have been pursued in more recent investigations. Table 4-2 summarizes one such study, which looks at the ability of factor requirements to explain an

Table 4-2. Factor Requirements and the Structure of U.S. Trade

Factor Requirement	Effect on Export Measure
Physical capital in dollars	Negative
Human capital in dollars	Positive
Labor in worker years	Negative

Source: Adapted from William H. Branson and Nikolaos Monoyios, "Factor Inputs in U.S. Trade," *Journal of International Economics*, 7 (May, 1977). Export measure is difference between exports and imports.

---

[5]Jaroslav Vanek, "The Natural Resource Content of Foreign Trade, 1870–1955, and the Relative Abundance of Natural Resources in the United States," *Review of Economics and Statistics*, 41 (May 1959).

[6]Donald B. Keesing, "Labor Skills and Comparative Advantage," *American Economic Review*, 56 (May 1966). Keesing also drew attention to the great intensity with which U.S. export industries employ scientific skills, thus linking the notion of skill intensity to the notion mentioned in Chapter 3 that the United States has enjoyed a comparative advantage in research-intensive products; see Donald B. Keesing, "The Impact of Research and Development on United States Trade," in P. B. Kenen and R. Lawrence, eds., *The Open Economy* (New York: Columbia University Press, 1968).

[7]Peter B. Kenen, "Nature, Capital and Trade," *Journal of Political Economy*, 73 (October 1965); reprinted in P. B. Kenen, *Essays in International Economics* (Princeton, N.J.: Princeton University Press, 1980).

export measure for each class of goods. (The export measure is the difference between exports and imports in that class.) Physical capital and raw labor are found to have negative effects on the export measure; industries intensive in these factors appear mainly on the import side rather than the export side. Human capital is found to have a positive effect; industries intensive in that factor appear mainly on the export side. This particular study, then, does not resolve the Leontief paradox. It tends instead to ratify Keesing's suggestion that the United States is abundantly endowed with skills or human capital.

Table 4-3 summarizes another study covering some 60 countries, which looks at the ability of factor endowments to explain cross-country differences in a similar export measure. Instead of asking how factor requirements affect the roles of various goods in U.S. foreign trade, it asks how various countries' factor endowments affect those countries' roles in various types of trade.

This study does not show clearly the influence of skills. Large endowments of professional and technical workers appear to contribute positively to a country's comparative advantage in temperate-zone agricultural commodities but negatively to its comparative advantage in three types of manufactured goods. Large supplies of literate workers appear to contribute negatively to comparative advantage in labor-intensive and capital-intensive manufactures, but negatively to comparative advantage in chemicals (which, like machinery, are not especially capital or labor intensive). The results *are* strongly consistent with Vanek's emphasis on the importance of natural resources. Comparative advantage in raw materials is positively associated within minerals production (standing for a country's raw-materials endowment) and negatively associated with capital and labor endowments. Comparative advantage in agricultural commodities is positively associated with large endowments of tropical and temperate-zone land, and the latter, in turn, are negatively associated with comparative advantage in most sorts of manufactures (because countries well endowed with land will tend to export agricultural goods and import manufactures).

The last word is not in. There is need for more work on trade theory itself and for new approaches to verification.

SUMMARY

In the Heckscher–Ohlin model, cross-country differences in relative prices are due to differences in factor endowments, which become the basic cause of trade. The factor-proportions version of the *Heckscher–Ohlin theorem* says that a country with much capital per worker will export capital-intensive goods, whereas a country with little capital per worker will export labor-intensive goods. The relative-price version of the theorem says that a country where the wage rate is high relative to the return on capital will export capital-intensive goods, while a country where the wage rate is relatively low will export labor-intensive goods.

Three other theorems can be extracted from the Heckscher–Ohlin model: The *Rybczynski theorem* describes the relationship between a country's factor endowment and its output mix at its full-employment point. An increase in the supply of one

Table 4-3. Factor Endowments and the Structure of World Trade

| | Effect on Export Measure | | | | | | |
| | | Agricultural Products | | Manufactured Products | | | |
National Endowment	Raw Materials	Tropical	Temperate Zone	Labor Intensive	Capital Intensive	Machinery	Chemicals
Capital	Negative	Negative	Negative	None	Positive	Positive	Positive
Professional and technical labor	None	None	Positive	Negative	Negative	Negative	None
Nonprofessional labor:							
Literate	Negative	None	Negative	Positive	Positive	None	Negative
Illiterate	None	None	None	None	Positive	None	None
Tropical land	None	Positive	Positive	None	None	None	Negative
Temperate-zone land	None	Positive	Positive	None	Negative	Negative	Negative
Minerals production	Positive	None	None	None	None	None	None

Source: Adapted from Edward E. Leamer, *Sources of International Comparative Advantage* (Cambridge, Mass.: MIT Press, 1986), Table 6.6 (1975 data). List of factors omits coal and oil production (which are not included in minerals production) and dry land; list of goods omits oil (which is not included in raw materials trade), forest products, and animal products, and it combines two categories of temperate-zone land (which is shown here as having a significant effect when either category has one); export measure is difference between exports and imports. (Effects are shown as "none" when *t*-statistics are lower than 2.0 in the original table.)

factor raises the country's output of the good intensive in that factor and reduces its output of the other good. The *Stolper–Samuelson theorem* describes the effect of trade on a country's factor prices. Trade raises the relative price of labor in the labor-abundant country and reduces the relative price of labor in the capital-abundant country. (It also raises the real wage and reduces the real return to capital in the labor-abundant country, and it has the opposite effects in the capital-abundant country.) The *factor-price-equalization theorem* carries these results to their logical limit. When there are no trade barriers or transport costs, trade will equalize completely the real earnings of the factors of production.

The Stolper–Samuelson theorem can also be used to predict the effects of a tariff. By raising the relative price of the imported good, it will raise the relative and real returns to the scarce factor of production and reduce the returns to the abundant factor of production.

The Heckscher–Ohlin model can be extended to cover many countries, goods, and factors. When this is done in one direction at a time, however, it is hard to make clear statements about outputs and trade flows or the influence of trade on factor prices. When we add a third country, the trade pattern is ambiguous. When we add a third good, production and trade patterns are both ambiguous. When we add a third factor, the model tends to break down because there are too few goods to determine factor prices. These difficulties do not arise when we add countries, goods, and factors simultaneously but maintain "evenness" among the numbers. It is not easy to interpret the conclusions, however, because the notions of factor abundance and factor intensity lose their simplicity.

Empirical work on the Heckscher–Ohlin model has produced surprises. Early work by Leontief suggested that the United States is a labor-abundant country rather than a capital-abundant country; its export production is more labor intensive than its import-competing production. This paradox is not adequately explained by demand reversals or factor reversals. It is perhaps explained by the omission of natural resources and of skills or human capital from Leontief's calculations.

RECOMMENDED READINGS

Many important contributions to the literature on the Heckscher–Ohlin model relate to the general version developed in Chapter 6, and some of them are listed at the end of that chapter. Here are some readings that do not relate specifically to that version and some that deal with quantitative work:

Most of the basic results in this chapter were stated or anticipated by Eli Heckscher and Bertil Ohlin; their contributions, newly translated, appear with an excellent introduction in Harry Flam and M. June Flanders, eds., *Heckscher–Ohlin Trade Theory* (Cambridge, Mass.: MIT Press, 1991).

The Leontief paradox was first reported in Wassily Leontief, "Domestic Production and Foreign Trade: The American Capital Position Reexamined," *Economia Internazionale*, 7 (February 1954), reprinted in American Economic Association, *Readings in International Economics* (Homewood, Ill.: Richard D. Irwin, 1968), ch. 30. (The paper cited in the source note to Table 4-1 contains revised calculations.)

Attempts to explain the Leontief paradox are surveyed in two papers, which also present important empirical work. See Robert E. Baldwin, "Determinants of the Commodity Structure of U.S. Trade," *American Economic Review*, 61 (March 1971), and "Determinants of Trade and Foreign Investment: Further Evidence," *Review of Economics and Statistics*, 61 (February 1979).

For more recent empirical work on U.S. foreign trade, see Robert M. Stern and Keith E. Maskus, "Determinants of the Structure of U.S. Foreign Trade, 1958–76," *Journal of International Economics*, 11 (May 1981), and Edward E. Leamer, *Sources of International Comparative Advantage* (Cambridge, Mass.: MIT Press, 1986).

QUESTIONS AND PROBLEMS

(1) When demand conditions are the same in all countries, the Rybczynski and Stolper–Samuelson theorems can be used to prove the Heckscher–Ohlin theorem. Explain. Why must demand conditions be the same?

(2) Sweden has 400 workers and 600 machines. Italy has 400 workers and 400 machines. Factor requirements per unit of output are fixed as follows:

	Workers	Machines
Ball bearings	4	10
Shoes	6	5

Calculate each country's full-employment output combination. Suppose that demand conditions are the same in both countries and that free trade leaves them at their full-employment output points. Which country will export shoes? Illustrate your answer using transformation curves and trade triangles.

(3) Working with the countries and numbers in (2), suppose that the Italian labor force grows but that Sweden and Italy remain at their full-employment output points after adjusting to the new situation. What will happen to Italy's terms of trade? What will happen to the relative and real wage in Italy? In Sweden? Use transformation curves to show the effect on Italian output.

(4) Modify the diagram you drew to answer (2) to show how a difference in demand conditions could reverse the trade pattern.

(5) Figure 4-6 illustrated two output possibilities involving the production of two goods—corn and steel at *T*, and blankets and steel at *T'*. Both outcomes used all of the country's labor and capital. There is one more such possibility. Illustrate it.

(6) With free trade between two countries, both countries can produce at their full-employment output points, or one can produce at its full-employment output point and the other at a different point on its transformation curve. But both countries cannot produce at points different from their full-employment output points. Explain.

(7) Labor and capital are the only factors of production. A $1 million increase in a country's exports raises its demand for labor by 10 workers per year and its demand for capital by $2.5 million. A $1 million increase in imports, matched by a reduction in import-competing production, reduces the country's demand for labor by 6 workers per year and its demand for capital by $3.0 million. What conclusions would you draw about the country's factor endowment? What assumptions must you make to draw those conclusions?

(8) Use the numbers in (7) to determine the annual wage and rate of return to capital in the country.

5

Factor Substitution and a Modified Ricardian Model

INTRODUCTION

Consumers gain from trade whenever supply conditions differ systematically from country to country. We have examined two trade models designed to account for those differences. The differences arise in the Ricardian model because technologies differ across countries. They arise in the Heckscher–Ohlin model because factor endowments differ across countries. The models are too simple to explain trade patterns fully but help us organize our thinking. Furthermore, the main hypotheses drawn from the models are partly verified by quantitative studies.

In the Ricardian and Heckscher–Ohlin models, trade affects the domestic economy profoundly. It alters the composition of output, the ways that factors of production are distributed across activities, and the real earnings of those factors. The effects on real earnings and the income distribution call for close attention, because they help us understand why governments adopt trade policies that appear to ignore the teachings of trade theory.

This chapter and the next look more closely at the domestic effects of trade by relaxing the assumption used in Chapters 3 and 4, where factor requirements were fixed. That assumption influenced the shapes of transformation curves and the ways that trade affected outputs and earnings. In the Ricardian model, the transformation curve was a straight line, and one trading country had to specialize completely. In the Heckscher–Ohlin model, the transformation curve had two straight-line segments and a single full-employment point, and a country starting at that point did not specialize at all.

This chapter introduces *factor substitution* into the Ricardian model by making factor requirements depend on factor prices. An increase in the relative price of labor, for example, leads employers to substitute capital for labor—to adopt more capital-intensive methods of production. The slope of the transformation curve changes with the output mix, and the effects of trade on outputs, earnings, and the income distribution differ from those in the simple Ricardian model.

86

The next chapter introduces factor substitution into the Heckscher–Ohlin model. Once again, the slope of the transformation curve changes with the output mix, and each point becomes a full-employment point. The effects of trade on real earnings do not differ greatly from those predicted by the simple Heckscher–Ohlin model, but the new version of the model is more realistic. Factor prices never fall to zero, and the Rybczynski theorem holds at every output point.

THE ISSUES

After introducing the techniques needed to allow for factor substitution, this chapter will study three issues:

- How trade affects the allocation of the factors of production and their real earnings.

- How tariffs modify the effects on real earnings and who might therefore favor tariffs.

- How economic growth affects production, the trade pattern, and the terms of trade.

We begin with the effects of factor prices on producers' behavior.

FACTOR PRICES AND FACTOR SUBSTITUTION

The Ricardian model was unrealistic in many ways, but one assumption should have bothered you more than the rest. Wine and cloth were made by labor—nothing else. Yet wine cannot be made without grapes, and grapes cannot be grown without land. Furthermore, cloth can be made in cottages, small shops, or factories, but cannot be woven without looms. We need to introduce more factors of production.

Production with Specific Factors

Suppose that Britain has a fixed supply of labor, as before, but has other factors, too. It has a fixed supply of land that is used to grow grapes for making wine. It has a fixed supply of capital that is invested in looms and other machines used for weaving cloth.[1] Labor is used by both industries and is perfectly mobile

---

[1]These assumptions take us only part way to reality. Yarn is needed to make cloth, cotton to make yarn, and land to grow cotton. Furthermore, there must be an industry somewhere in the world that produces the machines used to make cloth. The need to grow cotton could be met by supposing that there is a fixed supply of land that can be used for this purpose but not for growing grapes, and it would not be hard to include an additional industry to produce machines. When we move in this direction, however, new issues arise. What would happen if land could be used to grow cotton or grapes? What would happen if Britain could import cotton rather than grow its own? Advanced trade theory deals with these issues—the definition of comparative advantage and determination of the terms of trade in models that include "intermediate" goods.

between them. Land and capital are *specific factors*. Land is used only to make wine; capital is used only to make cloth; and the supply of each specific factor is fixed. A firm in the cloth industry may be able to bid machines away from other firms in that industry, just as firms can bid labor away from other firms, but it cannot bid them away from firms in the wine industry, because they are not used there.

If the production of a gallon of wine were to require a fixed quantity of land and the production of a yard of cloth were to require a fixed quantity of capital, outputs would be fixed completely. Britain's transformation curve would degenerate into a single point. It would show the quantity of wine that could be made with the quantity of land available and the fixed requirement per gallon of wine, and the quantity of cloth that could be made with the quantity of capital available and the fixed requirement per yard of cloth.[2]

This chapter, however, adopts a different supposition, which is used in most of economic theory. There are many ways for firms to combine the various factors of production. If labor is cheap relative to land, a winery will use a large quantity of labor per acre of land. If labor becomes more expensive, the winery will substitute land for labor and use less labor per acre of land. The factor intensity of each activity depends on the prices of the factors of production used in that activity.

Marginal Products and Employment

The implications of this supposition are shown in Figure 5-1, which describes the determination of employment in the wine industry. The curve MP_W measures the *marginal product* of labor in the wine industry. This is the additional wine output, measured in gallons, produced by employing an additional worker but holding all other things constant. The size of the marginal product of labor depends on the fixed quantity of land available and on the variable quantity of labor already employed by the industry. The marginal product of labor falls as employment rises in the wine industry. When employment rises from OL_1 to OL'_1, for example the marginal product of labor falls from OV to OV' gallons.

Strictly speaking, the marginal product of labor depends on the land-labor ratio of the wine industry. The larger the quantity of land per worker, the higher the marginal product of labor and the lower the marginal product of land.[3] This particular formulation is known as the *law of variable proportions*. It derives from an assumption made in Chapter 3 and carried over to this chapter. Returns to scale are constant in each industry. If land and labor inputs could be doubled, output would double, too, and the marginal products of labor and land would not change. When the labor input is doubled but the land input is kept constant, wine output rises but

---

[2]This statement assumes that Britain has enough labor to satisfy the needs of its wine and cloth industries. Suppose that 1 acre of land is required to make 1 gallon of wine, along with 6 workers, and that Britain has 20 acres. It can produce 20 gallons of wine but needs 120 workers to do so. Suppose that 2 machines are required to make 1 yard of cloth, along with 3 workers, and that Britain has 60 machines. It can produce 30 yards of cloth but needs 90 workers to do so. To use all its land and capital, then, Britain must have at least 210 workers.

[3]The marginal product of land is well defined conceptually even when the quantity of land is fixed. It is the increase in wine output that could be obtained if it were possible to increase the quantity of land, holding the quantity of labor constant.

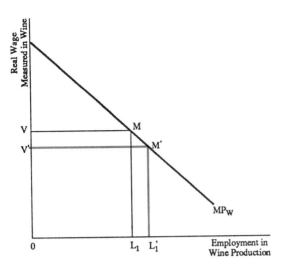

FIGURE 5-1
Demand for Labor in the Wine Industry
The MP_W curve depicts the marginal product of labor in the wine industry. The marginal product falls as employment rises. When employment is OL_1 workers, the marginal product of labor is OV gallons; when employment rises to OL'_1 workers, the marginal product falls to OV' gallons. The MP_W curve is also the demand curve for labor by the wine industry. When the real wage measured in wine is OV gallons, the demand for labor is OL_1 workers.

does not double. Furthermore, the marginal product of labor falls, and the marginal product of land rises. The changes in marginal products result from the fall in the land-labor ratio.

How much labor will the wine industry employ? A profit-maximizing firm will hire workers up to the point at which the marginal product of labor is equal to the real wage measured in terms of the firm's own output. This is shown algebraically in Section 4 of Appendix A, and the logic of the argument is easy to illustrate numerically.

Suppose that the wage rate is $4 per worker, that the marginal product of labor is 3 gallons of wine when the firm employs 10 workers, and that the price of wine is $2 per gallon. By employing one more worker, the firm can earn $6 of additional revenue; it can produce 3 more gallons of wine and sell them for $2 each. It can thus raise its profits by $2, because it has to pay only $4 for an additional worker. Therefore, the firm will hire an eleventh worker. When it does that, however, it reduces its land-labor ratio, and the marginal product of labor falls to 2 gallons. If it were to hire a twelfth worker, then, it could earn only $4 of additional revenue, and it could not raise its profits, as it would have to pay $4 for the worker. Hence, it has no incentive to hire a twelfth worker. In brief, the firm will hire labor up to the point at which

$$\text{Wage rate} = \text{price of wine} \times \text{marginal product of labor,}$$

or

$$\frac{\text{Wage rate}}{\text{Price of wine}} = \text{marginal product of labor.}$$

Returning to Figure 5-1, let the real wage measured in wine be OV gallons. The wine industry will then hire OL_1 workers.

When we know how much labor and land the wine industry uses, we know its output. Furthermore, we know the marginal product of land, which gives us the real rental rate for land measured in gallons of wine. If the marginal product of land were higher than the real rental rate, each firm in the industry would try to acquire more land. But the supply of land is fixed. Therefore, its rental rate would rise as firms bid against each other, and the real rental rate would not stop rising until it was equal to the marginal product of land.

Equilibrium in the Labor Market

To determine wine and cloth outputs together, the two industries' demand curves for labor must be put together in a single diagram to find the real wage at which the labor market will be in equilibrium. The real wage determines employment in each industry and, therefore, the output of each industry.

This exercise is illustrated in Figure 5-2. Employment is measured on the horizontal axis, as before, and the total quantity of labor in Britain is fixed at $O\bar{L}$. The real wage is measured on the vertical axis, but using yards of cloth rather than gallons of wine.

The curve E_C is the demand curve for labor in the cloth industry. It is the marginal-product curve for labor in the cloth industry, given the quantity of capital

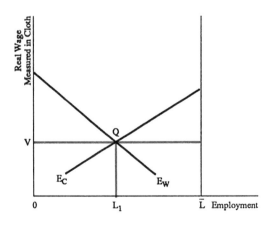

FIGURE 5-2
Equilibrium in the British Labor Market
The supply of workers is fixed at $O\bar{L}$. The E_C curve describes the demand for labor in the cloth industry. It shows the marginal product of labor in that industry measured in cloth. The E_W curve describes the demand for labor in the wine industry. It shows the marginal product of labor in that industry divided by the relative price of cloth and thus shows the marginal product measured in cloth. When labor is perfectly mobile within Britain, both industries must pay the same real wage. Therefore, the labor market is in equilibrium when OV is the real wage. The wine industry demands OL_1 workers; the cloth industry demands $\bar{L}L_1$ workers; the two demands add up to the fixed supply.

(machines) used in the industry, but is drawn to measure employment from $\bar{L}$. When the real wage measured in cloth is OV, the cloth industry demands $\bar{L}L_1$ labor. The curve E_W is the demand curve for labor in the wine industry; it plots the demand for labor in the wine industry against the real wage measured in cloth. It is obtained from the marginal-product curve for labor in the wine industry by taking one intermediate step. Divide both sides of the previous equation by the relative price of cloth:

$$\left(\frac{\text{Wage rate}}{\text{Price of wine}}\right)\Bigg/\left(\frac{\text{price of cloth}}{\text{price of wine}}\right) = \text{Marginal product of labor}\Bigg/\left(\frac{\text{price of cloth}}{\text{price of wine}}\right),$$

or

$$\frac{\text{Wage rate}}{\text{Price of cloth}} = \frac{\text{marginal product of labor}}{\text{relative price of cloth}}.$$

When the real wage in cloth is OV, the wine industry demands OL_1 labor.

Clearly, the real wage must be OV cloth for the labor market to be in equilibrium, because the two industries' demands for labor, $\bar{L}L_1$ and OL_1, add up to the total supply, $O\bar{L}$. If the real wage were higher than OV, each industry's demand would be smaller, and the total demand would be smaller than the fixed supply. The real wage would fall. If the real wage were lower than OV, each industry's demand would be larger, and the total demand would be larger than the fixed supply. The real wage would rise.

When the real wage is OV, moreover, we know employment in each industry and, therefore, the output of each industry, given the quantity of land used by the wine industry and the quantity of capital used by the cloth industry.

THE MODIFIED RICARDIAN MODEL

The point Q in Figure 5-2 corresponds to a point on Britain's transformation curve. Starting from that point, the British economy cannot make more cloth without sacrificing wine and cannot make more wine without sacrificing cloth. The location of Q depends on four variables: the fixed supply of labor in Britain; the fixed quantities of land and capital that determine the marginal products of labor, given the technologies available to Britain; and the relative price of cloth, which is needed to convert the marginal-product curve for the wine industry into the demand curve E_W in Figure 5-2.

Relative Prices and the Transformation Curve

To trace the whole transformation curve for Britain, we must ask what happens in the labor market when there is an increase in the relative price of cloth. The results are shown in Figure 5-3.

The demand curve for labor in the wine industry measures the marginal product of labor divided by the relative price of cloth. Therefore, an increase in the relative

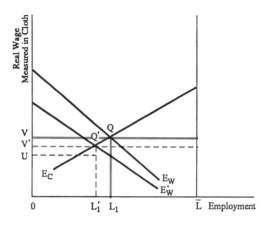

FIGURE 5-3
An Increase in the Relative Price of Cloth
The demand curve for labor in the wine industry is the marginal-product curve divided by the relative price of cloth. Therefore, an increase in the relative price of cloth shifts the demand curve downward from E_W to E'_W, displacing equilibrium from Q to Q'. Employment in the wine industry falls from OL_1 to OL'_1; employment in the cloth industry rises from $\bar{L}L_1$ to $\bar{L}L'_1$. The real wage falls in terms of cloth but rises in terms of wine. The real wage in terms of cloth falls by VV'/OV, and this is smaller than UV/OV, which measures the increase in the relative price of cloth. Hence, workers whose wages have fallen in terms of cloth can nevertheless buy more wine than before, which says that their real wage has risen in terms of wine.

price of cloth shifts the curve downward from E_W to E'_W. (The vertical distance UV/OV measures the price increase.) When this happens, however, the marginal product of labor in the wine industry falls below the real wage, OV, when both are measured in cloth, and firms in the wine industry lay off workers. The real wage falls in terms of cloth because of excess supply in the labor market, and firms in the cloth industry hire more workers. The new equilibrium point is Q'. Employment in the wine industry falls to OL'_1, and employment in the cloth industry rises to $\bar{L}L'_1$. Wine output falls and cloth output rises.

The movement from Q to Q' in Figure 5-3 traces a movement along Britain's transformation curve. But the shape of that curve is different from the Ricardian transformation curve. It looks like Z_1Z_2 in Figure 5-4, being bowed outward (convex) rather than a straight line. A formal proof is given in Section 4 of Appendix A, (along with a new proof of the familiar assertion that the slope of the transformation curve is equal at each point to the relative price of cloth). A moment's thought, however, should satisfy you on this point. When labor is transferred from wine to cloth production, the marginal product of labor falls in the cloth industry and rises in the wine industry. This is because the cloth industry becomes more labor intensive as it hires workers, while the wine industry becomes less labor intensive as it lays off workers. As more and more labor is transferred, then, cloth output expands at a decreasing rate, wine output contracts at an increasing rate, and the transformation curve gets steeper.

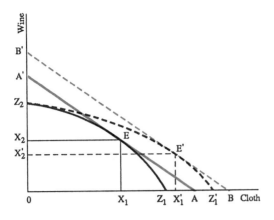

FIGURE 5-4
The British Economy in the Modified Ricardian Model
The labor-market equilibria shown in Figure 5-3 trace the transformation curve Z_1Z_2. (Point Q in Figure 5-3 corresponds to point E on the transformation curve.) The transformation curve gets steeper as cloth output rises. Its slope is equal at each point to the relative price of cloth. An increase in the quantity of capital used by the cloth industry displaces the transformation curve to Z'_1Z_2. When the relative price of cloth is given by the slopes of the lines AA' and BB', the output point shifts from E to E'. The value of national product measured in cloth rises from OA to OB, and actual cloth output rises from OX_1 to OX'_1, but actual wine output falls from OX_2 to OX'_2.

The Haberler Theorem

How does the movement from Q to Q' in Figure 5-3 affect the real earnings of the factors of production? We have already seen that the real wage falls in terms of cloth, going from OV to OV'. It rises, however, in terms of wine. This can be demonstrated in two ways: (1) The text attached to Figure 5-3 shows that the increase in the relative price of cloth is larger than the decrease in the real wage in terms of cloth. Hence, the increase in the purchasing power of cloth is large enough to raise the real wage in terms of wine, even though the real wage falls in terms of cloth. (2) If the real wage did not rise in terms of wine, firms in the wine industry would not lay off workers, which means that the cloth industry could not hire workers. Putting this point differently, the decrease of employment in the wine industry makes the industry less labor intensive and thus raises the marginal product of labor in the wine industry until it is equal in equilibrium to the real wage in terms of wine.

The decrease of employment in the wine industry tells us what happens to the real rental rate of land. The marginal product of land falls in the wine industry, which means that the real rental rate falls in terms of wine. And the purchasing power of wine falls, too, so that the real rental rate falls even further in terms of cloth.

The increase of employment in the cloth industry tells us what happens to the return to capital. The marginal product of capital rises in the cloth industry, which means that the real return rises in terms of cloth. And the purchasing power of cloth rises, too, so that the real return to capital rises even further in terms of wine.

These findings can be summarized in what we will call the Haberler theorem:[4]

> **A change in relative prices raises the real earnings of the factor used specifically in the industry whose output price has risen and reduces the real earnings of the factor used specifically in the industry whose output price has fallen. The real earnings of the mobile factor (labor) fall in terms of the good whose price has risen and rise in terms of the good whose price has fallen.**

This theorem will be used to show how trade affects the real earnings of land, capital, and labor in the specific-factor version of the Ricardian model.

Factor Supplies and the Transformation Curve

Figure 5-5 shows what happens when there is an increase in the supply of capital. The marginal product of labor rises in the cloth industry, because the industry becomes less labor intensive at each level of employment. Therefore, the demand curve for labor shifts upward from E_C to E'_C, displacing equilibrium from Q to Q'. Employment in the cloth industry increases to $\bar{L}L'_1$, and employment in the wine industry decreases to OL'_1. Cloth output rises due to the increase in the supply

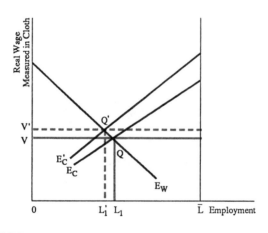

FIGURE 5-5
An Increase in the Supply of Capital Used in Cloth Production
An increase in the supply of capital used in making cloth raises the marginal product of labor in the cloth industry, shifting the demand curve for labor from E_c to E'_c, and displacing equilibrium from Q to Q'. Employment in the wine industry falls from OL_1 to OL'_1, reducing wine output, and employment in the cloth industry rises from $\bar{L}L_1$ to $\bar{L}L'_1$, raising cloth output. The real wage measured in cloth rises from OV to OV'.

---

[4]Haberler did not prove this theorem completely but was among the first economists to examine the behavior of real earnings in a specific-factor model; see Gottfried von Haberler, *The Theory of International Trade* (London: William Hodge, 1936), ch. xii.

of capital and the resulting increase in employment. Wine output falls due to the decrease in employment.

Returning to Figure 5-4, the increase in the supply of capital shifts Britain's transformation curve from Z_1Z_2 to Z'_1Z_2. The distance OZ_1 rises to OZ'_1, showing how the increase in the supply of capital would raise cloth output if all of Britain's workers were employed in making cloth. The distance OZ_2 does not change, because an increase in the supply of capital cannot affect wine output when Britain does not produce any cloth. Let the relative price of cloth be equal to the slopes of the parallel lines AA' and BB'. The economy will be at E initially, and the value of national product will be OA measured in cloth. The increase in the supply of capital shifts the economy to E'. Cloth output rises, wine output falls, and the national product rises to OB.

These output effects resemble those predicted by the Rybczynski theorem developed in connection with the Heckscher–Ohlin model. An increase in the supply of a specific factor raises the output of the industry using that factor and reduces the output of the other industry. This prediction holds for every set of goods prices at which the economy produces both goods.

What are the effects on the earnings of the factors of production? There is, of course, an increase in the real wage measured in cloth. It rises from OV to OV' in Figure 5-5. Furthermore, the real wage rises in terms of wine as well, because relative prices have not changed. There is a decrease in the real rental rate for land, whether measured in wine or cloth, because the wine industry becomes less labor intensive and the marginal product of land falls. There is a decrease in the real return to capital, whether measured in wine or cloth, because the cloth industry becomes less labor intensive, too, and the marginal product of capital falls. (The cloth industry uses more labor and more capital, but becomes less labor intensive, because of the increase in the real wage measured in cloth. This implies an increase in the marginal product of labor and, therefore, a decrease in the labor intensity of the cloth industry.) These effects on earnings are different from those in the Ricardian and Heckscher–Ohlin models, where real earnings cannot change unless goods prices change.

Factor Supplies and Trade

Suppose that Britain and Portugal have the same technologies and same supplies of labor. Let Britain have more capital than Portugal, however, and Portugal more land than Britain. What can we say about trade between them? When the relative price of cloth is the same in the two countries, which happens with free trade, Britain produces more cloth than Portugal, and Portugal produces more wine. If tastes are the same in the two countries, however, with unitary income elasticities of demand, their consumers will demand the same combinations of wine and cloth. Therefore, Britain must export cloth, and Portugal must export wine, just as they did in the simple Ricardian model.

How does trade affect the real earnings of land, capital, and labor? As Britain exports cloth, the relative price of cloth had to be lower in Britain before trade was opened. By implication, trade must raise that price in Britain and reduce it in Portugal, and the Haberler theorem tells the rest of the story.

Trade must raise the real return to capital in Britain and reduce it in Portugal. Conversely, trade must reduce the real rental rate for land in Britain and raise it in Portugal. These effects are similar to those predicted by the Stolper–Samuelson theorem developed in connection with the Heckscher–Ohlin model. Capital is abundant in Britain, and land is abundant in Portugal. The opening of trade, then, raises the real earnings of the abundant specific factor and reduces the real earnings of the scarce specific factor.

The effects on real wages are more complicated. As trade raises the relative price of cloth in Britain, the real wage must fall in terms of cloth but rise in terms of wine. As the relative price of cloth falls in Portugal, the real wage must rise in terms of cloth but fall in terms of wine. When tastes are the same in the two countries, then, trade is beneficial to workers in one country but harmful to workers in the other. If workers spend most of their incomes on cloth, trade makes them worse off in Britain but better off in Portugal. (In the simple Ricardian model, by contrast, trade makes workers better off in both countries, regardless of their tastes. The real wage rises in each country in terms of its import good and is constant in terms of its export good.)

In this example, trade is explained by differences in national endowments of specific factors rather than differences in technologies, using predictions about output that resemble those made by the Rybczynski theorem. Furthermore, the effect of trade on the real earnings of the specific factors resemble those predicted by the Stolper–Samuelson theorem. In consequence, many economists treat this specific-factor model as a version of the Heckscher–Ohlin model rather than a version of the Ricardian model. In the short run, they say, some factors of production are not mobile across industries. In the long run, all factors are perfectly mobile. Therefore, the specific-factor model can be used to describe the short-run behavior of an economy, and the factor-endowments model can be used to describe its long-run behavior.

Tariffs and Factor Prices

When looking at the impact of a tariff in the Heckscher–Ohlin model, we used the Stolper–Samuelson theorem to forecast the effects on real earnings. A tariff tended to reverse the effects of trade by raising the real earnings of the scarce factor and reducing the real earnings of the abundant factor.

Here, we can use the Haberler theorem. Suppose that Portugal imposes a tariff on imported cloth. The relative price of cloth will rise in Portugal. Hence, the tariff will raise the real return to capital in Portugal and reduce the real rental rate for land, whether they are measured in wine or cloth. It will also raise the real wage in terms of wine but reduce it in terms of cloth.

We would therefore expect owners of capital in Portugal to favor protection for the Portuguese cloth industry, owners of land to oppose it, and the views of workers to depend on their tastes. If they spend most of their incomes on cloth, we would expect them to oppose protection; if they spend most of their incomes on wine, we would expect them to favor it. Note that their views should not depend on the industry in which they work, because they can move freely from industry to industry. If workers cannot move at all, their views will depend on their jobs. Workers in the Portuguese cloth industry will join with the owners of capital in favoring protection for the cloth industry. Workers in the Portuguese wine industry will join with the owners of land in opposing protection for the cloth industry.

As a Portuguese tariff on imported cloth tends to reduce the relative price of cloth in Britain, the effects on real earnings will be opposite in sign to those in Portugal. We should therefore expect owners of capital in Britain to oppose protection for the Portuguese cloth industry and owners of land in Britain to favor it. We should expect the views of British workers to depend on their tastes, because the real wage will fall in terms of wine but rise in terms of cloth.

ECONOMIC GROWTH IN THE MODIFIED RICARDIAN MODEL

In previous chapters, we used the Ricardian and Heckscher–Ohlin models to show why trade takes place, how the terms of trade are determined and the gains from trade distributed, and how trade affects the earnings of the factors of production. We did not ask how trade patterns are altered by changes in factor supplies–capital formation and population growth–or by technological change. But we have done most of the work needed to deal with these matters. Therefore, let us look at economic growth.

Economic growth can reflect changes in factor supplies or changes in the quality of capital and labor and in the efficiency with which they are used. Changes in factor supplies are easiest to analyze, and we will focus on capital formation because it is less complicated than population growth. (When numbers of persons and workers change, the principal measures of economic growth may not move together; an increase in total output may not raise output per person or output per worker. Population growth and technological change are examined in Chapter 6, using the Heckscher–Ohlin model.)

We will not explore the underlying reasons for capital formation—the motives for saving and investment. Nor will we ask what happens while it is taking place and raising the demand for capital equipment—the looms needed to make cloth in this chapter and the mills and tractors needed to make steel and grow corn in the next chapter. In the spirit of earlier chapters, we will concentrate on the long-run effects of capital formation by asking how an increase in the capital stock, optimally allocated among industries, affects the terms of trade, the gains from trade, and the real earnings of labor, land, and capital.

To answer this question systematically, however, we must subdivide it into three: (1) How does capital formation affect the output mix and the income distribution in the growing country, before it has affected the terms of trade? (2) How does the change in the output mix affect the terms of trade and distribution of the gain from trade? (3) How does the change in the terms of trade affect the income distribution?

Effects on Outputs and Real Earnings at Constant Terms of Trade

We answered the first question completely when we showed how a change in the capital stock affects the transformation curve and the labor market. Our results are reproduced in Figures 5-6 and 5-7 and can be used to summarize our principal findings.

In Figure 5-6, the British transformation curve is Z_1Z_2 initially, and the relative price of cloth is given by the slope of the line AA'. The British economy produces at E. An increase in Britain's capital stock shifts the transformation curve to $Z_1'Z_2$. When the terms of trade remain unchanged, the British economy produces at E', so cloth output rises and wine output falls.

In Figure 5-7, labor-market equilibrium is at Q initially, and the real wage in terms of cloth is OV yards. Capital formation raises the marginal product of labor in the cloth industry, shifting its demand curve from E_C to E_C'. and labor-market equilibrium is displaced to Q'. Employment in the wine industry falls, employment in the cloth industry rises, and the real wage rises in terms of cloth to OV' yards, which means that it rises in terms of wine as well, because relative prices have not changed.

The remaining results follow directly. As the real wage has risen in terms of wine and cloth, the marginal products of labor must be higher in the wine and cloth industries. Therefore, the marginal products of land and capital must be lower. Capital formation reduces the real rental rate for land and the real return to capital.[5]

Effects on the Terms of Trade and Gains from Trade

If Britain were too small to influence world prices, the story would end here. Capital formation in Britain would not affect the terms of trade, and Britain would appropriate the entire gain in welfare resulting from domestic capital formation. In Figure 5-6, British consumers would move from point C on the indifference curve U_1 to point C' on the higher indifference curve U_2. Portuguese consumers would stay where they were initially.

When Britain is large enough to influence world prices, we must go on to answer questions (2) and (3), concerning the effect of capital formation on the terms of trade and its implications for the gains from trade and for real earnings in Britain and Portugal. This can be done most easily by making an assumption used frequently in economic theory, that consumers demand more of every good when their incomes rise (that no good is "inferior").

Return to Figure 5-6 to note the effect of capital formation on real national product in Britain. It starts at OA in terms of cloth and rises to OB with capital formation. As the number of consumers is constant, consumers' incomes rise in Britain, the consumption point moves from C to C', and consumers demand more wine and cloth. But capital formation reduces wine output and raises cloth output.

---

[5]These changes in the real earnings of the factors do not describe completely the changes in their *shares* (the changes in the income distribution). We can show what happens to the landlords' share. The amount of land is fixed and the real rental rate declines, so the real incomes of landlords fall. Furthermore, real national product rises. These events together reduce the landlords' share. But this is all we can say. The amount of labor is constant and the real wage rate rises, so the real incomes of workers rise. But we do not know whether they rise by more or less than real national product and thus cannot tell what happens to the workers' share. The amount of capital rises and the real return to capital falls, which means that the real incomes of capitalists can go up or down, and the change in their share is thoroughly ambiguous. As similar problems crop up later, the analysis in the text concentrates on real earnings rather than factor shares.

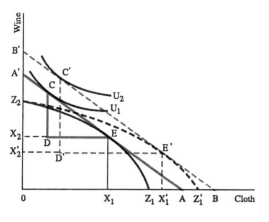

FIGURE 5-6
Capital Formation and the Demands for Cloth and Wine
The British transformation curve is Z_1Z_2. When the relative price of cloth is equal to the slope of AA', the output point is E, where cloth output is OX_1 and wine output is OX_2. Real national product is OA in terms of cloth. Consumption takes place at C, where the indifference curve U_1 is tangent to AA'. Britain exports ED cloth and imports DC wine. Capital formation shifts the transformation curve to $Z_1'Z_2$. When the relative price of cloth is unchanged and thus equal to the slope of BB', the output point is E', where cloth output rises to OX_1' and wine output falls to OX_2'. Real national product rises to OB in terms of cloth. Consumption takes place at C', where the indifference curve U_2 is tangent to BB'. Britain's export offer rises to $E'D'$ cloth, and its import demand rises to $D'C'$ wine. (When consumers demand more wine and cloth, C' is northeast of C, so $D'C'$ must exceed DC when output moves from E to E'.)

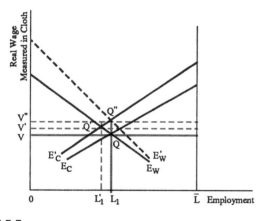

FIGURE 5-7
Capital Formation and Real Earnings
Capital formation in Britain raises the marginal product of labor in the cloth industry, shifting the demand curve for labor from E_C to E_C' and displacing equilibrium from Q to Q'. Employment in the wine industry falls from OL_1 to OL_1', and employment in the cloth industry rises from $\bar{L}L_1$ to $\bar{L}L_1'$. The real wage measured in cloth rises from OV to OV'. The corresponding increase in cloth output reduces the relative price of cloth, raising the demand for labor in the wine industry. It is shown here to rise from E_W to E_W', displacing equilibrium to Q'' and restoring employment in each industry to what it was initially. The real wage rises to OV'' measured in cloth and is unchanged when measured in wine.

Therefore, it generates an excess demand for wine matched by an excess supply of cloth at the initial terms of trade. The British demand for wine imports rises from DC to $D'C'$, and the supply of cloth exports rises from ED to $E'D'$.

The effects on Britain's terms of trade are shown in Figure 5-8, using offer curves. The British offer curve is OJ initially. The Portuguese offer curve is OJ^*. The two curves intersect at W, where Britain imports OZ wine and exports ZW cloth. Britain's terms of trade are given by the slope of OF, passing through W and measuring the relative price of cloth.

As capital formation in Britain generates an excess demand for wine and an excess supply of cloth at the initial terms of trade, Britain's demand for wine imports rises from OZ to OZ', but Britain's supply of cloth exports rises from ZW to $Z'Y$.[6] Therefore, the point Y must lie on the new British offer curve, which is OJ'. Equilibrium in trade between Britain and Portugal is displaced to W, and Britain's terms of trade deteriorate. The new terms of trade are given by the slope of OF', which is flatter than OF.

The effects on economic welfare in Britain are analyzed in Figure 5-9. It is based on Figure 5-6, showing once again the new transformation curve, Z'_1Z_2. If Britain's

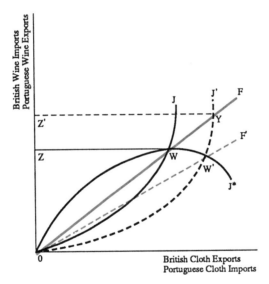

FIGURE 5-8
Capital Formation and the Terms of Trade
The British offer curve is OJ and the Portuguese offer curve is OJ^*. Equilibrium is established initially at W, where Britain imports OZ wine and exports ZW cloth. Britain's terms of trade (the relative price of cloth) are given by the slope of OF. Capital formation in Britain increases the British demand for wine imports to OZ' and the British supply of cloth exports to $Z'Y$. The British offer curve becomes OJ', and equilibrium is displaced to W'. Britain's terms of trade are given by the slope OF' and have therefore deteriorated.

---

[6]The slope of OF in Figure 5-8 corresponds to the slope of AA' in Figure 5-6; the distances OZ and OZ' correspond to the distances DC and $D'C'$; and the distances ZW and $Z'Y$ correspond to the distances ED and $E'D'$.

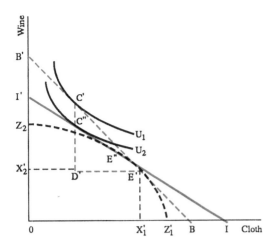

FIGURE 5-9
Capital Formation and the Gains from Trade
The transformation curve $Z_1'Z_2$ and trade triangle $E'D'C'$ are reproduced from Figure 5-6. They show the results of capital formation if there is no change in Britain's terms of trade. If the terms of trade deteriorate, three outcomes are possible. In the case shown here, the relative price of cloth falls until it is equal to the slope of II', displacing the output point from E' to E'' and displacing the consumption point from C' to C''. As C'' lies on the indifference curve U_1 (the one that British consumers reached before the increase in the capital stock), the gains from economic growth are exactly offset by the reduction in the gains from trade due to the deterioration in the terms of trade.

terms of trade do not change, capital formation will cause Britain to produce at E' and consume at C', and consumers will reach the indifference curve U_2. They will be better off than they were initially. When the terms of trade deteriorate, however, they may be better or worse off.

Consider the line II' in Figure 5-9. It is drawn to connect the transformation curve with the indifference curve U_1, the one on which British consumers began, before the increase in the capital stock. The slope of this line serves to classify three possibilities:

1. If the new terms of trade are equal to those given by II', the deterioration in the terms of trade is just large enough to offset the welfare gain from capital formation. British consumers are driven back to the indifference curve U_1, and they do not gain or lose from capital formation.

2. If the new terms of trade are more favorable than those given by II', the deterioration in the terms of trade is not large enough to offset the welfare gain from capital formation. British consumers cannot reach the indifference curve U_2 but can reach one higher than U_1, and they are better off than they were initially.

3. If the new terms of trade are less favorable than those given by II', the deterioration in the terms of trade more than offsets the welfare gain from capital formation. British consumers are driven back to an indifference curve lower than U_1, and they are worse off than they were initially.

The third case is described as *immizerizing growth*, and much theoretical work has been devoted to the conditions under which it can happen. It is most likely to occur when the Portuguese demand for British cloth is inelastic and when it is comparatively difficult for Britain to move from cloth to wine production. (It has been shown, moreover, that immizerizing growth testifies to poor trade policy. It cannot occur when a country imposes an "optimum" tariff on imports, a notion defined precisely in Chapter 9.)

Note that the increase in welfare occuring in the second case will not be realized fully unless incomes are redistributed within Britain. We have already seen that capital formation reduces the real return to capital in Britain, and we are about to see that the deterioration in the terms of trade reinforces that effect, even when it is not large enough to cause immizerizing growth. Hence, consumers whose incomes derive from the ownership of capital will be made worse off by growth, even when a "typical" consumer reaches an indifference curve higher than U_1. It is therefore most accurate to say that growth has the *potential* to raise welfare, contingent on a redistribution of income that compensates those consumers whose incomes are reduced by growth.

Additional Effects on Real Earnings

How does the deterioration in Britain's terms of trade affect the real earnings of the factors of production? The answer is given by Figure 5-7, where we saw that capital formation raised the marginal product of labor in Britain's cloth industry, shifting the industry's demand curve to E'_C and displacing labor-market equilibrium to Q'. Employment rose by $L_1 L'_1$ in the cloth industry and fell by the same amount in the wine industry. The real wage rose by VV' measured in cloth. We have now to add the effects of the deterioration in Britain's terms of trade, reflecting the reduction in the relative price of cloth.

At the start of this chapter, the demand curve for labor by the wine industry was obtained by dividing the relative price of cloth into the marginal product of labor. Therefore, a reduction in the relative price of cloth shifts that curve upward from E_W to E'_W in Figure 5-7. This shift displaces labor-market equilibrium to some such point as Q''. Employment rises in the wine industry, compared to the situation at Q', and falls in the cloth industry.[7] The effects of the movement to Q'' are described completely by the Haberler theorem. The deterioration in the terms of trade reduces the real return to capital and raises the real rental rate for land, whether they are measured in wine or cloth. It raises the real wage measured in cloth, but reduces the real wage measured in wine.

Combining these effects with those involved in the earlier movement from Q to Q', we get clear-cut results for the return to capital. The real return was lower at Q' than at Q and is even lower at Q''. Therefore, capital formation in Britain reduces the real return to British capital, whether it is measured in wine or cloth. One other result is also clear. The real wage in terms of cloth was higher at Q' than at Q and is even higher at Q''. Therefore, capital formation in Britain raises the real wage in terms of

---

[7]The shift from Q' to Q'' in Figure 5-7 corresponds to the shift of the output point from E' to E'' in Figure 5-9.

cloth, the good that uses capital. But the real wage in terms of wine can rise or fall, depending on the size of the reduction in the relative price of cloth, and the effect on the real rental rate for land is likewise ambiguous.

The reasons for these ambiguities are shown by the special case depicted by Figure 5-7. Point Q'' has been placed vertically above the initial point Q, which says that the relative price of cloth falls by just enough to restore the initial pattern of employment.[8] In this special case, the marginal products of labor and land in the wine industry are the same as they were initially, because the land-labor ratio is the same. Capital formation does not affect the real wage or real rental rate when they are measured in wine. But it raises the real rental rate measured in cloth, because of the reduction in the relative price of cloth.

In this special case, then, these are the combined effects of capital formation shown by the movement from Q to Q'' in Figure 5-7:

	In Terms of:	
Real Earnings of:	Wine	Cloth
Labor	Constant	Increase
Land	Constant	Increase
Capital	Decrease	Decrease

If the reduction in the relative price of cloth were larger than the reduction implied by the shift in the demand curve to E'_W, employment in the wine industry would exceed OL_1 workers. The real wage would fall in terms of wine (but would rise by more in terms of cloth), and the real rental rate for land would rise in terms of wine. If the reduction in the relative price of cloth were smaller than the reduction implied by the shift in the demand curve to E'_W, employment would not reach OL_1 workers. The real wage would rise in terms of wine (but would rise by less in terms of cloth), and the real rental rate for land would fall in terms of wine.

Effects on the Portuguese Economy

Capital formation in Britain can have important effects in Portugal, but only if it leads to a deterioration in Britain's terms of trade. If Britain is too small to influence world prices, the Portuguese economy is not affected.

A deterioration in Britain's terms of trade is, of course, an improvement in Portugal's terms of trade, and it raises economic welfare in Portugal. In effect, the deterioration in Britain's terms of trade redistributes from Britain to Portugal some of the welfare gains from capital formation in Britain.

The effects on real earnings are equally simple. They are described completely by the Haberler theorem. The real return to capital falls in Portugal, and the real

---

[8]By implication, wine output is what is was initially, because the same quantities of land and labor are used in wine production, but cloth output is larger, because more capital is used in cloth production along with the initial quantity of labor.

rental rate rises, whether measured in wine or cloth. The real wage falls in terms of wine and rises in terms of cloth. Capital formation in Britain makes Portuguese landlords better off and capitalists worse off, and it has an uncertain effect on Portuguese workers. If those workers consume much cloth and little wine, they benefit from capital formation in Britain. If they consume much wine and little cloth, they suffer.

Capital Formation in Portugal

We have dealt thus far with capital formation in Britain, which exports the good that uses capital. We found that it worsens Britain's terms of trade and gives rise to the possibility of immiserizing growth. Consider the effects of capital formation in Portugal, which imports the good that uses capital.

The effects on Britain's output mix are the same as before. The transformation curve for Portugal shifts outward in the manner described by Figure 5-6. If Portugal begins at a point such as E, capital formation moves it to a point such as E', where real national product is larger and cloth output is larger, too, but wine output is smaller. The increase in real national product raises consumers' incomes, and they demand larger quantities of wine and cloth. Accordingly, Portugal displays an excess demand for wine matched by an excess supply of cloth.

But Portugal exports wine and imports cloth. Therefore, an excess demand for wine reduces its supply of wine exports, and an excess supply of cloth reduces its demand for cloth imports. Portugal's offer curve shifts inward, instead of shifting outward as did the British offer curve in Figure 5-8. But an inward shift of the Portuguese offer curve has the same effect as an outward shift of the British offer curve. It depresses the relative price of cloth.

By implication, capital formation in Portugal improves the Portuguese terms of trade, adding to the increase in economic welfare that results directly from economic growth. It cannot produce immiserizing growth. By worsening the British terms of trade, moreover, it reduces economic welfare in Britain. Contrasting the effects of capital formation in Britain and Portugal we find:

Location of Capital Formation	Economic Welfare	
	Britain	Portugal
Britain	Ambiguous	Increase
Portugal	Decrease	Increase

As capital formation reduces the relative price of cloth whether it occurs in Britain or Portugal, the effects on the income distributions are symmetrical. The changes in the real earnings of labor, land, and capital that take place in Portugal when capital formation occurs in Portugal are the same as those that take place in Britain when capital formation occurs in Britain. Similarly, the changes that take place in Britain when capital formation occurs in Portugal are the same as those that take place in Portugal when capital formation occurs in Britain.

SUMMARY

In the modified Ricardian model, one factor is specific to each industry. Another factor, labor, is mobile across industries. The real wage of labor in each industry is equal to its marginal product in that industry. The requirements of equilibrium in the labor market determine the allocation of the labor force and, therefore, the output of each industry.

The effects of a change in relative prices are described by the *Haberler theorem*. An increase in the relative price of cloth raises employment in the cloth industry and reduces employment in the wine industry. Therefore, it raises the real wage in terms of wine but reduces it in terms of cloth. Furthermore, it raises the real return to capital, the factor specific to the cloth industry, and reduces the real rental rate for land, the factor specific to the wine industry. The Haberler theorem also serves to predict the distributional effects of a tariff.

An increase in the supply of one specific factor raises output in the industry using that factor and reduces output in the other industry. By implication, countries with different supplies of specific factors will have different transformation curves and will trade with one another. The country that is well supplied with capital will export cloth. The country that is well supplied with land will export wine.

The welfare effects of capital formation depend on the trade pattern. If the growing country exports the good that uses capital, the other country gains, and the growing country can gain or lose, depending on the size of the deterioration in its terms of trade compared to the direct welfare-raising effect of capital formation. If the growing country imports the good that uses capital, the other country loses, and the growing country gains, because capital formation improves its terms of trade.

Capital formation reduces the real return to capital in the growing country. Its effects on other real earnings, however, depend on the good in which they are measured and on the new employment pattern. The effects on real earnings in the other country are given by the Haberler theorem.

RECOMMENDED READINGS

The modern version of the specific-factor model is developed in Michael Mussa, "Tariffs and the Distribution of Income: The Importance of Factor Specificity, Substitutability, and Intensity in the Short and Long Run," *Journal of Political Economy*, 82 (November 1974).

On the use of the specific-factor model to describe short-run equilibrium and the factor-endowments model to describe long-run equilibrium, see J. Peter Neary, "Short-Run Capital Specificity and the Pure Theory of International Trade," *Economic Journal*, 88 (September 1978).

For a different and interesting combination of specific-factor and factor-endowments models, see Kalyan K. Sanyal and Ronald W. Jones, "The Theory of Trade in Middle Products," *American Economic Review*, 72 (March 1982).

On conditions likely to produce immiserizing growth, see Jagdish Bhagwati, "Immiserizing Growth: A Geometrical Note," *Review of Economic Studies*, 25 (June 1955), reprinted in American Economic Association, *Readings in International Economics* (Homewood, Ill.: Richard D. Irwin, 1968), ch. 18.

QUESTIONS AND PROBLEMS

(1) The Dutch tulip industry uses land and labor. The bicycle industry uses capital and labor. Labor is perfectly mobile across industries. Holland exports tulips and is "large" in world markets (a change in the supply of tulip exports affects the world price of tulips). Show how capital formation affects the terms of trade, Dutch outputs of tulips and bicycles, and the real earnings of the factors of production measured in tulips and bicycles. Can capital formation be immiserizing? Explain.

(2) Use the information in (1) but hold the terms of trade constant. Show how an increase in the Dutch labor force affects the outputs of tulips and bicycles and the real earnings of the factors of production measured in tulips and bicycles.

(3) Use your answer to (2) to explain why you would not be able to predict the sign of the change in the terms of trade if you were to let them change.

(4) Use the information in (1) but hold the terms of trade constant. Show how an invention that raises the marginal products of capital and labor in the Dutch bicycle industry affects the outputs of tulips and bicycles and the real earnings of the factors of production measured in tulips and bicycles.

(5) Use your answer to (4) to explain why you would be able to predict the sign of the change in the terms of trade if you were to let them change. Which way would they move? How would the change in the terms of trade affect the real return to land measured in tulips and bicycles?

(6) How would the change in the terms of trade predicted in your answer to (5) affect the real earnings of the factors of production in a country importing tulips and exporting bicycles? Who might be led to favor a tariff on Dutch tulips?

6

Factor Substitution and the Heckscher–Ohlin Model

THE ISSUES

Factor substitution does not change the Heckscher–Ohlin model as much as it changed the Ricardian model. Its main effect is to alter the shape of the transformation curve. Instead of having two straight-line segments, it becomes a smooth curve, and every point becomes a full-employment output point. Nevertheless, the methods used to illustrate factor substitution allow us to explore more thoroughly some of the issues raised in earlier chapters:

- How factor endowments influence production and trade.

- How trade and tariffs affect the real earnings of the factors of production.

- How capital formation, population growth, and changes in technology affect production, trade, and economic welfare.

We begin by introducing the techniques needed to depict factor substitution in the Heckscher–Ohlin model.

ANOTHER WAY TO DEPICT FACTOR SUBSTITUTION

In the modified Ricardian model, labor was perfectly mobile within the economy, and firms were able to combine various amounts of labor with fixed amounts of land or capital. In the Heckscher–Ohlin model, both factors of production, labor and capital, are perfectly mobile, and firms are able to combine various amounts of labor with various amounts of capital.

The choices confronting an individual firm are described by *isoquants* like the curve I_C in Figure 6-1. Each point on an isoquant defines a combination of labor and capital that can be used to grow a single bushel of corn. At Q, for example, the firm uses OL_1 labor and OK_1 capital. (We will come back to the assumption that corn is grown with labor and capital rather than labor and land.)

If the firm confronting the isoquant I_C wants to use less capital, it must use more labor. Otherwise, it cannot produce as much corn. But the shape of the isoquant makes a stronger statement. As the firm uses less and less capital, it must use increasingly large amounts of labor to hold corn output constant. The isoquant is bowed inward (concave). This proposition is proved algebraically in Section 4 of Appendix A. It follows from an assertion made in Chapter 5 that the marginal products of capital and labor depend on the capital-labor ratio, because the shape of the isoquant depends directly on those marginal products.

Suppose that the marginal product of capital is 4 bushels of corn and that the marginal product of labor is 2 bushels. If the firm reduces its use of capital by one bushel, its output of corn will fall by 4 bushels, and it must hire 2 more workers to keep corn output constant. Along any isoquant, then,

Decrease in capital × marginal product of capital

= increase in labor × marginal product of labor.

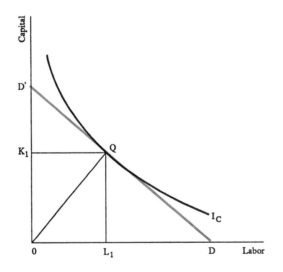

FIGURE 6-1
An Isoquant for the Corn Industry
The isoquant I_C shows the various combinations of labor and capital that a firm can use to produce a single bushel of corn. At Q, for example, the firm can use OL_1 labor and OK_1 capital to produce 1 bushel. As the slope of OQ measures the capital-labor ratio, it determines the marginal products of capital and labor when the firm produces at Q. The slope of I_C itself is equal to the ratio of marginal products, and the least-cost combination of capital and labor is given by the tangency between I_C and a line such as DD' having a slope equal to the relative price of labor (the wage rate divided by the return to capital).

Therefore,

$$\frac{\text{Decrease in capital}}{\text{Increase in labor}} = \frac{\text{marginal product of labor}}{\text{marginal product of capital}}.$$

The slope of the isoquant I_C, showing the rate at which capital can be replaced by labor without affecting output, is given by the ratio of marginal products. As production becomes more labor intensive, however, the marginal product of labor falls and the marginal product of capital rises. Therefore, the isoquant gets flatter.

Two more propositions follow from this one:

1. All corn isoquants will look just like I_C. To be precise, their slopes will equal the slope of I_C at points that lie on the same straight line drawn from the origin. Where they cross the line OQ, for example, all corn isoquants will have slopes equal to the slope of DD', which is tangent to I_C at Q.

2. A profit-maximizing firm will choose that factor combination at which the slope of an isoquant is equal to the relative price of labor. If the relative price of labor is given by the slope of DD', the firm will go to Q, where DD' is tangent to I_C.

The first proposition follows from the fact that marginal products depend entirely on the capital-labor ratio. When the firm produces at Q, however, the capital-labor ratio is given by the slope of the line OQ, which is, of course, the same at every point on OQ. Therefore, the ratio of marginal products is the same at every point on OQ. We have just seen, moreover, that the slope of an isoquant is equal to the ratio of marginal products. Therefore, the slopes of all corn isoquants must be the same where they cross OQ. The second proposition follows from a statement made earlier. A profit-maximizing firm uses those quantities of labor and capital at which the marginal product of labor is equal to the real wage and the marginal product of capital is equal to the real return. Therefore, we can substitute the real wage for the marginal product of labor and substitute the real return for the marginal product of capital:

$$\frac{\text{Decrease in capital}}{\text{Increase in labor}} = \frac{\text{real wage}}{\text{real return}}$$

$$= \frac{\text{wage rate}}{\text{price of corn}} \times \frac{\text{price of corn}}{\text{return to capital}}$$

$$= \frac{\text{wage rate}}{\text{return to capital}},$$

which is, of course, the relative price of labor.[1]

---

[1]This condition can be derived from the simple assumption that a firm will always minimize the cost of producing any output. Suppose that the slope of DD' in Figure 6-1 is equal to the relative price of labor and that the firm begins by using OL_1 labor and OK_1 capital to produce a single bushel of corn. The total cost of producing that bushel will be OD' in terms of capital:

Total cost = (quantity of capital × return to capital) + (quantity of labor × wage rate

Footnote 1 continued on next page

Working back from this last proposition, let us see what we can say about the behavior of the firm when we know the shape of the corn isoquant and the relative price of labor. We know what point the firm will choose on a corn isoquant—the amounts of labor and capital it will use to grow the quantity of corn corresponding to that isoquant. Therefore, we know the capital-labor ratio or capital intensity of corn production, and it will be the same at each level of corn output, because it depends entirely on the relative price of labor. We also know the marginal products of labor and capital, because they depend on the capital intensity of corn production. Therefore, we know the real wage of labor and the real return to capital. Finally, we know that an increase in the relative price of labor will cause the firm to substitute capital for labor, raising the capital intensity of corn production at each output level. This will raise the real wage and reduce the real return to capital.

Allocating Capital

Labor can move freely from industry to industry. Capital can move, too, given enough time.

Before capital can be employed to manufacture steel, it must be invested in machinery and buildings. Call those investments "mills" for brevity. Before it can be employed to grow corn, it must be invested in some other form. Land is needed to grow corn, but land must be improved by applying capital—cleared, irrigated, and fertilized—and it must be worked with the help of machinery. Suppose that the supply of land is fixed, but that the supply available for growing corn depends on the amount of capital invested in it. Call those investments "tractors" for brevity.[2]

At any moment in time, part of the economy's capital will be invested in mills, and

---

and total cost in terms of capital will be

$$\frac{\text{Total cost}}{\text{Return to Capital}} = \text{quantity of capital} + \text{quantity of labor} \times \frac{\text{wage rate}}{\text{return to capital}}.$$

But the quantity of capital is OK_1, the quantity of labor is OL_1, and the relative price of labor is $(L_1 Q / L_1 D) = (K_1 D' / K_1 Q) = (K_1 D' / OL_1)$. Therefore,

$$\frac{\text{Total cost}}{\text{Return to capital}} = OK_1 + \left(OL_1 \times \frac{K_1 D'}{OL_1} \right) = OK_1 + K_1 D' = OD'.$$

Suppose that the firm attempts to reduce its total cost below OD'. It cannot reach I_C. By implication, it cannot grow a bushel of corn at less cost than OD'. Suppose instead that the firm chooses a point on I_C other than Q. The total-cost line passing through that point will lie above DD', and total cost in terms of capital will exceed OD'. The combination of labor and capital shown at Q is the least-cost combination when the relative price of labor equals the slope of DD'.

[2]To be more realistic, we might want to assume that the supply of land available for growing corn rises by smaller and smaller amounts as additional tractors are used cultivate a fixed quantity of raw land (that the law of diminishing returns applies to investments in land). But we will assume for simplicity that the supply of land rises in proportion to the number of tractors, so the quantity of land used for growing corn can be represented by the quantity of capital invested in it.

the rest in tractors. The economy will resemble the modified Ricardian model. It will have one mobile factor (labor) and two specific factors (mills and tractors). But capital can be reallocated gradually. Mills and tractors depreciate with age and use, and their owners must set aside funds to replace them. If those funds are used in the amounts required to maintain the numbers of mills and tractors, the supply of capital will not change, and its allocation will not change. This is what will happen in long-run equilibrium, when a dollar of capital earns the same return in every potential use—whether invested in a mill or a tractor. If that equilibrium is disturbed, however, the number of mills and tractors will begin to change.

Let there be an increase in the relative price of corn. The Haberler theorem for the specific-factor model tells us what will happen in the short run. There will be an increase in the real return to tractors, the form of capital used specifically in growing corn, and a decrease in the real return to mills, the form used specifically in making steel. This will raise the rate of return to a dollar of capital invested in a tractor, compared to the rate of return to a dollar invested in a mill. Farmers will start to buy additional tractors. They can obtain the funds they need to increase the total number of tractors by borrowing from firms that manufacture steel, because they can pay more for the use of those funds than steel producers can earn by replacing their old mills. There need be no change in the quantity of capital—it is constant here—but it will be reallocated. The number of tractors will rise, and the number of mills will fall.

This way of looking at the role of capital is somewhat artificial, but it is more realistic than the approach adopted in many presentations of the Heckscher–Ohlin model. That approach assumes that there is a "machine" that can be used with equal ease to make steel or grow corn. The supply of capital is measured in machines and is freely transferable between the two activities. There is, of course, no such machine. When we treat capital more realistically, however, we must be very clear about our findings. They hold only in the long run, when the supply of capital is allocated optimally between mills and tractors (i.e., the return to a dollar of capital is the same in both uses).

Equilibrium in the Factor Markets

Figure 6-2 shows one way to describe long-run equilibrium in an economy of this sort. The isoquant I_C shows how labor and capital (tractors) can be combined to grow corn. The isoquant I_S shows how labor and capital (mills) can be combined to make steel. Represent the relative price of labor by the slope of the line DD', and give the economy enough time to allocate capital optimally between mills and tractors. Corn will be grown by the method shown at C. The capital intensity of corn production is given by the slope of OC, showing how much capital is invested in tractors for every worker growing corn. Steel will be manufactured by the method shown at S. The capital intensity of steel production is given by the slope of OS, showing how much capital is invested in mills for every worker making steel. As OS is steeper than OC, steel is the capital-intensive good, as it was in Chapter 4. The shapes of the isoquants in Figure 6-2 generate this ordering of factor intensities at every set of factor prices.

The economy is endowed with $O\bar{L}$ workers and $O\bar{K}$ dollars of capital. Therefore,

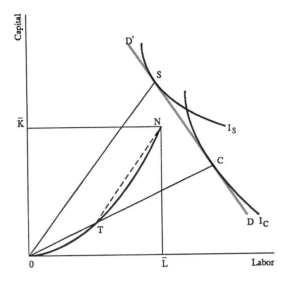

FIGURE 6-2
The Output Mix with Flexible Factor Intensities
Factor supplies are $O\overline{L}$ labor and $O\overline{K}$ capital. The relative price of labor is given by the slope of the line DD'. As that line is tangent to I_C at C, the slope of OC gives the capital-labor ratio in corn production. As it is tangent to I_S at S, the slope of OS gives the capital-labor ratio in steel production. Steel is more capital intensive than corn. The full-employment point is T, where the economy produces OT corn and NT steel. (The line NT is parallel to OS, measuring the capital intensity of steel production.) When factor intensities can vary, however, there are many full-employment points. They lie on the curve OTN.

it can employ both factors fully by producing at T. It can grow OT bushels of corn and can manufacture NT tons of steel. If factor intensities were fixed, T would be the only full-employment point. When factor intensities can vary, it is only one of many full-employment points that can be reached in the long run. They are the points on the curve OTN.

THE MODIFIED HECKSCHER–OHLIN MODEL

To show how the Heckscher–Ohlin model behaves with factor substitution, we have first to show how market forces generate the curve OTN, and then use it to derive the transformation curve for an economy having $O\overline{L}$ labor and $O\overline{K}$ capital.

Factor Prices and Factor Intensities

The curve OTN is produced by the influence of factor prices on firms' decisions about factor intensities. Figure 6-3 shows what they do. The corn isoquant I_C is drawn as before. The steel isoquant I_S is inverted, and its origin placed at N, so capital and labor used in making steel are measured from that point. Begin as

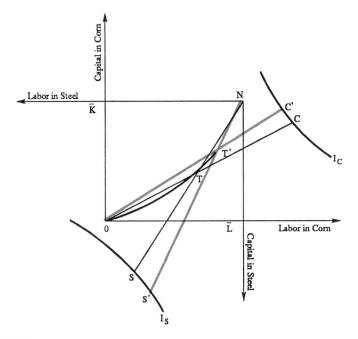

FIGURE 6-3
Factor Prices, Factor Intensities, and the Output Mix
The corn isoquant I_C is drawn as it was in Figure 6-2. The steel isoquant I_S is inverted; the factors used in making steel are measured from N. When the relative price of labor equals the slopes of I_C at C and I_S at S, the full-employment point is T. The economy produces OT corn and NT steel. When the relative price of labor equals the slopes of I_C at C' and I_S at S', the full-employment point is T'. Corn output rises to OT' and steel output falls to NT'. Thus, a shift from steel to corn output raises the demand for labor and reduces the demand for capital, because corn is the labor-intensive commodity. The relative price of labor rises, inducing both industries to substitute capital for labor and thus adopt more capital-intensive methods; OC is steeper than OC, and NS' is steeper than NS.

before by letting the relative price of labor equal the slope of I_C at C and the slope of I_S at S. The capital intensity of corn production is given by the slope of OC, and the capital intensity of steel production is given by the slope of NS. Both factors of production will be fully employed if the economy winds up at T. Now raise the relative price of labor by letting it equal the slope of I_C at C' and the slope of I_S at S'. The capital intensity of corn production is given by the slope of OC', and the capital intensity of steel production is given by the slope of NS'. Both factors of production will be fully employed when the economy winds up at T'. The points T and T' lie on the curve OTN, which traces the whole set of full-employment output points.

When the economy moves from T to T', both industries become more capital intensive. How can this happen when the supply of capital is fixed? A movement from T to T' raises the output of corn, the labor-intensive good, and reduces the output of steel, the capital-intensive good. This change in the output mix reduces the demand for capital, offsetting the shift by each industry to a more capital-intensive method of production.

The same point can be made by starting with a change in the output mix rather than a change in factor prices. Let there be an increase in corn output and a decrease in steel output. The demand for labor rises, because corn is more labor intensive than steel, and this raises the relative price of labor. Farmers are induced to substitute capital for labor and thus move along I_C from C to C', raising the capital intensity of corn production. Steel firms do so, too, and thus move along I_S from S to S', raising the capital intensity of steel production. Substitution of capital for labor takes place in each industry and makes way for the increase in the output of the labor-intensive good. With factor substitution, a change in the output mix leads to a change in factor prices that leads, in turn, to changes in factor intensities, which maintain equilibrium in the factor markets.

Goods Prices and Factor Prices

There is a relationship between the curve OTN and the transformation curve. It is depicted in Figure 6-4. The lower part shows what we have seen before: the fixed supplies of labor and capital, $O\bar{L}$ and $O\bar{K}$, and the curve OTN. It also shows the isoquants I_C and I_S that relate to the output levels obtained at T. The corn and steel isoquants are tangent to each other because the economy produces at T only when the slopes of both isoquants are equal to the relative price of labor, which means that their slopes are equal to each other. The upper part of the diagram shows the transformation curve Z_1QZ_2 that corresponds to OTN and the output point Q that corresponds to T. The transformation curve is bowed outward, because changes in output lead to changes in factor intensities that alter the marginal products of labor and capital. Furthermore, the slope of the transformation curve is equal in equilibrium to the relative price of corn.

The upper part of Figure 6-4 can be derived from the lower part. Details are provided in Note 6-1. The text attached to the diagram explains how to move from T to Q. The two parts of the diagram taken together provide a great deal of information about the behavior of the economy.

Let us summarize that information by setting the relative price of corn equal to the slope of the transformation curve at Q, causing the economy to produce at that point. Corn output is OX_1 bushels, and steel output is OX_2 tons. The text attached to the diagram tells us how to locate T, the counterpart of Q. The slopes of the isoquants at T tell us the relative price of labor, and the slopes of the lines OT and NT tell us the capital intensities chosen by corn and steel producers. Those intensities, in turn, give us the marginal products of labor and capital, which are equal to the real earnings of labor and capital. The real wage of labor measured in corn equals the marginal product of labor in the production of corn, and the real wage measured in steel equals the marginal product of labor in the production of steel. Similarly, the real return to capital measured in corn equals the marginal product of capital in the production of corn, and the real return measured in steel equals the marginal product of capital in the production of steel.

How does the economy respond to an increase in the relative price of corn? The output point Q travels down the transformation curve, as corn output rises and steel

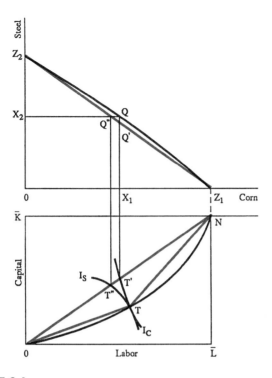

FIGURE 6-4
Equilibrium in Factor and Goods Markets
When $O\bar{L}$ labor and $O\bar{K}$ capital are used to grow corn, output is OZ_1 bushels. When they are used to make steel, output is OZ_2 tons. Output points on the straight line ON correspond to output points on the straight line Z_1Z_2, and this fact can be used to connect points on the curve OTN with those on the transformation curve Z_1QZ_2. Start at T on OTN. Hold corn output constant by moving along the corn isoquant I_C until it intersects ON at T'. As T' corresponds to Q', corn output at both T' and T is OX_1 bushels. Returning to T, hold steel output constant by moving along the steel isoquant I_S until it intersects ON at T''. As T'' corresponds to Q'', steel output at both T'' and T is OX_2 tons. These are the outputs at Q on the transformation curve Z_1QZ_2. The relative price of labor is given at T by the slopes of the isoquants. The relative price of corn is given at Q by the slope of the transformation curve. To move from Q to T, go first to Q', keeping corn output constant, then to T' to find the isoquant I_C corresponding to corn output at Q'. Move along that isoquant to T. (The movement between Q and Q' is equivalent to the movement along I_C between T and T'.)

output falls, causing T to travel up the curve OTN. The relative price of labor rises, and both industries substitute capital for labor, raising their capital-labor ratios. The marginal products of labor rise, raising the real wage of labor measured in corn or steel, and the marginal products of capital fall, reducing the real return to capital measured in corn or steel. This proves the Stolper–Samuelson theorem for the modified version of the Heckscher–Ohlin model. An increase in the price of corn, the labor-intensive good, raises the real wage of labor and reduces the real return to capital. (The theorem holds only in the long run, however, after the numbers of mills and tractors are fully adjusted to the new situation.)

NOTE 6-1
Deriving a Transformation Curve from Factor-Market Information

If the economy shown in Figure 6-4 specializes completely in corn, it will be at N in the lower part of the diagram, and its output will be some such quantity as OZ_1 bushels. (Point Z_1 is drawn to lie directly above N.) If the economy specializes completely in steel, it will be at O in the lower part of the diagram, and its output will be some such quantity as OZ_2 tons. (Point Z_2 is chosen arbitrarily.)

Draw the straight lines ON and Z_1Z_2 and note the relationship between them. If the economy produces at T', a point on ON, it will find itself at Q', the point on Z_1Z_2 that lies vertically above T'. This relationship derives from the assumption that returns to scale are constant in all industries. Suppose that the economy produces at the middle of ON, using half its labor and capital to grow corn and the rest to make steel. Its outputs will be half OZ_1 and half OZ_2, putting it at the middle of Z_1Z_2. Thus, movements along ON correspond to movements along Z_1Z_2.

Now, start at T on OTN and move along the corn isoquant I_C until you reach ON at T'. As corn output is constant at all points on I_C and the same at T' and Q', it must be OX_1 bushels at T. Next, return to T and move along the steel isoquant I_S until you reach ON at T''. As steel output is constant at all points on I_S and the same at T'' and Q'', it must be OX_2 tons at T. But OX_1 and OX_2 are the coordinates of Q, so Q is the point on the transformation curve Z_1QZ_2 that matches T on OTN.

By repeating this procedure for each point on OTN, you can trace out the whole transformation curve.

The information obtained from Figure 6-4 is summarized conveniently in Figure 6-5, where relative prices and capital intensities are shown as distances rather than slopes. The curve CC' on the left side of this diagram shows how the capital intensity of corn production responds to the relative price of labor. When that price is OW, for example, the capital intensity of corn production is OK_1. When it is higher than OW, farmers substitute capital for labor, raising the capital intensity of corn production above OK_1. The curve SS' shows how the capital intensity of steel production responds to the relative price of labor. When that price is OW, the capital intensity of steel production is OK_2. Steel is more capital intensive than corn, and this is always true in Figure 6-4, because CC' and SS' do not cross.

The curve HH' on the right side of the diagram shows the relationship between the relative price of labor and the relative price of corn. When the relative price of labor is OW, the relative price of corn is OP. When the relative price of labor rises, the relative price of corn rises too, because corn is the labor-intensive good.

There is another way to use this diagram, and that is the main reason for introducing it. It shows the whole set of output possibilities open to a country having a particular factor endowment and allows us to determine which one it will choose

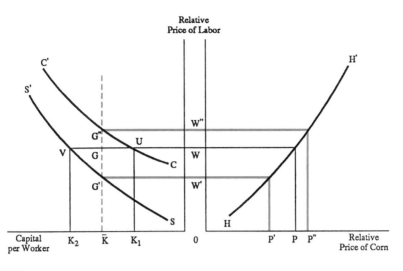

FIGURE 6-5
Goods Prices, Factor Prices, and Factor Intensities
The curve HH' connects the relative price of corn with the relative price of labor.
When the relative price of corn is OP, the relative price of labor is OW. An increase
in the relative price of corn raises the relative price of labor. The curve CC' describes
the relationship between the relative price of labor and the capital-labor ratio in corn
production. The curve SS' describes the corresponding relationship in steel production.
When the relative price of labor is OW, corn producers use OK_1 capital per worker,
and steel producers use OK_2 capital per worker. (Steel is more capital intensive than
corn.) A country that has $O\bar{K}$ capital per worker will produce at G' when the relative
price of corn is OP' (or lower); it will specialize completely in steel. It will produce at
G" when the relative price of corn is OP" (or higher); it will specialize completely in
corn. It will produce at G when the relative price of corn is OP; it will not specialize
completely but will instead produce both corn and steel. (When the economy
produces at G, the capital-labor ratio will be WU in corn production and WV in steel
production.)

when we know the relative price of corn. Suppose that an economy is endowed with
$O\bar{K}$ capital per worker. If the relative price of corn is OP', the relative price of labor
will be OW', and the economy will be at G', where all its labor and capital are used
to manufacture steel. If the relative price of corn is OP", the relative price of labor
will be OW", and the economy will be at G", where all its labor and capital are used
to grow corn. Therefore, the segment G'G" corresponds to the country's transformation curve. When the relative price of corn is OP, the economy will be at G,
producing corn and steel. When that price is higher than OP, the economy will move
to a point above G, producing more corn and less steel.[3]

---

[3]When the relative price of corn falls below OP', the economy continues to produce at G', and
the relative price of labor remains at OW'. This says that the curve HH' has no economic
meaning for this economy when the relative price of corn is lower than OP' or higher than
OP". The relative price of labor gets stuck once the economy is completely specialized. It can
go no lower than OW' and no higher than OW".

Factor Endowments and the Transformation Curve

Before making further use of Figure 6-5, let us answer one more question. How does an economy respond to an increase in the supply of capital? The Rybczynski theorem holds but must be reformulated. When factor intensities were fixed, that theorem told us what would happen to the full-employment point. When factor intensities vary, it tells us what happens to the whole transformation curve.

In Chapter 4, where factor requirements were fixed, the Rybczynski theorem was illustrated by Figure 4-3. Look back at that diagram. The capital intensity of corn production was given by the slope of OC, the capital intensity of steel production was given by the slope of OS, and the slopes of those lines were fixed. An increase in the supply of capital from $O\bar{K}$ to $O\bar{K}'$ shifted the full-employment point from T to T', raising steel output to $N'T'$ and reducing corn output to OT'.

When factor intensities can vary, they depend on decisions by producers, given the relative price of labor. But we have already seen that the relative price of labor depends on the relative price of corn. When the relative price of corn is equal to the slope of the transformation curve at Q in Figure 6-4, the relative price of labor is equal to the slope of I_C at T. Factor intensities are not fixed, but they do not change unless there is a change in the relative price of corn. Accordingly, the shift of the full-employment point shown in Figure 4-3 can be reinterpreted as describing the shift of a point such as T in Figure 6-4 and, therefore, the shift of the output point Q. It illustrates the shift of the whole transformation curve due to a change in the factor endowment. The point on the new transformation curve having the same slope as Q will lie to the northwest of Q. The value of national output will rise expressed in corn or steel, and steel output will rise, too, but corn output will fall.

Here we see clearly the major difference in behavior between the modified Ricardian model and the modified Heckscher–Ohlin model. In the modified Ricardian model, an increase in the supply of capital used in making cloth altered the real earnings of the factors of production even when there was no change in the relative price of cloth. It led to a reallocation of labor from wine to cloth production, but no reallocation of land or capital. In the Heckscher–Ohlin model, an increase in the supply of capital does not affect real earnings unless it leads to a change in the relative price of corn. It causes a reallocation of capital along with the reallocation of labor, so factor intensities are not affected by the increase in the supply of capital. of labor, so factor intensities are not affected by the increase in the supply of capital. Hence, there are no changes in marginal products or real earnings.

Factor Endowments and Trade

The Rybczynski theorem can be used as before to derive the Heckscher–Ohlin theorem. Consider once again Manymen and Fewmen, which differ only in their factor endowments. As Manymen has more labor and less capital, the Rybczynski theorem tells us what will happen when the two countries' markets are unified by trade. As the relative price of corn must be the same in the two countries after trade is opened, Manymen will grow more corn and Fewmen will make more steel. As demand conditions are the same in the two countries, however, they will want to consume the same collections of goods. Therefore, Manymen will export corn, the labor-intensive good, and Fewmen will export steel, the capital-intensive good.

The results are summarized by Figure 6-6. Manymen has $O\bar{K}_1$ capital per worker. Fewmen has $O\bar{K}_2$ capital per worker. Before trade is opened, the relative price of corn is OP_1 in Manymen, the relative price of labor is OW_1, and Manymen produces at M. The relative price of corn is OP_2 in Fewmen, the relative price of labor is OW_2, and Fewmen produces at F. The relative price of corn is lower in Manymen, and so is the relative price of labor. After trade is opened, the relative price of corn moves to some such level as OP, driving the relative price of labor to OW in both countries. Corn and labor become more expensive in Manymen but cheaper in Fewmen. The output point for Manymen moves from M to M', closer to the CC' curve and farther from the SS' curve. As the relative price of corn rises in Manymen, it moves along its transformation curve to grow more corn and make less steel. The output point for Fewmen moves from F to F', in the opposite direction. As the relative price of corn falls in Fewmen, it moves along its transformation curve to grow less corn and make more steel.

Figure 6-6 illustrates another theorem. Free trade can equalize the two countries' factor prices. When the relative price of labor is OW in Manymen and Fewmen, their

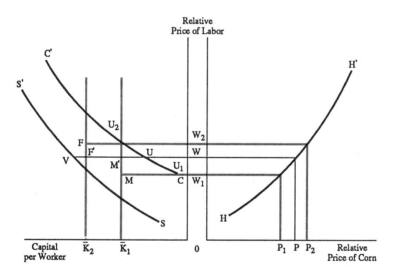

FIGURE 6-6

Free Trade Between Manymen and Fewmen

The capital-labor ratio is $O\bar{K}_1$ in Manymen and $O\bar{K}_2$ in Fewmen. Before trade is opened, the relative price of corn is OP_1 in Manymen, the relative price of labor is OW_1, and Manymen produces at M. The relative price of corn is OP_2 in Fewmen, the relative price of labor is OW_2, and Fewmen produces at F. The real wage is higher in Fewmen, and the real return to capital is higher in Manymen. When trade is opened, the relative price of corn goes to OP in both countries, and the relative price of labor goes to OW. Manymen produces at M', growing more corn and making less steel. Fewmen produces at F', growing less corn and making more steel. The real earnings of the factors have been equalized. The capital intensities of both industries are the same in both countries, having risen in Manymen and fallen in Fewmen. (In cloth production, for example, the capital-labor ratio is WU, having risen from W_1U_1 in Manymen and fallen from W_2U_2 in Fewmen.) Hence, the real wage has risen in Manymen and fallen in Fewmen, whereas the real return to capital has fallen in Manymen and risen in Fewmen.

industries must have the same capital intensities. (The capital intensity of corn output is given at U by the distance WU. The capital intensity of steel output is given at V by the distance WV.) Thus, the marginal products of labor and capital will be the same in the two countries, which means that the factors' real earnings will be equal, whether they are measured in corn or steel.

The factor-price-equalization theorem is a strong result, and it depends on strong assumptions. This is a useful point at which to recapitulate. All markets must be perfectly competitive. Both countries must have access to the same technologies and must produce both goods. There can be no trade barriers or transport costs. Returns to scale must be constant, and industries must differ in their factor intensities. These assumptions are unrealistic. They serve nonetheless to highlight an important implication of the Heckscher–Ohlin model: free trade tends to maximize world output.

Return to the pretrade situation in Figure 6-6. When the relative price of labor is OW_1 in Manymen and OW_2 in Fewmen, *both* industries are more capital intensive in Fewmen. Therefore, the marginal product of labor is lower in Manymen, and the marginal product of capital is lower in Fewmen.

Suppose that we could transfer factors of production from one country to the other. We could increase world output by moving labor from Manymen to Fewmen. Output would fall in Manymen but rise by more in Fewmen, because the marginal product of labor is higher in Fewmen. Similarly, we could increase world output by moving capital from Fewmen to Manymen. These transfers, however, would alter the marginal products. The marginal product of labor would rise in Manymen and fall in Fewmen; the marginal product of capital would fall in Manymen and rise in Fewmen. After the gaps were closed completely, we could not increase world output by moving more factors around. World output would be maximized.

Consider the role of trade from this same standpoint. Under the strong assumptions of the Heckscher–Ohlin model, free trade will equalize marginal products. The marginal product of labor will rise in Manymen and fall in Fewmen, closing the gap between marginal products without any transfer of labor. The marginal product of capital will fall in Fewmen and rise in Manymen without any transfer of capital. Therefore, free trade maximizes world output. It is a perfect substitute for factor movements from one country to another.

As factor-price equalization cannot be complete in the real world, free trade cannot maximize world output. Under much weaker assumptions than those made here, however, it does reduce differences between factor prices, narrowing the gaps between marginal products. Thus, it raises world output and is therefore a partial substitute for factor movements. This is another way to look at the gains from trade in the context of the Heckscher–Ohlin model.

ECONOMIC GROWTH IN THE HECKSCHER–OHLIN MODEL

As capital is used by both industries in the Heckscher–Ohlin model, we might expect the analysis of economic growth to be more complicated than it was in the modified Ricardian model. Fortunately, it is simpler, because the real earnings of the factors of production depend only on the terms of trade, and we do not have to worry about the good in which they are measured.

In the modified Ricardian model, labor was the only factor that moved between industries. Therefore, an increase in the relative price of cloth, inducing a shift of labor from wine to cloth production, increased the real wage in terms of wine but reduced it in terms of cloth. In the Heckscher–Ohlin model, labor and capital can move together, given enough time, and capital intensities can thus rise and fall together. An increase in the relative price of corn, the labor-intensive good, shifts labor and capital from steel to corn production, raising the capital intensities of steel and corn outputs. It thus raises the marginal products of labor in both industries and reduces the marginal products of capital. The real wage rises and the real return to capital falls whether they are measured in corn or steel.

In what follows, then, it will not be necessary to mention the good used to measure real earnings. It will be necessary, however, to remember that the results hold only in the long run, when capital has been optimally allocated between industries. We begin with capital formation; then we turn to other sources of economic growth.

Capital Formation in Fewmen

Consider the effects of capital formation in Fewmen, the capital-abundant country, which exports steel, the capital-intensive good. The output effects are given by the Rybczynski theorem. At the goods and factor prices prevailing initially, real national product will rise in Fewmen, steel output will rise, too, and corn output will fall.[4] But consumers in Fewmen will demand more corn and steel, so Fewmen will display an excess demand for corn matched by an excess supply of steel. Its offer curve will shift outward, because it exports steel, and its terms of trade will deteriorate. The story is the same one told by Figure 5-8 in Chapter 5, with steel and corn put in place of cloth and wine, Fewmen put in place of Britain, and Manymen put in place of Portugal. Fewmen's offer curve will shift from OJ to OJ', displacing equilibrium from W to W'. The relative price of steel will fall, which worsens Fewmen's terms of trade.

The effects on economic welfare resemble those obtained when capital formation took place in Britain in the modified Ricardian model. If the relative price of steel falls far enough, Fewmen can experience immiserizing growth. The deterioration in its terms of trade can wipe out the welfare gain conferred by capital formation, because consumers can be driven to an indifference curve lower than the one on which they started. Otherwise, Fewmen will gain from growth, but the gain will be smaller than the gain it would obtain if Fewmen were too small to influence world prices. By implication, Manymen is bound to gain. It will experience an improvement in its terms of trade.

How do real earnings change? They are not affected by capital formation until it reduces the relative price of steel. Once that happens, moreover, we have merely to

---

[4]The shift in the transformation curve is much like the one in Figure 5-6 of Chapter 5, with steel put in place of cloth and corn put in place of wine. But there is one difference. As capital is used by both industries, capital formation increases the distance OZ_2 as well as the distance OZ_1. The whole curve shifts outward.

apply the Stolper–Samuelson theorem. A reduction in the relative price of steel depresses the real return to capital, the factor used intensively in making steel. It raises the real wage of labor, the factor used intensively in growing corn. Furthermore, these same things happen in Fewmen and Manymen whenever free trade equalizes the two countries' factor prices.

The effects of capital formation in Fewmen are summarized by Figure 6-7. Manymen has $O\bar{K}_1$ capital per worker, and Fewmen has $O\bar{K}_2$ before the increase in its capital stock. The relative price of corn is OP in both countries, and the relative price of labor is OW. Manymen produces at M, and Fewmen produces at F. Capital formation in Fewmen raises the quantity of capital per worker to $O\bar{K}'_2$, shifting Fewmen's output point to F', where Fewmen makes more steel and grows less corn. This change in the output mix raises the relative price of corn to some such level as OP'. Therefore, it raises the relative price of labor to OW' and shifts both countries' output points. Fewmen moves from F' to F'', and Manymen moves from M to M'. Both countries grow more corn and make less steel to compensate for the shift in Fewmen's output mix when it moved initially from F to F'. Capital intensities rise

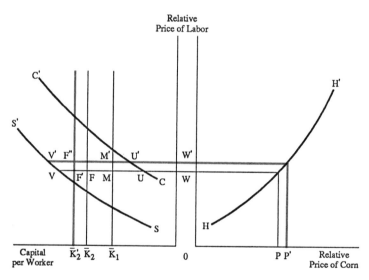

FIGURE 6-7

Capital Formation in Fewmen

Manymen has $O\bar{K}_1$ capital per worker, and Fewmen has $O\bar{K}_2$. With free trade between them, the relative price of corn is OP in both countries, and the relative price of labor is OW. Manymen produces at M, and Fewmen produces at F. The capital intensity of corn production is WU, and the capital intensity of steel production is WV. Capital formation in Fewmen raises capital per worker to $O\bar{K}'_2$ and shifts that country's output point from F to F', where it produces more steel and less corn. The reduction in total corn output raises the relative price of corn to OP', and the relative price of labor rises to OW'. The output point in Fewmen moves from F' to F'', and the output point in Manymen moves from M to M'. The capital intensities of corn and steel production rise to $W'U'$ and $W'V'$, respectively, raising the marginal products of labor in both industries and countries and reducing the marginal products of capital. Real wages rise and real returns to capital fall.

rise in both industries and countries, raising real wages in both countries and reducing real returns to capital.

Capital Formation in Manymen

You should be able to ascertain the effects of capital formation in Manymen. The effects on relative prices and real returns must be the same as when capital formation took place in Fewmen. But Manymen imports steel, which means that a reduction in the relative price of steel is an improvement in Manymen's terms of trade. Accordingly, capital formation in Manymen cannot be immiserizing, and its welfare effects are unambiguous:

Location of Capital formation	Economic Welfare	
	Fewmen	Manymen
Fewmen	Ambiguous	Increase
Manymen	Decrease	Increase

This tabulation is identical to the one for the modified Ricardian model.

Growth in the Supply of Labor

The long-run effects of growth in the supply of labor are given by the Rybczynski and Stolper–Samuelson theorems. It increases the supply of the labor-intensive good in the growing country and decreases the supply of the capital-intensive good. Therefore, it reduces the relative price of the labor-intensive good, worsening the terms of trade of the labor-abundant country. Furthermore, it raises the real return to capital in both countries and reduces the real wage. These effects are perfectly analogous to those obtained previously for capital formation. But a new problem arises. An increase in the supply of labor usually involves an increase in the number of consumers, which affects the measurement of economic welfare.

When studying capital formation in Fewmen, we saw that it raised real national product, which cushioned the effect of the deterioration in Fewmen's terms of trade. As the number of consumers was constant, the increase in real national product raised consumers' incomes and led to an increase in economic welfare at the initial terms of trade. There had to be a large deterioration in the terms of trade before Fewmen could experience immiserizing growth. With an increase in the supply of labor and no change in the supply of capital, real national product rises by less than the number of consumers (workers), and consumers' incomes fall. (Proof is offered in Section 4 of Appendix A.) Therefore, growth in the supply of labor reduces economic welfare at the initial terms of trade.

Accordingly, we come to dismal conclusions regarding the effects of growth in one country's population:

1. When population growth takes place in Manymen, which exports the labor-intensive good, it is bound to be immiserizing. The welfare-decreasing deterioration in Manymen's terms of trade is combined with a welfare-decreasing decline in consumers' incomes. But Fewmen gains, as usual, because its terms of trade improve.

2. When population growth takes place in Fewmen, which imports the labor-intensive good, it can still be immiserizing. The welfare-increasing improvement in Fewmen's terms of trade may not be large enough to offset the welfare-decreasing decline in consumers' incomes. Manymen loses, moreover, because its terms of trade deteriorate.

There is a difference, however, between the immiserizing growth that occurs with population growth and the sort that can occur with capital formation. Population growth is immiserizing in a closed economy; terms-of-trade effects can make matters worse or better, but they are not the primary cause of the welfare loss. Capital formation cannot be immiserizing in a closed economy; terms-of-trade effects are crucial for the outcome.

These assertions are illustrated in Figure 6-8, where outputs are divided by numbers of persons to show how capital formation and population growth affect the welfare of the typical consumer. The transformation curve is $Z_1 Z_2$ initially in both parts of the diagram, and it is tangent at E to an indifference curve U_0.[5] Real output per capita is OA measured in corn, and equals real income per capita. Corn output per capita is OX_1 and equals corn consumption per capita in a closed economy. Steel output per capita is OX_2 and equals steel consumption per capita.

The effects of capital formation are shown in the upper panel of the diagram, where the transformation curve shifts outward to $Z_1' Z_2'$. If the relative price of corn were constant, real product per capita would rise to OB measured in corn, shifting the output point to E'. As the Rybczynski theorem holds for outputs per capita, capital formation raises steel output per capita and reduces corn output per capita. But a portion of the new transformation curve lies above U_0, so the typical consumer can

---

[5]The outputs shown by this transformation curve can be obtained from equations. (3.4) in Section 3 of Appendix A. Factor L from the right side of each equation and divide both sides of each equation by N (population):

$$\frac{x_1}{N} = \frac{1}{D}\frac{L}{N}\left[b_2 - a_2\left(\frac{K}{L}\right)\right] \quad \text{and} \quad \frac{x_2}{N} = \frac{1}{D}\frac{L}{N}\left[a_1\left(\frac{K}{L}\right) - b_1\right],$$

where $D = a_1 b_2 - a_2 b_1 > 0$ when x_1 is the labor-intensive good (corn). Outputs per capita depend on L/N, which measures labor-force participation, on K/L, the capital-labor ratio for the whole economy, and on the capital and labor requirements, a_i and b_i ($i = 1, 2$). Output per capita of the labor-intensive good falls with an increase in the capital-labor ratio, and output per capita of the capital-intensive good rises. The Rybczynski theorem applies to outputs per capita. Furthermore, Section 4 of Appendix A shows that real product per capita rises with an increase in the capital-labor ratio. (The curve U_0, incidentally, is an individual indifference curve, not a community indifference curve of the sort used previously.)

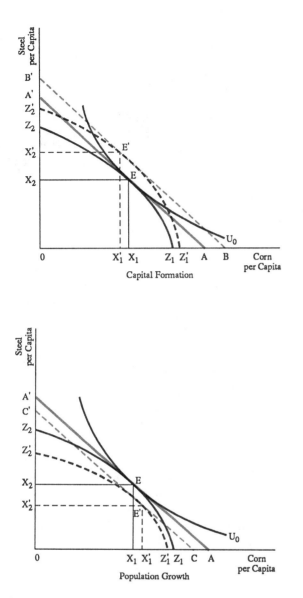

FIGURE 6-8
Capital Formation and Population Growth in a Closed Economy
The transformation curve Z_1Z_2 in the upper panel shows outputs per capita of corn
and steel. It is tangent to the indifference curve U_0 at E. Capital formation shifts the
transformation curve outward to $Z_1'Z_2'$. If relative prices remain unchanged, the output
point will go to E', where corn output per capita falls from OX_1 to OX_1' and steel
output per capita rises from OX_2 to OX_2'. Real product per capita will increase from
OA to OB measured in corn. As portions of $Z_1'Z_2'$ lie above U_0, the typical consumer can
reach a higher indifference curve. Capital formation cannot be immiserizing in a
closed economy. The situation is the same initially in the lower panel of the diagram.
But population growth shifts the transformation curve inward to $Z_1'Z_2'$. If relative
prices remain unchanged, the output point will go to E', where corn output per capita
rises from OX_1 to OX_1' and steel output per capita falls from OX_2 to OX_2'. Real product
per capita decreases from OA to OC measured in corn. As $Z_1'Z_2'$ lies entirely below U_0,
the typical consumer is driven to a lower indifference curve. Population growth is
always immiserizing in a closed economy.

reach a higher indifference curve. Therefore, capital formation raises welfare in a closed economy.[6]

The effects of population growth are shown in the lower panel of the diagram, where the transformation curve shifts *inward* to $Z'_1Z'_2$. If the relative price of corn were constant, real product per capita would fall to OC measured in corn, shifting the output point to E'. Population growth reduces steel output per capita and raises corn output per capita. In this case, however, the new transformation curve lies entirely below U_0, so the typical consumer is driven to a lower indifference curve. Therefore, population growth reduces welfare in a closed economy.

Growth in Supplies of Capital and Labor

What happens when the capital stock and population grow together? The long-run effects on economic welfare depend on their rates of growth. This can be shown clearly by treating the two examples already considered as limiting cases. When the supply of labor rises in Manymen, which exports the labor-intensive good, without any increase in the supply of capital, economic welfare falls in Manymen. It is reduced by the decline in consumers' incomes and the deterioration in the terms of trade. When the supply of capital rises without any increase in population, economic welfare rises in Manymen. It is raised by the increase in consumers' incomes and the improvement in the terms of trade. But one more case deserves attention, because it introduces an important point.

Suppose that there is *balanced growth* in a single country. Capital formation and population growth proceed at the same rate. The whole economy will grow at that rate, but quantities per capita will not change. The closed economy described in Figure 6-8 will remain where it was to start, and the typical consumer will stay on the indifference curve U_0. An open economy, however, will demand more imports and offer more exports. (Imports per capita will not change, but total imports will grow with the increase in population.) Therefore, the country's offer curve will shift outward, and its terms of trade will deteriorate. Balanced growth reduces economic welfare. Note that this result was obtained without knowing whether the growing economy exported the labor-intensive or capital-intensive good.

An Improvement in Economic Efficiency

Consider, finally, the effects of technological change. They depend on the nature of the change, the industry affected by it, and the country in which it occurs.

Increase the efficiency of steel production in Fewmen, the country that has its comparative advantage in steel. For simplicity, assume that the improvement is

---

[6]When consumers demand more of both commodities as their incomes increase, capital formation raises the relative price of corn. The increase in real product per capita from OA to OB raises the demands for corn and steel, but steel output rises and corn output falls as the output point goes from E to E'. There is thus an excess demand for corn that raises the relative price of corn. The final equilibrium position occurs on $Z'_1Z'_2$ to the southeast of E'. For analogous reasons, population growth reduces the relative price of corn. But these adjustments do not alter the principal results regarding the changes in economic welfare.

"factor neutral" in that it raises the efficiency with which the industry uses capital and labor without affecting the capital intensity chosen at each set of factor prices.[7]

The increase of efficiency has two effects. First, it raises the quantity of steel that Fewmen can produce with each allocation of labor and capital. Second, it reduces the cost of producing a ton of steel by reducing labor and capital requirements. The two effects together shift the transformation curve in the manner shown by Figure 5-6 in Chapter 5, with steel put in place of cloth and corn in place of wine. The output-increasing effect of the increase in efficiency will shift the output point to the right; steel output will exceed OX_1 when corn output is OX_2. The cost-reducing effect will make the new transformation curve flatter at each point, so the point on the new curve that has the same slope as the old curve at E is some point such as E', where steel output is larger than OX_1 but corn output is smaller than OX_2. The result resembles the prediction made by the Rybczynski theorem. An increase in the efficiency of one industry raises real national product, raises the output of the industry affected, and reduces the output of the other industry when the prices of goods do not change.

The welfare effects resemble those we encountered when studying capital formation in Fewmen. The increase in real national product generates an increase in consumers' incomes. But it also raises Fewmen's demand for corn imports, because domestic consumption rises and domestic production falls. Accordingly, the terms of trade move against Fewmen, and the welfare effect is ambiguous. An increase of efficiency in the export industry can reduce economic welfare if it leads to a large deterioration in the terms of trade. (There is, of course, an increase in welfare in Manymen, because its terms of trade improve.)

The increase in efficiency, however, differs from capital formation in one important way. By changing technology in Fewmen, it interferes with factor-price equalization. Figure 6-9 reproduces the initial free-trade equilibrium shown in earlier diagrams. Manymen has $O\bar{K}_1$ capital per worker, and Fewmen has $O\bar{K}_2$. With free trade between them, the relative price of corn is OP, and the relative price of labor is OW. The capital intensity of corn production is WU in both countries, and the capital intensity of steel production is WV. Therefore, factor prices are the same in both countries. But an increase of efficiency in Fewmen's steel industry changes the relationship between the relative prices of labor and corn. The cost-reducing effect of the change in technology shifts the HH' curve outward in Fewmen. The new curve is $H_FH'_F$. If the relative price of labor were to remain at OW, the relative price of corn would rise to OP'.

With free trade between the two countries, however, prices have to be the same in Fewmen and Manymen, and we already know what happens. The relative price of corn rises, because of the increase in Fewmen's demand for corn imports. It comes to rest at some such level as OP''. The relative price of labor rises in Manymen, raising the capital intensities of that country's industries. Hence, the marginal

---

[7]A factor-neutral improvement raises the marginal products of capital and labor to the same extent, shifting each isoquant inward without changing its shape. An improvement can be biased. It can raise one marginal product by more than the other and will then twist each isoquant when shifting it inward, affecting capital intensities and thus affecting the position of the SS' curve in Figure 6-9.

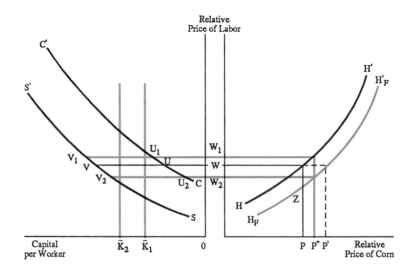

FIGURE 6-9
An Improvement in Efficiency in Fewmen's Steel Industry
The relative price of corn is *OP* initially, the relative price of labor is *OW*, the capital intensity of corn production is *WU*, and the capital intensity of steel production is *WV*. An increase of efficiency in Fewmen's steel industry shifts the curve connecting the relative price of labor to the relative price of corn. It was *HH'* initially for both countries. It is H_FH_F' for Fewmen after the improvement. The relative price of corn would rise to *OP'* if the relative price of labor remained at *OW*. But the improvement raises Fewmen's demand for corn imports, which raises the relative price of corn to *OP"* in both countries. In Manymen, the relative price of labor rises to OW_1, the capital intensity of corn production rises to W_1U_1, and the capital intensity of steel production rises to W_1V_1. In Fewmen, the relative price of labor falls to OW_2, the capital intensity of corn production falls to W_2U_2, and the capital intensity of steel production falls to W_2V_2. Hence, the real return to capital falls in Manymen and rises in Fewmen.

products of capital fall in both industries, reducing the real return to capital. But the relative price of labor falls in Fewmen, reducing the capital intensities of that country's industries and raising the real return to capital. Thus, the increase of efficiency in Fewmen's steel industry creates a difference between the two countries' technologies, interfering with factor-price equalization.

SUMMARY

In the modified Heckscher–Ohlin model, factor intensities depend on factor prices. An increase in the relative price of labor causes firms to substitute capital for labor, making each industry more capital intensive. The requirements of equilibrium in the factor markets determine the relative price of labor and actual factor intensities. An economy can thus use its factors fully at each point on its transformation curve. All the theorems of the Heckscher–Ohlin model hold in the modified version of the model.

An increase in the relative price of corn raises corn output and the demand for labor, the factor used intensively in growing corn. Therefore, it raises the relative price of labor. The marginal product of labor rises, raising the real wage. The marginal product of capital falls, reducing the real return. These statements lead directly to the *Stolper–Samuelson theorem*. In a labor-abundant country, trade raises the real wage of labor and reduces the real return to capital. In a capital-abundant country, trade raises the real return to capital and reduces the real wage of labor.

An increase in the supply of one factor raises the output of the product intensive in that factor at each set of goods and factor prices. This is the *Rybczynski theorem*. It leads directly to the factor-proportions version of the *Heckscher–Ohlin theorem*. The country that has little capital per worker will export the labor-intensive good, and the country that has much capital per worker will export the capital-intensive good. Finally, the *factor-price-equalization theorem* continues to hold and takes on an additional implication. By closing gaps between marginal products, free trade maximizes world output.

The welfare effects of capital formation are similar to those in the modified Ricardian model but must be stated differently. If the growing country imports the capital-intensive good, that country gains and the other country loses. If the growing country exports the capital-intensive good, it can gain or lose, but the other country gains. Capital formation reduces the real return to capital in both countries, regardless of the good in which it is measured, and raises the real wage.

Some of the effects of population growth are symmetrical to those of capital formation. But population growth is more likely to reduce economic welfare in the growing country. It causes immiserizing growth in a closed economy, and capital formation cannot. Therefore, population growth is necessarily immiserizing in an open economy unless the economy imports the labor-intensive good, so that its terms of trade improve; the terms-of-trade improvement can be large enough to offset the welfare-reducing effect of population growth.

The effects of an increase in efficiency depend on the nature of the increase and the industry and country in which it occurs. In the simplest case, it raises the output of the affected industry and reduces the output of the other industry. Therefore, an increase of efficiency in the export industry can raise or lower welfare at home, because it worsens the terms of trade, but it raises welfare abroad. An increase of efficiency in the import-competing industry raises welfare at home, by improving the terms of trade, but it lowers welfare abroad. The effects on real earnings likewise depend on the industry in which efficiency rises, and they will be different at home and abroad, because an increase of efficiency interferes with factor-price equalization.

RECOMMENDED READINGS

The Heckscher–Ohlin model as a whole is described concisely by Harry G. Johnson, "Factor Endowments, International Trade, and Factor Prices," *Manchester School of Economic and Social Studies*, 25 (September 1957), reprinted in American Economic Association, *Readings in International Economics* (Homewood, Ill.: Richard D. Irwin, 1968), ch. 5.

The Stolper-Samuelson theorem is developed with flexible factor intensities in Wolfgang F. Stolper and Paul A. Samuelson, "Protection and Real Wages," *Review of*

Economic Studies, 9 (November 1941), reprinted in American Economic Association, *Readings in the Theory of International Trade* (Philadelphia: Blakiston, 1949), ch. 15.

The factor-price-equalization theorem is set out clearly in Paul A. Samuelson, "International Factor-Price Equalisation Once Again," *Economic Journal*, 59 (June 1949), reprinted in American Economic Association, *Readings in International Economics* (Homewood, Ill.: Richard D. Irwin, 1968), ch. 3.

For a different treatment of the role of capital in the Heckscher–Ohlin model, see Peter B. Kenen, "Nature, Capital, and Trade," *Journal of Political Economy*, 73 (October 1965), reprinted in P. B. Kenen, *Essays in International Economics* (Princeton, N.J.: Princeton University Press, 1980).

On economic growth, trade, and welfare in the Heckscher–Ohlin model, see Harry G. Johnson, "Economic Development and International Trade," *Nationaløkonomist Tidskrift*, 97 (1959), reprinted in American Economic Association, *Readings in International Economics* (Homewood, Ill.: Richard D. Irwin, 1968), ch. 17.

For a survey of research on trade and growth in various trade models, see Ronald Findlay, "Growth and Development in Trade Models," in R. W. Jones and P. B. Kenen, eds., *Handbook of International Economics*, Vol. 1 (Amsterdam: North-Holland, 1984).

The treatment of growth in this chapter has asked how trade and the terms of trade are affected by capital formation and technological change that take place independently. New work on this subject asks how capital formation and technological change interact with trade. It uses models featuring economies of scale and imperfect competition, discussed in the next chapter, and recommended readings are listed at the end of that chapter.

QUESTIONS AND PROBLEMS

(1) Prove the assertion in the text—that you can work out for yourself the effects of capital formation in Manymen.

(2) Adapt Figure 6-6 to illustrate a case in which free trade between Manymen and Fewmen leads Manymen to specialize completely in corn and Fewmen to specialize completely in steel.

(3) Adapt Figure 6-6 to show what happens when Manymen imposes an import tariff on steel. How do factor prices, factor intensities, and the real earnings of labor and capital change in Manymen. How do they change in Fewmen?

(4) Adapt Figure 6-6 to show how a factor reversal interferes with factor-price equalization. (Redraw the CC' and SS' curves so they cross at some point, making corn more labor intensive than steel when the relative price of labor is low, but more capital intensive than steel when the relative price of labor is high. Then ask yourself how the reversal affects the shape of the HH' curve.)

(5) There is balanced growth in Manymen and Fewmen, but the rate of growth is higher in Manymen. Explain why the terms of trade will turn against Manymen. Why must this reduce economic welfare in Manymen and raise it in Fewmen?

(6) Trace the effects of a factor-neutral increase of efficiency in Fewmen's corn industry, taking account of the change in relative prices resulting from the change in Fewmen's demand for corn imports. Show how it will affect Fewmen's transformation curve, the output point at constant prices, and the actual output point. What will happen to economic welfare in Fewmen and Manymen?

(7) Using your answer to (6), adapt Figure 6-9 to show how the increase of efficiency in Fewmen's corn industry will affect factor intensities and factor returns in Fewmen and Manymen.

7

Imperfect Competition and International Trade

THE ISSUES

The trade models presented in previous chapters cannot explain two striking characteristics of the international economy. First, countries with similar factor endowments trade heavily among themselves, resulting in two-way trade between many pairs of countries in many classes of goods. Second, firms engaged in international trade also undertake international investment, resulting in multinational production.

These two features of the international economy can be shown to reflect two characteristics of modern industrial economies—imperfect competition and economies of scale. This chapter will show how these characteristics influence trade by focusing sharply on two issues:

- How firms with monopoly power at home compete with similar firms abroad.
- Why countries with similar factor endowments engage in two-way trade.

The next chapter will show why imperfect competition and economies of scale lead firms to engage in multinational production.

INTERINDUSTRY AND INTRAINDUSTRY TRADE

We need not dwell at length on the frequency and size of visible departures from perfect competition. Large parts of the manufacturing sector in every major country are dominated by small numbers of companies. You can count on your fingers the number of automobile manufacturers in the United States, Japan, or

Western Europe, and you will have fingers left over to count the worldwide total of companies that manufacture large commercial aircraft.

Nevertheless, these numbers overstate the degree of concentration and thus understate the intensity of competition. Firms producing in one country must compete with foreign firms, not just among themselves. That is one main gain from trade that was neglected in earlier chapters. Trade tends to intensify competition. Furthermore, the number of firms actually in business does not measure the intensity of competition when new firms—including foreign firms—can enter an industry easily. The mere threat of entry can deter monopolistic behavior.

Competition is still far from perfect, however, because there are significant barriers to entry. First, the products and technologies of existing firms are protected by patents. Second, those firms have cost and reputational advantages because they have acquired experience in making and marketing their products. Third, it is expensive to build and start up a new plant big enough to offer the economies of scale already enjoyed by established firms. We will cite these barriers to entry when we study the opening of trade between two countries whose national markets have each been dominated by a single firm and when we study two-way trade in differentiated products—those that have similar factor intensities but differ in function, quality, or style.

The aims of this chapter can be restated in terms of a distinction used increasingly by trade theorists. The models presented in previous chapters help us to explain *interindustry* trade: flows of goods with different factor intensities. Countries with large supplies of skilled labor tend to export sophisticated manufactures; those with large supplies of unskilled labor tend to export simple manufactures; and those with large supplies of land or natural resources tend to export agricultural or resource-intensive goods. But those models do not help us to explain *intraindustry* trade: flows of goods with similar factor intensities. Countries that are large net exporters of sophisticated manufactures are, of course, importers of simple manufactures, farm products, and raw materials. But they also trade among themselves, exporting similar sophisticated products to each other.

The extent of intraindustry trade is impressive. Look at Table 7-1, which lists selected manufactures that appear on both sides of the U.S. trade accounts. The United States exports about $1 billion of automotive engines, but its imports are almost three times as large. It exports many types of machinery but imports every one of them. And it exports $3.0 billion of books, records, disks, and tapes but imports $2.5 billion.

The two-way trade in automotive engines testifies to the importance of multinational production, because most such engines are bought by the foreign affiliates of the firm that makes them. Much intraindustry trade is also *intrafirm* trade. But that is a characteristic of such trade, not an explanation. Why do Japanese companies assemble cars in the United States, using engines made in Japan? Factor requirements play a role, as they are not the same at all stages of production. Tariffs and other trade barriers are also important. But a bigger question lies ahead. Why do Americans buy Japanese cars when they can buy less expensive American cars? For once, the obvious answer is also the right answer. The two countries' cars are not identical. And that answer covers many other cases. Clearly, American books and records are not identical to British, Dutch, or German books and records. Some

Table 7-1. Examples of Intraindustry Trade: U.S. Exports and Imports of Selected Manufactured Goods, 1988 (in millions of dollars)

Category	Exports	Imports
Motor vehicle engines	1,194	3,107
Gas turbines	2,250	1,142
Harvesting machinery	731	510
Metal-cutting machine tools	455	1,588
Airconditioning machinery	954	795
Lifting and loading machinery	970	773
Ball and roller bearings	413	962
Line telephone equipment	1,522	3,442
Electronic microcircuits	4,114	8,778
Film	1,430	1,285
Books	922	832
Sound recordings, disks, and tapes	2,050	1,683

Source: United Nations, *Yearbook of International Trade Statistics*, 1988.

cases are harder to explain, however, because the product differences are far smaller. We will soon see, in fact, that a country may export and import identical varieties of the same basic product, because the domestic and foreign firms that make the product will invade each other's market. Let us study that case first, before looking at trade in differentiated products.

TRADE BETWEEN MONOPOLIZED NATIONAL MARKETS

Consider two companies, Edo in Japan and Acme in America, that manufacture industrial robots. Let them be identical in every way and face identical national markets. To keep the analysis simple, suppose that they have constant marginal costs but that the fixed costs of making robots, including the costs of design and development, are high enough to prevent additional firms from entering the robot market. Edo and Acme will thus function as monopolists until trade is opened between their home markets.

Equilibrium in the Closed Economies

Because firms and markets are identical here, we can concentrate completely on one country's market, before and after trade is opened. The same things will happen in the other market.

Figure 7-1 describes the American market before trade is opened. The American demand curve for robots is *DD*. Although they are producer's goods, not consumers' goods the demand curve for robots is downward sloping, because their use will spread as their prices fall. The corresponding marginal-revenue curve is *MR*. It is a

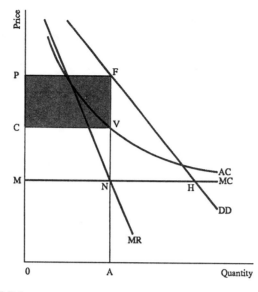

FIGURE 7-1
Acme's American Market Before Trade
The American demand curve for robots is *DD*, and the corresponding marginal-revenue curve is *MR* (which lies half way between *DD* and the vertical axis when *DD* is a straight line). Acme's marginal-cost curve is *MC*, and its average-cost curve is *AC*. As *MR = MC* at *N*, Acme maximizes its profits by selling *OA* robots in the American market. The price there is *OP*, Acme's total revenue is *OAFP*, its total cost is *OAVC* (*OANM* variable cost *plus* *MNVC* fixed cost), and profits are *CVFP*. Note that *OA = MN = (1/2)MH*.

straight line when *DD* is a straight line, but is twice as steep. Proof of this and other statements about Figure 7-1 are given in Section 5 of Appendix A (which handles a slightly more complicated case in which firms and markets are not identical). As the marginal cost of making a robot is constant here, the marginal-cost curve is the horizontal line *MC* (which also shows average variable cost). But there are fixed costs, too, so the average cost of making a robot is the downward-sloping curve *AC*.

Because Acme can act as a monopolist before trade is opened, it will maximize its profits by producing the output at which marginal revenue is equal to marginal cost and selling that output in the American market. Thus, it produces *OA* robots and sells them at the price *OP*. Its profits are *CVFP*. Note that Acme's strategy can be described without drawing the marginal-revenue curve, because *MR* must intersect *MC* at *N*, half way along *HM*. Therefore, marginal-revenue curves are omitted from subsequent diagrams.

The situation in the American market is replicated in the identical Japanese market, where Edo produces *OA* robots and sells them at *OP*.

The Opening of Trade

In previous models, a difference in prices was both necessary and sufficient to generate trade. That was the law of comparative advantage. Trade will take place here, however, even though prices are equal in the two countries' markets. Edo will invade the American market, and Acme will invade the Japanese market.

Before we can show what they will do, however, we must deal with a problem that does not arise under perfect competition or monopoly but is vital under *oligopoly*, where a few large firms dominate a market. With perfect competition, an individual firm does not worry about the behavior of other firms, because it is too small to provoke any change in their behavior; it takes prices as given. With monopoly, the individual firm does not have to worry about the behavior of others, because there are no others. With oligopoly, by contrast, each firm is large enough to influence the others and must forecast their behavior when planning its own strategy. How will the other firms respond? This example uses a simple supposition. Each firm expects its foreign rival to keep on selling the same quantity of robots, even when its own behavior leads to a change in the price of robots.

The effects of this supposition on Edo's behavior are shown in Figure 7-2, which reproduces the main features of Figure 7-1 but adds one fact. The marginal-cost curve has been relabeled to remind us that Acme and Edo have the same marginal costs.[1] As Acme has been selling OA robots in the American market and Edo expects it to keep on doing so, Edo knows that it cannot sell any robots in the American market if the price there remains at OP. At any lower price, however, it can invade the American market. In effect, Edo faces that portion of the American demand curve that lies to the right of the line AF. It thus faces a marginal-revenue curve that starts at F and crosses the marginal-cost curve at T, half way along NH. Therefore, Edo will export AE robots to the American market. This will drive down the price to OP', but Edo's total profits will rise by $NTGF'$. Acme's profits will fall by $P'F'FP$, however, until it changes the volume of its sales.

Acme will be doing the same thing in the Japanese market that Edo is doing in the American market, so each firm faces the same problem. What to do about the invasion of its domestic market?

We could use Figure 7-2 to show how Acme will respond, but that would be cumbersome. We would have then to trace Edo's answer to Acme's response, and so on. It is easier to use new tools, known as *reaction curves*, and not hard to derive them. We start with Figure 7-3, which reproduces the demand curve DD and shows how Edo will behave when Acme has chosen its level of sales in the American market and Edo expects Acme to keep to that level.

Suppose that Acme decides to sell OA robots. Edo will face that part of the demand curve that lies to the right of the line AF and will go to T, half way along NH, just as it did in Figure 7-2. It will sell AE robots in the American market. Suppose that Acme decides to sell OA' robots instead, driving down the price to OP'. Edo will face that part of the demand curve that lies to the right of the line $A'F'$ and

---

[1]The AC curve has been dropped from Figure 7-2, along with the MR curve, because it is not immediately relevant to Edo's behavior. Edo has been covering its fixed costs (and making a profit) from its sales in Japan. The AC curve would tell us whether Acme can continue to cover its fixed costs from its sales in America and, by implication, whether Edo can continue to cover its fixed costs from its sales in Japan. But that information would not be useful, because each firm will be selling in the other's market as well as its own. We do need to know that both firms can cover their fixed costs from their *total* sales when they reach equilibrium. Otherwise, the equilibrium will not be sustainable. (In this particular example, both firms can do so when one firm can, because their situations are identical, and both firms will take losses when one firm does. But we will ignore that last possibility.)

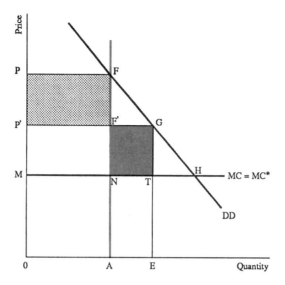

FIGURE 7-2
Edo Enters the American Market
The demand curve *DD* and Acme's marginal-cost curve *MC* are reproduced from Figure 7-1 (but the latter is also Edo's marginal-cost curve and is labeled accordingly). Acme's initial position is also reproduced from Figure 7-1; it sells *OA* robots in the American market at the price *OP*. Taking that level of Acme's sales to be fixed, Edo will enter the American market. Its marginal-revenue curve (not drawn) starts at *F* and passes through *T*, the midpoint of *NH*, so Edo will export *AE* robots to the American market, driving down the price to *OP'*. Edo's profits will rise by *NTGF'*, but Acme's profits will fall by *P'F'FP* until Acme changes the volume of its sales.

will go to *T'*, half way along *N'H*. It will sell *A'E'* robots in the American market. What is the relationship between the changes in the two firms' sales? The text attached to Figure 7-3 shows that Edo's sales will fall by half of any increase in Acme's sales. Reversing the procedure, we could start with an arbitrary level of sales by Edo, find Acme's sales, and show that Acme's sales in the American market will fall by half of any increase in Edo's sales.

These statements are repeated in Figure 7-4, using reaction curves for the two firms. Acme's reaction curve is *AA*. When Edo's exports to the American market are zero, Acme sells OX_0 robots in that market. (This was the quantity *OA* in Figure 7-2, which measured Acme's sales when there was no trade.) As Edo starts to sell robots in the American market, Acme reduces its sales; they fall by half of every increase in Edo's sales. Edo's reaction curve is *EE*. If Acme sold no robots in the American market, Edo would sell OX_0^*. (This is likewise the quantity *OA* in Figure 7-2, because the two firms have the same marginal costs.) As Acme starts to sell robots in that market, Edo reduces its sales; they fall by half of every increase in Acme's sales.

It is easy to depict the opening of trade and the subsequent adjustments made by the two firms until they reach an equilibrium. As Acme was selling OX_0 robots before trade was opened, Edo will go to Q_1 on its own reaction curve; it will start to sell OX_1^* robots in the American market. We have already seen however, that Edo's sales drive down the price of robots and Acme must alter its behavior. Because

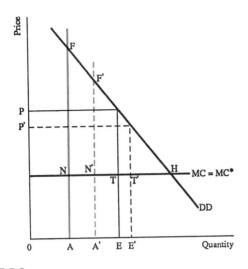

FIGURE 7-3
Deriving Edo's Reaction Curve
Let Acme sell *OA* robots in the American market. Taking that level to be fixed, Edo will export $(1/2)NH = NT = AE$ robots to the American market, and the price will be *OP*. Now let Acme sell *OA'* robots instead. Taking that level to be fixed, Edo will export $(1/2)N'H = N'T' = A'E'$ robots, and the price will be *OP'*. But $(1/2)N'H = (1/2)(NH - NN') = AE - (1/2)AA'$, so Edo will reduce its sales by half of any increase in Acme's sales.

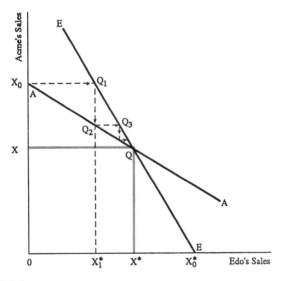

FIGURE 7-4
Oligopolistic Equilibrium in the American Market
Edo's reaction curve is *EE*, showing that Edo will decrease its sales in the American market by half of any increase in Acme's sales. Acme's reaction curve is *AA*, showing that Acme will decrease its sales in the American market by half of any increase in Edo's sales. Before trade was opened, Acme was selling *OX₀* robots in the American market. As soon as trade is opened, Edo moves to Q_1 on *EE*, selling *OX₁* robots in that market. This causes Acme to move to Q_2 on *AA*, which takes Edo to Q_3, and the two firms converge to equilibrium at *Q*, where Acme sells *OX* and Edo sells *OX** (and $OX = OX^*$).

Acme assumes that Edo will keep its sales at OX_1^*, Acme will go to Q_2 on its reaction curve, reducing its sales by half of Edo's sales. But that will cause Edo to adjust its sales; it will go to Q_3 and thus raise its sales by half of the reduction in Acme's sales. Eventually, the two firms will reach Q and will stay there. Acme has no cause to alter its sales when Edo sells OX^* robots, and Edo has no cause to alter its sales when Acme sells OX robots.

The equilibrium at Q has two characteristics. First, the market is divided evenly between the two firms, because they have identical costs. We will soon see that Acme's sales would be larger and Edo's sales smaller if Acme's cost were lower. (Transport costs would also favor Acme in the American market by making it more expensive for Edo to deliver goods to that market.) Second, the price in the American market is lower at Q than it was before the opening of trade. This is because the volume of sales is larger. The overall reduction in Acme's sales (from OX_0 to OX) is only half as large as the overall increase in Edo's sales (from zero to OX^*), so total sales have increased by half of Edo's sales.

The same diagram can be used to locate equilibrium in the Japanese market. The story starts differently, with Edo selling OX_0^* robots and Acme selling none, but ends at the same equilibrium point, because demand and cost conditions are identical (and there are no transport costs).

We have thus told a rather strange tale. Prices were the same in the two markets before trade was opened, but that did not keep trade from starting. Furthermore, both countries export robots, and their intraindustry trade is perfectly balanced. Edo exports OX^* robots to the American market, Acme exports OX robots to the Japanese market, and these quantities are equal. In Section 5 of Appendix A, moreover, we show that both companies wind up with lower profits, even though they were induced to invade each other's market by the prospect of raising their profits. International trade has introduced an element of competition into the two countries' markets, undermining each firm's monopoly of its own home market, reducing prices in both markets, and reducing the firms' profits. Their profits do not fall to zero, as they would with perfect competition, but oligopolistic competition is better than none. It is not hard to show that the gains to consumers due to lower prices are larger than the losses to producers due to lower profits.

Finally, our tale tells us why firms such as Edo and Acme are tempted to form market-sharing arrangements, called *cartels*, to protect their profits. If they can agree to stay out of each other's market or to divide their markets without letting total sales rise, prices and profits will not fall. But the gains from trade will be lost completely, which is why governments usually try to prohibit cartels.

Shifting the Reaction Curves

Having learned how to derive reaction curves, what more can we do with them? We can use them to show how a difference in marginal costs or change in one country's costs alters an oligopolistic equilibrium and the trade flows that go with it. We can also use them to show what happens when a government subsidizes exports and the other government retaliates.

Return to Figure 7-3 and draw a new marginal-cost curve for Edo below the common curve shown in the diagram. When Acme sells OA robots, Edo's new sales point will lie on a line lower and longer than NH and thus to the right of T. When Acme sells OA' robots, Edo's new sales point will lie on a line lower and longer than $N'H$ and thus to the right of T'. At each and every level of Acme's sales, Edo will sell more robots in the American market. Faced with an increase in Acme's sales, however, Edo will still reduce its own sales by half of the increase in Acme's sales. Therefore, Edo's reaction curve will lie to the right of the curve EE in Figure 7-4 but parallel to it. Similarly, a reduction in Acme's marginal costs will shift its reaction curve. It will lie above the curve AA but parallel to it. That is the shift shown in Figure 7-5, where Acme's curve moves from AA to $A'A'$, taking the equilibrium point to Q'.

When Acme's marginal costs are lower than Edo's, Acme sells more in the American market, and Edo sells less. But total sales are larger than before, because Edo reduces its sales by half of the increase in Acme's sales. Hence the price of robots is lower. As the same things happen in the Japanese market, intraindustry trade is not perfectly balanced. Acme's exports to the Japanese market are larger than Edo's exports to the American market.

Effects of Export Subsidies

Exports subsidies are instruments of commercial policy, and it would be logical to study them in Chapters 9 and 10, which examine the instruments and uses of commercial policy. The tools are at hand, however, and we can use them now.

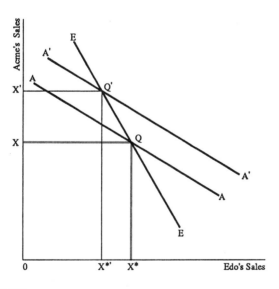

FIGURE 7-5
A Reduction in Acme's Costs
A downward shift in Acme's marginal-cost curve increases that firm's sales in both markets for every level of Edo's sales. Acme's reaction curve shifts upward from AA to $A'A'$, displacing equilibrium from Q to Q'. Acme's sales rise from OX to OX', and Edo's sales fall from OX^* to $OX^{*'}$. The same changes occur when the American government subsidizes Acme's exports.

To steer clear of complications, including the welfare effects of price changes on domestic robot buyers and the need to distinguish between export subsidies and production subsidies, let us change the setting slightly. Suppose that American and Japanese industries are fully supplied with robots; they do not want more at any price. But Brazilian industries still need robots, so the shipments shown in Figure 7-5 go only to Brazil, which does not produce any robots of its own.

When Acme and Edo have the same marginal costs, their reaction curves are AA and EE, as before, and an oligopolistic equilibrium is established at Q. Acme and Edo sell the same quantities of robots. There is only one-way trade, however, because Brazil does not make or export robots.

In this sort of situation, Acme's profits from its exports to Brazil add to American national income.[2] Therefore, an American government interested in maximizing American welfare will want to raise Acme's profits. It can do so by offering Acme an export subsidy that has the effect of reducting the marginal cost at which Acme can export robots to Brazil.[3] Acme's reaction curve shifts upward, as in Figure 7-5, raising Acme's exports and reducing Edo's exports. In Section 5 of Appendix A, moreover, it is shown that a carefully chosen subsidy will raise Acme's profits by more than the goverment spends on the subsidy—a condition that must be satisfied to increase American national income. (If the increase in profits were just as large as the amount spent on the subsidy, there would be no change in national income. All of Acme's gain would be the taxpayers' loss, as they must provide the revenue needed for the subsidy.)

Brazil's buyers of robots benefit from the American subsidy. The increase in Acme's exports is twice as large as the decrease in Edo's exports, so the subsidy drives down the price of robots. But Japanese national income falls, because Edo's profits fall; its sales are smaller and its price is lower. Therefore, the Japanese government will be tempted to retaliate by subsidizing Edo's exports.

If Japanese retaliation served merely to shift Edo's reaction curve in the way that the American subsidy shifted Acme's curve, we could end this story quickly. But something more will happen. The American government will respond to the Japanese subsidy by adjusting its own subsidy. Interdependence between the two firms' strategies makes for interdependence between their governments' policies.

This interdependence is described by the new reaction curves in Figure 7-6, which show how each government's subsidy depends on the other's subsidy. The policy reaction curves, WW and JJ, are derived in Section 5 of Appendix A, which proves that they are downward sloping. The governments do not keep on raising their subsidies, leapfrogging over each other. Instead, each government reduces its subsidy whenever the other raises its subsidy. This is because an increase in a subsidy raises the cost of the subsidy, and the increase in cost must be subtracted from the increase in profit (if any) to measure the change in national income. In fact, an increase in one country's subsidy causes the other to cut its subsidy by one-quarter of the

---

[2]The rest of its export revenues do not, because they represent costs of production and thus payments to American factors of production that could be used by other American industries.

[3]Acme could pursue this profit-raising strategy without a government subsidy, merely by reducing the price of its robots, but it would be exposed to losses if Edo retaliated. By allowing the American government to take the initiative, it shifts the risk of loss to the government.

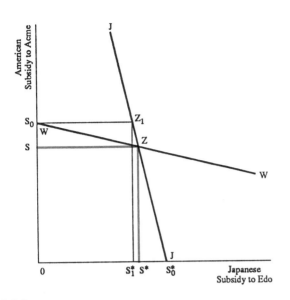

FIGURE 7-6
Policy Reaction Curves for Export Subsidies
The American policy reaction curve is *WW*, showing the optimal American export subsidy for every level of the Japanese subsidy. The Japanese policy reaction curve is *JJ*, showing the optimal Japanese export subsidy for every American subsidy. When Japan does not subsidize Edo's exports to Brazil, the optimal American subsidy is OS_0. When America does not subsidize Acme's exports, the optimal Japanese subsidy is OS_0^*. When each government responds to the other's subsidy, however, they wind up at Z, where the subsidies are *OS* and *OS**. Note that *OS* is smaller than OS_0. Japanese retaliation reduces the American subsidy.

increase in the first country's subsidy. (That is why *JJ* in Figure 7-6 is twice as steep as *EE* in Figure 7-5, while *WW* is half as steep as *AA*.)

Where will the two governments wind up? Let us start at the origin of Figure 7-6, where there are no subsidies, and assume that the American government acts first. It moves immediately to S_0, the point on its policy reaction curve *WW* that shows what the American subsidy should be when there is no Japanese subsidy. Hence, the initial American subsidy is OS_0. This step provokes retaliation by Japan, however, which moves to Z_1 on its policy reaction curve *JJ*. It sets its subsidy at OS_1^*. The American government responds, and events unfold much as they did in Figure 7-4, where Acme and Edo were reacting to each other. Eventually, an equilibrium is reached at Z, where the American subsidy is *OS*, and the Japanese subsidy is *OS**. The two subsidies are equal in size because Edo and Acme have identical costs and compete in the same Brazilian market.

The corresponding outcomes for Edo and Acme are shown in Figure 7-7, which replicates most of Figure 7-5, including the initial shift in Acme's reaction curve from *AA* to *A'A'* induced by the initial American subsidy. But we have seen that the equilibrium level of the American subsidy will be lower than the initial level. Therefore, Acme's reaction curve will be *A"A"*, which lies between *AA* and *A'A'*. Furthermore, Edo's reaction curve will shift in response to the equilibrium level of the Japanese subsidy. It will be *E"E"*. The two reaction curves will intersect at *Q"*,

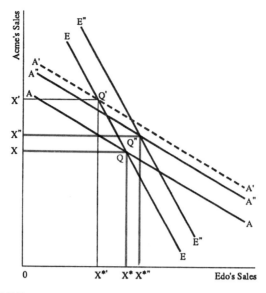

FIGURE 7-7
Export Subsidies and Sales
When America subsidizes Acme's exports to Brazil, the firm's reaction curve shifts
from *AA* to *A'A'*, raising American exports from *OX* to *OX'* and reducing Japanese
exports from *OX** to *OX*"*. When Japan retaliates, however, and the sequence of
reciprocal adjustments is completed, the American subsidy will be lower than it was
initially, shifting Acme's reaction curve to *A"A"*. But Edo's reaction curve will shift to
the same extent, from *EE* to *E"E"*. Hence, both countries' exports will rise by the same
amount. Acme's will rise from *OX* to *OX"*. Edo's will rise from *OX** to *OX*"*.

where each firm will export more robots than it did before the subsidies were
introduced. Acme's sales will rise to *OX"*, and Edo's sales will rise to *OX*"*. In fact,
they will rise by the same amounts in this particular case.

Clearly, Brazil is better off than it was before the subsidies; the fall in the price of
robots has improved its terms of trade. But both exporting countries are worse off.
Figure 7-8 shows what happens to them, using numbers obtained by assigning
particular values to the coefficients of the equations in Section 5 of Appendix A. The
columns of Figure 7-8 represent the policy options open to the American government. The rows represent the options open to the Japanese government. The first
number in each cell is the change in American national income, compared with the
situation in which there are no subsidies. The second is the change in Japanese
national income.

Look first at the upper right-hand cell, which shows what happens when the
American government subsidizes Acme but the Japanese government does not
subsidize Edo. American national income rises by 50, and Japanese national income
falls by 175. Look next at the lower right-hand cell, which shows what happens when
the governments reach the equilibrium described by the point *Z* in Figure 7-6. The
two countries' national incomes are 48 lower than they were without any subsidies.
Retaliation has allowed Japan to make good much of the loss it suffered from the
American subsidy and has "punished" America in the process by converting its gain
into a loss.

		American Options	
		No Subsidy	Subsidy
Japanese Options	No Subsidy	0, 0*	+50, -175*
	Subsidy	-175, +50*	-48, -48*

FIGURE 7-8
A Strategic Analysis of Export Subsidies
The columns represent policy options open to the American government. The rows represent options open to the Japanese government. The numbers in each cell represent the changes in national income compared to the situation in which there are no subsidies (which is why there are zeros in the upper left-hand cell). When the American government subsidizes exports and the Japanese government does not, American income rises by 50 and Japanese income falls by 175. When both countries subsidize exports, both countries' incomes fall by 48. When they make their decisions independently, however, both governments will subsidize exports, even though that will reduce both countries' incomes.

A Strategic Analysis of Export Subsidies

Thus far, we have assumed that each government chooses its subsidy on the supposition that the other government will not respond. That is how the American government chose its initial subsidy in Figure 7-6, how the Japanese government reacted, and how the two governments moved sequentially to the unsatisfactory equilibrium at Z. (It is unsatisfactory because both countries lose, but it is an equilibrium nevertheless. Neither government has any incentive to depart from it unilaterally. It is, in effect, a loss-minimizing equilibrium.) But this sequential process is not the only way in which governments can get into trouble.

Suppose that the American and Japanese governments are trying to decide individually whether to subsidize their exports and will not be able to reverse their decisions once they have announced them. (A government can change the size of its subsidy but cannot abandon the basic decision to subsidize once that decision is made.) Suppose that each government knows the numbers in Table 7-8 and thus the effects on its national income of the four possible outcomes but does not know in advance what the other government will do. Both governments will subsidize their exports and wind up with losses.

Look at the situation from the American government's standpoint. It must decide whether it should commit itself to subsidizing exports without knowing whether Japan will make a similar commitment. Reviewing its options, it will decide that it is safer to subsidize. If Japan decides not to subsidize, America will be better off for having decided to subsidize; its national income will rise by 50 rather than stay unchanged. If Japan decides instead to subsidize, America will still be better off for having decided to subsidize; its national income will fall by 48 rather than fall by 175. But Japan will make similar calculations and arrive at the same conclusion. Hence, both governments will commit themselves to subsidizing exports, and both countries' national incomes will fall.

This is the "noncooperative" solution to a famous problem in game theory, known as the Prisoner's Dilemma. It takes its name from an example in which two prisoners are held incommunicado. Each is told that he will be released if he accuses the other and no accusation is made against him, that he will be punished severely if he is accused by the other, and that both prisoners will be punished but less severely if they remain silent. Clearly, the two prisoners should "cooperate" by remaining silent; both will be treated leniently. Looking at his options by himself, however, each prisoner will find it safer to accuse the other, with the result that both are punished severely.

Governments would be better off if each country could promise not to subsidize its exports. And governments have found ways to do that. The General Agreement on Tariffs and Trade prohibits the use of export subsidies, although it tolerates several exceptions, most notably for agricultural exports. The major industrial countries have also agreed to limit the size of the export-credit subsidies they give to developing countries. These promises are frequently broken, however, sometimes by disguising export subsidies as production subsidies or as support for research and development. It is also difficult to punish cheating. If the American and Japanese governments agree not to subsidize their robot exports, but the American government breaks its promise, Japan will find it hard to punish the American transgression, except by subsidizing Japanese exports. Agreements of this sort are especially fragile when many countries are involved; small countries can cheat without being punished, because large countries do not want the whole agreement to unravel. Agreements tend to be more robust when the participating governments are linked by many other agreements; the threat to renounce the whole set of agreements may prevent a government from violating one of them.

TRADE WITH MONOPOLISTIC COMPETITION

In the example we have been examining, Acme and Edo produced identical goods, and each had the entire domestic market to itself before trade was opened. Economies of scale kept other firms from entering their markets. But trade replaced monopoly with oligopoly.

We turn now to a different framework, *monopolistic competition*, in which each country's market is served by many firms, but each firm makes a different version or variety of the same basic good. Economies of scale are important here. They determine the number of varieties each country will produce.

Equilibrium in the Closed Economy

To highlight the features of this model, suppose that widgets, the basic product, can be made in many shades. Think of them as lying along a line from light to dark. If there were no economies of scale in the widget industry, a very small country could produce every variety of widget. There could indeed be many firms making each variety, and the market for that variety would be perfectly competitive. When there are significant economies of scale, fewer varieties will be produced, fewer firms will make them, and markets will be less than perfectly competitive.

A large body of literature deals with the way that firms will choose their places on the line between light and dark widgets. Their behavior will depend in part on consumers' preferences and on the consumers' willingness to substitute one type of widget for another. In this example, we will assume that consumers are distributed evenly along the line; if every variety of widget were available and their prices were the same, the same number of consumers would buy each variety. But we will assume that our countries are too small to produce every variety of widget. Therefore, the varieties actually produced will be spread out along the line, with gaps between them. This will force some consumers to choose between buying no widgets at all and buying varieties that do not satisfy them perfectly.

We will deal with two countries, France and Italy. Each country produces n varieties, but France produces the odd-numbered varieties $(1, 3, 5, \ldots, 2n - 1)$, and Italy produces the even-numbered varieties $(2, 4, 6, \ldots, 2n)$. The initial situation looks like this:

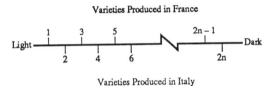

There will be one firm producing each numbered variety, and each will have its own cluster of consumers.[4]

The situation of the typical firm in long-run equilibrium is shown by Figure 7-9. The firm produces the jth variety, its average-cost curve is AC, and its demand curve is DD. The shape of the average-cost curve reflects the assumption made earlier, that there are economies of scale in the production of widgets. The demand curve is downward sloping because the firm can acquire additional customers by cutting its price. Some who have been buying the adjacent varieties, $j - 2$ and $j + 2$, will switch to the jth variety. The demand curve will be fairly flat if the adjacent varieties are close substitutes for the jth variety; a small reduction in the price of the jth variety will attract a large number of customers. The position of DD will depend on the prices of the other varieties, but especially those of adjacent varieties. If an adjacent firm reduces its price and attracts additional customers, the demand curve for the jth variety will shift to the left. The size of the shift will depend on the number of consumers who abandon the jth variety when the price of another variety falls.

The firm will have marginal-cost and marginal-revenue curves, but we do not need them to describe the situation. We have merely to locate E, the point of tangency between DD and AC, where the firm produces OQ widgets and sells them at the price

---

[4]There are technical difficulties with this linear arrangement of varieties and firms. The firm at each end of the line will have only one close competitor, and all other firms will have two. But the linear arrangement is a convenient approximation.

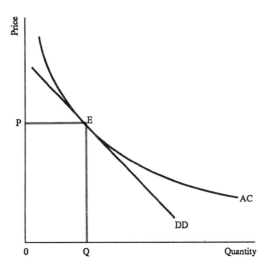

FIGURE 7-9
Equilibrium under Monopolistic Competition
The curve *DD* is the domestic demand curve for the *j*th variety of widget. The curve *AC* is the average-cost curve for the only firm making that variety. The firm sells *OQ* widgets at price *OP*. Its total revenues are *OQEP* and are equal to its total costs. If the firm were making profits, additional firms would enter the widget industry to produce close substitutes for the *j*th variety, and the firm's demand curve would shift to the left until it was just tangent to its average-cost curve, making the firm's profits disappear.

OP. Its total revenues are equal to its total costs. If its total costs were higher, the firm would show losses and would have to drop out of the industry; its customers would have to move to other varieties. If its total costs were lower, it would make profits and would attract new firms to the widget industry. These firms would produce additional varieties and the demand curve for the *j*th variety would shift to the left, reducing the firm's profits.

To sum up, France has *n* widget-making firms, and they produce odd-numbered varieties. Italy has the same number of firms, but they produce even-numbered varieties. Each firm in each country makes the same quantity of widgets and sells them at the same price. Each country has the same number of consumers, and some of them would like to buy every sort of widget. Before trade is opened, however, French consumers can buy only odd-numbered varieties and Italian consumers can buy only even-numbered varieties.

The Opening of Trade

Trade serves a very simple function in this model. It fills the gaps in the menu of widgets available to French and Italian consumers. But this can have a number of consequences. First, it will rearrange each country's consumption. Second, it may rearrange each country's production. Third, it may stimulate consumption and production.

The first effect is easily explained without an additional diagram. When consumers are evenly distributed and are given the opportunity to buy both odd-numbered and even-numbered widgets, half of those who used to buy odd-numbered widgets will switch to even-numbered widgets, and vice versa. Look at the outcome from the standpoint of the jth firm. The firm will lose half its domestic customers to the newly adjacent foreign firms making varieties $j - 1$ and $j + 1$, but it will gain just as many foreign customers from them. Therefore, it will continue to produce OQ widgets and obtain the price OP, but it will start to export half its output. Look at the outcome in terms of trade flows. France will export half its output of odd-numbered widgets, Italy will export half its output of even-numbered widgets, and trade in widgets will be balanced.

The second and third effects, which modify this outcome, reflect the indirect results of thickening the widget menu available to French and Italian consumers. Before trade was opened, the ability of the jth firm to attract additional customers was limited by the two-digit distance between the jth variety and the closest substitutes available domestically, $j - 2$ and $j + 2$. After trade is opened, the firm can more easily attract additional customers, because there is only a one-digit distance between the jth variety and its closest substitutes, $j - 1$ and $j + 1$, which come from the other country. Furthermore, consumers who did not buy widgets before will return to the widget market, attracted by the richer menu. The immediate effects are shown in Figure 7-10, where the demand curve shifts from DD to $D'D'$. It gets flatter because there are closer substitutes for the jth variety; it shifts upward because more consumers are attracted to the widget market.

Each firm will see this as an opportunity to raise its output and move to a point such as E', where its output is OQ' and its price is OP'. Its profits will be $CFE'P'$. But every other firm will see things the same way and try to raise its output. Hence, the prices of adjacent varieties will fall and the demand curve for the jth variety will shift to the left. A new long-run equilibrium will be established when the demand curve is $D*D*$, which is tangent to AC at $E*$. The firm will produce $OQ*$ widgets, its price will be $OP*$, and its profits will be zero, just as they were before trade. Important gains will accrue to consumers, however, as they can consume more widgets at lower prices.

The increase in widget consumption is due partly to the increase in demand resulting from the increase in the number of consumers—the return of those who were not buying widgets before trade was opened. But it is also due to another phenomenon—a reduction in the total number of varieties produced and thus the number of firms. Each of the remaining firms will produce more widgets and will thus be able to exploit more fully the economies of scale in widget production.

How does this reduction come about? Initially, each country's consumers had a menu comprising n varieties. The opening of trade doubled the number, allowing some consumers to pick widgets better suited to their preferences. But ask yourself what you would do if offered a variety quite close to your ideal type or one that was somewhat farther away but was priced at $OP*$ rather than OP. You might choose the cheaper widget, and that is what has happened in Figure 7-10. Think of the outcome this way: Before trade, France produced n odd-numbered varieties and Italy produced n even-numbered varieties; after the opening of trade and all of the resulting adjustments, France produces varieties 1, 4, 7, and so on, while Italy produces varieties 2.5, 5.5, 8.5, and so on. The number of varieties is larger than n

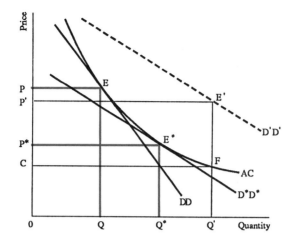

FIGURE 7-10
Trade under Monopolistic Competition
Before trade, *DD* is the domestic demand curve for the *j*th variety of widget, and *AC* is the average-cost curve for the firm making that variety. Output is *OQ*, and price is *OP*. By making additional varieties available, trade shifts the demand curve to *D′D′*. It becomes flatter because the firm can gain more customers by cutting its price; it shifts upward because more customers enter the widget market. The firm moves initially from *E* to *E′*, raising its output to *OQ′* and reducing its price to *OP′*. Its total revenues are *OQ′E′P′*, its total costs are *OQ′FC*, and its profits are *CFE′P′*. But all other firms do the same thing, so every demand curve shifts to the left. The new long-run equilibrium is established at *E**, where profits have vanished, output is *OQ**, and price is *OP**. The movement from *E′* to *E** is associated with a reduction in the number of widget-making firms. Each remaining firm produces more than it did initially (*OQ** is larger than *OQ*) and sells it at a lower price (*OP** is smaller than *OP*).

but smaller than $2n$, and they are 1.5 digits apart. They are thus closer together than they were before trade but farther apart than they would be without any rearrangement of production. Consumers benefit from more choice and lower prices, because costs are cut by reducing the number of firms and raising the output of each remaining firm.

Innovation, Growth, and Trade

Trade models with monopolistic competition are being used extensively to study economic growth and a large number of policy problems relating to trade and growth. Until recently, economists treated technological change as something that happens *exogenously*—outside the model being studied. That is how we viewed it in the previous chapter, when we asked how an improvement in economic efficiency affects production, trade, and economic welfare. Current work on technological change treats it as something that happens *endogenously*—within the model being studied. When products are differentiated and entry is limited by economies of scale, firms have an incentive to invest in research and development. They may find new ways to make old products, devise new varieties of old products, or invent completely new products. When entry is limited by economies of scale (or patent protection, for that matter), investing in research and development can be very profitable. Investors can capture some of the welfare gains obtained by reducing costs of production, improving product quality, or thickening the consumer's menu.

When seeking to maximize profits, then, firms must make the usual decisions about inputs and outputs, but they must also decide how much to invest in research and development. Their decisions will determine the growth rate of the economy and, more important for our purpose, the nature of a country's foreign trade. For these same reasons, however, governments are apt to look for ways to encourage investment in research and development. When they do this competitively, however, they run the risk of reducing economic welfare, much as they do when they subsidize their exports.

Let us return to the example considered earlier, in which Acme and Edo sold robots to Brazil. Suppose that Acme and Edo are trying to develop a new type of robot, that they are evenly matched and bound to succeed eventually, and that the first firm to succeed will capture the whole Brazilian market.

Let the value of the market for the new robot be $10 billion, measured by the profit to be made over the life of the product, and suppose that each firm is investing $1 billion in research and development. On these assumptions, each firm (and country) will value the Brazilian market at $4 billion. This is the value of the market *times* the probability of winning the race to develop the new robot *less* the firm's investment in research (i.e, $10 billion *times* 0.5 *less* $1 billion). This number is shown in the upper left-hand box of Figure 7-11, where the American and Japanese governments do not subsidize their companies' research.

Now suppose that a $1 billion subsidy from the American government can increase the probability that Acme will win the race; let it rise from 0.5 to 0.75. The value of the market from the American standpoint will rise to $5.5 billion ($10 billion *times* 0.75 *less* $2 billion of total spending on research), and the value from the Japanese standpoint will fall to $1.5 billion ($10 billion *times* 0.25 *less* $1 billion).[5] These numbers are shown in the upper right-hand box of Figure 7-11, where America subsidizes research and Japan does not. Because the situation is symmetrical here, the same numbers appear in the lower left-hand box, where Japan subsidizes research and America does not. Finally, the numbers in the lower right-hand box reflect the outcome when both firms are subsidized. They are evenly matched again, but $1 billion of additional expenditure on research must be deducted from the value that each country attaches to the Brazilian market.

Clearly, the governments have reason to agree that they will not compete by subsidizing research. If they do not trust each other, however, both will act defensively and subsidize their firms. If America decides not to subsidize, the value of the market will be $4 billion when Japan makes the same decision and $1.5 billion when Japan subsidizes. If America decides to subsidize, the value of the market will

---

[5] As additional research raises the value of the market from Acme's own standpoint, we must ask why it does not spend more on research without help from its government. The most plausible answer is that Acme cannot expect to recover all its expenditure. This would happen if it could not patent its discovery or could expect to lose scientists and engineers to other American firms willing to pay high salaries for their skills and knowledge of the work in progress in Acme's laboratories.

	American Options	
	No Subsidy	Subsidy
Japanese Options — No Subsidy	4, 4*	5.5, 1.5*
Japanese Options — Subsidy	1.5, 5.5*	3, 3*

FIGURE 7-11
A Strategic Analysis of Research Subsidies
The first number in each cell is the increase in American national income resulting from the corresponding pair of policies. The second (with an asterisk) is the increase in Japanese national income. Each number is the value of the Brazilian market *times* the probability of winning the market *less* the total expenditure on research. When the American and Japanese governments act defensively, each one will subsidize its company's research, even though that will reduce both countries' incomes.

be $5.5 billion when Japan does not subsidize and $3 billion when Japan subsidizes. If America cannot be sure that Japan will not subsidize, it makes sense for America to subsidize. But Japan will make the same comparisons and come to the same conclusion. Hence, both governments will subsidize and wind up in the lower right-hand box.

This example is far too simple. It ignores the effects of subsidies on the probability that the discovery will in fact be made, focusing instead on the probability that one country's firm will make it. It also ignores the difficult problem of deciding which firm to subsidize, as we have assumed that there is only one firm in each country. But it highlights the risk of competitive behavior by governments, which is very similar to the risk they court when they start to subsidize exports or production.

EMPIRICAL WORK ON INTRAINDUSTRY TRADE

Quantitative work on intraindustry trade underscores the importance of the variables featured in the models we have been examining. The level of intraindustry trade is usually measured by this index:

$$T = 1 - \frac{|x_{ijk} - x_{jik}|}{x_{ijk} + x_{jik}},$$

where x_{ijk} is the value or volume of the ith country's exports to the jth country in the kth product group, and x_{jik} is the trade flow in the opposite direction. This index is zero when trade goes only one way (when $x_{ijk} = 0$ or $x_{jik} = 0$); it is one when trade is perfectly balanced (when $x_{ijk} = x_{jik}$).[6]

One of the most ambitious empirical studies, covering 38 countries and 152 product groups, is summarized in Table 7-2. It tries to explain the value of T for each bilateral trade flow.

Table 7-2. Country and Product Characteristics Affecting Levels of Intraindustry Trade Between Pairs of Countries

Characteristic	Effect
Average of countries' incomes per capita	Positive
Difference in incomes per capita	Negative
Average of countries' total incomes	Positive
Difference in total incomes	Negative
Average trade orientation of countries	Positive
Distance between countries	Negative
Common border between countries	Positive
Common language between countries	Positive[a]
Membership in common trade bloc	Positive
Product differentiation within industry	Positive[b]
Economies of scale for firms in industry	Negative
Industrial concentration in industry	Negative
Multinational production by firms in industry	Negative[c]
Average tariff level for industry	None
Tariff dispersion within industry	Negative

Source: Adapted from Bela Balassa and Luc Bauwens, *Changing Trade Patterns in Manufactured Goods* (Amsterdam: North-Holland, 1988), Table 8-1. Effect is shown as "none" when not significant at the 0.05 level.
[a]Positive for English, French, German, and Portuguese but not for Spanish or Scandinavian languages.
[b]Three measures were used simultaneously: an index of export prices (unit values) within the industry, an index of dispersion for profits, and a measure of advertising expenditure. All three had positive effects.
[c]Two variables were used simultaneously: a measure of income received from foreign affiliates and a measure of trade with foreign affiliates. Both had negative effects.

---

[6]Returning to Table 7-1, we can compute T for U.S. trade in records, tapes, and disks:

$$T = 1 - \frac{|2050 - 1683|}{2050 + 1683} = 1 - \frac{367}{3733} = 0.902$$

which says that trade in this product group comes close to being pure intraindustry trade. The average value of T for trade in manufactured goods lies between 0.55 and 0.75 for most major industrial countries; see David Greenaway and Chris Milner, *The Economics of Intra-Industry Trade* (Oxford: Blackwell, 1986), Table 5-3.

The first five variables listed in the table pertain to the general characteristics of the trading countries, and each of them has the expected effect. Models of monopolistic competition suggest that countries with high incomes can be expected to engage heavily in intraindustry trade, because their consumers will spend large fractions of their incomes on sophisticated manufactured goods, which tend to be sharply differentiated. Conversely, countries with different income levels can be expected to have different tastes and thus to engage in less intraindustry trade. Similarly, large countries can be expected to produce many varieties of manufactured goods, and levels of national income are used to represent country size. Finally, countries that are outwardly oriented, with low trade barriers, are also shown to participate heavily in intraindustry trade.

The next four variables relate to the characteristics of the bilateral relationship between each pair of countries. Distance discourages intraindustry trade, as transport costs tend to reduce each country's share of its partner's market; this happened in the model of pure national monopoly that led to oligopolistic competition, and it can also be expected to happen in models of monopolistic competition. Information can be expected to flow freely between countries with a common border or common language, and this should promote intraindustry trade, because each country's consumers should be thoroughly familiar with the range and variety of goods available from neighboring countries. Membership in a common trade bloc, such as the European Community, also encourages intraindustry trade.

The last six variables relate to the characteristics of the industries and product groups rather than those of the countries. Measures of product differentiation have the positive effect predicted by models of monopolistic competition. But economies of scale and industrial concentration appear to have perverse effects. In both models studied in this chapter, economies of scale were used to limit entry and generate intraindustry trade. Furthermore, industrial concentration should produce the mutual penetration of national markets that took place in the model of oligopolistic competition. But forces working in the opposite direction appear to dominate. When there are significant economies of scale or large firms in an industry, there are opportunities for standardization as well as differentiation, and standardization leads to specialization rather than intraindustry trade. The extent of multinational production can likewise cut two ways. On the one hand, it displaces trade; firms that produce locally for a particular market do not have to export to that market. On the other hand, it creates trade; firms that produce locally often import parts and components from plants in other countries. In this particular study, the trade-displacing effect appears to dominate. Finally, tariffs and other trade barriers might be expected to limit intraindustry trade, but their effects are rather weak in this and other studies.

SUMMARY

Models with perfectly competitive markets cannot explain two-way trade within a single product group. Yet this *intraindustry trade* accounts for a large portion of all international trade, especially in manufactured goods. Models with inperfect markets are needed to explain it.

When two countries' domestic markets are monopolized, the opening of trade intensifies competition; oligopoly replaces monopoly, reducing prices and profits. Producers lose but consumers gain, and the gains are larger than the losses. Trade can occur even when the countries' firms produce identical goods and sell them at identical prices.

When two countries' markets are characterized by monopolistic competition involving differentiated products, the opening of trade raises the number of varieties available. It can also reduce the number produced in each country, along with the number of producers, allowing the survivors to exploit economies of scale and thus reduce their costs. Trade is beneficial for both of these reasons.

Under conditions of imperfect competition, there are incentives for governments to subsidize their exports or to subsidize research to develop new exports, in order to capture larger profits from foreign markets. When other governments retaliate, however, there are losses all around, and binding agreements may be needed to keep the process from starting.

Finally, it must be remembered that models of imperfect competition can explain intraindustry trade but cannot by themselves explain why particular countries are net exporters of certain manufactures, net importers of others, and net exporters or importers of other goods. Those models must be combined with others, such as the modified Ricardian model or Heckscher–Ohlin model, to explain the trade pattern completely.

RECOMMENDED READINGS

The model of oligopolistic competition developed in this chapter is based on the model in James A. Brander, "Intra-Industry Trade in Identical Commodities," *Journal of International Economics*, 11 (February 1981); the model of monopolistic competition is based on the model in Paul R. Krugman, "Increasing Returns, Monopolistic Competition, and International Trade," *Journal of International Economics*, 9 (November 1979). A good survey of theoretical work on these subjects is provided in David Greenaway and Chris Milner, *The Economics of Intra-Industry Trade* (Oxford: Blackwell, 1986), chs. 2–3.

For a survey of research on strategic aspects of trade policy, see Gene M. Grossman and J. David Richardson, *Strategic Trade Policy: A Survey of Issues and Early Analysis*, Special Papers in International Economics 15 (Princeton, N.J.: International Finance Section, Princeton University, 1985); for contrasting views on the same subject, see Paul R. Krugman, ed., *Strategic Trade Policy and the New International Economics* (Cambridge, Mass.: MIT Press, 1986), chs. 2–4, and Avinash Dixit, "How Should the United States Respond to Other Countries' Trade Policies?" in R. M. Stern, ed., *U.S. Trade Policies in a Changing World Economy* (Cambridge, Mass.: MIT Press, 1987), ch. 6.

On trade between countries in which economic growth results from investment in research and development, see Gene M. Grossman and Elhanan Helpman, "Comparative Advantage and Long Run Growth," *American Economic Review*, 80 (September 1990), and Luis A. Rivera-Batiz and Paul M. Romer, "International Trade with Endogenous Technological Change," *European Economic Review*, 35 (May 1991). For a more extensive and rigorous treatment, see Gene M. Grossman and Elhanan Helpman, *Innovation and Growth in the Global Economy* (Cambridge, Mass.: MIT Press, 1991).

For another way of using economies of scale and product differentiation to explain important economic issues, see Paul Krugman, *Geography and Trade* (Cambridge, Mass.: MIT Press, 1991).

QUESTIONS AND PROBLEMS

(1) Explain the statement in the text, that an agreement (cartel) between Acme and Edo to keep trade from reducing their profits would eliminate the gains from trade.

(2) Let the Japanese robot market be half as large as the American market. Adapt Figures 7-3 and 7-4 to show the equilibrium in each market after trade is opened; identify the equilibrium price in each market, Edo's exports to the American market, and Acme's exports to the Japanese market.

(3) Adapt Figures 7-3 and 7-4 to show what happens when the American government imposes an import tariff on robots. Show the changes in sales by Acme and Edo in the American market and the change in the equilibrium price. Is there any effect on their sales in the Japanese market? What happens to Acme's profits? (You may find it helpful to think of the tariff as being equivalent to an increase in the marginal cost of selling Edo's robots in the American market.)

(4) To illustrate the effects of research subsidies, the text assumed that a subsidy affects the probability that a particular firm will win the race to develop a new robot but not the probability that someone will develop it eventually. That was assumed to be certain. Suppose, instead, that the probability of succeeding is 0.4 when there are no subsidies and that it rises to 0.8 when both governments subsidize research. Assume that Acme and Edo are evenly matched and show that it will pay both governments to subsidize research.

(5) In the Ricardian trade model, a small country can appropriate most of the gains from trade. The same sort of thing can happen with trade under monopolistic competition, but for a different reason. It relates to the thickening of consumers' menus. Explain.

8

Trade and Factor Movements

THE ISSUES

This chapter examines two groups of issues. The first part of the chapter uses trade theory to show what happens when factors of production can move freely from one country to another. It concentrates on three issues:

- How factor movements affect the total outputs of the countries involved and the composition of each country's output.
- How factor movements affect the incomes of the factors of production.
- How factor movements affect trade flows, the terms of trade, and economic welfare.

The second part of the chapter deals with some major issues raised by the theory of factor movements but not treated fully by it:

- Why firms engage in *multinational production*, putting plants in many countries rather than one country.
- How multinational production affects the individual economies involved and the trade between them.

The chapter ends with a brief excursion into the theory of taxation. When firms and individuals reside in one country but earn income in another, what principles should govern the taxation of that income?

PERSPECTIVES AND OBJECTIVES

In most of our work thus far, we have focused on the nation state as the basic unit of analysis and have measured the effects of trade on the welfare of the typical consumer. When examining capital formation, for example, we compared the sizes of two changes affecting the welfare of the typical consumer in the growing country—the change in real income measured at initial prices and the change in the terms of trade resulting from the change in the output mix.

When dealing with movements of capital or labor from one country to another, it makes less sense to focus on the nation state and the typical consumer. It is hard, indeed, to define the typical consumer, because factor movements can involve movements of consumers, too. When workers move from Portugal to Britain, should we treat them as Portuguese or British consumers? When capital moves from Britain to Portugal, should we reclassify the owners of that capital?

Even when we can answer these questions clearly and can therefore define the typical consumer in each country, the concept itself can obscure some of the interesting issues. Why do most countries limit immigration? There are, of course, political and cultural reasons. To get at the economic reasons, however, we must distinguish the effects on the incomes of the immigrants from the effects on the incomes of others, not average the effects on immigrants and others.

We will continue to concentrate on long-run changes in outputs and incomes—those we can identify after a factor movement has been completed and the factors of production are optimally allocated. But we will classify them differently in this chapter. First, we will look at the effects on global output, defined as the sum of the outputs in the *host* and *source* countries, to see how a factor movement has affected the efficiency of the world economy. Second, we will look at the distributional effects by examining the changes in the incomes of three groups: those persons who move (or move their capital) from the source country to the host country, those who reside initially in the host country, and those who remain behind in the source country. It will be important, moreover, to look separately at the effects on the earnings of labor, capital, and land, which may be very different.

Although we will adopt a different classification of welfare effects, we will follow the same general approach adopted to study economic growth. We will concentrate on capital movements, which are easier to analyze than labor movements, and we will look at the effects of factor movements in both of the models used before—the modified Ricardian model and the Heckscher–Ohlin model.

It is easy to find reasons for factor movements in the modified Ricardian model and equally easy to analyze their consequences. We can ask how factor movements alter outputs and earnings when there are no other changes in the countries concerned, ask next how they influence the pattern of employment, and ask finally how the changes in employment affect real earnings in the host and source countries. We will see that factor movements tend to be *self-limiting* in the modified Ricardian model. The changes in earnings in the two countries remove the incentive for more factors to move.

It is harder to find economic reasons for factor movements in the Heckscher–Ohlin model, because free trade can equalize factor prices and thus deprive capital and labor of any economic incentive to move. We must therefore introduce an impediment to factor-price equalization so as to drive a wedge between the countries' factor prices. The effects of the resulting factor movement, however, depend on the nature of the impediment. In some cases, factor movements will remove the impediment itself, allowing trade to equalize the countries' factor prices and ending the incentive for factors to move. In other cases, factor movements cannot remove the impediment, and the factor movements will continue unabated until they have eliminated trade itself.

CAPITAL MOVEMENTS IN THE MODIFIED RICARDIAN MODEL

Recall the main characteristics of the countries in the modified Ricardian model. Britain and Portugal have the same quantities of labor, but Britain has more capital than Portugal, and Portugal has more land than Britain. When their tastes and technologies are the same and there is free trade between them, Britain exports cloth and Portugal exports wine. Yet free trade does not equalize the countries' factor prices. When their stocks of capital differ greatly, the marginal product of capital will be lower in Britain's cloth industry, so the real return to capital will be lower in Britain, whether it is measured in cloth or wine.[1] There is thus an incentive for capital to move from Britain to Portugal.

Primary Effects of a Capital Movement

The initial situation is described by Figure 8-1. The curve AC shows the relationship between the marginal product of capital in Britain's cloth industry and the quantity of capital in Britain, given the number of workers in the industry. When the quantity of capital is OK_1, the marginal product of capital is OR yards of cloth, which measures the real return to capital in terms of cloth. Therefore, the owners of capital earn $ORBK_1$ yards of cloth. The curve $A*C*$ shows the relationship prevailing in Portugal, given the number of workers in its cloth industry. (The British curve is higher and flatter than the Portuguese curve, because more workers are employed in Britain's cloth industry.) When the quantity of capital is OK_2 in Portugal, the marginal product of capital is $OR*$ yards of cloth, and the owners of capital earn $OR*PK_2$ yards of cloth.

An additional point about marginal-product curves is important here. The area under any marginal-product curve measures the total product of the industry. When the supply of capital is OK_1 in Britain, cloth output is $OABK_1$ yards. Hence, workers

---

[1]We can prove this assertion by recalling the results of capital formation obtained from the special case considered in Chapter 5, where the real wage remained constant in Britain when measured in wine. Let the marginal products of capital be equal initially in Britain and Portugal, then introduce capital formation in Britain. The real return to capital falls in both countries but falls further in Britain. The proof is in three steps: (1) Marginal products in each industry depend only on the industry's capital-labor ratio. If the marginal products of capital are equal in the countries' cloth industries, the capital-labor ratios must be equal, too, which means that the marginal products of labor must be equal. By implication, real wages must be equal, whether measured in wine or cloth. (2) Capital formation in Britain raises each country's real wage measured in cloth, but raises it more in Britain. Otherwise, the real wage measured in wine could not remain constant in Britain while falling in Portugal, and that is what happened in Chapter 5. (3) When the real wage rises by more in Britain, however, the marginal product of labor must rise by more in Britain's cloth industry. Therefore, the marginal product of capital must fall by more in Britain's cloth industry and be lower thereafter in Britain than in Portugal.

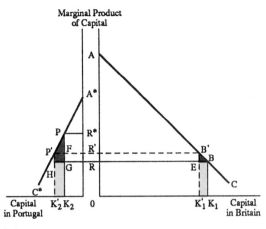

FIGURE 8-1
Effects of Transferring Capital from Britain to Portugal Before Reallocating Labor
The curve AC gives the marginal product of capital in Britain's cloth industry. With OK_1 capital invested in that industry initially, the marginal product is OR, and cloth output is $OABK_1$. Payments to capital are $OR \times OK_1$, or $ORBK_1$, and payments to labor are RAB. When K_1K_1' capital is transferred from Britain to Portugal, the marginal product rises to OR', and cloth output falls to $OAB'K_1'$. Payments to capital remaining in Britain rise from $OREK_1'$ to $OR'B'K_1'$, and payments to labor fall to $R'AB'$. Hence, the loss to British workers is EBB' bigger than the gain to capitalists remaining in Britain. The curve A^*C^* gives the marginal product in Portugal's cloth industry. With OK_2 capital invested in that industry initially, the marginal product is OR^*, and cloth output is OA^*PK_2. Payments to capital are OR^*PK_2, and payments to labor are R^*A^*P. When K_2K_2' capital is transferred to Portugal, the marginal product falls to OR', and cloth output rises to $OA^*P'K_2'$. Payments to capital initially in Portugal fall from OR^*PK_2 to $OR'FK_2$, and payments to labor rise to $R'A^*P'$. Hence, the gain to Portuguese workers is FPP' bigger than the loss to capitalists initially in Portugal.

in the British cloth industry earn RAB yards of cloth, the difference between total output and the payment made to the owners of capital. In Portugal, cloth output is OA^*PK_2 yards, and workers in the Portuguese industry earn R^*A^*P yards of cloth.

When the real return to capital is lower in Britain, owners of capital have an incentive to transfer some capital to Portugal. The primary effects show up in Figure 8-1. Suppose that K_1K_1' of British capital is transferred to Portugal, reducing the capital stock to OK_1' in Britain and raising it to OK_2' in Portugal (i.e., K_1K_1' $= K_2K_2'$). Five effects follow directly.

First, the transfer of capital eliminates completely the difference between marginal products in Britain and Portugal. The marginal product of capital rises in Britain to OR'. It falls in Portugal to OR'. (A smaller transfer of capital would reduce the difference but not eliminate it.) Therefore, the factor movement is self-limiting. By closing the gap between marginal products and thus the difference between real returns, it removes the incentive for owners of capital to transfer any more.

Second, the transfer raises global cloth output, increasing the efficiency of the world economy. Output falls to $OAB'K_1'$ in Britain and rises to $OA^*P'K_2'$ in Portugal. Note 8-1 shows, however, that the increase in Portuguese output exceeds the decrease in British output by $\frac{1}{2}(K_1K_1' \times RR^*)$ yards of cloth, where K_1K_1' is the capital transfer and RR^* is the initial gap between marginal products. If there were no such gap, the capital transfer would not raise global output. Without the gap, however, the owners of capital would not move it, because rates of return would not differ. Putting the same point in general terms, a factor movement activated by a difference in real returns raises the efficiency of the world economy.

Third, the transfer of capital raises the incomes of its owners, even though it removes the gap between marginal products. Their capital earned $K_1'EBK_1$ in Britain and will earn $K_2'P'FK_2$ in Portugal. Hence, their incomes rise by $HP'FG$ yards of cloth.

Fourth, the transfer redistributes income in Britain from labor to capital. Note 8-1 shows that the owners of capital remaining in Britain earn an additional $RR'B'E$ yards of cloth but that the earnings of British workers fall by $RR'B'B$ yards of cloth. Hence, British capitalists have reason to favor the capital movement from Britain to Portugal, and British workers have reason to oppose it. Furthermore, the British government cannot compensate the workers by taxing part of the gain accruing to the capitalists, because the workers' loss is bigger than the capitalists' gain.

Fifth, the transfer redistributes income in Portugal from capital to labor. Note 8-1 shows that the earnings of the owners of capital initially in Portugal fall by $R'R*PF$ yards of cloth but that Portuguese workers earn an additional $R'R*PP'$ yards of cloth. Hence, Portuguese workers have reason to favor the capital movement, but

---

Note 8-1
Measuring the Output and Income Effects of a Capital Movement from Britain to Portugal

The transfer of K_1K_1' capital from Britain to Portugal reduces output in Britain from $OABK_1$ to $OAB'K_1'$; it falls by $K_1'B'BK_1$ yards of cloth, which can be rewritten as $K_1'EBK_1 + EBB'$. The transfer raises output in Portugal from $OA*PK_2$ to $OA*P'K_2'$; it rises by $K_2'P'PK_2$ yards of cloth, which can be rewritten as $K_2'HGK_2 + HP'FG + FP'P$. But $K_1'EBK_1 = K_2'HGK_2$ (because $K_1K_1' = K_2K_2'$). Therefore, the increase in Portuguese output exceeds the decrease in British output by $HP'FG + FP'P - EBB'$. This is the increase in global output. But $HP'FG = GH \times GF$, while $FP'P = \frac{1}{2}(FP' \times FP)$, and $EBB = \frac{1}{2}(EB \times EB')$. Furthermore, $FP = GH = K_2K_2' = K_1K_1' = EB$, while $GF = RR' = EB'$, and $FP = R'R*$. Therefore, the increase in global output is $(K_1K_1' \times RR') + \frac{1}{2}(K_1K_1' \times R'R*) - \frac{1}{2}(K_1K_1' \times RR') = \frac{1}{2}(K_1K_1' \times RR') + \frac{1}{2}(K_1K_1' \times R'R*) = \frac{1}{2}(K_1K_1' \times RR*)$, because $RR' + R'R* = RR*$.

The earnings of capitalists remaining in Britain rise from $OREK_1'$ to $OR'B'K_1'$, an increase of $RR'B'E$ yards of cloth. The earnings of workers in Britain fall from RAB to $R'AB'$, a decrease of $RR'B'B$, and this exceeds the increase in the capitalists' earnings by EBB' yards of cloth.

The earnings of capitalists initially in Portugal fall from $OR*PK_2$ to $OR'FK_2$, a decrease of $R'R*PF$ yards of cloth. The earnings of workers in Portugal rise from $R*A*P$ to $R'A*P'$, an increase of $R'R*PP'$ yards of cloth, and this exceeds the decrease in the capitalists' earnings by $FP'P$ yards of cloth.

Portuguese capitalists have reason to oppose it. But the Portuguese government can compensate the capitalists by taxing part of the gain accruing to the workers, as the workers' gain is bigger than the capitalists' loss.

Secondary Effects of a Capital Movement

These five results, however, were derived with the help of a drastic simplification. The positions of the curves AC and A^*C^* depend on the initial levels of employment in the two countries' cloth industries. Yet our previous work with the modified Ricardian model showed that a change in the capital stock leads to a reallocation of labor. When allowance is made for this effect, the capital transfer shown in Figure 8-1 proves to be too small to eliminate the gap between marginal products, and the increase in global output understates the efficiency gain provided by the transfer. (By implication, the increase understates to a greater extent the efficiency gain that would be conferred by a transfer large enough to close the gap completely.)

These assertions are confirmed by Figure 8-2, which traces the effects of a capital transfer on the two countries' labor markets. The point B defines the initial equilibrium in Britain's labor market. The real wage measured in cloth is OV_1 yards, OL_1 workers are employed in the wine industry, and $\bar{L}L_1$ workers are employed in the cloth industry. Wine and cloth outputs are measured by the areas under the demand curves for labor (because they are marginal-product curves), but wine output is measured by its cloth equivalent at the free-trade prices prevailing initially. Thus, cloth output is $\bar{L}MBL_1$ yards in Britain, and the cloth equivalent of wine output is $OGBL_1$. The point P defines the initial equilibrium in Portugal's labor market. The real wage measured in cloth is OV_2 yards, OL_2 workers are employed the wine industry, and $\bar{L}^*L_2$ are employed in the cloth industry. Cloth output is $\bar{L}^*NPL_2$ yards, and the cloth equivalent of wine output is $OHPL_2$ yards.

The real wage expressed in cloth is higher in Britain than in Portugal, because the marginal product of labor is higher in Britain's cloth industry. Recall that the marginal products in a particular industry depend on factor proportions in that industry. As the marginal product of capital is lower initially in Britain than in Portugal, the capital-labor ratio must be higher in Britain's cloth industry, which means that the marginal product of labor must likewise be higher.

The transfer of capital from Britain to Portugal induced by the gap between rates of return is shown in Figure 8-2 by shifting the demand curves for labor. The capital stock falls in Britain, reducing the marginal product of labor in Britain's cloth industry and shifting its demand curve for labor downward from E_C to E'_C. The capital stock rises in Portugal, raising the marginal product of labor in Portugal's cloth industry and shifting its demand curve upward from E_C^* to $E_C^{*\prime}$.

These shifts in the demand curve have been drawn carefully to satisfy two requirements. First, the capital transfer in Figure 8-1 was just large enough to equalize the marginal products of capital in the two countries' cloth industries at the initial levels of employment. Therefore, it must also equalize the marginal products of labor. Accordingly, the shifts in the curves shown in Figure 8-2 must bring the marginal products of labor to the common level OV_0 when employment is $\bar{L}L_1$ in Britain's cloth industry and $\bar{L}^*L_2$ in Portugal's cloth industry. Second, the capital

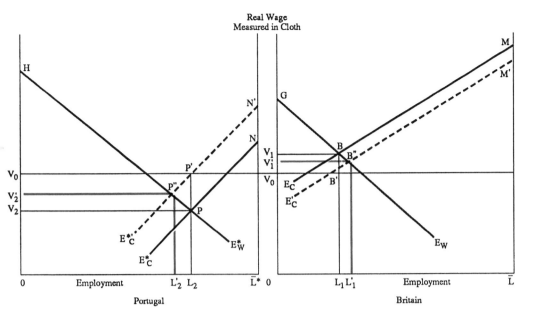

FIGURE 8-2
Effects of Transferring Capital from Britain to Portugal After Reallocating Labor
Initially the real wage is OV_1 in Britain, so OL_1 workers are employed in the wine industry and $\bar{L}L_1$ in the cloth industry. The transfer of capital shown in Figure 8-1 shifts the demand curve for labor downward, from E_C to E'_C, reducing the real wage to OV_0 and reducing cloth output by $MBB'M'$. Initially, the real wage is OV_2 in Portugal, so OL_2 workers are employed in Portugal's cloth industry and $\bar{L}L_2$ in the wine industry. The transfer of capital shifts the demand curve for labor upward, from E^*_C to $E^{*'}_C$, raising the real wage to OV_0 and raising cloth output by $NPP'N'$. When the real wage is OV_0 in Britain, however, the wine industry demands more workers; equilibrium cannot be established until $L_1L'_1$ workers have moved from the cloth industry to the wine industry and the real wage has risen to OV'_1. Cloth output falls by an extra $L_1B'B''L'_1$ yards, but the cloth equivalent of wine output rises by $L_1BB''K'_1$ yards, so the cloth value of national output in Britain rises by $B'BB''$ yards. Similarly, equilibrium cannot be established in Portugal until $L_2L'_2$ workers have moved from the wine industry to the cloth industry and the real wage has fallen to OV'_2. The cloth equivalent of wine output falls by $L_2PP''L'_2$ yards, but cloth output rises by an extra $L_2P'P''L'_2$ yards, so the cloth value of national output in Portugal rises by $PP'P''$ yards. As the marginal product of labor in the cloth industry is now higher in Britain than Portugal, the marginal product of capital must be higher in Portugal than Britain, and an additional transfer of capital is needed to equalize real returns.

transfer raised Portuguese cloth output by more than it reduced British cloth output. Accordingly, the area $NPP'N'$ in Figure 8-2, which measures the increase in Portuguese cloth output at the initial level of employment, must be larger than the area $MBB'M'$, which measures the corresponding decrease in British cloth output.

The new points B' and P', however, are not equilibrium points. If the real wage falls in Britain to OV_0, the wine industry will demand more labor, driving up the real wage. If the real wage rises in Portugal to OV_0, the wine industry will demand less labor, driving down the real wage. Equilibrium in Britain's labor market must be established at B'', with $L_1L'_1$ workers moving from the cloth to the wine industry.

Equilibrium in Portugal's labor market must be established at P'', with L_2L_2' workers moving from the wine to the cloth industry. What are the implications?

The real wage rises in Britain and falls in Portugal, which means that the difference between real wages has been reduced but not eliminated. Therefore, the transfer of capital has not eliminated the difference between the marginal products of capital. This proves the first assertion made previously. The transfer required to remove the gap is larger than the one shown in Figure 8-1.

There are secondary changes in output that augment the gain in global efficiency. In Britain, cloth output falls but wine output rises, and the increase in wine output is large enough to raise the value of national output by $B'BB''$ yards measured in terms of cloth. In Portugal, wine output falls but cloth output rises, and the increase in cloth output is large enough to raise the value of national output by $PP'P''$ yards measured in terms of cloth. Therefore, the ultimate increase in global output is bigger than the initial increase shown in Figure 8-1. (The decrease in the cloth value of British output is $MBB''M'$ rather than $MBB'M''$, and the increase in the cloth value of Portuguese output is $NPP''N'$ rather than $NPP'N'$.)

The complicated story told by Figure 8-2 does not contradict any basic lesson taught by Figure 8-1. A larger capital transfer would completely eliminate the difference between real wages and, therefore, the difference between real returns to capital. That transfer, moreover, would raise global output by more than the amount in Figure 8-2 (which is already larger than the amount in Figure 8-1). Furthermore, the labor-market changes shown in Figure 8-2 do not fundamentally alter the results obtained earlier concerning the earnings of labor and capital. The owners of capital remaining in Britain gain from the capital transfer, because the real return to capital rises. British labor loses, however, because the real wage falls.

Three more points should be made before ending this discussion. First, the output changes brought about by transferring capital from Britain to Portugal could alter relative prices (the terms of trade), which would alter the distribution of gains and losses within and between the countries. Second, a transfer of capital large enough to equalize marginal products in Britain and Portugal will also equalize the marginal products of labor and land. Therefore, it will *maximize* the efficiency of the world economy. There is no need to transfer any other factor.[2] Finally, a transfer of capital does not undermine the basis for trade. As Portugal has more land than Britain, it will continue to produce more wine, even when marginal products have been equalized. As Britain has more capital, even after the transfer, it will continue to produce more cloth.

CAPITAL MOVEMENTS IN THE HECKSCHER–OHLIN MODEL

In the modified Ricardian model, factor movements are required to equalize marginal products and thus maximize global efficiency. Trade alone cannot do so. In the Heckscher–Ohlin model, factor movements may not be needed. Trade alone

---

[2]This conclusion, however, depends on two basic assumptions: that returns to scale are constant, so that marginal products depend only on factor proportions, and that technologies are the same in both countries.

can equalize marginal products and maximize efficiency, because it can equalize factor prices.

The factor-price-equalization theorem, however, depends on a number of restrictive assumptions. All markets must be perfectly competitive, and trade must unify markets completely; there can be no transport costs, tariffs, or other trade barriers. All countries must produce a common set of traded commodities, and the number of commodities in that set must be no smaller than the number of factors of production; in the two-country, two-commodity, two-factor case, one country cannot specialize completely in a single commodity. Production functions must be the same in all countries, must display constant returns to scale, and must not give rise to factor reversals when factor prices change.

These strong assumptions have strong consequences. On the one hand, they give us a good reason for favoring free trade—for wanting to remove all trade barriers. Free trade maximizes global efficiency. On the other hand, they deprive us of any economic explanation for factor movements. By ruling out differences in real earnings, free trade removes the main economic motivation for factor movements.

To generate and analyze factor movements in the Heckscher–Ohlin model, we must modify one of the basic assumptions, in order to produce a situation in which trade cannot equalize factor prices, then trace the consequences of that situation. Two examples will be used to illustrate this strategy. In the first, a tariff will interfere with the unification of markets, preventing factor-price equalization. A capital movement will occur in response to the resulting difference in real earnings, and it will eliminate trade completely. In the second, factor intensities will be reversed; corn will be labor intensive in one country but capital intensive in the other. This will prevent factor-price equalization and induce a capital movement. But the capital movement will not eliminate all trade. Instead, it will eradicate the factor reversal, allowing trade to equalize factor prices.

Effects of a Tariff

We have seen that a tariff on Fewmen's corn imports raises the relative price of corn in Fewmen and also tends to lower it in Manymen. This is the situation shown in Figure 8-3. As usual, Manymen begins with $O\bar{K}_1$ capital per worker, and Fewmen begins with $O\bar{K}_2$. In the initial free-trade equilibrium, the relative price of corn is OP in both countries, the relative price of labor is OW, and factor intensities are the same in the two countries' industries. (The capital intensity of steel production, for example, is WV capital per worker.) Hence, the marginal products of capital and labor are the same in both countries, and their real earnings are the same, whether they are measured in corn or steel.

When Fewmen imposes a tariff on its corn imports, the relative price of corn rises to OP_2 in that country, and the relative price of labor rises to OW_2. Fewmen moves to F, producing more corn and less steel than it did with free trade, and firms adopt more capital-intensive methods of production. In Manymen, however, the relative price of corn falls to OP_1, and the relative price of labor falls to OW_1. Manymen moves to M, producing less corn and more steel, and firms adopt less capital-intensive methods. The gap between capital intensities implies a gap between marginal products and, therefore, a gap between real returns. The real return to

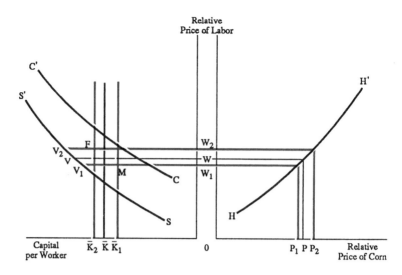

FIGURE 8-3
A Capital Movement Induced by a Tariff
Manymen has $O\bar{K}_1$ capital per worker, and Fewmen has $O\bar{K}_2$. Under free trade, the relative price of corn is OP, the relative price of labor is OW in each country, and the capital intensity of steel production is WV. Manymen exports corn and Fewmen exports steel. If Fewmen imposes a tariff on its corn imports, the relative price of corn will rise to OP_2 in Fewmen, and the relative price of labor will rise to OW_2. Fewmen will produce at F, and the capital intensity of steel production will rise to W_2V_2. The relative price of corn will fall to OP_1 in Manymen, and the relative price of labor will fall to OW_1. Manymen will produce at M, and the capital intensity of steel production will fall to W_1V_1. As the capital intensity of steel production is higher in Fewmen, the marginal product of capital must be lower, and capital will move from Fewmen to Manymen, driving both countries' factor endowments closer to $O\bar{K}$ capital per worker. This process can end only when the capital movement has eliminated trade completely by eliminating the difference between the countries' factor endowments.

capital is lower in Fewmen, whether it is measured in corn or steel. Therefore, capital will move from Fewmen to Manymen, reducing the quantity in Fewmen and raising it in Manymen.

If owners of capital are sufficiently responsive to the gap between real returns, they will continue to transfer capital to Manymen until the gap has vanished. This cannot occur, however, until all other gaps have vanished—the gaps between marginal products, factor intensities, relative prices of labor, and relative prices of corn. But the gap between relative prices cannot vanish until trade has vanished. For as long as any corn moves from Manymen to Fewmen, crossing Fewmen's tariff, the relative price of corn must be higher in Fewmen. The two countries' goods prices cannot be equalized until the influence of the tariff has been eliminated, and this can happen only when trade itself has been eliminated.

How does the transfer of capital eliminate trade? As capital moves from Fewmen to Manymen, it reduces the difference between their factor endowments. At some point in the process, determined in part by the level of the tariff, the difference in endowments becomes too small to furnish any basis for trade, and trade comes to an end. But the capital movement continues even after that. Going back to our earlier work on the opening of trade, recall how we proved the Heckscher–Ohlin theorem. When demand conditions are the same in Manymen and Fewmen but factor endowments are not, relative prices will differ before trade is opened. That is the situation here just after trade has ended. When relative prices differ, however, marginal products also differ, and the capital movement continues. It cannot cease until the countries' endowments have become identical. In Figure 8-3, the capital stock in Fewmen must fall to some such level as $O\bar{K}$ per worker and the capital stock in Manymen must rise to that same level.

Suppose that the two countries reach $O\bar{K}$, ending the capital transfer. What would happen if Fewmen repealed its tariff? Nothing. Trade would not resume, because there is no basis for it. Manymen and Fewmen are the same in all significant respects and cannot gain from trade. In the Heckscher–Ohlin model, then, trade and factor movements are perfect substitutes. When free trade equalizes factor prices, maximizing global efficiency, factor movements are not needed and do not occur. When trade is restricted, however, factor movements are required to maximize efficiency, and they wipe out trade.[3]

Note finally the effects of the capital transfer on the real earnings of labor and capital. By keeping the relative price of corn in Fewmen above its free-trade level, a tariff raises the real wage above its free-trade level and depresses the real return to capital. The capital transfer reduces the real wage and raises the real return to the capital remaining in Fewmen. If you were a worker in Fewmen, then, you would oppose the transfer. The situation is symmetrical in Manymen. The tariff keeps the relative price of corn below its free-trade level, depressing the real wage and raising the real return to capital. The capital transfer raises the real wage and reduces the real return to the capital in Manymen. If you were a worker in Manymen, you would favor the transfer.

Effects of a Factor Reversal

In Figure 8-3 and earlier diagrams, the SS' and CC' curves did not intersect. Steel was more capital intensive than corn at all sets of factor prices. In Figure 8-4, the two curves cross at Y, reversing the factor intensities. When the relative price of labor is below OW, steel is more capital intensive than corn. When the relative price of labor is above OW, corn is more capital intensive than steel. The shape of the HH' curve reflects this reversal. When the relative price of labor is below OW, so that steel is more capital intensive than corn, an increase in the relative price of labor raises the cost of producing corn compared to the cost of producing steel. This raises the

---

[3]There are two qualifications to this proposition. (1) If there are impediments to factor movements as well as to trade, factor movements may not wipe out trade completely. In Figure 8-3, the capital movement will drive the capital-labor ratios closer to $O\bar{K}$ but will stop before they reach $O\bar{K}$. The remaining difference between endowments may be large enough for trade to continue. The outcome depends on the cost of moving goods (the level of the tariff) compared to the cost of moving factors. (2) Those who move their capital from Fewmen to Manymen may not move with it. If they remain behind in Fewmen, the income they earn on their capital in Manymen must be brought back to Fewmen, and this requires trade. Manymen must sell some of its output to Fewmen to pay for the services of capital from Fewmen. This trade, however, is not the sort we have studied heretofore. Manymen will export corn *and* steel rather than export corn and import steel.

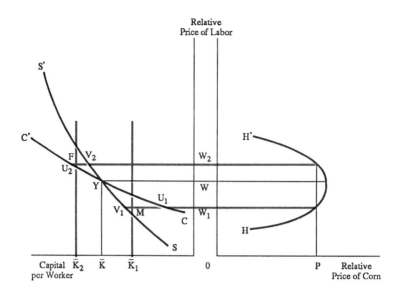

FIGURE 8-4
A Capital Movement Induced by a Factor Reversal
When the relative price of labor is lower than OW, steel is more capital intensive than corn; when it is OW_1, for example, the capital intensity of steel production is W_1V_1, and the capital intensity of corn production is W_1U_1. When steel is more capital intensive than corn, an increase in the relative price of labor raises the relative price of corn, and the HH' curve is upward sloping; when corn is more capital intensive than steel, an increase in the relative price of labor raises the relative price of steel, and the HH' curve is backward bending. Manymen begins with $O\bar{K}_1$ capital per worker, and Fewmen begins with $O\bar{K}_2$. When the relative price of corn is OP, the relative price of labor is OW_1 in Manymen, and it produces at M, but the relative price of labor is OW_2 in Fewmen, and it produces at F. Steel is more capital intensive than corn in Manymen but more labor intensive than corn in Fewmen. Yet the capital intensity of steel in Manymen is lower than its capital intensity in Fewmen; it is W_1V_1 in Manymen but W_2V_2 in Fewmen. Hence, the real return to capital is lower in Fewmen, and capital will move from Fewmen to Manymen. The movement will continue until both countries' factor endowments lie on the same side of $O\bar{K}$. The factor reversal will then be eliminated, and free trade can equalize thre two countries' factor prices.

relative price of corn. When the relative price of labor is above OW, so that factor intensities are reversed, an increase in the relative price of labor raises the cost of producing steel compared to the cost of producing corn. This reduces the relative price of corn.

Technologies determine the shapes of the SS' and CC' curves, excluding or allowing factor reversals. But factor endowments affect the actual result. When Manymen and Fewmen have capital stocks smaller than $O\bar{K}$ per worker, steel is more capital intensive than corn in both countries; when they have stocks larger than $O\bar{K}$, corn is more capital intensive than steel. In both cases, the trade pattern is easy to predict. In the first case, the country with the larger capital stock will export steel; in the second case, that country will export corn. In both cases, moreover, free trade can equalize factor prices, and there is no need or incentive for capital to move. Factor reversals occur and complicate the problem only when factor endowments straddle $O\bar{K}$.

When Manymen has $O\bar{K}_1$ capital per worker, steel is the capital-intensive commodity at all points on Manymen's transformation curve. When Fewmen has $O\bar{K}_2$ capital per worker, corn is the capital-intensive commodity at all points on Fewmen's transformation curve. It is therefore impossible to forecast the trade pattern merely by examining factor endowments. Looking at the situation in Manymen, we would be tempted to predict that it will import steel, because it has less capital per worker and steel is the capital-intensive commodity. But looking at the situation in Fewmen, we would be tempted to predict that it will import steel, too, because it has more capital per worker and steel is the labor-intensive commodity. The two predictions would be inconsistent. Both countries cannot import steel. More important for present purposes, free trade cannot equalize factor prices when a factor reversal occurs.

Suppose that the relative price of corn is OP in the initial free-trade equilibrium. The relative price of labor must be OW_1 in Manymen, and it produces at M, where the capital intensity of steel output exceeds the capital intensity of corn output. The relative price of labor must be OW_2 in Fewmen, and it produces at F, where the capital intensity of corn output exceeds the capital intensity of steel output. But both capital intensities are higher in Fewmen. Therefore, the marginal products of capital are lower in Fewmen, and the real return is thus lower . Free trade does not equalize factor prices, and capital will flow from Fewmen to Manymen in response to the gap between real returns.

As the flow of capital will not cease until it has closed the gap, it has to eliminate the factor reversal. Here are two ways in which this can happen:

1. Capital per worker can fall below $O\bar{K}$ in Fewmen before it has risen to that level in Manymen. Steel will become more capital intensive than corn in both countries. Fewmen will export steel, because it continues to have more capital per worker, and Manymen will export corn.
2. Capital per worker can rise above $O\bar{K}$ in Manymen before it has fallen to that level in Fewmen. Corn will become more capital intensive than steel in both countries. Fewmen will export corn, because it continues to have more capital per worker even in this instance, and Manymen will export steel.

The actual outcome will depend on the initial situation and on the sizes of the countries. If $O\bar{K}_2$ is close to $O\bar{K}$ but $O\bar{K}_1$ is far away, and the countries have the same quantities of labor, the capital movement is likely to drive $O\bar{K}_2$ below $O\bar{K}$, producing the first outcome. In both cases, however, the capital movement serves the same basic purpose. It permits trade to equalize factor prices, rather than eliminate trade itself, so free trade can maximize global efficiency.[4]

When factor movements are induced by factor reversals, they can have drastic effects on the trade pattern. If Fewmen exports corn initially, the first outcome will switch the trade pattern completely. Steel will become more capital intensive than corn in both countries, and Fewmen will export steel instead of corn. If Fewmen exports steel initially, the second outcome will switch the trade pattern. Corn will

---

[4]There is a third possibility. Both countries could wind up with $O\bar{K}$ capital per worker and would have identical transformation curves (which would be straight lines, like those in Chapter 3). There would be no basis for trade.

become more capital intensive than steel in both countries, and Fewmen will export corn instead of steel.

We do not have to know the trade pattern, however, or the way that it evolves, to predict the change in the relative price of corn. As corn is capital intensive in Fewmen when it produces at F, the fall in Fewmen's capital stock decreases its corn output and increases its steel output, pursuant to the Rybczynski theorem. As steel is capital intensive in Manymen when it produces at M, the rise in Manymen's capital stock increases its steel output and decreases its corn output. Steel outputs rise in both countries, and corn outputs fall. Therefore, the capital transfer raises the relative price of corn.

A worker in Fewmen has reason to oppose this sort of capital transfer. The transfer itself reduces the real wage in Fewmen by reducing the capital intensities of steel and corn production. The output effects of the transfer can compound or cushion the reduction in the real wage but cannot reverse it. If both countries wind up with capital stocks larger than $O\bar{K}$ per worker, corn will be more capital intensive than steel in both countries. Hence, the increase in the relative price of corn resulting from the transfer will reduce real wages in both countries, compounding the reduction that took place in Fewmen because of the capital transfer itself. If both countries wind up with capital stocks smaller than $O\bar{K}$ per worker, corn will be less capital intensive than steel in both countries. Hence, the increase in the relative price of corn will raise real wages in both countries, cushioning the reduction that took place in Fewmen because of the capital transfer. When capital stocks are smaller than $O\bar{K}$ per worker, however, capital intensities must be lower than WY in both industries and countries, and they must therefore be lower than they were in Fewmen before the capital transfer. Therefore, the real wage in Fewmen must be reduced by the transfer, even after the reduction is cushioned by the output effect of the transfer. Symmetrical reasoning should convince you that a worker in Manymen has reason to favor the capital transfer.

CAPITAL MOVEMENTS AS TRANSFERS OF CLAIMS

Thus far, international capital movements have been represented by altering stocks of capital equipment. In the Heckscher–Ohlin model, for example, Manymen ends up with more mills to make steel and more tractors to grow corn, and Fewmen ends up with fewer mills and tractors. There are two ways of making these adjustments, by shipping equipment from one country to the other or by financing internal changes in supplies.

When the return to capital is higher in Manymen, that country's firms can afford to borrow at interest rates higher than those that Fewmen's firms can afford to pay. Hence, residents of Fewmen will lend to firms in Manymen rather than firms in Fewmen. Manymen's firms will be able to acquire more mills and tractors, and Fewmen's firms will be forced to run down their holdings.

If mills and tractors can be shipped from one country to the other, firms in Manymen will buy them from firms in Fewmen. If they cannot be transferred, the adjustment process is more complicated. New mills and tractors must be manufactured in Manymen, using factors of production ordinarily employed to make steel and grow corn. To maintain its consumption of steel and corn, Manymen must then export less corn to Fewmen and import more steel. But fewer mills and tractors are needed in Fewmen to replace those that wear out, so Fewmen can divert factors of production to make more steel and grow more corn. It can export more steel to Manymen and import less corn. When mills and tractors are not traded, flows of other goods adjust, permitting the countries involved in a capital transfer to alter their stocks of mills and tractors.[5]

A capital movement, however, need not alter stocks of capital goods (mills and tractors in the Heckscher–Ohlin model). It may serve merely to accommodate a change in consumption. Suppose that Manymen suffers a drought that reduces its corn crop temporarily. The relative price of corn will rise on world markets, but something else may happen, too. Residents of Manymen may borrow from residents of Fewmen to compensate for the loss of real income resulting from the drought. This is an international capital movement, even though it does not affect stocks of capital equipment. Residents of Manymen will issue bonds to residents of Fewmen, mortgaging a portion of their country's future output in exchange for some of Fewmen's current output. Alternatively, residents of Manymen will sell shares to residents of Fewmen, transferring the ownership of firms in Manymen and thus the future earnings of those firms; mills and tractors in Manymen will come under foreign control without any changes in location or quantity.

This example leads to a general statement about the nature of capital movements:

> **International capital movements are transfers of claims that raise the future income of the country acquiring them.**

The country that issues the claims can use the proceeds to buy or build capital goods or to consume more currently than it can produce. The claims themselves may convey information about the issuer's motives, but this is not always the case.

The many forms that capital movements can take are shown by Table 8-1, which lists the claims on other countries held by U.S. residents and the claims on the United States held by foreigners. The numbers are large and changed dramatically in the 1980s. At the end of 1980, U.S. residents held about $936 billion of claims and foreigners held about $544 billion. The difference between the totals, known as the net investment position, was $392 billion. This difference says that gross capital outflows from the United States were larger in previous decades than gross capital inflows into the United States. In the 1980s, however, the net investment position

---

[5]When we come to national-income accounting, we will derive this equation:

$$\text{Investment} - \text{saving} = \text{imports} - \text{exports}$$

When Manymen invests more in mills and tractors but the level of saving does not change, Manymen must import more, export less, or both. It need not import mills and tractors, but it will then have to import more or export less of other goods so as to release the resources needed to produce more mills and tractors. The resulting gap between imports and exports will be filled by borrowing or transferring securities. The same sort of thing will happen in a case described below, when Manymen suffers a drought and its corn crop fails. In that case, the gap between imports and exports will correspond to a reduction in saving—a fall in output and income without a fall in consumption—rather than an increase in investment.

Table 8-1. International Investment Position of the United States, 1980, 1990, and 1991 (billions of dollars)

Type of Claim	1980	1990	1991
Claims held by U.S. residents	936.3	1,884.2	1,960.3
Held by U.S. government:			
Monetary reserves[a]	171.4	174.7	159.2
Loans and other claims	63.9	82.2	78.7
Held by other U.S. residents:			
Direct investments[b]	396.2	623.6	655.3
Foreign bonds	43.5	131.7	147.6
Foreign stocks	18.9	110.0	158.3
Other claims:			
Reported by U.S. banks	203.9	652.1	656.7
Reported by U.S. corporations, etc.	38.4	109.8	104.4
Claims held by foreigners	543.7	2,179.0	2,321.8
Held by foreign governments:			
U.S. government securities	118.2	297.0	318.0
Other claims	57.9	74.1	78.6
Held by other foreigners:			
Direct investments[b]	125.9	466.5	487.0
U.S. government securities	16.1	130.7	154.7
Corporate and other bonds	9.5	240.7	277.0
Corporate stocks	64.6	231.2	282.6
Other claims:			
Reported by U.S. banks	121.1	693.4	680.1
Reported by U.S. corporations, etc.	30.4	45.4	43.8
Net investment position (claims by U.S. residents *less* claims by foreigners)	392.5	−294.8	−361.5

Source: U.S. Department of Commerce, *Survey of Current Business*, June 1992. Detail may not add to total because of rounding.
[a]Includes U.S. gold stock valued at market price.
[b]Valued at replacement cost of tangible assets.

turned negative. Capital outflows were large, raising the claims of U.S. residents by $948 billion through 1990, but capital inflows were very much larger, raising the claims of foreigners by $1,635 billion. This striking change was due largely to the budget and trade deficits of the United States, but a full explanation must be postponed until we have examined the relationship between those two deficits and the roles of the exchange rate and capital movements in maintaining that relationship. The table is important here because it shows the wide variety of capital movements.

Claims and liabilities of governments bulk large in Table 8-1. At the top of the table, for example, we find the foreign claims of the U.S. government. It held about $159 billion of monetary reserves at the end of 1991 and about $79 billion of loans and other claims on foreigners. The reasons for holding monetary reserves are examined in subsequent chapters. The other claims of the U.S. government include loans to developing countries to finance their development, loans by the Export-Import Bank to finance U.S. exports, and subscriptions to international institutions such as the World Bank. Later in the table, we find that foreign governments held $318 billion of U.S. government securities and $79 billion of other claims, including large deposits with U.S. banks. These claims are the monetary reserves that other countries hold in dollars, reflecting the prominent role of the dollar in the international monetary system.

Claims held by corporations, financial institutions, and individuals take three forms: direct investments, portfolio investments, and loans to finance capital formation or consumption.

Direct investments by U.S. firms totaled almost $655 billion at the end of 1991. They reflect the growth of multinational production. American companies own factories and other facilities in many foreign countries. General Motors, for example, has plants in Canada, Britain, Germany, Spain, Australia, Brazil, Mexico, and two dozen other countries. Some of these facilities serve foreign markets, producing goods and services that the parent companies would otherwise export from the United States. Some serve the U.S. market, producing raw materials, parts and components, and finished goods for use or sale in the United States. Foreign direct investments in the United States have increased hugely in recent years, rising from $126 billion in 1980 to $487 billion in 1991, and the trade names of the firms involved involved are household words. Honda is Japanese, Volkswagen is German, Shell is Dutch, Nestlé is Swiss, and Michelin is French.[6]

Portfolio investments are holdings of stocks and bonds designed to earn dividends and interest rather than exercise control over the use of foreign facilities. At the end of 1991, Americans held about $306 billion of foreign stocks and bonds, and foreigners held about $714 billion of American securities. The very large size of foreign holdings, compared to American holdings, is linked to the budget and trade deficits mentioned earlier, but there was a similar (though smaller) difference in 1980, before those deficits emerged. There are many reasons, including the size of the American economy. American firms are larger than their foreign counterparts and issue larger quantities of stocks and bonds, and there are active markets for those securities, making it easy to buy and sell them. Furthermore, American firms must disclose more information than most other countries' firms, which makes it somewhat easier for investors to assess their risks and prospects.

Some of the "other claims" in Table 8-1 also represent portfolio investments. Claims of foreign residents reported by U.S. banks include deposits and short-term securities held by foreign banks and corporations, and some of the corresponding claims of U.S. residents represent deposits held at foreign banks. But most of the claims reported by U.S. banks are the banks' own loans to foreigners. These loans began to grow in the 1960s but became much larger in the 1970s, when many foreign countries borrowed heavily to deal with financial problems brought on by higher oil prices. We will say more about them when we look at the resulting debt crisis and subsequent efforts to deal with it.

---

[6]The direct investments of U.S. and foreign firms are listed in the table at replacement cost rather than the actual cost of acquisition. It is therefore impossible to match up precisely the annual amounts of direct investment with the year-to-year change in the amounts outstanding.

MULTINATIONAL PRODUCTION AND TRANSNATIONAL TAXATION

The multinational company is not a new phenomenon. Some American firms had plants in other countries before World War I. Singer Sewing Machine and the Ford Motor Company are well-known examples. The phenomenon became much more common after World War II, however, and it is hard to find a major company today that does not have affiliates in other countries.

The U.S. government gathers detailed data on the foreign affiliates of American firms and U.S. affiliates of foreign firms. A summary is reproduced in Table 8-2,

Table 8-2. Multinational Investment and Production, 1989 (assets and sales in billions of dollars, employment in thousands of workers)

Category	Assets	Sales	Employment
Foreign affiliates of U.S. firms	$1,314	$1,266	6,621
Location of affiliate:			
Europe	658	659	2,708
Canada	192	183	945
Japan	133	138	388
Latin America	163	113	1,301
All other countries	168	173	1,279
Industry of affiliate:			
Manufacturing	491	641	4,189
Petroleum	193	224	291
Trade	132	261	1,162
Finance and real estate[a]	403	59	160
Other	94	81	820
U.S. affiliates of foreign firms	1,402	1,041	4,440
Location of parent:			
Europe	686	538	2,636
Canada	201	117	755
Japan	328	267	504
All other countries	187	119	545
Industry of affiliate:			
Manufacturing	367	347	2,123
Petroleum	91	92	135
Trade	180	415	1,209
Finance and real estate[a]	642	112	243
Other	122	75	729

Source: U.S. Department of Commerce, *Survey of Current Business*, July 1991 and October 1991. Detail may not add to total because of rounding.
[a]Except banking.

which shows total assets, total sales, and numbers of employees, classified by region and activity.

The assets of the foreign affiliates of American firms totaled $1,314 billion in 1989, a figure more than twice as large as the figure for direct investments in Table 8-1. This is because the figures in Table 8-2 relate to the total assets of the foreign affiliates, whereas those in Table 8-1 relate to the amounts of financing provided by their parent companies. Foreign affiliates of American firms raise some of their capital by issuing securities and borrowing from banks; they do not rely entirely on their parent companies. Measured by assets, sales, and employment, the foreign affiliates of U.S. firms are concentrated heavily in manufacturing and are also concentrated in developed countries (in Western Europe, Canada, and Japan), which have the largest markets. The distributions are somewhat different for the U.S. affiliates of foreign firms. Most of them come from other developed countries, but manufacturing is less important than trade, finance, and real estate, when measured by assets or sales. Foreign direct investment in the United States has included large purchases of commercial property, including office buildings, shopping centers, and hotels, and foreign firms are involved in a wide range of financial activities, including insurance and banking.

The economic importance of multinational production is demonstrated by some simple comparisons. Sales by the foreign affiliates of U.S. firms, listed at $1,266 billion in Table 8-2, can be compared with sales by their U.S. parents, which amounted to $3,133 billion.[7] Thus, the affiliates accounted for nearly 30 percent of total sales by the parents and affiliates. Furthermore, the affiliates accounted for about 80 percent of the combined sales outside the United States; in other words, the affiliates' sales in foreign markets were about four times as large as their parents' exports. They were, indeed, far larger than total U.S. exports. The numbers of workers employed by the foreign affiliates, listed at 6.6 million in Table 8-2, can likewise be compared with the numbers employed by their parent companies, which amounted to 18.7 million. The affiliates accounted for more than a quarter of the global total. Put differently, one foreign worker was employed by an affiliate for every three workers employed by its parent in the United States, and the corresponding figure for manufacturing was closer to one foreign worker for every two in the United States.[8] These numbers have been fairly stable for more than a decade.

Many American firms derive more than a quarter of their earnings from their foreign affiliates, including Coca-Cola, Colgate-Palmolive, Ford, General Electric, IBM, and Xerox. A number of these firms, such as IBM and Xerox, produce goods using new technologies, and many of them, such as Coca-Cola and Colgate-Palmolive, market consumer goods with well-known brand names. This point will come up again.

---

[7] The parents' sales are not shown in Table 8-2 but come from the same source as the figures in the table.

[8] When sales and employment figures are compared with those for the whole U.S. economy, not just for the parent companies, the numbers are smaller but still impressive. In 1989, all nonbank businesses in the United States (other than the U.S. affiliates of foreign firms) employed 87.5 million workers, compared with the 6.6 million employed by the foreign affiliates of U.S. firms, and manufacturing firms employed 17.6 million workers, compared with the 4.2 million employed by the foreign affiliates. In manufacturing, then, one foreign worker was employed for every four in the United States.

When we look at the United States as a host country, it becomes much harder to compare the activities of parents and affiliates, because the parents come from many countries, and we do not have comparable numbers for sales or employment by the parent companies. But we can compare the figures for their U.S. affiliates with the corresponding figures for the whole U.S. economy. Thus, the 4.4 million workers employed by the U.S. affiliates of foreign firms in 1989 amounted to 4.8 percent of total business employment in the United States, and the percentage has been growing rapidly. In 1977, for example, the U.S. affiliates of foreign firms employed only 1.2 million workers, or 1.7 percent of total U.S. business employment. Furthermore, the 2.1 million workers employed by affiliates in manufacturing amounted to 10 percent of the corresponding total for the whole U.S. economy.

Reasons for Multinational Production

Why do firms acquire or build facilities in other countries rather than expand their facilities at home? Simple reasons come to mind, and they fit some cases easily.

You cannot produce oil in countries without oil fields. You cannot produce copper or aluminum in countries without ores. Firms in extractive industries will go where they can find the minerals they need. Similar arguments can be adduced to explain the international migration of manufacturing. Firms producing labor-intensive goods will migrate to labor-abundant countries, where labor costs are low even after allowing for differences in productivity. Firms producing goods that have high shipping costs, such as processed foods and household supplies, which are bulky compared to their value, will build plants close to their large markets. A firm that faces a high tariff or some other barrier limiting its access to a major foreign market can often leap over the barrier by building a plant on the other side, even when costs of production are higher there. Thus, Honda, Nissan, and Toyota began to make cars in the United States to overcome restrictions on the number of cars that they can bring in from Japan.[9]

The preceding explanations are helpful, but they are incomplete. They explain why economic activity will concentrate in certain places—countries with large markets, scarce natural resources, or abundant quantities of inexpensive labor. They do not explain why foreign firms have been more successful than local firms in exploiting markets and developing resources, despite differences in language, law, and customs that should tend to favor local firms. Why have Japanese automobile firms been so successful in the American market? Why were the oil fields of the Middle East developed by American, British, French, and Dutch companies, rather than local companies?

Clearly, the foreign firms involved must have specific advantages over their local

---

[9]This result, however, has changed the form of the debate about imports of Japanese cars. By inducing Japanese firms to assemble cars in North America and Europe, using large numbers of parts and components produced in Japan, American and European restrictions on imports of Japanese cars have led to demands for restrictions on imports of parts and components. We shall return to this development and some of its strange consequences when we review recent issues in trade policy.

competitors. They may have easier access to capital from home and foreign sources. They may sometimes be subsidized by their own national governments. But other advantages are more important. Scanning the names of the companies listed earlier, it is not hard to spot them. Some firms have technological advantages—better products, processes, or combinations of the two. Other firms have well-known product lines. They built up their foreign markets by exporting products made at home, then turned to multinational production when their foreign markets became large enough to let them exploit economies of scale.

An explanation of multinational production must focus on the same phenomena that were used to explain intraindustry trade in Chapter 7. Differentiated products, technological advantages, and economies of scale give large, established firms a competitive advantage over smaller, newer local firms. Returning to the widget case considered in Chapter 7, an Italian firm may be able to manufacture widgets in France, for sale in Italy as well as France, because its widgets are sufficiently different from those of all other producers. Replace widgets with automobiles, and you can tell the story of Honda, Nissan, and Toyota in the American market. A firm's specific advantage need not be permanent. It has merely to last long enough for the firm to establish itself by exploiting effectively the special features of its product or those of the local environment—access to raw materials, low labor costs, or the protection afforded by trade barriers.

Costs and Benefits of Multinational Production

The rapid growth of multinational production has led to much controversy and many policy problems. Multinational firms encounter vocal criticism in host and home countries alike, and some of the criticism that used to be leveled at U.S. firms in other countries is now being leveled at foreign firms in the United States.

Viewed from a cosmopolitan perspective, the advantages of multinational production appear to dominate the disadvantages. The activities of multinational firms tend to increase the efficiency and flexibility of the world economy by making resource use and, therefore, trade patterns more sensitive to relative costs. When costs rise in one country compared to others, all firms have the same incentive to find alternative sources of supply. But multinational firms may be able to move faster and farther than others. A firm that does not have foreign affiliates must start by searching for new suppliers and then place orders with them. It must also weigh the costs of breaking relations with old suppliers, which it might want to reestablish if cost conditions were to change again. Multinational firms do not have these problems. They can switch orders and production from one affiliate to another. Furthermore, they are apt to keep close watch on relative costs and prices, because they do business in many places.

The firms' flexibility is not unlimited. A multinational firm may hesitate to close down a plant in a high-cost country or lay off workers, because it fears punitive action by the country's government. As managers of multinational firms emphasize these difficulties, some observers have concluded that multinational firms are actually insensitive to cost conditions and may fail to make appropriate adaptations. But testimony can be marshalled on the other side. Labor leaders claim that multinational firms have unusual bargaining power in wage negotiations precisely because they *can* close plants when labor costs get out of line; they can relocate production without interrupting it. As usual, the truth lies between extremes. Multinational firms have more flexibility than localized producers but less than their critics and admirers believe. On balance, then, they probably contribute to global efficiency by raising the responsiveness of output and trade flows to changes in comparative costs and by fostering the international mobility of capital, technology, and managerial talent.

Governments express concerns much like those of labor leaders, because multinational firms can act in ways that limit a government's ability to pursue certain policy objectives. The development of multinational banking, for example, has enhanced the international mobility of capital, and we will soon see that high capital mobility reduces the effectiveness of monetary policy under pegged exchange rates and of fiscal policy under floating rates. Furthermore, "footloose" firms can frustrate a government's attempt to regulate or tax domestic business more heavily than other countries regulate or tax it, because firms can move to more congenial environments. This option is most readily available to a multinational firm because of its experience in linking plants and markets at distant points around the world.

Multinational firms do not always have to move in order to minimize the impact of cross-country differences in policy regimes. They can manipulate *transfer prices*, the prices at which goods pass from plant to plant within a single firm. A firm with an affiliate in a high-tax country can instruct it to charge low prices for goods sold to the firm's affiliate in a low-tax country. When the goods are sold again to final buyers, with or without additional processing, the profits accrue to the affiliate in the low-tax country and thus escape taxation by the high-tax country. Some governments try to regulate transfer pricing, but they rarely have enough information to do it effectively.

Trade policies can have unexpected consequences when multinational firms are involved. A tariff designed to protect domestic firms from foreign competition may attract foreign firms to the domestic economy. This happened in the 1960s when U.S. firms built plants in Europe to serve the large internal market of the European Economic Community (EEC). Tariffs were not raised in that particular instance, but U.S. firms were placed at a competitive disadvantage compared to European firms and sought to overcome it by investing in Europe. Similarly, in the 1980s Japanese firms began to manufacture cars in the United States because the United States had restricted the number of cars that could be imported from Japan.

When outsiders jump over trade barriers by building plants inside them, the barriers can still protect the incomes of the factors of production used intensively by the protected industry. But the barriers will cease to protect the incomes of domestic firms and their stockholders, which is often the main policy objective.

Differences between national policies may cause firms to *become* multinational. In the 1960s and 1970s, American banks established branches in London and other financial centers to escape the effects of interest-rate ceilings and other regulations in the United States that put them at a competitive disadvantage when bidding for foreign deposits and making foreign loans. The banks' migration had two effects. First, it put pressure on the U.S. authorities to relax or remove the restrictions that were causing the banks to migrate. Second, it led them to permit the establishment of International Banking Facilities (IBFs) in the United States, which domestic and foreign banks can use to conduct international business without meeting some of the requirements imposed on banks that operate domestically in the United States.

When firms operate in many countries, another problem arises. Governments clash over jurisdiction. Several such clashes occured because of efforts by the United States to limit trade with the Soviet Union. Washington tried to impose its regulations on the operations of U.S. firms in Europe, and European governments objected strongly. The French affiliate of a U.S. firm, they argued, must obey French law but lies beyond the reach of U.S. law. A famous clash occurred in 1979, after Iranian militants seized the American embassy in Teheran. The United States instructed U.S. banks to freeze the accounts of their Iranian depositors, including those at foreign branches of the U.S. banks. The British government objected, maintaining that the London branches of U.S. banks are subject only to its orders, not those of Washington.

Additional concerns are heard in many host countries, where critics charge that foreign firms impair economic and political independence. When asked what they mean, some critics retreat into rhetoric about neocolonialism and the subversion of indigenous values. Others are more precise. Multinational firms, they say, resist guidance or control by host-country governments, interfering with the execution of national policies and development plans, and they evade host-country taxes by manipulating transfer prices. Multinational firms, they say, exploit their host countries' natural resources unfairly. They perpetuate an "unequal" division of labor by mining raw materials in developing countries but processing them in developed countries. They use their bargaining power to wring one-sided concessions from host-country governments, paying too little for the raw materials they take away and depriving future generations of their rightful inheritance by taking them away too rapidly.[10] These concerns about exploitation, transfer pricing, and the depletion of raw materials have been expressed for many years in countries ranging from Canada to Australia and from Venezuela to Nigeria. Governments have responded by canceling petroleum and mining concessions, requiring local participation in the new affiliates of foreign firms, and taking over foreign affiliates. Saudi Arabia, Venezuela, Iran, and Libya have taken over the local affiliates of foreign oil companies, paying full or partial compensation. Mexico took them over decades ago, provoking a long and bitter dispute with the United States.

Concerns about transfer pricing and tax evasion are now heard in the United States itself, where the incomes of foreign firms have risen far less rapidly than their total sales, leading some to charge that distorted transfer prices are being used by foreign firms to evade U.S. taxes. Concerns about the exploitation of raw materials and the heritage of future generations are being voiced in Russia and the other republics of the former Soviet Union, where there is strong opposition to foreign investment in the oil industry. Elsewhere in Central and Eastern Europe, concerns have been expressed that state-owned enterprises are being privatized by selling them to foreigners at bargain prices.

---

[10]This complaint invokes an important proposition. The more oil we lift today, the lower the current price and the higher the future price (because less oil will be available in the future). There is, then, an optimal rate of extraction that depends on current and future demands and on the weights that consumers attach to future income compared to current income.

There have been significant changes, however, in the views and policies of many developing countries, which have started to welcome and actively attract foreign direct investment. They give three reasons. First, foreign direct investment adds to the capital stock in the host country, creating employment and raising wages. Second, it provides on-the-job training for the domestic labor force, supplying the skilled workers and managers needed by domestic firms. Third, it helps to shift the host country's economy and its economic policies from an inward-looking orientation, emphasizing the protection of domestic markets, to an outward-looking orientation, emphasizing the development of export markets, including those of the multinational firms.

We may indeed have reached a point at which multinational firms are criticized more harshly in their own home countries than in most host countries. Labor unions charge that multinational firms destroy jobs at home when they go abroad, whether to serve foreign markets or bring goods back to the home country. These complaints are easy to understand but hard to evaluate. Workers who lose their jobs when a company closes a plant in Michigan or California and opens one in Spain or South Korea cannot be blamed for saying that the company has destroyed their jobs. Companies reply, however, that their home-country costs were too high—that they could not have saved their workers' jobs even if they had not opened plants abroad. They say that they protect domestic jobs, moreover, when they import low-cost parts from their foreign affiliates in order to compete more effectively with imports of finished products.

Economists looking at these issues call attention to indirect effects neglected by workers and companies alike. The building of a plant abroad can raise foreign incomes and augment the demand for exports from the home country. This effect is often overlooked because the additional exports may be manufactured by a different company and the jobs they create may be located in a different town or region. Furthermore, the full effects of multinational production on employment and wage rates depend on the factor intensities of the goods involved—those produced in the plants that are closed and those for which foreign demand is raised.

Problems of Transnational Taxation

One additional issue deserves study here, because it arises directly from our work on capital movements and introduces a distinction we will need again. Who should tax incomes arising from capital movements, including those arising from direct investments, and what tax rates should be chosen?

Most governments claim and exercise the right to tax incomes generated in their countries. This right is rarely contested. It arises in part from the basic relationship between taxes collected and services supplied. The relationship is loose. A government that takes a dollar of your income does not necessarily give you a dollar's worth of services. Yet those who live and work within a country or hold property protected by its laws do receive some value for their taxes.

Applying this principle pervasively, most governments claim tax jurisdiction over all individuals and firms residing inside their borders, including the local affiliates of foreign firms. Typically, they tax those affiliates just as they tax domestic firms. Some treat them preferentially, however, to attract foreign capital, and some have been known to discriminate against them, despite attempts by the home countries' governments to prevent discrimination.

The main problem in transnational taxation has to do with the rights of the *home* country. Should it tax the foreign earnings of its own citizens, including those remitted by the foreign affiliates of domestic firms? Most countries claim and exercise this right, saying that they furnish protection and services to *all* their citizens, even those residing abroad. If foreign tax rates are lower than their own, moreover, and they do not tax their citizens' foreign earnings, their citizens will have inappropriate incentives to invest in other countries rather than invest at home.

Once we concede this possibility, however, we have to answer another question. What is an "inappropriate" incentive? The answer depends on the government's perspective. In Chapter 1, we encountered two perspectives, cosmopolitan and national. They can be applied to transnational taxation.

Consider a competitive model of the sort used earlier to study the effects of capital movements. (We can use a modified Ricardian model or a Heckscher–Ohlin model. It does not matter here.) As the real return to capital in each country will equal the marginal product of capital, we can use real returns to measure the effects of capital movements on each country's output and on global output.

If governments adopt a cosmopolitan perspective and thus seek to maximize global output regardless of its distribution, they will not want to discourage capital movements resulting from differences in real returns. When the return to capital is higher in country A than country B, a capital movement from country B to country A will raise output in country A by more than it reduces output in country B. Therefore, it will raise global output. Conversely, governments will want to discourage capital movements that do not reflect differences in real returns, because they will reduce global output. Such movements may occur, however, whenever tax rates differ from country to country.

Suppose that $100 of capital can earn $10 in each country, but the income tax is 50 percent in country A and 20 percent in country B. If country A does not tax its citizens' foreign-source incomes, a citizen of country A can earn $5 by investing in country A but $8 by investing in country B:

Investment of $100 in Country A		Investment of $100 in Country B	
Income before tax	$10	Income before tax	$10
Tax paid to country A	5	Tax paid to country B	2
Income after tax	5	Income after tax	8

There is an "inappropriate" incentive for citizens of country A to invest in country B, and country A must adopt a different tax policy. It must impose its own tax rate on its citizens' incomes from country B but give them a *credit* for taxes paid to country B. This is shown algebraically in Note 8-2 and illustrated by the following calculations:

Investment of $100 in Country B	
Income before tax	$10
Tax paid to country B	2
Tax paid to country A:	
Provisional tax (at 50 percent)	5
Less credit for tax paid to	
country B	−2
Actual tax	3
Income after tax	5

This tax regime is *neutral* from a cosmopolitan standpoint, because after-tax earnings are the same in both countries when pretax earnings are the same.

The government of country A, however, may adopt a national perspective instead and seek to maximize its own country's income. It will then want to discourage its citizens from investing in country B unless investments in country B add more to the national income of country A than do investments in country A itself. As taxes paid to country B add nothing to the income of country A, the government of country A will not want its citizens to invest in country B unless they can earn more *after* paying taxes to country B than they can earn *before* paying taxes on income earned at home.

Suppose that $100 of capital can earn $8 in country A and $10 in country B and that tax rates are the same as before (50 percent in country A and 20 percent in country B). A citizen of country A can earn $4 by investing in country A but $8 by investing in country B:

Investment of $100 in Country A		Investment of $100 in Country B	
Income before tax	$8	Income before tax	$10
Tax paid to country A	4	Tax paid to country B	2
Income after tax	4	Income after tax	8

Citizens of country A will want to invest in country B, but the government of country A will want them not to do so, because an investment in country B adds only $8 to the national income of country A, no more than an investment in country A itself.

A credit for taxes paid to country B will not serve the purpose here. Income after tax from investing in country B would be $5, as before, $1 more than income after tax from investing in country A, and citizens of country A would still want to invest in country B. Country A must impose its own tax rate on its citizens' incomes from country B but give them a *deduction* rather than a credit for taxes paid to country B. This is shown in Note 8-2 and illustrated by these calculations:

Investment of $100 in Country B		
Income before tax		$10
Tax paid to country B		2
Tax paid to country A:		
Income from country B	10	
Less deduction of tax paid to country B	−2	
Income taxable by country A	8	
Actual tax (at 50 percent)		4
Income after tax		4

This regime is neutral from the standpoint of country A, because after-tax earnings are the same whenever earnings from country A before paying taxes to country A are equal to earnings from country B after paying taxes to country B.

What is the actual tax policy of the United States? It is cosmopolitan, not national, in that it allows investors to credit foreign taxes against taxes due to the U.S. government. In fact, it goes further. A firm with earnings from a foreign affiliate does not have to pay U.S. taxes on those earnings if it reinvests them in its affiliate. Tax payments are *deferred* until income is brought home. By reinvesting its foreign-source income in its foreign affiliate, then, a firm can obtain what amounts to an interest-free loan from the U.S. Treasury. The size of this implicit subsidy, however, depends on the size of the difference between U.S. and foreign tax rates. When those rates are equal, the firm does not owe any tax to the U.S. government, thanks to the tax credit, and there is no subsidy. As corporate tax rates in other industrial countries are not very different from U.S. rates, the subsidy is small.

SUMMARY

When analyzing international factor movements, we must distinguish effects on the factors that move from effects on factors remaining in the source country and factors residing initially in the host country. In the modified Ricardian model, for example, a capital movement raises the real return to the capital that moves and to capital remaining in the source country, but reduces the return to capital residing initially in the host country. It reduces the real wage in the source country but raises the real wage in the host country. When factor movements are induced by differences in real earnings, which are due in turn to differences in marginal products, factor movements raise global output, contributing to global efficiency. They raise output in the host country by more than they reduce it in the source country.

To induce and analyze factor movements in the Heckscher–Ohlin model, we must modify the assumptions of the model to keep trade from equalizing factor prices. The effects of the factor movements, however, depend on the particular impediment used to separate factor prices. A tariff can cause factor movements that wipe out all trade; the host and source countries wind up with identical factor endowments. A reversal

Note 8-2
The Taxation of Foreign-Source Income

When citizens of country A invest at home, they earn r_A on each dollar and pay taxes to country A at the rate t_A. Their after-tax return is $r_A(1 - t_A)$. When they invest in country B, they earn r_B on each dollar and pay taxes to country B at the rate t_B. Because they reside in country A, however, they owe taxes to that country, too, and the rate they pay is t'_A, so their after-tax return is $r_B(1 - t_B - t'_A)$. We can define the difference between the after-tax returns as:

$$D = r_b(1 - t_B - t'_A) - r_A(1 - t_A).$$

Citizens of country A will invest in country B whenever D is positive. What rate t'_A should country A adopt, given the other two tax rates?

If country A seeks to maximize global income, it should encourage its citizens to invest in country B whenever r_B exceeds r_A. Therefore, it should impose the rate t_A on its citizens' earnings from country B but allow them to *credit* taxes paid to country B against taxes owed to country A. They will then pay $r_B t'_A = r_B t_A - r_B t_B$ to country A, so that $t'_A = t_A - t_B$. Substituting into the definition of D,

$$D = r_B[1 - t_B - (t_A - t_B)] - r_A(1 - t_A)$$
$$= (r_B - r_A)(1 - t_A).$$

D will be positive, inducing investment in country B, whenever r_B exceeds r_A.

If country A seeks to maximize its own national income, it should encourage its citizens to invest in country B only when $r_B(1 - t_B)$ exceeds r_A, because an investment in country B adds only $r_B(1 - t_B)$ to national income in country A. Therefore, it should impose the rate t_A on its citizens' earnings from country B but allow them to *deduct* taxes paid to country B before they calculate the taxes owed to country A. They will then pay $r_B t'_A = r_B(1 - t_B)t_A$ to country A, so that $t'_A = (1 - t_B)t_A$. Substituting into the definition of D,

$$D = r_B[1 - t_b - (1 - t_B)t_A] - r_A(1 - t_A)$$
$$= [r_B(1 - t_B) - r_A](1 - t_A).$$

D will be positive, inducing investment in country B, whenever $r_B(1 - t_B)$ exceeds r_A.

of factor intensities, by contrast, can cause self-limiting factor movements that do not eliminate trade; they eliminate the factor reversal instead, allowing trade to equalize factor prices. In both cases, however, factor movements have the same effects on real earnings, and the effects resemble those obtained in the modified Ricardian model.

The results summarized thus far come from cases in which capital movements are linked to capital formation. The capital stock rises in the host country and falls in the source country. These are special cases. Capital movements take place whenever residents of one country acquire claims on residents of another country. Those who issue the claims are mortgaging some of their future income in order to invest or consume more now.

When firms in one country buy or build facilities in another, the capital movement is described as direct investment. It leads to multinational production. Explanations for this phenomenon emphasize competitive advantages enjoyed by large firms— superior technologies and well-known product lines—that give them a competitive advantage over local firms. Multinational production raises the efficiency and flexibility of the international economy and can help to open up inward-looking national economies. In host countries, however, multinational firms are accused of resisting indigenous policies, manipulating transfer prices to minimize taxes, and using their bargaining power to obtain concessions from host-country governments. In home countries, they are accused of taking plants and jobs abroad and weakening trade unions.

When firms and individuals earn incomes abroad, their governments must decide how to tax them. What allowances should be made for taxes paid to foreign governments? If governments adopt a cosmopolitan perspective and thus seek to maximize global income, they should allow their citizens to credit foreign taxes paid against taxes owed at home. If they adopt a national perspective and seek to maximize domestic incomes, they should be less generous and grant deductions rather than credits.

RECOMMENDED READINGS

The effects of capital movements are studied from the standpoint of host countries in G. D. A. MacDougall, "The Benefits and Costs of Private Investment from Abroad," *Economic Record*, Special Issue (March 1960), reprinted in American Economic Association, *Readings in International Economics* (Homewood, Ill.: Richard D. Irwin, 1968), ch. 10.

The causes and effects of factor movements in the Heckscher–Ohlin model are examined in Robert A. Mundell, "International Trade and Factor Mobility," *American Economic Review*, 57 (June 1957), reprinted in American Economic Association, *Readings in International Economics* (Homewood, Ill.: Richard D. Irwin, 1968), ch 7.

On movements of labor rather than capital, see Peter B. Kenen, "Migration, the Terms of Trade, and Economic Welfare in the Source Country," in J. N. Bhagwati et al., eds., *Trade, Balance of Payments and Growth* (Amsterdam: North-Holland,f 1971), ch. 11, reprinted in P. B. Kenen, *Essays in International Economics* (Princeton, N.J.: Princeton University Press, 1980).

On the role and behavior of the multinational firm, see Wilfred J. Ethier, "The Multinational Firm," *Quarterly Journal of Economics*, 101 (November 1986), and Elhanan Helpman, "A Simple Theory of International Trade with Multinational Corporations," *Journal of Political Economy*, 92 (June 1984).

The characteristics and policy implications of foreign direct investment in the United States are examined in Edward M. Graham and Paul R. Krugman, *Foreign Direct Investment in the United States* (Washington, D.C.: Institute for International Economics, 1991). Proposals for reforming the tax treatment of foreign-source income are set forth in Gary G. Hufbauer, *U.S. Taxation of International Income* (Washington, D.C.: Institute for International Economics, 1992).

QUESTIONS AND PROBLEMS

(1) How will the labor-market adjustments shown in Figure 8-2 affect the real incomes of landlords in Britain and Portugal? How would you modify your answer if the capital transfer from Britain to Portugal had been big enough to equalize the real returns to capital?

(2) The text says that Britain will have more capital than Portugal even after a capital transfer to Portugal large enough to equalize the real returns to capital. It also says that Britain will continue to produce more cloth than Portugal. Explain both statements. (You will find it helpful to recall two assumptions: Portugal has more land than Britain, but both countries have the same amounts of labor.)

(3) Modify Figure 8-4 by making the CC' curve steeper than the SS' curve and then redrawing the HH' curve. Show that steel will be more capital intensive than corn in Fewmen but less capital intensive than corn in Manymen. Does this modification affect the direction in which capital will move? Does it alter the output effects of the capital movement? Does it alter the effects on real wages? Explain.

(4) When two countries are completely specialized, free trade cannot equalize factor prices, and capital will move from the country with much capital per worker to the country with little capital per worker. Illustrate this proposition.

(5) An American firm exporting pharmaceutical products to Japan plans to build an additional plant and is examining three locations: California, Japan, and Thailand. How might its decision be affected by the characteristics of its product, the characteristics of the three countries, and the tax and tariff policies of those countries?

(6) An investment in country A will yield $30 per year; an investment in country B will yield $40. The tax rate is 30 percent in country A and 20 percent in country B. Where will a citizen of country A invest if country A adopts a cosmopolitan perspective, giving a credit for foreign taxes paid? Where will the citizen invest if country A adopts a national perspective, giving a deduction for foreign taxes paid? How would your results be altered if the tax rate in country B were 40 percent?

(7) A Swedish firm wants to buy an American firm that is the only producer of a sophisticated guidance system used by the Defense Department. Should the U.S. government forbid the sale? Are there other ways to safeguard the technology involved?

9

Instruments and Uses of Trade Policy

THE ISSUES

The trade models developed in earlier chapters illustrated two basic propositions. Under competitive conditions, free trade can maximize the value of global output. Furthermore, it is beneficial to each participating country. It relaxes the constraints imposed by a country's endowment of labor, capital, and natural resources, premitting households to consume collections of commodities better than those the country can produce on its own. Look around the world, however, and you will find that every country uses import tariffs, and many use other trade barriers as well. In most countries, moreover, important economic and political groups want even more protection from foreign competition. Is something wrong with the case for free trade?

The answer to this question has two parts. Some well-known arguments for protection are fallacious and easily refuted by economic analysis. Nevertheless, their superficial plausibility and political popularity gives them immunity from economic logic. Other arguments stand up to analysis, but they must be carefully qualified, and it is almost always possible to show that there are less costly ways of achieving the same policy objective. Tariffs and other trade barriers usually prove to be *second-best* policy instruments.

To develop these propositions convincingly, we must acquire the tools we will need to represent and analyse tariffs and other trade barriers, then use them to study the principal arguments for protection. The first part of this chapter will therefore be concerned with the representation of tariffs and other trade barriers. It will focus on these issues:

- How tariffs affect prices, output and trade patterns, and economic welfare at home and abroad.

- How tariffs on one product can affect producers of other products.

- How the effects of quotas and other trade barriers differ from those of tariffs.

The rest of the chapter will analyze some of the best-known arguments for tariffs and show why tariffs tend to be second-best policy instruments. It will focus on these issues:

- How tariffs can affect the distribution of the gains from trade.
- How tariffs can affect the distribution of domestic income.
- How tariffs can compensate for structural rigidities.

Subsequent chapters will trace the evolution of trade policy in the United States and other major countries, then look at current issues in trade policy.

THE INSTRUMENTS OF TRADE POLICY

Governments have many trade-policy instruments and many uses for them. Some are used to raise revenue or influence the terms of trade. Some are used to limit imports or encourage exports.

When tariffs are imposed on imported goods that are not produced at home, they are clearly aimed at raising revenue rather than protecting a domestic industry. European countries, for example, have tariffs on coffee and other tropical products. The same intent is clear when an imported commodity is taxed in the same way as its local counterpart. Taxes on imported wine, liquor, and tobacco products are good examples of these compensatory tariffs. Without them, the taxes on domestic goods would handicap domestic producers. A number of countries use export tariffs for this same revenue-raising purpose. The practice is common in developing countries, because tariffs on exports are relatively easy to collect (The U.S. Constitution prohibits the United States from using export tariffs. The Southern states feared that the federal government would finance itself by putting export tariffs on tabacco and other Southern exports.) Most tariffs, however, are protective in purpose and effect. They are meant to stimulate production in domestic import-competing industries.

Tariffs affect quantities by affecting prices. Subsidies operate in the same way, and they are sometimes used to stimulate exports. The General Agreement on Tariffs and Trade, the basic code of conduct governing trade policies, attempts to outlaw export subsidies. That is because subsidies can cancel the protective effects of existing import tariffs (and because they can lead to competitive subsidization of the welfare-reducing sort illustrated in Chapter 7). But the prohibition is not fully effective. Many countries subsidize exports indirectly. They offer export credits at low interest rates, treat export earnings preferentially when taxing business profits, and subsidize production in their export industries instead of directly subsidizing the exports themselves.

Imports quotas affect quantities directly rather than affecting them indirectly by altering prices. A quota is an absolute limitation on the volume of an imported good. At one time, the United States had quotas on oil imports. It still has quotas on several agricultural commodities covered by domestic price supports. If there were no such quotas, it would be impossible to support the domestic prices of farm products without also supporting their world prices, and the benefits of price supports could not be confined to domestic farmers.

Like other schemes that ration quantities directly, quotas interfere with economic efficiency; changes in prices reflecting changes in scarcity cannot have their usual effects on quantities. Furthermore, quotas are hard to administer fairly. If you happen to be at the head of the line when "tickets" are handed out, giving you a share of an import quota, you can reap large windfall profits. If you are the one who hands them out, you may be tempted to grab some of the profits for yourself. Quotas breed corruption. If quotas are distributed to foreign suppliers, using base-period market shares, old suppliers obtain an advantage over new suppliers, even when the new suppliers are more efficient.

Because they interfere with efficiency and produce inequities, quotas are prohibited by the GATT. But there are important exceptions to the prohibition, including one involved by the United States to justify its quotas on farm products. Furthermore, some countries, including the United States, have persuaded their trading partners to impose "voluntary" export restrictions, which resemble import quotas in most of their effects (apart from the distribution of the windfall profits).

Tariffs, subsidies, and quotas are fairly transparent. Although it may be hard to measure their effects on prices, outputs, and trade flows, it is not hard to identify them and their purposes. Other forms of intervention are less transparent.

Most countries regulate products and processes for reasons of health, safety, and environmental quality, and they regulate imports for the same reasons. All too often, however, the regulations are written or administered in ways that discriminate against imports, so that the regulations become protective. Restrictions on imports of meat products and plants, meant to keep out diseases and pests, are used to protect domestic farmers. Rules about packaging and labeling are used to make it costly for foreign producers to enter domestic markets.

Governments grant significant advantages to domestic firms when buying goods and services for themselves, and these may be the most important barriers to trade. Governments are the biggest buyers of many manufactured goods, especially in countries where mass transportation, communications, and electricity are provided by the public sector. They buy motor vehicles, aircraft, telecommunications equipment, and power plants, along with military hardware. In the United States, federal and state agencies have "Buy American" regulations that favor domestic firms bidding for government contracts. A foreign firm can win a contract only if the lowest domestic bid exceeds the lowest foreign bid by more than a fixed margin, and the margins are quite high. They are fixed at 50 percent under some federal programs, a number more than twice as high as the typical tariff rate shown later in this chapter. Matters are worse in many foreign countries; contracts can be awarded without competitive bidding, and, even when bids are solicited, margins of preference are not fixed or publicized. To complicate the problem of the foreign bidder, specifications can be rigged deliberately to favor domestic firms.

Although tariffs are transparent, compared to these devices, their impact can depend on decisions made at dockside by the customs inspector. A product may be taxed at a high or low rate, depending on the way in which the inspector classifies it. How will an inspector classify a wooden box filled with chocolates? Is it a wood product or a food product? As the box is probably worth more than the candy, the inspector is likely to treat it as a wood product. He must go farther, however, to decide what sort of wood product. And decisions made by one inspector are not binding on the next. You may get your first box through as a food product, only to be told that the next one is a wood product and subject to a higher tariff.

Tariffs, Prices, and Protection in a Single Market

In Chapter 2, we used supply and demand curves to show how an import tariff raises the domestic price of an imported good, increases import-competing production, and reduces economic welfare. In subsequent chapters, we said that a tariff could also reduce the foreign price of the imported good, with effects on the exporting country as well as the importing country. Before showing how that happens, let us review and recast the results obtained in Chapter 2.

The diagram used in Chapter 2 is reproduced on the left side of Figure 9-1 (but small changes in notation have been made to simplify the story). The curves S_H and D_H are the domestic supply and demand curves, and the line S_W is the world supply curve, which is drawn to keep the world price at OP. With free trade, production is OQ, consumption is OC, and the quantity of imports is QC. By raising the domestic price to OP', a tariff raises production to OQ', reduces consumption to OC', and reduces the quantity of imports to $Q'C'$. The tariff revenue is $F'FHH'$, and the welfare loss is $S'F'H'$ *plus* SFH.

The same results are shown on the right side of the diagram, using the demand curve for imports, D_M. It is derived by subtracting domestic supply from domestic demand at each domestic price. When the price is $OP*$, for example, domestic demand is equal to domestic supply on the left side, and no imports are demanded on the right side. When the price is OP, demand exceeds supply by QC on the left side and thus by the equal amount ON on the right side. Once again, the tariff raises the domestic price to OP', reducing the quantity of imports by $N'N$, which is, of course, the sum of the two effects shown on the left side of the diagram—the production effect, QQ', and the consumption effect $C'C$. The tariff revenue is $PRR'P'$, and the welfare loss is RVR'. Note 2-1 of Chapter 2 showed that the welfare loss can be written as $\Delta W = -\frac{1}{2} \times \Delta M \times tp_W$, where ΔM is the change in the quantity of imports, p_W is the world price, and t is the tariff rate (so that tp_W equals PP', the price-raising effect of the tariff).

This new presentation will allow us to study cases too hard to analyze using supply and demand curves of the ordinary sort. When using the curve D_M, however, we must always remember that movements along a demand curve for imports represent changes in production *and* consumption and that the corresponding welfare changes are the differences between changes in producer surplus and changes in consumer surplus.

Note, finally, that Figure 9-1 can be used to compare an import quota with an import tariff. Start again with free trade and suppose that the government imposes a quota that has the same import-restricting effect as the tariff shown in Figure 9-1. It limits the volume of imports to ON'. The domestic price must rise to OP' to clear the domestic market, raising domestic production and reducing domestic consumption. The production and consumption effects of a quota are, in fact, identical to those of a tariff when the two devices are equally restrictive. But there is one major difference between the quota and the tariff. The tariff yields revenue, and the quota does not. The revenue equivalent, $PRR'P'$, goes as a windfall to the

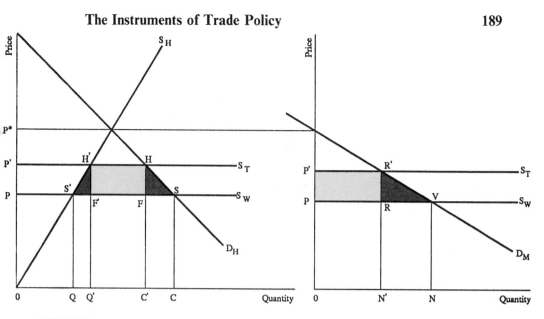

FIGURE 9-1

A Tariff on a Single Good with a Fixed World Price

The curves D_H and S_H on the left side of the diagram are the domestic demand and supply curves. The line S_w is the world supply curve; it is drawn to keep the world price at OP. With free trade, the country produces OQ, consumes OC, and imports QC. A tariff that raises the domestic price to OP' raises production to OQ', reduces consumption to OC', and reduces the quantity of imports to $Q'C'$. The decrease in consumer surplus exceeds the increase in producer surplus by $S'SHH'$, but the tariff revenue, $F'FHH'$, is remitted to consumers, reducing the welfare loss to $S'F'H'$ plus SFH. The same effects are shown on the right side of the diagram, where the curve D_M is the demand curve for imports. It is obtained by subtracting domestic supply from domestic demand at each price. When the price is OP^*, demand is equal to supply, and no imports are demanded. When the price is OP, demand exceeds supply by QC, which equals ON. A tariff that raises the domestic price to OP' reduces imports to $Q'C'$, which equals ON'. The tariff revenue is given by $PRR'P'$, and the welfare loss is given by RVR', which combines the losses due to the production and consumption effects of the tariff.

importers standing at the head of the line when the import tickets are handed out. Under the assumptions adopted here, however, this difference does not matter much. When tariff revenues are returned to consumers, they get back what they paid. When a quota is used instead of a tariff, importers collect what consumers pay out, but importers are consumers, too. Therefore, the welfare loss resulting from the quota remains at RVR', just what it was with the tariff.

The basic equivalence between a tariff and a quota breaks down in two cases: when markets are not perfectly competitive, and when the various supply and demand curves shift up and down. Under a tariff, for example, shifts in the foreign supply curve affect domestic production. Under a quota, they do not. Furthermore, shifts in supply and demand have different welfare effects under tariffs and quotas.

Figure 9-2 shows how a tariff can reduce the world price of an imported good, affecting welfare in the exporting country. The demand curve for imports is drawn as before, but the foreign supply curve, S_W, is upward sloping, not horizontal,

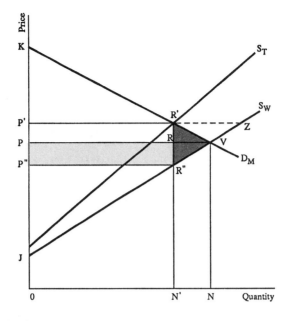

FIGURE 9-2
A Tariff on a Single Good with a Variable World Price
The demand curve for imports is D_M. The foreign supply curve is S_W and is upward sloping. Equilibrium with free trade is established at V, where world and domestic prices are OP, and imports are ON. Consumer surplus exceeds producer surplus by KVP in the importing country; producer surplus exceeds consumer surplus by JVP in the exporting country. An import tariff at the *ad valorem* rate $P'P''/OP''$ reduces the quantity supplied by foreign producers. If they received the price OP', they would go to Z on the curve S_W, supplying the quantity $P'Z$. With the tariff, however, they receive the lower price OP'' and go to R'' on the curve S_W, supplying the smaller quantity $P''R''$. This supply-reducing effect of the tariff is represented by drawing the new supply curve S_T. Equilibrium is established at R', where the domestic price rises by PP', the world price falls by PP'', the quantity of imports falls by $N'N$, and total tariff revenue is $P''R'R'P'$. The exporting country experiences a welfare loss; the lower world price reduces producer surplus by $P''R''VP$ more than it raises consumer surplus. The welfare effect on the importing country is ambiguous. The higher domestic price reduces consumer surplus by $PVR'P'$ more than it raises producer surplus. But consumers in the importing country receive $P''R''R'P'$ of tariff revenue from their government, so welfare rises whenever $P''R''RP$ exceeds RVR'. The world as a whole experiences a welfare loss, because $P''R''RP$ of the loss to the exporting country represents a gain to the importing country, leaving a net loss of $R''VR'$.

because the importing country is big enough to affect world prices. The free-trade equilibrium occurs at V, where the two curves intersect, and the quantity of imports is ON. In the importing country, consumer surplus exceeds producer surplus by KVP. In the exporting country, producer surplus exceeds consumer surplus by OVP. Suppose that an import tariff is imposed at the *ad valorem* (percentage) rate $P'P''/OP''$. If the domestic price of the product rises to OP', the tariff will be $P''P'$ on each unit, and foreign producers will receive OP'' per unit. Therefore, they will supply ON' units, and we can represent this outcome by shifting the foreign supply curve to S_T. The new equilibrium will be established at R', the world price will fall to OP'', the domestic price will rise to OP', and the quantity of imports will fall to ON'.

In the exporting country, the fall in the world price causes a welfare loss equal to $P''R''VP$; the decrease in producer surplus exceeds the increase in consumer surplus. In the importing country, the rise in the domestic price causes a welfare loss equal to $PVR'P'$; the decrease in consumer surplus exceeds the increase in producer surplus. But something else happens in the importing country; the government distributes $P''R''R'P'$ of tariff revenue to consumers. There will thus be a welfare gain in the importing country if $P''R''RP$ exceeds RVR'. The effect on world welfare is the sum of the effects in the two countries, and it is a loss of $R''VR'$. Note 9-1 shows that this welfare loss can be written as $\Delta W_T = -\frac{1}{2} \times \Delta M \times t(p_W - \Delta p_W)$, where $(p_W - \Delta p_W)$ is OP'', the new world price. This formula resembles the one for the welfare loss in Figure 9-1. The only difference between then is the term Δp_W, reflecting the reduction in the world price.

Note 9-1
Measuring the Welfare Effects of a Tariff with a Variable World Price

The welfare loss for the exporting country in Figure 9-2 is the area $P''R''VP = P''R''RP$ *plus* $R''VR$. But $P''R''VP$ is $P''P \times P''R''$, which we can write as $\Delta p_W \times M'$, where Δp_W is $P''P$, the fall in the world price, and M' is $P''R''$ or ON', the new quantity of imports. And $R''VR$ is $\frac{1}{2} \times P''P \times RV$, which we can write as $\frac{1}{2} \times \Delta p_W \times \Delta M$, where ΔM is RV or $N'N$, the fall in the quantity of imports. Therefore, the loss for the exporting country is

$$\Delta W_X = -[(\Delta p_W \times M') + (\tfrac{1}{2} \times \Delta p_W \times \Delta M)].$$

The welfare gain for the importing country is the area $P''R''RP$ *less* RVR' (being a gain if positive and loss if negative). But $P''R''RP$ is $\Delta p_W \times M'$, and RVR' is $\frac{1}{2} \times RR' \times RV$, which we can write as $\frac{1}{2} \times \Delta p_H \times \Delta M$, where Δp_H is RR' or PP', the rise in the domestic price. Furthermore, Δp_H can be written as $(1 + t)(p_W - \Delta p_W) - p_W$, because $(1 + t)(p_W - \Delta p_W)$ is the new domestic price and p_W is the old one (as world and domestic prices were equal before the tariff was imposed). But $(1 + t)(p_W - \Delta p_W) - p_W = t(p_W - \Delta p_W) - \Delta p_W$, so Δp_H is $\frac{1}{2} \times [t(p_W - \Delta p_W) - \Delta p_W] \times \Delta M$. Therefore, the welfare gain to the importing country is

$$\Delta W_M = \Delta p_W \times M' - \tfrac{1}{2} \times [t(p_W - \Delta p_W) - \Delta p_W] \times \Delta M.$$

The welfare effect on the whole world is the sum of the effects on the two countries. Canceling common terms,

$$\Delta W_T = -\tfrac{1}{2} \times \Delta M \times t(p_W - \Delta p_W),$$

which measures the welfare loss shown as $R''VR'$ in Figure 9-2.

Three conclusions emerge from Figure 9-2. First, the protective effect of a tariff depends on the size of the country imposing the tariff, because it depends on the size of the increase in the domestic price. In Figure 9-1, where the importing country is small, the domestic price rises by the full amount of the tariff; in Figure 9-2, where the country is large, the domestic price rises by less than the amount of the tariff, because the tariff reduces the world price. Second, a tariff imposes a welfare loss on the outside world whenever the importing country is large enough to affect world prices. Third, a tariff can raise welfare in the importing country, because part of the loss to the outside world represents a gain to the importing country. When a tariff reduces the world price of the imported product, some of the tariff revenue is "extracted" from the foreigner—the rectangle $P''R''RP$ in Figure 9-2. That amount can be big enough to offset the welfare loss represented by the triangle RVR'.

The third result anticipates an important point developed later in this chapter. Free trade may not be the best regime for a single country if the country can use tariffs to influence the terms of trade and thus manipulate the gains from trade. By doing so, however, it reduces world welfare.

Tariffs, Prices, and Production in General Equilibrium

When the foreign supply curve is perfectly elastic, as in Figure 9-1, the foreign offer curve is a straight line, and a tariff cannot alter the terms of trade. This point was made in Chapter 2, which examined the effects of a tariff on camera imports when the importing country was small. The relative price of a camera rose in the importing country but did not fall in the exporting country, and the effects on the tariff were not influenced by the way the government spent its tariff revenue.

When the foreign supply curve is less than perfectly elastic, as in Figure 9-2, the foreign offer curve is not a straight line, and a tariff is bound to affect the terms of trace. Furthermore, the effects of the tariff will depend on the way the government spends the revenue.

In Figure 9-3, the British offer curve is OJ, the Portuguese offer curve is OJ^*, and the free-trade equilibrium occurs at W. The relative price of cloth is given in both countries by the slope of the line OP_W. Suppose that Portugal imposes an import tariff at the rate $W'Z'/Z'V'$ and spends the tariff revenue entirely on wine. The relative price of cloth rises in Portugal; it is given by the slope of the line OP_H. The Portuguese economy is displaced to W', where Portuguese consumers demand OV' cloth imports and Portuguese producers supply $V'W'$ wine exports. The relative price of cloth falls in Britain; it is given by the slope of the line OP_F. The British economy is displaced to Z', where British producers supply OV' cloth exports and British consumers demand $Z'V'$ wine imports. The diagram describes an equilibrium in trade between Britain and Portugal, but only because the tariff revenue is used entirely to buy wine. That revenue is worth $W'Z'$ wine. When it is spent on wine, the supply of wine exports is cut by that amount, falling to $Z'V'$, which is equal to the British demand for wine imports. Hence, the wine market clears, and so does the cloth market.

The tariff improves Portugal's terms of trade by reducing the relative price of cloth in the outside world, the price at which Portugal buys cloth from Britain. The tariff

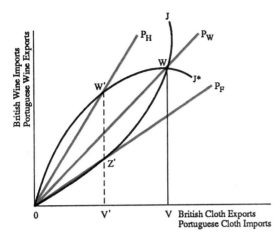

FIGURE 9-3
A Tariff in a Two-Good World with Large Countries
The Portuguese offer curve is OJ^*. The British offer curve is OJ. In the initial free-trade equilibrium at W, the relative price of cloth is given in both countries by the slope of OP_W, and Portugal imports OV cloth in exchange for VW wine. When Portugal imposes an import tariff and spends the tariff revenue on wine, the relative price of cloth is given in Portugal by the steeper slope of OP_H. It is given in Britain by the flatter slope of OP_F. The tariff rate is $W'Z'/Z'V'$. Equilibrium in Portugal is displaced from W to W', where Portugal's supply of wine exports is $V'W'$ and its demand for cloth imports is OV'. Tariff revenue is $Z'W'$ measured in wine. Because it is spent entirely on wine, Portugal's offer of wine exports is reduced to $V'Z'$. Equilibrium in Britain is displaced to Z', where Britain's supply of cloth exports is OV' and its demand for wine imports is $V'Z'$, which equals Portugal's supply of wine exports.

protects the Portuguese cloth industry by raising the relative price of cloth inside Portugal. (The welfare effects of the tariff are examined later in this chapter.)

When Portugal was too small to influence its terms of trade, the spending of the tariff revenue did not affect the final outcome. Here, by contrast, it affects the size of the change in the terms of trade and, therefore, the change in the relative price of cloth in Portugal, the change that gives protection to the Portuguese cloth industry. There are two ways to illustrate this assertion. (1) We can hold the tariff rate constant and show how relative prices are affected by the way the tariff revenue is spent. (2) We can hold one of the price effects constant and show how the tariff rate must change with changes in the way the revenue is spent. The first method goes directly to the point at issue, but the diagram gets very complicated. Therefore, Figure 9-4 uses the second method. It fixes the relative price in Portugal, which fixes the protective effect of the Portuguese tariff, and it asks how the tariff rate must change when the revenue is spent on cloth instead of wine.

The offer curves OJ and OJ^* are drawn as before, along with the price lines OP_H and OP_F, giving the relative prices of cloth in Portugal and Britain when the revenue is spent on wine. The new price line, OP_F' shows what happens to the relative price of cloth in Britain (the Portuguese terms of trade) when the revenue is spent on cloth and the tariff rate is adjusted to prevent the relative price of cloth from changing in Portugal.

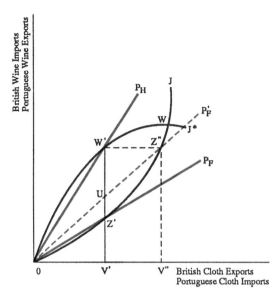

FIGURE 9-4
Tariffs, Spending Patterns, and Relative Prices
The offer curves and prices lines OP_F and OP_H and drawn as before, showing the effects of a Portuguese tariff when the tariff revenue is spent on wine. The tariff rate is $W'Z'/Z'V'$, equilibrium in Portugal occurs at W', and equilibrium in Britain occurs at Z'. When the tariff revenue is spent on cloth instead, the price of cloth rises in both countries. Alternatively, Portugal can obtain the same change in the domestic price of cloth by imposing a lower tariff. If it is set at the rate $W'U/UV'$, the relative price of cloth in Portugal is still given by the slope of OP_H, keeping Portugal's supply of wine exports at $V'W'$ and its demand for cloth imports at OV'. Tariff revenue is UW' measured in wine. As the revenue is spent on cloth, however, Portugal's demand for cloth imports rises by $W'Z''$, becoming OV''. Equilibrium in Britain is displaced to Z'', where Britain's supply of cloth exports is OV'' and its demand for wine imports is $V''Z''$.

The rate required for this purpose is $W'U/UV'$, which is lower than the rate $W'Z'/Z'V'$. As the relative price of cloth in Portugal is still given by the slope of OP_H, the Portuguese economy goes to W', where consumers demand OV' cloth imports and producers supply $V'W'$ wine exports. As the relative price of cloth in Britain is equal to the slope of OP'_F, the British economy goes to Z'', where producers supply OV'' cloth exports and consumers demand $Z''V''$ wine imports. The tariff revenue, however, is worth $W'U$ wine, which can buy $W'Z''$ cloth. (The Portuguese government does not have to pay its own tariff on cloth; it can import cloth at the world price, given by the slope of OP'_F.) When the revenue is spent entirely on cloth, then, the demand for cloth imports rises to OV'', which is equal to the British supply of cloth exports. The cloth market clears, and do does the wine market.

The outcome in Figure 9-4 is different in two ways from the outcome in Figure 9-3. The tariff rate is lower, and the change in the terms of trade is smaller. There is a simple explanation. When the Portuguese government spends its revenue on cloth, it raises the global demand for cloth and thus raises the price of cloth in both Britain and Portugal. (It raises *both* countries' prices because they can differ only by the tariff rate.) Therefore, it reduces the improvement in Portugal's terms of trade but gives more protection to Portuguese cloth producers. If the government does not want to give them more protection, it can reduce the tariff rate.

The same point can be made in another way. When the Portuguese government spends its revenue on wine, it drives up the price of wine, increasing the improvement in Portugal's terms of trade but decreasing the amount of protection given to Portuguese cloth producers. There is, in fact, one case in which the producers are injured, not aided, by the tariff: when the revenue is spent entirely on wine and the British demand for wine imports is inelastic.

This perverse case is illustrated by Figure 9-5, where Britain's offer curve bends backward because the British demand for wine imports is inelastic.[1] When Portugal imposes a ratiff at the rate $W'Z'/Z'V'$ and spends the revenue on wine, the Portuguese economy moves to W', and the relative price of cloth in Portugal, given

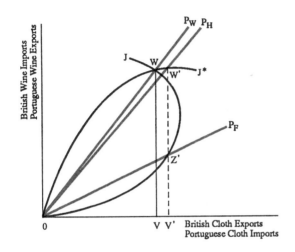

FIGURE 9-5
A Perverse Case
In the neighborhood of the free-trade equilibrium at W, the British offer curve OJ bends backward. The British demand for wine imports is inelastic. When Portugal imposes a tariff on its cloth imports and spends the revenue on wine, the relative price of cloth can move perversely in Portugal, reducing cloth output rather than raising it. When the tariff rate is $W'Z'/Z'V'$ and the revenue $W'Z'$ is spent on wine, Portugal's export offer is $Z'V'$. Equilibrium in Britain is established at Z', and the British price line is OP_F. As usual, the relative price of cloth falls in Britain. Equilibrium in Portugal is established at W', and the Portuguese price line is OP_H. As OP_H is flatter than OP_W, the relative price of cloth falls in Portugal, too. Therefore, the tariff works perversely to reduce Portuguese cloth output.

---

[1] When the demand for a product is inelastic, an increase in its price reduces the quantity demanded but raises the amount spent on the product. In Figure 9-5, increases in the relative price of wine are shown by drawing flatter price lines from the origin. (An increase in the relative price of wine is a decrease in the relative price of cloth.) On the backward-bending segment of OJ, price increases reduce the quantity of wine imported by Britain but raise the cloth equivalent of the payment for it. When the relative price of wine is given by the slope of OP_W, the quantity imported is WV, and the payment is worth OV cloth. When the relative price of wine is given by the slope of OP_F, the quantity imported falls to $Z'V'$, but the payment is worth OV' cloth.

by the slope of OP_H, is lower than it was with free trade, so cloth output falls in Portugal. The reason is the large improvement in the terms of trade. It is given by the slope of OP_F, which is much flatter than OP_W.

Nominal and Effective Tariffs

By using offer curves to trace the effects of tariffs, we are able to show how a tariff on a single product can alter output levels in other industries and countries. In Figures 9-3 and 9-4, for example, a Portuguese tariff on imported cloth raised the relative price of cloth in Portugal. As a result, it raised Portuguese cloth production and reduced Portuguese wine production. But it also reduced the price of cloth in Britain, reducing British cloth production and raising British wine production.

There is another way in which a tariff on one product can affect output levels in other industries. By raising the domestic price of steel, a tariff on imported steel will tend to reduce output in the automobile industry and every other steel-using industry. If the tariff on steel is high enough, it can more than offset the protective effects of tariffs on automobiles and other steel-using products. Economists allow for these indirect effects by computing the *effective tariff rate* for each economic activity. This rate measures more precisely the protection given to each activity and thus the way in which a country's tariff schedule affects the allocation of domestic resources.

To illustrate the calculation of an effective rate, let us look at the iron industry in a small economy. Suppose that it uses 1 ton of domestic coal and 2 tons of imported ore to manufacture a ton of iron. Because the economy is small, it faces fixed prices in world markets:

Iron	$100 per ton
Coal	35 per ton
Ore	20 per ton

If the country has no tariffs, the costs of the materials needed to make iron will total $75 per ton. Therefore, the iron industry will suffer losses if wage and other factor costs total more than $25 per ton.

What happens when the country imposes a 50 percent tariff on imported iron? The domestic price of iron will rise from $100 to $150 per ton, and the iron industry will not suffer losses unless wage and other factor costs total more than $75 per ton. Putting the same point differently, a 50 percent tariff on imported iron is equivalent to a 200 percent tariff on the *value added* by the iron industry. It raises the amount available for meeting wage and other factor costs from $25 to $75 per ton, an increase of $50, or 200 percent. The tariff rate on value added is the *effective* rate for the iron industry. This example shows that it can be quite different from the nominal (ordinary) tariff rate on imported iron.

What happens, however, when the country imposes a 50 percent tariff on imported ore together with the tariff on imported iron? The costs of the materials required to make iron will rise to $95 per ton, and the iron industry will suffer losses if wage and other factor costs total more than $55 per ton. The addition of the tariff on imported ore reduces the effective rate for the iron industry from 200 to 120 percent. The amount available for meeting wage and other factor costs rises from $25 to $55 per ton, an increase of $30 rather than $50.

Two points emerge from these calculations. First, we should concentrate on effective rates when asking how tariffs affect profits and production in each domestic industry. Second, the effective rate for a particular industry depends on the nature of its costs and on a variety of nominal rates, those on the industry's outputs and those on its inputs.

The formula employed to calculate effective rates is derived in Note 9-2. It shows what we have just discovered. The effective rate will rise with the nominal rate on an industry's output. It will fall with an increase in the nominal rates on the industry's inputs.[2]

How large are the differences between effective and nominal tariffs? Data for the United States, Europe, and Japan are reproduced in Table 9-1. Effective rates are higher than nominal rates in many cases, because tariffs on outputs are higher than tariffs on inputs. They are more than three times as high for apparel and footwear in Japan and for nonferrous metals in Europe; they are about twice as high for food, beverages, and tobacco in the United States and Japan, for textiles and apparel in the United States, and for steel in Europe. They are lower in some instances, however, because tariffs on inputs are higher than tariffs on outputs, and nine effective rates are actually negative. The structure of protection damages these industries; they would be better off with free trade. Instances of this sort crop up quite frequently in the tariff schedules of developing countries, where tariffs on manufactured inputs are so high that the industries dependent on those inputs are handicapped severely.

The calculation of effective rates was popular some years ago but has lost popularity for two reasons. First, the formula used to calculate effective rates is based on many restrictive assumptions. It assumes that the country under study is too small to alter world prices. It assumes that the industry under study is unable to substitute one input for another—that the coefficients in the formula are fixed. It neglects the influence of quotas, subsidies, and other trade controls that may be more important than tariffs in determining effective rates. Second, there have been significant advances in the design, estimation, and solution of large econometric models that shed light directly on protective effects. Those models show what happens to each and every industry when a single tariff rate is raised or reduced.

The concept of effective protection is still needed, however, to warn against errors in analysis and policy. It warns that the influence of any tariff depends on many

---

[2]Here is how to apply the formula in Note 9-2 to the case of the iron industry: The value of t is 50 percent (the nominal rate on iron). The value of t_i is zero for coal (there is no tariff), and the value of c_i is 0.35. The value of t_i for ore is 50 percent, and the value of c_i is 0.40. Therefore, the effective rate for iron is

$$T = \frac{50 - [(0 \times 0.35) + (50 \times 0.40)]}{1 - (0.35 + 0.40)} = \frac{50 - 20}{0.25} = 120,$$

which is the number given in the text.

Note 9-2
Computing the Effective Tariff Rate

An imported good, x, is produced by labor, L, whose wage is w, and capital, K, whose rate of return is r, using intermediate goods in amounts y_i. The world price of the good is p, and the world prices of the intermediate goods are p_i. Under competitive conditions,

$$px = wL + rK + \Sigma p_i y_i.$$

Value added in the production of x is defined by

$$V = wL + rK = px - \Sigma p_i y_i.$$

Let a_i be the fixed amount of y_i required per unit of output, so that $y_i = a_i x_i$ and

$$V = (p - \Sigma p_i a_i)x.$$

Define value added per unit of output by

$$v = \frac{V}{x} = p - \Sigma p_i a_i.$$

Impose a tariff, t, on imports of x and tariffs, t_i, on imports of the intermediate goods. Value added per unit of output becomes

$$v' = (1 + t)p - \Sigma(1 + t_i)p_i a_i = v + (tp - \Sigma t_i p_i a_i),$$

so $v' - v = tp - \Sigma t_i p_i a_i$. Dividing this difference by v, we obtain the effective tariff rate, T, for the x industry:

$$T = \frac{v' - v}{v} = \frac{tp - \Sigma t_i p_i a_i}{p - \Sigma p_i a_i} = \frac{t - \Sigma t_i c_i}{1 - \Sigma c_i},$$

where $c_i = (p_i a_i / p)$, the share of the ith intermediate good in the price of x. Subtracting t from both sides of this equation,

$$T - t = \frac{\Sigma(t - t_i)c_i}{1 - \Sigma c_i}.$$

When all t_i equal t (a uniform tariff), the effective rate equals the nominal rate. When many t_i are higher than t, the effective rate is lower than the nominal rate. When many t_i are lower than t, the effective rate is higher.

Table 9-1. Nominal and Effective Tariff Rates After Reductions Negotiated in the Tokyo Round

Product Group	United States		European Community		Japan	
	Nominal	Effective	Nominal	Effective	Nominal	Effective
Food, beverages, and tobacco	4.7	10.2	10.2	17.8	25.4	50.3
Textiles	9.2	18.0	7.2	8.8	3.3	-2.4
Apparel	22.7	43.3	13.4	19.3	13.8	42.2
Leather products	4.2	5.0	2.0	-2.2	3.0	-14.8
Footwear	8.8	15.4	11.6	20.7	15.7	50.0
Wood products	1.7	1.7	2.5	1.7	0.3	-30.6
Furniture and fixtures	4.1	5.5	5.6	11.3	5.1	10.3
Paper and paper products	0.2	-0.9	5.4	8.3	2.1	1.8
Printing and publishing	0.7	0.9	2.1	-1.0	0.1	-1.5
Chemicals	2.4	3.7	8.0	11.7	4.8	6.4
Petroleum and petroleum products	1.4	4.7	1.2	3.4	2.2	4.1
Rubber products	2.5	2.0	3.5	2.3	1.1	-5.0
Nonmetallic mineral products	5.3	9.2	3.7	6.5	0.5	-0.5
Glass and glass products	6.2	9.8	7.7	12.2	5.1	8.1
Iron and steel	3.6	6.2	4.7	11.6	2.8	4.3
Nonferrous metals	0.7	0.5	2.1	8.3	1.1	1.7
Metal products	4.8	7.9	5.5	7.1	5.2	9.2
Nonelectrical machinery	3.3	4.1	4.4	4.7	4.4	6.7
Electrical machinery	4.4	6.3	7.9	10.8	4.3	6.7
Transport equipment	2.5	1.9	8.0	12.3	1.5	0.0

Source: Adapted from Alan V. Deardorff and Robert M. Stern, "The Effects of the Tokyo Round on the Structure of Protection," in R. E. Baldwin and A. O. Krueger, eds., *The Structure and Evolution of Recent U.S. Trade Policy* (Chicago: University of Chicago Press, 1984), Tables 10-1 through 10-3.

other tariffs. It warns that an increase in the nominal tariff on one product can reduce the effective rate on another. It may thus be impossible to give more protection to one industry without taking protection away from another industry.

ANALYZING ARGUMENTS FOR TARIFFS

Many familiar arguments for tariffs cannot stand up to close scrutiny. Others are logically sound but are aimed at objectives that can often be achieved by other, less costly forms of intervention. Tariffs and other trade barriers tend to be second-best policy instruments because they violate a simple rule:

> **To minimize the welfare loss or maximize the welfare gain associated with a particular policy objective, governments should intervene at the point in the economy closest to the policy objective at issue.**

If the government seeks to change the income distribution, it should alter income taxes. If it seeks to change the composition of production, it should tax or subsidize production. If it seeks to change the composition of consumption, it should tax or subsidize consumption. It should not tax or subsidize imports or exports to influence the income distribution, production, or consumption, even when trade taxes or subsidies can achieve these purposes.

We begin our survey of arguments for tariffs with two of the oldest arguments, stemming from the threat of competition from cheap foreign labor and the risk of damage to defense-related industries. Thereafter, we turn to arguments concerned with the distribution of the gains from trade, the distribution of domestic income, and the rectification of distortions in domestic markets.

The Hardiest Fallacy

The oldest and hardiest argument for tariffs says that they are needed to protect domestic workers against cheap foreign labor. Its advocates cite lots of numbers about low foreign wages, but they draw the wrong inference from those numbers. We answered them, in fact, when we showed how wage rates are determined in the simple Ricardian model of Chapter 3.

When wages in Britain and Portugal were equal before trade was opened, the prices of wine and cloth were higher in Britain, because British labor was less efficient. Wages had to fall in Britain and rise in Portugal before Britain could specialize in cloth and Portugal could specialize in wine. The wage changes were achieved by the process of adjustment to the opening of trade, which translates comparative advantage into market prices. Protectionists who make alarming comparisons between high wages in the United States and low wages elsewhere do not allow for the crucial relationship between wages and efficiency. Differences in wage rates, they assert, make for unfair competition. Those differences, however, are produced by competition, and trade cannot occur without them when levels of efficiency differ greatly.

Some version of the argument are more subtle. Low wages, it is said, may testify to low levels of efficiency in a country as a whole, but efficiency may be very high in its export industries. The methods used to make textiles in Hong Kong and Singapore are similar to those used in the United States, yet wages are much lower in those countries, even in their textile industries. Surely, textile workers in the United States are exposed to unfair competition. The answer should be obvious enough. Textile workers in the United States suffer from intense foreign competition, but it is not unfair competition. It is competition that has to be tolerated if countries are to realize the gains from trade.

Return to the example used in Chapter 3. Workers in Portugal's cloth industry might be expected to complain of unfair competition from Britain. The British cloth industry was less efficient than the Portuguese industry, but the efficiency gap was smaller than the wage-rate gap. If this were not so, however, Britain could not export cloth. To realize the gains from trade between the two countries, cloth output must contract in Portugal in the face of British competition, and wine output must contract in Britain in the face of Portuguese competition. The gains from trade based on these adjustments, moreover, are large enough to compensate those who are hurt in the process.

The logic of this argument is impeccable. Yet it gives little comfort to American textile workers who have lost their jobs on account of competition from Hong Kong, Singapore, and other countries, and more jobs would be lost if tariffs and other trade barriers were removed completely. Some who lose their jobs have trouble finding new ones and suffer in other important ways. They lose seniority and thus job security. Some have to move from one city to another to find new jobs and may take large losses when they sell their homes. Furthermore, those who keep their jobs may take cuts in real wages, and these cuts may not be confined to the workers in the import-competing industries. In the modified Ricardian model, the opening of trade reduces the real wage measured in terms of the export good, and the reduction occurs throughout the economy. In the Heckscher–Ohlin model, it reduces the real wage, whether measured in terms of the export good or the import-competing good, whenever the export good is more capital intensive than the import-competing good. Reductions in tariffs have these same effects.

Economists who make the strong case for free trade do not always pay enough attention to these costs, and they weaken their case by neglecting them. It is not enough to demonstrate that the gains from trade are larger than the adjustment costs and the permanent income losses suffered by some groups. Ways must be found to make compensation. This problem is taken up in Chapter 10, which looks at techniques that have been used to help those who are hurt by tariff cuts and other trade-related shocks.

Tariffs and the National Defence

Another hardy argument for protection appeals to the needs of national defense, the importance of maintaining domestic industries able to produce planes, tanks, and guns in the event of war. This argument goes back to Adam Smith:[3]

---

[3]Adam Smith, *The Wealth of Nations*, 1776, bk. iv, ch. ii. The second exception admitted by Smith is the case for a compensatory revenue tariff, mentioned earlier in this chapter.

There seem, however, to be two cases in which it will generally be advantageous to lay some burden upon foreign [industry] for the encouragement of domestic industry.

The first is, when some particular sort of industry is necessary for the defence of the country. The defence of Great Britain, for example, depends very much upon the number of its sailors and shipping. The act of navigation, therefore, very properly endeavours to give the sailors and shipping of Great Britain the monopoly of the trade of their own country...

The act of navigation is not favourable to foreign commerce, or to the growth of that opulence which can arise from it.... As defence, however, is of much more importance than opulence, the act of navigation is, perhaps, the wisest of all the commercial regulations of England.

The same argument is made today to justify the subsidies received by merchant ships that fly the U.S. flag, although the connection between national security and the health of the maritime industry was tenuous even when Smith accepted it and is far more tenuous today. The argument, moreover, is easily abused. Here is language used by Congress some years ago, in legislation instructing the president to impose trade barriers for reasons of national defense:

...the President shall, in the light of the requirements of national security and without excluding other relevant factors, give consideration to domestic production needed for projected national defense requirements, the capacity of domestic industries to meet such requirements, existing and anticipated availabilities of the human resources, products, raw materials, and other supplies and services essential to the national defense, the requirements of growth of such industries... the importation of goods in terms of their requirements, availabilities, character, and use as those affect such industries and the capacity of the United States to meet security requirements.

Then Congress went even further, saying that the president

... shall further recognize the close relation of the economic welfare of the Nation to our national security, and shall take into consideration the impact of foreign competition on the welfare of individual domestic industries; any substantial unemployment, decrease in revenues of government, loss of skills, or investment, or other serious effects resulting from the displacement of any domestic products by excessive imports shall be considered.

Fortunately, the president did not apply these criteria literally. Otherwise, he might have been obliged to restrict all sorts of imports—from cameras and cars to textiles and toys—because of their effects on employment, revenues, and so on. The legislation was invoked, however, to limit oil imports. Oil prices were low at the time, and import quotas were seen as a way to keep domestic oil prices above world prices and thus encourage exploration in the United States. Exploration would add to domestic reserves and thus reduce future dependence on imports. The quotas, however, had the opposite effect. They tended to accelerate the exploitation of existing domestic reserves by more than they fostered the discovery of new reserves.

What would Adam Smith say about the language adopted by Congress? He was quick to denounce self-serving arguments and would surely ask whether Congress was wrapping the flag around all sorts of industries that wanted protection against import competition but contributed little to the national defense. Furthermore, he would probably concede that imports restrictions are less useful today than they were in his own time, because of changes in the nature of warfare and of the national-security problem. The case for protecting "essential" industries depends on their ability to convert to military production when war breaks out. Smith wanted to be sure that Great Britain would have the shipyards to build men-of-war and the trained seamen to sail them. Congress wanted to make sure that the United States would have the factories to make planes and tanks. But there are two objections.

The first objection is strategic. Although the threat of global war has receded with the collapse of the Soviet Union, the nature of the military problem has not changed. The United States might have to fight two types of war—a limited war on foreign soil, like those in Korea, Vietnam, and the Persian Gulf, or a major war for survival. The first sort of war, limited in area and the sorts of weapons used, is not likely to require massive mobilization of the domestic economy. The second sort of war would not provide the time required for mobilization It would be ended quickly and terribly by nuclear weapons built before it began.

The second objection is tactical. Concede for the sake of analysis that the United States might have the need and time for industrial mobilization. Experience during the Second World War suggests that the conversion of civilian firms and facilities may not be the best method. The Unites States built a huge cargo fleet after the war began and was able eventually to launch ships faster than German submarines could sink them. The shipyards that built them were new ones, however, and used mass-production methods that older shipyards could not adopt. Studies by the Defense Department have also shown that workers trained specifically to produce advanced weapons do better than workers with broadly similar skills who try to adapt to new tasks. Makers of watches used to argue that they should be protected against import competition because they can make fuses needed by the military. The Defense Department found, however, that newly trained workers did the job more efficiently and that they could be trained quite quickly.

Go one more step. Concede the need to maintain "essential" industries but ask how this should be done. Tariffs to protect them from import competition are not the best way to maintain them. A tariff has two main effects. It encourages domestic production and discourages domestic consumption. The consumption effect reduces economic welfare, and the loss is borne by the peacetime users of the products made by the protected industry. Therefore, the tariff is inequitable. The costs of national defense should be borne by the nation as a whole, not by one group of consumers. Furthermore, the tariff is inefficient. Subsidies to domestic producers make more sense, on the basic principle stated earlier. They do not distort consumers' choices.

The needs of national defense cannot be neglected, and events abroad could impair the national security of the United States. If the war in the Persian Gulf had shut down oil production in Saudi Arabia, as well as Kuwait and Iraq, the United States would have been hurt directly, because it depends on imported oil, and it would have been hurt indirectly, because the world economy would have contracted sharply.

Trade theory warns us, however, that self-sufficiency is the wrong response. It makes more sense to import oil and thus conserve domestic reserves than to search for new reserves or develop substitutes regardless of cost. The short-run effects of a major crisis in the Middle East can be met by using reserves set aside for that purpose. This is the approach actually adopted by the United States, which holds a Strategic Petroleum Reserve, financed by the federal government. In the event of a crisis, it can be used to buy time for reducing domestic consumption and switching to imports from other sources.

Many other noneconomic reasons are given for protecting domestic industries. National prestige may be just as potent as national security in rallying political support for protection. How else can we explain why small, poor countries insist on having their own international airlines? But let us turn to arguments that make more economic sense.

TARIFFS AND THE DISTRIBUTION OF THE GAINS FROM TRADE

We have already seen that a tariff can raise economic welfare in the importing country when the revenue extracted from the exporting country is large enough to offset the welfare losses resulting from the consumption and production effects of the tariff. This proposition, however, can be put more strongly:

> **A country large enough to affect its terms of trade can impose an optimum tariff that will raise its economic welfare above the free-trade level but will reduce world welfare.**

The size of the optimum tariff depends on domestic demand conditions and on the shape of the foreign offer curve.

A Special Case

The optimum-tariff argument is easy to illustrate when a country is completely specialized, because its own output mix is not affected by the tariff. Let us return to the simple Ricardian model, where Britain specialized completely in cloth and imported wine from Portugal. The situation seen from the British standpoint is shown in Figure 9-6. Britain's transformation curve is BB', and Britain produces at B. Portugal's offer curve is BJ^*, which is drawn with its origin at B. The free-trade equilibrium occurs at W, where the price line BP_W cuts the Portuguese offer curve and is also tangent to a British indifference curve. Britain produces OB cloth, consumes OV, and exports VB, and it imports VW wine from Portugal.

As the indifference curve U_1 is tangent to the price line BP_W rather than the Portuguese offer curve, it is not the highest curve accessible to Britain. The highest curve is U_2, which is tangent to the Portuguese offer curve at W'. Britain can reach that indifference curve by cutting its wine imports from VW to $V'W'$. It can use an import quota but can also use a tariff. To measure this optimum tariff, we need to

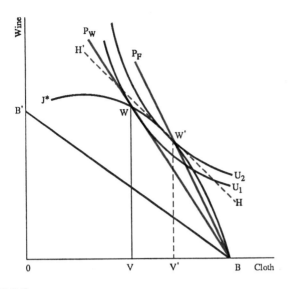

FIGURE 9-6
The Optimum Tariff with Complete Specialization
The British transformation curve is BB'. The Portuguese offer curve is BJ^*. The free-trade equilibrium occurs at W, where the price line BP_W cuts the Portuguese offer curve and is also tangent to the British indifference curve U_1. The relative price of cloth is given in both countries by the slope of BP_W. Britain specializes completely in cloth, producing OB, and exports VB cloth in exchange for VW wine. As U_1 is tangent to the price line but not to the Portuguese offer curve, a higher indifference curve, U_2, is tangent to the offer curve. Britain can reach U_2 by imposing a tariff. The new price of cloth will then be given in Portugal by the slope of BP_F, which is steeper than BP_W. Britain will improve its terms of trade. The new price of cloth in Britain will be given by the slope of U_2 at the new equilibrium point, W'. It is the slope of HH', which is flatter than BP_F. The relative price of cloth will be lower in Britain, and the difference between the countries' prices measures the British tariff.

know what prices will take the two countries to W'. To take the Portuguese economy to W', the relative price of cloth in Portugal must equal the slope of the line BP_F. To take the British economy to W', the relative price of cloth in Britain must equal the slope of the indifference curve U_2 and, therefore, the slope of the line HH'. The gap between those prices measures the optimum tariff for Britain. It is derived algebraically in Note 9-3.

The General Case

When Britain does not specialize completely in cloth, a tariff will alter its output mix. This does not undermine the argument but complicates the presentation. The left side of Figure 9-7 shows the free-trade situation seen from the British standpoint. The British transformation curve is BB', and Britain produces at Q, where its cloth output is OX_1 and its wine output is OX_2. The Portuguese offer curve is QJ^*, which is drawn with its origin at Q. The free-trade equilibrium occurs at W, and the relative price of cloth is equal to the slope of the line FF', which is tangent to the British transformation curve at Q and to a British indifference curve at W. As

---

Note 9-3
Measuring the Optimum Tariff

When Britain imposes a tariff on Portuguese wine,

$$p^* = (1 + t)p,$$

where p is the relative price of cloth in Britain, p^* its relative price in Portugal, and t is the tariff rate. Therefore,

$$t = \frac{p^* - p}{p} \quad \text{or} \quad t = \frac{p^*}{p} - 1.$$

In Figure 9-6, p^* is given by the slope of BP_F and p by the slope of HH'.

The optimum tariff rate is related to the elasticity of Portuguese demand for British cloth. Portugal's offer curve can be viewed as Britain's total-revenue curve; it shows how much wine Britain can earn by exporting cloth to Portugal. In Figure 9-6, Britain's total revenue is $W'V'$ wine when it exports $V'B$ cloth. Therefore, Britain's average revenue is $W'V'/V'B$, which equals the slope of BW' and thus equals p^*. Britain's marginal revenue is the slope of Portugal's offer curve, which equals the slope of HH' and thus equals p. Therefore, the ratio of average to marginal revenue is p^*/p, which equals $1 + t$. That same ratio, however, is related to e_d, the elasticity of demand:

$$\frac{\text{Average revenue}}{\text{Marginal revenue}} = \frac{e_d}{e_d - 1}.$$

Hence, $(1 + t) = [e_d/(e_d - 1)]$, and $t = 1/(e_d - 1)$. Note that $t > 0$ only when $e_d > 1$. Britain's optimum-tariff point must lie on the elastic portion of Portugal's demand curve. A country using market power to maximize economic welfare is much like an ordinary monopolist using market power to maximize profits. Both operate on the elastic portions of the demand curves for their products.

---

before, Britain can move to an indifference curve higher than U_1. When it does so in this instance, however, it will reduce the relative price of cloth in Britain, which will move the output point along the transformation curve. The output point also serves as the origin for the Portuguese offer curve, which means that the offer curve must move too. The whole diagram begins to disintegrate as soon as we disturb it.

The new equilibrium is not hard to draw, however, once it has been located. It is shown on the right side of Figure 9-7, where the relative price of cloth in Britain is given by the slopes of the two lines HH'. The output point is Q', where the solid line HH' is tangent to the British transformation curve; the consumption point is W', where the broken line HH' is tangent to a British indifference curve. The Portuguese

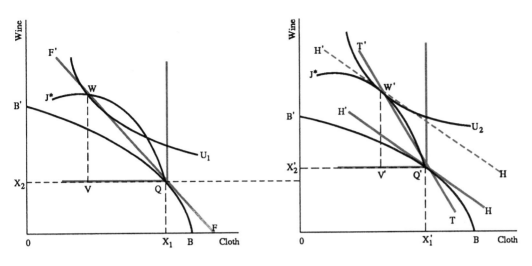

FIGURE 9-7
The Optimum Tariff with Incomplete Specialization
The free-trade equilibrium is shown on the left. The British transformation curve is
BB', and the Portuguese offer curve is QJ^*. Britain produces at Q, where the slope of
the price line FF' equals the slope of its transformation curve. Its cloth output is OX_1,
and its wine output is OX_2. Britain consumes at W, where the slope of FF' equals the
slope of the indifference curve U_1. It exports QV cloth and imports VW wine, which
match the quantities that Portugal imports and exports when the price line cuts the
Portuguese offer curve at W. The optimum-tariff equilibrium is shown on the right.
The relative price of cloth is given in Britain by the slopes of the price lines HH'. Britain
produces at Q', where the slope of the (solid) line HH' equals the slope of its
transformation curve. As HH' is flatter than FF', the relative price of cloth has fallen
in Britain, reducing cloth output to OX_1' and raising wine output to OX_2'. Britain
consumes at W', where the slope of the (broken) line HH' equals the slope of the
indifference curve U_2. It exports $Q'V'$ cloth and imports $V'W'$ wine, which match the
quantities that Portugal imports and exports when it faces the price line TT'. As TT'
is steeper than FF', Britain has improved its terms of trade. As U_2 is tangent to the
Portuguese offer curve, Britain has chosen the optimum tariff.

offer curve is $Q'J^*$, which is drawn with its origin at Q', the British output point, and
is tangent to the British indifference curve at W'. To take the Portuguese economy
to W', the relative price of cloth in Portugal must equal the slope of the line TT',
and the gap between prices in Britain and Portugal measures the tariff rate. As the
indifference curve U_2 is tangent to the Portuguese offer curve, it is the highest
indifference curve accessible to Britain. Therefore, the tariff rate implicit in this
outcome is the optimum tariff for Britain.

As the optimum tariff improves Britain's terms of trade in Figures 9-6 and 9-7, the
optimum-tariff argument is sometimes called the terms-of-trade argument. Do not
be misled by this language. An improvement in Britain's terms of trade is necessary
but not sufficient to raise economic welfare in Britain. Recall the result obtained from
Figure 9-2. A tariff can reduce economic welfare in the country imposing it even
when some of the revenue is extracted from the foreigner. Now, look again at Figure
9-6. If the terms-of-trade line were steeper than BP_F, it would intersect the
Portuguese offer curve below W'. It might even intersect the offer curve below the

point at which the offer curve is cut by the indifference curve U_1. In that case, of course, the tariff would take Britain to an indifference curve lower than U_1, making Britain worse off than with free trade. The tariff rate must be chosen carefully. Bigger is not necessarily better.

Retaliation

Thus far, we have ignored the possibility of retaliation. When Britain imposes its optimum tariff, economic welfare falls in Portugal. The reason is familiar. Any departure from free trade reduces world welfare. Hence Portugal must lose when Britain gains. Portugal can minimize its loss, however, by imposing its own optimum tariff, taking account of the British tariff. The two countries may get into a tariff cycle, raising and lowering their rates sequentially, without reaching an equilibrium. Alternatively, they may move to a tariff-ridden equilibrium that can have any one of three properties: (1) Britain is better off, but Portugal is worse off. (2) Portugal is better off, but Britain is worse off. (3) Both countries are worse off.

The last of these outcomes, in which both countries lose, resembles one in Chapter 7, when America and Japan subsidized their robot exports to Brazil, and it can be interpreted in the same manner.[4] Both governments know that their citizens will suffer welfare losses if they reach this sort of tariff-ridden equilibrium. When they do not trust each other, however, both will be tempted to use tariffs. To preserve free trade or a less restrictive tariff-ridden regime, the governments must make a binding agreement to refrain from starting the process. This may be one reason why governments participate in the GATT, which prevents them from raising their tariffs unilaterally.

The optimum-tariff argument is analytically sound. Yet, a tariff is a second-best policy instrument for redistributing the gains from trade because it reduces world welfare. Suppose that Britain gives notice to Portugal that it is about to adopt its optimum tariff. Portugal can threaten to retaliate but has another option. It can offer Britain an annual "bribe" just large enough to put British consumers on the indifference curve they would reach with the optimum tariff. The bribe would redistribute world welfare without reducing it, and Portugal would suffer a welfare loss smaller than the loss it would endure if Britain imposed its optimum tariff.

There is, of course, a practical objection. It would be hard for the Portuguese government to carry out its promise. Its citizens would probably object, urging retaliation instead. National self-esteem would probably dominate national self-interest. The first-best policy would not be feasible, and Britain could increase its welfare only by imposing its optimum tariff.

In the cases considered hereafter, however, it is easy to define and use a first-best policy. The cases deal with domestic policy objectives and, thus, the domain of a single government. The treatment of each case will emphasize the welfare costs of using a tariff and will show how another policy instrument can be used instead. In

---

[4]The two examples are very similar indeed, because the example in Chapter 7 can be modified to generate the three possibilities listed above. Both countries lose in that particular example because they produce identical robots under identical cost conditions. Under less symmetrical conditions, one country can gain and the other can when both use export subsidies.

each case, moreover, the country imposing the tariff will be too small to influence its terms of trade. This assumption will exclude optimum-tariff gains and thus focus attention on the welfare costs involved. (It will also exclude the perverse case described by Figure 9-5; a tariff will not lower the domestic price of the import-competing product.)

TARIFFS AND THE DISTRIBUTION OF DOMESTIC INCOME

A tariff can alter the income distribution within a single country, because it can affect the real earnings of labor, capital, and land. Its impact, however, depends on the structure of the national economy.

Effects in the Modified Ricardian Model

In Chapter 5 on the modified Ricardian model, the effects of a change in relative prices on the real earnings of the factors of production were summarized by the Haberler theorem, which also describes the effects of a tariff. When Britain imposes a tariff on its wine imports, the relative price of wine rises in Britain. The owners of land gain, because land is used in making wine, and the owners of capital lose, because capital is used in making cloth. The effects on British workers depend, of course, on the good in which the real wage is measured. The real wage rises in terms of cloth and falls in terms of wine.

These outcomes are reviewed in Figure 9-8, along with some we have not yet seen. The curve E_C is the demand curve for labor used in making cloth; it measures the marginal product of labor in Britain's cloth industry. The curve E_W is the demand curve for labor used in making wine; it measures the marginal product of labor in Britain's wine industry divided by the relative price of cloth. Let the free-trade equilibrium occur at F, where the real wage is OV cloth in both industries, OL_1 workers are employed in the wine industry, and $\bar{L}L_1$ workers are employed in the cloth industry.

When Britain imposes an import tariff on wine, the relative price of wine rises in Britain, reducing the relative price of cloth. The demand curve E_C is not affected, but the demand curve E_W shifts upward to E'_W. The size of the shift is equal to the *ad valorem* tariff.[5]

Consider first a case we have not yet examined. Suppose that there is *no* labor mobility. Employment in the wine industry is fixed at OL_1, fixing the marginal products of labor and land used in making wine. Employment in the cloth industry is fixed at $\bar{L}L_1$, fixing the marginal products of labor and capital used in making cloth. A tariff cannot alter *own* real earnings, those measured in terms of the goods

---

[5]Using notation developed in Appendix A, the free-trade wage, OV, can be written as f_L^w/p, where f_L^w is the marginal product of labor in the wine industry and p is the relative price of cloth in Britain. With free trade, p is equal to p^*, the relative price of cloth in Portugal. When Britain imposes a tariff, however, $p^* = (1 + t)p$, as in Note 9-3, so $p = p^*/(1 + t)$, and the new wage, OV', is $f_L^w(1 + t)/p^*$. Therefore, $(OV' - OV)/OV = V'V/OV = t$.

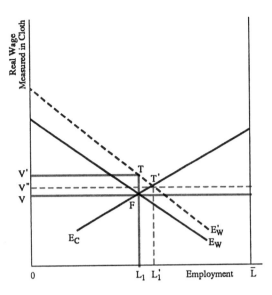

FIGURE 9-8
A Tariff and the Income Distribution When Some Factors Are Not Mobile
Under free trade, equilibrium in Britain occurs at *F*, where the real wage measured in cloth is *OV* in both industries. When Britain imposes a tariff on wine imports, the demand curve for labor by the wine industry shifts upward by the full amount of the tariff. It shifts from E_W to E'_W when the tariff rate is *VV'/OV*. If labor is completely immobile, employment remains at OL_1 in the wine industry, and equilibrium is displaced to *T*. The real wage measured in wine does not change in the wine industry, but the real wage measured in cloth rises by the full amount of the tariff, going from *OV* to *OV'*. The real wage measured in cloth does not change in the cloth industry, but the real wage measured in wine falls by the full amount of the tariff. If labor is perfectly mobile, equilibrium is displaced to *T'*, and employment in the wine industry rises to OL'_1. The real wage measured in cloth rises in both industries but by less than the amount of the tariff; it goes from *OV* to *OV''* but not all the way to *OV'*. Therefore, the real wage measured in wine falls in both industries.

produced by the factors earning them, because own real earnings are equal to marginal products. But a tariff can alter *cross* real earnings, those measured in terms of the other good, by altering relative prices.

Let us spell this out. Although the earnings of the land and labor used in the wine industry are fixed in terms of wine, they rise together in terms of cloth, because the tariff reduces the relative price of cloth. In Figure 9-8, labor-market equilibrium for the wine industry is shifted to *T*, raising the real wage measured in cloth by the full amount of the tariff. The earnings of the capital and labor used in the cloth industry are fixed in terms of cloth; labor-market equilibrium for the cloth industry remains at *F*. But those earnings fall together in terms of wine, because the tariff raises the relative price of wine.

Consider next the case studied in Chapter 5. When labor is perfectly mobile in Britain, the tariff leads to equilibrium at *T'*. The real wage rises in terms of cloth, but not by enough to prevent it from falling in terms of wine. Employment rises in the wine industry, increasing the marginal product of land, which raises the real rental rate for land whether measured in wine or cloth. Employment falls in the cloth industry, decreasing the marginal product of capital, which reduces the real return to capital measured in wine or cloth.

Effects in the Heckscher–Ohlin Model

In Chapter 6, on the Heckscher–Ohlin model, the effects of a change in relative prices on the real earnings of the factors of production were summarized by the Stolper–Samuelson theorem. An increase in the relative price of corn raised the real wage of labor, the factor used intensively in growing corn, and reduced the real return to capital. But the theorem depended on the basic assumption that all factors can move freely from industry to industry, which means that it can hold only in the long run, because it takes time to transform capital from mills into tractors.

The Stolper–Samuelson theorem was developed initially to answer the question at issue here. How does a tariff affect the income distribution in the Heckscher–Ohlin model? As corn is the labor-intensive product, Manymen is the labor-abundant country, and tastes are the same in Manymen and Fewmen, we know that Manymen exports corn and imports steel. By implication, Manymen can use an import tariff to redistribute income from labor to capital. A tariff raises the relative price of steel in Manymen. Over the long run, then, it raises the real return to capital and reduces the real wage of labor. Fewmen can use a tariff for the opposite purpose. By raising the relative price of corn in Fewmen, a tariff raises the real wage of labor and reduces the real return to capital, redistributing income from capital to labor.

The Crucial Role of Factor Mobility

Before looking at the costs of using a tariff to alter the income distribution, note that the exercises we have just conducted make different forecasts about attitudes toward tariffs:

1. When there is no factor mobility whatsoever, your attitude should depend entirely on the industry from which you obtain your income, not the nature of that income. If you earn your income from the British wine industry, whether it be rental or wage income, you should favor an import tariff. It will raise your real income by raising your cross real earnings. If you earn your income from the British cloth industry, you should oppose an import tariff.

2. When labor is perfectly mobile but land and capital are not, your attitude should depend in part on the nature of your income, not the industry from which you obtain it. If you own land in Britain, you should favor an import tariff. If you own capital in Britain, you should oppose it, If you are a worker in Britain, your attitude should depend in part on the way you spend your income. If you dress much and drink little, you should favor a tariff, as it will raise your real wage in terms of cloth but reduce it in terms of wine. If you dress little and drink much, you should oppose a tariff.

3. When all factors of production are perfectly mobile, as in the Heckscher–Ohlin model, your attitude should depend entirely on the nature of

your income, not the industry from which you earn it nor the way you spend it. If you own capital in Manymen, you should favor a tariff. If you are a worker in Manymen, you should oppose it.

We will return to these differences in Chapter 10 when looking at the sources of political support for tariffs and other trade barriers.

Welfare Costs and Alternative Policies

To measure the welfare costs of a tariff and compare them with the costs of other redistributive policies, let us look again at the modified Ricardian model and examine the goods-market equilibria shown in Figure 9-9. Britain's transformation curve is BB', and Britain's terms of trade are given by the slope of the line FF'. In the initial free-trade situation, the output point is Q and the consumption point is C.

When Britain imposes an import tariff to redistribute income from the owners of capital to the owners of land, the relative price of wine rises in Britain, reducing the

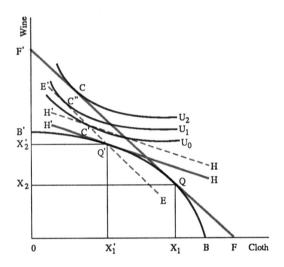

FIGURE 9-9
Comparing a Tariff with a Production Subsidy
Britain's terms of trade are given by the slope of FF'. Under free trade, Britain produces at Q on the transformation curve BB' and consumes at C on the indifference curve U_2. Cloth output is OX_1, and wine output is OX_2. A tariff on wine imports raises the relative price of wine in Britain (reduces the relative price of cloth). This effect is represented by the slope of HH'. Britain will produce at Q', where cloth output is OX_1' and wine output is OX_2', and will trade along EE' (parallel to FF') until it reaches C', where the slope of the indifference curve U_0 equals the slope of the broken line HH'. A subsidy to wine production financed by a tax on cloth production can have the same effect on the output point. The slope of HH' can be taken to represent the effects on prices received by British producers, causing them to move to Q'. But the prices paid by British consumers are still given by the slopes of FF' and EE', just as they were under free trade. Therefore, Britain will trade to C'', where the slope of the indifference curve U_1 is equal to the slope of EE'. As U_1 lies above U_0, the subsidy reduces economic welfare by less than a tariff that has the same effects on outputs and the income distribution.

relative price of cloth. Represent the new relative price of cloth by the slope of the lines HH'. The output point moves to Q', where the transformation curve is tangent to the solid line HH'. The consumption point moves to C' on the indifference curve U_0, where the indifference curve is tangent to the broken line HH' and the line EE', parallel to FF', connects Q' with C'. The tariff reduces welfare because U_0 is lower than U_2.

There are other ways to redistribute income that avoid or reduce the welfare loss. The first-best policy goes directly to the heart of the matter. If Britain wants to redistribute imcome from owners of capital to owners of land, it should raise taxes on income from capital and reduce taxes on income from land. This policy would leave production at Q, avoiding the protective effect. It would leave consumption at C, avoiding the consumption effect. Therefore, it would leave economic welfare at the free-trade level.

The next-best policy would tax cloth output and subsidize wine output, changing the net prices received by producers. It would set the ratio of those prices equal to the slope of HH', moving the output point to Q'. The rental rate for land would rise, the return to capital would fall, and real income would be redistributed just as it is by a tariff. But the prices paid by British consumers would not change; the ratio of those prices would still equal the slopes of FF' and EE'. The consumption point would move to C'', where an indifference curve U_1 is tangent to EE'. As this indifference curve lies between U_0 and U_2, the tax-subsidy scheme would cause a smaller welfare loss than the tariff. There would be a welfare-reducing protective effect, but no consumption effect. In this particular case, a tariff is a third-best policy. It is dominated by income-tax adjustments and by the tax-subsidy scheme.

TARIFFS AND DOMESTIC DISTORTIONS

An economy may differ in many ways from the models we have studied. Markets may not be perfectly competitive. Product and factor prices may be rigid in nominal or real terms. Uncertainty may influence producers and consumers. Certain products and processes may be harmful to health or the environment.

These possibilities have led economists to study ways of using tariffs and other trade controls to compensate for welfare-reducing distortions. They have spent much time modeling the distortions themselves and ranking policies to compensate for them. Their methods and conclusions can be illustrated by looking at the consequences of a rigid real wage in the modified Ricardian model.

Figure 9-10 shows the British labor market once again. Before the opening of trade, equilibrium occurs at D, where the real wage is $O\bar{V}$ measured in cloth. Employment is OL_1 in the wine industry and $\bar{L}L_1$ in the cloth industry. The opening of trade reduces the relative price of wine in Britain, and the demand curve for labor in the wine industry shifts downward from E_W to E'_W. When the real wage is flexible, equilibrium is displaced to F, and the real wage falls to OV^*. Employment falls to OL_1^* in the wine industry and rises to $\bar{L}L_1^*$ in the cloth industry. When the real wage is rigid in terms of cloth, however, it remains at $O\bar{V}$. Employment falls to OL_1' in the

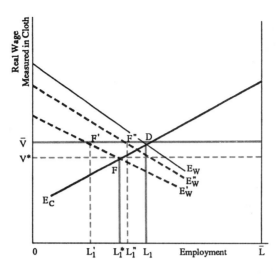

FIGURE 9-10
Labor-Market Equilibrium when the Real Wage Is Rigid
Before trade, E_C is the demand curve for labor in the British cloth industry, and E_W is the demand curve in the British wine industry. Equilibrium occurs at D, where the real wage is $O\bar{V}$ measured in cloth. Trade raises the relative price of cloth in Britain, shifting E_W downward to E'_W. If the real wage is flexible, it falls to OV^*, and equilibrium occurs at F, where employment in the wine industry falls from OL_1 to OL_1^*, and employment in the cloth industry rises from $\bar{L}L_1$ to $\bar{L}L_1^*$. If the real wage is rigid at $O\bar{V}$, however, employment in the wine industry falls to OL'_1, and employment in the cloth industry remains at OL_1. There is unemployment. A tariff on wine imports raises the relative price of wine and shifts the wine industry's demand curve from E'_W to E''_W, raising employment to OL''_1. It does not affect employment in the cloth industry (so it cannot establish equilibrium at F). A tariff could shift the demand curve all the way to E_W, raising employment to OL_1 and eradicating unemployment. But the relative price of wine would return to what it was before trade, and trade itself would be eliminated. A wage subsidy could take the labor market to F, offsetting the effects of wage rigidity. The requisite subsidy measured in cloth would be $V^*\bar{V}$ per worker in both industries.

wine industry but remains at $\bar{L}L_1$ in the cloth industry. There is unemployment amounting to DF' workers.

The output and welfare effects of this wage rigidity are shown in Figure 9-11. Before trade, equilibrium occurs at Q, where the transformation curve BB' is tangent to the indifference curve U_0. The opening of trade is represented by introducing the price line FF', steeper than U_0 at Q. The relative price of cloth rises in Britain.

When the real wage is flexible, the output point moves to Q^*. Cloth output rises and wine output falls, matching the reallocation of labor shown in Figure 9-10. Britain trades along FF' to some such point as C^*, reaching an indifference curve higher than U_0. When the real wage is rigid, by contrast, Britain cannot move along its transformation curve. The cloth industry will continue to employ the $\bar{L}L_1$ workers shown in Figure 9-10, so cloth output will remain at OX_1. But the wine industry will employ only the $O\bar{L}$ workers shown in Figure 9-10, fewer than before the opening of trade, so wine output will fall to OX'_1 in Figure 9-11. The new output

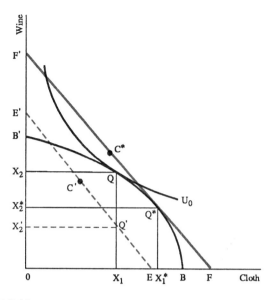

FIGURE 9-11
Production and Welfare When the Real Wage Is Rigid
Before trade, Britain produces and consumes at Q, on the transformation curve BB' and the indifference curve U_0. When trade is opened, the terms of trade are given by the slope of FF'. If the real wage is flexible, production moves to Q^*, where cloth output rises to OX_1^*, wine output falls to OX_2^*, and Britain trades along FF' to some such point as C^* on an indifference curve higher than U_0. If the real wage is rigid, cloth output cannot rise, and wine output falls all the way to OX_2'. The production point is Q', and Britain trades along EE' (parallel to FF') to some such point as C' on an indifference curve lower than U_0. The opening of trade reduces welfare. If employment is subsidized in both industries, however, firms can reach Q^*, the point they would reach if the real wage were flexible.

point is Q', and Britain must trade to some such point as C', which will lie on an indifference curve below U_1 when the output loss is sufficiently large. Free trade can reduce economic welfare when the real wage is rigid.

How can a tariff compensate for a rigid real wage? By raising the relative price of wine in Britain, it can shift the wine industry's demand for labor from E_W' to E_W'' in Figure 9-10, raising employment in that industry from OL_1' to OL_1''. (It cannot raise employment in the cloth industry because it cannot affect the rigid real wage.) The implications for output and welfare are shown in Figure 9-12, which reproduces the output points Q, Q^*, and Q' from Figure 9-11, along with the consumption points C^* *and* C'. The increase of employment in the wine industry is shown by the increase in wine output from OX_2' to OX_2'' and the corresponding movement of the output point to Q''. Britain trades to C'', where the indifference curve U_1 is tangent to the line HH', which reflects the effect of the tariff on the relative price of cloth in Britain. As U_1 is above U_0, the tariff has converted a welfare loss into a welfare gain. British consumers are better off with the tariff than they were before trade was opened and, therefore, far better off than they were with free trade.

Look back at Figure 9-10, however, and note that some workers are still unemployed in Britain. Unemployment has fallen from DF' with free trade to DF''

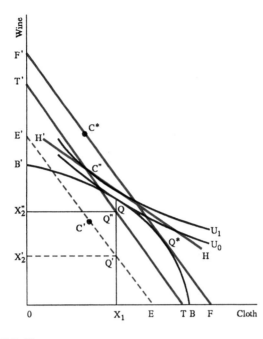

FIGURE 9-12
Using a Tariff to Compensate for a Rigid Real Wage
The production points Q, Q', and Q^* are reproduced from Figure 9-11. With free trade and a rigid wage, Britain produces at Q' rather than Q^*, and it trades along EE' to C', on an indifference curve below U_0 (the indifference curve reached before trade is opened). By raising wine output above OX_2', a tariff can raise economic welfare above the level reached at C'. If it raises wine output to OX_2'' (the level corresponding to employment at OL_1'' in Figure 9-10), it shifts the production point to Q'', and Britain can trade along TT' (parallel to FF' and EE') until it reaches a point such as C'', where the indifference curve U_1 is tangent to HH', the slope of which is equal to the relative price of cloth in Britain. As U_1 is higher than U_0, the tariff raises welfare above the level reached before trade was opened. As U_1 is lower than the indifference curve tangent to FF' at C^*, however, the tariff cannot raise welfare to the level that would be reached by subsidizing employment to produce at Q^* and consume at C^*.

with an import tariff, but it has not been eradicated. Britain could reach full employment by imposing a tariff high enough to shift the wine industry's demand curve for labor all the way back to E_W. In that case, however, the relative price of cloth in Britain would have to be what it was before trade was opened, which means that the tariff would eliminate all trade. The output point in Figure 9-12 would move all the way back to Q, where the relative price of cloth in Britain would equal the slope of the indifference curve U_0. Hence, Britain would consume at Q, and economic welfare would be what it was before trade was opened. As in the optimum-tariff case, a higher tariff is not necessarily better, even though it can eradicate unemployment.

As the tariff cannot stimulate employment in Britain's cloth industry, it cannot establish labor-market equilibrium at F in Figure 9-10, the point that would be reached with a flexible real wage. That is why it cannot eliminate unemployment while raising welfare at the same time. Furthermore, the tariff has a costly consumption effect. Because consumers' choices are governed by the slope of the price line

HH' in Figure 9-12, they go to C'' on U_1 rather than a point on a higher indifference curve. As usual, the tariff is a second-best policy.

Can Britain find a form of intervention that does not have these defects—one involving intervention closer to the problem? As wage rigidity arises in the labor market, intervention directly in that market is apt to give better results. Return to Figure 9-10 and suppose that the government subsidizes firms to hire workers. Let the subsidy be $V^*\bar{V}$ per worker, which reduces the firm's cost of hiring a worker from $O\bar{V}$ to OV^*. That is what the cost would be with wage flexibility, and the labor market will reach equilibrium at F. The output point will move to Q^* in Figure 9-12, and Britain can reap the full gains from trade.

SUMMARY

Many popular arguments for tariffs are fallacious. Differences in wage rates, for example, do not justify protection. They are required for trade to take place when levels of productivity differ across countries. Tariffs can protect domestic industries essential for the national defense, but this argument is rarely compelling; the maintanance of a mobilization base may not be very helpful in the nuclear age. Furthermore, protection is the wrong way to maintain such a base. Tariffs tax consumers of the peacetime products of the protected industries rather than distributing the costs across the whole population. It would be more equitable and efficient to use production subsidies.

The same point can be made against many other arguments, even those that are analytically sound. Because they distort consumer's choices, tariffs are *second-best* policy instruments compared to other ways of redistributing income, increasing output in domestic industries, or dealing with domestic distortions. Yet tariffs are better instruments than most other trade controls, because they are less rigid and more transparent. Quotas are formally equivalent to tariffs under perfectly competitive conditions, but quotas do not allow imports to increase when domestic demand rises, and they give windfall profits to the quota holders.

By raising the domestic price of the imported good, a tariff raises the production of domestic substitutes (the protective effect) and reduces domestic demand (the consumption effect). Both effects impose welfare losses on the domestic economy. Tariffs have a third effect when the country imposing them is large enough to influence world prices. They can improve its terms of trade. When they do so, however, they impose welfare losses on the outside world. As these are always larger than the welfare gains extracted from foreign suppliers, there is a welfare loss for the world as a whole. The size of the improvement in the terms of trade varies with the way the tariff revenue is spent. It is largest when the revenue is spent on the export good.

To measure the protective effects of tariffs, we must examine the whole tariff schedule. The protective effects increase with the sizes of the tariffs on products that compete with an industry's output. The effects decrease with the sizes of the tariffs on products the industry purchases. The net effects can be approximated by the *effective tariff rate* for the industry. This rate can be higher or lower than the nominal rate. It can even be negative, in which case the industry would be better off with completely free trade.

Three uses of tariffs reviewed in this chapter show why tariffs and other trade controls are rarely first-best policy instruments.

A country large enough to influence its terms of trade can use a tariff to improve them and capture larger gains from trade at the expense of other countries. The size of its *optimum tariff* depends on the shape of the foreign offer curve. If other countries retaliate, however, the country that initiates the process may wind up worse off than with free trade. Furthermore, the departure from free trade reduces world welfare, which means that there must be a less costly way to redistribute welfare. It is possible in principle to "bribe" a country to dissuade it from imposing an optimum tariff.

A tariff can be used to redistribute income internally. If all factors of production are immobile internally, a tariff will benefit factors employed in the import-competing industry and harm those employed in the export industry. Real earnings in the import-competing industry will rise in terms of the export good; real earnings in the export industry will fall in terms of the import-competing good. If some factors are mobile and others are not, as in the modified Ricardian model, the Haberler theorem applies. A tariff will raise the real earnings of the factor specific to the import-competing industry and reduce those of the factor specific to the export industry. It will raise the real earnings of the mobile factor (labor) in terms of the export good but reduce them in terms of the import-competing good. If all factors are mobile internally, as in the Heckscher–Ohlin model, the Stolper–Samuelson theorem applies. A tariff will raise the real earnings of the factor used intensively in the import-competing industry and reduce those of the factor used intensively in the export industry. In every case, however, a tariff is a third-best way to redistribute income. Income taxes are the first-bet way; they do not distort production or consumption. Production taxes and subsidies are the second-best way; they distort production but not consumption.

When a country's goods or factor markets do not function perfectly, free trade may reduce economic welfare. When real wages are rigid, for example, the opening of trade can cause unemployment, and the resulting welfare loss can exceed the welfare gain obtainable through trade. By raising employment in the import-competing industry, a tariff can reduce the welfare loss resulting from the rigid wage. But it cannot compensate completely for a rigid wage, and it distorts consumers' choices. It would be better for the government to intervene at a point closer to the problem by subsidizing firms to hire workers at the rigid wage.

RECOMMENDED READINGS

This chapter has concentrated on import tariffs, but export tariffs have identical effects on relative prices and outputs. See Abba P. Lerner, "The Symmetry between Import and Export Taxes," *Economica*, 3 (August 1936), reprinted in American Economic Association, *Readings in International Economics* (Homewood, Ill.: Richard D. Irwin, 1968), ch. 11.

On comparing tariffs with quotas when markets are not perfectly competitive, see Jagdish Bhagwati, *Trade, Tariffs, and Growth* (Cambridge, Mass.: MIT Press, 1969), ch. 9; on comparing them when demand and supply curves are subject to random shocks, see Michael D. Pelcovits, "Quotas Versus Tariffs," *Journal of International Economics*, 6 (November 1976).

For ways of extending and applying the concept of effective protection, see W. Max Corden, "The Structure of a Tariff System and the Effective Protective Rate," *Journal of Political Economy*, 74 (June 1966), reprinted in J. N. Bhagwati, ed., *International Trade: Selected Readings* (Cambridge, Mass.: MIT Press, 1981), ch. 9.

Attempts have been made to measure the welfare costs of trade restrictions using the concepts of consumer and producer surplus. For an example, see Stephen P. Magee, "The Welfare Effects of Restrictions on U.S. Trade," *Brookings Papers on Economic Activity*, 1972 (3); for a compilation of more recent calculations, see Gary Clyde Hufbauer and Howard F. Rosen, *Trade Policy for Troubled Industries*, Policy Analyses in International Economics, 15 (Washington, D.C.: Institute for International Economics, 1986).

On optimum tariffs and retaliation, see Tibor de Scitovszky, "A Reconsideration of the Theory of Tariffs," *Review of Economic Studies*, 9 (Summer 1942), reprinted in American Economic Association, *Readings in the Theory of International Trade* (Philadelphia: Blakiston, 1949). For more on retaliation, see Harry G. Johnson, "Optimum Tariffs and Retaliation," *Review of Economic Studies*, 21 (1953–54), reprinted in H. G. Johnson, *International Trade and Economic Growth* (London: George Allen & Unwin, 1958), ch. 2.

On tariffs and the income distribution, see Michael Mussa, "Dynamic Adjustment in the Heckscher–Ohlin–Samuelson Model," *Journal of Political Economy*, 86 (August 1978), and the paper by Stolper and Samuelson, "Protection and Real Wages" (full citation at the end of Chapter 6).

There has been much work on tariffs to deal with domestic distortions. Three papers are especially relevant to this chapter: Harry G. Johnson "Optimal Trade Intervention in the Presence of Domestic Distortions," in R. E. Caves et al., eds., *Trade, Growth and the Balance of Payments* (Chicago: Rand McNally, 1965); Jagdish N. Bhagwati, "The Generalized Theory of Distortions and Welfare," in J. N. Bhagwati et al., eds., *Trade, Balance of Payments and Growth* (Amsterdam: North-Holland, 1971), ch. 4; and Richard A. Brecher, "Optimum Commercial Policy for a Minimum-Wage Economy," *Journal of International Economics*, 4 (May 1974). All three are reprinted in J. N. Bhagwati, ed., *International Trade: Selected Readings* (Cambridge, Mass.: MIT Press, 1981), chs. 11–13.

QUESTIONS AND PROBLEMS

(1) Interpret Figure 9-2 as showing the effects of an import quota rather than a tariff. How large is the quota? What significance, if any, do you attach to the area $P''R''VRP'$ and to each of its four components? Do the welfare effects of the quota differ from those of the tariff? Explain.

(2) Adapt Figure 9-3 to show the effects of an import tariff imposed by Britain when Britain spends the tariff revenue on wine. Identify the tariff rate. Does the tariff rate shown for Britain differ from the rate shown for Portugal? Explain.

(3) Using your answer to (2), interpret your adaptation of Figure 9-3 as representing an export tariff on wine imposed by Portugal, then as an export tariff on cloth imposed by Britain, with the revenue spent on wine on both instances. What conclusion do you draw concerning the price effects of export and import tariffs? Is it sensible to say that an export tariff has a protective effect?

(4) Using your answer to (2), interpret Figure 9-5 as showing the effects of an import tariff imposed by Britain. In what sense is this outcome perverse?

(5) Figure 9-4 analyzed the effects of spending patterns by fixing the relative price of cloth in Portugal and showing how the spending pattern affects the size of the Portuguese tariff rate required to keep that price constant. Make the same point by fixing the relative

price of cloth in Britain (the Portuguese terms of trade), making sure you show how the Portuguese tariff rate and spending pattern affect the relative price of cloth in Portugal.

(6) The assembly of a lefthanded widget requires 1 hour of labor and two parts. The U.S. wage is $6.00 per hour. The world price of a lefthanded widget is $20.00, and the U.S. tariff is 30 percent. The world price of the first part is $4.00, and the U.S. tariff is 50 percent; the world price of the second part is $3.00, and the U.S. tariff is 25 percent. What is the profit per widget to a U.S. firm that assembles lefthanded widgets. What is the effective tariff rate on widget assembly?

(7) Using your answer to (6), show what happens to the effective tariff rate on widgets when the tariffs on the first and second parts are eliminated separately. Explain the difference in the effect of eliminating the two tariffs.

(8) Adapt Figure 9-11 to show that free trade can be better than no trade, even when the real wage is rigid, if the opening of trade does not cause a large fall in employment and output. Could the opening of trade lead to any unemployment if the real wage were rigid in terms of the import-competing good rather than the export good?

(9) Show how an import tariff on cloth affects the real earnings of Portuguese workers and real returns to capital and labor when there is no labor mobility in Portugal.

10

The Evolution of
Trade Policy

THE ISSUES

Chapter 9 reviewed some of the well known arguments for restricting trade and showed that trade restrictions often prove to be inefficient instruments. Nevertheless, governments continue to use them, and many new trade barriers have been erected recently. This chapter examines the long-term evolution of trade policy and deals with four issues:

- How trade theory has influenced trade policy.
- Why and how the influence of trade theory has varied from time to time and place to place.
- How the process of trade liberalization has been organized.
- How the process of liberalization has changed and why it is threatened.

The next chapter will focus on recent developments, including the attempt to broaden trade liberalization by extending it from goods to services and the attempt to deepen trade liberalization by forming regional trading blocs.

TARIFF THEORY AND TARIFF HISTORY

At one time or another, every argument for tariffs has been invoked in debates about trade policy. Tariff history is also the history of tariff theory and shows how theory can influence policy.

Divergent Trends: 1816-1860

In the United States, trade policy was dominated by the *infant-industry argument* during the first half of the nineteenth century, and tariffs rose more or less steadily. Trade policy in Great Britain was dominated by distributional arguments, and tariffs were reduced dramatically.

The infant-industry argument is analyzed extensively in the next chapter, which examines its use and abuse in developing countries. Basically, it argues that new industries should be protected if they give promise of competing successfully with imports after being helped to grow. The future gains from growth, it says, will more than compensate for the welfare-reducing effects of temporary protection. There are two versions of the infant-industry argument. The first claims that young industries will achieve economies of scale when protection gives them preferential access to the domestic market. The second claims that young industries will achieve economies of experience when protection gives them time for learning by doing. Both versions were advanced by Alexander Hamilton in his *Report on Manufactures*, urging industrial development in the United States and the use of tariffs to promote it, and the argument acquired enormous influence.

The United States had taxed imports from the start. But its early tariffs, although protective in effect, were designed mainly to raise revenue for the federal government. Because there was no income tax, the government relied on excise taxes and tariffs. Imports tariffs were fairly easy to collect; one had merely to police the ports and coastline. It would have been even easier to tax the country's major exports, cotton and tobacco, but the Southern states that grew them had insisted that the U.S. Constitution prohibit export taxes. They feared that the federal government would be dominated by the more populous Northern states and would pay its bills by taxing Southern exports.

After the War of 1812, however, manufacturers in New England and the Middle Atlantic states demanded additional protection. Transatlantic trade had been disrupted for more than a decade. Jefferson's Embargo had tried to prevent the impressment of American sailors by keeping them from going to sea and had cut off imports of British textiles and hardware. The embargo and the War of 1812 had effects equivalent to *prohibitive* tariffs on imported manufactures. With the coming of peace and resumption of trade, British goods began again to cross the Atlantic, and American producers lost ground. Despite opposition from the South, which wanted to import cheap foreign manufactures, Congress imposed higher tariffs on textiles in 1816 and on iron, cutlery, and glass in 1824.

The North-South controversy over tariffs reached a peak in 1828. Southern Congressmen tried to outmaneuver their Northern opponents by amending a pending tariff bill; they added high tariffs on raw wool and other crude materials, hoping that Northern manufacturers, who used those materials, would reject the whole bill. Today, we would say that they were trying to reduce effective tariffs on Northern manufactures. Their strategem failed, however, and the bill became law. Its effect is shown clearly in Figure 10-1. Tariff rates soared, and the bill was promptly dubbed the Tariff of Abominations. It inspired South Carolina's Ordinance of Nullification, which proclaimed a state's right to abrogate federal legislation, asserting that "the tariff law of 1828, and the amendment to the same of 1832, are

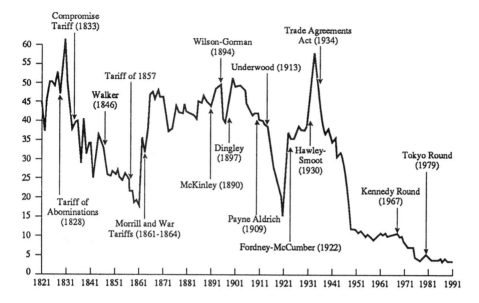

FIGURE 10-1
Average U.S. Tariff Rates on Dutiable Imports, 1820–1990
Legislation raising U.S. tariffs is usually reflected in an increase in the average rate of duty, and legislation reducing them is usually reflected in a decrease. *Source:* U.S. Department of Commerce, Bureau of the Census, *Historical Statistics of the United States,* and *Statistical Abstract of the United States.*

null and void and no law, nor binding upon this State, its officers and citizens." The Constitutional issue was not settled until the Civil War, but the furor over tariff policy died down with the passage of a compromise tariff in 1833.

In the 1840s, the federal government developed an embarrassing budget surplus, and Congress cut tariffs to reduce tax revenues. The average rate of duty fell toward 25 percent as tariffs were cut sharply in 1846 and again in 1857. But the United States was still out of step with Europe, which was moving toward free trade.

The free-trade movement started in Great Britain as part of a broader assault on the powers of the aristocracy. It sought to end the political dominance of the rural gentry, who were the main beneficiaries of the tariffs on imported grain, known as the Corn Laws. As in the United States, the British debate about tariffs policy was entangled in constitutional questions, including the issue of parliamentary reform. But the free-trade movement was also inspired by the arguments of the classical economists. It invoked the *allocative* argument for free trade that Adam Smith had formulated 50 years before and David Ricardo had refined just before the debate on the Corn Laws:[1]

---

[1]David Ricardo, *On the Principles of Political Economy and Taxation,* 1817, ch. vii. Ricardo had attacked the Corn Laws in an earlier work, *An Essay on the Influence of a Low Price of Corn on the Profits of Stock,* published in 1815, which set out the *distributive* argument we will discuss shortly.

> Under a system of perfectly free commerce, each country naturally devotes its capital and labour to such employments as are most beneficial to each. This pursuit of individual advantage is admirably connected with the universal good of the whole. By stimulating industry, by rewarding ingenuity, and by using most efficaciously the peculiar powers bestowed by nature, it distributes labour most effectively and most economically.... It is this principle which determines that wine shall be made in France and Portugal, that corn shall be grown in America and Poland, and that hardware and other goods shall be manufactured in England.

The free-trade movement relied even more heavily on a *distributive* argument against the Corn Laws. It can be extracted from the modified Ricardian model developed in Chapter 5. Suppose that Great Britain produces corn using land and labor and produces hardware using capital and labor. Land and capital are specific factors, but labor is perfectly mobile between industries. Suppose that Great Britain imports corn and has a tariff on it. Finally, assume that workers consume corn but little or no hardware, an assumption used frequently by classical economists. If Great Britain removed its tariff on corn, the relative price of corn would fall. Therefore, landlords' rents would fall in terms of cloth and hardware, and capitalists' profits would rise. Workers' wages would rise in terms of corn and fall in terms of hardware, but workers would gain because they consume mainly corn. Ricardo and his colleagues went further, saying that workers would gain in *two* ways. First, free trade would raise real wages directly by making corn cheaper. Second, it would increase the demand for labor by raising profits and encouraging investment.

Great Britain had started toward free trade in the eighteenth century, and the Tory government continued the process after the Napoleonic Wars. It abolished tariffs on many raw materials without provoking the rural gentry, who did not produce those materials. During the next decade, however, attention turned to grain, a more explosive issue. In 1842, the Tory government of Sir Robert Peel refused to repeal the Corn Laws, taking the side of the gentry. But the Irish famine of 1845–1846 forced Peel to reverse himself and allow cheaper imports of grain. He suspended the Corn Laws in 1845, and he split the Tory party by repealing them permanently a year later.

The Triumph and Decline of Free Trade: 1860-1914

To move further toward free trade, Great Britain turned to diplomacy. In the Cobden-Chevalier Treaty of 1860, Britain and France agreed to *reciprocal* tariff cuts, including a reduction in British taxes on French wines. The French, in turn, negotiated tariff treaties with other European countries and with the *Zollverein*, the German customs union. (A customs union is a group of countries that have no tariffs on trade among themselves and a common tariff on their trade with the outside world. We will encounter another one shortly.)

The treaties of 1860–1870 had two effects. First, they made new tariff cuts, enlarging world markets. Second, they generalized those tariff cuts, because they included the *most-favored-nation clause*, the key provision in commercial treaties. This clause commits the parties to give each other *all* of the concessions they give to any other country.[2] Under the most-favored-nation clause, France gave the *Zollverein* the concessions it had given to Great Britain under the Cobden–Chevalier Treaty. The *Zollverein* was not obliged to make concessions in return but had to give France all of the concessions it had given or would give to any other country.

Within 10 years, however, the free-trade movement was reversed by shifts in political and economic circumstances. The 1870s witnessed a sharp change in European views concerning the benefits and costs of colonies. Imperialist sentiment had died down after the Napoleonic Wars, and no new colonies were acquired during the next 50 years, apart from French acquisitions in North Africa. In the 1870s, however, European governments started again to scramble for tropical real estate. The partition of Africa was completed in two decades, and new rivalries arose in the Near East and Orient. Bellicose nationalism captured European politics and soon led to the use of tariffs to protect domestic industries, especially those needed to make armaments.

At about the same time, European agriculture began to face new competition. Railroads and steamships brought wheat from the United States, Argentina, and Russia to compete with German and French grain. Germany had long been an exporter of grain but became an importer when farm prices fell. European farmers and landlords had favored free trade, just like their counterparts in the American South. They changed their minds, however, when they encountered import competition, and the balance of political power swung toward protection.

The tide turned first in Germany in 1879. Six years earlier, Bismarck had abolished the tariff on imported iron and announced that tariffs on iron products would be abolished soon. He was forced to backtrack, however, when landlords in Prussia and farmers in Bavaria united to support manufacturers in the Ruhr and Rhineland, Bismarck introduced a new tariff law in 1879, giving more protection to industry and agriculture.

German protectionists invoked the infant-industry argument. In fact, a German, Friedrich List, produced the most elaborate version of that argument. List had lived in the United States and was impressed by the growth of American industry behind high tariff walls. He returned to Germany a passionate advocate of protection. List conceded that free trade is best from a cosmopolitan standpoint, but he said that a nation should not be guided by allocative arguments until it has developed its domestic industries and can export manufactures instead of raw materials. Only then can it prosper by benefiting fully from the international division of labor.

List's views about the gain from trade are easily refuted. Countries such as Denmark, Australia, and New Zealand export agricultural products but have higher living standards than many other countries. Furthermore, List's argument contains a contradiction. If all countries were to export manufactures, the terms of trade would turn against them; the prices of raw materials would rise, and some countries

---

[2] The name of the clause is a bit misleading. It sounds like a promise of preferential treatment. It is, instead, a promise that no *other* country will be given preferential treatment (i.e., that the partner will receive treatment no less favorable than that given to any other country). The clause is the basis of modern commercial diplomacy and appears in the General Agreement on Tariffs and Trade, discussed later in this chapter.

would find it advantageous to export raw materials. Nevertheless, List's argument won the day in Germany.

France was quick to follow Germany. Manufacturers and farmers united to enact the Meline Tariff of 1892 designed to promote industrial development. The French economy grew rapidly thereafter, but the Meline Tariff cannot take credit. It may instead have handicapped the iron and steel industry by levying a high tax on coal and thus raising the costs of producing iron. In other words, the new tariff on coal reduced the effective tariff on iron.

The resurgence of protectionism was followed by tariff warfare. In 1902, for example, Germany raised its tariffs to increase its bargaining power, and it peppered its tariff schedule with artificial distinctions to conserve that power. To distinguish Swiss from Danish cattle, the 1902 tariff had a separate category applying to 'brown or dappled cows reared at a level of at least 300 metres above sea level and passing at least one month in every summer at an altitude of at least 800 metres." As Danish cattle cannot graze at those altitudes, German negotiators were able to reduce the German tariff on Danish cattle without automatically reducing the tariff on Swiss cattle *via* the most-favored-nation clause.

American tariffs did not come down as far as European tariffs, and they turned upward earlier. In 1861, Congress passed the Morrill Tariff Act, raising rates on iron and steel products; in 1862 and 1864, it raised other duties. The new rates were not meant to be protective but merely to deny foreign producers an unfair advantage over domestic producers. To finance the Civil War, Congress had imposed high excise taxes on many domestic products and then raised tariffs to offset them. When the war ended, government spending fell, and the domestic taxes were allowed to lapse, but the wartime tariffs were not repealed. Therefore, they came to be highly protective, and the McKinley Tariff of 1890 raised rates to a postwar peak. (Tariffs were brought down slightly during Grover Cleveland's second term, when control of Congress passed briefly to the Democrats, but the Republicans raised them as soon as they regained control.)

After 1900, the Republican party seemed to edge away from the extreme protectionism that had been one of its chief tenets. Its 1908 platform declared that

> the true principle of protection is best maintained by the imposition of such duties as would equalize the difference between the cost of production at home and abroad, together with a reasonable degree of profit.

This formula looked rather reasonable and was reflected in the Payne–Aldrich Tarifff of 1909, which cut some duties slightly. But trade theory points to the obvious flaw in this "scientific" principle. Differences in costs of production are the very basis for trade, and a tariff designed to offset them will therefore prohibit trade, except in farm products, which need special climates, and in raw materials, which can be produced only where nature puts them. If costs of production are equalized, transport costs will usually suffice to prohibit trade in manufactures.

Collapse and Reconstruction: 1914-1939

On the eve of World War I, the Wilson administration cut tariffs sharply and added many items to the "free list," including iron, coal, wool, lumber, and newsprint. But the war, the peace settlement, and shortsighted policies disrupted trade patterns and burdened many countries with heavy debts. Protectionist pressures began to build up everywhere.

The peace settlement lengthened Europe's frontiers by more than 12,000 miles by cutting up the Hapsburg Empire into a half-dozen states—Austria, Czechoslovakia, Hungary, and the rest—and tariff walls were built all along the new borders. Great Britain had sold foreign assets during the war to pay for imports of arms and food and was therefore deprived of the earnings and assets that had offset the gradual decline in the competitive position of British industry. Furthermore, Britain and France had borrowed heavily in the United States to pay for war material, and Germany had been saddled with huge reparation payments by the Versailles Treaty. In the United States, industries that had expanded during the war feared foreign competition with the coming of peace. Farmers were apprehensive, too, not only in the United States but in many other countries. They had been encouraged to grow large crops during the war, confronted intense competition when it ended, and experienced adverse terms of trade throughout the 1920s.

One by one, governments erected new trade barriers. Some raised their tariffs. Others used quotas and other nontariff barriers. The new nations of Central Europe led the way, but they were not alone. Germany imposed high tariffs on farm products in 1925. Countries in Latin America, burdened by debts and adverse terms of trade, used tariffs and quotas more freely than before. Great Britain abandoned free trade in 1919 and succumbed completely to protectionism in 1931, amidst the worldwide economic crisis.

The United States should have lowered its tariffs after World War I to allow other countries to earn the dollars they needed to service their debts. Instead, Congress voted to increase tariffs during the first postwar recession. The Fordney–McCumber Tariff of 1922 was designed to help farmers, but it also helped "war babies" such as the chemicals industry. Eight years later, Congress passed the Hawley–Smoot Tariff, once called the "Holy-Smoke Tariff" by a student with keener insight than memory. Hearings on tariff reform began in 1929, concerned once again with helping the farmers. But then the economy started its sickening slide into the Great Depression, and one industry after another demanded protection to stimulate domestic production. When the new tariff bill came before Congress, there was an orgy of logrolling. Congressmen traded votes, seeking higher tariffs for their own constituents, and when they were done, the United States had the highest tariffs in its history.

The early 1930s gave birth to more trade barriers. Shut out of American markets by the Hawley-Smoot Tariff and concerned to defend their own economies from the spread of the depression, governments restricted imports. Each country frustrated its neighbors' efforts; a cut in one country's imports was, of course, a cut in other countries' exports. As a result, trade recovered from the Depression less vigorously than did production. Indeed, the slowing down of trade was a drag on economic recovery. World imports in 1938 were only half as large as they had been in 1928.

U.S. tariffs started to decline after 1932. Part of the reduction was due to the gradual increase in prices that took place with recovery. Many U.S. tariffs were *specific* duties, fixed in cents per pound, dollars per dozen, and so on; when the prices of dutiable products rose, their *ad valorem* (percentage) equivalents fell.[3] But some of the reduction in U.S. tariffs reflected a major turnabout in policy. Seeking ways to stimulate production and employment, the Roosevelt administration turned to world markets, launching a campaign to reduce trade barriers in order to expand U.S. exports.

In 1934, President Roosevelt asked Congress for the power to negotiate bilateral trade agreements. The United States would cut its tariffs by as much as 50 percent in return for equivalent cuts by other countries. The president told Congress:

> A resumption of international trade cannot but improve the general situation of other countries, and thus increase their purchasing power. Let us well remember that this in turn spells increased opportunity for American sales.... Legislation such as this is an essential step in the program of national economic recovery which the Congress has elaborated during this past year.

Roosevelt promised that reciprocal tariff cuts would not hurt American producers by opening domestic markets to competitive imports. In effect, he foreswore the allocative gains from freer trade; he was looking instead for the output and employment effects of expanded exports. Having made a mess of tariff policy in 1930, when the legislative process got out of control, and deeply worried about the depression, Congress gave the president the power he requested.

The United States negotiated 31 reciprocal trade agreements before World War II and extended the concessions to many other countries under the most-favored-nation clause. The Trade Agreements Program resembled the network of trade treaties that spread out from France after 1860. Unlike that earlier network, it did not bring the world very close to free trade. Nevertheless, it helped to arrest the worldwide increase in trade barriers that was choking world trade. Furthermore, it broke an historic pattern. U.S. tariffs had risen after every other major war, but the Trade Agreements Program held them down after World War II.

THE MULTILATERAL APPROACH
TO TRADE LIBERALIZATION

During World War II, governments put strict controls on trade and payments to keep their citizens from spending foreign currencies needed to buy food and war materiel. Many carried their controls into the postwar period to save scarce foreign currencies for reconstruction. Early in the war, however, they began to draw up plans for liberalizing peacetime trade and payments. Even before the fighting ceased, they established two new institutions, the International Monetary Fund

---

[3] A $2 tariff on a $20 product works out at 10 percent *ad valorem*; if the price of the product rises to $40, the tariff falls to 5 percent *ad valorem*.

(IMF) and the International Bank for Reconstruction and Development (IBRD), commonly known as the World Bank, to manage the monetary system and encourage international lending. They also made plans to reduce trade barriers.

The American Initiative: Universality and the GATT

The wartime planners drew on American experience with the Trade Agreements Program but tried to correct its flaws. Under that program, for example, bargaining took place bilaterally and thus sequentially, and governments were fearful of making large tariff cuts because they had to hoard their bargaining power. Therefore, the wartime planners adopted a *multilateral* approach. When bargaining takes place multilaterally and thus simultaneously, countries have less incentive to hoard their bargaining power; each participant can keep track of the concessions it is likely to receive directly in exchange for its own and those it is likely to receive indirectly under the most-favored-nation clause. The prewar program, moreover, had dealt mainly with tariffs, and the wartime planners wanted to eliminate quotas and other nontariff barriers. Quotas block imports absolutely, preventing price changes from affecting trade patterns, and they had been used in the 1930s to nullify negotiated tariff cuts by keeping out the imports attracted by those cuts. Therefore, the wartime planners sought to design a more comprehensive approach to trade liberalization.

The new approach found its first expression in wartime agreements between the United States and Great Britain—the Atlantic Charter and the Lend-Lease Agreement under which the United States gave aid to Britain before its own entry into the war. It was then embodied in a charter for an International Trade Organization (ITO) to be affiliated with the United Nations. But the charter was not ratified by the U.S. Senate, and the ITO never came into being. Its charter had antagonized foes of international cooperation, who charged that the new organization would meddle in domestic economic matters. It had disappointed advocates of cooperation, who warned that no country would be bound by the rules because exceptions and qualifications had swamped the basic principles.

In 1947, however, the major trading countries agreed on rules for reducing tariffs and convened the first of many tariff-cutting conferences. That agreement has survived as the General Agreement on Tariffs and Trade (GATT). Its heart is the most-favored-nation clause, under which each tariff bargain made at a GATT meeting is extended to all members. Its rules discourage withdrawals of concessions, because countries injured by an increase in another country's tariffs are entitled to retaliate by withdrawing their concessions to the offending country. Unfortunately, the practices and language of the GATT perpetuate an ancient fallacy. Because government have to contend with protectionist pressures at home, they treat reductions in their tariffs as concessions made to foreigners, rather than achievements for their own consumers and for the efficient use of their own resources. Mercantilist notions about national advantage interfere with clear thinking about comparative advantage.

The rules of the GATT outlaw discriminatory practices and prohibit the use of import quotas except by countries experiencing balance-of-payments problems or by those imposing comparable quotas on domestic producers—crop ceilings on farmers, for example, imposed in conjunction with domestic price-support programs. There are exceptions, moreover, for developing countries that permit them to protect infant industries. In addition, GATT members have drawn up codes of conduct to deal with dumping, subsidies, and other "unfair" practices. These are discussed later in this chapter.

Congress passed another Trade Agreements Act in 1945, authorizing the president to cut U.S. tariffs in GATT negotiations, and five rounds of bargaining were completed between 1947 and 1961. The largest cuts were made in 1947 and 1948, and they are reflected in Figure 10-1. But they used up most of the president's powers, and Congress became increasingly reluctant to give him more when it was asked periodically to extend the Trade Agreements Act.

When President Roosevelt proposed the Trade Agreements Program in 1934, he promised that no injury would befall American industry. Accordingly, an *escape clause* was written into the bilateral trade agreements of the 1930s, allowing the United States to withdraw tariff cuts when American firms were injured by imports. President Truman promised to continue this practice when he asked for more tariff-cutting powers in 1945. But Congress was not satisfied, and the president had to introduce formal procedures for dealing with injury from import competition. The Tariff Commission, now known as the International Trade Commission (ITC), would hold hearings whenever American producers charged that tariff cuts had exposed them to injury. When the commission found evidence of injury, it would recommend a higher tariff or some other way to limit imports. The president could set aside its recommendations, but this would put him on the defensive, because he would be seen to be allowing injury.

In the 1950s, however, protectionist pressures intensified in the United States. With the reconstruction of war-damaged industries in Europe and Japan, American producers began to experience vigorous foreign competition for the first time in decades. Furthermore, a major political shift had occurred in Congress, reminiscent of the shifts in Germany and France during the 1870s. Industrial development had spread to the South, and Southern Congressmen began to retreat from their historic opposition to high tariffs. In 1951, Congress wrote an escape clause into the Trade Agreements Act itself, tightening procedures and listing the criteria that should be employed when judging a complaint of injury from import competition:

> In arriving at a determination... the Tariff Commission, without excluding other factors, shall take into consideration a downward trend of production, employment, prices, profits, or wages in the domestic industry concerned, or a decline in sales, an increase in imports, either actual or relative to domestic production, a higher or growing inventory, or a decline in the proportion of the domestic market supplied by domestic producers.

An increase in imports was to be regarded as a *measure* of injury, not just a cause, and it did not have to be an absolute increase. A company could petition for additional protection if its sales had grown but imports had grown faster.

Congress broadened the escape clause thereafter, making it harder for the president to reject advice from the Tariff Commission. It also passed the National Defense Amendment quoted in Chapter 9. Furthermore, a number of tariffs were raised in response to recommendations by the Tariff Commission. Yet trade policy did not become a front-page issue in the United States until developments in Europe raised its importance and led to new round of liberalization.

The European Initiative: Regionalism and the EEC

Soon after the end of World War II, the United States adopted the Marshall Plan, an unprecedented commitment to the reconstruction of Western Europe. At the same time, the United States urged European governmments to combine their economic and political resources in pursuit of an age-old dream, a united states of Europe. Washington was concerned to strengthen Western Europe against the threat of Soviet aggression and also to bind Germany into a democratic federation so that it could never again wage war against its neighbors.

At first, the Europeans adopted a *sectoral* approach to economic integration. They created the European Coal and Steel Community, freeing trade in coal and steel and creating a supranational agency to regulate pricing polices and commercial practices. Then they changed their tactics and began work on a full-fledged customs union–an arrangement under which they would abolish all barriers to internal trade and adopt a common external tariff. In 1957, six countries (Belgium, France, Germany, Italy, Luxemborg, and the Netherlands) signed the Treaty of Rome, establishing the European Economic Community (EEC), or Common Market, and committing themselves to go much further. They undertook to harmonize domestic policies, lift restrictions on internal movements of labor and capital, and eventually to unify their monetary systems. In other words, they agreed to a blueprint for comprehensive economic integration, not just for a customs union.

For many Europeans, and Washington as well, ultimate political unification was the chief rationale for the EEC. But its members also hoped to reap economic benefits. They expected to intensify internal competition and thus foster more efficient resource use. They expected to capture economics of scale often associated with large markets and thus to strengthen European firms vis-à-vis their large American competitors.

The transition was not painless. There was rapid progress initially, and the customs union was completed in 1968, two years ahead of schedule. But the early history of the EEC was punctuated by disputes and crises. The first crisis occurred in 1963, when France vetoed a British application for membership, and this issue was not resolved until 1973, when Great Britain and two other countries were admitted.[4] The EEC adopted a Common Agricultural Policy (CAP) in 1968, setting uniform prices for farm products and imposing *variables levies* on imports to keep world prices from undercutting higher support prices in the EEC. But this agreement led new disputes about the financing of the CAP and other budgetary matters. The EEC did not start moving rapidly toward its long-term objective until 1986, when its members approved the Single European Act, allowing many important decisions to be made by weighted majority voting, instead of giving each member a veto by

---

[4]At the beginning of 1993, Belgium, Denmark, France, Germany, Greece, Ireland, Italy, Luxembourg, the Netherlands, Portugal, Spain, and the United Kingdom were members, and other countries had applied for membership, including Austria, Finland, and Sweden.

requiring unanimity. That decision paved the way for an ambitious program aimed at unifying European markets for goods, services, capital, and labor by the end of 1992.

The European Economic Community, the Coal and Steel Community, and the European Atomic Energy Authority are known collectively as the European Communities (EC). They are governed by a single Commission whose members are appointed by the member governments, but most of the Commission's decisions must be approved by a Council of Ministers representing the member governments. A European Parliament is elected directly by the voters of the member countries, but its powers are quite limited. In December 1991, the EC countries agreed to a major revision of the Treaty of Rome. It will unite the communities into a single European Community and extend its domain to foreign and defense policies. The agreement also provides for monetary union by 1999. Its monetary aspects are examined in Chapter 20.

The United States encouraged the creation of the EEC but was concerned about the economic impact. Although the common external tariff was not higher than the separate national tariffs of the member countries (it was, in fact, an average of those tariffs), it threatened to divert demand from American exports. Previously, exports from the United States to France paid the same French tariff as exports from Germany or Italy; once the EEC was formed, however, goods from Germany and Italy paid no tariff, whereas goods from the United States had to pay the common external tariff. There was concern about the CAP, too, because it could reduce American exports of farm products.

The United States had two options. It could treat the EEC as a threat and respond by retreating to protection. Alternatively, it could treat the EEC as an opportunity and respond by reviving trade liberalization.

The American Response: The Kennedy Round

In 1961, the Kennedy administration chose trade liberalization and asked Congress for new legislation. A year later, Congress passed the Trade Expansion Act, which gave the president broader tariff-cutting powers. In previous negotiotions, the United States has bargained on a product-by-product basis; henceforth, it could make more sweeping offers. The president could cut *all* U.S. tariff rates in half if the EEC and other countries were willing to make similar across-the-board cuts. Furthermore, the Trade Expansion Act modified the basic "no injury" rule that had limited the process of trade liberalization.

First, it tightened the criteria to be used when deciding whether domestic producers had been injured by import competition. An increase of imports, by itself, would no longer be regarded as a form of injury. The International Trade Commission was authorized to "take account of all economic factors which it considers relevant," but told to pay particular attention to the "idling of productive facilities, inability to operate at a level of reasonable profit, and unemployment or underemployment." Furthermore, petitioners had to show that "increased imports have been the major factor in causing, or threatening to cause, such injury," and that the increase in imports was "in major part" the result of tariff cuts.

Second, it introduced a new way to deal with injury. Instead of raising tariffs, the president could give *trade adjustment assistance* directly to companies and workers. Companies could obtain tax benefits and low-cost loans to diversify or modernize their operations. Workers could receive supplementary unemployment benefits and assistance in finding new jobs. The benefits for workers are listed in Table 10-1 (which also shows how benefits were liberalized by the Trade Act of 1974). We will look at experience with adjustment assistance later in this chapter. The main point to note here is the change in principle. Instead of renouncing the allocative gains from trade by restricting imports, the new law sought to capture them by encouraging new uses of capital and labor. Adjustment assistance can also be viewed as an attempt to compensate those who are hurt by trade liberalization—to redistribute some of the gains from freer trade along lines mentioned in earlier chapters.

New GATT negotiations, known as the Kennedy Round, got under way soon after passage of the Trade Expansion Act, but they were not completed until 1967. They were interrupted by internal crises in the EEC, and their success was in doubt until the very end, because of disputes between Europe and the United States. Disputes about the tariff-cutting process were resolved by agreeing that countries could submit *exceptions lists* showing those tariffs they would not reduce by the full 50 percent adopted as the target for the Kennedy Round, and most of the subsequent bargaining focused on those lists. Disputes about agricultural issues were harder to resolve. The Europeans had just adopted the CAP and were not ready to modify it.

Table 10-1. Benefits to Workers Under the Trade Adjustment Assistance Programs

Item	Trade Act of 1962	Trade Act of 1974
Finding of eligibility Requirement for individual eligibility	International Trade Commission Employment in 78 of prior 156 weeks and with affected firm in 26 of prior 52 weeks	Department of Labor Employment with affected firm in 26 of prior 52 weeks
Cash payments	65% of previous weekly earnings but not more than 70% of average weekly earnings in manufacturing	70% of previous weekly earnings but not more than 100% of average weekly earnings in manufacturing
Benefit period	Up to 52 weeks (65 if worker over age 60)	Up to 52 weeks (78 if worker over age 60)
Other benefits: 　Job training and counseling	No special services but access to all other federal programs	Same
Job search allowance	None	$500 maximum
Relocation payments	Reasonable and necessary expenses plus 2.5 *times* average weekly earnings in manufacturing	80% of reasonable and necessary expenses plus 3.0 *times* worker's own average weekly wage

Source: Adapted from George R. Neumann, "Adjustment Assistance for Trade Displaced Workers," in D. B. H. Denoon, ed., *The New International Economic Order* (New York: New York University Press, 1979).

The United States wanted to maintain its share of Europe's grain market. The two sides agreed to disagree so that the Kennedy Round would not collapse.

In the end, the Kennedy Round was quite successful in reducing tariffs on manufactured products. Two-thirds of the reductions were as large as 50 percent and covered the major industrial countries. Average tariffs on manufactures fell by about 33 percent (because the exceptions lists kept the average cut below 50 percent). But many trade problems had still to be faced, and protectionist pressures were building up again.

Broadening Liberalization: The Tokyo Round

Soon after the Kennedy Round, Congress began to consider bills that would have put import quotas on many products, ranging from textiles to steel. Forty years of trade liberalization were threatened by a new outbreak of congressional initiatives, reminiscent of the 1930 outbreak that led to the Hawley–Smoot Tariff.

The Johnson and Nixon administrations tried at first to mollify the protectionists by negotiating "voluntary" restrictions on Japanese and other exports to the United States. In 1971, however, the Nixon administration adopted a different strategy. In the midst of a monetary crisis described later in this book, it called for a new round of GATT negotiations aimed at ending trade practices "unfair" to the United States, and it promised to pay particular attention to the concerns of American farmers. In the Trade Act of 1974, Congress gave the president more bargaining power and made other changes in trade policy. Workers were given easier access to adjustment assistance. Companies seeking relief from import competition had no longer to show that imports were the major cause of their problems or that increased imports were due to tariff cuts.

A meeting in Tokyo in 1973 agreed to an ambitious agenda for the new GATT round. There were to be more tariff cuts, special efforts to liberalize trade in farm products, an attempt to reduce nontariff barriers and prepare codes of conduct to bar unfair trade practices, and an effort to give "special and differential" treatment to exports from the developing countries. The Tokyo Round lasted until 1979 and covered a large part of its agenda. Some of its failures are examined in the next chapter, which will deal with agricultural trade and the special problems of developing countries. We concentrate here on the reductions in tariffs and in certain nontariff barriers.

The tariff cuts were similar to those of the Kennedy Round. They are summarized in Table 10-2. Cuts were made across the board, using a formula designed in part to meet complaints made by the Europeans at the start of the Kennedy Round; it called for the largest cuts in the highest tariffs. Had the new formula been applied uniformly, it would have cut tariffs by 60 percent, a more ambitious target than that of the Kennedy Round. As in that earlier round, however, each country proposed exceptions, and average tariff rates on manufactured goods fell by only 34 percent, a figure close to the average for the Kennedy Round, even though the Tokyo target cut was bigger.

Attempts have been made to estimate the employment effects of the tariff cuts. One of them is summarized in Table 10-3. Reductions in U.S. tariffs reduce employment in import-competing domestic industries (and in industries that sell them raw

Table 10-2. Average Tariff Rates Before and After the Tokyo Round

Category	All Industrial Countries[a]	United States	European Community	Japan[b]
Raw materials				
Before	0.8	0.9	0.7	1.5
After	0.3	0.2	0.2	0.5
Percentage cut	*64.0*	*77.0*	*69.0*	*67.0*
Semimanufactures				
Before	5.7	4.5	5.8	6.6
After	4.0	3.0	4.2	4.6
Percentage cut	*30.0*	*33.0*	*27.0*	*30.0*
Finished manufactures				
Before	9.8	8.0	9.7	12.5
After	6.5	5.7	6.9	6.0
Percentage cut	*34.0*	*29.0*	*29.0*	*52.0*
All industrial products				
Before	7.1	6.4	6.6	5.5
After	4.7	4.4	4.7	2.8
Percentage cut	*34.0*	*31.0*	*29.0*	*49.0*

Source: International Monetary Fund, *Developments in International Trade Policy* (Washington, D.C.: International Monetary Fund, 1982), Table 49. Averages are weighted by imports.
[a]Austria, Canada, Finland, Japan, Norway, Sweden, Switzerland, the United States, and the EEC.
[b]Tariff rates are those to which Japan agreed in the Kennedy and Tokyo Rounds. Between the two rounds, however, Japan made unilateral tariff cuts, and the actual reductions to which Japan agreed in the Tokyo Round were therefore smaller than those shown here.

Table 10-3. Trade and Employment Effects of Tariff Reductions in the Tokyo Round: Results for the United States When Exchange Rates are Adjusted to Balance Trade Changes

Sectors	Trade (in millions of dollars)			Employment (in thousands of jobs)		
	Exports	Imports	Net	Exports	Imports	Net
All sectors	2,900	2,900	0	147.9	148.2	−0.3
Primary agriculture	47	7	39	6.2	2.9	3.3
Mining	−4	8	−12	1.5	1.7	−0.2
Manufacturing	2,858	2,885	−27	92.6	95.8	−3.2
Services	—	—	—	47.6	47.8	−0.2

Source: U.S. Department of Labor, Bureau of International Labor Affairs, *Trade and Employment Effects of Tariff Reductions Agreed to in the MTN*, 1980, Table C.1. Employment changes in each sector include those induced by tariff cuts on products made by other sectors.

materials, parts, and services). But reductions in other countries' tariffs raise U.S. exports and thus raise employment in domestic export industries. To focus on the compositional effects and the resulting need to reallocate resources, the study assumes that exchange-rate adjustments prevent any change in the overall trade balance, so that the increase in total exports balances the increase in total imports. It then looks at the resulting changes in employment in the major sectors of the U.S. economy.

Because the trade balance does not change in this particular study, the change in

Table 10-4. Employment Effects of Tariff Reductions in the Tokyo Round: Detail for Selected U.S. Industries

Industry	Change in Number of Jobs			Net Change as Percentage of Industry Labor Force
	Exports	Imports	Net	
Office machinery	9,572	2,345	7,227	2.25
Electrical components	11,793	3,393	8,400	1.96
Aircraft and parts	10,158	5,077	5,081	0.94
Electrical machinery	3,552	1,609	1,943	0.43
Paper products	2,566	1,086	1,480	0.31
Chemicals	2,762	1,899	863	0.28
Metalworking machinery	2,920	2,369	551	0.16
Printing and publishing	3,801	2,066	1,735	0.16
Scientific instruments	3,160	2,738	422	0.13
Miscellaneous metal products	2,151	2,664	−513	−0.10
Primary iron and steel	3,514	4,585	−1,071	−0.12
Rubber and miscellaneous plastics	1,781	2,932	−1,151	−0.17
Electrical lights and wiring	2,281	2,863	−582	−0.27
Lumber products	1,378	2,973	−1,595	−0.27
Radio and television equipment	3,771	5,745	−1,978	−0.33
Apparel	698	8,737	−8,039	−0.56
Fabrics, yarn, and thread	1,777	5,303	−3,526	−0.60
Stone and clay products	791	5,234	−4,452	−0.90
Miscellaneous manufacturing	2,010	10,230	−8,220	−1.84

Source: U.S. Department of Labor, Bureau of International Labor Affairs, *Trade and Employment Effects of Tariff Reductions Agreed to in the MTN*, 1980, Tables C.2 and C.3 Industries listed are those in which the change due to exports or imports exceed 2,500 jobs; employment changes in each industry include those induced by tariff cuts on products made by other industries.

total exployment is tiny, a loss of 300 jobs. But the study predicts large shifts in employment within and between sectors. Cuts in other countries' tariffs on farm products create an additional 3,300 jobs in American agriculture, but the number of jobs in manufacturing falls. What happens within manufacturing? Answers are given in Table 10-4. Large numbers of jobs are created in some industries, such as those producing office equipment and aircraft, but there are job losses in other industries, including those producing textiles and apparel. Few gains and losses, however, are larger than 1 percent of the total labor force in the affected industry.

In Chapter 9, we saw that tariffs are more transparent than other trade barriers, yet decisions made at dockside about classification and valuation can greatly affect the duties that importers must pay. Uncertainty about valuation can inhibit trade by more than the level of the tariff rate itself. One of the GATT codes of conduct deals with this problem. It calls for the use of prices "actually paid or payable" when valuing goods for tariff purposes.

Chapter 9 called attention to another problem. Governments discriminate against foreign firms when buying goods and services for themselves. In the United States, for example, a foreign firm can win a federal contract only when the lowest bid by a domestic firm exceeds by some percentage the lowest bid by a foreign firm. For military procurement, the allowable cost margin can be as large as 50 percent. In many other countries, government contracts are awarded without bidding, and even when there is competitive bidding, cost margins are not fixed.

During the Tokyo Round, American negotiators pressed for a code of conduct on government procurement, because governments buy large quantities of goods in which the United States has a comparative advantage, such as transport and telecommunications equipment. After hard bargaining, a code was drafted. In countries whose governments adopt the code, specified lists of government agencies must employ competitive bidding and cannot discriminate against firms from countries whose governments apply the code on a comparable basis. But the code does not cover military procurement or purchases by state and local governments, and some governments do not apply the code to state-owned entities, such as telephone and electricity companies, airlines, and railroads. Nevertheless, the code makes a start.

THE RETREAT FROM TRADE LIBERALIZATION

By launching the Tokyo Round and promising to win "fair" treatment for American producers, the Nixon administration kept Congress from imposing import quotas. During and after the Tokyo Round, however, there was a worldwide retreat from liberal trade policies. Responding to complaints of injury from imports and charges of unfair practices by foreigners, governments imposed import quotas, persuaded other countries to accept "voluntary" export restraints, and subsidized domestic industries. They promised repeatedly to refrain from these practices but broke their promises with increasing frequency. By 1981, Japanese exports of automobiles had been restricted or restrained by countries that then accounted for two-thirds of those exports, including the United States. In 1982, the United States put quotas on imports of steel from Europe, and the EEC extended or tightened its restrictions on steel imports from Japan, Brazil, Korea, and many other countries. In addition, most of the developed countries maintained or imposed import quotas on textiles and apparel from developing countries. Why did protectionist pressures mount so sharply? Why did governments respond by imposing quotas instead of raising tariffs?

Import Competition and Protectionist Pressures

The pressures testify in part to the poor performance of the world economy in the 1970s and the early 1980s. Growth rates of gross domestic product fell sharply in the major industrial countries, and unemployment rose steeply, especially in Europe. When economies grow slowly, adjustments are difficult. Those who lose their jobs or markets because of changes in demand, technology, or comparative advantage have trouble finding new ones. Therefore, they seek to protect themselves from dislocation, and they find it easier to mobilize political support for actions aimed at import competition than to take steps to remedy the other causes of their plight. Furthermore, firms compete aggressively for foreign markets when domestic markets shrink or stagnate, which makes it even easier for their foreign competitors to mobilize support for trade restrictions.

The new protectionism also testifies to the success of previous trade liberalization. Economies have become more open and more sensitive to global competition. Old industries, in particular, have been exposed to intense competition from new producers and new products. The three cases mentioned above—textiles, steel, and automobiles—provide illustrations.

Textiles and Apparel

The makers of clothing and other textile products tend to be small firms and to use large amounts of unskilled labor. Therefore, textile production has migrated gradually from high-wage to low-wage regions. This happened within the United States several decades ago, when the textile industry moved from New England to the South, and it has also happened internationally. Production grew rapidly in Japan after World War II, when Japan was a low-wage country; it then moved to developing countries, ranging from India and Hong Kong to Mexico and Brazil.

In 1957, the United States sought to limit textile imports by persuading Japan to impose voluntary export restraints. But imports from other countries, expecially Hong Kong, began to replace imports from Japan, and the United States called for an international agreement on trade in cotton textiles. A short-term agreement was concluded in 1961, put on a long-term basis in 1962, and replaced in 1974 by a comprehensive scheme covering all textiles and known as the Multifibre Agreement (MFA). Its stated objective is

> to ensure the expansion of trade in textile products, particularly for the developing countries, and progressively to achieve the reduction of trade barriers and the liberalization of world trade in textile products while, at the same time, avoiding disruptive effects on individual markets and on individual lines of production in both importing and exporting countries.

In fact, the MFA serves as an "umbrella" under which importing countries negotiate bilateral agreements with exporting countries to limit trade in textiles and apparel on a country-by-country, product-by-product basis. The United States and EC have agreements of this type with more than twenty developing countries.

The MFA has not stopped trade from growing or kept the developing countries from raising their share of world exports; their share of world textile exports rose from 17 percent in 1973 to 28 percent in 1988, and their share of clothing exports rose from 30 percent to 45 percent. But it has slowed the growth of trade, and developing countries have objected strongly to the way it is interpreted. They charge that the developed countries have failed to meet the long-term objective of liberalizing trade in textiles and that the MFA violates the spirit of the GATT because it is discriminatory. They have sought to phase it out completely in the Uruguay Round of trade negotiations, discussed in the next chapter. They will still face high tariffs, however, and some importing countries may erect new trade barriers to replace the MFA. The industry is too important to many industrial countries. It is, in fact, the largest industrial employer in the world and still accounts for more than 10 per cent of total industrial employment in the developed countries.

The MFA establisued an important precedent. In the Trade Act of 1974, Congress authorized the use of *orderly marketing agreements*, modeled on the bilateral agreements negotiated under the MFA, to deal with injury from import competition. Such agreements have been used in one form or another to protect a number of important industries, including the steel industry.

Steel

The problems of the American steel industry go back many years, just like those of the textile industry, and they likewise reflect in part the migration of the industry to developing countries such as Brazil and Korea. But they also reflect slow growth in the demand for steel and the slow pace at which the industry has adapted to technological change. The slow growth in demand was due partly to the problems of the major steel-using industries, including the automobile industry, and partly to the use of lighter metals and plastics in place of steel. The American industry retired many of its old mills, reducing excess capacity, but it was reluctant to build new ones using new technologies. Therefore, productivity grew less rapidly in the United States than in the newer steel-producing countries. The European industry has had similar problems.

The American industry began to seek protection in the 1960s and was increasingly successful. In 1968, Japan and seversl European countries were persuaded to impose "voluntary" export restraints (VERs) on basic carbon steel. In 1976, Japan accepted an orderly market agreement on stainless and other specialty steels. Nevertheless, the industry sought additional relief, saying that foreign producers were dumping steel in the American market—selling it below its normal market price. The Carter administration responded by devising a mechanism to put a floor beneath the prices of imported steel products and succeeded temporarily in holding down the volume of imports.

In the early 1980s, however, a worldwide recession cut production deeply in most steel-producing countries, and mills were working far below capacity. And the end of the recession did not solve the problems of American producers. For reasons examined in later chapters, the dollar began to *appreciate* hugely, which reduced the dollar prices of foreign steel products relative to those of domestic products, and stimulated imports. The American industry petitioned for relief under the escape clause and filed numerous complaints against dumping by foreign producers and subsidies by foreign governments. Some of these complaints were dismissed, but others were found to be valid, and the United States threatened to impose *antidumping duties* to offset abnormally low foreign prices and *countervailing duties* to offset foreign subsidies. Rather than confront these higher tariffs, the EC agreed in 1982 to limit exports of steel products to the United States and thus reduce Europe's share of the American market. Quotas were imposed on other steel products in 1983, when the ITC found that the industry was being injured, and the Reagan administration adopted a "comprehensive" approach when the ITC made another such finding in 1984.

The president rejected the specific recommendations of the ITC and announced, instead, a program to deal with "unfair" competition. It aimed at limiting imports to 18.5 percent of the American market. Countries whose exports to the United States had "surged" in previous years were invited to sign bilateral agreements with the United States, limiting their shares of the American market in exchange for promises by U.S. firms that they would cease to file complaints of unfair competition. Agreements were signed with many countries, including Japan, Korea, Brazil, and Mexico, and the United States extended and broadened its 1982 agreement with the European Community.

These agreements were allowed to lapse at the end of the decade and were followed by negotiations to deal with dumping and subsidies. When those talks broke down, however, American firms began to file numerous complaints of unfair competition. At the end of 1992, the United States started to impose countervailing and antidumping duties on imported steel.

Automobiles

The automotive industry offers another illustration of the tendency to limit imports when domestic firms have been slow to adjust to changing circumstances. In 1980, the United Auto Workers and Ford Motor Company petitioned the ITC to recommend relief from import competition. The ITC turned them down, ruling that the problems of the industry were due to the shift in demand to small, fuel-efficient cars induced by higher gasoline prices, a shift which the industry had failed to anticipate. But the industry would not take no for an answer. It appealed to the Carter administration, which authorized payments to workers under the Trade Adjustment Assistance program but refused to limit imports, despite the introduction of bills in Congress that would have put quotas on Japanese cars.

In the face of mounting congressional pressure, however, the Reagan administration began talks with Japan, which led to an agreement in 1981. Japan would limit its exports to 1.68 million cars per year, a number 8 percent below its actual exports to the United States in 1981. The agreement was renewed annually until 1985. When it expired, moreover, Japan announced that it would continue to limit its automobile exports, hoping to discourage restrictive legislation. This self-imposed limit has lost most of its importance, however, because the large Japanese manufacturers, Honda, Nissan, and Toyota, have opened plants in the United States, and their sales from these plants are now larger than their shipments from Japan. But the growth of "transplanted" production has led to new disputes. Japanese plants in the United States depend heavily on parts and components made in Japan (or made in the United States but by other "transplanted" Japanese firms). Therefore, American producers of automotive parts have lobbied for legislation or agreements with Japan to require that the Japanese automobile industry buy more parts from American suppliers. Transplanted production also threatens to cause a trade dispute between the United States and the European Community. The EC has reached an agreement with Japan limiting sales of Japanese cars in the European market. Under that agreement, Japanese cars made in Europe will be treated as Japanese, not European, and will thus be limited. The EC has also indicated, however, that Japanese cars made in the United States will be treated as Japanese, which means that they will be limited, too. The United States insists that these cars should be treated as American and thus excluded from the limit.

The migration of the Japanese automobile industry to the United States was the most dramatic consequence of the 1981 agreement limiting Japanese exports to the United States. The migration might have taken place eventually, without the agreement, as the growing American demand for Japanese cars made it possible for Japanese firms to build American plants large enough to capture economies of scale. But the process was surely accelerated by the 1981 agreement.

Another more subtle effect took place very quickly. Japanese firms redesigned their cars. Because the limit on exports to the United States was defined in terms of vehicles, not values, the Japanese firms began to export larger cars on which they could earn bigger profits, and to include as standard features many that used to be optional. One study calculates that these changes raised the prices of Japanese cars by an average of $1,000 per car.[5] These should not be viewed as welfare-improving quality improvements; they limited consumers' choices and forced them to buy options they did not really want.

Trade Theory and Trade Politics

The automobile case has another interesting feature. It appears to contradict conventional trade theory. In 1980, the union and the second-largest company took the same side of the trade question, asking for relief from import competition. Most trade models, by contrast, predict that labor and capital will take opposite sides.

In the two-factor, two-sector Heckscher–Ohlin model, trade policies that benefit one factor of production are bound to hurt the other. When a country imports capital-intensive goods, an increase in tariffs raises the real return to capital

---

[5]Charles Collyas and Steven Dunaway, "The Cost of Trade Restraints: The Case of Japanese Automobile Exports to the United States, *International Monetary Fund Staff Papers*, 34 (March 1987), Table 10. This sort of quality upgrading has been observed in other cases, too; see Randi Boorstein and Robert C. Feenstra, "Quality Upgrading and Its Welfare Cost in U.S. Steel Imports, 1969–74," in E. Helpman and A. Razin, eds., *International Trade and Trade Policy* (Cambridge, Mass.: MIT Press, 1991).

throughout the economy and reduces the real wage. Therefore, owners of capital should favor protection, regardless of the industry in which they have invested, and workers should oppose protection, regardless of the industry in which they are employed.

In the modified Ricardian model, trade policies benefit some specific factors, injure others, and have mixed effects on labor, the mobile factor. An increase in tariffs raises the real return to capital invested in the import-competing industry and reduces its real return in the export industry. The effect on labor depends in part on workers' tastes, because a tariff raises the real wage in terms of the export product but lowers it in terms of the import-competing product.

In the world described by the Heckscher–Ohlin model, unions and companies should disagree decisively about protection. In the world described by the modified Ricardian model, two outcomes are possible: (1) If workers consume large quantities of import-competing goods, they will be hurt by higher tariffs, and unions should oppose protection, together with companies in the export sector. They should thus disagree with companies in the import-competing sector. (2) If workers consume large quantities of export goods, they will benefit from higher tariffs, and unions should favor protection, together with companies in the import-competing sector. They should disagree with companies in the export sector. In both instances, however, unions should agree among themselves; they should not divide along industry lines.

As a matter of fact, unions and companies agree far more frequently than they disagree. Here are the results of a study by based on congressional hearings:[6]

Industry in which unions and companies		
Agreed about trade policy		19
Favored protection	14	
Opposed protection	5	
Industries in which unions and companies		
disagreed about trade policy		2

The evidence is thus inconsistent with the forecast made by the Heckscher–Ohlin model; unions and companies agreed overwhelmingly. But the evidence is likewise inconsistent with the forecast made by the modified Ricardian model, because the unions were not unanimous. They tended to divide along industry lines:

Unions favoring protection		16
In import-competing industries	11	
In export industries	5	
Unions opposing protection		5
In import-competing industries	1	
In export industries	4	

[6]Stephen P. Magee, "Three Simple Tests of the Stolper–Samuelson Theorem," in P. Oppenheimer, ed., *Issues in International Economics* (London: Oriel, 1978), Tables 3 and 5.

The evidence may favor a version of the modified Ricardian model discussed briefly in Chapter 9, in which *all* factors of production, including labor, are somewhat immobile (specific). In such a model, an increase in tariffs raises the real incomes of labor and capital employed in import-competing industries and reduces the real incomes of labor and capital employed in export industries.[7]

Trade Politics and Trade Adjustment Assistance

There are two sets of obstacles to labor mobility. First, there are obstacles to *occupational mobility*. Jobs are not alike, and workers cannot move from job to job without learning new skills. Second, there are obstacles to *geographic mobility*. Table 10-4 said that the Tokyo Round was expected to create 5,000 jobs in the aircraft industry and eliminate 4,000 jobs in the apparel industry. But much of the aircraft industry is on the West Coast, and much of the apparel industry is on the East Coast. Workers cannot always move from job to job, even when they have the necessary skills, without moving from place to place, and moving is expensive in both monetary and nonmonetary terms. Furthermore, workers who change jobs may lose many benefits, including the seniority that is often crucial for future job security. Most workers want to stay put, with the same firm in the same place.

Trade adjustment assistance was introduced in 1962 to compensate workers for some of these costs and to raise labor mobility itself. It was meant to win support from labor unions for the Trade Expansion Act and the forthcoming Kennedy Round. The benefits to labor were summarized in Table 10-1. Eligible workers received extended unemployment-compensation payments, job-search and relocation payments, and access to existing job-training programs. But the program did not work as well as its advocates had promised, and it was not successful politically. One labor leader called it "burial insurance," and the American labor movement became more strongly protectionist in the 1970s.

The program had two defects. First, it was hard for workers to qualify for benefits. Second, the program helped to maintain workers' incomes when they lost their jobs but was not very effective in promoting adjustment.

Under the program introduced in 1962, workers and companies had to prove to the ITC that they had been injured by import competition resulting from earlier tariff cuts; they had to satisfy the tight criteria introduced by the Trade Expansion Act. These criteria made good economic sense, but they had an unintended consequence. Few workers and firms could meet them completely. Hence, trade adjustment assistance was not given a fair test and could not accumulate political support. From 1962, when it was introduced, through 1974, when it was liberalized, the ITC certified fewer than 54,000 workers and a very small number of firms.

The first defect was corrected by the Trade Act of 1974, which put the Labor Department in charge of the program for workers and made access easier. More than 1.3 million workers were certified for benefits in the next few years, and outlays rose

---

[7]There is another possibility, that unions enjoy some monopoly power and can therefore expect to capture for their members part of the increase in their employers' profits conferred by a tightening of import restrictions.

hugely. But much of the increase in numbers and dollars represented aid to workers in a single industry. Although the auto workers failed to persuade the ITC that they had been injured by import competition, they were able to qualify for adjustment assistance under the program run by the Labor Department.

Studies of the program tend to confirm the assertion that adjustment assistance was more helpful in compensating workers for the costs of unemployment than in finding them new jobs. One such study interviewed workers who received trade adjustment assistance (TAA) and compared their histories with those of workers who received ordinary unemployment insurance benefits (UI).[8] If found that TAA workers were unemployed for longer periods than were UI workers and that they were more likely to leave the labor force. They were less likely to change occupations or industries when they did find new jobs, and they were more likely to suffer pay cuts. Finally, TAA recipients received less training than did UI recipients; only one in 30 took job training, and only one in 200 received a job-search allowance.

Recipients made more use of these services in the early 1980s, but fewer workers found new jobs after they completed training. The number of workers certified for benefits also fell in the 1980s, when the Reagan administration tightened the standards for workers. It also reduced the level of benefits in its effort to curtail domestic programs; workers could not qualify for trade adjustment assistance until they had exhausted their unemployment benefits.

The Clinton administration has emphasized the need for improving the skills of the labor force and raising labor mobility. It is likely to revive trade adjustment assistance in one form or another. To succeed in economic and political terms, however, the new program will have to pay close attention to the particular problems and characteristics of workers displaced by trade liberalization and import competition.

The Costs of Protection

An effective approach to adjustment assistance is badly needed, because the costs of protection are quite high, viewed from the consumers' standpoint. Table 10-5 draws on a compilation of studies that estimate the total cost to the consumer and the cost per job saved in the domestic industry. The costs reflect the higher prices paid for domestic goods, as well as for imports, because trade barriers permit domestic producers to raise their prices on goods that compete with imports. The figure for automobiles, $105 thousand per job saved, is lower than other estimates for the auto industry, because methodologies differ from study to study. It is also lower than several other figures in the table, most notably those for steel products. But most of the numbers, including those for automobiles, are much higher than the annual incomes of the workers whose jobs were protected.

It should be noted, moreover, that the sorts of trade barriers imposed on textiles, steel, and automobiles are particularly expensive. When we studied the welfare effects of tariffs and quotas in Chapter 9, we saw that the tariff revenues collected by the

---

[8]J. David Richardson, "Trade Adjustment Assistance Under the United States Trade Act of 1974: An Analytical Examination and Worker Survey," in J. N. Bhagwati, ed., *Import Competition and Response* (Chicago: University of Chicago Press, 1982).

Table 10-5. Cost to the American Consumer of Special Protection, Selected Product Groups

Industry	Starting Year	Annual Cost to Consumers	
		Total (in millions)	Per Job Saved (in thousands)
Specialty steel	1976	520	1,000
Nonrubber footwear	1977	700	55
Color TV sets	1977	420	42
Bolts, nuts, and large screws	1979	110	550
Automobiles	1981	5,800	105
Textiles and apparel	1982	27,000	42
Carbon steel	1982	6,800	750
Motorcycles	1983	104	150

Source: Adapted from Gary C. Hufbauer, Diane T. Berliner, and Kimberly A. Elliott, *Trade Protection in the United States: 31 Case Studies* (Washington, D.C.: Institute for International Economics, 1986), Tables 1.1 and 1.2.

government and the quota profits collected by the importers offset in part the losses suffered by consumers. The welfare cost was the loss of consumer surplus *less* the gain in producer surplus *less* the tariff revenue or quota profit. When a quota is administered by the exporting country, however, the quota profits typically accrue to the foreign producers. Hence, the welfare loss to the importing country is much higher.

THE CHANGING NATURE OF PROTECTION

The developments described in the previous section call attention to two trends—the growing use of nontariff barriers to protect domestic industries and the frequency with which dumping by foreign firms and subsidies by foreign governments have been used to justify protection.

The Use of Nontariff Barriers

The United States has not been alone in using nontariff barriers to protect domestic industries. These barriers have been used extensively by the EC and Japan, and they have been applied to a wide variety of products—not only to textiles, steel, and automobiles, but to television sets, other electronic products, and many agricultural commodities. Table 10-6 shows how broadly nontariff barriers are used and how heavily they apply to the exports of developing countries. Table 10-7 focuses more narrowly on the number of export-restraining arrangements. It tells a story similar to that of Table 10-6, even though it excludes the large number of MFA arrangements. It also shows that these export-restraining arrangements are being

Table 10-6 Imports of Major Industrial Countries Covered by Non-tariff Barriers in 1990, Selected Product Groups

Product Group	Percentages of Imports from		
	Developed Countries	Developing Countries	Eastern Europe and USSR
Food	41.8	28.7	56.7
Iron and steel	56.8	40.6	67.1
Fuels	23.8	12.6	43.8
Textiles	17.0	61.6	69.3
Clothing	27.6	71.6	75.1
Vehicles	58.6	0.7	11.1
All imports	17.1	19.9	30.4

Source: International Monetary Fund, *Issues and Developments in International Trade Policy* (Washington, D.C.: International Monetary Fund, 1992), Table A7; uses "broad" group of nontariff barriers and covers Australia, Austria, Canada, the EC, Finland, Japan, New Zealand, Norway, Sweden, Switzerland, and the United States.
[a]Includes products not listed above.

Table 10-7 Export-Restraining Arrangements, 1987 and 1989

Category	1987	1989
Total number in effect	135	289
Classified by protected market		
United States	48	69
European Community[a]	69	173
Japan	6	13
All other countries	12	34
Classified by restrained exporter		
Japan	25	70
Other industrial countries	23	57
Developing countries	66	121
Eastern Europe	20	41

Source: International Monetary Fund, *Issues and Developments in International Trade Policy* (Washington, D.C.: International Monetary Fund, 1992), Table A8; excludes MFA arrangements.
[a]Includes arrangements initiated by individual EC countries (which rose from 20 in 1987 to 96 in 1989).

used more frequently. There are three reasons for concern about the growing use of nontariff barriers.

First, such barriers are more rigid than tariffs, because they do not allow changes in relative costs to influence trade patterns. If an exporter's costs of production fall, the volume of its exports cannot rise, nor can it capture part of the ongoing growth of demand in the importing country unless the restrictions on exports are cast in terms of market share.

Second, they tend to be discriminatory, because they are usually imposed on a country-by-country basis. The United States and the EC do not restrict each other's exports of textiles and apparel, but both of them restrict imports from developing countries. This selectivity, incidentally, helps to explain why quotas tend to spread; countries that are not covered initially expand their exports at the expense of those that are covered, until quotas are applied to them, too. That is how the MFA began.

Third, nontariff barriers are often applied outside the GATT framework, and they limit or nullify the effects of previous tariff cuts, just as they did in the 1930s, when they were used to nullify the effects of tariff cuts under the Trade Agreements Program. As their use is not supervised by the GATT, they are not made to comply with international guidelines. Furthermore, they undermine the authority of the GATT as the watchdog of the trading system.

Dumping and Subsidies

We have little reason to believe that dumping by foreign firms and subsidies by foreign governments have become more common. Yet antidumping and counter-vailing duties are being used with greater frequency. In the case of the United States, the number of antidumping and countervailing actions rose from 131 in 1981 to a record high of 289 in 1989, before falling slightly in 1990 and 1991.

When an American firm asks for action against dumping or subsidies, the U.S. government must undertake an investigation. The Commerce Department must look into the facts, and the ITC must then determine the extent of injury to domestic firms. If there is adequate evidence of dumping or the use of subsidies and domestic firms are being injured, additional tariffs must be imposed.

A prohibition against dumping–selling below normal market price–was included in the GATT because dumping is often viewed as a *predatory* practice. By selling at low prices, even taking losses, a strong firm can drive weaker rivals out of business and increase its market power. Consumers enjoy low prices in the short run, but they may lose in the long run, when the predatory firm exploits its market power. Like many other unfair practices, however, predatory dumping is hard to identify. Firms may charge low export prices for many benign reasons, not to drive competitors out of business. Two tests of dumping are employed by U.S. law and the GATT anti-dumping code:

> For the purpose of this Code a product is to be considered as being dumped, i.e., introduced into the commerce of another country at less than its normal value, if the export price of the product... is less than the comparable price, in the ordinary course of trade, for the like product when destined for consumption in the exporting country....

> When there are no sales of the like product in the ordinary course of trade in the domestic market of the exporting country or when, because of the particular market situation, such sales do not permit a proper comparison, the margin of dumping shall be determined by a comparison with... the cost of production in the country of origin plus a reasonable amount for administrative, selling and any other costs and for profits.

The flaws in the two tests are easy to illustrate by cases in which exporters would violate then without any predatory purpose.

Consider a firm that sells its product in two markets and tries to maximize its long-run profits. Suppose that it has constant costs of production but faces a downward-sloping demand curve in each market. Its situation is described by Figure 10-2. The firm's marginal-cost curve is MC. The demand curve in its home market is AR_h, and the corresponding marginal-revenue curve is MR_h. The demand curve in its export market is AR_f, and the marginal-revenue curve is MR_f. The firm will maximize its total profits when its sales in each market equate the marginal revenue from that market with the firm's (constant) marginal cost. Therefore, it will sell OQ_h

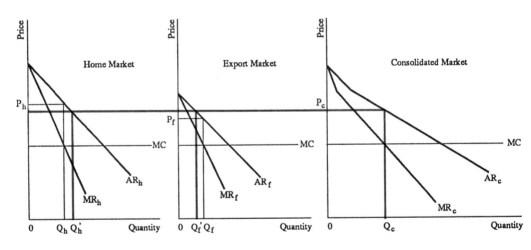

FIGURE 10-2
Dumping by a Firm with Monopoly Power
A firm has constant costs of production, so its marginal-cost curve is MC in each panel of the diagram. The firm has monopoly power in each market and will therefore maximize profits when its sales in that market equate marginal revenue with marginal cost. The panel on the left represents the firm's home market; the demand curve is AR_h, the marginal-revenue curve is MR_h, and the firm will sell OQ_h at the price OP_h. The panel in the center represents the firm's export market; the demand curve is AR_f, the marginal-revenue curve is MR_f, and the firm will sell OQ_f at the price OP_f. As OP_f is lower than OP_h, the firm will be accused of dumping, even though it is not exporting at a loss to undercut foreign competitors. If forced to charge the same price in both markets, it will operate in the manner described by the panel on the right. The curve AR_c is the (horizontal) sum of the home and foreign demand curves, and MR_c is the corresponding marginal-revenue curve. The firm will sell OQ_c and charge OP_c. (It will sell OQ_h' in the home market and OQ_f' in the export market.) The price OP_c is below the profit-maximizing home price OP_h but above the profit-maximizing export price OP_f.

in the home market by setting its domestic price at OP_h, and it will sell OQ_f in the export market by setting its export price at OP_f. The firm is not a predator. The prices OP_h and OP_f are long-run profit-maximizing prices. Nevertheless, the firm is violating the first test in the GATT code, because its export price is lower than the price it charges normally in its home market.[9]

What would the firm do if it could not "dump" its product? It would add up its foreign and domestic demand curves to obtain the consolidated demand curve AR_c and the corresponding marginal-revenue curve MR_c. It would then sell OQ_c and charge the price OP_c. Note that OP_c is higher than OP_f and lower than OP_h. In this instance, the rule against dumping has the odd effect of hurting the firm's foreign customers but helping its domestic customers.

The cost-of-production test has a different defect. It penalizes firms that follow the right short-run pricing rule when demand is depressed temporarily. Consider a firm that has high fixed costs of production typical of steel firms and those in other capital-intensive industries. When demand is depressed by a recession or events in the firm's own industry, the firm may be unable to cover its full costs. It should not shut down, however, if it can cover its *variable* costs and have anything left over to meet some of its fixed costs. If it were to shut down completely, it would still have to cover all its fixed costs (by borrowing or drawing down cash balances). If it goes on operating, even at low prices, and can cover some of its fixed costs, it will minimize its losses. Nevertheless, it can be charged with dumping because its export prices will be lower than its total unit costs.

To make matters worse, the cost-of-production rule is frequently interpreted unfairly. Foreign firms are assumed to have higher fixed costs and profit margins than domestic firms. Hence, the cost-of-production rule overstates the normal price in the foreign firms' domestic market and makes it more likely that they will be charged with dumping. The rule against dumping has thus become a popular route for domestic firms to obtain protection against import competition.

A prohibition against export subsidies was written into the original GATT, for the reason given in Chapter 9. When a government cuts its tariffs, it is entitled to expect that other governments will not nullify the tariffs that remain, and that is what an export subsidy can do. If the United States has a 10 percent tariff on imported steel, but Brazil gives a 10 percent export subsidy to its steel industry, Brazilian steel will enter the United States at its free-trade price, and the American steel industry will not be protected. Widespread use of export subsidies can undermine the framework for trade liberalization established by the GATT and thus lead to tariff warfare.

Yet, many countries subsidize their exports indirectly. Examples listed in Chapter 9 included low interest rates on export credits, preferential tax treatment for profits from exports, and output subsidies to export industries (typically in the form of wage subsidies and investment incentives). These practices were not prohibited by the

---

[9]A firm cannot charge different prices in two markets unless there are barriers to trade between them. If goods could be shipped freely from one to the other, someone would buy the firm's products in its export market and ship them back for sale in the firm's home market. There are, of course, such barriers, including transport costs and tariffs. (In this instance, tariffs protect the firm against itself by sheltering its home market from the firm's own goods.)

GATT, and they have spread widely. Furthermore, most governments use subsidies to achieve domestic goals—to aid depressed communities or regions, encourage adaptation or modernization in declining industries, retrain unemployed workers, reduce environmental hazards, and encourage research and development. The European subsidies that prompted complaints by the American steel industry were part of a "crisis" plan adopted by the EC to modernize the European steel industry. They were not outright export subsidies.

The Tokyo Round adopted a new code on export subsidies. It broadens the GATT prohibition on export subsidies and tries to deal with domestic subsidies that have similar effects. Such subsidies, it says, may injure an industry in other countries or nullify GATT benefits accruing to them. Governments are not barred from using them but must try to avoid adverse effects on other countries. When other countries' industries are injured by subsidies, their governments can still impose countervailing duties, even when the subsidies are not export subsidies narrowly defined.

Two sorts of export subsidies are still permitted, but they have become increasingly controversial. First governments may subsidize their exports of farm products unless these give their exports "more than an equitable share of world trade" in those products. The interpretation of this phrase gave rise to the bitter dispute between the United States and the EC discussed in the next chapter. Second, a developing country may subsidize its manufactured exports but must reduce or eliminate its subsidies when they have become "inconsistent with its competitive development needs." The United States claims that some developing countries have ignored this requirement. It has imposed countervailing duties on exports from Argentina, Brazil, Mexico, and other developing countries, saying that they have outgrown the need to use export subsidies.

Measures to Open Foreign Markets

As more and more American industries experienced import competition in the 1970s and early 1980s, the domestic political coalition supporting trade liberalization began to collapse. Three steps were taken to build a new coalition by attracting support from industries seeking to increase their exports. First, the United States undertook to negotiate trade-policy rules for services analogous to the GATT rules for goods and then to liberalize trade in services by bargaining down barriers. Second, Congress insisted that future trade negotiations redeem the promise made repeatedly to liberalize agricultural trade. Third, Congress adopted measures aimed at opening foreign markets to U.S. exports and investments. The results of the first two steps will be examined in the next chapter, when we study the Uruguay Round of trade negotiations. We take up the third step here, because it represents a controversial departure from the traditional practice of trade policy.

Unlike import-competing industries, exporters are not usually given ways to petition for industry-specific relief from injury or from "unfair" foreign practices. As tariff levels have fallen, however, exporters have become increasing aware of governmental and business practices that limit their access to foreign markets and have sought ways to eliminate them.

Congress responded to exporters' concerns in the 1974 Trade Act. It adopted Section 301, which gave the president the power to retaliate against foreign countries that limit U.S. exports by nontariff barriers and restrictive business practices. In effect, it encouraged the president to act unilaterally rather than use GATT rules and procedures for settling trade disputes. Proponents of Section 301 viewed the threat of retaliation as the great trade-policy can opener, which the president could use to pry open foreign markets. Critics viewed it as a grave threat to the rule of international law in matters of trade policy. The United States would play the part of the dog, Fury, in the tale of the mouse in *Alice in Wonderland*. "I'll be judge. I'll be jury, said cunning old Fury; I'll try the whole cause, and condemn you to death."

But nothing happened—not right away. More than 100 complaints were filed under Section 301, but the president took retaliatory measures in fewer than 10 percent of them. Others were dismissed or handled informally by agreements with the foreign governments concerned—agreements that were not always satisfactory to U.S. exporters and were not always honored fully. Accordingly, Congress adopted a tougher approach in the 1988 Trade Act. It tightened Section 301 and adopted a new provision, commonly known as Super 301, which *required* the president to identify unfair foreign practices, not wait for U.S. firms to make complaints, and to take retaliatory measures in the absence of an adequate response by the foreign government. Most importantly, Super 301 introduced a "results-oriented" standard for judging the implementation of a foreign government's promise to end an unfair practice. Success would be judged by the size of the increase in U.S. exports, not by the actions of the foreign government.

Very few cases were pursued decisively under Super 301, and it was allowed to lapse in 1990. The principles embodied in it, however, including the "results-oriented" standard, enjoy strong support in Congress and even among some economists, who see it as the only effective way to deal with certain trade-policy problems facing the United States, especially the need to open Japanese markets.

Trade disputes with Japan have played a prominent role in shaping U.S. trade policy, partly because Japan has run large trade surpluses and partly because it is seen to be "different" from other market economies.

In the 1950s and 1960s, foreign attention focused on Japanese industrial policy. The Ministry of International Trade and Industry (MITI) was accused of *targeting* new products for Japan to export and then helping Japanese companies to make them. No one would deny that MITI tried to guide industrial development and that it paid particular attention to the use of new technologies. But MITI made some big mistakes, and its influence is probably exaggerated. Furthermore, some of its efforts were designed to compensate for defects in the Japanese economy:[10]

> Most Japanese high-technology companies obtain their financing from
> banks and government finance agencies, which tend to be very conservative,
> rather than from the equity markets. In the United States..., venture

---

[10]Congressional Budget Office, *The GATT Negotiations and U.S. Trade Policy* (Washington, D.C.: 1987), pp. 53–55.

capitalists compete with each other to turn [new] technology into new products, signaling to the rest of the economy that this is an area of potential rewards. MITI plays an equivalent role in Japan, signaling to bankers and corporations through its "visions," as its plans are called, that it favors certain investments....

The cooperative R&D projects sponsored by MITI... are similarly misperceived, according to this view. The Japanese educational system, combined with lifetime employment guarantees, produces researchers who are not as well-rounded in their technical background as U.S. personnel.... [The] movement of personnel among firms, and the informal exchanges that are typical among employees in U.S. high-technology firms, do not occur in Japan. Technological cross-pollinization has been central to U.S. advance. In order to imitate it, MITI has encouraged firms to participate in cooperative research....

Government subsidies to Japanese industry, either through credit or the tax system, have been relatively small. In both Europe and the United States, subsidy programs are much larger. Moreover, the larger Japanese subsidies go to declining industries....

The principal function of Japanese targeting has been to prevent foreign access to a [local] market until the domestic industry has reached the point at which it no longer needed this level of protection. Even here, however, the role of the government should not be overstated.

In the 1970s and 1980s, however, attention turned to the policies and practices that limit access to Japan's own markets. Some of them probably reflect cultural and institutional differences between Japan and other industrial societies that baffle foreigners trying to do business in Japan. Others reflect official and business practices that discriminate against imports. The government and trade associations apply quality and safety standards that foreigners find unneccessarily rigid, and goods that are tested abroad must be tested again in Japan. Some of the standards are silly and obviously designed to handicap foreigners. It was said, for example, that Japanese snow is "different" and requires the use of Japanese skis! And Japanese baseball players had to use Japanese bats! But other rules and practices have more serious consequences. The Japanese government has been slow to apply and extend the GATT code on government procurement, and Japanese firms frequently favor local suppliers, particularly those that belong to their own *keiretsu*–the families of closely affiliated companies that organize Japanese business activity.

Issues like these have been under discussion for mamy years, in sector-specific negotiations between Washington and Tokyo and in the more general framework of the Structural Impediments Initiative (SII), the bilateral talks begun by the Bush administration in response to the pressure applied by Congress when it adopted Super 301. Progress has been slow, however, as the Japanese government and business commmunnity believe that the Japanese economy has worked very well, and they are unwilling to make major changes merely to make life easier for foreigners— especially for those whose own economies are deemed to be less successful.

SUMMARY

There have been long swings in national trade policies. In the United States, tariffs rose sharply during the first three decades of the nineteenth century, fell for the next three, but rose rather steadily from the start of the Civil War until the eve of World War I. Great Britain, by contrast, moved rapidly toward free trade during the first half of the nineteenth century, a process that was dramatized by the repeal of the Corn Laws, and it did not lapse back to protection until the depression of the 1930s. France and Germany participated briefly in the movement toward free trade, which spread out from Britain by way of trade treaties containing the most-favored-nation clause. But they raised their tariffs during the last quarter of the century, when French and German farmers encountered import competition and joined with factory owners to demand protection.

After World War I, tariffs rose sharply on both sides of the Atlantic, and American tariffs reached their peak in 1930 with the passage of the Hawley–Smoot Tariff. In addition, many countries started to use quotas and other controls to protect their economies against the spread of the depression. Trace liberalization began again when the Roosevelt administration started the Trade Agreements Program. It was interrupted by World War II but resumed in 1947 with the signing of the General Agreement on Tariffs and Trade and first rounds of GATT negotiations. During the 1950s, protectionist pressures in the United States slowed down trade liberalization, but it regained momentum with the formation of the European Economic Community, the passage of the Trade Expansion Act, and the Kennedy Round of tariff cuts. In the 1970s, trade liberalization took a new tack. In the Tokyo Round, governments attempted to reduce nontariff barriers, along with tariffs, and agreed on codes of conduct dealing with government purchases and with subsidies and dumping.

But protectionist pressures built up strongly in the 1970s and became more intense in the early 1980s, when economic growth slowed down and unemployment rose. In the United States, large industries and labor unions began to experience import competition and sought protection, despite the introduction of trade adjustment assistance and of quantitative limits on many manufactured imports, including textiles, steel, and cars. These limits have been very costly to consumers and have not always solved the industries' problems.

Growing protectionist pressures have also led to the more frequent use of antidumping and countervailing duties and to the introduction of market-opening measures in place of more traditional GATT procedures for settling trade disputes. The "results-oriented" test of effectiveness used in Super 301 is the most radical feature of this new approach.

RECOMMENDED READINGS

On trade-policy debates in the United States from 1815 to 1930, see Frank W. Taussig, *The Tariff History of the United States* (New York: Capricorn, 1964); on the free-trade movement in Europe, see Charles P. Kindleberger, "The Rise of Free Trade in Western Europe, 1820–1874," *Journal of Economic History*, 35 (March 1975).

The politics of trade policy in the United States are examined in I. M. Destler, *American Trade Politics: System Under Stress* (Washington, D.C.: Institute for International Economics, 1992), and Robert E. Baldwin, *The Political Economy of U.S. Import Policy* (Cambridge, Mass.: MIT Press, 1985).

Trade adjustment assistance is discussed in C. Michael Aho and Thomas A. Bayard, "Costs and Benefits of Trade Adjustment Assistance," in R. E. Baldwin and A. O. Krueger, eds., *The Structure and Evolution of Recent U.S. Trade Policy* (Chicago: University of Chicago Press, 1984), ch. 5.

For a more formal but rather unorthodox analysis of dumping, see Wilfred Ethier, "Dumping," *Journal of Political Economy*, 90 (June 1982). On the use of antidumping duties for protective purposes, see J. Michael Finger, "Dumping and Antidumping: The Rhetoric and the Reality of Protection in Industrial Countries," *World Bank Research Observer*, 7 (July 1992).

A thoughtful history of Japanese industrial policy is provided by Kozo Yamamura, "Caveat Emptor: The Industrial Policy of Japan," in P. R. Krugman, ed., *Strategic Trade Policy and the New International Economics* (Cambridge, Mass.: MIT Press, 1986); on the import-restricting effects of Japanese *keiretsu*, see Robert Z. Lawrence, "Efficient or Exclusionist? The Import Behavior of Japanese Corporate Groups," *Brookings Papers on Economic Activity*, 1991 (1).

On the implications of Super 301, see Robert Hudec, "Thinking About the New Section 301: Beyond Good and Evil," in J. Bhagwati and H. Patrick, eds., *Aggressive Unilateralism: America's 301 Trade Policy and The World Trading System* (Ann Arbor: University of Michigan Press, 1990), and Rudiger Dornbusch, "Policy Options for Freer Trade: The Case for Bilateralism," in R. Z. Lawrence and C. L. Schultze, eds., *An American Trade Strategy* (Washington, D.C.: The Brookings Institution, 1990).

QUESTIONS AND PROBLEMS

(1) "Like Britain's enthusiasm for free trade in the nineteenth century, America's support for trade liberalization after World War II reflected America's faith in its industrial dominance and sought to perpetuate that dominance by keeping other countries from protecting their home markets, where they might develop their own industries. When the strategy failed, America abandoned it." Comment.

(2) "Multinational production raises questions about the basic purpose of protection and of efforts to reduce other countries' trade barriers. Should the United States try to open Japanese markets to telecommunications equipment sold by an American firm but manufactured in Taiwan? Should it oppose restrictions on European imports of Japanese cars made in the United States when these would compete with cars made by the European affiliates of Ford and General Motors?" Comment.

(3) "The migration of the Japanese automobile industry to the United States is sometimes said to show that import restrictions on Japanese cars were ineffective. In fact, the restrictions were successful precisely because they promoted that migration." Comment.

(4) Estimates of the costs of protection given in Table 10-5 are based on a formula adapted from the one derived in Note 2-1 to Chapter 2. Why must it be adapted? What information would you need to make a numerical estimate from it?

(5) "Trade adjustment assistance should focus on firms rather than workers. Firms injured by import competition should be helped to modernize their plants and products; other firms should be encouraged to open plants in communities where jobs have been lost to import competition. It may be better, indeed, to think in terms of regional policy than industrial policy." Comment.

(6) Modify Figure 10-2 to produce a case in which profit-maximizing pricing would cause a firm to charge higher prices in its export market than in its domestic market.

(7) Develop arguments in favor and against a "results-oriented" standard for judging a country's implementation of a promise to eliminate hidden trade barriers.

11

The Future of
the Trading System

INTRODUCTION

Events in the 1970s and 1980s posed new threats and challenges to the trading system constructed in the decades after World War II. Some of these were studied in Chapter 10. Trade liberalization exposed older industries to new import competition, producing protectionist pressures in the United States and the European Community and leading to the frequent use of nontariff barriers, as well as antidumping and countervailing duties. It also reduced political support for the existing trade regime, especially in the United States. It thus produced a new trade-policy agenda, with an emphasis on opening foreign markets by threatening retaliation, a promise to liberalize agricultural trade, and a promise to extend the trade-policy regime to international trade in services.

Other major changes in the world economy posed more challenges. The rapid growth of multinational production raised questions about the aims and effects of traditional trade policies. When Japanese firms make automobiles in the United States, who is protected by trade barriers that limit the number of automobiles imported from Japan? How should the EC treat Japanese automobiles made in the United States—as Japanese or American? How can trade policies contribute effectively to economic development in Asia, Africa, and Latin America? Should the developing countries continue to pursue inward-looking strategies, which shelter their domestic markets from foreign competition, or should they shift to outward-looking strategies, which expose their industries to global competition? How should the countries of Central and Eastern Europe, including those of the old Soviet Union, be integrated into the world economy? How closely and rapidly should they be associated with the European Community? Which ones should be viewed as potential EC members?

The evolution of the European Community and the signing of the North American Free Trade Agreement, linking the United States, Canada, and Mexico,

256

raise another set of questions. Do regional arrangements threaten the GATT system and portend an era of rivalry and conflict between trade blocs? Or are those arrangements a promising way to extend and deepen trade liberalization?

Other issues loom on the horizon. How far must countries go to harmonize their domestic policies in order to reap the benefits of trade liberalization and avoid trade conflicts? Must the Japanese become "more like us" by ending business practices that would be illegal in the United States or Europe? Or must we become "more like them" by forming partnerships between government and industry to develop new technologies and products? Are environmentalists right to charge that international trade and investment threaten to undermine environmental standards?

THE ISSUES

It would be impossible to cover all these questions in a single chapter, even if we had clear answers to them. But we will touch on most of them as we study four broad issues:

- What can be expected from the Uruguay Round if and when it is completed.
- Whether regional blocs will contribute to global trade liberalization or work to reverse it.
- How trade can contribute to economic growth in the developing countries and to economic transformation in Central and Eastern Europe.
- What problems should figure most importantly on the long-term agenda for U.S. trade policy and on the global trade-policy agenda.

THE URUGUAY ROUND

As protectionist pressures mounted in the 1980s and new policy problems came to the fore, governments began to plan a new GATT round of trade negotiations. They knew they could not finish it for several years but relied on the process itself to keep the situation from deteriorating. The Tokyo Round had served this purpose. Because governments could promise that the round would deal with their industries' concerns, they could postpone taking steps to limit import competition and pry open foreign markets.

The United States was the main advocate of a new GATT round, and it had an ambitious agenda. It sought to liberalize agricultural trade, to develop a trade-policy regime for services, to improve the GATT codes on government procurement, dumping, subsidies, and safeguards against injury, and to strengthen the GATT processes for settling trade disputes, in order to meet Congressional criticism and avoid the need for acting unilaterally under Section 301 of the 1974 Trade Act.

Australia, Canada, and other large exporters of farm products joined the United States in wanting to liberalize agricultural trade; they shared U.S. objections to the

Common Agricultural Policy of the EC. Japan wanted to find better ways of dealing with disputes, because it has been the principal target of other countries' VERs and similar trade barriers. But Japan was opposed to the liberalization of agricultural trade, because it protects its farmers heavily; it had prohibited rice imports completely and had high tariffs on wheat, meat, and other agricultural products, although it depends heavily on imports of those products. It was also apprehensive about liberalizing trade in financial services, which would force it to open Tokyo's financial markets to foreign banks and securities firms.

The developing countries had an agenda of their own. They complained, with good reason, that previous tariff-cutting rounds had not paid enough attention to their needs. In fact, those rounds had *raised* effective rates of protection on some of their exports; tariffs on many raw materials had been cut more sharply than tariffs on the manufactured goods that use those raw materials, including textiles and other products exported by many developing countries. They also hoped to terminate the MFA. They objected to freeing trade in services, however, because foreign banks and insurance companies might come to dominate their markets. Furthermore, they objected to measures aimed at protecting copyrights, patents, and other forms of intellectual property. Some of them feared that these measures could keep them from acquiring new technologies; others feared losing a lucrative business—the pirating of books, tapes, computer software, and designer fashions.

The strongest resistance to the new round, however, came from the EC, which had two reasons for concern. First, it was just starting to create its single internal market and wanted to finish that task before opening new negotiations with the outside world. Its concerns were reinforced by the belief that other countries wanted a new GATT round to prevent the EC from creating a "Fortress Europe" as it built its single market. Second, the EC feared correctly that its Common Agricultural Policy was the main target of U.S. plans to liberalize agricultural trade.

After many meetings devoted to planning future meetings, agreement was reached in 1986 at Punta del Este, Uruguay, to start the new GATT round, which is thus called the Uruguay Round. Governments promised not to take new trade measures that might disrupt the negotiations, and they adopted an ambitious agenda. There were to be new tariff cuts, including cuts on products of particular interest to the developing countries and cuts by the developing countries themselves, the liberalization of agricultural trade, improvements in the GATT codes on dumping, subsidies, and safeguards against injury, and the design of better methods for resolving trade disputes.[1] The bargaining on services was to take place separately, in deference to the concerns of Brazil, India, and other developing countries, which feared being forced to liberalize trade in services to get what they wanted on trade in goods.

The Uruguay Round was supposed to be finished by the end of 1990, and the U.S. Congress undertook to consider the agreement as a single package, under a *fast track* procedure that would keep the Congress from altering the agreement in ways that

---

[1]As tariffs on many goods are already low, governments agreed to consider a *zero-for-zero* option, which would *eliminate* some tariffs completely, but they did not agree in advance to eliminate VERs and other nontariff barriers. The agenda covered several other issues, including trade-related measures affecting foreign investors and measures to protect intellectual property.

could upset the balance struck in the negotiations. As the deadline approached, however, the round came to a halt, blocked by disagreements about trade in farm products. Washington sought to abolish *all* trade-distorting agricultural policies—an unrealistic position that would have been opposed by American farmers; the EC was willing to make changes in the CAP but not to abandon it; and Japan refused to end its prohibition on rice imports. Talks continued on other subjects, including services, and many tentative agreements were reached, including an agreement in principle to phase out the MFA over a ten-year period. But the hard bargaining on tariff cuts was not even started, as everyone waited for an end to the *impasse* on agricultural trade.

Liberalizing Agricultural Trade

Twenty years ago, disputes about agricultural policies focused mainly on barriers to imports of temperate-zone farm products—the measures used by the United States and the EC to support the domestic prices of grains, meat, dairy products, and other commodities. Washington feared that the CAP would reduce the American farmers' share of European markets. These disputes were not resolved, but new ones began to attract more attention. High prices for farm products created huge surpluses in Europe, and the EC used export subsidies to sell them on world markets. American and European farmers were competing in third markets more intensely than in each other's markets and were displacing other countries' exports from those markets. To complicate matters, a number of food-importing countries, such as India, became self-sufficient in many food products. There is famine in Africa but no global shortage of food.

The effects of EC policies are reflected clearly in Table 11-1. The EC has become

Table 11-1. Self-Sufficiency of the European Community in Selected Agricultural Commodities (production as percentage of consumption)

Product	1968/69	1978/79	1988/89
Wheat	94	108	123
Rye	100	108	106
Corn	45	60	95
Sugar	82	124	124
Vegetables	98	94	106
Beef and veal	90	100	104
Poultry	101	105	105

Source: Margaret Kelly, Anne Kenny McGuirk, and others, *Issues and Developments in International Trade Policy* (Washington, D.C.: International Monetary Fund, 1992); data for 1968/69 cover Belgium, France, Italy, Germany, Luxembourg, and the Netherlands; data for 1978/79 add Denmark, Ireland, and the United Kingdom; data for 1988/89 cover all 12 EC countries (i.e., those listed above *plus* Greece, Portugal, and Spain).

self-sufficient in most agricultural products, and it has large exportable surpluses of wheat and several other commodities. The impact of its export subsidies are shown in Table 11-2, which traces the evolution of the principal exporters' shares of global trade in cereals. The EC share rose from an average of 8.7 percent in 1978–1983 to an average of 13.7 percent in 1987–1991. The U.S. share fell sharply from 1978–1983 to 1983–1987, but it recovered thereafter, when the United States began to subsidize its own grain exports. Nevertheless, the U.S. share was lower in 1987–1991 than in 1978–1983. In fact, the fall in the U.S. share over the whole period exactly matched the rise in the EC share.

The conflict over agricultural trade was deep-seated, because it arose from basic differences between the farm policies of the United States and Europe. Both used "target prices" to determine the amounts by which they would support their farmers' incomes, but they provided support in different ways.

In the United States, farmers receive *deficiency payments* whenever the market prices for wheat and other grains are below their target prices. The government does not prop up market prices by purchasing grain, so it does not accumulate surpluses. The cost of the program is kept down by imposing acreage reductions, which require farmers to set aside some of their land.[2]

In Europe, the EC has bought up wheat and other grains whenever the market prices for those products have been lower than their target prices. As target and market prices in Europe have been higher than world prices, the EC has used tariffs

Table 11-2. Cereal Exports as Percentages of World Total

Exporter	Crop Years		
	1978–1983	1983–1987	1987–1991
Australia and Canada	18.2	22.7	18.5
European Community	8.7	11.6	13.7
United States	53.4	42.0	48.4
Other Europe	2.9	4.6	3.5
Developing countries	16.8	19.1	15.9
Thailand	2.9	3.9	3.0
Argentina	7.7	8.5	4.5
All other	6.2	6.7	8.4

Source: Same as Table 11-1; "Other Europe" includes Eastern Europe and the Soviet Union.

---

[2]A different method of support remains available. The Commodity Credit Corporation (CCC) can make loans to farmers, which they can repay in cash or kind. When market prices are lower than the prices at which farmers can repay in kind, they will turn their crops over to the CCC. In recent years, however, the CCC has set loan repayment prices below market prices. In the 1991 crop year, for example, the target price was set at $4.00 per bushel of wheat, the average market price was $2.61 per bushel, and the loan repayment price was only $1.95 per bushel. (The bulk of the difference between target and market prices was offset by deficiency payments, which averaged $1.28 per bushel.) The CCC system is still used for several other products, such as oilseeds and certain dairy products, but beef and sugar prices are propped up by tariffs and quotas.

(so-called variable levies) to keep imports from undercutting EC prices; without those tariffs, the EC would have found itself supporting world prices, not just European prices. The EC subsidized exports to limit the size of its surpluses, and the budgetary cost of those subsidies rose by more than 65 percent during the 1980s, exceeding $10.5 billion in 1991.

As EC target prices have been quite high, the cost of the CAP has been far larger than the cost of the corresponding U.S. program, and more of the cost has been borne by consumers, in the form of higher prices. Table 11-3 compares the levels of support for farmers' incomes in Europe, Japan, and the United States by using a common measure—the subsidy farmers would have to receive to keep their incomes constant if all other forms of support were eliminated.[3] Table 11-4 divides the costs of the European and American programs between consumers and taxpayers and also shows the costs per capita. The share paid by consumers has been almost twice as high in Europe, and the cost per capita has been higher by a third.

The rising cost of the CAP worried European governments for many years, and some of them welcomed the confrontation with the United States as an opportunity

Table 11-3. Agricultural Programs Measured in Terms of Producer Subsidy Equivalents (percentages of total agricultural product)

| Country | Averages | | | |
	1983–1985	1986–1988	1989	1990
European Community	35	48	41	48
Japan	65	75	71	68
United States	25	39	29	30

Source: Same as Table 11-1.

Table 11-4. Total Transfers to Agriculture, 1990 (billions of dollars for total and components; dollars for cost per capita)

| Country | Total | Paid by | | Cost per Capita |
		Consumers	Taxpayers	
European Community	133.4	85.1	48.3	405
United States	74.1	27.9	46.2	295

Source: Same as Table 11-1; duties on farm products deducted from costs to taxpayers.

---

[3]The 1990 subsidy equivalents were higher in other European countries, ranging from 46 and 59 percent in Austria and Sweden, respectively, to 72 percent in Finland, 77 percent in Norway, and 78 percent in Switzerland. These high levels of support may be the hardest political issue facing the countries concerned when they begin to negotiate admission to the EC.

to deal with a problem that would need attention even without the Uruguay Round. But France and a few other EC countries opposed any reduction in the level of support and any basic change in method. French farmers enjoy political influence hugely disproportionate to their numbers. In 1992, however, the EC agreed in principle to reform the CAP by reducing target prices and shifting to the use of deficiency payments and acreage reductions rather than price supports, and this agreement paved the way for an agreement with the United States.[4] Dropping its earlier demand for the abolition of all trade-distorting farm policies, Washington accepted the main provisions of the CAP reform, together with cuts in the volume of subsidized EC exports and limits on the budgetary cost of the subsidies. The EC, in turn, agreed to work with the United States in persuading other countries, including Japan, to modify their farm policies—to substitute tariffs for quotas and reduce farm-price supports.

With the breaking of the deadlock on farm trade, the rest of the talks began again in earnest, but many other issues had still to be resolved, such as disagreements about cutting tariffs, eliminating other barriers to trade, and revising the GATT codes. Much work has also to be done on the framework for liberalizing trade in services.

Liberalizing Trade in Services

When we think about international trade, we usually focus on trade in goods. But look at Table 11-5, on U.S. trade in services. In 1991, the United States earned $152 billion from sales of services (other than the services of capital, which earn dividends and interest); this amount was more than a quarter of total U.S. earnings from goods and services combined. Furthermore, trade in services has grown more rapidly than trade in goods. Receipts from trade in goods rose by 75 percent between 1981 and 1991, but receipts from trade in services rose by 230 percent. The numbers in Table 11-5, moreover, understate the importance of services, because they deal only with cross-border trade. Some services have to be provided locally, in the buyers' own factory or office. Hence, U.S. exports of those services must by supplied by the foreign affiliates of U.S. firms, and imports must be supplied by the U.S. affiliates of foreign firms. These are shown in Table 11-6.[5]

---

[4]The agreement was delayed and nearly derailed by a confrontation over EC subsidies for oilseeds. Two GATT panels had found that these contravened GATT rules, but such findings are not binding, and the EC had refused to reduce the subsidies. In November 1992, however, the United States threatened to impose retaliatory tariffs on white wines, and there was talk of a "trade war" between the United States and Europe. The other EC countries prevailed on France to agree to a compromise on oilseeds and the larger farm-trade issues. (The ultimate fate of the compromise will, of course, depend on the outcome of the Uruguay Round as a whole. If it is not sufficiently attractive to the EC countries, France may persuade them to repudiate the farm-trade compromise.)

[5]The transactions shown in Table 11-6 are not included in Table 11-5, but the income generated by them will appear eventually as investment income payments—the incomes paid to U.S. firms by their foreign affiliates and those paid to foreign firms by their U.S. affiliates. These are discussed in Chapter 12, which explains balance-of-payments accounting; they are also shown in Table 19-1 of Chapter 19, which traces the history of the U.S. balance of payments. Table 11-6 uses 1989 data, because the more recent data do not provide as much detail. When small

Table 11-5. U. S. Trade in Services, 1991 (billions of dollars)

Item	Receipts	Payments
Travel and transportation:		
Travel	48.8	37.0
Passenger fares	15.6	10.6
Freight	7.2	11.9
Port services	15.3	10.4
Other transportation	1.1	0.9
Royalties and license fees:		
Between affiliated businesses	14.0	2.9
Between other parties	3.8	1.1
Other private services:		
Between affiliated businesses	14.6	9.6
Between other parties	31.8	15.6
Education	5.7	0.7
Finance and insurance	6.8	5.1
Telecommunications	2.8	5.6
Business, professional, and technical	10.4	2.6
All other	6.1	1.6
Total	152.2	100.0

Source: U.S. Department of Commerce, *Survey of Current Business*, September 1992; transactions between affiliated businesses are cross-border payments only, not the total service sales of the businesses concerned.

The barriers to trade in services are quite different from the barriers to trade in goods. Few services are subject to tariffs or quotas. They are subject instead to various restrictions deeply imbedded in domestic legislation. Some of these are outright prohibitions; foreign ships, for example, are not allowed to carry cargoes from one American port to another, and American vessels must be used to carry goods sold or subsidized by the U.S. government. Foreign banks and other financial institutions may not set up branches in some countries or engage in certain lines of business. Foreign insurance companies may not sell policies to other countries' citizens. Engineers, lawyers, accountants, and other professionals may not sell their services in foreign countries, even to the local affiliates of their countries' own firms. Many services are closely regulated. International air transport, for example, is governed by a network of bilateral agreements. One country's airlines may use another country's airports only if the other's airlines are given comparable rights; fares and frequencies are tightly controlled; and foreign airlines may not carry passengers between domestic destinations.

As barriers to trade in services take so many forms, the liberalization of trade in

numbers of firms report statistics to the U.S. Department of Commerce, it combines the numbers in ways that protect the confidentiality of the individual reports. This was done with the 1990 data to avoid revealing the sales of individual Canadian firms selling insurance in the United States and of certain foreign firms engaged in retail trade. It was not done with the 1989 data, because larger numbers of firms were involved.

Table 11-6. Sales of Services by Foreign Affiliates of U.S. Firms and U.S. Affiliates of Foreign Firms, 1989 (billions of dollars)

Industry of Affiliate	By Foreign Affiliates of U.S. Firms	By U.S. Affiliates of Foreign Firms
Petroleum	6.0	2.3
Manufacturing	13.3	7.9
Wholesale and retail trade	15.0	3.4
Finance except banking	8.9	4.6
Insurance	18.2	32.6
Real estate	1.1	11.3
Computer and data processing	5.6	1.6
Motion pictures and TV tape	3.6	3.6
Engineering and management	7.4	3.2
Transportation	3.7	6.5
Other service sectors	12.8	12.6
All other[a]	3.6	4.4
Total	99.2	94.2

Source: Same as Table 11-5; detail may not add to total because of rounding.
[a]Includes agriculture, mining, construction, communications, and public utilities.

services cannot be conducted by the same techniques used to liberalize trade in goods. The problem is made more complicated because some countries have more barriers than others. In fact, countries such as the United States, which seek to sell more services, and thus favor liberalization, have fewer barriers to trade in services than do most other countries. It is therefore hard to define reciprocity and even harder to achieve it. Finally, some countries want to exclude certain sectors from the negotiations. The United States, for example, has sought to exclude maritime services in order to keep foreign vessels out of U.S. coastal trade.[6]

The Uruguay Round has produced a two-part agreement on services. One deals with basic principles. The other contains specific sector-by-sector commitments covering trade in financial services, telecommunications, airline travel, and certain professional services provided by individuals. The basic agreement embodies three principles. The first is the most-favored-nation clause, aimed at avoiding discrimina-

---

[6]The liberalization of trade in banking services is also complicated by the need to make sure that participating countries will abide by international guidelines pertaining to bank supervision. In 1975, the major industrial countries, acting under the auspices of the Bank for International Settlements (BIS), entered into a "concordat" on banking supervision, under which banks engaged in international activity are supervised on a consolidated basis; the country in which the bank has its head office is responsible for examining the bank's global activities. This agreement was tightened in 1992, after the failure of the Bank for Credit and Commerce International (BCCI), which had its head office in Luxembourg but did much of its business in London and the Cayman Islands. The bank engaged in massive fraud to cover up its losses and avoided detection by exploiting gaps in the supervisory network. Furthermore, the major countries have agreed on a common standard for measuring the adequacy of bank capital.

tion between trading partners (but it will apply only to countries that ratify the agreement on services, not to all GATT members). The second and third principles reflect the special nature of many services, which cannot be shipped across borders but must be supplied locally in the importing country. The agreement guarantees the *right of establishment* and the *principle of national treatment*. The two together define the right of a foreign firm or individual to set up a business on the same terms as a resident, without suffering discrimination under the host country's laws and regulations or being treated differently by its courts.

A separate agreement deals with the protection of intellectual property. It extends patent and copyright protection, including patent protection for computer chips and copyright protection for computer programs, and prohibits unauthorized use of well-known brand names.

The ultimate success of these new agreements will depend on the number of countries that ratify them and then take steps to liberalize their own regulations. Unfortunately, some will not.

Settling Trade Disputes

The obligations of governments under the GATT are legally binding. How are they enforced? When a governmen acts in ways that appear to violate its obligations, other governments can ask for the appointment of a GATT panel to investigate and make recommendations. The panel reports to the GATT Council, which typically adopts its recommendations. But the "defendant" must also agree to the creation of the panel and to its recommendations, even when the panel recommends retaliation against the defendant. This is the story of Fury and the mouse turned upside down. The defendant chooses the judge and jury and can veto their decisions. Furthermore, the process can take years.

The decision of the U.S. Congress to adopt Section 301 reflected its dissatisfaction with the GATT process, and it served to convince other governments of the need for reform. Better to strengthen the GATT than let the United States take matters into its own hands. In 1989, the GATT adopted new procedures, pending the completion of the Uruguay Round and a more thorough reform. It limited the ability of a defendant to block the creation of a panel but not its ability to block retaliation. The Uruguay Round has gone further, however, by limiting a defendant's ability to prevent retaliation. It has also drafted a charter for a Multilateral Trade Organization (MTO) to administer the GATT more effectively.

THE REGIONAL APPROACH TO TRADE LIBERALIZATION

The European Community has been mentioned frequently in this and earlier chapters, and a second regional arrangement, the North American Free Trade Agreement, was mentioned at the start of this chapter. Other regional arrangements are being formed or discussed in Latin America and Asia, and several more countries may join the EC before the end of the decade.

Why do countries form regional arrangements? How do those arrangements affect outsiders? Are we moving toward a world of trade blocs? Would that sort of world help or hinder global trade liberalization? Economists have answers to some of these questions, but others are hotly debated.

The Theory of Customs Unions

The European Community is a full-fledged customs union. There are no trade barriers between its members; they have a commom external tariff on their trade with other countries; and they speak with a single voice in GATT negotiations.

Customs unions are intriguing analytically because they can be studied from several points of view—the standpoint of each member separately, the membership collectively, outside countries, and the whole world. They are important historically and politically, because they have played key roles in the formation and consolidation of nation states, including the United States. The U.S. Constitution established a customs union by giving Congress the power to "regulate Commerce with foreign Nations, and among the several States," and denying the states the right to "lay any Imposts or Duties on Imports or Exports..."[7] Bismarck used a customs union, the *Zollverein*, to bring the petty states of Germany under Prussian dominance. And the Treaty of Rome, which established the European Economic Community, was seen as a first step toward the economic and political unification of Europe. In each instance, the customs union was a means to a larger end, but it had important economic consequences, too.

The first rigorous analysis of customs unions was provided by Jacob Viner, an American economist, who identified two ways in which a customs union can affect trade patterns and resource allocation:[8]

> There will be commodities... which one of the members of the customs union will now newly import from the other but which it formerly did not import at all because the price of the protected domestic product was lower than the price at any foreign source plus the duty. This shift in the locus of production as between the two countries is a shift from a high-cost to a lower-cost point, a shift which the free-trader can properly approve, as at least a step in the right direction, even if universal free trade would divert production to a source with still lower costs.
>
> There will be other commodities which one of the members of the customs union will now newly import from the other whereas before the customs

---

[7]In *Hood* vs. *Du Mond* (336 U.S. 525, 1949), Supreme Court Justice Jackson noted that: "The sole purpose for which Virginia initiated the movement which ultimately produced the constitution was 'to take into consideration the trade of the United States; to examine the relative situations and trade of the said states; to consider how far a uniform system in their commercial relations may be necessary to their common interest and their permanent harmony' and for that purpose the General Assembly of Virginia in January of 1786 named commissioners and proposed their meeting with those from other states.... The desire of the Forefathers to federalize regulation of foreign and interstate commerce stands in sharp contrast to their jealous preservation of power over their internal affairs. No other federal power was so universally assumed to be necessary, no other state power was so readily relinquished."

[8]Jacob Viner, *The Customs Union Issue* (New York: Carnegie Endowment for International Peace, 1950), p. 43.

union it imported them from a third country, because that was the cheapest possible source of supply even after the payment of duty. The shift in the locus of production is not now as between the two member countries but as between a low-cost third country and the other, high-cost member country. This is a shift of the type which the protectionist approves, but it is not one which the free-trader who understands the logic of his own doctrine can properly approve.

Viner called the first outcome *trade creation* and the second, *trade diversion*. When trade creation is dominant, he said, a union raises the welfare of its members collectively and raises world welfare, too. One member of the union may suffer a welfare loss, but the gain to the others will exceed that loss. Outside countries must suffer welfare losses, but the gain to the union will exceed them. When trade diversion is dominant, by contrast, a union may reduce the welfare of its members collectively and the welfare of the whole world.

Much of the large literature on customs unions that developed in the wake of Viner's contribution was concerned to rectify three defects. Viner did not show how to weigh trade creation against trade diversion. Furthermore, the distinction between them tends to break down when we drop an assumption implicit in his reasoning, that all goods are produced under constant returns to scale. Finally, his analysis took no account of the consumption effects that played so large a role in our analysis of tariffs. The main lines of the amended analysis can be illustrated by returning to a case examined earlier. Let us look at a customs union between Britain and Portugal, focusing on trade in wine.

Figure 11-1 shows a situation in which the union leads to trade diversion. The British demand curve for wine imports is D_M. (Remember that this sort of curve plots differences between domestic demand and supply, so a downward movement along D_M involves an increase in consumption, which raises consumer surplus, and a decrease in production, which reduces producer surplus.) The supply curve of wine from Portugal is S_P, and the supply curve of imports from the rest of the world (ROW) is S_W. Before the formation of the customs union, Britain imposes a tariff at the rate $P_T P_W / O P_W$. It displaces the supply curve of imports from Portugal to S_P' and displaces the supply curve of imports from the ROW to S_T. Hence, the price in Britain is OP_T, total imports are ON, and imports from Portugal are OM. Britain's tariff revenue is $P_W H T P_T$.

When Britain and Portugal form a customs union, Portuguese wine enters duty free. Therefore, S_P becomes the relevant supply curve, because Portuguese producers receive the price of wine in Britain, rather than the British price *less* the tariff. If the union adopts the British tariff on wine imports, the supply curve of imports from the ROW remains at S_T. In this particular case, then, the price of wine in Britain does not change, so domestic consumption and production do not change, and total imports remain constant. But imports from Portugal rise to OM^*, displacing an equal quantity from the ROW. Finally, Britain's tariff revenue falls by $P_W G K P_T$.

Why do these results represent trade diversion? The resource cost of the extra imports from Portugal can be measured by the area under the Portuguese supply curve. It is $MJKM^*$. The resource cost of the imports they displace is the corresponding area under the ROW supply curve. It is $MJGM^*$, which is JKG

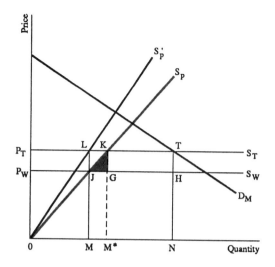

FIGURE 11-1
Trade Diversion in a Customs Union
The British demand curve for wine imports is D_M. The supply curve of wine from Portugal is S_P, and the supply curve from the rest of the world (ROW) is S_W. Britain's tariff rate is $P_T P_W / O P_W$, which displaces the Portuguese supply curve to S_P' and the ROW supply curve to S_T. The price in Britain is $O P_T$, total imports are ON, and imports from Portugal are OM. Britain collects $P_W HTP_T$ of tariff revenue, $P_W JLP_T$ on imports from Portugal and $JHTL$ on imports from the ROW. Britain and Portugal form a customs union, and they adopt the British tariff on wine. Hence, S_P becomes the relevant supply curve of wine from Portugal. As the price does not change in Britain, total imports remain at OM, but imports from Portugal rise from OM to OM^*, displacing an equal quantity of imports from the ROW. Britain's tariff revenue falls by $P_W GKP_T$, because Britain collects only $GHTK$ on imports from the ROW. The resource cost of the extra imports from Portugal is $MJKM^*$. The resource cost of the imports they displace is $MJGM^*$, which is JKG smaller. The reduction in tariff revenue is the welfare loss to Britain; the increase in Portuguese producer surplus, $P_W JKP_T$, is the welfare gain to Portugal; and JKG is the welfare loss to the union. There are no changes in consumer or producer surplus in the ROW, so its welfare does not change.

smaller than the cost of the extra imports from Portugal. The customs union diverts demand from a low-cost source to a high-cost source. In this special case, moreover, the increase in total resource cost measures the welfare loss to the world as a whole. These are the various welfare effects:

    1. As consumption and production are constant in Britain, there are no changes in consumer or producer surplus. But tariff revenue falls by $P_W GKP_T$. This measures the welfare loss to Britain.

    2. There is an increase in Portuguese producer surplus because of the increase in exports to Britain and the price paid to Portuguese suppliers. It is $P_W JKP_T$, and it measures the welfare gain to Portugal.

    3. The welfare effect on the members collectively is the sum of the effects on them individually. It is therefore the gain to Portugal *less* the loss to Britain, which amounts to a loss of JKG.

4. As the world price of wine is constant in this particular case, there are no changes in consumer or producer surplus in the ROW, and there is no change in its welfare.

5. The welfare effect on the whole world is the sum of the effects on the union and the ROW. In this example, then, it equals the loss to the union.

Note 11-1 reformulates these welfare effects in terms of prices, quantities, and the British tariff rate.

To measure the welfare effects of the union comprehensively, we would have to look at the market for cloth as well as the market for wine. If circumstances were similar in that market, the results would resemble those obtained from Figure 11-1. Britain would gain, Portugal would lose, and the union would lose. There would be no change in ROW welfare, so that the effect on the whole world would equal the loss to the union. Taking the two markets together, we would come close to the result obtained by Viner. When a union leads to trade diversion, one or both members must lose, the union as a whole must lose, and the whole world must lose.

Trade creation takes place whenever the formation of a customs union reduces high-cost domestic production in one of the member countries. This will happen when the formation of the union reduces the domestic price of the product, and there

---

Note 11-1
Welfare Effects of a Customs Union with Trade Diversion

In Figure 11-1, the welfare loss to Britain is $P_W GKP_T$, which can be written as $P_W P_T \times P_W G$. But $P_W P_T$ is tp_w, where t is the tariff rate and p_w is the world price, and $P_W G$ is OM^* or $M_P + \Delta M_P$, where M_P is OM, the initial quantity of imports from Portugal, and ΔM_P is MM^*, the change in that quantity. Therefore, the welfare change in Britain is

$$W_B = -p_w(M_P + \Delta M_P)t.$$

The welfare gain to Portugal is $P_W JKP_T$, which can be written as $P_W JLP_T$ *plus* JLK. But $P_W JLP_T$ is $P_W P_T \times P_W J$, where $P_W J$ equals OM, and JLK is $\frac{1}{2}(P_W P_T \times LK)$, where LM equals MM^*. Therefore, the welfare change in Portugal is

$$W_P = p_w(M_P + \tfrac{1}{2}\Delta M_P)t.$$

The welfare effect on the union as a whole is the sum of the effects on Britain and Portugal:

$$W_U = W_B + W_P = -p_w(\tfrac{1}{2}\Delta M_P)t.$$

This is also the effect on world welfare, as ROW welfare does not change.

are two ways in which a union can do that. First, the members can agree on a common external tariff lower than the previous national tariff of the importing country. Second, the displacement of imports from the outside world can reduce the world price of the imported product and thus depress the domestic price. The second possibility is more interesting. It involves an improvement in the union's terms of trade, which redistributes world welfare in favor of the union. It is harder to illustrate, however, because there are many more components to the welfare changes. Let us therefore concentrate on the first possibility.

Figure 11-2 reproduces the initial situation described by Figure 11-1. Britain imports ON wine, with OM coming from Portugal and the remainder coming from the ROW, and Britain's tariff rate is $P_T P_W / OP_W$. When Britain and Portugal form a customs union, they set their common tariff at the lower rate $P_T^* P_W / OP_W$, and the price of wine in Britain falls to OP_T^*. Therefore, total British imports rise to ON^*. As imports from Portugal pay no tariff, they rise to OM^*, which involves trade diversion; the extra imports from Portugal are produced at a higher resource cost than imports from the ROW. (The difference in cost is $JK'G'$, which is smaller than JKG in Figure 11-1, because the fall in the British price of wine limits the increase in imports from Portugal.) Imports from the ROW can rise or fall, depending on the size of the increase in total British imports and of the increase in imports from Portugal. They rise in Figure 11-2, where total British imports rise by more than imports from Portugal. The increase in total British imports reflects the usual production and consumption effects, and the production effect involves trade creation; the imports that displace domestic production are produced at lower cost, whether they come from Portugal or the ROW. Tariff revenue is $G'K'T'H'$. These are the various welfare effects:

> 1. The welfare effect in Britain has two components. The first is the gain $P_T^* T'TP_T$, which is the difference between the increase in consumer surplus and the fall in producer surplus; it can be rewritten as $P_T^* BTP_T$ plus BTT'. The second is the change in tariff revenue, which is the difference between $P_W HTP_T$ and $G'K'T'H'$; it can be rewritten as $HH'T'B$ less $P_T^* BTP_T$ less $P_W G'K'P_T^*$. Adding the two components, we obtain the total change in British welfare, $T'TB$ plus $HH'T'B$ less $P_W G'K'P_T^*$, which can be positive or negative.
>
> 2. The welfare effect in Portugal is the increase in producer surplus, $P_W JK'P_T^*$, so Portugal gains from the union.
>
> 3. The welfare effect on the members collectively is the sum of the effects in Britain and Portugal. But the gain to Portugal can be rewritten as $P_W G'K'P_T^*$ less $JK'G'$, and $P_W G'K'P_T^*$ is part of the loss to Britain. Therefore, the welfare effect on the union is $T'TB$ plus $HH'T'B$ less $JK'G'$, which can be positive or negative. Notice, however, that $HH'T'B$ must be larger than BTT' whenever HH' is at least as large as JG', and this will be true whenever total British imports increase by at least as much as British imports from Portugal. By implication, the members must gain collectively whenever the trade-creating and consumption effects of the union dominate the trade-diverting effect.

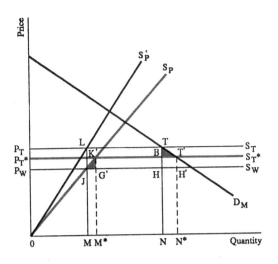

FIGURE 11-2
Trade Creation and Diversion in a Customs Union
The initial situation is the same as in Figure 11-1. When Britain and Portugal form a customs union, however, they adopt a lower tariff on imports from the ROW. It is $P_T^* P_W / OP_W$. The price of wine in Britain falls to OP_T^*, and total British imports rise from ON to ON^*. But imports from Portugal rise from OM to OM^*, because they pay no tariff. These extra imports are produced at a higher resource cost than imports from the ROW; the cost difference is $JK'G'$. Imports from the ROW will rise if NN^*, the increase in total imports, exceeds MM^*, the increase in imports from Portugal. The increase in total British imports has the usual production and consumption effects, and the imports that displace British production are produced at lower resource cost, whether they come from Portugal or the ROW. Tariff revenue is $G'K'T'H'$. The welfare effect in Britain has two parts. The first is the gain $P_T^* T'TP_T$, which is the difference between the rise in consumer surplus and the fall in producer surplus. The second is the change in tariff revenue, which is $P_W HTP_T$ less $G'K'TH'$. But $P_T^* T'TP_T$ can be written as $P_T^* BTP_T$ plus $T'TB$, and the change in tariff revenue can be written as $HH'T'B$ less $P_T^* BTP_T$ less $P_W G'K'P_T^*$. Adding these terms, we obtain the total change in British welfare. It is $T'TB$ plus $HH'T'B$ less $P_W G'K'P_T^*$, which can be positive or negative. The welfare effect in Portugal is the increase in producer surplus, $P_W JK'P_T^*$, so Portugal gains from the union. Its gain can be rewritten as $P_W G'K'P_T^*$ less $JK'G'$, and $P_W G'K'P_T^*$ is a loss to Britain. Therefore, the welfare effect on the union is $T'TB$ plus $HH'T'B$ less $JK'G'$, and it can be positive or negative. But $HH'T'B$ must exceed $T'TB$ when HH' is at least as large as JG', which will be true whenever total British imports rise by as least as much as British imports from Portugal. There is no change in ROW welfare, because there is no change in the world price of wine.

4. There is no change in ROW welfare, because there is no change in the world price of wine.

5. As ROW welfare does not change, the change in world welfare equals the change in union welfare, which can be positive or negative.

Note 11-2 reformulates these welfare effects in terms of prices, quantities, and the change in the tariff rate.

Note 11-2
Welfare Effects of a Customs Union with Trade Creation and Trade Diversion

In Figure 11-2, the welfare change in Britain is $T'TB$ *plus* $HH'T'B$ *less* $P_WG'K'P_T^*$. But $T'TB$ is $\frac{1}{2}(BT \times BT')$ or $\frac{1}{2}(P_TP_T^* \times NN^*)$, which is $\frac{1}{2}(\Delta tp_w \times \Delta M)$, where Δt is the change in the tariff rate, p_w is the world price, and ΔM is the change in total British imports. And $HH'T'B$ is $BH \times HH'$ or $P_T^*P_W \times NN^*$, which is $(t - \Delta t)p_w \times \Delta M$, where t is the initial tariff rate. Finally, $P_WG'K'P_T^*$ is $P_T^*P_W \times OM^*$, which is $(t - \Delta t)p_w(M_P + \Delta M_P)$, where M_P is the initial level of imports from Portugal, and ΔM_P is the increase. Therefore, the welfare change in Britain is

$$W_B = \tfrac{1}{2}(\Delta tp_w \times \Delta M) + (t - \Delta t)p_w \times \Delta M - (t - \Delta t)p_w(M_P + \Delta M_P)$$
$$= p_w[(t - \tfrac{1}{2}\Delta t)\Delta M - (t - \Delta t)(M_P + \Delta M_P)].$$

The welfare change in Portugal is $P_WJK'P_T^*$ or $P_WG'K'P_T^*$ *less* $JG'K'$. But $P_WG'K'P_T^*$ is $(t - \Delta t)p_w(M_P + \Delta M_P)$, as before, and $JG'K'$ is $\frac{1}{2}(P_WP_T^* \times MM^*)$, which equals $\frac{1}{2}(t - \Delta t)p_w\Delta M_P$. Thus, the welfare change in Portugal is

$$W_P = p_w[(t - \Delta t)(M_P + \tfrac{1}{2}\Delta M_P)].$$

Therefore, the change in the welfare of the union is

$$W_U = W_B + W_P = p_w[(t - \tfrac{1}{2}\Delta t)\Delta M - (t - \Delta t)\Delta M_P + (t - \Delta t)\tfrac{1}{2}\Delta M_P].$$

But $\Delta M = \Delta M_P + \Delta M_W$, where ΔM_W is the increase in imports from the outside world. Hence,

$$W_U = p_w[\tfrac{1}{2}t\Delta M_P + (t - \tfrac{1}{2}\Delta t)\Delta M_W],$$

which is positive whenever ΔM_W is positive (when imports from the outside world rise).

Effects of the European Community

Many economists have tried to measure the welfare effects of the European common market. The CAP was clearly trade diverting and harmful to the outside world, because it raised the level of agricultural protection and thus reduced imports from low-cost producers such as the United States. The effects on trade in manufactures were less clear. The EC countries were large enough collectively in world markets to affect their terms of trade by forming a customs union. But the adverse terms-of-trade effects on the outside world were mitigated by the import-raising effects of more rapid economic growth in Europe. Furthermore, the common external tariff was not higher, on average, than the member countries' national tariffs,

Table 11-7. Effects of the Common Market on U.S. Trade with Europe (billions of dollars at 1988 prices)

Effect	U.S. Gain	U.S. Loss
Trade creation in manufactures	45.0	—
Trade diversion in manufactures	—	18.5
Net trade diversion in agriculture	—	7.5

Source: Adapted from Gary C. Hufbauer, "An Overview," in G. C. Hufbauer, ed., *Europe 1992: An American Perspective* (Washington, D.C.: The Brookings Institution, 1990); calculations include effects of both EC enlargements.

because it was constructed by averaging those tariffs. In consequence, most studies found that the trade-creating effects exceeded the trade-diverting effects. One such study, focusing on U.S. trade with Europe, is summarized by Table 11-7.

Proponents of the common market emphasized its long-run political benefits, but they also stressed a number of economic benefits different from those emphasized by Viner's analysis. The tearing down of tariff walls between European countries would intensify competition by depriving national firms of monopoly power and would thus induce a more efficient allocation of resources. Furthermore, it would create European markets big enough to provide economies of scale. These efficiency-enhancing effects would raise productivity, furnishing a once-for-all increase in output and income, and they would also encourage European firms to invest in new plant and equipment, promoting economic growth. These gains would be reinforced by an increase of foreign investment in Europe. Firms in the United States and other outside countries would seek to overcome the trade-diverting effects of the customs union by building plants in Europe.

When told that a new policy will not have large "static" benefits, its proponents often promise huge "dynamic" benefits. Economists tend to be skeptical of such claims. Yet recent research on the sources of economic growth has led economists to attach more importance to the growth-promoting effects of economies of scale and other "dynamic" phenomena like those cited on behalf of the common market.

Nevertheless, the common market did not by itself fully integrate European markets. Tariffs were eliminated rapidly, but many nontariff barriers remained, and goods moving between EC countries were still subject to border controls. Furthermore, restrictive business practices continued to limit competition within and between national markets, and there were large price differences from country to country. As recently as 1992, a Japanese car priced at $15,547 in Germany was priced at $18,285 in Italy—and these were pre-tax prices, unaffected by any difference between German and Italian tax rates.

Little was done, moreover, to harmonize rules and standards. Each EC country continued to apply its own rules for licensing and supervising banks and other financial institutions, its own technical and safety standards for pharmaceuticals, electrical appliances, building materials, and many other goods, and its own rules for certifying doctors, lawyers, accountants, and teachers. The EC Commission in Brussels worked on the difficult problem of harmonizinng technical standards but did not make much progress. Even the seemingly simple task of defining "pasta" led to a bitter dispute between Italy and other EC countries.

In 1985, however, the EC Commission produced a document, *Completing the Internal Market*, with a plan to create a single European market aimed at achieving the efficiency gains that the customs union could not deliver. The plan tried to identify all of the remaining barriers to the free movement of goods, services, capital, and labor, and it listed some 300 legislative measures that would be needed to eliminate those barriers. The governments then took three major steps. First, they agreed that the legislative measures would not require unanimous approval but could be adopted by weighted majority voting. Second, they agreed to adopt the necessary legislation by the end of 1992, although some of it might not be implemented fully for several years thereafter. Third, they agreed to adopt common rules and standards when required for reasons of health, safety, or technical efficiency, but to depend on the *mutual recognition* of national rules whenever that was possible.

The principle of mutual recognition is very different from the principle of national treatment used to liberalize trade in services in the Uruguay Round. Suppose that a British bank wants to establish branches in Frankfurt and New York. Under the principle of mutual recognition, the German authorities must allow it to open the branch in Frankfurt if the bank meets the requirements of British law and practice, even if it does not meet German requirements. Under the principle of national treatment, the U.S. authorities cannot discriminate against the British bank but need not allow it to open a branch in New York unless it meets the requirements of U.S. law and practice. Clearly, the use of mutual recognition greatly simplified the task of the EC countries; they did not have to adopt huge numbers of common rules in order to unify European markets.

Nevertheless, the drafting of the legislation for the single market involved hard bargaining and occasional disputes with outside countries, including the United States.[9] Furthermore, some EC countries objected to ending border controls on movements of people; they were not willing to let their partners decide who would be allowed to enter Europe and thus to enter their own countries *via* other EC countries. On January 1, 1993, however, the barriers to movements of goods were abolished completely. Trucks now move from France to Germany as easily as they move from Indiana to Ohio.

---

[9] At one point in the drafting of the banking legislation, the EC seemed to be insisting that the United States substitute mutual recognition for national treatment. Pointing out that EC banks may deal in European securities markets, the EC argued that the U.S. branches of EC banks should be allowed to deal in American securities markets, even though American banks may not do so. If the United States did not agree, the EC might forbid American banks to establish new branches in Europe. The EC was really trying to put pressure on Japan to open its financial markets, but Americans warned that this missile aimed at Tokyo was likely to land in New York and explode in Washington. The EC backed off.

Effects of the North American Free Trade Agreement

Although the United States supported the creation of the EC, it was skeptical of other regional arrangements. It favored the multilateral GATT approach to trade liberalization. In 1965, however, the United States and Canada entered into a bilateral agreement eliminating tariffs on automobiles and automotive parts, and 20 years later, in 1985, they agreed to examine more general ways to integrate the U.S. and Canadian economies. Soon thereafter, Canada expressed interest in devising "the broadest possible package" of reductions in trade barriers, and the two countries agreed to establish a free trade area at the start of 1989. They would eliminate their tariffs gradually over a ten-year period, liberalize trade in services, and adopt new ways to deal with disputes about dumping, subsidies, and similar matters. They would not adopt a common external tariff, however, which is why the agreement is said to create a free trade area, not a customs union.

The agreement was controversial in Canada, where many industries worried about their ability to cope with import competition, but its advocates saw it as the best way to defend Canadian export industries from protectionist tendencies in the United States. It was less controversial in the United States, although it represented a major departure from traditional U.S. trade policy. It was, in fact, supported by some critics of that policy, who had come to believe that the GATT approach was not serving U.S. interests effectively, and by some exponents of the GATT approach, who wanted to warn the EC that the United States was losing patience with European opposition to the Uruguay Round.

In 1990, however, fewer than two years after the starting date for the agreement with Canada, the United States began to discuss a similar agreement with Mexico, and those talks were soon broadened to cover Canada, too. In December 1992, the three governments signed the North American Free Trade Agreement.

Like the agreement with Canada, which built on the earlier free-trade agreement in automobiles, the NAFTA built on a limited free-trade arrangement between Mexico and the United States, under which certain Mexican factories, known as *maquiladora*, assemble manufactured goods from parts and components made in the United States and export them to the United States without paying tariffs on the parts or finished goods. Furthermore, the NAFTA is similar to the 1989 agreement with Canada. Tariffs will come down gradually; trade in financial services will be liberalized completely by the year 2000; and there will be new procedures for settling trade disputes. But the NAFTA has other important provisions. As soon as the NAFTA takes effect, the United States will eliminate its quotas on Mexican textiles and apparel, and Mexico will start to remove its barriers to U.S. and Canadian investment in Mexico (but not to investments in its oil industry).

The agreement introduces a number of arrangements designed to meet the concerns of certain U.S. industries and of labor unions and environmentalists. The automobile industry was worried about the possibility that Japanese companies would build plants in Mexico to assemble cars for the American market. Accordingly, the NAFTA contains *rules of origin*, which say that cars produced in Mexico will still pay the U.S. tariff if less than $62\frac{1}{2}$ percent of their value was added in Mexico. Even tighter rules of origin apply to textiles and apparel.

The NAFTA is expected to create new jobs in all three member countries, but it will displace large numbers of workers. Furthermore, American labor unions have expressed concerns about Mexican rules on occupational health and safety; rules less strict than those in the United States would confer an unfair advantage on Mexican producers and could encourage American firms to move their plants to Mexico. Environmentalists have voiced similar concerns about Mexican rules on air and water pollution. Accordingly, supplemental agreements were attached to the NAFTA, and the Clinton administration strengthened them before asking Congress to approve the NAFTA.

Under the revised agreements, a group or individual in each country may file a complaint with that country's government charging it with failing to enforce its standards, and representatives of the three governments will then try to negotiate a solution. If they fail, a panel of independent experts will investigate the complaint. If the panel endorses the complaint, the offending government will have 60 days to develop a plan for enforcing its standards adequately. If the government does not produce a satisfactory plan, it can be fined as much as $20 million. The agreements also provide for U.S. assistance to Mexico in improving the enforcement of Mexico's labor and environmental standards and for joint efforts by the two countries to combat water pollution along the Mexican border. But labor unions and environmentalists say that the agreements do not go far enough, while business groups that favored the NAFTA initially believe that the agreements go too far. The outcome was in doubt when this book went to press.

The NAFTA would *not* relax restrictions on movements of people and might actually reduce Mexican migration to the United States by creating more jobs in Mexico. In fact, proponents of the NAFTA argue that the United States must choose between admitting Mexican goods and admitting Mexican workers. Freer trade in goods, they say, is the more sensible option, politically and economically. In Mexico, the NAFTA is seen as a way to "lock in" a number of recent reforms by tying the hands of future Mexican governments. Mexico has already cut its tariffs sharply and taken many other steps to improve the functioning of Mexico's economy, promote economic growth, and create new jobs.

Regional Arrangements and the GATT System

Several European countries have applied to join the EC, and more will probably apply before the end of the 1990s. The United States may decide to enlarge the NAFTA or make separate free-trade agreements with other countries. There is talk about closer trade links among the countries of Southeast Asia and about an Asian free-trade area that might even include Japan. Is this regional approach a good way to continue with trade liberalization? How would it affect the GATT?

Advocates of regional arrangements believe that groups of countries with many common interests are more likely to liberalize trade dramatically than the large, heterogeneous group of countries involved in GATT negotiations. That may be true. But the mere extent of liberalization is not a good guide to the welfare effects when liberalization takes place on a regional rather than a global basis. Recall Figure 11-2, which showed that a customs union—the most intensive regional arrangement—can be beneficial or harmful to its members. Had we analyzed more complicated cases, moreover, we would have seen that a customs union can be beneficial or harmful to the outside world, including the members of other customs unions, but that it is unlikely to be beneficial unless it has large trade-creating effects. It is far harder to predict the welfare effects of regional arrangements that are less intensive than full-fledged customs unions.

When looking at matters from a global standpoint, the extent of internal liberalization within a region or trade bloc may be less important than its members' willingness to engage in external liberalization. We have therefore to ask whether membership in a trade bloc will make a country more or less willing to liberalize trade with outsiders. Does membership in the EC make France more or less willing to engage in GATT rounds of tariff cuts? How will the NAFTA affect the attitudes of Canada, Mexico, and the United States? These questions have no simple answers, but two considerations suggest that the members of trade blocs may not be greatly interested in global liberalization. First, the members of such blocs may not gain large economies of scale from global liberalization; their blocs may be large enough to meet their needs completely. Second, the members of such blocs may want to invest their political energies in building and managing their regional arrangements rather than invest them in global bargaining. That was true of the EC in the 1980s, when it wanted to complete the single market and viewed the Uruguay Round as a troublesome distraction.

A world of trade blocs, moreover, would make the GATT more valuable rather than reduce the need for global trade rules. It can perhaps be argued that trade blocs will be careful to avoid trade policies that injure other blocs, because such policies could provoke retaliation. It may be far safer, however, to rely on a global institution like the GATT to resolve trade conflicts than rely on the risk of mutual damage to prevent those conflicts from causing trade warfare.

TRADE AND ECONOMIC DEVELOPMENT

At a number of points in Chapter 10, we touched on the trade problems of developing countries. We saw that the trade barriers imposed by the advanced industrial countries have been particularly harmful to developing countries. They have been the chief targets of the MFA, and some of them have been hard hit by countervailing and antidumping duties on steel and other products. It is not easy for old producers to make room for new competitors; they are more likely to strike back than to move aside. Their resistance, however, has made it harder for the developing countries to change their own policies—to abandon inward-looking development strategies based largely on infant-industry protection in favor of outward-looking strategies based on export growth and trade liberalization.

In Chapters 5 and 6, we examined the effects of economic growth on a country's foreign trade but not the other side of the coin, the effects of trade on growth. Those effects may be much more important, with extensive policy implications. Trade played a large role in the nineteenth century. It served as an "engine of growth" for many countries, including the United States, shaping their factor endowments and furnishing investment opportunities for foreign as well as domestic capital. John

Williams of Harvard put the point this way:[10]

> The development of international trade has been a process in which the countries outside the centre have owed the development of their trade, and indeed their very existence, to the movement, not merely of goods but of capital, labour, and enterpreneurship from the centre; and the centre countries have in turn owed their further development primarily to this movement. Western Europe created the modern world and was in turn remade by it. Any theory of international trade that does not approach the subject-matter in this way must have very serious limitations as a guide to policy.

Another economist, Ragnar Nurkse, dwelt on the same theme:[11]

> The industrial revolution happened to originate on a small island with a limited range of natural resources, at a time when synthetic materials were yet unknown. In these circumstances economic expansion was transmitted to less-developed areas by a steep and steady increase in Britain's demand for primary commodities which those areas were well suited to produce. Local factors of production overseas, whose growth may in part have been induced by trade, were thus largely absorbed in the expansion of profitable primary production for export. On top of this, the center's increasing demand for raw materials and foodstuffs created incentives for capital and labor to move from the center to outlying areas, accelerating the process of growth-transmission from the former to the latter.

Most economists continue to believe that trade is the most promising engine of growth for the developing countries, and they argue that the doctrine of comparative advantage applies with particular force to those countries, which should attempt to make the best possible use of their scarce skills and capital.

For many years, however, economists and governments in the developing countries rejected this advice. They argued that their countries are quite different from the young economies of the nineteenth century. The United States, Canada, and Australia had temperate climates and unusual factor endowments—vast quantities of land and small amounts of labor. They could therefore supply cotton, wheat, and other staples needed at the center of the world economy. Furthermore, the new countries of the nineteenth century were peopled by recent immigrants from Europe, who brought with them institutions and traditions conducive to the growth of a modern economy. Many developing countries of our day, by contrast, are tropical or semitropical, are densely populated, and lack the institutions and traditions conducive to economic growth.

Trade patterns, it was argued, are different today from those of the nineteenth century. Production at the center of the world economy tends to be resource saving

---

[10]John H. Williams, *Trade, Not Aid: A Program for World Stability* (Cambridge, Mass.: Harvard University Press, 1953), p. 10.

[11]Ragnar Nurkse, "Patterns of Trade and Development," in *Equilibrium and Growth in the World Economy* (Cambridge, Mass.: Harvard University Press, 1961), p. 285.

instead of resource using, and synthetics have replaced many raw materials. Furthermore, the trade policies of today's center countries are less liberal than those of the nineteenth century, which had no MFA, no CAP, and no countervailing duties on Brazilian steel.

Finally, many developing countries did not welcome private foreign capital because it had colonial overtones. Nor were they willing to serve forever as suppliers of raw materials. They feared the instability of raw-materials prices and wanted to draw back from export dependence. Above all, they identified economic development with industrialization and sought to build modern factories to symbolize their independence and assert their maturity. Invoking the infant-industry argument, countries in Asia and Latin America engaged in systematic *import substitution*. They protected their import-competing industries, penalized their export industries, and tended to neglect agricultural development.

The Infant-Industry Argument

The infant-industry argument was introduced in Chapter 10, which traced it back to Alexander Hamilton and noted that there are two versions of the argument. The first version looks to economies of scale; the second version looks to economies of experience.

The argument invoking economies of scale is based on strong assumptions about the way that costs of production vary with output. Costs rise steeply at first, but start to fall once output becomes large enough to justify the use of mass-production methods. As a tariff can raise the outputs of import-competing firms, it can be used to capture economies of scale. Once firms are on the downward-sloping parts of their cost curves, the tariff can be removed. The same argument can be put differently. Tariffs can reserve domestic markets for domestic goods until those markets are big enough to absorb the output levels at which economies of scale begin. Once that happens, local firms will not need protection. They may indeed begin to export.

This argument makes most sense analytically when the economies of scale attach to an industry as a whole rather than an individual firm. When economies of scale attach to a firm, it can capture them by expanding its own output until costs start to fall. It can undercut its domestic competitors and does not need a tariff. When economies of scale attach to an industry as a whole, a single firm cannot capture them by itself. Consider firms that assemble finished products from parts supplied by other firms, and suppose that mass-production methods can reduce the costs of making the parts. A single firm that expands its output of the finished product cannot induce its suppliers to use mass-production methods; its demand for parts is not large enough. If all such firms expand, however, they can induce their suppliers to adopt those methods and thus reduce the costs of parts and of the finished product. Economies of scale attaching to the firms that make the parts show up as economies of scale to the industry that assembles them. As firms that make the parts move along their downward-sloping cost curves, firms that assemble the parts experience a downward shift in their cost curves. A tariff on the finished product would be effective here.

The argument invoking economies of experience is based on the notion of *learning by doing*. An infant industry may be less efficient than an older industry because it lacks seasoned managers, skilled workers, and reliable suppliers of equipment and materials. Therefore, protection may be justified temporarily, until the industry matures, cuts back its costs, and can compete with imports. Recent statements of this argument put much emphasis on the time and effort needed to train workers, invoking the point made in Chapter 4 that labor skills are important determinants of comparative advantage.

This last version of the argument amounts to the assertion that temporary tariffs can induce a permanent outward shift of the transformation curve, leading to an increase in output that raises future welfare by more than the tariff reduces current welfare. Consider the economy depicted by Figure 11-3. It transformation curve is AA' initially, and it produces at Q_1, where the slope of its transformation curve is equal to the slope of $F_1F'_1$, which gives the relative price of coffee on the world market. It consumes at some such point as C_1, exporting coffee and importing trucks. When it imposes a tariff on trucks, the relative price of coffee in the domestic market is given by the slope of a line such as $H_1H'_1$, flatter than $F_1F'_1$. The production point moves to Q'_1, where the country produces more trucks and less coffee. Economic

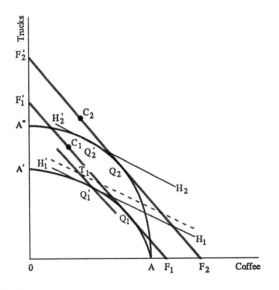

FIGURE 11-3
The Infant-Industry Argument
A country faces fixed terms of trade equal to the slope of $F_1F'_1$. Before imposing a tariff, it produces at Q_1 on the transformation curve AA'. It trades to a point such as C_1, where an indifference curve (not shown) is tangent to $F_1F'_1$. It exports coffee and imports trucks. An import tariff shifts production to Q'_1, where AA' is tangent to the flatter domestic price line $H_1H'_1$. The economy trades along a line with the same slope as $F_1F'_1$ to a point such as T_1, where an indifference curve (not shown) is tangent to the line having the same slope as $H_1H'_1$. The tariff raises the production of trucks but reduces welfare (T_1 lies on an indifference curve lower than C_1). With the passage of time, however, protection increases the efficiency of firms or factors engaged in making trucks. The transformation curve shifts outward to AA'', and production moves to Q'_2, where AA'' is tangent to $H_2H'_2$. The output of trucks at Q_2 is lower than at Q'_2, but higher than at Q'_1 or Q_1. The economy trades along $F_2F'_2$ to C_2 and reaches an indifference curve higher than it did at C_1.

welfare falls because consumers move to some such point as T_1, which lies on a lower indifference curve than C_1. With the passage of time, however, productivity rises in the domestic truck industry, because the increase in output fostered by the tariff encourages learning by doing. The transformation curve shifts outward to AA'', and the output point moves to Q_2'. When the tariff is removed, the output point moves to Q_2, and consumers can move to some such point as C_2, where welfare is higher than it was at C_1. Truck output falls when the tariff is removed but is higher than it was initially.

There are several answers to the infant-industry argument. Some come from trade theory, others from the histories of developing countries.

Trade theory tells us that there are better ways to help an infant industry. A production subsidy would be better than a tariff, because it would get closer to the policy objective, an increase in domestic output, without having costly consumption effects. A production subsidy, however, does not get to the heart of the problem. If a firm can expect to raise its future profits by training its workers and managers, it should be able to borrow in the capital market to cover the training costs and other losses suffered in its infancy; it can repay what it borrows when it reaches maturity. If capital markets are competitive and lenders are not strongly averse to risk, the interest rate at which the firm can borrow will reflect the social rate of return on capital. A firm that cannot borrow at that competitive rate does not have a good claim to protection or any other help from the government. The real resources used by that firm should go instead to firms that can afford to pay the competitive interest rate—those that can expect to earn the social rate of return on capital.

To justify infant-industry assistance, then, one must show that the capital market does not function efficiently. There are two possibilities. First, capital markets may not be perfectly competitive, and a firm may be forced to pay more than the social rate of return or be unable to borrow at all. When this is the case, however, the government should make loans to the infant industry rather than protect or subsidize its output. Second, a firm may be reluctant to borrow because it cannot expect to recover the costs of training workers. Once they have been trained, the workers may take jobs with other firms. If labor markets were perfectly competitive, the firm could expect to recover its costs by paying lower wages to trainees—by shifting the costs of training to the workers themselves. But labor-market imperfections and minimum-wage laws get in the way. In this case, however, the government should subsidize training rather than protect the industry involved.

The histories of developing countries that have used infant-industry protection teach us three general lessons. First, it is hard to choose the right industries. If protection is granted very freely, some of it will go to industries that cannot reap economies of scale or experience. Second, firms obtaining infant-industry protection are reluctant to give it up. They do not want to suffer cuts in output like the one described by the movement from Q_2' to Q_2 in Figure 11-3, and they frequently acquire enough political influence to block trade liberalization. Third, infant-industry protection can hurt other industries, even when it is confined to promising candidates. By attracting resources to the import-competing sector and raising the costs of imported equipment and materials, import substitution has handicapped export production in many developing countries. It has imposed negative effective protection on the export sector.

Trade Liberalization in Developing Countries

Import substitution seemed to be a promising strategy initially but ran into diminishing returns eventually. Opportunities for import substitution were exhausted, and economies were saddled with high-cost industries producing in small inefficient plants. Several developing countries began therefore to look for export opportunities. Singapore and Hong Kong relied on large supplies of low-cost labor and specialized in labor-intensive products—textiles, apparel, and light electronics. Korea and Taiwan began that way but went on to develop heavier industries—shipbuilding, steelmaking, and automobiles. Some countries subsidized their exports extensively.

These outward-looking strategies have been very successful. In 1973, developing countries accounted for only 6.9 percent of total manufactured exports; in 1989, they accounted for 15.1 percent. The shares of developing countries in various product groups are shown in Table 11-8. Furthermore, countries that adopted outward-looking strategies have tended to grow faster than other developing countries. Table 11-9 summarizes a study by the World Bank that classified the trade regimes of developing countries and then compared their growth rates. Most countries grew more slowly from 1973 to 1983 than from 1963 to 1973, but the countries that pursued outward-looking strategies grew faster in each period.

Evidence of this sort has been influential and has been reinforced by strong pressure from the World Bank and the International Monetary Fund. The IMF has identified no fewer than 36 developing countries that liberalized their trade regimes in the 1980s, including 31 that it describes as having had "tight" or "significant" trade controls initially. Of these 31 countries, moreover, 17 adopted reforms extensive enough for the IMF to describe them as having moved to "open" or "relatively open" trade regimes. Examples are listed in Table 11-10. In many cases, the countries also adopted extensive domestic reforms; they began to liberalize their capital markets and privatized large state-owned firms, including their national airlines and telephone companies. In several instances, however, the permanence and ultimate success of the reforms was cast in doubt by growing trade deficits reflecting the effects of trade liberalization and failure to control domestic inflation.

Table 11-8. Shares of Developing Countries in World Exports of manufactures (percentage of world exports in each product group)

Product Group	1973	1989
All manufactured goods	6.9	15.1
Textiles	17.3	28.0
Clothing	30.3	45.4
Other consumer goods	13.1	20.5
Iron and steel	3.3	13.0
Chemicals	4.4	9.0
Other semi-manufactured goods	11.7	17.1
Machinery and transport equipment	3.1	11.2

Source: Same as Table 11-1; "other consumer goods" excludes vehicles.

Table 11-9. Growth Rates of Per Capita Output in Developing Countries Classified by Trade Regime

Trade Regime	1963–1973		1973–1983	
	Number	Growth Rate	Number	Growth Rate
Strongly outward oriented	3	7.4	3[a]	6.1
Moderately outward oriented	10	3.7	8[b]	1.8
Moderately inward oriented	12	2.5	16[c]	0.7
Strongly inward oriented	16	1.7	14[d]	−1.0

Source: World Bank, *World Development Report* (Washington, D.C.: World Bank, 1987), Figure 5.3.

[a]Hong Kong, Korea, and Singapore.

[b]Brazil, Chile, Israel, Malaysia, Thailand, Tunisia, Turkey, and Uruguay.

[c]Cameroun, Colombia, Costa Rica, El Salvador, Guatemala, Honduras, Indonesia, Ivory Coast, Kenya, Mexico, Nicaragua, Pakistan, Philippines, Senegal, Sri Lanka, and Yugoslavia.

[d]Argentina, Bangladesh, Bolivia, Burundi, Dominican Republic, Ethiopia, Ghana, India, Madagascar, Nigeria, Peru, Sudan, Tanzania, and Zambia.

Table 11-10. Trade Liberalization in Developing Countries that Began the 1980s with "Tight" Trade Controls

Country	Highest Tariff Rate		Quantitative Controls Eliminated[a]
	Before	After	
To Open Trade Regimes:			
Argentina	100	22	Import licensing (60)
Bolivia	60	10	Import licensing (90)
Ghana	100	25	Import licensing (100)
Mexico	100	20	Import licensing (38)
To Relatively Open Trade Regimes:			
Jamaica	75	60	Foreign-exchange control (50)
Kenya	125	100	Foreign-exchange control (58)
Venezuela	80	20	Foreign-exchange control (65)

Source: Same as Table 11-1 (adapted from Tables 11 through 13).

[a]Figures in parentheses are percentages of imports previously covered by import licensing or exchange control.

Developing Countries and the GATT

In the era of inward-looking development strategies, the developing countries were exempted from GATT rules that ban the use of quotas and other nontariff barriers. They were also exempted from any obligation to reduce their own tariffs in exchange for tariff cuts by the developed countries. When they began to export manufactured goods, however, they became less concerned with exemptions for themselves and more concerned with access to other countries' markets, especially to those of the large developed countries.

They had won what seemed to be a major victory in 1968, at the second United Nations Conference on Trade and Development (UNCTAD), when the developed countries agreed to introduce a Generalized System of Preferences (GSP) for manufactured exports from developing countries. In 1973, moreover, at the start of the Tokyo Round, the developed countries promised to provide a "better balance" between developed and developing countries in sharing the gains from trade liberalization and to offer "special and more favorable treatment" to the developing countries. But both victories turned out to be small.

We have already seen how trade preferences work. Figure 11-1 was used to describe a trade-diverting customs union between two small countries, but it also tells the story of preferential treatment. When Portuguese wine is granted duty-free access to the British market, the relevant supply curve for Portugal is S_P rather than S'_P, and Portuguese wine exports to Britain rise from OM to OM^* at the expense of exports from the rest of the world. Portugal's export earnings rise, and there is an increase of Portuguese economic welfare.

Each developed country introduced its own version of the GSP, and most of them were quite limited in scope. Under the U.S. version, for example, eligible imports enter duty free, but many important products are not eligible (textiles, apparel, shoes, and several other "import-sensitive" goods). Furthermore, eligible quantities are limited on a country-by-country and product-by-product basis, and several developing countries have been "graduated" from the program to make room for exports from less-advanced countries. In practice, then, GSP benefits have been quite small, and the developing countries have been disappointed by them.

They were also disappointed by the Tokyo Round, which failed to give them "more favorable" treatment. Whereas tariff cuts on manufactured goods, taken as a group, averaged 34 percent, the tariff cuts on exports by developing countries averaged only 26 percent. In many cases, moreover, the cuts were not effective in opening markets to the developing countries. The goods in question were covered by the MFA and other nontariff barriers. To make matters worse, the developed countries have imposed a number of countervailing and antidumping duties on the manufactured exports of developing countries.

At the start of the Uruguay Round, the developing countries had to decide whether they should seek to liberalize the GSP or concentrate on other issues. They chose in the end to bargain for general tariff cuts on goods of particular interest to them and for elimination of the MFA, rather than to seek more preferences.

TRADE AND ECONOMIC REFORM
IN CENTRAL AND EASTERN EUROPE

The countries of Central and Eastern Europe face the most challenging task ever contemplated by economists—the transformation of their centrally planned economies into market economies. It is easier to privatize large state firms in developing countries than in Poland, Bulgaria, or Russia. Property rights are well defined in most developing countries, managers understand their duties, and capital markets work reasonably well. These conditions do not hold in Central and Eastern Europe. In large parts of that region, markets for goods and services, including labor, have just begun to function, and prices are just starting to take on the task of guiding production, consumption, and investment, replacing the planners' commands.

The trade problems of the region resemble those of the developing countries but are far more difficult. The countries of Central and Eastern Europe must reorient their trade flows completely and upgrade the quality of their exports to meet the high standards of the world market.

When they were dominated by the Soviet Union, the countries of Central Europe were tied tightly to the Soviet economy. Production and trade in the region as a whole were conducted in accordance with a "socialist division of labor" organized by the Council of Mutual Economic Assistance (CMEA). It was an artificial division of labor, however, which was predicated on a naive faith in economies of scale and paid scant attention to the principle of comparative advantage. Huge factories were built in strange places, and their output was shipped to captive customers in other countries of the region. Furthermore, the payments system of the region forced each country to balance its trade bilaterally with every other country, instead of running surpluses with some partners and using them to finance deficits with other partners. Trade with outsiders was heavily restricted.

These arrangements are reflected in Table 11-11, which looks at the trade of the CMEA countries, and in Table 11-12, which looks at trade among the republics of the former Soviet Union. Although the CMEA countries as a group accounted for a very small fraction of world trade, each country traded heavily with the others, especially with the Soviet Union. This is most vividly illustrated by the Bulgarian case; exports to the other CMEA countries accounted for 57 percent of Bulgaria's total exports, and exports to the Soviet Union accounted for almost 85 percent of

Table 11-11. Trade among the CMEA Countries, 1989

Country	CMEA as Percentage of Total		U.S.S.R. as Percentage of CMEA	
	Exports	Imports	Exports	Imports
Bulgaria	57.3	42.4	84.9	80.4
Czechoslovakia	40.9	40.9	64.8	63.2
Hungary	35.8	33.9	70.7	66.9
Poland	39.7	33.4	67.9	65.5
Romania	19.9	30.5	68.3	68.7

Source: Peter B. Kenen, "Transitional Arrangements for Trade and Payments Among the CMEA Countries," *International Monetary Fund Staff Papers*, 38 (June, 1991), Table 2; figures understate the concentration of trade on CMEA partners because they omit trade with East Germany.

Table 11-12. Intraregional Trade in the Former Soviet Union, the European Community, and Canada (average for region)

Region	Total Trade as Percentage of GDP	Intraregional Trade as Percentage of Total Trade
Republics of Former Soviet Union (1988)	29.4	71.8
Countries of European Community (1990)	23.1	59.2
Provinces of Canada (1984)	44.6	44.1

Source: International Monetary Fund, *Common Issues and Interrepublic Relations in the Former U.S.S.R.* (Washington, D.C.: International Monetary Fund, 1992). Total trade includes intraregional trade; averages for total trade are weighted by GDP for each republic, country, or province, averages for intraregional trade are weighted by total trade.

Note: Shares of intraregional trade in the former Soviet Union range from 57.8 percent for Russia to 89.1 percent for Armenia and Turkmenistan; shares in the EC range from 51.2 percent for Denmark to 74.3 percent for Belgium–Luxembourg; shares in Canada range from 33.9 percent for Ontario to 78.0 percent for the Yukon. The largest shares in the EC and Canada, however, are smaller than any share in the former Soviet Union except that of Russia.

Bulgaria's exports to all of the CMEA countries. But the other cases are not very different, except, perhaps for that of Romania (which had large exports to developing countries outside the CMEA). Trade among the republics of the former Soviet Union was much larger relative to their total trade than trade among the EC countries or trade among the Canadian provinces. In the Soviet case, indeed, the share of interrepublican trade was bigger for every republic (other than Russia) than the share of inter-EC trade for any EC country or the share of interprovincial trade for any Canadian province.

With the collapse of the Soviet empire, these tight trade links were cut, and the resulting reduction in intraregional trade was compounded by a collapse of output due in part to the abandonment of central planning. Within the former Soviet Union, moreover, disintegration of the currency area based on the ruble interfered with payments between republics and made trade even harder.

Governments in Central Europe were quick to recognize that they would have to seek new markets and sources of supply in the West and that the reform of their trading arrangements could contribute to the reform of their domestic economies. By dismantling their trade barriers, they could import world prices to replace the distorted domestic prices inherited from the days of central planning. They could thus force domestic industries to use resources more efficiently. The reforms adopted by the leaders in this process are summarized by Table 11-13. Together with other domestic reforms, they were quite successful in switching and raising exports to Western markets and in attracting foreign direct investment, especially to Hungary.

For economic and political reasons, these same countries, and others as well, seek close links with Western Europe and eventual membership in the European Community. The EC has endorsed this objective in principle and has granted these countries a limited form of associate membership. Nevertheless, the EC has been

Table 11-13. Price and Trade Reforms in Three Central European Countries

Category	Czechoslovakia	Hungary	Poland
State planning	Abolished	Abolished	Abolished
Domestic prices	Controls remain on 5% of wholesale and retail turnover	About 90% of all prices liberalized	Over 80% of consumer and 90% of producer prices liberalized
State trade monopoly	Abolished	Abolished	Abolished
Import controls	Licenses needed only for petroleum, gas, beef, and butter	Over 90% freed from licensing but global quota on consumer goods	Licenses needed only for trade under bilateral agreements
Import tariffs	Unchanged from 1989 but 15% surcharge on consumer goods	Unchanged from 1989 but about 80% of rates bound under GATT	Reformed with rates averaging 14% including surcharge
Export controls	Abolished but licenses needed to export energy and certain raw materials[a]	About 30% need licenses[a]	Quotas retained for 5 items and licenses needed for 20 items when sold for convertible currencies
Currency regime	Single fixed exchange rate; convertible for most current transactions	Single fixed exchange rate; convertible for most current transactions	Single fixed exchange rate for trade by firms but multiple rates for other transactions; individuals may buy foreign currencies on on free market

Source: Same as Table 11-1 (adapted from Table 6); information pertains to the situation prevailing in mid-1991. All three countries permit the repatriation of income and principal by foreign investors.

[a]Licenses also needed for goods subject to other countries' "voluntary" export restraints.

slow to open its markets to their exports, because the goods involved—textiles, steel, and meat—compete with the products of domestic sectors experiencing serious economic problems. In fact, the EC has erected new barriers to many of those exports, including antidumping duties on certain steel products. The United States had done so, too, along with other industrial countries.[12] Similar trade problems are likely to arise when the republics of the former Soviet Union start to reform their trade patterns and policies.

---

[12]Tables 10-6 and 10-7 in Chapter 10 show that the exports of Central and Eastern Europe to the major industrial countries are subject to many nontariff barriers and that the number of barriers has risen sharply in recent years.

THE LONG-TERM TRADE AGENDA

Most of the issues already discussed will remain on the trade-policy agenda for many years to come. It will take time for developing countries to complete and consolidate the shift to outward-looking trade policies. Some of them, including India and Pakistan, are far behind and moving rather slowly. Others will retreat if the developed countries are unwilling to make the domestic adjustments required to absorb more imports from developing countries. Some developing countries may refuse to liberalize trade in services. That process, moreover, has barely begun. Although the Uruguay Round has defined the task and ways to attack it, the actual freeing of trade in services will take much more bargaining.

Economic reforms in Central and Eastern Europe are starting to pay off, but huge problems lie ahead. The reformers are meeting political resistance, not only in Russia and other republics of the former Soviet Union but in Central Europe, too. As with the developing countries, moreover, the outcome will depend on the willingness of the industrial countries to open their own markets and find ways to promote domestic adjustment, rather than resist it by restricting imports.

Finally, the nature of the trading system will be affected crucially by decisions facing the United States—whether it will choose to pursue a global or regional approach to future trade liberalization, and whether it will rely on GATT rules and procedures to settle trade disputes or seek to act as judge and jury all by itself. The future of the trading system will also depend on economic and political developments across the Pacific—whether the countries of Southeast Asia will move toward regional free trade, whether Japan will be involved in any such arrangement, and the speed with which China will emerge as a major trading nation.

Three other issues will figure prominently on the long-term trade agenda—reconciling trade and environmental policies, regulating rivalry in high-technology trade, and harmonizing competition policies.

Trade and the Environment

Environmental issues are having two effects on trade policies. First, concerns have been expressed about freer trade between countries that have different environmental standards. Recall the objections to the NAFTA by American labor unions and environmentalists. Once goods made in Mexico can enter the United States without paying tariffs, American firms may migrate to Mexico to avoid the costs of meeting U.S. rules against industrial pollution. Second, many environmentalists favor the use of trade restrictions against countries that fail to adopt strict environmental standards. They persuaded the U.S. Congress to prohibit imports of tuna fish caught with drift nets, which kill or injure dolphins. They persuaded the EC to prohibit imports of furs from countries where animals are caught with leg-hold traps.

These are hard issues. Environmental protection is vital. Yet, serious risks attach to the use of trade restrictions for enforcing environmental standards, and very grave risks attach to unilateral action, whether by the United States or any other country, rather than collective action based on international agreements.

The NAFTA case seems simple at first glance. No one would want American workers to lose their jobs because employers can avoid the costs of meeting high environmental standards by moving their plants to Mexico. What would we say, however, if we were told that firms may move to Mexico or, for that matter, to Brazil or Thailand, because wages, taxes, and other costs are lower in those countries than in the United States? If tariffs and other trade barriers were used to offset *all* cost differences, trade would be obliterated. Some jobs would be "saved" but others would be lost, and the gains from trade would vanish completely.

It can perhaps be argued that the NAFTA case is special, because Mexican goods will have tariff-free access to the U.S. market, and the other costs of shipping goods across the Rio Grande are relatively small. To that extent, however, a special solution is needed, and it is foreshadowed in the NAFTA itself. Fines may be imposed on the Mexican government if it does not enforce its environmental standards—and the standards themselves are quite high. It should be sufficient for the purpose, moreover, to apply the standards quickly to new plants and firms; that will discourage American firms from migrating to Mexico. Mexico can move more slowly to upgrade old plants and clean up earlier environmental damage, in line with Mexico's own priorities. It may be more urgent for Mexico to improve its schools, hospitals, and other social services than to deal immediately with all of its environmental problems.

The problem posed by the dolphin and fur cases—whether import barriers should be used to punish a country that fails to adopt strict environmental rules—is part of a more general problem. When should a country use trade barriers to punish another country for *any* offense against commonly accepted standards of conduct? From time to time, the international community has acted collectively to punish behavior that violates international law. The United Nations imposed a trade embargo on Iraq after the invasion of Kuwait, because the invasion was an act of aggression, and the embargo had the force of law because it was imposed by the Security Council. The U.N. General Assembly recommended restrictions on trade with South Africa to protest against *apartheid*–the systematic segration of South Africa's black population. In many instances, however, the United States has taken matters into its own hands or has been urged to do so. Congress recommended that the Soviet Union be deprived of most-favored-nation treatment until it relaxed its restrictions on Jewish emigration, and it sought to withhold most-favored-nation treatment from China to protest the Tiananmen Square massacre.

Experts debate the effectiveness of these measures. In some cases, trade restrictions have probably stiffened the resistance of the country affected and helped its government mobilize domestic political support by charging foreign interference in its internal affairs. In other cases, they may have persuaded a government to modify its policies. Students of the subject agree, however, that trade restrictions will be most effective when they are adopted by large numbers of countries, and this is most likely to happen when the policies they aim to punish represent clear violations of international law.

This conclusion suggests in turn that governments should extend the rule of law by adopting treaties and other agreements to define acceptable conduct and to permit the use of trade restrictions when a country engages in unacceptable conduct. Governments are moving in this direction. The Montreal Protocol, aimed at banning chemicals that deplete the ozone layer, allows the use of trade restrictions against countries that violate the ban. The treaties signed at the Earth Summit in Rio de Janeiro do not go that far, but they start to build a body of environmental law for the world as a whole.

It is easiest to obtain international agreement on rules to prohibit policies or practices that injure other countries. It should thus be possible to make more progress on environmental issues than on human rights, free elections, or occupational safety. But impatience is dangerous. Governments live in glass houses and should not throw stones. Some countries have higher environmental standards than those of the United States, and some have better records in other important areas. Finally, governments must not abuse environmental standards by citing them to limit trade for less high-minded reasons.

High-Technology Trade

The infant-industry argument is usually heard in countries that seek to catch up with more advanced industrial countries. It is invoked for domestic producers of textiles, steel, and other manufactured goods, which are said to need protection temporarily, until they have learned to emulate more efficient foreign firms. Recently, however, a similar argument has been heard in the industrial countries themselves. It is invoked on behalf of high-technology industries, which are said to need protection because of the risks and costs faced by firms producing goods involving new technologies.

This argument is heard most frequently in the United States and Europe, which are seen to be falling behind in the race to develop and exploit new technologies. There is some evidence to that effect. Table 11-14 shows that the American and EC shares of global high-technology exports declined in the 1970s and 1980s, and their "revealed comparative advantage" fell in machinery and electronics.[13] It is easy to scare people with these numbers. Most of us take personal pride in owning the newest, most modern products, and we also take national pride in our own country's ability to make them. Why should we be content to make textiles and steel when we can focus on super computers, fiber optics, and biotechnology? How can a major power like the United States expect to command international respect if it is losing the technological race? Surely, something should be done. But the case for "doing something" does not stand on pride alone. There are legitimate issues here and much debate about them.

The conventional infant-industry argument is based in part on the belief that new, small firms are saddled with high costs because the firms supplying them with raw materials and parts are too small to capture economies of scale. If "downstream" industries are protected temporarily and can increase their production, their "upstream" suppliers can increase their production, too, and thus supply their "downstream" customers more efficiently, ending the need to protect them.

The high-technology variant of the argument turns this reasoning on end. It

---

[13]The American advantage in aircraft fell too, but that of the EC rose, as Airbus succeeded in competing with U.S. producers of commercial jets. (In electronics, moreover, some of the gains of the Asian countries reflect rising exports of consumer goods that use high-technology parts imported from Japan.)

Table 11-14. Trade in High-Technology Goods

Index of Performance	United States	European Community[a]	Japan	East Asian Countries[b]
Share in World Exports of High-Technology Goods:				
1970–1973	29.5	46.4	7.1	1.3
1979–1982	25.1	44.1	10.1	4.1
1988–1989	20.6	37.4	16.1	8.8
Index of Comparative Advantage in High-Technology Goods:				
All product groups				
1970–1973	219	99	80	54
1986–1989	192	91	133	110
Chemicals and drugs				
1970–1973	111	123	86	45
1986–1989	124	130	47	46
Mechanical equipment				
1970–1973	156	108	93	21
1986–1989	145	97	144	68
Electronic goods				
1970–1973	212	95	110	132
1986–1989	168	71	200	190
Aircraft and parts				
1970–1973	440	63	6	16
1986–1989	416	91	7	19
Scientific instruments				
1970–1973	217	103	86	15
1986–1989	208	109	100	43

Source: Adapted from Laura D'Andrea Tyson, *Who's Bashing Whom? Trade Conflict in High-Technology Industries* (Washington, D.C.: Institute for International Economics, 1992), Tables 2.3 and 2.4; the index of comparative advantage is the ratio of a country's share in world exports of the product group to its share in world exports in all manufactured goods.

[a]Excluding Greece, Portugal, and Spain.

[b]Hong Kong, Korea, Singapore, and Taiwan.

stresses the gains to the downstream firms and to the whole economy that can be obtained from promoting and protecting the upstream producers of high-technology goods. There are said to be synergistic links between the makers of computers and the makers of microchips. It is therefore better to make chips *and* computers than import chips to make computers. Furthermore, a country that does not make its own chips will be at the mercy of foreign suppliers, who may favor their own country's computer industry by meeting its needs more faithfully.

The industries developing and using new technologies may in fact confer significant benefits on the whole economy. They train engineers and workers, whose skills can then be used for many other tasks. And they cannot always count on recovering fully their investments in their workers; other firms can hire them away. Nor can they count on recovering fully their investments in research; the newer the product or process involved, the larger the risk of technical or economic failure.

These same uncertainties, however, raise serious questions about the wisdom of using trade policies or, for that matter, other selective policies to protect or promote the production of high-technology goods. There are two reasons for concern.

First, recall the practical objection to the traditional infant-industry argument. It is hard to decide which infants to protect. Clearly, it is even harder to decide which technologies to protect, precisely because they are new and untested. Furthermore, tariffs and other trade barriers provide protection by raising prices, and this price-raising effect must be weighed against the gain to the rest of the economy provided by protecting high-technology firms. In 1986, the United States and Japan made an agreement designed to raise the prices of Japanese micro chips; it was inspired by charges of dumping brought by American chip producers. The computer industry objected strongly, because the higher prices were hurting them. Finally, a selective, sector-by-sector approach to promoting innovation may go very wrong in the United States. Political pressures will be brought to bear on behalf of individual firms or sectors, not because they are particularly innovative, but because they are major employers in individual communities or regions. A senator from California will want to support high-technology firms in Silicon Valley, not because they enhance the efficiency of the whole economy but because there are votes in the Valley.

Second, trade measures or subsidies for high-technology sectors invite retaliation. Recall the example in Chapter 7, where an American firm, Acme, and a Japanese firm, Edo, were racing to develop a new product, and each firm was subsidized by its government. Because the firms were identical, the subsidies canceled each other completely, leaving the firms unaffected. The countries' citizens suffered, however, as they had to pay the taxes required to finance the subsidies.

Proponents of assisting high-technology firms acknowledge these and other objections:[14]

> Even if one accepts the notion that competitive advantage in such industries can be created by government action, one need not conclude that such action is warranted—it all depends on the costs and benefits. And these are devilishly difficult to measure with any precision....
> [Most] of the firms in such industries are global players, with extensive sales, production, and even research operations scattered around the world Increasingly, they are also linked with their foreign competitors through a web of strategic alliances and joint ventures. Does a national trade and domestic policy agenda for such industries make sense?... Should policies to promote a domestic high-technology production base be limited to American owned companies, or should they include the American subsidiaries of foreign companies?

[14]Laura D'Andrea Tyson, *Who's Bashing Whom? Trade Conflict in High-Technology Industries* (Washington, D.C.: Institute for International Economics, 1992), pp. 12–13.

Nevertheless, the author of these paragraphs favors an active industrial policy for high-technology firms, including the use of trade measures to protect domestic markets and the use of unilateral market-opening measures to capture foreign markets:

> Under some circumstances, the costs of inaction for American economic welfare are unacceptably high. We must not be hoodwinked by the soothing notion that, in the absence of U.S. intervention, the fate of America's high-technology industries will be determined by market forces. Instead, they will be manipulated by the trade, regulatory, and industrial policies of our trading partners.

Many economists favor subsidies for research, which would help high-technology sectors to develop new products. Many favor subsidies for training scientists, engineers, and workers. Some might also favor policies aimed at helping small, innovative firms to raise venture capital. But most economists are skeptical of efforts to pick individual "winners" and are especially skeptical of using trade policies to foster innovation or investment by high-technology firms.

Competition Policies

Some of those who favor trade measures and subsidies for high-technology sectors say that they might change their minds if all such practices were outlawed globally or regulated by GATT rules. But many of the most objectionable practices are private-sector practices, like those of the Japanese *keiretsu*, mentioned earlier. They are not government practices. A more comprehensive trade regime would be required to regulate those practices effectively, and that may be the largest task on the long-term agenda.

Trade liberalization has focused mainly on the policies of governments. As it has proceeded, however, liberalization has revealed many private-sector practices that prevent further liberalization and even threaten to reverse it by inducing retaliation. It is becoming increasingly clear, moreover, that private-sector pressures for conventional protection and for antidumping duties frequently reflect the efforts of domestic firms to defend their own collusive arrangements,[15] and that large firms sometimes prevent their suppliers and customers from doing business with their foreign competitors. Furthermore, the privatizations of the 1980s, involving telecommunications firms and other public utilities, have reduced the coverage of the GATT code on government procurement. Finally, the operations of multinational firms have altered the workings of traditional trade policies, and the firms themselves are affected in turn by laws and regulations that prevent them from buying into local firms or force them to meet local-content requirements.

Traditional trade policies are thus interacting broadly with various industrial

---

[15]An EC study, for example, found that half of the firms in the European chemical industry that were seeking relief from foreign price cutting *via* antidumping duties were also being charged with engaging in collusive price-fixing arrangements. The EC study also found that antidumping duties provided a high level of protection, facilitated cartelization of the industry, and reduced incentives for structural adjustment.

policies and, more importantly, with national policies on mergers and acquisitions, monopolistic practices, and the exercise of contract and property rights. These competition policies, like the GATT rules, seek to promote economic efficiency by making markets more competitive and preventing various forms of discrimination. Nevertheless, competition and trade rules can come into conflict and need to be harmonized. Freer trade, for example, raises the number of actual or potential competitors in any single national market and should thus make a government more willing to approve mergers between domestic firms—mergers that would have monopolistic consequences under a less liberal trade regime.

Governments are starting to study these matters and even to cooperate in limited ways. The United States has made agreements with the EC, Canada, and others to avoid jurisdictional conflicts and apply a common approach to problems of joint concern. Hard issues lie ahead, however, especially between Washington and Tokyo, and they will lead to trade disputes if the two governments cannot agree on ways to regulate private-sector practices that are seen by U.S. firms as obstacles to entering the Japanese market.

SUMMARY

The Uruguay Round of trade negotiations took up trade-policy problems left over from previous rounds, including the liberalization of agricultural trade, the need to accept more imports from the developing countries, and the need to improve the GATT rules for settling trade disputes. But it also took up a number of new problems, including the freeing of trade in services and the protection of intellectual property. The agenda was strongly influenced by the United States, which sought to generate domestic support for the GATT system by stressing the concerns of American farmers, the service sector, and other domestic groups dissatisfied with previous GATT rounds.

The agricultural issue was the largest obstacle to the completion of the Uruguay Round. It pitted the Unites States, which sought to end all trade-distorting agricultural policies, against the European Community, which was reluctant to change its Common Agricultural Policy. The disagreement held up the round for two years, but it was resolved at the end of 1992, after the EC agreed to reform the CAP by reducing farm-price supports and using deficiency payments to maintain farmers' incomes. The reform allowed the EC to limit its subsidized exports of farm products and thus to meet the chief demand made by the United States.

With the breaking of the deadlock on agricultural trade, the rest of the Uruguay Round began to go forward. If it is concluded successfully, it will lead to the gradual abolition of the MFA, one of the main targets of the developing countries, remove many other nontariff barriers, and reduce or eliminate many tariffs. It will also create a framework for liberalizing trade in services, strengthen the GATT process for resolving trade disputes, and establish a Multilateral Trade Organization to administer the GATT more effectively.

Nevertheless, the GATT system faces many challenges. The advent of new trading arrangements, such as the NAFTA, represents a significant shift from global to regional trade liberalization, and it poses a challenge to the principle of nondiscrimination on which the GATT is based. The trade reforms of the developing countries will require that the advanced industrial countries, including the United States, take more imports from them and make painful adaptations. The historic changes in Central and Eastern Europe pose a similar challenge, especially for Europe, and come at a time when the EC is deeply preoccupied with its own internal problems.

Economists have developed a rigorous framework for analyzing the effects of regional arrangements, including full-fledged customs unions, looser free-trade areas, and less extensive preferential arrangements. The welfare effects on the members and on the outside world can be shown to depend on the nature and size of the production and consumption effects. A customs union or free-trade area is more likely to raise its members' welfare, and raise world welfare, too, when the production effects are trade creating rather than trade diverting—when goods from low-cost countries replace goods from high-cost countries. That is more likely to happen, in turn, when a customs union adopts a low external tariff.

The EC began as a customs union. In 1985, however, its members agreed to go further—to create a single internal market by the end of 1992, with no restrictions whatsoever on movements of goods, services, capital, or labor. To achieve this objective without adopting uniform laws and regulations, the EC countries have applied the principle of mutual recognition. They have come remarkably close to reaching their ambitious goal and may go even further.

In 1989, the United States and Canada agreed to establish a free-trade area. Shortly thereafter, they undertook to include Mexico in a comprehensive North American Free Trade Agreement, which was signed in 1992. Supplementary agreements between Mexico and the United States seek to meet objections raised by labor unions and environmentalists. In Mexico, the NAFTA is seen as a way to "lock in" recent economic reforms; in the United States, it is seen as a way to promote economic development in Mexico, create additional jobs, and reduce the incentive for Mexican workers to migrate to the United States.

The recent economic reforms in Mexico reflect a trend in many developing countries—a shift from import substitution and infant-industry protection to export promotion, trade liberalization, and a friendlier attitude to foreign direct investment. The policy shift acknowledges that international trade has been a powerful "engine of growth" for many countries. For the shift to succeed, however, developing countries must be able to increase their exports, and this has led them to participate actively in the Uruguay Round, where they have sought to terminate the MFA and remove other barriers to their exports.

The countries of Central and Eastern Europe have had to alter their trade policies and patterns to move from planned to market economies. They have been obliged to move very rapidly because of the collapse of the Soviet Union, to which their trade was tightly tied. Some of them have made much progress, but the reluctance of the EC and other Western countries to accept their exports has made their task more difficult. The republics of the former Soviet Union face harder problems. The artificial division of labor imposed by Soviet central planning made them unusually interdependent, and the collapse of interrepublican trade, caused by monetary and political disorder, has led to sharp cuts in production, employment, and living standards. These hardships are now threatening the prospects for reform.

More trade issues lie ahead. Many environmentalists believe that liberal trade policies interfere with the pursuit of strict environmental standards, and some of them advocate the punitive use of trade restrictions to force adherence to those standards. Technological competition has become the rationale for new forms of the old infant-industry argument. The success of trade liberalization has revealed the need to regulate private-sector practices that tend to restrict trade. Governments are starting to understand the complex links between their trade policies and competition policies.

RECOMMENDED READINGS

This chapter has drawn heavily on the survey by Margaret Kelly, Anne Kenny McGuirk, and others, *Issues and Developments in International Trade Policy* (Washington, D.C.: International Monetary Fund, 1992).

On the issues faced by the Uruguay Round, see Jeffrey J. Schott, ed., *Completing the Uruguay Round* (Washington, D.C.: Institute for International Economics, 1990), and Robert E. Baldwin and J. David Richardson, eds., *The Uruguay Round and Beyond: Problems and Prospects* (Cambridge, Mass.: National Bureau of Economic Research, 1991).

The modern theory of customs unions is presented in Robert G. Lipsey, "The Theory of Customs Unions: A General Survey," *Economic Journal*, 70 (September 1960); recent theoretical innovations are reviewed and extended in Peter J. Lloyd, "3 × 3 Theory of Customs Unions," *Journal of International Economics*, 12 (February 1982).

The problems posed by the formation of the single European market are examined in Gary C. Hufbauer, ed., *Europe 1992: An American Perspective* (Washington, D.C.: The Brookings Institution, 1990); those posed by the North American Free Trade Agreement are examined in Gary C. Hufbauer and Jeffrey J. Schott, *NAFTA: An Assessment* (Washington, D.C.: Institute for International Economics, 1993). The implications of trade blocs for the GATT and the trading system are examined in Robert Z. Lawrence, "Emerging Regional Arrangements: Building Blocks or Stumbling Blocks?," in Richard O'Brien, ed., *Finance and the International Economy: 5* (Oxford: Oxford University Press, 1991).

The infant-industry argument is analyzed critically in Robert E. Baldwin, "The Case Against Infant-Industry Tariff Protection," *Journal of Political Economy*, 77 (May/June 1969). The trade policies of developing countries are surveyed by Anne O. Krueger, "Trade Policies in Developing Countries," in R. W. Jones and P. B. Kenen, eds., *Handbook of International Economics* (Amsterdam: North-Holland, 1984), ch. 12. The effects of inward-looking and outward-looking policies are compared by the World Bank, *World Development Report* (Washington, D.C.: World Bank, 1987). The benefits, costs, and problems of trade reform in the developing countries are debated by Rudiger Dornbusch and Dani Rodrik, "Trade Liberalization and Development," *Journal of Economic Perspectives*, 6 (Winter, 1992).

On the effects of trade preferences, see Tracy Murray, *Trade Preferences for Developing Countries* (New York: John Wiley, 1977); also Andre Sapir and Lars Lundberg, "The U.S. Generalized System of Preferences and Its Impacts," in R. E. Baldwin and A. O. Krueger, eds., *The Structure and Evolution of Recent U.S. Trade Policy* (Chicago: University of Chicago Press, 1984).

On trade problems and policies in Central and Eastern Europe, see Carl B. Hamilton and L. Alan Winters, "Opening Up International Trade with Eastern Europe," *Economic Policy*, 14 (April, 1992), and Oleh Havrylyshyn and John Williamson, *From Soviet disUnion to Eastern Economic Community?*, Policy Analysis in International Economics 35 (Washington, D.C.: Institute for International Economics, 1991); see also Constantine Michaelopoulos and David Tarr, *Trade and Payments Arrangements for the States of the Former USSR* (Washington, D.C.: World Bank, 1992).

For studies of competition and trade in high-technology sectors, see Laura d'Andrea Tyson, *Who's Bashing Whom? Trade Conflict in High-Technology Industries* (Washington, D.C.: Institute for International Economics, 1992). The whole range of future trade-policy issues is examined by Geza Feketekuty, *The New Trade Agenda* (Washington, D.C.: Group of Thirty, 1993).

QUESTIONS AND PROBLEMS

(1) Use supply and demand curves to show why a country that would export wheat if it had no domestic agricultural program must use import tariffs or quotas when it supports domestic farm prices above world prices.

(2) Use supply and demand curves for a closed economy to show that deficiency payments are better than price supports for maintaining farmers' incomes above the level that would prevail without either policy.

(3) A customs union violates the most-favored-nation clause, because its members eliminate their tariffs on imports from each other but not on imports from the outside world. Yet the GATT permits customs unions while banning other violations of the most-favored-nation clause. Is there any analytical justification for this apparent inconsistency?

(4) In Figure 11-1, on a trade-diverting customs union, Britain loses and Portugal gains from eliminating the tariff on wine, and it can likewise be shown that Britain gains and Portugal loses from eliminating the tariff on cloth. Does this mean that the union has no net effect on welfare?

(5) Show that the expressions in Note 11-2 for the changes in British, Portuguese, and union welfare become identical to those in Note 11-1 when the external tariff on wine does not change.

(6) Suppose that the United States imposes an "effluent tax" on firms that pollute the air or water. Use supply and demand curves like those in Figure 9-1 to show what will happen to consumption, production, and imports. Then show what will happen if the United States uses a tariff to offset the effect of the effluent tax on domestic production. Should it do so? Explain.

(7) "It is better to produce micro chips than potato chips. Hence, high-technology industries deserve protection from import competition." Comment.

(8) Consider a question posed by a passage quoted in the text. Should policies aimed at promoting high-technology sectors be limited to American-owned firms, or should they include the American affiliates of foreign firms?

(9) Governments adhering to the GATT code on government procurement cannot discriminate against foreign firms when buying goods and services. Would you favor a similar rule to prevent companies from discriminating against foreign firms when buying capital equipment, parts, or services?

PART THREE

INTERNATIONAL MONETARY THEORY AND POLICY

12

The Balance of Payments and the Foreign-Exchange Market

INTRODUCTION

When looking at the microeconomics of the open economy, we concentrated on the allocation of resources and the distribution of income. We saw how international transactions affect the way an economy deals with the problems of efficiency and equity. When looking at the macroeconomics of the open economy, we will concentrate on the utilization of resources. We will see how international transactions affect the way an economy deals with the problem of stability. We will examine three issues:

- How international transactions affect output and price levels, money stocks, interest rates, and other variables important for macroeconomic theory and policy.

- How international transactions affect the freedom and effectiveness with which governments can use monetary and fiscal policies to achieve and maintain economic stability.

- How international monetary arrangements, especially exchange-rate arrangements, influence the answers to these questions.

These are complicated issues, and we will devote nine chapters to them.

Introducing International Transactions

How should international transactions be introduced into macroeconomic models? Can we merely add them to familiar closed-economy models, or must we reach deeply into those models to modify the basic behavioral relationships determining income, prices, and interest rates? For many years, economists simply opened up their models by adding international transactions, without reworking the basic relationships. But trade and other international transactions affect the domestic economy profoundly, even the U.S. economy, which is less open than many others. We cannot capture the effects of international transactions without revising our models completely.

It is impossible, for example, to analyze completely the effects of a change in a country's exchange rate without allowing for *feedback effects* on its domestic economy. Some feedback effects are direct. The change in the foreign demand for a country's exports caused by an exchange-rate change will affect aggregate demand in domestic markets and will therefore affect output, income, and the price level. The income and price changes will in turn affect the domestic demand for foreign (imported) goods, and the price changes will also affect the foreign demand for domestic (exported) goods. Other feedback effects are indirect but can be even more important than the direct effects. A change in the exchange rate can induce financial flows that affect conditions in domestic asset markets, including interest rates. Therefore, an exchange-rate change can affect saving and investment in ways that alter aggregate demand, the supply of exports, and the demand for imports.

Analyzing Macroeconomic Policies

The second issue posed above asks how international interdependence limits or modifies national autonomy in the execution of economic policies. The problem has two aspects. On the one hand, an open economy has an additional policy target. Its international transactions must be balanced over time. This requirement may limit its freedom to pursue other important policy targets. On the other hand, the instruments of macroeconomic policy operate differently in an open economy.

To complicate matters, monetary and fiscal policies operate quite differently when exchange rates are pegged than when they are flexible. In a small economy with a pegged exchange rate, monetary policy cannot have any permanent effect on output, employment, or prices. In an economy with a flexible exchange rate, monetary policy can have larger effects than in a closed economy, because it affects the exchange rate itself. Furthermore, the effectiveness of monetary policy is influenced jointly by the exchange-rate regime and the degree of financial integration—the tightness of the links between national markets for bonds and other securities. Under a pegged exchange rate, tight links between national markets raise the speed at which monetary policy loses its influence. Under a flexible exchange rate, tight links enhance the influence of monetary policy.

We will prove these assertions about monetary policy in subsequent chapters. They are introduced here to show why we must consider the third issue posed earlier about the implications of exchange-rate arrangements. That issue, however, has many more dimensions. We must ask how exchange-rate arrangements affect the functioning of fiscal policy. We must ask how they affect the way an economy responds to a change in the foreign demand for its exports, a change in the foreign inflation rate, and other external shocks.

Cosmopolitan and National Perspectives Once Again

The international monetary system must be studied from a cosmopolitan as well as a national perspective. A simple example makes this clear. If the German government decides to peg the U.S. dollar price of the Deutsche mark, using techniques described later in this chapter, it will automatically peg the Deutsche mark price of the U.S. dollar. If it fixes the price of its currency at $0.60 per Deutsche mark, it will fix the price of the U.S. dollar at DM 1.67 per dollar. Putting the point in general terms, a world with n countries has only $n-1$ independent exchange rates. If every government other than the U.S. government pegs the dollar price of its own currency, the price of the dollar will be pegged automatically in terms of every foreign currency.

This point involves simple arithmetic, but it raises a major problem in political economy. Governments can come into conflict if they try simultaneously to pursue independent exchange-rate policies. The conflict can show up in foreign-exchange markets if governments intervene at cross purposes. It can also show up at the highest political levels, and the conflict can then interfere with international relationships of the greatest diplomatic and strategic importance.

How can international monetary arrangements avoid conflicts of this sort? We will use this question as an organizing principle in Chapter 19, when we review the evolution of the monetary system. We will see that the United States did not try to pursue an independent exchange-rate policy in the first decades following World War II. Because of its great economic strength and comparative self-sufficiency, it was content to be the nth country in the system. During that time, moreover, the dollar became the main international currency. It was the international *unit of account*, in that foreign governments used it to define their exchange rates. It was the international *means of payment*, in that foreign governments used it when they intervened on foreign-exchange markets to keep exchange rates close to their official values. It was an international *store of value*, in that foreign governments held dollars as reserves, to be used when they had to finance balance-of-payments deficits.

The central role of the dollar came under political attack in the 1960s, when the United States began to have balance-of-payments problems of its own. The French president, Charles de Gaulle, castigated the United States for abusing the "exorbitant privilege" conferred by the special role of the dollar. Matters were made worse a few years later when an American secretary of the Treasury told foreign officials that "the dollar is our currency but your problem." Eventually, the U.S. government decided the United States could no longer act as the nth country, and it started to pursue an active exchange-rate policy. The decision produced dramatic changes in international monetary arrangements, which have not really ended.

What Lies Ahead

A number of new terms have appeared in this introduction, such as *intervention* on foreign-exchange markets, *reserves* that countries hold to finance intervention, and *balance-of-payments* problems. The text has also referred to pegged and flexible exchange rates. Before answering the questions with which the chapter started, we must pause for definitions. We face indeed a larger task—showing how international transactions fit into a country's balance-of-payments accounts, how those accounts relate to conditions in foreign-exchange markets, and how transactions in those markets affect a country's banking system.

BALANCE-OF-PAYMENTS ACCOUNTS

A country's balance-of-payments accounts summarize its dealings with the outside world. To introduce the concepts and conventions used in those accounts, we will construct a hypothetical balance-of-payments table for the United States. We will then consider ways of balancing the cash flows that show up at the bottom of the table.

The balance-of-payments table is usually divided into two main parts, and each part has several subdivisions:

I. *The Current Account* shows all flows that directly affect the national-income accounts. It includes:
   Exports and imports of merchandise
   Exports and imports of services
   Inflows and outflows of investment income
   Grants, remittances, and other transfers

II. *The Capital Account* shows all flows that directly affect tha national balance sheet. It includes:
   Direct investments by foreign firms in their U.S. affiliates and by U.S. firms in their foreign affiliates
   Portfolio investments, which include:
      Net purchases by foreigners of U.S. securities and net lending to U.S. residents
      Net purchases by U.S. residents of foreign securities and net lending to foreigners
   Changes in cash balances, which include:
      Changes in balances held by banks and other foreign-exchange dealers, resulting from current and capital transactions
      Changes in reserves held by official institutions, resulting from intervention on foreign-exchange markets

All transactions are classified as credits ($+$) or debits ($-$). The method of classification may seem puzzling at first, but it is based on a few simple rules. If you accept them at face value, rather than try to attach deep meaning to them, you should have no trouble. Clear your mind of the notion that credits are good and debits bad. The notion is silly, because every transaction appears *twice* in the balance-of-payments table, once as a credit and once as a debit.

The Current Account

Merchandise exports appear in the first instance as credit items, because they give rise to claims on the outside world that foreigners must discharge by making payments to Americans. Merchandise imports appear in the first instance as debit items because they give rise to claims by the outside world that Americans must discharge by making payments to foreigners.

Exports and imports of services are treated analogously. When a foreign airline pays for baggage handling and aircraft maintenance at Kennedy Airport in New York, it is doing much the same thing as a foreign firm that buys machinery in the United States. It is using the services of American factors of production and incurring an obligation that must be discharged by payments to Americans. When American tourists buy tickets from that foreign airline, they are doing much the same thing as an American firm that buys steel in Brazil. They are using the services of foreign factors of production and incurring an obligation that must be discharged by payments to foreigners. (Exports and imports of services are sometimes described as *invisible* trade, because they cannot be seen to cross the border but have the same effects as visible merchandise trade. Some of the important services were described in Chapter 11.)

Inflows and outflows of investment income are put in the current account because they share two characteristics with exports and imports of goods and services. First, they give rise to claims that must be discharged by payments. Second, they reflect the use by one country of another country's capital, a factor of production, and add to the national income of the country owning the capital. A dividend paid to an American company by its Spanish affiliate is an inflow of investment income and appears in the first instance as a credit item; it represents compensation for the use by Spain of American capital, and it adds to U.S. national income. Interest paid by the U.S. Treasury to the Saudi Arabian Monetary Authority, which holds U.S. Treasury bills, is an outflow of investment income; it represents compensation for the use by the United States of Saudi Arabian capital, and it adds to Saudi Arabia's national income.

All of the credit items described thus far represent foreign payments to domestic factors of production. American exports of goods and services correspond to American spending on current output in the United States. They measure the immediate impact of foreign demand on production and employment in the United States. American imports of goods and services correspond to American spending on current output in other countries. They measure the immediate impact of American demand on production and employment in the outside world. Flows of investment income do not measure the effects of one country's demand on another country's output. Nevertheless, inflows represent additions to U.S. national income earned by American capital "working" in other countries, and outflows represent additions to other countries' national incomes earned by foreign capital "working" in the United States.

Grants, remittances, and other transfers, which appear at the foot of the current account, do *not* represent additions to income. As their names imply, they represent redistributions of income. When the U.S. government makes a grant for disaster relief or military aid, it transfers income from U.S. residents to the residents or government of another country. (Pension payments appear here, too, because they likewise represent transfers of income rather than payments for current services.) Transfers are included at this point so that the current-account balance, discussed later, will measure accurately the net change in U.S. claims on the outside world. If wheat donated to Bangladesh for famine relief were included in merchandise exports (as a credit) but the corresponding grant were not included in the current account (as a debit), we would mistakenly infer that the shipment had increased U.S. claims on Bangladesh.

There is another way to look at credits and debits, which will be especially useful when we turn to the capital account. Credits give rise to U.S. claims on foreigners that must be discharged by foreign payments to Americans. Therefore, we can think of credits as creating a foreign demand for dollars in the foreign-exchange market. Debits give rise to foreign claims on the United States that must be discharged by American payments to foreigners. Therefore, we can think of debits as creating an American demand for foreign currencies in the foreign-exchange market. The correspondence is not perfect. Some Americans may choose to be paid in foreign currencies, and some foreigners may choose to be paid in dollars. But it is close enough to be quite useful in sorting out debits and credits.

The Capital Account

Every transaction in the current account is an income-related flow. Every transaction in the capital account is an asset-related flow. Those flows that add to U.S. claims on foreigners are described as *capital outflows* and appear as debits. Those flows that add to foreign claims on the United States are described as *capital inflows* and appear as credits.[1]

These conventions are hard to assimilate. Two devices can be helpful. We can think in terms of trade in paper—deeds to real property, corporate securities, and various other debt instruments. When an American company acquires a plant in Spain, it is "importing" the deed to the plant. When an American pension fund buys bonds in Tokyo, it is "importing" securities. In each instance, the "importer" must make payment to a foreigner, just like an importer of goods or services. Alternatively, we can look at matters from the standpoint of the foreign-exchange market. When a company acquires a plant in Spain, it adds to the American demand for Spanish pesetas. When a pension fund buys shares on the Tokyo Stock Exchange, it adds to the American demand for Japanese yen. Conversely, when a Canadian insurance company buys bonds in New York, the transaction adds to foreign claims on the United States and appears as a credit in the U.S. balance of payments. The transaction is an "export" of securities, and it adds to the foreign demand for dollars.

We have already studied the first type of transaction in the capital account. Direct investments create, extend, or facilitate control over productive facilities in other countries. They are the building blocks of multinational enterprises, and we examined them in Chapter 8. (Notice, however, that U.S. direct investments include *all* increases in the claims of U.S. firms on their foreign affiliates. When Ford makes a loan to its British affiliate to finance the affiliate's purchase of steel from Belgium, the loan appears as a direct investment, even though there is no increase in the total productive capacity owned or controlled by Ford.)

All other transactions in claims to property, equities, and debt instruments appear

---

[1]Transactions that add to U.S. claims on foreigners are sometimes described as capital exports, but this terminology can be confusing. (It describes a debit as an export.) We will avoid it.

as portfolio investments. These are *arm's-length* transactions between independent entities. They are undertaken for financial or commercial reasons—to earn income, to capture capital gains or hedge against losses, or to finance trade in goods and services. They do not create or facilitate control. Portfolio investments take many forms. Corporations issue stocks and bonds abroad, and they borrow from foreign banks. Insurance companies, pension funds, and other institutional investors buy foreign securities to diversify their assets. Governments borrow from international institutions, from other governments, and from commercial banks.

The cash component of the capital account does not appear separately in published balance-of-payments tables for the United States. Its contents are scattered across the portfolio component, and they can be pulled together only with some difficulty. Nevertheless, it is helpful conceptually to collect in this one place all changes in bank balances and similar cash flows. These changes are crucial to the functioning of foreign-exchange markets and to the interpretation of the balance-of-payments accounts.

Recording Individual Transactions

Balance-of-payments accounts are built on the principles of double-entry book-keeping. Each transaction appears once as a credit and once as a debit. Most transactions appear for the first time in the current or capital account and then for the second time in the cash component of the capital account.

A German firm that buys machinery from the United States can pay for it by running down its dollar balance at an American bank or by buying dollars from a German bank and thus running down the dollar balance held by the German bank. Alternatively, it can obtain credit from the manufacturer or borrow dollars from an American bank.[2] In each case, the export of machinery will appear first as a credit in the current account. If the firm runs down its dollar balance or that of a German bank, the second entry will be a debit in the cash component of the capital account. If it borrows from its American supplier or an American bank, the second entry will be a debit in the portfolio component of the capital account. In both instances, however, the debit will testify to an increase in the *net* claims of the United States, the difference between its gross claims and gross liabilities. If the firm runs down its dollar balance or that of a German bank, it will reduce gross U.S. liabilities to foreigners. If it borrows instead, it will raise gross U.S. claims on foreigners.

These principles are illustrated in Table 12-1, which is a hypothetical balance-of-payments table for the United States. It contains seven transactions, worked out step by step:

(a) An American firm buys $240,000 worth of tin from a Malaysian company. It pays with pounds bought with dollars from a New York bank.

---

[2]It can also borrow dollars from a foreign bank—from a German bank in Frankfurt or its branch in Luxembourg, from the London branch of an American bank or, for that matter, the London branch of a Brazilian bank. We will examine some of these possibilities when we review the growth of international bank lending and of the Eurocurrency markets.

Table 12-1. Hypothetical Balance of Payments for the United States (thousands of dollars)

Item	Credit	Debit
Merchandise exports and imports		
Tin from Malaysia (a)		240
Antibiotics to Venezuela (b)	300	
Jet aircraft to India (g)	200	
Service exports and imports		
Shipping (c)	50	
Investment income		
Profit from German subsidiary (d)	75	
Balance on current account	*385*	
Direct investment		
Plant in Spain (f)		400
Portfolio investment		
U.S. Government loan (g)		200
Sale by foreigners of U.S. securities (e)		175
Cash component*		
Increase (+) in dollars held by foreign banks		
Venezuelan bank (b)		300
German bank (d)		75
Spanish bank (f)	400	
Net increase (+)	*25*	
Increase (−) in foreign currencies held by U.S. banks		
New York bank in pounds (a)	240	
Chicago bank in pounds (c)		50
Boston bank in yen (e)	175	
Net increase (−)	*365*	
Balance on capital account		*385*

*Note carefully the signs of the items in the cash component. As increases in U.S. liabilities to foreigners are credit items in the capital account, increases in the dollar balances of foreign banks show up as credits (+) in the cash component, and decreases show up as debits (−). As increases in U.S. claims on foreigners are debit items in the capital account, increases in the foreign-currency balances of U.S. banks show up as debits (−) in the cash component, and decreases show up as credits (+).

The purchase of tin appears as a merchandise import in the current account. The transfer of pounds to pay for it appears in the cash component of the capital account. The purchase of tin is a debit because it gives rise to a foreign claim on the United States. The transfer of pounds is a credit because it discharges the foreign claim by reducing the foreign-currency holdings of the U.S. bank that supplied the pounds. How will the transaction be executed? The American firm will write a check for $240,000 (plus a small commission) against its own bank account, hand the check over to the New York bank, and receive a *draft* for the equivalent in pounds. (If the exchange rate is $1.60 per pound, the draft will be for £150,000.) The American firm will endorse the draft to the Malaysian firm, which will sell it to its own bank in Kuala Lumpur and obtain the equivalent of £150,000 in Malaysian ringitt. The bank in Kuala Lumpur will send the draft to London, where the British bank on which it was drawn will deduct £150,000 from the pound (sterling) balance of the New York bank that issued it.

(b) An American firm sells $300,000 worth of antibiotics to Venezuela. It is paid with dollars bought from a bank in Caracas.

The sale of antibiotics appears as a merchandise export in the current account. The transfer of dollars to pay for it appears in the cash component of the capital account. The sale of antibiotics is a credit because it gives rise to a U.S. claim on the outside world. The dollar transfer is a debit because it discharges the U.S. claim by reducing the dollar holdings of the bank in Caracas. In this case, the Venezuelan importer will buy a $300,000 draft from the bank in Caracas, paying with a check for the equivalent in Venezuelan bolivares. The importer will endorse the draft to the U.S. firm supplying the antibiotics, and the firm will deposit the draft in its own bank account. Finally, the draft will be sent to the New York bank where the bank in Caracas keeps its dollar balance, and $300,000 will be deducted from that balance.

(c) A British firm pays $50,000 to lease an American ship to carry frozen beef from Buenos Aires to Liverpool. It pays with pounds bought from a British bank.

This transaction is similar to an export sale. The American owner of the ship provides a service using American resources. Therefore, the rental fee appears as a credit in the current account. If the British firm pays in pounds and the American recipient sells them to a bank in Chicago, the transaction appears as a debit in the cash component of the capital account. It raises the pound (sterling) balance of the Chicago bank, adding to U.S. claims on foreigners.

(d) The German subsidiary of an American firm remits $75,000 in profits to its American parent. It pays with dollars bought from a German bank.

This transaction is also similar to an export sale. The parent company in the United States is being paid for the services of capital and technology put to work in Germany, and the payment appears as a credit in the current account. The offsetting entry appears in the cash component of the capital account, where the dollar holdings of the German bank fall by $75,000. This is, of course, a debit, because there is a reduction in foreign claims on the United States.

(e) A Canadian insurance company sells $175,000 of IBM stock to an American investor and uses the proceeds to buy bonds in Tokyo. It employs a Boston bank to execute the whole transaction.

Both parts of this transaction appear in the capital account. The sale of stock appears as a debit in the portfolio component of the capital account, reflecting a reduction in foreign claims on the United States—in foreign holdings of American securities. The Canadian insurance company, however, needs Japanese yen to purchase bonds in Tokyo and buys them from the Boston bank handling the transaction. Its purchase of yen appears as a credit in the cash component of the capital account, reflecting a reduction in U.S. claims on the outside world—in the foreign-currency (yen) holdings of the Boston bank.

(f) An American company spends $400,000 to build a new factory in Spain. It uses a Spanish bank to execute the foreign-exchange transaction.

This transaction appears in the balance-of-payments table even though no goods, services, or securities cross the U.S. border. Both parts appear in the capital account. The building of the factory is a direct investment and appears as a debit in the capital account. It is an "import" of the title to the plant. The payment for the plant appears as a credit in the cash component. The American company must buy pesetas from a Spanish bank, and the bank builds up its dollar holdings with the American bank where it keeps its dollar balance.

(g) The Export-Import Bank, an agency of the U.S. government, lends $200,000 to the Indian government to buy jet aircraft from an American manufacturer.

This transaction does not appear in the cash component of the capital account, because the dollars lent to India come back immediately to pay for the jet aircraft. The export of aircraft appears, as usual, as a credit in the current account. The loan increases the claims of the United States and appears as a debit in the portfolio component of the capital account.

Totaling the entries in Table 12-1, we find that credits are equal to debits. There is $385,000 *surplus* on current account, and it is matched by a $385,000 *deficit* on capital account. This equality must always hold, because every transaction enters once as a credit and once as a debit.[3] By grouping certain credits and debits, however, we can learn a lot about a country's international transactions.

THE CURRENT ACCOUNT AND NATIONAL INCOME

The current-account surplus in Table 12-1 says that trade in goods and services and investment-income flows contributed more to the national income of

---

[3]In actual balance-of-payments accounts, there is usually a gap between recorded credits and debits, and it is covered by an item called errors and omissions. The gap arises because the accounts are not built up transaction by transaction, with each one entered twice. They are built up from data on each *type* of transaction. Data on trade flows are collected when goods cross the frontier; data on services are collected from shippers, travelers, and others who supply or buy the services; data on capital flows are collected from companies, securities dealers, banks, and other institutions. There are errors in each category, and large errors in some categories. Data on services and investment income are hard to collect, and data on capital flows are likewise incomplete. If you purchase foreign stocks and bonds through a broker in London or Zurich, the statisticians in Washington will not know it. They may catch the corresponding transfer of bank balances (a credit) but not the transfer of securities (a debit). Statisticians are often asked how much of the gap measured by errors and omissions is due to statistical error and how much is due to statistical omission. The question betrays misunderstanding. The errors-and-omissions entry is an accounting device; it is not a measure of statistical *quality*.

Table 12-2. Changes in the International Investment
Position of the United States (thousands of dollars)

Assets held by U.S. residents	+235
Held by U.S. government	
Loans and other claims	+200
Held by other U.S. residents	
Direct investments	+400
Foreign securities	—
Claims reported by U.S. banks	−365
Assets held by foreigners	−150
Held by foreign governments	—
Held by other foreigners	
Direct investments	—
U.S. securities	−175
Claims reported by U.S. banks	+25

Note: In Table 12-1, increases in assets held by U.S. residents were debits (−), and their signs are reversed here; increases in assets held by foreigners were credits (+), and their signs are the same here. The decrease in U.S. claims reported by U.S. banks is the decrease in the banks' own deposits with foreign banks; the increase in foreign claims reported by U.S. banks is the increase in the deposits of foreign banks.

the United States than to the national incomes of other countries. Furthermore, it says that the United States "paid its way" in the world. Indeed, it did more. It increased its claims on the outside world. In Chapter 8, we examined the international investment position of the United States. In Table 12-2, we see how the seven balance-of-payments transactions affect that position. A current-account surplus is necessarily reflected by an increase in domestic claims on the outside world, a decrease in foreign claims on the domestic economy, or a combination of the two, as in Table 12-2.

Remember an earlier warning, however, that credits are not "good" nor debits "bad" from any economic point of view. A current-account surplus represents an addition to national income, but a deliberate attempt to run a current-account surplus may not be a good way to stimulate income and employment. In Chapter 9, we saw that a tariff could be used to raise employment when the real wage was rigid. But a tariff is an inefficient instrument, inferior to a production or wage subsidy, because of its consumption effects. Furthermore, it is a "begger-thy-neighbor" remedy for unemployment, because it can reduce employment in other countries and provoke retaliation. An attempt to run or raise a current-account surplus is likewise inefficient and uncertain. The policy instruments used may interfere with efficiency and reduce economic welfare even though they raise output and employment. They may also reduce employment in the outside world, which is unneighborly and can also invite retaliation.

Another point will come up in Chapter 13. Although a current-account surplus says that trade in goods and services and investment-income flows have added more to domestic income than to foreign income, an increase in a current-account surplus does not necessarily reflect an increase in domestic income. It may indeed result from a fall in domestic income that has reduced the demand for imports.

Finally, a current-account surplus says that the domestic economy is not spending its entire income. To see why this is so, we must open up the basic relationship used in national-income accounts.

In a closed economy, there are three sources of demand for domestic output: consumption (C), government spending (G), and domestic investment (I). Therefore,

$$Y = C + G + I, \tag{1}$$

where Y is gross domestic product.[4] In an open economy, there is an additional source of demand and an additional source of supply. Exports of goods and services (X) constitute the additional source of demand for domestic output. Imports of goods and services (M) supplement supplies in domestic markets. Therefore, the open-economy equation is

$$Y + M = C + G + I + X. \tag{2}$$

Rearranging this equation,

$$X - M = Y - (C + G + I). \tag{3}$$

Define domestic *absorption* (A) as the sum of consumption, government spending, and investment, so that

$$X - M = Y - A. \tag{4}$$

But X *minus* M is the current-account balance when there are no transfers (we neglect them here), and Y *minus* A is the gap between output or income and absorption or expenditure. Therefore, equation (4) says that a country with a current-account surplus is not absorbing all of its own output. It is using some to build up claims on the outside world.

---

[4]In a closed economy, Y can be interpreted as gross *domestic* product (GDP) or as gross *national* product (GNP). There is no difference between them. In an open economy, they can differ significantly. GDP is the value of output originating within a country's borders. GNP is the value of output accruing as gross income to its residents. A country that pays investment income to foreigners must deduct it from GDP to obtain GNP. One that employs foreign workers who are not counted as permanent residents must likewise deduct their wages from GDP to obtain GDP. As we will interpret Y as GDP rather than GNP, exports of goods and services in equation (2) must be deemed to exclude investment income earned from foreigners, and imports of goods and services must be deemed to exclude investment income paid to foreigners. Hence, the difference between them in equation (3) will not measure the current-account balance exactly. Until recently, the U.S. national accounts were organized to feature GNP, but they have been revised to feature GDP, because of the growing importance of investment-income flows between the United States and the outside world. Other countries likewise feature GDP in their national accounts.

Rich countries can afford to do this. Poor countries cannot. They should indeed be trying to acquire additional resources for capital formation in order to promote economic development. Therefore, they should run current-account deficits and build up debt to the outside world. This is what most developing countries do. The United States did it, too, for most of the nineteenth century. It borrowed in foreign financial markets, mainly London, to finance its own development, especially the building of the railroads, and the proceeds covered its current-account deficits.

A current-account deficit does not become worrisome if it can be financed on acceptable terms and the proceeds of the borrowing are used well. A country can run into trouble, however, if it has to cover its current-account deficit by short-term borrowing (or running down reserves) and must then repay its debts before it can eliminate its deficit. It can also run into trouble if it has to borrow at high interest rates or refinance its debts at interest rates higher than those at which it borrowed initially. Finally, it can run into trouble if it fritters away borrowed resources by consuming rather than investing them. Its capital stock will not rise rapidly enough to yield the "growth dividend" it needs to repay its debt.

The connections between borrowing, consumption, and investment can be illustrated clearly by carrying the algebra one step further. Recall another basic statement made by the national-income accounts. Income can be used for three purposes: consumption (C), tax payments (T), and saving (S). Thus,

$$Y = C + T + S. \tag{5}$$

This statement is equally true for open economies, and it can be used to replace Y in equation (3):

$$X - M = (C + T + S) - (C + G + I)$$
$$= (S - I) + (T - G). \tag{6}$$

A current-account surplus $(X > M)$ must be matched by a private-sector surplus $(S > I)$ or a public-sector surplus $(T > G)$. A current-account deficit must be matched by a private-sector deficit or public-sector deficit.[5]

When a country starts to run a current-account deficit, a thoughtful observer will want to look at the right side of equation (6) to see whether there has been a decrease in saving, increase in investment, or increase in the budget deficit. There is reason to worry about the country's long-term prospects if the onset of a current-account deficit reflects smaller saving or a larger budget deficit. In both cases, the country is borrowing abroad or running down its foreign assets to sustain or raise consumption, whether by the private or public sector. There is less cause to worry when the onset of a current-account deficit reflects an increase in investment. In this case, the country is building up its capital stock more quickly and, therefore, increasing its future output.

---

[5]In a closed economy, X and M vanish, so $(S - I) + (T - G) = 0$. If the government balances its budget, moreover, $T = G$, so that $S - I = 0$ and $S = I$. Saving must equal investment, the assertion made in elementary macroeconomic models.

All of these issues will come up again when we look at the debt problems of the developing countries and at the current-account deficits of the United States.

CASH FLOWS AND THE FOREIGN-EXCHANGE MARKET

A country that runs a current-account surplus, building up net claims on the outside world, is adding to its wealth. However, we must pay attention to the composition of those claims. Look again at Table 12-1. The United States added to its income-producing claims (the direct investment in Spain and the load to India). It also redeemed a claim previously held by a foreigner (the Canadian investment in IBM stock). In the process, however, foreign banks built up their cash balances with U.S. banks by $25,000, and U.S. banks ran down their cash balances with foreign banks by $365,000. Let us look more closely at these changes in cash balances.

Banks supplied the currencies required for most of the transactions in Table 12-1. In the first transaction, for example, a New York bank sold $240,000 worth of pounds to the American firm purchasing tin from Malaysia. In other words, the bank served as a foreign-exchange dealer. Looking at matters from this standpoint, we can treat changes in the banks' cash balances as changes in their inventories. And when we see a change in any dealer's inventory, we are bound to ask whether the dealer will try to reverse it.

It is easy to concoct cases in which banks will not want to reverse a change in their cash balances. When interest rates in the United States are higher than in other countries, banks and other foreign-exchange dealers will want to hold more dollars and fewer pounds, marks, and yen. Foreign banks might be quite happy with the $25,000 increase in their dollar balances caused by their dealings with their customers, and U.S. banks might likewise be happy with the $365,000 decrease in their foreign-currency balances. When banks and other dealers expect the dollar to appreciate (to become more valuable in terms of other currencies), they will want to hold more dollars. In this case, too, they might be happy with the changes shown in Table 12-1.

There are clear limits, however, to the changes that banks can tolerate. If they do not have adequate inventories of foreign currencies, they cannot meet their customers' needs and cannot continue to function effectively as foreign-exchange dealers. Hence, banks may try to reverse large changes in their inventories.

It is useful at this point to distinguish between two parts of the foreign-exchange market. Heretofore, we have been concerned with the "retail" market, where banks meet the needs of their customers. Most transactions in that market take place at exchange rates (prices) posted by the banks, although large customers can sometimes shop around to get more favorable rates. When banks want to adjust their inventories, however, they turn to the "wholesale" market, where foreign-exchange dealers do business with each other. This market is nothing more than a network of telephone connections linking the banks' trading rooms. But it is like any other wholesale market. Variations in supply and demand lead to price changes.

Suppose that the Boston bank listed in Table 12-1 wants to rebuild its holdings of yen, which fell by the equivalent of $175,000 when it sold yen to the Canadian insurance company. The bank will place a bid in the wholesale market, saying how many yen it wants to buy and the price it is willing to pay. Its bid for yen is also an offer of dollars, and the price it is bidding for yen is therefore the price it is asking for dollars.

If it can find a seller at its quoted price, the Boston bank will make a contract right away. Suppose that it finds a Seattle bank that wants to sell yen. The Boston bank will deliver dollars to the Seattle bank, which will deliver yen to the Boston bank. The transfer of dollars can take place anywhere in the United States—on the books of a New York bank, for example, where the Boston and Seattle banks keep working balances. The transfer of yen can take place in Tokyo or some other trading center such as London, where banks can hold foreign-currency deposits.

There may be no other bank, however, willing to sell yen at the price quoted by the Boston bank. That bank will have then to raise its bid until it finds a buyer (or decides to withdraw temporarily from the market). This is how exchange rates change in the wholesale market, and rates in the retail market follow them closely. But it is not the end of the story. It is time to introduce the fundanental distinction between flexible and pegged exchange rates.

MONETARY ARRANGEMENTS AND THE ADJUSTMENT PROCESS

When no one comes forward to offer yen at the exchange rate quoted by the Boston bank, there is an *excess demand* for yen in the foreign exchange-exchange market (and thus an *excess supply* of dollars). Under a system of flexible exchange rates, the yen will *appreciate* (the dollar will *depreciate*). Under a system of pegged exchange rates, governments will intervene to stabilize the yen-dollar rate. The Japanese government will sell yen in exchange for dollars to meet the excess demand and prevent the yen from appreciating. The excess demand for yen will show up as an increase in the Japanese government's dollar holdings. Those holdings are described as *reserves*, and changes in reserves are frequently used to measure the *overall* surplus or deficit in a country's balance of payments:

> **A country is said to have a surplus in its balance of payments if there is an increase in the difference between its official reserves and its liabilities to foreign official institutions. It is said to have a deficit if there is a decrease.**

The surplus or deficit measured this way is sometimes called the balance on official settlements. In this particular example, the Japanese balance of payments displays a surplus, measured by the increase in Japanese reserves, and the U.S. balance of payments displays a deficit, measured by the increase in U.S. liabilities to the Japanese government.

At the end of World War II, governments adopted arrangements closely resembling a system of pegged exchange rates. The arrangements were not as simple or mechanical as those we use below to illustrate a pegged-rate system. First, the pegs were not permanent. From time to time, a government *devalued* its currency, decreasing its official value; less frequently, a government *revalued* its currency, increasing its official value. Second, most governments interfered systematically with the changes in money supplies that play a central role in balance-of-payments adjustment under pegged rates.

In 1971, the pegged-rate system broke down. Two years later, after unsuccessful attempts to rehabilitate it, the major industrial countries went over to arrangements closely resembling a system of flexible exchange rates. Once again, the arrangements were not as simple as those described below. Some countries continued to peg their currencies. Others intervened from time to time to combat erratic fluctuations in exchange rates or reduce the speed with which they were changing.

The monetary systems described and examined more thoroughly in subsequent chapters should be regarded as prototypes of actual exchange-rate regimes. They will help us to identify and analyze the main ingredients of the balance-of-payments adjustment process and the policy problems that arise under each regime.

Adjustment Under Flexible Exchange Rates

Under a system of flexible exchange rates, prices of currencies fluctuate freely in response to changes in supply and demand. There can be large fluctuations from week to week and month to month, as in Figure 12-1, which shows daily changes in the dollar prices of the yen and Deutsche mark. There can be long swings in rates, as in Figure 12-2, which shows movements in the value of the dollar measured by a weighted average of national exchange rates.

Changes in flexible exchange rates are normally initiated by banks' attempts to regulate their inventories. But the inventory changes to which they are reacting reflect more fundamental forces—changes in supply and demand that come from the households, firms, and financial institutions that buy and sell goods, services, and assets. When the Boston bank attempted to buy yen to rebuild its inventory and drove up the value of the yen in terms of the dollar, it was responding to the demand for yen that came from the Canadian insurance company.

Changes in exchange rates, moreover, modify behavior by households, firms, and financial institutions. They alter the demands for goods, services, and assets that have prices denominated in different currencies. An appreciation of the yen in terms of the dollar makes Japanese goods and services more expensive for American households and firms, which will reduce their purchases. The corresponding depreciation of the dollar in terms of the yen makes American goods and services less expensive for Japanese households and firms, which will raise their purchases. The fall in American purchases will reduce the demand for yen in the foreign-exchange market: the rise in Japanese purchases will raise the demand for dollars.

This adjustment process is described by Figures 12-3 and 12-4. The left side of Figure 12-3 shows the American demand for yen. The price of the yen is measured in dollars on the vertical axis; the quantity of yen demanded is measured on the horizontal axis. The demand curve DD is negatively sloped because an appreciation of the yen (an increase in its dollar price) raises the dollar prices of Japanese goods and services, reducing the American demand for them and thus the American demand for yen. When the dollar price of the yen is OP, the quantity demanded is OU. When the yen appreciates to OP', the quantity demanded falls to OU'. The position of the American demand curve depends on prices in Japan and the

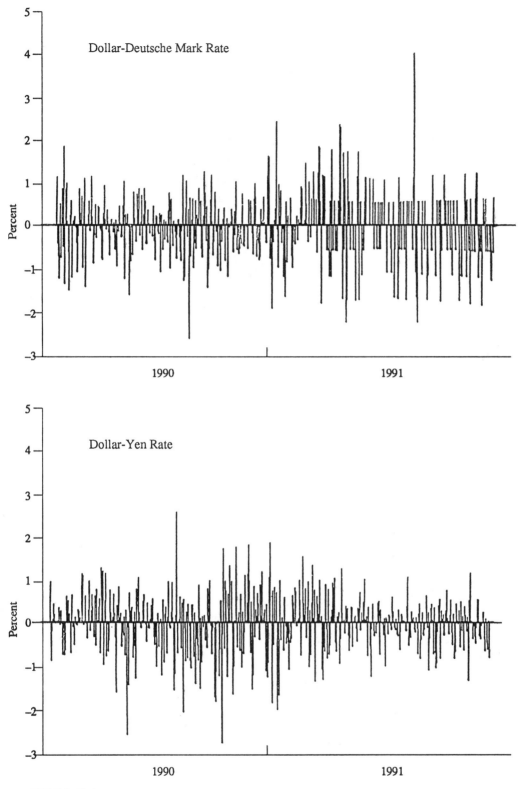

FIGURE 12-1
Daily Fluctuations in Exchange Rates, 1990—1991
Percentage changes from one day to the next in the dollar values of the yen and
Deutsche mark. *Source:* International Finance Section data bank, Princeton University.

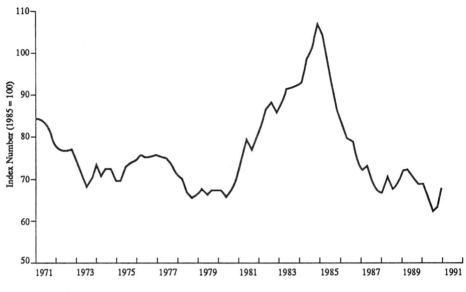

FIGURE 12-2
Average Value of the Dollar in Terms of Foreign Currencies, 1971—1991
Scales have been chosen so that increases represent appreciations of the U.S. dollar
against a weighted average of other currencies. *Source:* International Monetary Fund,
International Financial Statistics.

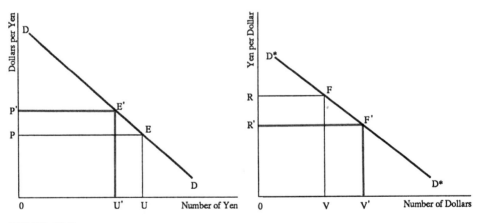

FIGURE 12-3
Demand Curves for Yen and Dollars
The curve *DD* on the left shows the American demand for yen. The price of the yen
is measured on the vertical axis and the quantity demanded on the horizontal axis.
An appreciation of the yen from *OP* to *OP'* reduces the quantity demanded from *OU*
to *OU'*. The curve *D*D** on the right shows the Japanese demand for dollars. The price
of the dollar is measured on the vertical axis and the quantity demanded on the
horizontal axis. The appreciation of the yen from *OP* to *OP'* shown on the left appears
on the right as a depreciation of the dollar from *OR* to *OR'*, and the quantity
demanded rises from *OV* to *OV'*. The Japanese demand curve *D*D** can be used to
derive a supply curve for yen. When the dollar price of the yen is *OP*, so that the yen
price of the dollar is *OR*, Japanese supply *OVFR* yen. When the yen appreciates, to *OP'*
so that the dollar depreciates to *OR'*, Japanese supply *OV'F'R'* yen. When *D*D** is
elastic, *OV'F'R'* will be larger than *OVFR*, and the supply curve of yen will be positively
sloped; when *D*D** is inelastic, *OV'F'R'* will be smaller than *OVFR*, and the supply
curve of yen will be negatively sloped.

318

United States, income in the United States, and all of the other variables affecting American demands for Japanese goods, services, and assets. The right side of Figure 12-3 shows the Japanese demand curve for dollars. The price of the dollar is measured in yen on the vertical axis; the quantity of dollars demanded is measured on the horizontal axis. The demand curve $D*D*$ is negatively sloped for the same reason that DD is negatively sloped. When the dollar price of the yen is OP on the left side, the yen price of the dollar is OR on the right side, and the Japanese demand or dollars is OV. When the yen appreciates to OP' on the left side, the dollar depreciates to OR' on the right side, and the Japanese demand for dollars rises to OV'. The position of the Japanese demand curve depends on all of the other variables affecting Japanese demands for American goods, services, and assets.

The two demand curves in Figure 12-3 cannot be used directly to determine the market-clearing exchange rate between the yen and dollar. Their axes measure different things. But the Japanese demand curve for dollars can be used to derive a Japanese supply curve of yen, which can then be combined with the American demand curve for yen to determine the exchange rate. The supply of yen is the quantity that Japanese will offer when they bid for dollars:

$$\text{Supply of yen} = \text{demand for dollars} \times \text{yen per dollar.}$$

When the dollar price of the yen is OP, the yen price of the dollar is OR, and the supply of yen is $OR \times OV$ or $OVFR$ yen. When the dollar price of the yen rises to OP', the yen price of the dollar falls to OR', and the supply of yen is $OV'F'R'$ yen. The quantity of yen supplied can rise or fall when the price of the yen rises. It rises when the demand curve $D*D*$ is *elastic*. It falls when $D*D*$ is *inelastic*.

In Figure 12-4, we copy the demand curve for yen, DD, from the left side of Figure 12-3 and add the supply curve of yen derived in the manner just described. The supply curve SS is positively sloped when the Japanese demand curve $D*D*$ is elastic, so that an increase in the price of the yen raises the quantity supplied. The supply curve is negatively sloped when $D*D*$ is inelastic, so that an increase in the price reduces the quantity supplied. The supply and demand curves intersect at E. This point gives the exchange rate that clears the foreign-exchange market.[6] When the price of the yen is OP, Americans demand OU yen, and Japanese supply them.

To see how flexible exchange rates function, consider the effects of an increase in the American demand for Japanese goods. It will raise the American demand for yen and shift the demand curve from DD to $D'D'$. American banks may run down their holdings of yen to satisfy their customers, but they will have to replenish those holdings eventually and will have to enter the foreign-exchange market to buy yen. There will be an excess demand for yen equal to UU'' at the initial exchange rate OP, and the yen will start to appreciate. As it does so, however, Americans will

---

[6]We will call it a market-clearing rate, rather than an equilibrium rate, because E may not denote a full-fledged equilibrium. We will soon see that exchange rates can affect domestic prices and other variables. When this happens, the curves DD and SS will move to new positions, changing the market-clearing rate. We should not describe E as an equilibrium point (and OP as an equilibrium exchange rate) unless we are sure that all the effects of the exchange rate OP have worked themselves out in each country so that the exchange rate will be self-perpetuating.

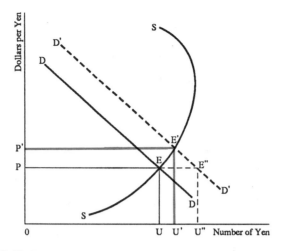

FIGURE 12-4
Supply and Demand Curves for Yen
The demand curve *DD* is copied from the left side of Figure 12-3. The supply curve *SS* is derived from the demand curve *D*D** on the right side of Figure 12-3. (The supply curve is positively sloped when the demand curve *D*D** is elastic; it is negatively sloped when the demand curve is inelastic.) As *DD* and *SS* intersect at *E*, *OP* will be the market-clearing exchange rate. If the demand for yen increases from *DD* to *D'D'*, there will be excess demand at the price *OP*. Under a flexible exchange rate, the yen will appreciate to *OP'*. Under a pegged exchange rate, governments will have to supply *UU"* yen to keep it from appreciating. The distance *UU"* is the surplus in the Japanese balance of payments measured in yen. The area *UEE"U"* is the deficit in the American balance of payments measured in dollars.

reduce their purchases from Japan, moving along *D'D'* toward *E'*, and Japanese will raise their purchases from the United States, moving along *SS* toward *E'* (i.e., moving along *D*D** from *F* toward *F'* in Figure 12-3). When they meet at *E'*, the excess demand for yen is eliminated, and the exchange rate stabilizes at *OP'*.

Adjustment under Pegged Exchange Rates

Under a system of pegged exchange rates, banks regulate their inventories much as they do with flexible rates, but their purchases and sales of currencies can have only small effects on exchange rates. Governments announce and maintain official prices for their currencies, known as *parities*, and keep actual exchange rates close to those official rates. When there is a pegged rate between the dollar and yen, and the Boston bank begins to bid for yen, one of the two governments will intervene on the foreign-exchange market. It will prevent the yen from appreciating by providing the yen demanded by the Boston bank and accepting the dollars offered.

The immediate effects of intervention show up in the balance-of-payments accounts. Table 12-3 reproduces a summary of the cash component from Table 12-1 and adds a new transaction:

(h) The Boston bank buys $175,000 worth of yen, and the U.S. Treasury supplies them, drawing on its balance with the Bank of Japan.

Table 12-3. Cash Component of the Balance of Payments for the United States (thousands of dollars)

Item	Credit	Debit
Increase (+) in dollars held by foreign banks		
Transactions (a) through (g)	25	
Increase (−) in foreign currencies held by U.S. banks		
Transactions (a) through (g)	365	
Boston bank in yen (h)		175
Net increase (−)	190	
Increase (−) in U.S. reserve assets		
Balance in yen with Bank of Japan (h)	175	

The Boston bank's purchase appears as a debit in the cash component (an increase in foreign currencies held by U.S. banks). The U.S. Treasury's sale appears as a credit on a new line, showing changes in official reserves.

The two new entries have no net effect on the cash component or the capital account. Changes in official reserves, however, have great significance. First, they differentiate a pegged-rate system from a flexible-rate system. Second, they have important consequences for national money supplies. That is why changes in reserves are used to measure overall surpluses and deficits in the balance-of-payments accounts. In this particular case, the United States has an overall deficit because it has lost reserves. Note that there can be no balance-of-payments surplus or deficit under a freely flexible exchange rate. Changes in reserves do not occur unless some government intervenes to influence exchange rates.

Intervention can be shown in Figure 12-4. Suppose that the dollar price of the yen is pegged officially at OP. When DD and SS intersect at E, the foreign-exchange market clears without intervention, and there is no surplus or deficit in the balance of payments. When DD shifts to $D'D'$, however, there is an excess demand for yen, and one of the governments must intervene to keep the exchange rate pegged at OP. It must sell UU'' yen and take up $UEE''U''$ dollars.

If the U.S. authorities intervene, U.S. yen reserves will fall, and the U.S. balance-of-payments deficit will be $UEE''U''$ dollars. There will be no change in Japanese reserves, but Japan will still show a balance-of-payments surplus of UU'' yen. The reduction in U.S. reserves appears in the Japanese cash account as a reduction in Japanese liabilities to a foreign official institution, which is treated as being equivalent to an increase in Japanese reserves. If the Japanese authorities intervene, Japanese dollar reserves will rise, and the Japanese surplus will still be UU'' yen. There will be no change in U.S. reserves, but the United States will still show a balance-of-payments deficit, because the increase in Japanese reserves appears in the U.S. cash account as an increase in U.S. liabilities to a foreign official institution and is treated as being equivalent to a decrease in U.S. reserves.

When exchange rates are pegged permanently, they cannot contribute to the adjustment process. What can take their place? Clearly, the supply and demand curves in Figure 12-4 must be made to move. The demand curve must be driven to the left or the supply curve to the right, until they intersect at a point on the line *PE''*. They will then eliminate the excess demand for yen and the need for further intervention, without any change in the exchange rate.

Many forces can contribute to this adjustment process. The mix will depend in part on the reasons for the initial increase in the American demand for yen. But money-supply changes induced by intervention will play a key role. The American money supply will fall, raising American interest rates, reducing American income and absorption, and reducing prices in the United States. The Japanese money supply will rise, reducing Japanese interest rates, raising Japanese income and absorption, and raising prices in Japan. All these events will contribute to the requisite shifts in the demand and supply curves. They are examined in subsequent chapters. This introduction concludes by showing why official intervention affects the American money supply.

Intervention and the Money Supply

When the U.S. Treasury sells yen to a Boston bank to keep the dollar from depreciating, it will receive instructions from the Boston bank to deposit the yen at the Japanese commercial bank where the Boston bank holds its working balance. The Boston bank will receive instructions from the Treasury to deposit the corresponding dollars in the Treasury's account at the Federal Reserve Bank of Boston. Therefore, the Treasury will instruct the Bank of Japan to transfer $175,000 worth of yen to the Japanese commercial bank, and the Boston bank will instruct the Federal Reserve Bank of Boston to transfer $175,000 to the Treasury's account. The Federal Reserve Bank will deduct $175,000 from the Boston bank's *member-bank balance* at the Federal Reserve Bank, and add it to the Treasury's account.

The U.S. Treasury will hold more dollars and fewer yen. These are the changes in its balance sheet (measured in thousands of dollars):

U.S. TREASURY

Assets		Liabilities
Reserves (yen) at		
Bank of Japan	−175	
Balance at FRB		
of Boston	+175	

The Federal Reserve Bank of Boston has larger liabilities to the U.S. Treasury but smaller liabilities to the Boston commercial bank:

FEDERAL RESERVE BANK OF BOSTON

Assets		Liabilities	
		Treasury balance	+175
		Member-bank balance	
		of Boston bank	−175

The Boston commercial bank has fewer dollars on deposit with the Federal Reserve Bank but more yen in its account with a Japanese commercial bank:

BOSTON COMMERCIAL BANK

Assets		Liabilities
Member-bank balance at FRB of Boston	−175	
Balane (yen) at Japanese bank	+175	

The most important change, however, is yet to come.

The member-bank balance held by the Boston bank at the Federal Reserve Bank is part of the cash reserve that it must hold against its own deposit liabilities. If that balance falls, and the bank does not have any excess reserves, it must cut back its loans and investments to replenish its cash reserves. This will trigger a complicated process that can lead to a contraction in the money supply many times larger than the initial cut, with the size of the multiple depending on the quantity of excess reserves held by the whole banking system and the *reserve requirement* imposed by the Federal Reserve System. If banks have no excess reserves and the reserve requirement is 20 percent, the reduction in the Boston bank's member-bank balance will produce a fivefold reduction in the American money supply.

A similar process will occur in Japan but will run the other way. When the Bank of Japan transfers yen to a Japanese commercial bank at the request of the U.S. Treasury, it adds to the commercial bank's cash reserves, and the bank can start to increase its loans and deposits. The Japanese money supply will start to grow.

Adjustment Under the Gold Standard

If currencies were pegged to gold, as they were before World War I, exchange rates would be pegged, too, and money-supply changes would take place automatically, without official intervention on foreign-exchange markets.

Under the gold standard, each government defined the value of its currency in grains or ounces of gold metal, then stood ready to buy and sell gold for its currency. Some governments went further, issuing gold coins, but this was not vital. The gold-standard mechanism worked equally well when governments issued paper money in exchange for gold, so that any change in official gold holdings caused an equal change in the supply of paper money.

When currencies were pegged to gold and governments were willing to deal in gold with private citizens as well as with other governments, gold could be used to trade one currency for another, and an implicit exchange rate was established between each pair of currencies. If the French franc was redeemable in gold at 140 francs per ounce, and the U.S. dollar was redeemable at $35 per ounce, $35 could be used to buy an ounce of gold, which could be used in turn to buy 140 francs. Therefore, a dollar would buy 4 francs. Actual exchange rates could fluctuate a bit, because governments charged small commissions, and traders had to pay the costs of shipping gold from one country to another. When an exchange rate moved outside the boundaries set by those commissions and costs, however, someone could profit by engaging in *arbitrage*.

An *arbitrageur* would buy gold with the currency that was priced below its gold parity in the foreign-exchange market, sell the gold for the currency that was priced above its gold parity, and then sell the second currency for the first. Suppose that the franc rose from $0.25 to $0.27 and that it cost $0.10 in commissions and freight to ship an ounce of gold from New York to Paris. An arbitrageur could buy 1,000 ounces of gold from the U.S. Treasury and ship them to Paris at a total cost of $35,100 ($35,000 for the gold and $100 in transactions costs). He could sell the gold to the Bank of France for 140,000 francs and could then sell the francs for dollars in the foreign-exchange market for $0.27 × 140,000 or $37,800. His profit would be $37,800 *less* $35,100 or $2,700. The arbitrageur would earn nearly 7 percent on capital in a matter of days! In the process, moreover, the arbitrageur would help to reduce the price of the franc by selling francs for dollars at the end of the three-part transaction.He would thus help to keep the actual exchange rate close to its gold parity. Finally, the arbitrageur's transactions would alter national money supplies. In this example, they would increase the supply of francs and decrease the supply of dollars, and these are the changes needed for balance-of-payments adjustment.

Every so often, someone calls for a return to the gold standard. But practice was messier than theory, even in the nineteenth century. Governments went on and off the gold standard, back and forth between pegged and flexible exchange rates. Furthermore, they interfered with the money-supply effects that gold flows were supposed to produce automatically. Most economists are convinced that the gold standard can be no better than most other methods of pegging exchange rates.

SUMMARY

The macroeconomic analysis of open economies is concerned with the effects of international transactions on output, employment, and the price level and the effects of these in turn on the balance of payments and exchange rate. It is also concerned with the implications of openness and of exchange-rate arrangements for the functioning of monetary and fiscal policies.

A country's international transactions are described by its balance-of-payments accounts. Purchases and sales of goods and services appear in the current account, as do investment-income flows. Credit items in the current account are those that raise domestic income; debit items are those that raise foreign income. Purchases and sales of real and financial assets appear in the capital account, along with changes in cash balances, including officially held balances described as reserves. Credit items in the capital account (capital inflows) are those that increase foreign claims on the domestic economy or decrease domestic claims on foreigners; debit items (capital outflows) are those that decrease foreign claims or increase domestic claims.

All transactions appear twice in the balance-of-payments accounts, once with each sign. Therefore, total credits equal total debits, and the balances on current and capital accounts always add up to zero. It is useful, however, to single out changes in official reserves to measure the overall surplus or deficit in the balance of payments. They reflect official intervention in foreign-exchange markets to peg or influence exchange rates. Under a freely flexible exchange rate, there can be no such surplus or deficit because there is no intervention. Under a pegged exchange rate, the surplus or deficit measures the amount of official intervention that was needed to prevent the exchange rate from changing.

Most transactions that appear in balance-of-payments accounts show up in the foreign-exchange market. Typically, those that appear as credits are reflected in the foreign demand for the domestic currency, and those that appear as debits are reflected in the domestic demand for foreign currency. These demands, moreover, depend on the exchange rate. A depreciation of the domestic currency reduces the domestic demand for foreign currency by raising the domestic-currency prices of foreign goods, services, and assets. It raises the foreign demand for the domestic currency by reducing the foreign-currency prices of domestic goods, services, and assets. The foreign demand for the domestic currency can be expressed as the foreign supply of the foreign currency, which can be used together with the domestic demand for that currency to identify the market-clearing exchange rate.

Under a flexible exchange rate, the domestic currency will depreciate in response to an excess demand for foreign currency. The depreciation, in turn, will reduce the domestic demand for foreign goods, services, and assets, curbing the demand for foreign currency, and will raise the foreign demand for domestic goods, services, and assets, boosting the supply of foreign currency. These adjustments will eliminate the excess demand.

Under a pegged exchange rate, official intervention will prevent any change in the exchange rate, but it will initiate monetary changes that also eliminate the excess demand. The domestic money supply will fall, reducing domestic expenditure and the domestic demand for foreign currency. The foreign money supply will rise, stimulating foreign expenditure and the foreign demand for the domestic currency. A gold standard is one way to peg exchange rates and induce these monetary changes automatically.

Transactions that appear in the current account of the balance of payments also appear in the national-income accounts. Exports add to the demand for domestic goods and services. Imports supplement supplies on domestic markets. The current-account balance is equal to the difference between output and absorption. It is also equal to the sum of two internal balances, the private-sector surplus (saving *minus* investment) and the public-sector surplus (tax revenue *minus* government spending).

RECOMMENDED READINGS

Some matters covered in this chapter are treated more thoroughly in subsequent chapters, and lists of readings are appended to those chapters. Here are readings that deal with balance-of-payments accounts, the foreign-exchange market, and the links between them:

On the problem of defining surpluses and deficits in the balance-of-payments accounts, see *The Balance of Payments Statistics of the United States: Report of the Review Committee for Balance of Payments Statistics* (Washington, D.C.: Government Printing Office, 1965), ch. 9. Several years ago, the U.S. government decided not to publish any measure of surplus or deficit; for reactions and comments, see Robert M. Stern et al., *The Presentation of the U.S. Balance of Payments: A Symposium*, Essays in International Finance 123 (Princeton, N.J.: International Finance Section, Princeton University, 1977). On the problems of collecting and improving balance-of-payments statistics, see Anne Y. Kester, ed., *Behind the Numbers* (Washington, D.C.: National Academy Press, 1992). The workings of the gold standard are analyzed in Barry Eichengreen, ed., *The Gold Standard in Theory and History* (New York and London: Methuen, 1985).

QUESTIONS AND PROBLEMS

(1) Organize the transactions listed below into a balance-of-payments table for Japan and show how they affect the balance sheet of Japanese commercial banks.

(a) A Japanese firm sells ¥200 million of microchips to a French firm, which pays in yen bought from a French bank that keeps a deposit with a bank in Tokyo.

(b) A Japanese insurance company buys ¥150 million worth of U.S. government securities, paying in dollars bought from a Japanese bank that keeps a deposit with a bank in New York.

(c) A Japanese subsidiary of a German firm pays a ¥50 million dividend to that firm, which, uses the yen to buy Deutsche marks from a German bank that keeps a deposit with a bank in Tokyo.

Can you identify a surplus or deficit in the Japanese balance of payments?

(2) Suppose that the German bank in transaction (c) does not want to hold more yen and seeks to sell them for Deutsche marks on the foreign-exchange market. The Bank of Japan intervenes to keep the exchange rate from changing, using its holdings of Deutsche marks at the German central bank. Add this transaction to the Japanese capital account and the Japanese banks' balance sheet. How does it affect the balance sheet of the Bank of Japan? What has happened to the reserves of Japanese commercial banks? What has happened, if anything, to the surplus or deficit in the Japanese balance of payments?

(3) Organize the transactions listed below into a balance-of-payments table for the United States, attaching appropriate signs to the entries. (If you get the signs right, total credits will equal total debits and you will not need to add an errors-and-omissions item.)

Merchandise imports	110
Foreign direct investment by U.S. firms	40
Interest payments to foreigners	25
Merchandise exports	140
Increase in foreign-currency holdings of U.S. banks	60
Increase in dollar holdings of foreign official institutions	30
Foreign purchases of U.S. corporate securities	50
Foreign tourist spending in the United States	15

Compute the balances on current and capital accounts and the official-settlements balance.

(4) Use the relevant numbers in your answer to (3) and some or all of the numbers shown below to calculate U.S. national income:

Consumption	400
Government spending	150
Saving	80
Investment	75

Is the government running a budget surplus or deficit?

(5) Use supply and demand curves to describe a foreign-exchange market in which U.S. dollars are traded against Deutsche marks. Begin with a market-clearing situation, showing the exchange rate and the quantities of dollars and Deutsche marks traded. Then show how an increase in the German demand for U.S. goods affects the situation when the exchange rate floats freely. Is the exchange-rate change an appreciation or depreciation of the dollar? If the German government intervenes to keep the exchange rate from changing, will it buy or sell dollars? How many?

13

Incomes and the Current Account

THE ISSUES

This chapter begins with an overview of the adjustment process and goes on to introduce some strategic assumptions that will help us sort out the principal elements in that process. Thereafter, it examines three issues:

- How the processes determining income and output are modified by international trade.
- How trade leads to economic interdependence.
- How trade can produce policy conflicts within and between individual countries.

This chapter will not analyze these issues completely. We will return to them frequently in subsequent chapters.

ELEMENTS IN THE ADJUSTMENT PROCESS

Chapter 12 used supply and demand curves to show how balance-of-payments adjustment is reflected in the foreign-exchange market. Under a flexible exchange rate, movements along the curves play the leading role. Under a pegged exchange rate, movements of the curves themselves play the leading role.

To review the main lines of the analysis, consider the effects of an increase in the domestic demand for foreign goods, services, or assets. It raises the domestic demand for foreign currencies, depleting dealers' inventories. Dealers enter the foreign-exchange market to rebuild those inventories and cause an outward shift in the demand curve for foreign currency. There is an excess demand for foreign currency at the initial exchange rate and, therefore, an excess supply of domestic currency.

If the exchange rate is flexible, the domestic currency depreciates. Foreign goods, services, and assets become more expensive in domestic markets, because the currency needed to buy them has become more expensive, and domestic buyers cut back their purchases, reducing the domestic demand for foreign currency. Domestic goods, services, and assets become cheaper in foreign markets, and foreign buyers step up their purchases, raising the foreign demand for domestic currency. These events show up as movements along the supply and demand curves.

If the exchange rate is pegged, an excess demand for the foreign currency must be met by official intervention on the foreign-exchange market. One or both of the governments concerned must sell the foreign currency, meeting the excess demand, and thus buy the domestic currency, absorbing the excess supply. Intervention typically reduces the cash reserves of domestic banks and raises those of foreign banks. The domestic money supply contracts, depressing aggregate domestic demand and reducing the domestic demand for imports. The foreign money supply expands, stimulating aggregate foreign demand and raising the foreign demand for imports. The demand for the foreign currency falls, and the demand for the domestic currency rises, even though the exchange rate does not change. These events show up as shifts of the supply and demand curves.

But these are not the only elements in the adjustment process. A complete analysis must look first at the reason for the increase in demand for the foreign currency.

Suppose that the increase in demand is caused by a change in tastes—a switch in domestic demand from domestic to foreign goods. This will depress aggregate domestic demand, which will reduce the domestic demand for imports. Similarly, it will raise aggregate foreign demand, which will raise the foreign demand for imports. The income effects of the disturbance will work directly to reduce the excess demand for the foreign currency caused by the initial change in tastes.

Suppose that the increase in demand for the foreign currency is caused by a change in asset preferences—a switch by domestic asset holders from domestic to foreign bonds. As those asset holders sell domestic bonds, the prices of those bonds will fall, which will raise the domestic interest rate. This will depress aggregate domestic demand and thus reduce the domestic demand for imports. As asset holders buy foreign bonds, the prices of those bonds will rise, which will reduce the foreign interest rate. That will stimulate aggregate foreign demand and raise the foreign demand for imports. Once again, the income effects of the disturbance will reduce the excess demand for the foreign currency caused by the initial disturbance.

Therefore, we must trace carefully the ramifications of any disturbance, showing its direct effects on supply and demand conditions in the foreign-exchange market and its effects on all of the other variables that impinge indirectly on that market. The character of the adjustment process will depend on the nature of the disturbance, the exchange-rate regime, the extent of integration between home and foreign markets, especially between asset markets, and the policies adopted by the governments concerned in response to the disturbance. It would be tiresome to trace in detail all the effects of every disturbance, but that is not necessary. We can learn a great deal by looking at a few disturbances and a small number of responses.

In this chapter and the next, we will concentrate on two disturbances, *switches* in demand between home and foreign goods and *shifts* in the level of aggregate demand. We will also concentrate on two responses, income effects and price effects. These are the chief ingredients of the adjustment process affecting the current account. In Chapter 15, we will go on to examine capital flows and interest-rate effects and combine them with income and price effects to describe the workings of domestic policies in an open economy. In Chapter 16, we will extend the analysis by examining the influence of expectations on capital movements and exchange rates.

STRATEGIC SIMPLIFICATIONS

In recent work on the balance of payments and on exchange-rate behavior, economists have emphasized the implications of economic integration. When national economies are tightly linked, one country's markets for goods and assets are influenced heavily by events in other countries' markets. Prices and interest rates are determined jointly at home and abroad, and domestic policies have rather limited effects on the domestic economy. There has been a tendency, moreover, to focus on long-run equilibria, in which wage rates have adjusted fully to changes in the demand for labor, and stocks of assets, including money, have adjusted fully to the corresponding flows.

These analytical strategies reflect recent experience, notably the discovery that national price levels are strongly affected by price changes in international markets. Changes in the world price of oil afford the most dramatic examples. Those strategies likewise reflect recent developments in macroeconomic theory, which has come to stress, too strongly perhaps, the limited effectiveness of macroeconomic policies, even in a closed economy. Some economists argue that monetary policy cannot have any permanent effect on the real side of the economy—on output or employment. Going further, some say that monetary policy cannot even have temporary effects unless a change in policy comes as a surprise to the private sector (or contractual arrangements prevent workers, firms, and households from adjusting their behavior right away). This new view depends in part on the strong assumption that workers, firms, and households have *rational expectations;* they are assumed to anticipate correctly the economy's response to any disturbance or policy change and neutralize the consequences by their own behavior.

Some of this new work will be examined in subsequent chapters, which present macroeconomic models in which markets are very closely integrated. Those chapters will not adopt the central thesis of the "new" macroeconomics, that policies are neutralized by private behavior. Nevertheless, they will show how economic integration can dilute the effects of monetary and fiscal policies, even in the absence of rational expectations, and how it can cause their effects to wear off eventually.

For a while, however, we will adopt an older and simpler approach. We will add international transactions to a closed economy without changing to any significant degree the ways in which its markets work. Furthermore, we will concentrate on the short or medium run, in which wages and prices tend to be rigid and stocks of assets do not change appreciably. Let us state these suppositions more precisely.

The Size of the Foreign Sector

Foreign transactions will be small compared with the size of the national economy, which will be small compared with the world economy. Putting these assumptions very strongly,

1. Home and foreign prices will be fixed, and thus unaffected by disturbances or policies or by the adjustment process set in motion by them. The price effects studied in the next chapter will come from changes in exchange rates, not in the home prices of home goods or foreign prices of foreign goods.

2. The economy itself will be too small to influence aggregate demand, output, or employment in the outside world. In other words, we will disregard the *foreign repercussions* of domestic events.

The first assumption is unrealistic, even as an approximation to short-run price rigidity. It is very useful, however, because it allows us to equate nominal with real changes. When a disturbance raises gross domestic product at current prices, we will be able to say that it raises *real* gross domestic product to the same extent and, by implication, that it raises domestic employment. The second assumption is less extreme but clearly inappropriate for studying relationships among large economies like those of the United States, Western Europe, and Japan. We will therefore abandon it later in this chapter, when we study interactions between economies.

Intervention and Sterilization

Official intervention in foreign-exchange markets will not be allowed to affect national money supplies. We can thus ignore temporarily the money-supply effects of surpluses and deficits invoked in Chapter 12 and in the opening paragraphs of this chapter. We will return to them in Chapter 15, where they will play a major role in explaining the long-run effects of monetary and fiscal policies, and they will be vital in Chapter 17, which presents the *monetary approach* to balance-of-payments theory and exchange-rate behavior.

There are two ways to insulate the money supply from the effects of intervention. First, we can pretend that the amounts of intervention are too small to have much cumulative impact in the short or medium run. Second, we can assume that central banks *sterilize* the money-supply effects of intervention.

When a central bank sells foreign currency and thus buys domestic currency to keep the domestic currency from depreciating, it reduces the cash reserves of domestic banks, which triggers a contraction of the money supply. To replenish the banks' cash reserves and prevent that contraction, the central bank can make an open-market purchase of domestic bonds. Conversely, when a central bank buys foreign currency and thus sells domestic currency to keep the domestic currency from appreciating, it can make by an open-market sale of domestic bonds to prevent an expansion of the money supply.

The mechanics of sterilization can be illustrated by extending an example used in Chapter 12, where a Boston bank bought yen for dollars and the U.S. Treasury intervened to keep the dollar from depreciating. The main monetary consequence was, of course, the $175,000 reduction in the member-bank balance of the Boston commercial bank, a reduction that could trigger a contraction of the American money supply. To offset it completely, the Federal Reserve System can buy $175,000 of government bonds on the open market, paying with a check drawn on itself (i.e., on the Federal Reserve Bank of Boston). To keep matters simple, suppose that the seller of the bonds deposits that check with the commercial bank involved in the original foreign-exchange transaction. That bank will credit the seller's account and send the check to the Federal Reserve Bank of Boston, which will credit the commercial bank's member-bank balance.

Let us look at the changes in the balance sheet of the Federal Reserve Bank of Boston, beginning with those shown in Chapter 12. After the U.S. Treasury has intervened in the foreign-exchange market, the Federal Reserve Bank has larger liabilities to the Treasury but smaller liabilities to the Boston commercial bank:

FEDERAL RESERVE BANK OF BOSTON

Assets	Liabilities	
	Treasury balance	+175
	Member-bank balance	
	of Boston bank	−175

The open-market purchase in the bond market adds to its assets and its liabilities:

FEDERAL RESERVE BANK OF BOSTON

Assets		Liabilities	
U.S. government bonds	+175	Member-bank balance	
		of Boston bank	+175

Consolidating the two transactions,

FEDERAL RESERVE BANK OF BOSTON

Assets		Liabilities	
U.S. government bonds	+175	Treasury balance	+175

There is no net change in the member-bank balance of the Boston commercial bank and, therefore, no cause for contraction of the money supply.

When domestic and foreign financial markets are closely integrated, central banks may not be able to engage in sterilized intervention, which means that they will not be able conduct independent monetary policies if they peg exchange rates. This possibility is examined in Chapter 15. In this and the next chapter, however, we will assume that central banks can engage in sterilization. We will go further, indeed, and assume that they have enough monetary independence, even under pegged exchange rates, to regulate interest rates by open-market operations. This will allow us to treat the interest rate as the chief instrument of monetary policy; it will be used to influence aggregate demand and, at times, to influence capital movements.[1]

INCOME, IMPORTS, AND THE MULTIPLIER

In Chapter 12, we examined the national-income accounts for an open economy. Exports of goods and services were added to consumption, investment, and government spending to define aggregate demand in the domestic market, and imports of goods and services were subtracted from aggregate demand to define gross domestic product. Using the same notation as before,

$$Y = C + I + G + X - M \tag{1}$$

We also saw that the current-account balance is equal to the sum of two domestic balances:

$$X - M = (S - I) + (T - G) \tag{2}$$

The first term on the right side is the private-sector balance, the difference between saving and investment; the second is the public-sector balance, the difference between tax revenue and government spending.

The discussion in Chapter 12 did not distinguish between nominal and real amounts; it derived the equations shown above without saying whether the variables are measured at current or constant prices. In this chapter, they are measured at constant prices, because we have assumed that prices do not change. Therefore, they refer to quantities produced, consumed, and traded. Furthermore, the second assumption made above, that there are no foreign repercussions, allows us to show how production and employment are determined in a small open economy.

We will start with the familiar case of a closed economy but will introduce some new notation and use methods slightly different from those in elementary textbooks.

The Multiplier for a Closed Economy

A closed economy has no exports or imports ($X = M = 0$). Therefore, equation (2) can be rewritten as

$$S = I + (G - T). \tag{3}$$

To simplify it further, use D to define the public-sector (budget) deficit:

$$D = G - T,$$

---

[1]To raise its country's interest rate, a central bank will make an open-market sale. The sale will reduce the supply of money but raise the supply of bonds available to the public. Accordingly, it will reduce bond prices, raising the interest rate.

so that

$$S = I + D. \tag{3a}$$

Finally, convert equation (3a) into a statement about changes,

$$dS = dI + dD, \tag{4}$$

where dS is the change in saving, and so on.

In closed and open economies alike, saving rises with income and with the interest rate, denoted here by r, but it can also change *autonomously* (i.e., for reasons unrelated to the behavior of the other variables under study). Therefore,

$$dS = sdY + S_r dr + dS^a. \tag{5}$$

Here, s is the *marginal propensity to save*, the fraction of any increase in income that goes to saving rather than consumption, S_r is the increase in saving induced by an increase in the interest rate, and dS^a is an increase in saving that takes place autonomously, for reasons unrelated to income and the interest rate.[2]

Investment depends on many variables, including the size of the capital stock, the intensity with which it is utilized, and the rate at which it depreciates. It also depends on the interest rate, which is the only variable included here:

$$dI = I_r dr + dI^a, \tag{6}$$

where I_r is the decrease in investment induced by an increase in the interest rate, and dI^a is an autonomous increase in investment (taking account implicitly of other variables that affect investment). Note that I_r is negative, whereas S_r is positive. An increase in the interest rate reduces investment but raises saving.

The size of the budget deficit depends on many decisions and events. An increase in income, for example, raises tax revenues even when tax rates are fixed. It is hard to forecast the budget deficit, let alone control it. But we will assume that D changes only when the government decides to change it. Politicians would laugh—or cry—at this assumption, but it is the easiest way to include fiscal policy in the analysis.

Returning to equation (4), substitute the right sides of equations (5) and (6) for the changes in saving and investment:

$$sdY + S_r dr + dS^a = I_r dr + dI^a + dD. \tag{4a}$$

Move $S_r dr$ and dS^a to the right side of this equation and divide both sides by the

---

[2]In many models, saving depends on disposable income (income after taxes) rather than total income. That specification may be more realistic, but it complicates the exposition in unnecessary ways. The specification in equation (5) has two implications. First, an increase in taxes is matched fully by a decrease in consumption, rather than falling partly on consumption and partly on saving. Second, an increase in government spending balanced by an increase in taxes has no effect on income; the "balanced-budget multiplier" is zero. (In Chapter 18, saving will depend on wealth in addition to income and the interest rate.)

marginal propensity to save:

$$dY = \left(\frac{1}{s}\right)[(dI^a - dS^a) + dD - (S_r - I_r)dr].\qquad(7)$$

Finally, simplify equation (7) by defining two new terms:

$$dA^a = dI^a - dS^a$$
$$dA^g = dD - (S_r - I_r)dr.$$

The first term is the autonomous change in domestic expenditure (absorption); it will be positive when there is an autonomous increase in investment larger than the autonomous increase in saving. (An autonomous increase in saving is independent of income, by definition, and must therefore be matched by a reduction in consumption. That is why it reduces autonomous expenditure.) The second term is the change in domestic expenditure induced by government policies. It will be positive when the government raises its budget deficit (runs a less restrictive fiscal policy) or when the central bank reduces the interest rate (runs a less restrictive monetary policy). Putting these terms into equation (7),

$$dY = \left(\frac{1}{s}\right)(dA^a + dA^g).\qquad(7a)$$

This formulation may look new, because of the notation, but it makes a familiar statement. Output, income, and employment, represented by Y, increase by a *multiple* of any autonomous or policy-induced increase in expenditure. The *multiplier* is $1/s$, which is larger than 1 because s is smaller than 1.[3]

The story told by equation (7a) is illustrated in Figure 13-1. The line OS describes the relationship between changes in saving and changes in income; its slope equals the marginal propensity to save. When autonomous and policy-induced expenditures add up to OA, income is OY. When they rise to OA', income rises to OY'.

The Multiplier for an Open Economy

When analyzing an open economy, we must work with equation (2), containing X and M, exports and imports of goods and services. It can be rewritten as

$$S + M = I + D + X.\qquad(2a)$$

Converting it into a statement about changes,

$$dS + dM = dI + dD + dX,\qquad(8)$$

---

[3]Equation (7a) may look more familiar when put differently. Write $c + s = 1$, where c is the marginal propensity to consume. As $s = 1 - c$, equation (7a) becomes

$$dY = \left(\frac{1}{1 - c}\right)(dA^a + dA^g).$$

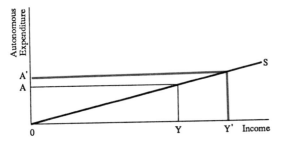

FIGURE 13-1
Income Determination in a Closed Economy
The slope of *OS* is the marginal propensity to save. When autonomous and policy-induced expenditure total *OA*, income is *OY*. When they rise to *OA'*, income rises to *OY'*. The increase in income, *YY'*, is larger than the increase in autonomous expenditure, *AA'*.

which contains the changes in imports and exports in addition to the terms for the closed economy.

A country's imports of goods and services depend on prices at home and abroad, the exchange rate, and the country's income. Prices are constant here, however, and we will hold the exchange rate constant temporarily. Therefore, the change in imports of goods and services can be written as

$$dM = mdY + dM^a, \tag{9}$$

where *m* is the *marginal propensity to import*, the fraction of any increase in income that is spent on imports, and dM^a is an autonomous increase in imports. Note that an autonomous increase in imports reduces the demand for domestic goods. Because it takes place independently of income, it cannot affect absorption directly. When absorption is unchanged, however, an increase in the demand for imports necessarily involves a switch from home to foreign goods.

A country's exports of goods and services depend on prices, the exchange rate, and foreign income, so our price and exchange-rate assumptions allow us to write

$$dX = m^*dY^* + dX^a, \tag{10}$$

where m^* is the foreign marginal propensity to import, dY^* is the change in foreign income, and dX^a is an autonomous increase in exports, a switch in foreign demand from foreign to home goods.

Returning to equation (8), substitute the right sides of equation (5) and (6) for the changes in saving and investment, and substitute the right sides of equations (9) and (10) for the changes in imports and exports:

$$(sdY + S_r dr + dS^a) + (mdY + dM^a) = (I_r dr + dI^a) + dD + (m^*dY^* + dX^a). \tag{8a}$$

Move $S_r dr$, dS^a, and dM^a to the right side of this equation, collect the income terms, and divide both sides by the sum of the marginal propensities to save and import:

$$dY = \left(\frac{1}{s+m}\right)[(dI^a - dS^a) + dD - (S_r - I_r)dr + (dX^a - dM^a) + m^*dY^*]. \quad (11)$$

This equation can be simplified by using the expressions for autonomous and policy-induced changes in expenditure and by introducing one more expression:

$$dN^a = (dX^a - dM^a) + m^*dY^*.$$

This is the autonomous change in net exports of goods and services and thus the autonomous change in the current-account balance. It contains the autonomous switches in domestic and foreign demands and the income-induced change in foreign demand. (We can treat an income-induced change as being autonomous here because we have assumed that the domestic economy is too small to influence other countries' incomes.) Putting this expression into equation (11),

$$dY = \left(\frac{1}{s+m}\right)(dA^a + dA^g + dN^a). \quad (11a)$$

This equation differs in two important ways from equation (7a), its closed-economy counterpart. First, the multiplier is $1/(s+m)$, which is smaller than $1/s$. There are two "leakages" from the domestic income stream, one into saving and the other into imports. Second, there as an additional influence on income—the autonomous change in net exports reflecting switches in domestic and foreign demand and changes in foreign income.

Income Changes and the Current Account

How do income changes affect the current-account balance? Use N to denote net exports of goods and services,

$$N = X - M, \quad (12)$$

so that

$$dN = dX - dM. \quad (13)$$

Now use the right sides of equations (9) and (10) to replace the changes in imports and exports:

$$dN = (m^*dY^* + dX^a) - (mdY + dM^a) = dN^a - mdY. \quad (13a)$$

Finally, use the right side of equation (11a) to replace the change in income,

$$dN = dN^a - m\left(\frac{1}{s+m}\right)(dA^a + dA^g + dN^a), \quad (13b)$$

which can be rewritten as

$$dN = \left(\frac{s}{s+m}\right)dN^a - \left(\frac{m}{s+m}\right)(dA^a + dA^g). \quad (13c)$$

This equation makes two statements: First, an autonomous increase in net exports improves the current-account balance. The improvement, however, is smaller than the autonomous increase itself; it is multiplied by $s/(s + m)$. The autonomous increase in net exports raises domestic income, which means that it raises imports, reducing the improvement in the current-account balance. Second, an autonomous or policy-induced increase in domestic expenditure worsens the current-account balance. By raising income, it raises the demand for imports.

These results are illustrated in Figure 13-2, which builds on Figure 13-1. The slope of OS is the marginal propensity to save. The slope of OF is the sum of the marginal propensities to save and import. (The difference between their slopes is therefore the marginal propensity to import.) When OE is the sum of autonomous and policy-induced expenditures, including the autonomous component of net exports, income is OY. When that sum rises to OE', income rises to OY'. The increase in income is smaller than in Figure 13-1, because the multiplier is $1/(s + m)$ rather than $1/s$. The line NX shows the relationship between income and net exports (the current-account balance); its slope is equal in absolute value to the marginal propensity to

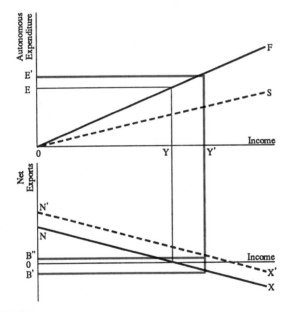

FIGURE 13-2
Income Determination in an Open Economy
The slope of *OS* is the marginal propensity to save. The slope of *OF* is the sum of the marginal propensities to save and import. When *OE* is the sum of autonomous and policy-induced expenditures, including autonomous net exports, income is *OY*. When the sum rises to *OE'*, income rises to *OY'* (by less than in Figure 13-1). The line *NX* shows the relationship between income and net exports; its slope is equal (absolutely) to the marginal propensity to import. When income is *OY*, net exports are zero. When *EE'* is an autonomous or policy-induced increase in domestic expenditure, net exports fall to *OB'*. When *EE'* is an autonomous increase in net exports (a switch in expenditure from foreign to home goods), *NX* shifts upwards to *N'X'* (*NN'* equals *EE'*), and net exports rise to *OB"*. But *OB"* is smaller than *NN'*, the autonomous increase that caused it (because *NN'* also equals *B'B"*, which is larger than *OB"*).

import. When the autonomous component of net exports is *ON* and income is *OY*, the current account is exactly balanced.

When income rises to *OY'*, net exports are affected, but we must know *why* income rises if we are to know *how* they are affected. When *EE'* represents an autonomous or policy-induced increase in domestic expenditure, net exports fall to *OB'*. The increase in income raises imports, driving the current account into deficit. But when *EE'* represents an autonomous increase in net exports, *NX* shifts upward to *N'X'*, and net exports rise to *OB"*. The switch in expenditure raises net exports, driving the current account into surplus. That surplus is smaller than the autonomous increase in net exports.

This last example illustrates a point made in Chapter 12. The nature of balance-of-payments adjustment depends on the type of disturbance involved. Turning the previous example around, consider an autonomous switch in expenditure from home to foreign goods. Taken by itself, that would reduce net exports by the full amount of the switch in expenditure. The actual reduction will be smaller, however, because domestic income falls, reducing the demand for imports. The induced fall in income contributes to balance-of-payments adjustment.

The same point is made in Figure 13-3, which shows what happens in the foreign-exchange market. A switch in expenditure from American to foreign goods increases the American demand for foreign currency. The demand curve for yen shifts outward from *DD* to *D'D'*, producing an excess demand for yen at the initial exchange rate and a corresponding excess supply of dollars. The excess supply of dollars also measures the autonomous decrease in net exports and the current-account deficit that would appear initially in the American balance of payments. But

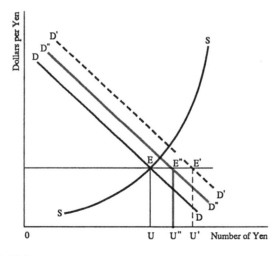

FIGURE 13-3
A Switch in Expenditure from Home to Foreign Goods
A switch in American expenditure from home to foreign goods increases the demand for foreign currency (yen) in the foreign-exchange market. The demand curve for yen shifts from *DD* to *D'D'*. The excess demand for yen is *UU'*, and the excess supply of dollars is *UEE'U'* (which also measures the autonomous change in net exports). But the switch in expenditure reduces American income, reducing the demand for imports and for foreign currency. The demand curve for yen falls to *D"D"* . The excess demand for yen drops to *UU"*, and the excess supply of dollars drops to *UEE"U"*.

American income falls, reducing the demand for imports and the demand for yen. The demand curve for yen drops back to $D''D''$, cutting the excess demand for yen and the excess supply of dollars.

Income changes of this sort contribute to balance-of-payments adjustment, but they are too small to do the whole job. In Figure 13-2, an increase in income offset part of the autonomous increase in net exports but left a current-account surplus equal to OB''. In Figure 13-3, a decrease in income offset part of the autonomous decrease in net exports but left a current-account deficit equal to $UEE''U''$.

These results raise two questions: (1) What would happen if we took account of income changes in the outside world? Would they do the rest of the job, eliminating completely the surplus or deficit that is reduced but not removed by the change in one country's income? (2) What should be done to deal with a surplus or deficit if it is not removed completely by automatic income changes? The first question can be answered briefly, using a two-country model. The answer to the second will take up the rest of this chapter and all of the next.

A TWO-COUNTRY MODEL

The United States is not a small country. Therefore, a switch in American expenditure from home to foreign goods will raise income in Japan and thus raise the Japanese demand for imports. In Figure 13-3, the supply curve SS will shift outward, as Japanese consumers demand additional imports and offer more yen to buy more dollars. This shift in the supply curve will reduce the excess demand for yen and the excess supply of dollars. But the imbalance will not disappear completely. The increase in Japanese income makes an additional contribution to the adjustment process but cannot eradicate the American current-account deficit.

Adjustment with Interdependent Incomes

A formal proof of this assertion is given in Section 1 of Appendix B, which derives equations for the changes in the two countries' incomes and their current-account balance. Illustrations are given in Figures 13-4 and 13-5.

The curve $I_1 I_1$ in Figure 13-4 shows how income in the United States depends on income in Japan; an increase in Japanese income raises U.S. income by raising the Japanese demand for U.S. exports. The position of the curve depends on autonomous expenditure in the United States and the autonomous component of net exports. The slope of the $I_1 I_1$ curve depends on the marginal propensities to save and import for the United States and the marginal propensity to import for Japan.[4]

---

[4]The curve $I_1 I_1$ comes from the first equation for U.S. income in Section 1 of Appendix B. Increases in A_1^q, A_1^q, and N_1^q would raise U.S. income by the small-country multiplier, $1/(s_1 + m_1)$, if they did not influence Japanese income; that is why they shift $I_1 I_1$ to the right. An increase in Japanese income raises U.S. income by the small-country multiplier *times* the Japanese marginal propensity to import; that is why the slope of $I_1 I_1$ depends on the U.S. marginal propensity to save and the U.S. and Japanese marginal propensities to import. The curve $I_2 I_2$ comes from the first equation for Japanese income, and its properties are similar. It is easy to show that $I_1 I_1$ is steeper than $I_2 I_2$ and that the curve BB, discussed later, lies between $I_1 I_1$ and $I_2 I_2$.

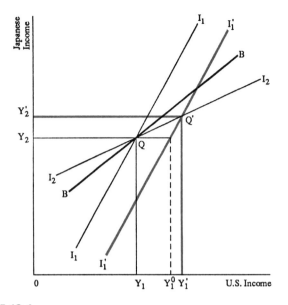

FIGURE 13-4
An Autonomous Increase in U.S. Expenditure in a Two-Country World
The curve I_1I_1 shows how U.S. income depends on Japanese income; when Japanese income is OY_2, U.S. income must be OY_1. The curve I_2I_2 shows how Japanese income depends on U.S. income; when U.S. income is OY_2, Japanese income must be OY_2. The two countries' actual incomes are thus given at Q. The curve BB shows the sets of income levels at which the current account is balanced; the U.S. current account is in surplus above BB and in deficit below it. An autonomous increase in U.S. expenditure shifts $I_1'I_1'$ to $I_1'I_1'$; if there were no change in Japanese income U.S. income would rise to OY_1^0. The new equilibrium point is Q', However, where U.S. income is OY_1', Japanese income is OY_2', and the U.S. current account is in deficit (because Q' lies below BB). The increase in U.S. income is Y_1Y_1', which exceeds $Y_1Y_1^0$, the increase that would occur in a small-country model, because the increase in Japanese income raises Japanese imports and thus amplifies the increase in U.S. income.

The curve I_2I_2 shows how income in Japan depends on income in the United States; an increase in U.S. income raises Japanese income by raising the U.S. demand for Japanese exports. Its position depends on autonomous expenditure in Japan and the autonomous component of net exports. Its slope depends on the marginal propensities to save and import for Japan and the marginal propensity to import for the United States.

The two countries' incomes are given at Q, because it is the only point where income levels are consistent. (When Japanese income is OY_2, the I_1I_1 curve says that U.S. income must be OY_1. When U.S. income is OY_1, the I_2I_2 curve says that Japanese income must be OY_2.)

The BB curve shows how the two countries' incomes affect the U.S. current account. Its position depends on the autonomous component of net exports. Its slope depends on the countries' marginal propensities to import. The current account is balanced at all points on BB.[5] At points above BB, the U.S. current account is in surplus (the Japanese account is in deficit); Japanese income is higher, relative to U.S. income, than it is along the BB curve, so Japanese imports are too large to balance the U.S. current account. At points below BB, the U.S. current account is in deficit (the Japanese is in surplus); Japanese income is lower, relative to U.S. income, than along the BB curve, so Japanese imports are too small to balance the U.S. current account.

There is a basic conceptual difference between the countries' income curves and the BB curve. The income curves depict the interdependence between the two countries' incomes. Their incomes are always given by points such as Q, where $I_1 I_1$ and $I_1 I_2$ intersect. The BB curve, by contrast, shows the relationship between the two countries' incomes, taken together, and a third variable, the current-account balance. Hence, the BB curve does not have to pass through points such as Q, because the current account does not have to balance at all times. (It does pass through Q in Figure 13-4, but that is for simplicity, not by necessity.)

What happens when there is an autonomous increase in U.S. expenditure? The $I_1 I_1$ curve shifts outward to $I_1' I_1'$. The other curves do not shift. If the United States were a small country, unable to affect incomes in the outside world, U.S. income would rise to OY_1^0, and the United States would have a current-account deficit. (The results would be the same as in Figure 13-2.) As the United States is not a small country, changes in its income affect other countries' incomes. The new equilibrium lies at Q', where $I_1' I_1'$. intersects $I_2 I_2$. Japanese income rises to OY_2', raising the demand for U.S. exports and thus raising U.S. income further, all the way to OY_1'. The multiplier for a large economy is bigger than the multiplier for a small economy. But Q' lies below BB, which says that the United States continues to run a current-account deficit. The increase in Japanese income reduces the current-account deficit but does not make it disappear completely.

Figure 13-5 deals with a more complicated case, a switch in expenditure from U.S. to Japanese goods. There are shifts in all three curves. The U.S. income curve shifts inward to $I_1' I_1'$, because the switch in expenditure reduces the demand for U.S. goods. The Japanese income curve shifts upward to $I_2' I_2'$, because the switch in expenditure raises the demand for Japanese goods. The current-account curve shifts upward to $B'B'$, because the switch in expenditure would drive the U.S. current account into deficit if there were no changes in the two countries' incomes. (It can be shown that $B'B'$ must intersect $I_1' I_1'$, vertically above Q, and must intersect $I_2' I_2'$, horizontally

---

[5]The BB curve is based on the first equation for the U.S. current-account balance in Section 1 of Appendix B. As net exports are zero all along BB, set $dN_1 = 0$ and solve that equation for the change in Japanese income required to keep the current account balanced when there is a change in U.S. income or an autonomous change in net exports:

$$dY_2 = \frac{m_1}{m_2} dY_1 - \frac{1}{m_2} dN_1^a.$$

An increase in U.S. income requires an increase in Japanese income to raise the demand for U.S. exports and balance the current account. Therefore, BB is positively sloped. An autonomous increase in U.S. net exports would put the U.S. current account in surplus if it did not increase U.S. income, and elimination of the surplus would require a reduction in Japanese income to reduce the demand for U.S. exports. Therefore, an autonomous increase in net exports shifts BB downward.

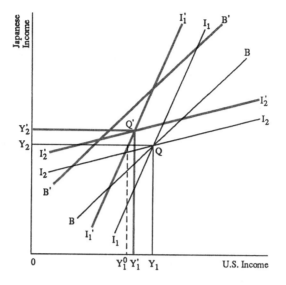

FIGURE 13-5
An Autonomous Switch in Expenditure from Home to Foreign Goods
in the initial equilibrium at Q, U.S. income is OY_1, Japanese income is OY_2, and the current account is balanced (because BB is drawn through Q). A switch in expenditure from U.S. to Japanese goods shifts the U.S. income curve from I_1I_1 to $I_1'I_1'$. If there were no change in Japanese income, U.S. income would fall to OY_1^0. But the switch in expenditure also shifts the Japanese income curve from I_2I_2 to $I_2'I_2'$, so the new equilibrium point is Q', where U.S. income is OY_1' and Japanese income is OY_2'. The fall in U.S. income is reduced, because the increase in Japanese income raises the demand for U.S. exports. The switch in expenditure, however, shifts the BB curve all the way to $B'B'$, and Q' lies below $B'B'$. Therefore, the U.S. current account moves into deficit.

across from Q.) The new equilibrium is at Q', where $I_1'I_1'$ and $I_2'I_2'$ intersect. Income falls to OY_1' in the United States, by less than it would if there were no increase in Japanese income. Income rises to OY_2' in Japan, by less than it would if there were no decrease in U.S. income. The fall in U.S. income is limited by the increase in Japanese income and the resulting increase in the Japanese demand for U.S. goods; the rise in Japanese income is limited by the decrease in U.S. income and the resulting decrease in the U.S. demand for Japanese goods. Nevertheless, the U.S. current account moves into deficit. The new equilibrium point, Q', lies below $B'B'$, the curve on which the U.S. current account would be balanced after the autonomous switch in expenditure.

We have thus answered the first question posed above, concerning the effects of income changes in the outside world. Although they contribute to adjustment, they cannot eliminate imbalances completely.

Measuring Interdependence

Econometric models of national economies rarely allow explicitly for the interdependence of national incomes. Best guesses about exports are fed into the models, not made by the models themselves. In recent years, however, national

Table 13-1. Interdependence among the Seven Economic Summit Countries: Income Changes Induced by Fiscal-Policy Changes (measured by third-year percentage changes in real gross domestic product)

Country Where Fiscal Policy Changes	Effect on Income in:						
	United States	Japan	Germany	France	United Kingdom	Italy	Canada
United States	*3.29*	0.53	0.37	0.44	0.70	0.34	1.41
Japan	0.03	*2.38*	0.16	0.18	0.17	0.11	0.18
Germany	0.00	0.24	*1.77*	0.84	0.33	0.56	0.18
France	0.03	0.11	0.32	*2.63*	0.23	0.30	0.09
United Kingdom	0.01	0.14	0.26	0.38	*0.65*	0.22	0.15
Italy	0.00	0.12	0.34	0.53	0.17	*1.68*	0.12
Canada	0.09	0.11	0.11	0.12	0.09	0.07	*1.84*

Source: John F. Helliwell and Tim Padmore, "Empirical Studies of Macroeconomic Interdependence," in R. W. Jones and P. B. Kenen, eds., *Handbook of International Economics* (Amsterdam: North-Holland, 1985), ch. 21. The estimates are those obtained using the EPA model for Japan, which gives rather large effects to U.S. fiscal policy. (It likewise gives lower estimates of the effects of foreign fiscal policies on U.S. income and an unusually low estimate of the own-country multiplier for the United Kingdom.)

models have been put together to show how disturbances and policy changes in one country affect other countries' incomes. The results of one such effort are shown in Table 13-1, which deals with changes in government spending. The numbers are not exactly comparable to the income multipliers we have been examining. They show the third-year effects of the policy changes rather than the full multiplier effects; they include the effects of changes in the countries' prices resulting from the changes in their incomes; and they include the effects of the changes in third countries' incomes. Nevertheless, the numbers are indicative of the degree to which events in a single country affect incomes elsewhere.

How do we read this table? Let there be an increase in government spending in the United States. Set it equal to 1 percent of real gross domestic product. The effect on U.S. income is shown on the first line of the table, in the column for the United States; real gross domestic product rises by 3.29 percent. The effect on Japanese income is shown on the same line, in the column for Japan; real gross domestic product rises by 0.53 percent. The *own-country* effects are italicized so that you can spot them easily. They are larger than the *cross-country* effects. But some of the cross-country effects are impressive, especially those of U.S. fiscal policy and, within Europe, those of German fiscal policy. Interdependence is far from negligible.

These linked simulations can be very useful. When governments exchange official forecasts, they frequently find that the forecasts are not mutually consistent. Each country is forecasting an increase in its exports different from the other countries' forecasts of their imports. When the relevant national models are linked, they produce consistent forecasts, not only of trade flows but also of incomes. Here is an example. The Japanese econometric model that was combined with other national models to generate the numbers in Table 13-1 can be used by itself to forecast the change in Japanese income resulting from an increase in Japanese government spending. The second-year increase in income turns out to be 12 percent lower than the forecast obtained when the Japanese model is combined with other countries' models. When used by itself, the Japanese model cannot allow for the increase in Japanese income induced by the increase in Japanese exports resulting from the increases in other countries' incomes.

COMPLETING THE ADJUSTMENT PROCESS

As income changes at home and abroad are not large enough to eradicate current-account deficits, we must turn to the second question posed earlier. What can be done about those deficits?

A current-account deficit can be *financed* by adopting policies capable of attracting a capital inflow—by borrowing abroad in one form or another. It can be met by intervention on foreign-exchange markets—by running down reserves. But these are not apt to be permanent solutions. A country that continues to run a current-account deficit may find it increasingly difficult to borrow abroad; its creditors may start to doubt the country's ability to manage and repay its debts. A country cannot run down reserves indefinitely because it will run out of them.

Therefore, a country with a current-account deficit may have to eliminate it sooner or later. It can tighten its monetary or fiscal policy to reduce domestic expenditure and thus reduce its imports. It can devalue its currency to switch expenditure from foreign to home goods. Alternatively, it can allow market forces take the lead in reducing or switching expenditure. If it stops sterilizing reserve losses, its money supply will shrink, and that will cut expenditure. If it stops intervening altogether, its currency will depreciate, and that will switch expenditure.

Chapter 14 will explain how a change in the exchange rate contributes to adjustment by switching expenditure. Here, let us examine the underlying choice between reducing and switching expenditure to end a current-account deficit, using the equations for a small economy developed earlier in this chapter.

Introducing the Theory of Optimal Policy

Consider an economy with a pegged exchange rate that starts out in a blissful state. Its income is at the full-employment level, defined as some desired fraction of the labor force or as a level consistent with long-run price stability. This condition is described hereafter as *internal balance*. Its current account is balanced or financed exactly by capital flows that can be expected to continue. In other words, there is no deficit or surplus in the country's balance of payments. This condition is described hereafter as *external balance*.

The government of this lucky country will want to prevent any change in income. An increase would cause inflation; a decrease would cause unemployment. It will also want to prevent any change in net exports. An increase would produce a balance-of-payments surplus; a decrease would produce a deficit.

Suppose that the initial situation is disturbed by an autonomous increase in domestic expenditure ($dA^a > 0$). Incomes rises and net exports fall, as shown by equations (11a) and (13c) and by Figure 13-2. What can the government do to restore internal and external balance? It can, of course, restore external balance by adopting policies to switch expenditure from foreign to home goods. This strategy, however, would drive the economy further from internal balance, because it would add to the increase in income.[6] Therefore, the government should restore internal balance by adopting policies to bring domestic expenditure down to its initial level. By doing so, moreover, it will bring net exports back to their initial level and thus restore external balance as well as internal balance.

Suppose that the initial situation is disturbed by an autonomous decrease in net exports ($dN^a < 0$). Income and net exports fall. The government can restore external balance by reducing domestic expenditure. But that is the wrong strategy in this instance; it drives the economy further from internal balance by reducing income. The government can restore internal balance by raising expenditure. But that is a bad strategy, too; it drives the economy further from external balance by raising net exports. Therefore, the government should adopt an expenditure-switching policy. By reversing the autonomous decrease in net exports, it can restore external and internal balance.

These examples illustrate a general principle. An *optimal pairing* of disturbances and policy responses can maintain internal and external balance. Facing an autonomous change in expenditure, a government should adopt an expenditure-changing policy. Facing an autonomous switch in expenditure, it should adopt an expenditure-switching policy.

Complications in the Two-Country Case

The same principle applies in the two-country model outlined earlier, but the applications are more complicated. We must distinguish between policy responses that are optimal from a global standpoint and those that are optimal only

---

[6]Using equation (13c), set $dN = 0$ and solve for the autonomous switch in expenditure that would exactly offset an autonomous change in domestic expenditure:

$$dN^a = \frac{m}{s} dA^a.$$

Using equation (11a), compute the effect on income:

$$dY = \frac{1}{s+m}(dA^a + dN^a) = \frac{1}{s+m}\left[dA^a + \left(\frac{m}{s}\right)dA^a\right] = \frac{1}{s}dA^a,$$

which is larger than the income change caused by the autonomous change in expenditure. (It is, in fact, equal to the income change that takes place in a closed economy, because the expenditure-switching policy offsets the leakage into imports.) The same method can be used to prove assertions made later in the text about policy-induced expenditure changes designed to achieve internal or external balance in the face of an autonomous switch in expenditure.

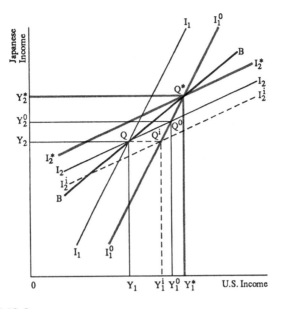

FIGURE 13-6
Effects of Japanese Expenditure Policies.
An autonomous increase in U.S. expenditure shifts the U.S. income curve from I_1I_1 to $I_1^0I_1^0$, raising U.S. income to OY_1^0, raising Japanese income to OY_2^0, and driving the U.S. current account into deficit (because Q^0 lies below BB). To restore internal balance by changing domestic expenditure, Japan must tighten its monetary or fiscal policy to shift its income curve from I_2I_2 to $I_2^iI_2^i$. The new equilibrium point is Q^i, where Japanese income returns to OY_2. U.S. income falls from OY_1^i, which takes the United States closer to internal balance, but the current-account deficits gets larger (because Q^i is farther from BB). To restore external balance by changing domestic expenditure, Japan must relax its monetary or fiscal policy to shift its income curve to $I_2^*I_2^*$. The new equilibrium point is Q^*, which lies on BB. But both countries move further from internal balance. Income rises to OY_1 in the United States and to OY_2 in Japan.

from a national standpoint. Algebraic illustrations are offered in Section 1 of Appendix B. A diagrammatic illustration is offered in Figure 13-6.

As in earlier diagrams, the two economies begin at Q. Income is OY_1 in the United States and OY_2 in Japan, and the current account is balanced. The initial situation is disturbed, however, by an autonomous increase in U.S. expenditure, which shifts the U.S. income curve to $I_1^0I_1^0$, as in Figure 13-4. Both countries' incomes rise, and the U.S. current account moves into deficit.

We can see at once the globally optimal response. By tightening monetary or fiscal policy, the United States can reduce domestic expenditure, shifting the U.S. income curve back to I_1I_1. This strategy restores internal balance in both countries and restores external balance for the two together. Suppose, however, that the United States does nothing. What options are available to Japan?

Japan can restore internal balance by tightening its monetary or fiscal policy. It can shift its income curve to $I_2^iI_2^i$ and thus bring Japanese income back to OY_2. By doing so, moreover, it brings the United States closer to internal balance by limiting the increase in U.S. income. But the new equilibrium point, Q^i, lies farther from the BB curve. An expenditure-changing policy for internal balance carries both economies further from external balance. Alternatively, Japan can restore external balance by relaxing its monetary or fiscal policy. It can shift its income curve to $I_2^* I_2^*$, so that the new equilibrium point, Q^*, lies on the BB curve. By doing so, however, it takes both economies further from internal balance: U.S. income rises all the way to OY_1^*, and Japanese income rises all the way to OY_2^*. These options, then, are not globally optimal. They are not even nationally optimal for Japan.

Japan should adopt an expenditure-switching policy. By changing the exchange rate between the yen and dollar, or letting it adjust automatically under the influence of market forces, Japan can achieve internal and external balance. It can thus *insulate* Japanese income and the balance of payments from the change in foreign expenditure. A proof is given in Section 1 of Appendix B (it could be given in Figure 13-6, but the diagram gets cluttered). The proof also shows, however, that the strategy is not globally optimal, because it raises U.S. income, driving the United States further from internal balance. It can be argued, however, that the U.S. government has itself to blame, for failing to reduce U.S. expenditure, which would be the globally optimal policy response.

Consider one more case, an autonomous switch in expenditure from U.S. to Japanese goods. We saw in Figure 13-5 that this disturbance reduces U.S. income, raises Japanese income, and drives the U.S. balance of payments into deficit. The optimal response from a global standpoint is, of course, a U.S. or Japanese policy to switch expenditure back again. Expenditure-changing policies are not optimal in this case, even from a national standpoint. If the United States raises domestic expenditure to restore internal balance, it will drive its balance of payments into deeper deficit. If it reduces domestic expenditure to restore external balance, it will carry its economy further from internal balance. Japan faces a symmetrical dilemma. Nevertheless, an odd result emerges from the algebra of Appendix B. If the United States reduces expenditure to achieve external balance, it will bring Japanese income back to its initial level. Japan will enjoy external and internal balance. An expenditure-changing policy for external balance is nationally optimal, but in an *altruistic* way. It confers internal balance on the *foreign* economy.

National Policies and International Polemics

When exchange rates are pegged and difficult to change, governments cannot easily achieve the switches in expenditure that are globally or nationally optimal for dealing with certain disturbances. (There are other ways to switch expenditure, including tariffs, but these have real welfare costs and can provoke retaliation.) The resulting conflicts can cause nasty arguments.

If one country's spending changes autonomously and its government fails to correct the situation by pursuing appropriate domestic policies, other countries will experience internal and external problems, which they cannot solve completely by changing their own policies. They will confront the dilemmas faced by Japan in Figure 13-6 and will therefore demand a change in policy by the country in which the disturbance occured. That country is the only one that can make a globally optimal response.

An autonomous switch in expenditure can cause trouble, too. Each government will want the other to adopt an expenditure-changing policy for external balance, the altruistic policy mentioned earlier. Japan may thus wait for the United States to act, the United States may wait for Japan, and each will blame the other for its plight. Blame is hard to fix in a case of this sort, however, because of the nature of the disturbance and the dilemma that both countries face.

These examples are too simple to explain completely the disputes of recent years, especially those involving U.S. fiscal policies. The disputes have been compounded by the effects of the capital flows produced by monetary and fiscal policies. Nevertheless, these simple examples show how controversies can arise when economies and policies are interdependent.

SUMMARY

This chapter has developed the theory of income determination for an open economy, beginning with a country that is too small to affect other countries' incomes. Prices were fixed throughout the chapter, the exchange rate was pegged, and the country's central bank sterilized reserve flows and used its control of the money supply to influence the interest rate. Changes in the interest rate represented changes in monetary policy. Changes in tax rates represented changes in fiscal policy. The two together were described as expenditure-changing policies.

Using the basic equations of national-income accounting and simple behavioral relationships connecting a country's income with its demands for home and foreign goods, we were able to derive the national-income multiplier for an open economy and an additional equation linking the current-account balance to autonomous changes and switches in expenditure.

The national-income multiplier is smaller for an open economy than for a closed economy, because there are two leakages from the income stream, one into saving and the other into imports. An autonomous or policy-induced increase in domestic expenditure raises income and worsens the current-account balance. An autonomous switch in expenditure from foreign to home goods raises income, too, but improves the current-account balance. The increase in income induced by an autonomous switch in expenditure raises the demand for imports and limits the improvement in the current-account balance, but it does not eliminate the whole improvement.

When we allow for changes in other countries' incomes, an autonomous increase in domestic expenditure leads to a larger increase in domestic income, because it raises other countries' incomes and imports. An autonomous switch in expenditure, however, leads to a smaller increase in domestic income, because it reduces other countries' incomes and imports. Even in this multicountry case, however, the resulting income changes cannot eliminate completely the current-account deficit or surplus produced by an autonomous change or switch in expenditure.

A country confronting an autonomous increase in domestic expenditure can restore internal and external balance by an expenditure-reducing policy—tightening its monetary or fiscal policy. A country confronting an autonomous switch in expenditure can restore internal and external balance by an expenditure-switching policy—changing the exchange rate. These policies are optimal from both national and global standpoints. Other policies may be optimal from a national standpoint but not a global standpoint. Confronting an autonomous change in foreign expenditure, for example, a government can restore internal and external balance by an expenditure-switching policy. A change in the exchange rate will insulate the economy from the external disturbance, but it will drive the foreign country further from internal balance.

RECOMMENDED READINGS

The subjects treated in this chapter are examined at greater length in James E. Meade, *The Balance of Payments* (London: Oxford University Press, 1951), pts. I–IV. On the multiplier and its uses, see Lloyd A. Metzler, "Underemployment Equilibrium in International Trade," *Econometrica*, 10 (April 1942); for a more thorough geometric treatment of the two-country case, see Romney Robinson, "A Graphical Analysis of the Foreign Trade Multiplier," *Economic Journal*, 62 (September, 1952).

The vital distinction between shifts and switches in expenditure comes from a famous paper by Harry G. Johnson, "Towards a General Theory of the Balance of Payments," in H. G. Johnson, *International Trade and Economic Growth* (Cambridge, Mass.: Harvard University Press, 1961), reprinted in American Economic Association, *Readings in International Economics* (Homewood, Ill.: Richard D. Irwin, 1968), ch. 23.

Econometricians have done much work on the links between national models; for a review and assessment, see Ralph C. Bryant, et al., eds, *Empirical Macroeconomics for Interdependent Economies* (Washington, D.C., The Brookings Institution, 1988).

The problems of policy interdependence are explored more thoroughly in Chapters 19 and 20, and additional readings are listed there.

QUESTIONS AND PROBLEMS

(1) An economy that is too small to affect other countries' incomes experiences a $1 billion increase in domestic expenditure. Its marginal propensity to import is 0.10, and its marginal propensity to save is 0.15. Tax receipts do not vary with income. By how much does its national income change? By how much does its current-account balance change? If the economy had been closed to foreign trade, by how much would the increase in expenditure have changed its national income? Explain the difference in results.

(2) The same economy experiences a $2 billion decrease in the foreign demand for its exports. What happens to its national income and current-account balance?

(3) A small open economy experiences a switch in domestic expenditure from foreign to domestic goods. Using equations (11a) and (13c) in the text, compare the effects on national income and the current-account balance of these four policy responses:

(a) An expenditure-changing policy for external balance;
(b) An expenditure-changing policy for internal balance;
(c) An expenditure-switching policy for external balance;
(d) An expenditure-switching policy for internal balance.

Summarize your results in a general statement about the optimal policy response to an expenditure-switching disturbance.

(4) Adapt Figure 13-4 to illustrate the following assertion: If all countries seek to raise their incomes by expenditure-changing policies but each ignores the others' policies, they are likely to make excessive changes in their policies and thus overshoot their income targets. You will not need the *BB* curve and may omit it from your diagram.

(5) Your answer to (4) illustrates the case for coordinating national policies, and there has been much discussion of this subject in recent years. Looking at the numbers in Table 13-1, what would you say about the incentives of the United States to coordinate its policies with those of other countries, compared with the others' incentives to coordinate with the United States? What about the case for coordination among the European countries?

(6) Adapt Figure 13-4 to show what happens to U.S. income and the current-account balance when Japan tries to raise its income by an expenditure-changing policy. Go on to show what happens to Japanese income and the current-account balance when the United States responds with an expenditure-changing policy for internal balance.

14

Exchange Rates and the Current Account

THE ISSUES

At several points in the previous chapter, changes in exchange rates were said to cause switches in expenditure between domestic and foreign goods. This chapter provides the explanation and examines the implications for economic policy and for the choice between exchange-rate regimes. It explores three issues:

- How an exchange-rate change switches expenditure and the conditions that must be fulfilled for it to improve the current account.
- How macroeconomic policies must be managed to make an exchange-rate change effective.
- When it would be sensible for a country to give up using the exchange rate for balance-of-payments adjustment and to fix its exchange rate irrevocably.

The first part of the chapter works through the expenditure-switching effects of an exchange-rate change; it sets out the *elasticity approach* to the analysis of exchange-rate changes. The next part looks at the implications for incomes and prices at home and abroad; it develops the *absorption approach* and examines the role of the exchange rate as a policy instrument. The final part of the chapter introduces the *theory of optimal currency areas*; it examines some of the benefits and costs of fixing exchange rates irrevocably.

The chapter uses the same basic assumptions made in Chapter 13. Home and foreign prices are fixed. The economy under study is too small to influence economic activity in other countries. The central bank sterilizes the monetary effects of intervention on foreign-exchange markets and uses its control of the money supply to set the domestic interest rate.

THE ELASTICITIES APPROACH

In Chapter 12, which introduced exchange-rate theory, we were already dealing with switches in expenditure. When a change in the exchange rate led to movements along the demand and supply curves for currencies, they reflected switches in demand between domestic and foreign goods.[1] Additional conditions must be satisfied, however, before we can be sure that a depreciation or devaluation of the domestic currency will improve the current account and raise domestic income—the assertions made in the previous chapter.

The Marshall-Lerner-Robinson Condition

On such condition involves the price elasticities of the domestic and foreign demands for imports. It is known as the Marshall-Lerner-Robinson (MLR) condition, after the three economists who derived it independently.

Consider two countries in which prices and incomes are constant. Neglect trade in services and investment-income flows so that the current-account balance equals the trade balance, and assume that trade is balanced initially. The MLR condition states that:

A depreciation or devaluation of a country's currency will improve its current-account balance if the sum of the price elasticities of domestic and foreign demands for imports is larger than unity.

This condition is derived algebraically in Section 2 of Appendix B. It is illustrated diagrammatically in Figure 14-1.

The upper panels of Figure 14-1 show demand curves for exports and imports plotted against prices in domestic currency. The lower panels show them plotted against prices in foreign currency. The home-currency price of exports, p_1, is constant. Therefore, the supply curve S_1 in the upper left panel is perfectly elastic and cannot shift. Its foreign-currency counterpart, however, depends on the exchange rate, π. The supply curve in that panel is also infinitely elastic, but it shifts downward as π rises. The foreign-currency price of imports, p_2^*, is constant, too, so the supply curve S_2 in the lower right panel is perfectly elastic and cannot shift. Its home-currency counterpart, however, depends on π. It shifts upward as π rises.

The curve D_1 in the lower left panel is the demand curve for the home country's

---

[1]Another form of switching is frequently emphasized. A depreciation of the domestic currency tends to raise the domestic prices of *traded* goods relative to those of *nontraded* goods. Therefore, it switches domestic demand from traded to nontraded goods, releasing additional goods for export, as well as reducing imports. Symmetrical effects occur in the outside world. Some say that this is the most important expenditure-switching effect, because the prices of traded goods are determined in international markets and are not affected by changing the exchange rate. The form of substitution does not matter much, however, when we are dealing with the broad macroeconomic effects of an exchange-rate change. We have merely to show that there is *some* form of substitution, so that the exchange-rate change *can* switch expenditure.

exports (i.e., the foreign demand curve for imports). It is plotted against the price facing the foreign consumer. That price begins at Oa, and the quantity demanded is Oc. Therefore export receipts in foreign currency begin at $Oabc$. A depreciation or devaluation of the domestic currency raises π and reduces the price facing foreign consumers. Let it fall to Oa', shifting the supply curve downward from S_1 to S_1'. Foreign consumers move along D_1, raising export volume to Oc'. Export receipts in foreign currency go to $Oa'b'c'$. This outcome is translated into domestic currency in the upper left panel. The export price remains at OA in domestic currency, so the supply curve does not shift. But export volume rises to OC' (CC' equals cc'). Seen from the standpoint of domestic suppliers, the outcome is an outward shift in the demand curve to D_1', an increase in sales, and an increase in home-currency receipts to $OAB'C'$.

The curve D_2 in the upper right panel is the domestic demand curve for imports plotted against the price facing the domestic consumer. That price begins at OE, and the quantity demanded is OG. Import payments in domestic currency begin at $OEFG$. A depreciation or devaluation of the domestic currency raises the home-currency price. Let it rise to OE', shifting the supply curve upward from S_2 to S_2'. (The ratio EE'/OE must equal absolutely the ratio $a'a/Oa$, as both measure the same change in π.) Domestic consumers move along D_2, and import volume falls to OG'. Import payments in domestic currency go to $OE'F'G'$. This outcome is translated into foreign currency in the lower right panel. The import price remains at Oe in foreign currency, so the supply curve does not shift. But import volume falls to Og' (gg' equals GG'). Seen from the standpoint of foreign suppliers, the outcome is an inward shift in the demand curve to D_2', a decrease in sales, and a decrease in their foreign-currency receipts to $Oef'g'$.

Let trade be balanced initially (so that $OABC$ equals $OEFG$, and $Oabc$ equals $Oefg$). Suppose that the price elasticity of the foreign demand curve is 1 in the neighborhood of point b. The revenue-reducing effect of the decrease in price is exactly equal to the revenue-raising effect of the increase in quantity, so export revenues stay constant in foreign currency. Suppose that the price elasticity of the domestic demand curve is greater than zero. The quantity of imports falls (gg' is not zero), reducing import payments in foreign currency. The values chosen for the two price elasticities satisfy the MLR condition, because their sum is greater than unity. Hence, the depreciation or devaluation improves the current-account balance measured in foreign currency.

What about the balance measured in home currency? It must also improve. When export proceeds are unchanged in foreign currency, their value in home currency must rise in proportion to the change in the exchange rate ($OAB'C'/OABC$ must equal OF'/OF). When import payments fall in foreign currency, they may rise or fall in domestic currency, but they cannot rise in proportion to the change in the exchange rate ($OE'F'G'/OEFG$ must be smaller than OE'/OE). Therefore, export proceeds must rise by more than the largest possible increase in import payments, and the current-account measured in home must improve.

Figure 14-1 can be used to work through other cases. Suppose, for example, that the price elasticity of domestic demand is 1 and that the elasticity of foreign demand is greater than zero, assumptions that also satisfy the MLR condition. It is easy to show that import payments will be constant in domestic currency, export receipts

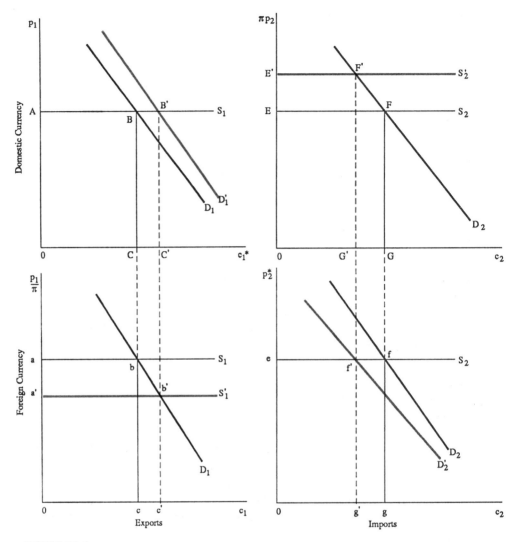

FIGURE 14-1
Devaluation and the Current-Account Balance
The upper panels show prices and outlays in home currency. When the home-currency price of exports is OA, foreign demand is OC, and export proceeds are $OABC$. When the home-currency price of imports is OE, domestic demand is OG, and import payments are $OEFG$. Let $OABC$ equal $OEFG$ initially, so that the current account is balanced. The lower panels show prices and outlays in foreign currency. When the foreign-currency price of exports is Oa, foreign demand is Oc, and export proceeds are $Oabc$. When the foreign-currency price of imports is Oe, domestic demand is Og, and import payments are $Oefg$. When $OABC$ equals $OEFG$, then $Oabc$ equals $Oefg$. A devaluation or depreciation of the domestic currency reduces the foreign-currency price of exports from Oa to Oa', raising quantity from Oc to Oc'. Export proceeds in foreign currency become $Oa'b'c'$. Domestic suppliers see this as an increase in demand—an outward shift in the demand curve from D_1 to D_1' in the upper export panel. Quantity rises by CC' (equal to cc'), and export proceeds in home currency rise to $OAB'C'$. The devaluation raises the home-currency price of imports from OE to OE', reducing quantity from OG to OG'. Import payments in home currency become $OE'F'G'$. Foreign suppliers see this as a decrease in demand — an inward shift in the demand curve from D_2 to D_2' in the lower import panel. Quantity falls by gg'

will rise, and the current-account balance will improve, regardless of the currency in which it is measured.[2]

The MLR condition is a sufficient condition for an improvement in the current-account balance. It is not a necessary condition. If supply curves are less than infinitely elastic, a depreciation or devaluation of the domestic currency can improve the current-account balance even when demand elasticities are too low to satisfy the MLR condition.

But the MLR condition appears to be satisfied for most major industrial countries. Estimates of price elasticities are shown in Table 14-1. In all but the British case, the elasticities of domestic and foreign demand sum to numbers much larger than unity. There is just one difficulty. These elasticities relate to long-run responses; they describe the effects of an exchange-rate change after enough time has passed for consumers and producers to work through old commitments and find new suppliers and customers. The short-run elasticities are lower and do not always satisfy the MLR condition. Therefore, the current-account balance may trace a J-shaped curve through time, getting worse before it improves in response to a depreciation or devaluation.

This J-curve effect poses no serious problem when a government devalues a pegged exchange rate, provided the government has enough reserves to finance the temporary deterioration of the current-account balance. It does pose a problem for the functioning of a flexible exchange rate. If the current account gets worse when the domestic currency depreciates, the currency may go on depreciating under the pressure of excess supply in the foreign-exchange market. The market may be unstable. If this instability is to be avoided, foreign-exchange markets must be inhabited by speculators farsighted enough to know that exchange-rate movements

---

[2]It can also be shown that the current-account balance measured in foreign currency will improve by a larger amount if it begins in deficit, and this is an important result. A country is more likely to devalue its currency when it has a deficit. Return to the example in the text. When the elasticity of foreign demand is 1, $Oa'b'c'$ equals $Oabc$; there is no change in foreign-currency export proceeds. But foreign-currency import payments fall by $g'f'fg$, which is gg' times Oe. Furthermore, gg'/Og is equal to the elasticity of domestic demand, e_2, *times* the exchange-rate change: $gg'/Og = -e_2(EE'/OE)$. Therefore, $gg' = -e_2(Og)(EE'/OE)$, while $gg' \times Oe = -e_2(Og \times Oe) \times (EE'/OE)$, and $g'f'fg = -e_2(Oefg) \times (EE'/OE)$. The reduction in import payments increases absolutely with the size of $Oefg$, the initial import bill.

(equal to GG'), and import payments in foreign currency fall to $Oef'g'$. Let the elasticity of D_1 be unity in the range bb' (so that $Oa'b'c'$ equals $Oabc$); export receipts are constant in foreign currency. Let the elasticity of D_2 be greater than zero in the range FF' (so that $Oef'g'$ is smaller than $Oefg$ because gg' is not zero); import payments fall in foreign currency. The current-account balance improves in foreign currency. When export proceeds are constant in foreign currency, moreover, they must rise in home currency by an amount proportional to the exchange-rate change ($OAB'C'/OABC$ must equal OE'/OE). When import payments fall in foreign currency, they may rise or fall in home currency ($OE'F'G'$ can be larger or smaller than $OEFG$), but they cannot rise by an amount proportional to the exchange-rate change ($OE'F'G'/OEFG$ must be smaller than OE'/OE). Hence, the increase in export proceeds must exceed the largest possible increase in import payments ($OAB'C'$ must exceed $OE'F'G'$ when $OABC$ equals $OEFG$ initially), and the current-account balance also improves in home currency.

Table 14-1. Price Elasticities of Demand for the Major Industrial Countries

Country	Price Elasticities of Demand for Imports	
	Domestic	Foreign
Canada	1.30	0.79
France	1.08	1.31
Germany	0.88	1.11
Italy	1.03	0.93
Japan	0.78	1.11
Britain	0.65	0.48
United States	1.66	1.41

Source: Adapted from Robert M. Stern et al., *Prince Elasticities in International Trade* (London: Macmillan, 1976), Table 2.2.

Note: These are "consensus" estimates, based on many studies, rather than the outcomes of one study. Estimates from individual studies vary widely, depending on the concepts, econometric methods, price data, and time periods employed.

tend to go too far and that profits can therefore be made by purchasing a currency that has been depreciating, because it can be expected to appreciate when the current account begins to improve. Their purchases will finance the temporary current-account deficit and limit the depreciation of the domestic currency. We will illustrate this outcome in Chapter 16.

Nominal and Real Exchange Rates

The main limitations of the elasticities approach reside in the assumptions about prices and incomes that were used to derive the MLR condition. In Figure 14-1, a depreciation of the domestic currency improved the current-account balance because it affected relative prices. It raised the home-currency price of the foreign (imported) good relative to that of the domestic (exported) good, inducing domestic consumers to switch from foreign to domestic goods. It lowered the foreign-currency price of the domestic good relative to that of the foreign good, inducing foreign consumers to switch in that same direction. A change in the *nominal* exchange rate, the price of foreign currency in terms of domestic currency, altered the *real* exchange rate, the price of foreign output in terms of domestic output.

A country's real exchange rate can be defined as the relative purchasing power of domestic output:

$$v = \frac{\pi p_2^*}{p_1},$$

where v is the real exchange rate, π is the nominal exchange rate, p_2^* is the foreign-currency price of the foreign good, and p_1 is the home-currency price of the domestic good. The real exchange rate is thus the *reciprocal* of the terms of trade.

Section 2 of Appendix B proves that the MLR condition relates fundamentally to the effect of a change in the real exchange rate. A change in the nominal exchange rate can affect the current-account balance only by changing the real exchange rate. That is what happened throughout Chapter 13, where p_1 and p_2^* were constant, but it is easy to build cases in which prices are not constant.

One such case arises when real wage rates are completely rigid—when workers have the market power to raise the money wage in a manner that offsets completely every increase in the cost of living or when the money wage is *indexed* automatically to the cost of living. Suppose that the real wage is fixed institutionally in terms of the imported good. Furthermore, suppose as before that domestic output (income) is kept constant, keeping the marginal product of labor constant and thus fixing the real wage in terms of the domestic good.

To put these assumptions precisely, let w be the money wage rate. Then $w/\pi p_2^*$ will be constant at some level $\bar{w}_2$ when the real wage is fixed institutionally in terms of the imported good, and w/p_1 will be constant at some level $\bar{w}_1$ when the marginal product of labor is fixed by keeping output constant. Dividing $\bar{w}_1$ by $\bar{w}_2$,

$$\frac{\bar{w}_1}{\bar{w}_2} = \frac{w/p_1}{w/\pi p_2^*} = \frac{\pi p_2^*}{p_1} = v.$$

The real exchange rate will be constant when the real wage is constant. Any change in the nominal exchange rate will be offset completely by a change in the money wage that prevents the real exchange rate from changing, and the change in the nominal rate cannot affect the current-account balance even when the MLR condition is satisfied.[3] But the real exchange rate cannot be constant unless prices change; an increase in π must raise v unless p_1 rises or p_2^* falls. Accordingly, the constant-price assumption used to derive the MLR condition rules out rigidity in the real wage. Conversely, rigidity in the real wage contradicts the constant-price assumption.

When the real wage is rigid or sticky in the short run, any shock or policy that raises the price level can touch off a wage-price spiral. Wages will be raised to offset the increase in the cost of living, and prices will be raised again to offset the resulting increase in the cost of labor. Once an inflationary process has begun, moreover, it is hard to stop. It sets up expectations of continuing inflation that permeate behavior in labor and goods markets and thus prolong the process. Therefore, a single exchange-rate change can lead to a vicious circle. If it raises wages, costs, and prices, it produces the need for another devaluation, which generates another round of wage, cost, and price increases. An inflationary process can be halted by tightening

---

[3]The same problem arises when the real wage is fixed institutionally in terms of a price index containing both domestic and foreign goods. Define a *geometric* price index, $p_i = p_1{}^a(\pi p_2^*)^{1-a}$, where a and $1-a$ are the weights attached to the home-currency prices of domestic and foreign goods, and define $\bar{w}_i = w/p_i$. Then, $\bar{w}_1/\bar{w}_i = (\pi p_2^*/p_1)^{1-a} = v^{1-a}$. The real exchange rate is still rigid when $\bar{w}_1$ and $\bar{w}_i$ are fixed.

monetary and fiscal policies, but the output and employment costs can be very high. The inflationary consequences of devaluation are, of course, most serious in a small economy, where a change in the exchange rate is bound to have a large effect on the cost of living. For this reason, among others, exchange-rate arrangements in Western Europe have tended to "harden" in recent years. We will return to this point shortly.

Another form of price behavior can prevent a change in the nominal exchange rate from changing the real rate to the same extent. Figure 14-1 assumed implicitly that the home-currency price of each country's export good was determined in its own home market. That is apt to happen when a country's home market is large, compared to its foreign markets. When the opposite is true, however, firms may adjust their home-currency prices to offset exchange-rate changes and thus prevent those changes from affecting the prices of their exports expressed in foreign currency.

Recent studies of export pricing by firms in major industrial countries support this hypothesis. The pricing policies of U.S. firms are influenced mainly by conditions in their own domestic markets. Therefore, a depreciation of the dollar reduces the foreign-currency prices of their exports. The pricing policies of Japanese firms are heavily influenced by conditions in foreign markets, especially in American markets. The firms are said to engage in "pricing to market" to insulate their export markets from exchange-rate changes. When the dollar depreciates, for example, they reduce the yen prices of their exports to hold down their dollar prices and thus maintain their market shares in the United States. The dollar prices of Japanese cars have risen substantially in recent years, but not by as much as they would have risen if Japanese manufacturers had kept their yen prices constant and allowed the depreciation of the dollar to raise their dollar prices.[4]

The pursuit of "pricing to market" reduces profitability. When Japanese manufacturers reduce their yen prices, their profit margins fall, because their wage and other costs are expressed in yen. That is one reason why Japanese firms began to manufacture cars and other products in the United States. Nevertheless, "pricing to market" is an attractive strategy when firms expect exchange-rate changes to be reversed in the near future; a profit squeeze will be more acceptable if it is thought to be temporary, especially when the alternative is a loss of market share and a wastage of previous investments made to acquire foreign markets. Consider a Japanese firm that has invested in a network of dealerships in the United States. If it allows a depreciation of the dollar to raise the dollar prices of its exports, its U.S. sales will decline, and some of its dealers will go out of business, making it hard for the firm to expand its sales after the depreciation has been reversed.

The Income Effects of Changing Exchange Rates

The expenditure-switching effects of a depreciation or devaluation increase the total demand for the domestic good and decrease the total demand for the foreign good. These changes in demand can have two consequences. First, they can

---

[4]For evidence to this effect, see Richard C. Marston, "Pricing to Market in Japanese Manufacturing," *Journal of International Economics*, 29 (November 1990). Note that pricing to market can often be interpreted as dumping and may be one reason for the recent increase in the number of antidumping actions described in Chapter 11.

raise prices at home and depress them abroad and thus limit the initial switch in expenditure by limiting the change in the real exchange rate. Second, they can raise real income and imports at home and reduce them abroad, eroding the improvement in the current-account balance.

The demand-increasing effect of a depreciation or devaluation was predicted by equations (11a) and (13c) in Chapter 13. Those equations were derived under our constant-price assumption, which allowed a depreciation or devaluation to affect the real exchange rate and thus switch expenditure. The switch is equivalent to an autonomous increase in net exports ($dN^a > 0$). Therefore, it raises real income Y, and the ultimate improvement in the current-account balance is only a fraction, $s/(s + m)$, of the initial expenditure switch.

The same demand-increasing effect can be detected in Figure 14-1. That diagram was constructed by aasuming that incomes are constant. But interest rates and taxes are also constant, so total consumption is constant in each country. When consumption is constant, moreover, a change in spending on one good must be marched by an equal but opposite change in spending on the other. This statement points to a contradiction lurking in Figure 14-1.

Look first at expenditure on the home good measured in home currency. Foreign expenditure on that good rises by an amount proportional to the exchange-rate change. Domestic expenditure on the foreign good can rise or fall, depending on the elasticity of the domestic demand for imports. We saw before, however, that it cannot rise by an amount proportional to the exchange-rate change, because of the reduction in the quantity demanded. By implication, domestic expenditure on the home good cannot fall by an amount proportional to the exchange-rate change. Therefore, foreign expenditure on the home good must rise by more that the largest possible decrease in domestic expenditure, and there must thus be an increase in *total* expenditure on the home good, which shows up as an increase in the quantity demanded when the domestic price is constant.

Look next at expenditure on the foreign good measured in foreign currency. Domestic expenditure falls. Foreign expenditure is constant, because there is no change in foreign spending on the domestic good when the elasticity of foreign demand is unity. Accordingly, there must be a decrease in *total* expenditure on the foreign good, which shows up as a decrease in the quantity demanded when the foreign price is constant.

Therefore, Figure 14-1 contains a contradiction. It was constructed by assuming that incomes and prices are constant at home and abroad. Yet they cannot stay constant when a depreciation or devaluation improves the current-account balance. Demand for the home good rises and demand for the foreign good falls. There must then be an increase in domestic output (income) or in the price of the home good to clear the market for the home good. There must be a decrease in foreign output (income) or in the price of the foreign good to clear the market for the foreign good.

When prices change to clear goods markets, the outcome is the first result mentioned previously, a smaller switch in expenditure, because the real exchange rate does not change by as much as the nominal rate. When outputs and incomes change to clear those markets, the outcome is the second result, an income-induced change in trade flows that offsets some of the switch in expenditure.

In some situations, there can be *no* switch in expenditure and no improvement in the current-account balance, because there can be no change in the real exchange rate. Recall the Ricardian model in Chapter 3, where employment was fixed at its full-employment level and the terms of trade were determined in international markets. A depreciation or devaluation of the Portuguese currency cannot affect the real exchange rate. It raises the money wage and price level in Portugal, reduces them in Britain, and can have no effect on the current-account balance. Similar results obtain in the simple monetary model examined in Chapter 17.

Measuring the Impact of Exchange-Rate Changes

Whole books have been written about individual devaluations, and many cross-country comparisons have been made in an effort to determine when devaluations are most likely to work well. Table 14-2 summarizes the results of one such comparative study, which covers 36 devaluations by 24 developing countries. (The table itself shows the average outcome for each group of cases, followed by examples from each group.) It focuses on two questions: (1) Does a permanent change in the nominal exchange rate lead to a long-lasting change in the real rate? (2) Does a change in the real exchange rate affect the current-account balance?

To answer the first question, the table examines the path of the real exchange rate in the wake of each devaluation and identifies three groups of outcomes. In the first 20 cases, devaluation of the nominal exchange rate led to a long-lasting depreciation of the real rate at least half as large as the nominal devaluation.[5] In 1972, for example, Pakistan devalued its currency by 130 percent against the U.S. dollar, causing the real exchange rate to depreciate by almost 127 percent; during the two years following the devaluation, however, inflation reduced the real depreciation to 77 percent. In the next nine cases, the devaluations were less successful; there were long-lasting depreciations of the real exchange rate, but they were less than half as large as the devaluations of the nominal rate. In the last seven cases, the outcomes were perverse; the real exchange rate appreciated soon after the nominal devaluation.

To answer the second question, the table examines the change in the current-account balance during the first full year after the devaluation. The current account improved in 17 of the first 29 cases, where real depreciations lasted for at least two years, and longer-lagged improvements took place in some other cases, too.

Evidence of this sort cannot be decisive. One would like to know what would have happened to the real exchange rate had there been no devaluation. One would also like to know what would have happened to the current-account balance if the real exchange rate had not changed. (In many of the cases covered by Table 14-2, the real rate would have appreciated, because of domestic inflation, and the current account would have worsened if the real exchange rate had not depreciated. Conditions were bad and getting worse—which is why the governments resorted to devaluation.) Econometric work can illuminate these issues. Thus, the study summarized in Table 14-2 showed that the behavior of the real exchange rate is affected

---

[5]In several of these cases, however, the real depreciation was fortified by additional devaluations in the two years after the initial devaluation; the government allowed the nominal exchange rate to "crawl" in order to prevent domestic inflation from eroding the influence of the initial devaluation.

Table 14-2. Nominal and Real Devaluations in Developing Countries

Country and Year	Nominal Devaluation	Real Devaluation k Years after Nominal Devaluation			Change in Current Account
		$k = 0$	$k = 1$	$k = 2$	
I. Large Real Devaluation Achieved					
Average for					
20 cases	41.1	35.2	31.9	35.7	1.0
Pakistan (1972)	130.1	126.8	88.6	76.8	2.5
Chile (1982)	88.2	74.7	65.7*	107.4*	4.0
India (1966)	58.6	46.8	29.5	30.1	0.7
Ecuador (1970)	38.8	36.9	30.7	26.6	−5.4
Kenya (1981)	35.9	32.6	38.9*	36.8*	7.7
Pakistan (1982)	29.6	24.9	25.3*	36.9*	3.3
Egypt (1962)	23.9	27.7	26.5	22.2	−0.8
Malta (1967)	16.6	16.6	16.7	18.7	−3.9
Israel (1967)	16.6	13.1	15.5	16.2	−4.4
Guyana (1967)	15.9	13.2	13.2	16.6	7.4
II. Small Real Devaluation Achieved					
Average for					
9 cases	69.5	42.1	28.1	19.6	1.8
Mexico (1982)	267.8	136.1	76.7*	46.3*	3.3
Israel (1962)	66.6	51.2	43.9	31.9	4.2
Peru (1967)	44.4	31.7	13.5	11.4	4.6
Costa Rica (1974)	28.8	17.6	10.2	10.6	5.6
Jamaica (1967)	15.9	13.2	10.2	7.4	−1.8
III. No Real Devaluation Achieved					
Average for					
7 cases	40.1	13.8	14.3	−18.3	0.4
Bolivia (1972)	66.6	8.2	34.5	−9.5	1.4
Nicaragua (1979)	43.0	8.7	−8.3	−19.2	−3.2
Argentina (1970)	25.0	14.2	−12.5	−42.3	−1.1
Israel (1971)	20.0	9.8	2.9	−3.4	2.9

Source: Adopted from Sebastian Edwards, *Real Exchange Rates, Devaluation, and Adjustment: Exchange Rate Policy in Developing Countries* (Cambridge Mass.: MIT Press, 1989), Tables 6.1, 7.1, and 7.8. The nominal and real devaluations are percentage changes in U.S. dollar values (not effective rates) from the full year before the devaluation to the kth year after it; the current-account change is the improvement in the current-account balance measured as a percentage of gross domestic product from the full year before the devaluation to the full year after it.

*Includes effects of subsequent devaluations.

strongly by the monetary policy followed in the wake of a devaluation; when monetary policy was very restrictive, the devaluation typically produced a large, long-lasting depreciation of the real rate. Furthermore, the study showed that the real exchange rate had large expenditure-switching effects on the current-account balance, but those effects were overwhelmed when domestic absorption was allowed to rise after a devaluation.

THE ABSORPTION APPROACH AND OPTIMAL POLICY

We can draw three general conclusions from our work thus far:

1. A change in the exchange rate is the appropriate policy response to an autonomous switch in expenditure.

2. For that very reason, however, a depreciation or devaluation designed to improve the current account can drive an economy out of internal balance.

3. The departure from internal balance caused by an exchange-rate change can undermine the effectiveness of the exchange-rate change by altering domestic and foreign prices in ways that reduce or reverse the corresponding change in the real exchange rate.

The third conclusion poses the basic policy problem faced by any government that contemplates a change in the nominal exchange rate. It can be restated as the fundamental postulate of the absorption approach:

> **When resources are fully employed, a change in the nominal exchange rate cannot affect the current-account balance unless absorption is adjusted to accommodate the expenditure-switching effect of the exchange-rate change.**

Using language introduced in Chapter 12, an improvement in the current-account balance calls for an increase in the private-sector surplus (the difference between saving and investment) or an increase in the public-sector surplus (a decrease in the budget deficit).

This proposition has inspired two strands of analysis. The first was developed by economists who sought to show that a change in the exchange rate can affect absorption automatically and that the automatic changes in absorption are the chief way in which an exchange-rate change improves the current-account balance. Some of them argued that a devaluation reduces real income by worsening the terms of trade and that the resulting reduction in real income will reduce absorption. Others argued that devaluation raises the price level, which reduces absorption by raising the amounts that households want to save or by raising the amounts of money that they want to hold. The cash-balance version of this argument is central to the monetary approach presented in Chapter 17.

The second strand of analysis was developed by economists who held that the absorption approach was complementary to the elasticities approach, rather than a substitute for it. They constructed policy-oriented models to show how monetary and fiscal policies should be adjusted to make room for the expenditure-switching effects of an exchange-rate change—to make sure that the MLR condition can translate a depreciation or devaluation of the nominal exchange rate into an improvement in the current-account balance. That is the tack taken in the rest of this chapter.

Optimal Policy Once Again

Consider the small open economy examined in Chapter 13. Its prices are fixed or change only slowly when it moves away from internal balance. Its government pegs the exchange rate but is free to change the peg—to devalue or revalue the domestic currency from time to time. Its central bank controls the money supply to influence the domestic interest rate.

Such a country is described by Figure 14-2. The vertical axis measures the restrictiveness of expenditure policy, which rises with the tax rate and interest rate. An upward movement along the vertical axis represents a tightening of fiscal or monetary policy, which reduces policy-induced expenditure. The horizontal axis measures the nominal exchange rate and thus measures the real rate, too, because goods prices do not change without prolonged departures from internal balance.

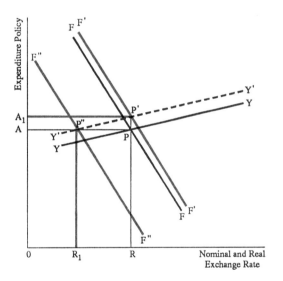

FIGURE 14-2
Policy Responses to Autonomous Changes and Switches in Expenditure
Points on the curve YY show combinations of expenditure policy and the exchange rate that maintain internal balance. Points on the FF curve show combinations that maintain external balance. The economy starts at the policy point P. An autonomous increase in expenditure that shifts the internal-balance curve to Y'Y' will shift the external-balance curve to F'F'. The new policy point is P', where expenditure policy must be tightened from OA to OA₁, but the exchange rate need not change. An autonomous switch in expenditure to domestic goods that shifts the internal-balance curve to Y'Y' will shift the external-balance curve to F"F". The new policy point is P", where expenditure policy need not change but the domestic currency must be revalued from OR to OR₁.

The YY curve shows how the exchange rate can be combined with expenditure policy to maintain internal balance. It is upward sloping because a devaluation switches domestic and foreign demand to domestic goods and thus requires a more restrictive expenditure policy to reduce absorption and restore internal balance. There is unemployment above the YY curve and inflationary pressure below it. The FF curve shows how the exchange rate can be combined with expenditure policy to maintain external balance. It is downward sloping because a devaluation improves the current-account balance and thus requires a less restrictive expenditure policy to raise imports and restore external balance. There are balance-of-payments surpluses above the FF curve and deficits below it. The intersection of the YY and FF curves at P defines an optimal policy combination conferring internal and external balance simultaneously.[6]

An autonomous increase in domestic expenditure shifts YY upward, because a more restrictive expenditure policy is needed to maintain internal balance. It shifts FF upward, too, because a more restrictive expenditure policy is likewise needed to maintain external balance. In fact, the curves shift up together, to $Y'Y'$ and $F'F'$, displacing the policy point to P' and reproducing a result we encountered before. When an economy experiences an autonomous increase in expenditure, a tightening of expenditure policy can maintain internal and external balance without a change in the exchange rate.

An autonomous switch in expenditure to domestic goods (or an increase in foreign expenditure) shifts YY upward, because a more restrictive expenditure policy is needed to maintain internal balance. Let it go to $Y'Y'$, just as before. This

---

[6]To obtain the YY curve, set $Y = Y^t$, the income level required for internal balance. Then $dY = dY^t$. But dY is given by equation (11a) in Chapter 13, with one modification. Separate the autonomous change in net exports into two components: $dN^a = dN^{a'} + dN^{a''}$. Here, $dN^{a'}$ is truly autonomous and $dN^{a''}$ is the expenditure-switching effect of an exchange-rate change:

$$dN^{a''} = (p_1 c_1^*) e_\pi (d\pi/\pi),$$

where e_π is the expression for the MLR condition used in Appendix B. Substituting into equation (11a) and solving for the policy-induced change in expenditure,

$$dA^g = -(p_1 c_1^*) e_\pi (d\pi/\pi) - dA^a - dN^{a'} + (s + m) dY^t.$$

As $e_\pi > 0$ when the MLR condition is satisfied, A^g must fall with a rise in π, which means that the tax rate or interest rate must rise and the YY curve must be upward sloping. (A^g must likewise fall with a rise in A^a or $N^{a'}$ but rise with a rise in Y^t.) To obtain the FF curve, set $N + K = 0$, where N is the current-account balance and K is an autonomous capital inflow. When $N + K = 0$, the economy is in external balance (there is no balance-of-payments surplus or deficit). Then $dN + dK = 0$, where dN is given by equation (13c) in Chapter 13 modified in the same way as equation (11a). Substituting into equation (13c) and solving for the policy-induced change in expenditure,

$$dA^g = (p_1 c_1^*) \left(\frac{s}{m}\right) e_\pi (d\pi/\pi) - dA^a + \left(\frac{s}{m}\right) dN^{a'} + \left(\frac{s + m}{m}\right) dK.$$

As $e_\pi > 0$, A^g must rise with a rise in π, which means that the tax rate or interest rate must fall and the FF curve must be downward sloping. (A^g must likewise rise with a rise in $N^{a'}$ or K, but fall with a rise in A^a.) Note that the FF curve gets flatter as the economy becomes more open (i.e., as m increases).

disturbance, however, shifts FF downward, because a less restrictive expenditure policy is needed for external balance. It goes to $F''F''$, displacing the policy point to P'', and thus reproduces another result encountered before. When an economy experiences an autonomous switch in expenditure, a change in the exchange rate can maintain internal and external balance without a change in expenditure policy.

Both episodes illustrated in this diagram appear to violate a basic proposition in the theory of economic policy. Normally, the number of policy instruments must be at least as large as the number of policy targets. Two targets are represented in the diagram, internal and external balance. In each episode, however, it was sufficient to alter one policy instrument—expenditure policy in the first and the exchange rate in the second. But these were special cases. The economy began at an optimal policy point, and each disturbance that drove it from that point had properties that paired it with a single policy instrument. The first was an increase in expenditure, which could be offset by a more restrictive expenditure policy; the second was a switch in expenditure, which could be offset by an expenditure-switching policy. When disturbances do not have this special property, both instruments must be adjusted. Figure 14-3 supplies two illustrations.

Suppose that the labor force grows. The target level of income rises, because income and output must be raised to maintain full employment. The YY curve shifts to $Y'Y'$, as a less restrictive expenditure policy is needed for internal balance, but the FF curve stays in place. The policy point goes to P'. There must be an easing of expenditure policy, and the domestic currency must be devalued.

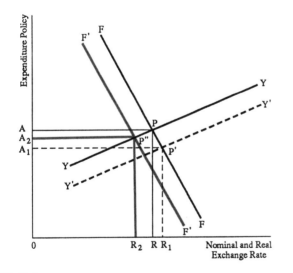

FIGURE 14-3
Policy Responses to Changes in Policy Targets
The economy begins at the policy point P, in internal and external balance. An increase in the labor force raises the target level of income, shifting the internal-balance curve to $Y'Y'$. The policy point goes to P', where expenditure policy must be eased to A_1 and the domestic currency must be devalued to OR_1. An increase in capital inflows requires a reduction in net exports, shifting the external-balance curve to $F'F'$. The policy point goes to P'', where expenditure policy must be eased to OA_2 and the domestic currency must be revalued to OR_2.

Suppose that capital inflows increase permanently. Net exports must be reduced to maintain external balance. The FF curve shifts to $F'F'$, as a less restrictive expenditure policy is needed for external balance, but the YY curve stays in place, and the policy point goes to P''. The domestic currency must be revalued, and expenditure policy must be eased.

The Assignment Problem

When working with Figure 14-2, we were able to pair each disturbance with a single policy instrument. When working with Figure 14-3, it is tempting to pair each target with an instrument. If the labor force grows, for example, it seems natural to say that expenditure policy should be used to raise income and exchange-rate policy should be used to prevent a deterioration in the balance of payments. But the pairing of targets and instruments is tricky. It is known as the *assignment problem*, and it is solved by using a rule that its author, Robert Mundell, described as the principle of effective market classification:

> **Each policy instrument should be assigned to the target variable on which it has the greatest relative effect.**

The use of this principle is illustrated by Figure 14-4, which deals with a somewhat artificial case in which the policy instruments are adjusted sequentially.

Let the economy begin at P_0, above the YY and FF curves. It has unemployment and a balance-of-payments surplus. Assign the task of maintaining external balance to the manager of the exchange rate, and assign the task of maintaining internal balance to the manager of expenditure policy. Assume arbitrarily that the manager of the exchange rate is the first to act.

To pursue external balance, the manager of the exchange rate will revalue the domestic currency to OR_1, taking the economy back to the FF curve. But the new policy point, P_1, lies above the YY curve, so there will still be unemployment. Therefore, the manager of expenditure policy will ease expenditure policy to OA_1, taking the economy back to the YY curve. But this step drives the balance of payments into deficit, because the new policy point, P_1'; lies below the FF curve. Accordingly, the domestic currency must be devalued to OR_2, which will trigger another change in expenditure policy. The policy path is described by the *cobweb* P_0, P_1, P_1'; P_2, P_2'; and so on and converges on P, where YY and FF intersect.

This decentralized procedure seems wasteful. The exchange rate goes up and down. So does expenditure policy. To move directly to the optimal point P, however, policymakers must possess all the information needed to construct the YY and FF curves and know where those curves lie. Policymakers do not claim to know this much. But they can most certainly recognize a balance-of-payments surplus or deficit, incipient unemployment, and incipient inflation. By pairing each policy instrument with a symptom of departure from internal or external balance, they can wend their way through the cobweb shown in Figure 14-4 without knowing the whole structure of the economy or the nature of every disturbance affecting it.

It is nevertheless essential to get the assignment right. In Figure 14-4, exchange-rate policy is assigned to external balance and expenditure policy to internal balance.

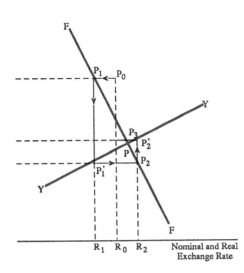

FIGURE 14-4
A Stable Assignment of Instruments to Targets
The economy starts at P_0. There is unemployment, because P_0 is above the YY curve, and a balance-of-payments surplus, because it is above the FF curve. As exchange-rate policy is assigned to external balance, its manager revalues the domestic currency from OR_0 to OR_1, taking the economy to P'_1. As expenditure policy is assigned to internal balance and there is still unemployment at P'_1, its manager eases expenditure policy from OA_0 to OA_1, taking the economy to P_2. But the balance of payments is in deficit there, so the domestic currency must be devalued from OR_1 to OR_2, taking the economy to P'_2 and producing inflationary pressure. Expenditure policy is then tightened from OA_1 to OA_2, taking the economy to P_2. The policy path is the cobweb that leads to P, the optimum policy point. The assignment is stable.

This is the conventional assignment, but it is the right assignment only because the FF curve is steeper absolutely than the YY curve. If the configuration were reversed, the conventional assignment would be unstable. The policy point would move further and further from P. This could happen in a very open economy, with a marginal propensity to import larger than the marginal propensity to save. As the marginal propensity to import rises, expenditure policy acquires more influence over the balance of payments, because a change in income produces a larger change in imports. When the marginal propensity to import is very large, the principle of effective market classification says that expenditure policy should be assigned to external balance and the exchange rate assigned to internal balance.

Optimal Policy with a Flexible Exchange Rate

In the story told by Figure 14-4, the exchange rate was pegged and thus adjusted periodically. The same sort of diagram can be used to describe policy optimization under a flexible exchange rate and the resulting behavior of the exchange rate itself. The exchange rate is the price that clears the foreign exchange market. Throughout this chapter, moreover, the only flows that cross that market are those that come from the current account or from autonomous capital movements. Accordingly, the FF curve can be regarded as the market-clearing curve for the foreign-exchange market. It supplies information about the exchange rate.

In Figure 14-5, the economy begins at P_0, which lies on the initial FF curve. The economy cannot leave the FF curve, even momentarily, because the balance of payments cannot be in surplus or deficit with a freely flexible exchange rate. An autonomous increase in capital inflows shifts FF to $F'F'$, as before, because it requires an appreciation of the domestic currency to clear the foreign-exchange market. The exchange rate moves at once from OR_0 to OR_1, as the foreign-exchange market does the job previously assigned to a policymaker. But the location of the point P_1 says that there is unemployment in the new situation, and expenditure policy must be eased to restore internal balance. Suppose that it is eased immediately to OA_1, the full amount required to achieve internal balance at the exchange rate OR_1. The economy does not move to P'_1, as it did in Figure 14-4. It moves along the $F'F'$ curve directly to P_2, because the domestic currency depreciates immediately to OR_2. Unemployment is replaced by inflationary pressure, and expenditure policy must then be tightened to OA_2. The policy path is P_0, P_1, P_2, and so on, rather than a cobweb. Nevertheless, the policy point converges to P.

In this particular diagram, the slopes of YY and FF describe the effects of managing expenditure policy to maintain internal balance. If the marginal propensity to import is low, YY will be flatter than FF, and the economy will converge to

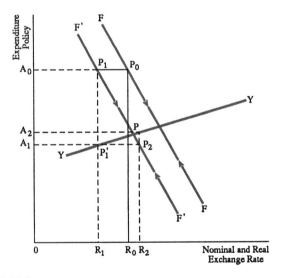

FIGURE 14-5
Optimal Policy under a Flexible Exchange Rate
When the exchange rate is flexible, the economy cannot depart from its external-balance curve, and the initial policy point, P_0, must thus lie on that curve. An autonomous increase in the capital inflow shifts the curve to $F'F'$, moving the economy immediately to P'_1, because the domestic currency appreciates from OR_0 to OR_1. An easing of expenditure policy from OA_0 to OA_1, designed to achieve internal balance, takes the economy to P_2 rather than P'_1, because the domestic currency depreciates from OR_1 to OR_2. The economy converges to P by successively smaller movements up and down the $F'F'$ curve.

P even under the extreme assumption used in the diagram, that expenditure changes by the very large amounts needed to achieve internal balance at the existing exchange rate, without allowing for the exchange-rate effects. The economy will oscillate but not explosively. If the marginal propensity to import is high, however, *YY* will be steeper than *FF*, and the economy cannot converge to *P* when expenditure policy is managed in this fashion. The economy will oscillate explosively.

But policymakers are not as dumb as those who inhabit this diagram. They can take account of the exchange-rate changes resulting from adjustments in expenditure policy. Because an increase in expenditure raises imports and causes the domestic currency to depreciate, it has two effects on income: a direct expenditure-raising effect and an indirect expenditure-switching effect. By taking account of the indirect effect as well as the direct effect, policymakers can use small changes in expenditure policy to maintain internal balance. They can therefore prevent explosive oscillations. (Matters become more difficult, however, when exchange-rate changes have long-lagged effects on the current account, producing a J-curve and making it hard to predict the ultimate expenditure-switching effect of each exchange-rate change.)

OPTIMAL POLICY AND THE EXCHANGE-RATE REGIME

The theory of optimal policy developed in this chapter raises an interesting question. If a change in the exchange rate is the most appropriate policy response to an expenditure-switching shock, why should countries—or regions within countries—be willing to forgo that policy option by fixing the exchange rates connecting their currencies or by participating in a full-fledged *monetary union* with a single currency? Might Michigan or Texas be better off having its own currency, so that it could change its exchange rate or let market forces change it?

The question is interesting analytically, because it makes us think about the benefits and costs of monetary sovereignty. But it is much more important than that. It is one of the principal questions being debated in Europe today. In Western Europe, the countries of the European Community have agreed to move to full-fledged monetary union before the end of the 1990s; a single European central bank will assume responsibility for the conduct of monetary policy, and a single currency, the ECU, will replace the members' national currencies. In Eastern Europe, the republics of the former Soviet Union face the choice between using the ruble as their common currency and issuing new currencies of their own. Ukraine and the Baltic republics—Estonia, Latvia, and Lithuania—have decided to issue their own currencies, but some of the other republics have chosen to stay with the ruble, at least temporarily.

The issues involved are complicated, because monetary sovereignty has many dimensions. When countries have separate currencies, businesses and households face the costs of converting one currency into another and the risks associated with exchange-rate changes, even when the rates are not altered frequently. A tourist starting with $100, visiting all 12 EC countries, and buying each country's currency in turn, will wind up with only $30 without spending a penny on food or anything else. A firm doing business in the EC countries must quote prices in all of their national currencies and take steps to protect itself against the risk of exchange-rate changes, which could turn profits into losses. Furthermore, the benefits and costs of monetary sovereignty must be assessed realistically. We will soon see that high capital mobility can force a government to choose between a stable exchange rate and an independent monetary policy. In other words, exchange-rate flexibility may be the price of meaningful monetary sovereignty.

We will return to these issues in Chapter 20, after examining the role of capital movements in the balance-of-payments adjustment process, the evolution of exchange-rate arrangements among the major industrial countries, and exchange-rate arrangements in Western Europe. At this point, we will focus on a narrower question. Suppose that two countries, East and West, adopt a single currency or fix the nominal exchange rate connecting Eastern and Western dollars in a way that eliminates completely the costs and risks of exchange-rate changes.[7] How will their economies adjust to a switch in demand from Eastern to Western goods?

If both countries' prices were perfectly flexible, there would be no adjustment problem. The switch in demand would raise Western prices and reduce Eastern prices, making Western goods more expensive relative to Eastern goods and reversing the switch in demand. When prices are not perfectly flexible, the switch in demand will raise the Western demand for labor and other factors of production and will reduce the Eastern demand; factor mobility can thus act as a substitute for price flexibility. Movements of labor and capital from East to West will raise Western output to match the larger demand for Western goods and will reduce Eastern output to match the smaller demand. Factor movements will not be perfect substitutes for price flexibility if the two countries' goods have different factor requirements. Furthermore, the costs of adjustment will be differently distributed with factor movements than with price flexibility; it is costly for workers to move from job to job and even more costly to move from place to place. Finally, factor movements take time, particularly when they involve building up one country's capital stock and letting the other's run down.

Some of the costs can be redistributed, however, and the need for adjustment can be reduced when the countries involved belong to a fiscal union as well as to a monetary union. Suppose that East and West are regions or states within a single country and that all of its citizens pay some of their taxes directly to a central government. The switch in demand to Western goods will raise Western tax bills by raising Western incomes, and it will reduce Eastern tax bills by reducing Eastern incomes. The changes in tax payments will serve two purposes. First, they will transfer purchasing power from West to East, reducing the income effects of the switch in demand. Second, they will help to finance the current-account imbalance between East and West. The increase in Western exports due to the switch in demand will be partly offset by the increase in Western tax payments; the decrease in Eastern exports will be partly offset by the decrease in Eastern tax payments.

---

[7]We have in fact accomplished that in the United States, where each of the 12 Federal Reserve Banks issues its own dollar bills but accepts the others' bills at *par*. Look at the bills in your wallet. You will see that each one has a number and letter corresponding to the Federal Reserve Bank that issued it. Because the system works so smoothly, however, no one hesitates to accept a dollar bill issued in a different Federal Reserve District.

These considerations lead economists to ask three questions when examining the optimality of a monetary union: (1) How closely are the countries' factor markets integrated? (2) How closely are their fiscal systems integrated? (3) What types of disturbances do they face? On all three counts, the states and regions of the United States come closer to being an *optimal currency area* than the national economies of the European Community. Labor mobility is fairly high among U.S. states and regions; it is lower among EC countries, because of differences in language and culture. Fiscal transfers are remarkably large in the United States and nearly negligible in Europe. According to one recent study, the automatic workings of the U.S. fiscal system offset almost a third of any short-run change in regional income, but the budget of the European Community is too small and rigid to work that way.[8] Finally, U.S. states and regions seem less apt to suffer the sorts of disturbances represented earlier by a switch in demand from East to West.

This last point deserves more attention. Instead of supposing that East and West experience a simple switch in demand, introduce a third country, South, and suppose that it suffers a recession, reducing its demand for Eastern and Western goods. If the recession affects East and West *symmetrically*, their governments will have no reason to change the East-West exchange rate—although they may want to change the exchange rate connecting their currencies jointly to the Southern currency. But if it affects Eastern exports more severely and there are no factor movements or fiscal transfers between East and West, their governments may want to change the East-West exchange rate, and the monetary union will be burdensome. It is therefore important to ask whether the members of a monetary union experience similar or different disturbances—symmetrical or asymmetrical shocks.

Several recent studies have tried to measure and characterize the shocks experienced by U.S. states and regions and those experienced by EC countries. Some of the studies fail to distinguish between the shocks themselves and subsequent responses to them. (They focus on changes in real exchange rates, forgetting that a change in the real exchange rate reflects not only the initial shock but also the nature and speed of the adjustment to it.) One study is fairly successful in avoiding this pitfall, however, and some of its findings are shown in Table 14-3. The shocks affecting U.S. regions are larger on average than those affecting EC countries, but they are more symmetrical. The shocks affecting the New England, Great Lakes, and Plains states, in particular, are highly correlated with those affecting the Mid-Atlantic states. By contrast, the shocks affecting Germany's closest neighbors, France, Belgium, the Netherlands, and Denmark, are not highly correlated with those affecting Germany; the correlations for the other EC countries are even lower.

Other considerations bear importantly on the feasibility and optimality of a monetary union. We have already noted, for example, that small countries may want to avoid exchange-rate changes because of their effects on the cost of living, and countries with histories of high inflation have sought to "import" price stability by pegging their currencies to those of low-inflation countries. On the three criteria

---

[8]Tamin Bayoumi and Paul R. Masson, "Fiscal Flows in the United States and Canada: Lessons for Monetary Union in Europe" (Washington, D.C.: International Monetary Fund, 1991, processed).

Table 14-3. The Size and Symmetry of Measured Demand Shocks in U.S. Regions and EC Countries

Region or Country	Sizes of Shocks	Correlations with Shocks in First Region or Country
U.S. Regions:		
Mid-Atlantic	0.019	1.00
New England	0.025	0.79
Great Lakes	0.033	0.60
Plains	0.022	0.51
South East	0.018	0.50
South West	0.018	0.13
Rocky Mountains	0.015	−0.28
Far West	0.017	0.33
European Countries:		
Germany	0.014	1.00
France	0.012	0.35
Belgium	0.016	0.33
Netherlands	0.015	0.17
Denmark	0.021	0.39
United Kingdom	0.017	0.16
Italy	0.020	0.17
Spain	0.015	−0.07
Ireland	0.034	−0.08
Portugal	0.028	0.21
Greece	0.016	0.19

Source: Adapted from Tamin Bayoumi and Barry Eichengreen, "Shocking Aspects of European Monetary Unification," Working Paper 3949 (Cambridge, Mass.: National Bureau of Economic Research, 1992), Tables 4 and 6. The sizes of the shocks are the standard deviations of the measured disturbances.

considered here, however, the European Community is not as close as is the United States to being an optimal currency area.

SUMMARY

Using the assumptions made in Chapter 13 concerning incomes, prices, and policies, one can show how exchange-rate changes switch expenditure. But several conditions must be satisfied.

The Marshall–Lerner–Robinson condition is the basis of the elasticities approach to the analysis of exchange-rate changes. A devaluation or depreciation of the domestic currency improves the current-account balance when the price elasticities of domestic and foreign demands for imports sum to a number larger than unity.

Statistical evidence suggests that this condition is satisfied for most major countries, although there may be difficulties in the short run.

When the MLR condition is satisfied, however, a devaluation or depreciation raises income at home and reduces it abroad, and these income changes have expenditure effects that diminish the improvement in the current-account balance. If home and foreign prices are rigid, the expenditure effects will operate by way of the multiplier process. If prices are flexible, the expenditure effects will operate by raising prices at home and reducing them abroad, and these changes will limit the change in the real exchange rate brought about by a devaluation or depreciation of the nominal exchange rate. Empirical research suggests that price changes can offset a large fraction of any devaluation or depreciation unless the government maintains close control over domestic expenditure.

These findings lead directly to the basic postulate of the absorption approach. A devaluation or depreciation will not improve the current-account balance unless absorption is adjusted to make room for the expenditure-switching effects of an exchange-rate change. This postulate has inspired attempts to show that a devaluation or depreciation reduces absorption automatically. It has also led to the development of policy-oriented models showing how monetary and fiscal policies must be used jointly with exchange-rate changes to maintain internal and external balance—that the absorption and elasticities approaches are complementary.

Policy models can also be used to show how each policy instrument should be assigned to a policy target. To obtain an optimal policy combination by successive approximations, each instrument should be assigned to the target on which it has the greatest relative effect. We would therefore expect the exchange rate to be used for external balance and expenditure policies to be used for internal balance. In highly open economies, however, with large marginal propensities to import, the conventional assignment should be reversed.

The same policy models can be used to describe the behavior of a flexible exchange rate. Because it clears the foreign-exchange market automatically, it is in effect assigned to external balance, and expenditure policies must then be assigned to internal balance. In a very open economy, however, large changes in monetary or fiscal policy can cause explosive oscillations if the policy changes are made without allowing for their exchange-rate effects.

When two countries fix their exchange rate firmly or form a monetary union, they cannot use exchange-rate changes to offset expenditure-switching disturbances and other asymmetrical shocks. But labor and capital mobility are helpful in fostering adjustment to such shocks, and fiscal transfers can reduce the costs of adjusting to them. Therefore, economists seeking to assess the benefits and costs of monetary unions examine the extent of labor and capital mobility, the degree of fiscal integration, and the size and character of the shocks affecting the participants. Studies of this sort suggest that the states and regions of the United States come closer to being an optimal currency area than do the member countries of the European Community.

RECOMMENDED READINGS

Some readings recommended at the end of Chapter 13, including the book by Meade and the article by Johnson, deal with issues covered in this chapter. Here are additional suggestions:

The derivation of the Marshall–Lerner–Robinson condition in Figure 14-1 comes from a paper by Gottfried Haberler, "The Market for Foreign Exchange and the Stability of the Balance of Payments," *Kyklos*, 3 (1949); that paper also shows how supply elasticities affect the outcome and the importance of the MLR condition for the stability of the foreign-exchange market.

On the expenditure-switching effects of exchange-rate changes in a variety of models and the importance of wage flexibility, see Neil Bruce and Douglas D. Purvis, "The Specification and Influence of Goods and Factor Markets in Open-Economy Macroeconomic Models," in R. W. Jones and P. B. Kenen, eds., *Handbook of International Economics* (Amsterdam: North-Holland, 1985), ch. 16.

Lags in responses to exchange-rate changes and "pricing to market" are examined in Paul R. Krugman and Richard E. Baldwin, "The Persistence of the U.S. Trade Deficit," *Brookings Papers on Economic Activity*, 1987(1), and their implications for the adjustment process are assessed in Paul R. Krugman, *Has the Adjustment Process Worked?*, Policy Analyses in International Economics 34 (Washington, D.C., Institute for International Economics, 1991).

The absorption approach is implicit in Meade's analysis but is set out explicitly by Sidney S. Alexander, "Effects of Devaluation on a Trade Balance," *International Monetary Fund Staff Papers*, 2 (April, 1952), reprinted in American Economic Association, *Readings in International Economics* (Homewood, Ill.: Richard D. Irwin, 1968), ch. 22.

For the effects of exchange-rate changes on saving and absorption, see Svendt Laursen and Lloyd A. Metzler, "Flexible Exchange Rates and the Theory of Employment," *Review of Economics and Statistics*, 32 (November, 1950); and the reformulation by Lars E. O. Svensson and Assaf Razin, "The Terms of Trade, Spending, and the Current Account," *Journal of Political Economy*, 91 (February, 1983).

On the assignment problem and the principle of effective market classification, see Robert A. Mundell, "The Monetary Dynamics of International Adjustment under Fixed and Flexible Exchange Rates," *Quarterly Journal of Economics*, 74 (May, 1980); on the notion of an optimal currency area and the contribution of labor mobility, see his "A Theory of Optimum Currency Areas," *American Economic Review*, 51 (November, 1951). Both papers are reprinted in Robert A. Mundell, *International Economics* (New York: Macmillan, 1968), chs. 11–12.

Subsequent work on the theory of optimal currency areas and recent empirical studies are surveyed in Barry Eichengreen, *Should the Maastricht Treaty Be Saved?*, Princeton Studies in International Finance 74 (Princeton, N.J.: International Finance Section, Princeton University, 1992).

QUESTIONS AND PROBLEMS

(1) Adapt Figure 14-1 to show how a revaluation or appreciation of the domestic currency affects the home-currency and foreign-currency values of the trade balance using the assumptions in the text concerning the sizes of the price elasticities.

(2) Reinterpret the trade-balance effects of the devaluation shown in Figure 14-1 when the price elasticity of the domestic demand curve is 1 and the elasticity of the foreign demand curve is greater than zero. Be sure to trace the effects separately in domestic and foreign currencies.

(3) Using your answer to (2), trace the effects of the devaluation on total expenditure in both countries. Be sure to work in home currency when tracing the effects on expenditure in the domestic economy and in foreign currency when tracing the effects on expenditure in the foreign economy.

(4) Adapt Figure 14-2 to show what must happen to the exchange rate and to expenditure policy when there is an autonomous switch in expenditure to foreign goods.

(5) Adapt Figure 14-3 to show what must happen to the exchange rate and to expenditure policy when there is an autonomous decrease in capital inflows.

(6) Adapt Figure 14-4 to show what happens when the marginal propensity to import is very high, so that the *FF* curve is flatter than the *YY* curve. Then show how the problem can be solved by reversing the assignment of instruments to targets.

(7) "When two countries have highly diversified economies, with similar patterns of production, it will not be costly to fix the exchange rate between their currencies." Explain and comment. Do the correlations in the second column of Table 14-3 lend any support to this statement?

15

Interest Rates and the Capital Account

INTRODUCTION

The theory of balance-of-payments adjustment in Chapters 13 and 14 originated in the 1950s, when many countries had tight controls on international capital movements. Therefore, the theory said very little about the capital account; it emphasized income and exchange-rate changes affecting the current account. Questions were raised occasionally about the effects of autonomous capital flows on the policies required for internal and external balance. But economists paid little attention to the role of capital flows in the adjustment process or to the implications of capital mobility for choosing optimal policies.

During the 1950s and 1960s, capital controls were liberalized, and other changes in the economic environment reduced the risks and costs of capital movements. There was thus an increase in capital mobility, and balance-of-payments theory began to take notice. Two economists, J. Marcus Fleming and Robert Mundell, made large contributions, and the model used in the next section of this chapter is thus known as the Fleming–Mundell model.

The 1970s brought another change in the monetary system, the shift in 1973 from pegged to flexible exchange rates. Having shown how capital movements can affect the adjustment process and the behavior of a flexible exchange rate, economists had now to show how a flexible exchange rate can affect capital movements.

When exchange rates are flexible, you must answer two questions before choosing between domestic and foreign assets: (1) Are rates of return higher at home or abroad? (2) Which way will the exchange rate go? Suppose that an asset denominated in foreign currency bears a higher rate of return than a comparable asset denominated in domestic currency. Before deciding to buy the foreign asset and hold it for a year, you must forecast the exchange rate at which you can expect to bring your money home. If the price of the foreign currency will be lower a year from now, your loss on the exchange-rate change can swamp your profit on the simple difference between rates of return. Thus, an analysis of capital movements must take account of ways in which investors form their expectations about future exchange rates and of the uncertainty surrounding all such expectations. Both can affect capital movements and the behavior of a flexible exchange rate.

Asset holders are not the only ones affected by future exchange-rate changes. Trade takes time. A firm that signs a contract to sell goods to a foreigner and agrees to take payment in the foreigner's currency may not be paid for many months, until the goods have been delivered. How can the firm protect itself against a change in the exchange rate? There are several ways, but one of them involves the *forward* foreign-exchange market. The firm can sell foreign currency in that market at a price determined now, but it will not deliver the foreign currency to the buyer until a stated future date.

THE ISSUES

This chapter and the next look at many issues and arrangements produced by international capital mobility, by expectations and uncertainty about exchange rates, and by transactions in the forward market. This chapter introduces capital movements into the simple balance-of-payments model constructed in earlier chapters, turning it into the Fleming–Mundell model. It uses the Fleming–Mundell model to study four issues:

- How capital mobility contributes to balance-of-payments adjustment.
- How capital mobility affects the behavior of a flexible exchange rate.
- How capital mobility affects the theory of optimal policy.
- How capital mobility alters the functioning of monetary and fiscal policies under pegged and flexible exchange rates.

We will also look at empirical work that tries to measure capital mobility and the effects of removing controls on international capital movements.

The next chapter introduces expectations and uncertainty and shows how they affect capital mobility and a flexible exchange rate. We will see that expectations about future exchange rates can affect the present rate. Under certain circumstances, they can indeed determine the present rate completely. We will examine transactions in the forward market and see how traders and investors can *hedge* against uncertainty and how that market can be used for purposes of speculation.

THE FLEMING—MUNDELL MODEL

In Chapters 13 and 14, monetary and fiscal policies were lumped together. They were described as expenditure policies, because they were used to regulate absorption, which is how they affected the balance of payments. When interest rates at home and abroad influence capital movements, we cannot lump those policies together. Both policies continue to affect absorption and thus affect the current account by affecting imports, but monetary policy affects the capital account as well. By raising the domestic interest rate, the central bank can encourage capital inflows, discourage capital outflows, and improve the balance of payments. Two propositions follows: (1) When monetary policy is combined with a flexible exchange rate, the risk of instability is intensified. (2) A government can use monetary and fiscal policies to pursue external and internal balance without changing the exchange rate.

Interest Rates and Capital Flows

Let us go back to the economy studied earlier. It is too small to influence incomes and prices in other countries. It is likewise too small to influence their interest rates. Domestic prices are fixed, as before, and the central bank controls the domestic interest rate.

In language used extensively hereafter, domestic and foreign bonds are *imperfect substitutes* viewed from an investor's standpoint. If the domestic interest rate rises and the foreign rate does not, an investor will switch partially from foreign to domestic bonds but not switch completely from one bond to the other. Therefore, the switch in demand for bonds will not be large enough to obliterate the interest-rate difference, and the central bank can influence the domestic interest rate by open-market operations. It can raise the domestic interest rate by open-market sales, which increase the supply of domestic bonds and decrease the money supply. It can reduce the rate by open-market purchases, which decrease the supply of bonds and increase the money supply.

In the Fleming–Mundell model, moreover, a permanent interest-rate difference causes a permanent capital flow. Suppose that the central bank raises the domestic interest rate. It makes domestic bonds more attractive, compared with foreign bonds, causing domestic and foreign investors to build up their holdings of domestic bonds. In the Fleming–Mundell model, they continue to build them up for as long as the interest-rate incentive persists, and the additional flow demand for domestic bonds shows up as a continuing capital inflow.

This flow formulation is illustrated in Figure 15-1. Interest rates are shown on the vertical axis and capital flows on the horizontal axis. The foreign interest rate is fixed at Or^*. When the domestic interest rate is equal to the foreign rate, there is no net capital flow. When the domestic rate is raised to Or_1, there is a continuing capital inflow equal to OK_1. When it is reduced to Or_2, there is a continuing capital outflow equal to OK_2.

The slope of the KK curve depends on the degree of substitutability between domestic and foreign bonds. If there were no substitutability whatsoever, the curve would be vertical. An interest-rate difference could not cause investors to switch between domestic and foreign bonds; it would not cause a capital flow. If there were perfect substitutability, the curve would be horizontal. The tiniest interest-rate difference would lead investors to switch completely from one bond to the other, which would drive the interest-rate difference back to zero. The central bank would have no control over the domestic interest rate. When there is imperfect substitutability, the KK curve is upward sloping. The central bank retains control over the

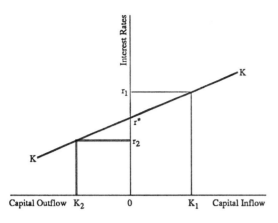

FIGURE 15-1
Interest Rates and Capital Flows
The *KK* curve shows the relationship between interest rates and capital flows in the Fleming–Mundell model. When the foreign interest rate is fixed at Or^*, the capital flow depends on the domestic interest rate. When it is raised to Or_1, there is a net inflow equal to OK_1. When it is reduced to Or_2, there is a net outflow equal to OK_2. The slope of *KK* depends on the substitutability between domestic and foreign bonds. When they are close substitutes, *KK* is quite flat. A small difference between domestic and foreign interest rates causes a large switch in demand between domestic and foreign bonds and a large capital flow.

domestic interest rate, and the size of the continuing capital flow depends on the interest-rate difference. (The higher the degree of substitutability, however, the larger are the open-market operations required to maintain a given interest-rate difference and prolong the corresponding capital flow. In Chapter 16, substitutability is related to investors' attitudes toward risk.)

The flow formulation in the Fleming–Mundell model has been strongly criticized, and the critics have produced better formulations. In Chapter 18, for example, we will develop a model in which an increase in the domestic interest rate generates a one-time shift in asset holdings from foreign to domestic bonds, causing a temporary capital flow. The Fleming–Mundell model is still useful, however, expecially for short-run analysis, and most of the conclusions drawn from it have been shown to hold in models with more complicated formulations.

Capital Mobility and Exchange-Rate Flexibility

How do capital movements affect the behavior of a flexible exchange rate? The greater the influence of interest-rate differences, the greater is the likelihood of instability like that illustrated by Figure 14-5 in the previous chapter.

Figure 15-2 is another version of that earlier diagram. The interest rate replaces expenditure policy on the vertical axis. Interest rates and exchange rates that confer internal balance are shown by the $Y_i Y_i$ curve, which is a variant of the YY curve in Figure 14-5. It is upward sloping because a devaluation or depreciation of the domestic currency switches expenditure to the domestic good and requires an increase in the domestic interest rate to offset it (assuming that there is no change in fiscal policy). Interest rates and exchange rates that confer external balance are shown by the F_iF_i curve, which is a variant of the earlier FF curve. It is downward sloping, because a depreciation of the domestic currency improves the current account and requires a decrease in the interest rate to offset it.[1]

A lower interest rate has two effects on the balance of payments. It worsens the current account by raising absorption and imports. It worsens the capital account by inducing investors to switch from domestic to foreign bonds. Therefore, the slope of the F_iF_i curve is affected by two characteristics of the economy that do not affect the slope of the Y_iY_i curve: the marginal propensity to import and the interest sensitivity of capital movements. An increase in either one makes the F_iF_i curve flatter. It diminishes the size of the reduction in the interest rate needed to offset a depreciation of the domestic currency. (If domestic and foreign bonds were perfect substitutes, the curve would be horizontal and the domestic interest rate could not be different from the foreign rate.)

In Chapter 14, the external-balance curves were steeper absolutely than the internal-balance curves. We assumed that the marginal propensity to import was smaller than the marginal propensity to save and that capital movements were not affected by the interest rate. In Figure 15-2, by contrast, the external-balance curve

---

[1]To obtain the Y_iY_i curve in Figure 15-2 and the UU curve in Figure 15-3, reproduce the equation for the YY curve from footnote 6 of Chapter 14, omitting for simplicity the autonomous changes and switches in expenditure:

$$dA^g = -(p_1c_1^*)e_\pi(d\pi/\pi) + (s + m)dY^t.$$

Then reproduce from Chapter 13 the definition of the policy-induced change in expenditure, omitting the change in government expenditure (so that $dD = -dT$):

$$dA^g = -dT - (S_r - I_r)dr,$$

where $(S_r - I_r) > 0$ because an increase in r raises saving and reduces investment. Substituting into the YY equation and solving for the change in r,

$$dr = [1/(S_r - I_r)][(p_1c_1^*)e_\pi(d\pi/\pi) - dT - (s + m)dY^t].$$

The Y_iY_i curve in Figure 15-2 is obtained by plotting the change in r against the change in π (and is thus upward sloping). The UU curve in Figure 15-3 is obtained by plotting the change in r against the change in T (and is thus downward sloping). Note that both curves shift downward with an increase in Y^t, the target level of income. To obtain the F_iF_i curve in Figure 15-2 and the XX curve in Figure 15-3, reproduce the equation for the FF curve from footnote 6 of Chapter 14, making the same omissions and making the change in the capital inflow depend on the change in the interest-rate difference, $dK = k(dr - dr^*)$:

$$dA^g = (s/m)(p_1c_1^*)e_\pi(d\pi/\pi) + [(s + m)/m]k(dr - dr^*)].$$

Substituting for the change in A^g and solving for the change in r,

$$dr = -[1/(S_r - I_r + K_r)][(s/m)(p_1c_1^*)e_\pi(d\pi/\pi) + dT - (K_r)dr^*],$$

where $K_r = [(s + m)/m]k$. The F_iF_i curve in Figure 15-2 is obtained by plotting the change in r against the change in π (and is thus downward sloping). The XX curve in Figure 15-3 is obtained by plotting the change in r against the change in T (and is also downward sloping). Note that both curves shift upward with an increase in r^*, the foreign interest rate. Note further that UU is steeper than XX, because the change in r produced by a change in T is $-[1/(S_r - I_r)]$ in the case of UU but only $-[1/(S_r - I_r + K_r)]$ in the case of XX.

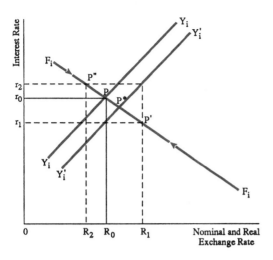

FIGURE 15-2
Behavior of a Flexible Exchange Rate with High Capital Mobility
The Y_iY_i curve shows the combinations of the interest rate and exchange rate required for internal balance. The F_iF_i curve shows the combination required for external balance. High capital mobility makes the F_iF_i curve flatter absolutely than the Y_iY_i curve. When the exchange rate is flexible, the economy cannot depart from the F_iF_i curve. Growth in the labor force shifts the Y_iY_i curve to $Y_i'Y_i'$ because a lower interest rate is needed to raise income and employment. As there would be unemployment at the initial point P, because P is above $Y_i'Y_i'$, the central bank reduces the interest rate from Or_0 to Or_1, but the economy moves directly to P', because the domestic currency depreciates from Or_0 to OR_1. As there is inflationary pressure at P', because P' is below $Y_i'Y_i'$, the central bank raises the interest rate to Or_2, but the economy moves directly to P'' because the currency appreciates to OR_2. The policy path is P, P', P'', and so on, and it does not converge to $P*$.

is flatter absolutely than the internal-balance curve, because we assume that capital movements are highly sensitive to interest rates. This can introduce instability.

Because a flexible exchange rate clears the foreign-exchange market automatically, is is assigned implicitly to external balance, and monetary policy must then be assigned to internal balance. When F_iF_i is flatter than Y_iY_i, however, the central bank must be careful. If it does not take adequate account of the exchange-rate changes resulting from changes in monetary policy, it can cause explosive oscillations in the exchange rate and in domestic income.

Let there be growth in the labor force once again, raising the income level required to achieve internal balance. The Y_iY_i curve shifts downward to $Y_i'Y_i'$, saying that the interest rate should be reduced to stimulate aggregate demand. If it is cut immediately from Or_0 to Or_1, the interest rate needed for internal balance at the initial exchange rate, the policy point moves at once to P', because the exchange rate goes to OR_1. Unemployment gives way to inflationary pressure, and the central bank must tighten monetary policy. If it raises the interest rate to Or_2, the rate needed for internal balance at the new exchange rate, the policy point moves to P'', because the exchange rate goes to OR_2. Inflationary pressure gives way to unemployment, and the central bank must alter its policy again. The policy path is P, P', P'' and so on, and the economy moves farther and farther from $P*$, the optimal policy point.

This instability does not condemn exchange-rate flexibility but reminds us of a point made in Chapter 14. The central bank must not focus exclusively on domestic targets, disregarding the exchange-rate effects of its actions. Clearly, this warning is made more important by the introduction of capital mobility.

Why not use fiscal policy for internal balance? We will soon show that fiscal policy loses its effectiveness when the exchange rate is flexible and capital mobility is high. When the exchange rate is pegged, however, high capital mobility opens up a new possibility.

Capital Mobility and Optimal Policy Under a Pegged Exchange Rate

When monetary and fiscal policies have different effects on the balance of payments, they can be assigned to different targets, using the principle of effective market classification defined in Chapter 14. As monetary policy has an extra influence on the balance of payments, because it affects capital flows, it can be assigned to external balance, and fiscal policy can then be assigned to internal balance. Therefore, both targets can be achieved without changing the exchange rate.

This strategy is illustrated in Figure 15-3. Monetary policy is represented by the domestic interest rate, measured on the vertical axis. Fiscal policy is represented by the tax rate, measured on the horizontal axis. The UU curve shows how monetary and fiscal policies can be combined to maintain internal balance. It is downward sloping because an increase in the tax rate reduces domestic expenditure and requires an offsetting decrease in the interest rate. There is unemployment above UU and inflationary pressure below it. The XX curve shows how the two policies can be combined to maintain external balance. It is downward sloping, too, because an increase in the tax rate improves the balance of payments by reducing imports and likewise requires an offsetting decrease in the interest rate. There is a balance-of-payments surplus above XX and a deficit below it.

If capital movements were not sensitive to interest rates, the UU and XX curves would be identical Monetary and fiscal policies would affect the balance of payments only by affecting absorption, and there would be no way to distinguish between the two policies, apart from their different effects on the composition of aggregate demand, an important issue for domestic purposes, but not important here. When capital movements are sensitive to interest rates, the XX curve is flatter than the UU curve. To see why, assume that the economy begins in internal and external balance and raise the tax rate arbitrarily. Absorption will fall, reducing imports, and the balance of payments will move into surplus. Next, reduce the interest rate by enough to restore absorption to its initial level and thus restore internal balance. Imports will return to their initial level, but the balance of payments will move from surplus into deficit because the interest-rate reduction will cause a capital outflow. Putting the point differently, the cut in the interest rate required for external balance is smaller than the cut required for internal balance, making XX flatter than UU.

Suppose that the economy starts at P, the optimal policy point. Let the labor force grow, raising the income level needed for internal balance. The UU curve shifts downward to $U'U'$. Less restrictive policies are needed to maintain internal balance. The policy point goes to P, which says that the tax rate should be reduced to Ot_1,

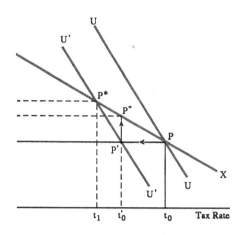

FIGURE 15-3
Fiscal and Monetary Policies for Internal and External Balance
The *UU* curve shows the tax rates and interest rates that maintain internal balance; it is downward sloping because a decrease in the interest rate is needed to offset an increase in the tax rate. The *XX* curve shows the tax rates and interest rates that maintain external balance; it is downward sloping for the same reason. But the *XX* curve is flatter than the *UU* curve, because a smaller decrease in the interest rate is needed for external balance than for internal balance. As the interest rate affects capital flows, it has an additional influence on the balance of payments. An increase in the labor force calls for an increase in income to maintain internal balance; the *UU* curve shifts to *U'U'*, and the policy point shifts from *P* to *P**. The tax rate must be cut to stimulate absorption and increase employment. The interest rate must be raised to attract a capital inflow and offset the increase in imports produced by the increase in absorption. If fiscal policy is assigned to internal balance and monetary policy to external balance, the assignment will be stable. When the *UU* curve shifts to *U'U'*, the tax rate must be cut from Ot_0 to Ot_0' to restore internal balance, taking the economy to *P'*. As *P'* lies below *XX*, the interest rate must be raised from Or_0 to Or_0' to restore external balance, taking the economy to *P''*. The policy path will wind up at *P**.

to stimulate income and employment, and the interest rate should be raised to Or_1, to induce the capital inflow needed for external balance (to offset the increase in imports resulting from the increase in income).

The same result can be obtained by assigning the tax rate to internal balance and the interest rate to external balance, and this assignment will be stable. When the labor force grows, producing unemployment, the finance ministry will cut the tax rate to Ot_0'. This will restore internal balance, but the balance of payments will move into deficit. Hence, the central bank will raise the interest rate to Or_0' to restore external balance, and unemployment will reappear. The finance ministry will cut the rax rate again, producing a new deficit in the balance of payments, and the central bank will raise the interest rate again. The policy point will move to *P* eventually.[2]

_____

[2]There is one difference between this stepwise movement and that in Figure 14-4, where expenditure policy and the exchange rate were adjusted sequentially. The policy instruments, income, and the balance of payments all move *monotonically* in Figure 15-3 (i.e., without any oscillations).

The assignment, however, may not work well in the long run. The first reason, mentioned earlier, has to do with the effect of an interest-rate difference. Instead of producing a permanent capital flow, it may merely produce a one-time switch in demand between foreign and domestic bonds. In that case, the central bank would have to raise the interest rate over and over again to produce a continuing capital inflow—to induce investors to make repeated shifts from foreign to domestic bonds. The second reason has to do with interest payments. These were left out of the model developed in earlier chapters and were not put back when capital flows were added. When they are included in the current-account balance, interest rates affect that balance in a way that diminishes the case for assigning monetary policy to external balance. An increase in the domestic interest rate raises interest payments to foreigners on all of the domestic bonds that they held initially, and the capital inflow induced by a higher interest rate adds further to those payments. Taken together, these effects reduce the net improvement in the balance of payments produced by raising the interest rate. Indeed, the balance of payments can deteriorate.[3] In any case, reliance on high domestic interest rates to maintain external balance involves large interest payments to the outside world and corresponding income losses to the domestic economy.

CAPITAL MOBILITY, EXCHANGE RATES, AND DOMESTIC POLICIES

Under a flexible exchange rate, capital movements affect the domestic economy directly. Whenever they produce exchange-rate changes, they have expenditure-switching effects on income, output, and employment, and they can also alter domestic prices. Under a pegged exchange rate, capital movements do not affect the economy directly but may affect it indirectly by altering the money supply, interest rates, and so on. With high capital mobility, indeed, the central bank is unable to control the money supply and thus loses control of the domestic interest rate—an assertion made at the very beginning of this book.

It is time to examine this possibility by abandoning the assumption introduced in Chapter 13, that the monetary effects of official intervention are sterilized completely. Let us go to the opposite extreme. Assume that there is *no* sterilization. Capital mobility acquires important implications for the workings of monetary and fiscal policies, but has different implications under pegged and flexible exchange rates.

---

[3] Let the domestic interest rate be 10 percent initially, and suppose that foreigners hold $1 billion of domestic bonds. Interest payments start at $100 million. Raise the interest rate to 12 percent and suppose that this induces a $200 million increase in foreign holdings of domestic bonds. Interest payments rise to $144 million ($1.2 billion *times* 12 percent), worsening the current-account balance by $44 million. As the capital inflow is $200 million, the balance of payments improves by only $156 million. Now change one number. Suppose that foreigners start out with $10 billion. With the increase in the interest rate, interest payments rise to $1.224 billion ($10.2 billion *times* 12 percent), worsening the current-account balance by $224 million. The balance of payments deteriorates by $24 million! (The two effects mentioned in the text can guarantee disaster when put together. If the interest rate must be raised repeatedly to produce a continuing capital inflow and each increase worsens the current-account balance by raising interest payments, the balance of payments must deteriorate sooner or later.)

New Tools

Two new tools of analysis are helpful in tracing these implications. They are the *IS* and *LM* curves in Figure 15-4.

The *IS* curve shows how the interest rate affects the real income of a small economy with fixed domestic prices. It is downward sloping because a reduction in the interest rate stimulates absorption, raising real income. It will be fairly flat—the increase in income will be large—when absorption is very sensitive to the interest rate or the multiplier is large (the marginal propensities to save and import are low). The position of the *IS* curve depends on all of the other variables affecting absorption. Two are important here. A depreciation or devaluation of the domestic currency shifts the curve to the right by switching expenditure from foreign to home goods. A tax cut shifts it in the same direction by raising absorption.

The *LM* curve shows the relationship between income and the interest rate required for monetary equilibrium. The demand for money increases as income rises,

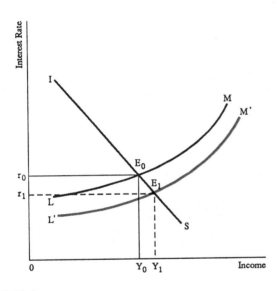

FIGURE 15-4
Monetary Policy under a Pegged Exchange Rate
This *IS* curve shows how a change in the interest rate affects real income. Its slope depends on the interest sensitivity of absorption and the size of the multiplier. Its position depends on the exchange rate and tax rate. The *LM* curve shows the relationship between income and the interest rate required for monetary equilibrium. It is upward sloping because the demand for money rises with income and falls with the interest rate, so an increase in the interest rate is needed to offset an increase in income. Its position depends on the supply of money. The economy begins at E_0, where income is OY_0 and the interest rate is Or_0. An increase in the money supply shifts it from *LM* to *L'M'*, displacing equilibrium from E_0 to E_1. Income rises from OY_0 to OY_1, and the interest rate falls from Or_0 to Or_1. In an open economy with a pegged exchange rate, however, these income and interest-rate changes drive the balance of payments into deficit, which reduces the money supply. The *LM* curve moves back to its initial position, taking income back to OY_0 and the interest rate back to Or_0. The effects of monetary policy wear off. They wear off faster with high capital mobility, because the initial reduction in the interest rate leads to a larger balance-of-payments deficit.

because transactions rise with income. It decreases as the interest rate rises, because holders of money are induced to switch from cash to interest-bearing assets (bonds) when they can earn more on those assets. When the supply of money is fixed by central-bank policy, monetary equilibrium can be maintained only when the demand-raising effect of an increase in income is offset by the demand-reducing effect of an increase in the interest rate. This is the relationship shown by the *LM* curve, which is thus upward sloping. The position of the curve depends on the supply of money. An increase in the money supply shifts it downward because a lower interest rate is needed to maintain monetary equilibrium at each and every income level.

In earlier exercises, we represented changes in monetary policy by changing the domestic interest rate. In the rest of this chapter, we represent them by changing the money supply. An easier monetary policy is represented by raising the money supply and shifting the *LM* curve downward. A tighter policy is represented by reducing the money supply and shifting the curve upward. A balance-of-payments deficit is also represented by shifting the curve upward, because a deficit reduces official reserves, which reduces the money supply when the central bank does not engage in sterilization. In each exercise that follows, we will assume that the balance of payments is in equilibrium at the initial levels of income and the interest rate; this will keep the money supply from changing until we introduce a policy change.

Monetary Policy Under a Pegged Exchange Rate

Under a pegged exchange rate, the domestic effects of monetary policy wear off eventually when the central bank does not sterilize reserve flows, and they wear off faster with high capital mobility. This story is told by Figure 15-4.

The economy begins at E_0, where the *IS* and *LM* curves intersect. Let the central bank make an open-market purchase, increasing the money supply and shifting the *LM* curve downward to $L'M'$. The economy is displaced to E_1. Income rises to OY_1, and the interest rate falls to Or_1. This is the permanent result for a closed economy. It is the *initial* result in an open economy with a pegged exchange rate. An increase in income worsens the current account, and a decrease in the interest rate worsens the capital account. The balance of payments moves into deficit, and reserves start to fall. If the central bank were to sterilize reserve flows indefinitely, the economy would remain at E_1. Otherwise, the money supply starts to fall and must go on falling until the balance-of-payments deficit is eliminated. Accordingly, the money supply must return eventually to what it was before the open-market purchase, taking the *LM* curve back to its starting point. Income must return to OY_0, and the interest rate must return to Or_0. The effects of the change in monetary policy must wear off completely.

Capital mobility is important here mainly for the speed at which the economy returns to its starting point. With no capital mobility, the balance-of-payments deficit is equal to the current-account deficit induced by the increase in income. With the introduction of capital mobility, the deficit is widened by the capital outflow resulting from the reduction in the interest rate, and the money supply falls faster. Capital mobility accelerates the rate at which the economy "exports" additional money created by an open-market purchase.

In the limiting case of *perfect capital mobility* (i.e., perfect substitutability between domestic and foreign bonds), monetary policy has *no* influence whatsoever in a small economy, not even temporarily. The domestic interest rate cannot fall in Figure 15-4, because it must equal the foreign interest rate. The economy must stay at E_0. By implication, the *LM* curve must snap back immediately after an open-market purchase. The whole effect of the purchase is offset instantaneously by a capital outflow. Investors buy foreign bonds to replace the domestic bonds purchased by the central bank, and the central bank loses reserves in an amount equal to its additional holdings of domestic bonds. The money supply does not change.

Fiscal Policy Under a Pegged Exchange Rate

The workings of fiscal policy are described in Figures 15-5 and 15-6. The initial effect of a tax cut is shown in both diagrams by shifting the *IS* curve to $I'S'$. Equilibrium is displaced to E_1. Income rises to OY_1, and the interest rate rises to Or_1. This is, again, the permanent result for a closed economy, or for an open economy in which the central bank sterilizes reserve flows. It is not the whole story when those flows affect the money supply. In the fiscal-policy case, however, the rest

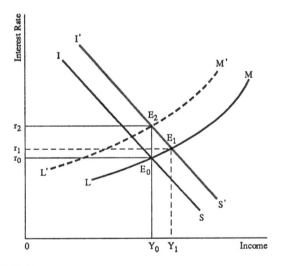

FIGURE 15-5
Fiscal Policy under a Pegged Exchange Rate with Low Capital Mobility
A tax cut shifts the *IS* curve to $I'S'$, displacing equilibrium from E_0 to E_1. Income rises from OY_0 to OY_1, and the interest rate rises from Or_0 to Or_1. With no capital mobility, the deterioration in the current account drives the balance of payments into deficit, and the money supply falls. The *LM* curve goes gradually to $L'M'$, displacing equilibrium to E_2, where income has gone back to OY_0, the interest rate has risen to Or_0, and the balance-of-payments deficit has ended. The effects of fiscal policy wear off gradually. With low capital mobility, the increase in the interest rate from Or_0 to Or_1 induces a capital inflow that offsets part of the deterioration in the current account, reducing the balance-of-payments deficit. It is brought to an end, moreover, at a point on the $I'S'$ curve between E_1 and E_2, where income is between OY_0 and OY_1 and the interest rate is between Or_1 and Or_2. The current account stays in deficit, but the deficit is covered by a continuing capital inflow. Reserves and the money supply are stabilized. The effects of the tax cut are reduced in the long run but do not wear off completely.

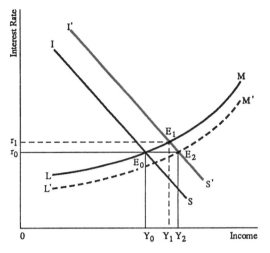

FIGURE 15-6

Fiscal Policy under a Pegged Exchange Rate with High Capital Mobility

The initial effects of a tax cut are the same as before. The *IS* curve shifts to *I'S'*, raising income from OY_0 to OY_1, and raising the interest rate from Or_0 to Or_1. With high capital mobility, however, the capital inflow induced by the higher interest rate is larger than the deterioration in the current account, and the balance of payments moves into surplus. The money supply rises, driving the *LM* curve downward. With perfect capital mobility it would drop immediately to *L'M'*, because the interest rate would remain at Or_0. The equilibrium point would be diaplaced to E_2, and income would rise to OY_2. Otherwise, the balance-of-payments surplus is brought to an end at a point on the *I'S'* curve between E_1 and E_2, where income is between OY_1 and OY_2 and the interest rate is between Or_0 and Or_1. The current account remains in deficit, as before, and the deficit is covered by a capital inflow. But the effects of the tax cut are reinforced by high capital mobility.

of the story depends crucially on capital mobility, which affects the *direction* in which variables move, not merely the speed at which they move. Outcomes with no and low mobility are shown in Figure 15-5. Outcomes with perfect and high mobility are shown in Figure 15-6.

When there is no capital mobility, the long-run outcome resembles the outcome after a change in monetary policy, because income returns eventually to its initial level. A tax cut produces a balance-of-payments deficit; it is equal to the current-account deficit induced by the initial increase in income. Reserves fall, reducing the money supply, and the *LM* curve moves gradually upward. It cannot stop moving until the payments deficit has ended, which means that it must move to *L'M'* in Figure 15-5. Income is brought bck to OY_0, and the current-account deficit is eliminated. This result is achieved by the increase in the interest rate, which rises to Or_2 and "crowds out" enough domestic spending to offset the stimulus provided by the tax cut. The effect of fiscal policy wears off completely.

When capital mobility is low, fiscal policy raises income permanently but by less than the increase to OY_1. The initial increase in the interest rate induces a capital inflow that offsets part of the current-account deficit. Therefore, the balance-of-payments deficit is smaller initially, and it is brought to an end before the increase in income has been reversed completely. In Figure 15-5, the *LM* curve comes to rest at a point on *I'S'* somewhere between E_1 and E_2. The permanent level of income lies between OY_1 and OY_0, and the permanent level of the interest rate lies between Or_1 and Or_2. There is still a current-account deficit, because income is above its initial level, but the remaining deficit is offset by the larger capital inflow induced by the additional increase in the interest rate. The effect of fiscal policy is weakened but does not disappear.[4]

Clearly, there is some degree of capital mobility that would keep the economy at E_1 permanently. The capital inflow induced by the increase in the interest rate to Or_1 would just match the current-account deficit induced by the increase in income to OY_1. When capital mobility is lower, the results are those described by Figure 15-5. When capital mobility is higher, the results are those described by Figure 15-6.

Start with the limiting case of perfect capital mobility. The domestic interest rate cannot change because it must equal the foreign rate. Therefore, the tax cut must take the economy all the way to E_2, raising income to OY_2. By implication, the capital inflow must be very large, because it must produce a balance-of-payments surplus large enough to shift the *LM* curve downward immediately to *L'M'* and to prevent the domestic interest rate from rising. The increase in income is large, too, because there is no increase in the interest rate to "crowd out" the stimulus provided by the tax cut. In general, high capital mobility makes fiscal policy more effective. The interest rate rises initially, as it did in Figure 15-5, but the increase induces a capital inflow larger than the current-account deficit. The balance of payments moves into surplus, and the money supply grows. The *LM* curve moves downward and comes to rest at a point on *I'S'* between E_1 and E_2. The permanent level of income lies between OY_1 and OY_2, and the permanent level of the interest rate lies between Or_0 and Or_1. (There is a permanent deficit on current account, but it is exactly offset by a capital inflow, as it was with low capital mobility.)

Let us sum up. When the exchange rate is pegged and the central bank does not sterilize reserve flows, we can assert that:

1. If there is no capital mobility, the effects of monetary and fiscal policies wear off completely.

2. As capital mobility rises, the effectiveness of monetary policy is reduced more speedily. With perfect capital mobility, monetary policy is completely ineffective.

3. As capital mobility rises, the effectiveness of fiscal policy is restored. With high capital mobility, the total effect of fiscal policy is larger than its initial effect.

All three propositions however, abstract from the effects of capital flows on

---

[4]Note that this outcome resembles closely the outcome in Figure 15-3, where fiscal policy was used for internal balance and monetary policy was used for external balance. In that example, however, the outcome was obtained immediately; the money supply was reduced abruptly by an open-market sale. In this example, it is obtained by a gradual reduction in the money supply produced by a transitory balance-of-payments deficit.

interest-income payments,[5] and the third proposition depends crucially on the underlying assumption of the Fleming–Mundell model, that an interest-rate difference induces a continuing capital flow. If capital flows taper off eventually, the effects of fiscal policy must wear off, too. The economy must start to run a balance-of-payments deficit in the wake of a tax cut, and it must move eventually to E_2 in Figure 15-5. The interest rate must rise, and income must fall back to what it was before the tax cut.

Monetary Policy Under a Flexible Exchange Rate

Under a pegged exchange rate, the position of the LM curve is determined in part by the balance of payments. If the central bank does not sterilize reserve flows, it cannot control the money supply. Under a flexible exchange rate, there are no reserve flows, and the position of the LM curve is determined completely by monetary policy. This is one basic difference between the two regimes, and it is often used as an argument for exchange-rate flexibility. But there is another difference. Under a pegged exchange rate, the position of the IS curve is determined by domestic economic conditions, including fiscal policy. Under a flexible rate, its position depends in part on the real exchange rate, which affects the division of expenditure between domestic and foreign goods. Both differences are relevant for the workings of domestic policies under pegged and flexible exchange rates.

A flexible exchange rate enhances the effectiveness of monetary policy, and capital mobility compounds the increase in effectiveness. These propositions are illustrated in Figure 15-7.

An open-market purchase shifts the LM curve downward to $L'M'$, just as with a pegged exchange rate, and equilibrium is displaced to E_1. Income rises immediately to OY_1, and the interest rate falls to Or_1. This is the outcome for a closed economy but not for an open economy with a flexible exchange rate, not even initially. Something more must happen right away. Because an increase in income raises imports, and a decrease in the interest rate causes a capital outflow when there is any capital mobility, the domestic currency must depreciate to clear the foreign-exchange market. The expenditure-switching effect of the depreciation shifts the IS curve to some such position as $I'S'$. The equilibrium point goes to E_2, and income rises to OY_2. The size of the shift in the IS curve depends on the size of the depreciation, which increases with the size of the capital outflow. Hence, high capital

---

[5]To illustrate the implications of interest-income payments, consider the effects of an increase in the money supply that reduces the domestic interest rate initially. Asset holders will sell domestic bonds and buy foreign bonds (there will be a capital outflow on the way to the new long-run equilibrium). Interest payments to foreigners will fall because of the change in bond holdings, and this will improve the current-account balance. Therefore, the long-run equilibrium cannot be at E_0 in Figure 15-4. The permanent level of the interest rate must be Or_0, just as it was before; otherwise, capital flows would continue, and the level of interest payments would go on changing. But the permanent level of income must be higher than OY_0, because the economy must run a permanent trade deficit just large enough to match the reduction in interest payments and thus to bring the current account into balance. (In effect, the IS curve will shift slightly to the right, because the reduction in interest payments will raise the permanent level of income.) Monetary policy will then have a small effect on income, even in the long run. Statements made later about flexible exchange rates have to be amended in similar ways to make allowance for interest-income payments.

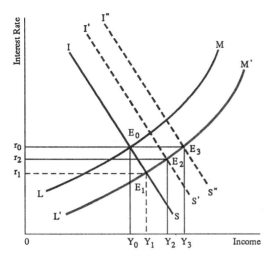

FIGURE 15-7
Monetary Policy under a Flexible Exchange Rate
An increase in the money supply shifts the *LM* curve to *L'M'*, displacing equilibrium from E_0 to E_1. The domestic currency depreciates at once, even in the absence of capital mobility, because an increase in income from OY_0 to OY_1 raises imports. The expenditure-switching effect of the depreciation shifts the *IS* curve to some such position as *I'S'*, displacing equilibrium to E_2 and raising income to OY_2. Capital mobility strengthens this effect, because the reduction in the interest rate induces a capital outflow, causing a larger depreciation of the domestic currency. With perfect capital mobility, the interest rate must stay at Or_0, and equilibrium is displaced to E_3. The *IS* curve shifts all the way to *I"S"*, and income rises all the way to OY_3. Under a flexible exchange rate, monetary policy is effective permanently, and capital mobility raises its effectiveness.

mobility adds to the increase in income. Look at the limiting case of perfect capital mobility. As the interest rate must stay at Or_0, the *IS* curve must shift all the way to *I"S"*, and income must rise to OY_3.

Fiscal Policy Under a Flexible Exchange Rate

A flexible exchange rate can reduce the effectiveness of fiscal policy, and high capital mobility is to blame. The reasons are shown in Figure 15-8. A tax cut shifts the *IS* curve to *I'S'*, as in Figures 15-5 and 15-6, displacing equilibrium to E_1. This is again the outcome for a closed economy, but not for an open economy with a flexible exchange rate. We must allow for the change in the exchange rate, and the outcome depends on the degree of capital mobility.

When there is no mobility or low mobility, the domestic currency depreciates. The current account deteriorates because of the increase in income, and the capital inflow, if any, is too small to cover the deterioration. The expenditure-switching effect of the depreciation amplifies the shift in the *IS* curve, taking it beyond *I'S'* to some such position as *I'₁S'₁*. Therefore, income rises all the way to OY'_1. The flexible exchange rate adds to the income-raising effect of the tax cut, making fiscal policy more effective.

When there is perfect mobility or high mobility, however, the domestic currency

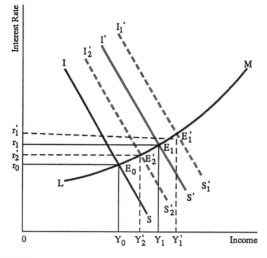

FIGURE 15-8
Fiscal Policy under a Flexible Exchange Rate
A tax cut shifts the *IS* curve to *I'S'*, displacing equilibrium from E_0 to E_1. Income rises from OY_0 to OY_1, and the interest rate rises from Or_0 to Or_1. With no capital mobility or low mobility, the domestic currency must depreciate at once. The expenditure-switching effect of the depreciation shifts the *IS* curve to some such position as $I_1'S_1'$, displacing equilibrium to E_1' and raising income permanently to OY_1'. The tax cut is more effective. With high capital mobility, the domestic currency must appreciate instead, because of the large capital inflow induced by the increase in the interest rate. The expenditure-switching effect shifts the *IS* curve to some such position as $I_2'S_2'$, displacing equilibrium to E_2' and reducing income to OY_2'. The tax cut is less effective. With perfect mobility, the interest rate must stay at Or_0, and the appreciation of the domestic currency must be large enough to drive the *IS* curve back to its starting point. There is no increase in income, and the tax cut is completely ineffective.

appreciates. The current account deteriorates, but the capital inflow is more than sufficient to cover the deterioration. The expenditure-switching effect of the appreciation limits the shift in the *IS* curve, taking it to some such position as $I_2'S_2'$. Income rises but only to OY_2'. With perfect mobility, fiscal policy is completely ineffective. As the interest rate must stay at Or_0, the economy must stay at E_0. By implication, the appreciation of the domestic currency must snap the *IS* curve right back to its starting point, and income cannot change at all.

The outcomes under a flexible exchange rate can be summarized most easily by starting with perfect capital mobility:

1. With perfect capital mobility, the effectiveness of monetary policy is maximized, but fiscal policy is deprived of any effect on the domestic economy.

2. As capital mobility falls, the effectiveness of monetary policy diminishes, but its effect on income is always larger than the effect obtained with a pegged exchange rate and complete sterilization.

3. As capital mobility falls, the effectiveness of fiscal policy grows, and its effect on income can be larger than the effect obtained with a pegged exchange rate and complete sterilization.

Note that *all* these results depend in part on the Fleming–Mundell supposition about the permanence of capital flows. If capital movements taper off, the influence of monetary policy is reduced gradually. But the permanent change in income is nonetheless larger than the change to OY_1 in Figure 15-7; the domestic currency must still depreciate to eliminate the current-account deficit. The influence of fiscal policy is raised gradually, and the permanent change in income is also larger than the change to OY_1 in Figure 15-8, because the domestic currency depreciates.

ASSESSING THE EXTENT OF CAPITAL MOBILITY

International capital movements grew very rapidly during the 1980s under the influence of two developments. First, many governments removed or relaxed their controls on capital movements. Second, the use of computers and other innovations helped investors manage their assets more adroitly and led banks and other institutions to devise new financial instruments that made it easier for investors to shift funds from country to country or currency to currency. Much has been written about the *globalization* of financial markets, and the lives of those who deal in those markets changed dramatically.

Many economists represent the present situation by assuming perfect capital mobility in their analytical models and empirical work. There is some tendency, however, to exaggerate the basic economic significance of recent innovations in the technology of trading and investing. Richard Cooper of Harvard University has noted that the laying of the first Atlantic cable in 1866 shortened the time required to communicate between London and New York by more than all subsequent innovations combined. Furthermore, recent empirical work has raised questions about the degree of capital mobility.

The important effects of liberalizing capital controls are illustrated vividly by Figure 15-9. It shows the difference between interest rates on domestic and foreign deposits denominated in French francs. Domestic deposits are those held with banks in France; foreign deposits are those held with banks in other countries. In the early 1980s, the interest rate on foreign deposits was much higher than the rate on domestic deposits, because French capital controls prevented most French residents from making deposits in foreign banks. But those controls were liberalized gradually and removed completely at the end of the decade, and this reduced the interest-rate difference. Interest rates on domestic deposits rose relative to those on foreign deposits as French banks had to offer interest rates competitive with those available from foreign banks.

In the next chapter, however, we will see that the lifting of capital controls does not remove all of the costs and risks of investing in another country or currency, and one recent study of capital mobility suggests that it is far from perfect. To understand the strategy adopted by that study, let us reinterpret Figure 15-8, which dealt with fiscal policy under a flexible exchange rate. Suppose that the initial shift in the *IS* curve reflects an increase of investment, rather than a change in fiscal policy, and consider two extreme cases.

In the absence of any capital mobility, the increase of investment raises income

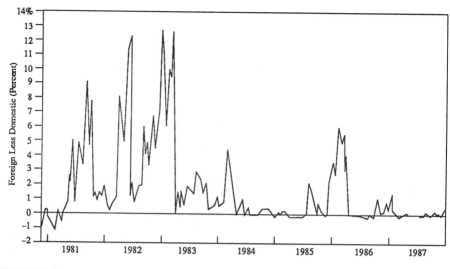

FIGURE 15-9
Difference Between Interest Rates on Bank Deposits in French Francs
In the early 1980s, French capital controls prevented French residents from holding deposits with foreign banks. As the controls were relaxed, French residents began to move their funds to foreign banks, forcing French banks to offer higher interest rates and reducing the interest-rate difference. The very large differences from 1981 to 1983 reflect speculative pressures against the franc. Foreign banks had to offer high interest rates to discourage depositors from shifting into other currencies, but French banks did not, because French capital controls prevented French residents from shifting into other currencies. *Source:* Adapted from Francesco Giavazzi and Alberto Giovannini, *Limiting Exchange Rate Flexibility: The European Monetary System* (Cambridge, Mass.: MIT Press, 1989).

permanently, and the increase in income is amplified by the depreciation of the domestic currency needed to offset the increase of imports resulting from the increase in income. The IS curve shifted initially to $I'S'$ because of the increase in investment but then shifted to $I'_1S'_1$ because of the expenditure-switching effects of the depreciation. Income rose all the way to OY'_1. In the absence of capital mobility, the current account must be balanced in the new equilibrium at E'_1. Hence, the increase of investment must be matched by an increase in saving, an increase in tax payments, or the two together. Accordingly, there should be a high correlation between changes in investment and the sum of changes in saving and tax payments.[6]

At the opposite extreme, with perfect capital mobility, the increase in investment produces a very large capital inflow, which causes the domestic currency to appreciate. The expenditure-switching effects of the appreciation drive the IS curve all the way back to its starting point, and income returns to OY_0, but the new equilibrium at E_0 is different from the initial equilibrium. Saving and tax payments have not changed, because income has not changed. Yet investment is higher than

---

[6]The increase in the interest rate to Or'_1 will, of course, cut back the increase in investment, but the increase actually observed in the end must be matched by the sum of the increases in taxes and saving if the current account must be balanced. That was the basic point made by equation (8) in Chapter 13.

it was initially, and there is a current-account deficit, which is financed by a capital inflow. With perfect capital mobility, then, there should be *no* correlation between changes in investment and the sum of changes in saving and tax payments.

What do the data show? The study that proposed this particular test found high correlations between investment and saving and concluded that capital mobility is low. Subsequent studies have used different methods and data but have also found high correlations. One study actually found higher correlations for the 1967–1984 period than for the 1953–1966 period, when capital controls were used more widely and enforced more rigorously. The issue has not been resolved.[7]

Nevertheless, the experience of the United States in the 1980s suggests that the high-mobility outcome in Figure 15-9 fits the facts more closely than the low-mobility outcome. We will study that experience carefully in Chapter 19, when reviewing the history of the monetary system. It is sufficient to note here that there was a large shift in U.S. fiscal policy at the start of the 1980s, when the Reagan administration cut taxes and began to raise military spending. The process of adjustment to the new fiscal policy was much like the one described at point E'_2 in Figure 15-8. There was a large capital inflow, the dollar appreciated hugely, and the current account moved into deficit. But other forces were at work, including shifts in expectations about future exchange rates. Hence, we must introduce exchange-rate expectations before we can analyze that episode completely.

SUMMARY

When capital movements are responsive to interest rates, monetary policy acquires additional influence on the balance of payments and on the behavior of a flexible exchange rate. It is therefore necessary to amend the theory of optimal policy developed in earlier chapters. Under a flexible exchange rate, for example, capital mobility adds to the risk of instability. When monetary policy is used to achieve internal balance and the central bank does not take account of the large exchange-rate changes resulting from high capital mobility, there can be explosive oscillations in income and the exchange rate.

Under a pegged exchange rate, moreover, monetary policy can be used to maintain external balance while fiscal policy is used to maintain internal balance. The two targets can be reached simultaneously without changing the exchange rate, and the policy assignment is stable. But there are two objections to this strategy. An increase in the domestic interest rate induced by a tightening of monetary policy may produce a one-time switch in investors' portfolios, rather than an ongoing capital inflow, and this will not improve the balance of payments permanently. Furthermore, an increase in the interest rate can lead to a progressive deterioration in the current-account balance, because it raises interest payments to the outside world.

---

[7] For the first study of this type, see Martin S. Feldstein and Charles Horioka, "Domestic Saving and International Capital Flows," *Economic Journal*, 90 (*June* 1980); for the 1953–66 and 1967–84 correlations, see Maurice Obstfeld, "How Integrated Are World Capital Markets? Some New Tests," in G. Calvo et al., *Debt, Stabilization and Development* (New York: Harper & Row, 1989).

Capital mobility has additional effects on the workings of domestic economic policies. These are seen most clearly when we cease to assume that central banks sterilize the money-supply effects of intervention in the foreign-exchange market.

If the exchange rate is pegged and there is no capital mobility, the domestic effects of monetary and fiscal policies must wear off eventually. An easing of monetary policy or a tax cut leads to an outflow of reserves that gradually undermines the influence of the policy change. As capital mobility rises, the effectiveness of monetary policy is reduced more speedily, and it has no influence whatsoever with perfect capital mobility. By contrast, the effectiveness of fiscal policy is enhanced by capital mobility, and the permanent effects of fiscal policy are larger with high mobility than its initial effects with no mobility.

If the exchange rate is flexible and there is no capital mobility, the effectiveness of fiscal policy is reinforced; a tax cut induces a depreciation of the domestic currency, and the expenditure-raising effect of the tax cut is supplemented by the expenditure-switching effect of the depreciation. When capital mobility is high, however, the effectiveness of fiscal policy is low; a tax cut induces an appreciation of the domestic currency by producing a large capital inflow. Fiscal policy is utterly ineffective with perfect capital mobility. The consequences for monetary policy go the other way. Monetary policy is always more effective with a flexible rate than with a pegged rate, and its effectiveness is enhanced by capital mobility.

The liberalization of capital markets in the 1980s and the removal of capital controls have increased capital mobility; it has also been enhanced by innovations in technology, which have transformed the functioning of financial markets and offered investors new ways to manage and diversify their assets. But recent research on capital mobility warns us that we do not have perfect capital mobility.

RECOMMENDED READINGS

The Fleming–Mundell model owes its name to one paper by Fleming and two by Mundell: J. Marcus Fleming, "Domestic Financial Policies Under Fixed and Under Floating Exchange Rates," *International Monetary Fund Staff Papers*, 9 (November 1962), reprinted in J. M. Fleming, *Essays in International Economics* (Cambridge, Mass.: Harvard University Press, 1971), ch. 9; Robert A Mundell, "The Appropriate Use of Monetary and Fiscal Policy Under Fixed Exchange Rates," *International Monetary Fund Staff Papers*, 9 (March 1962), and "Capital Mobility and Stabilization Policy Under Fixed and Flexible Exchange Rates," *Canadian Journal of Economics and Political Science*, 29 (November 1963), reprinted in R. A. Mundell, *International Economics* (New York: Macmillan, 1968), chs. 16, 18.

Subsequent contributions include Jeffrey Sachs, "Wages, Flexible Exchange Rates, and Macroeconomic Policies," *Quarterly Journal of Economics*, 94 (June 1980), which shows how wage rigidity alters the effects of the exchange-rate regime on the workings of monetary and fiscal policies; see also Richard C. Marston, "Stabilization Policies in Open Economies," in R. W. Jones and P. B. Kenen, eds., *Handbook of International Economics* (Amsterdam: North-Holland, 1985), ch. 17, which synthesizes a large body of research.

For an assessment and restatement of the Fleming–Mundell model, see Jacob A. Frenkel and Assaf Razin, "The Mundell–Fleming Model A Quarter Century Later: A Unified Exposition," *International Monetary Fund Staff Papers*, 34 (December 1987).

Recent research on the measurement of capital mobility is reviewed in Jeffrey A. Frankel, "International Financial Integration, Relations among Interest Rates and Exchange

Rates, and Monetary Indicators," in *International Financial Integration and U.S. Monetary Policy* (New York: Federal Reserve Bank of New York, 1989); related references are given at the end of Chapter 16.

QUESTIONS AND PROBLEMS

(1) Adapt Figure 15-3 to show how the tax rate and interest rate must change to maintain internal and external balance when there is an autonomous switch of expenditure from domestic to foreign goods. Bear in mind that this disturbance affects the positions of the *UU* and *XX* curves. Suppose that the current account was balanced before the expenditure switch. Is it balanced after the switch and the policy changes? Explain.

(2) Adapt Figure 15-4 to show how an open-market sale affects income and the interest rate when the exchange rate is pegged and there is less than perfect capital mobility. Distinguish short-run from long-run effects. How would perfect capital mobility alter your answer?

(3) Show how a tax increase affects income and the interest rate when the exchange rate is pegged and there is high capital mobility. Suppose that the current account was balanced before the tax increase. Is it balanced after the increase? Explain.

(4) Consider an economy with a flexible exchange rate and high capital mobility. The government wants to raise income but does not want the exchange rate to change. Use *IS* and *LM* curves to show how it must change its monetary and fiscal policies. The policy changes should resemble those shown in Figure 15-3. Why?

(5) Adapt Figure 15-6 to show how an open-market sale affects income, the interest rate, and the exchange rate when the exchange rate is flexible and there is perfect capital mobility. Is it necessary to distinguish between short-run and long-run effects? Explain.

(6) Suppose that there is an increase in the foreign interest rate. Use *IS* and *LM* curves to show what will happen in the domestic economy when there is perfect capital mobility and the exchange rate is pegged.

(7) Repeat your answer to (6) for a flexible exchange rate.

16

Expectations, Exchange Rates, and the Capital Account

THE ISSUES

Most investments are uncertain. They must be based on forecasts about future earnings, and forecasts can be wrong. Foreign investments are especially uncertain, because they involve forecasts about changes in exchange rates, as well as forecasts about earnings. International capital movements depend not only on interest-rate differences but also on investors' expectations about future exchange rates. Furthermore, they are influenced by attitudes toward risk, which affect the investors' willingness to make commitments in an uncertain world.

This chapter introduces expectations and uncertainty into the analysis of capital movements. It begins by examining three issues:

- How exchange-rate expectations affect an investor's choice between foreign and domestic bonds.

- How that choice is influenced by attitudes toward risk.

- How speculation based on expectations about future exchange rates affects the functioning of the foreign-exchange market.

We will see that speculation links the actual exchange rate today with the rate expected in the future and that it can contribute to exchange-rate stability.

Thereafter, the chapter looks at the *forward* foreign-exchange market and examines two more issues:

- How traders and investors use the forward market to protect themselves against exchange-rate risk.

- How speculators use the forward market to place "bets" on their views about the future by deliberately incurring exchange-rate risk.

We will see that the forward market allows traders and investors to shift risk to speculators.

EXPECTATIONS AND RATES OF RETURN

Let there be two bonds, a domestic bond bearing an interest rate r and denominated in domestic currency, and a foreign bond bearing an interest rate r^* and denominated in foreign currency. The exchange rate between the two currencies is π, the number of units of domestic currency needed to buy a unit of foreign currency. To keep matters simple, suppose that r and r^* are known in advance and that the two bonds are identical in every other way—maturity, likelihood of default, and the rest.

The Open Interest Differential

If you invest a unit of domestic currency in the domestic bond, you can expect to come out with $1 + r$ units of that currency after a year. If you invest a unit of domestic currency in the foreign bond, you will obtain $1/\pi$ foreign-currency units of that bond and can therefore expect to come out with $(1/\pi)(1 + r^*)$ units of foreign currency after a year. This is where exchange-rate expectations enter the story. To compare the two returns, you must forecast the exchange rate that is likely to prevail a year from now. Denote that *expected* exchange rate by π^e and use it to convert the foreign-currency return on the foreign bond. It is $(1/\pi)(1 + r^*)\pi^e$ units of domestic currency. Then use u to define the difference between the two returns:

$$u = \frac{1}{\pi}(1 + r^*)\pi^e - (1 + r). \tag{1}$$

This is the *open interest differential* between foreign and domestic investments. If you are indifferent to risk, the possibility of being wrong about the future exchange rate, you will buy the foreign bond whenever u is positive.

The equation for u can be simplified by defining a new term, $\hat{\pi}$, the *expected rate of change* of the exchange rate:

$$\hat{\pi} = \frac{\pi^e - \pi}{\pi}. \tag{2}$$

A positive value of $\hat{\pi}$ signifies an expectation that the domestic currency will depreciate during the coming year; a negative value signifies an expectation that it will appreciate. As $\pi^e = (1 + \hat{\pi})\pi$, equation (1) can be rewritten as

$$u = (1 + r^*)(1 + \hat{\pi}) - (1 + r) = (r^* - r) + (1 + r^*)\hat{\pi}$$
$$\approx (r^* - r) + \hat{\pi}, \tag{1a}$$

because $(1 + r^*)\hat{\pi}$ is approximately equal to $\hat{\pi}$.

There are two ways to look at equation (1a). Viewed from the perspective of an investor concerned primarily with the advantage of holding one bond instead of the other, it says that an additional gain or loss can come from investing in the foreign bond. It is the capital gain or loss resulting from a change in the exchange rate. Viewed from the perspective of a speculator concerned primarily with the advantage of holding one currency instead of the other, the equation says that an additional gain or loss can come from purchasing the foreign currency in the belief that $\hat{\pi}$ is positive. It is the interest gained or lost by holding the foreign bond.[1]

But perspectives do not matter fundamentally. An investor who buys the foreign bond is also a speculator; part of the return expected from that purchase depends on $\hat{\pi}$, the investor's forecast of the change in the exchange rate. A speculator who buys the foreign currency is also an investor; part of the return expected from that purchase depends on the interest rate that can be earned by holding foreign-currency assets. Whenever u is positive, moreover, an investor-speculator will want to hold *some* foreign-currency bonds. We can show this clearly by rearranging equation (1a):

$$u \approx (r^* + \hat{\pi}) - r. \tag{1b}$$

The first term is the rate of return expected on the foreign bond; the second is the rate of return on the domestic bond. If the first is larger than the second, regardless of the reason, an investor-speculator will hold some foreign bonds. Furthermore, an increase in u will raise the demand for the foreign bond and reduce the demand for the domestic bond. It will thus cause a capital flow from the domestic to the foreign economy, raising the demand for foreign currency in the foreign-exchange market.

An Illustration

As equation (1a) plays an important role in much of this chapter, let us illustrate its use. Suppose that the U.S. interest rate is 8 percent, that the British interest rate is 6 percent, and that the current exchange rate is $1.75 per pound. You are an American investor and calculate your wealth in dollars. You expect the dollar to depreciate (the pound to appreciate) to $1.85 per pound during the coming year. You should therefore invest in British bonds, even though they pay a lower interest rate. You will sacrifice 2 percent in interest by investing in British bonds. If you are right about the future exchange rate, however, you will gain 10 cents on every pound invested in British bonds, and 0.10/1.75 is 5.7 percent, which is 3.7 percent more than the interest you will sacrifice. Working with equation (1b), r^* is 6 percent, r is 8 percent, and $\hat{\pi}$ is 5.7 percent, so

$$u \approx (6.0 + 5.7) - 8.0 = 11.7 - 8.0 = 3.7.$$

---

[1]Both interpretations assume that investors and speculators measure gains and losses in domestic currency. They will be concerned, however, with the *real* values of their assets, not *nominal* values in domestic or foreign currency. Real values depend in turn on the prices of the goods they consume. When we deal with real values, however, the analysis grows complicated, because we must take account of expectations about prices, as well as expectations about exchange rates, and the main conclusions do not differ greatly from those in the text, which continues to deal with nominal values.

You can go further, by borrowing dollars at 8 percent in the United States, buying pounds at $1.75, and investing the pounds in Britain at 6 percent. If the exchange rate goes to $1.85 a year from now, as expected, the transaction will cost you 2 percent in interest but give you a 5.7 percent capital gain on the exchange-rate change. There are many ways to exploit an open interest differential. Whenever u is positive, however, they all involve purchasing pounds now and selling pounds later.

UNCERTAINTY AND ATTITUDES TOWARD RISK

In the previous example, you decided to buy pounds, because the expected gain from the exchange-rate change was larger than the sacrifice of interest income. But you can be wrong about the exchange rate.

Errors, Uncertainty, and Risk

Suppose that interest rates are the same in the United States and Britain, so that there are no interest gains or losses. You believe that there is a 75 percent chance that the pound will appreciate from $1.75 to $1.90 per pound during the coming year but a 25 percent chance that it will depreciate from $1.75 to $1.70 per pound. The expected exchange rate, π^e, is $1.85 per pound, as before. It is defined formally as a weighted average of the possibilities with their probabilities used as weights:

$$\pi^e = (0.75 \times \$1.90) + (0.25 \times \$1.75) = \$1.85.$$

It still makes sense for you to buy some British bonds. When interest rates are equal, u is equal to $\hat{\pi}$, which is still 0.10/1.75, or 5.7 percent. You will earn more, of course, if the pound appreciates to $1.90; the gain will be 0.15/1.75, or 8.6 percent. You will incur a loss, however, if the pound depreciates to $1.70; the loss will be 0.05/1.75, or 2.8 percent. Accordingly, you may not want to invest your whole portfolio in British bonds. Your exposure to the risk of loss rises with the fraction invested in those bonds.[2]

Two propositions can be drawn from this illustration: (1) The open interest differential measures the expected gain or loss from shifting to the foreign bond. (2) the size of the shift may be influenced by the uncertainty surrounding investors' expectations.

---

[2]To see why π^e is defined as the weighted average of the possibilities, suppose that you could "bet" repeatedly on those possibilities. You would make an 8.6 percent gain on 75 percent of your "bets" but would lose 2.8 percent on the other 25 percent. Your average gain would be $(0.75 \times 8.6) - (0.25 \times 2.8)$, or 5.7 percent, and you would come out ahead in the long run. You could suffer a series of losses, however, that could put you out of business. That is why you might not invest entirely in British bonds.

Risk Neutrality and Open Interest Parity

Some investors may be indifferent to uncertainty. We describe them as being *risk neutral*. When the open interest differential favors investment in Britain, those investors will shift completely into British bonds, regardless of the risk of loss. In other words, they will be guided only by expected gains and losses and can therefore be said to treat domestic and foreign bonds as *perfect substitutes*.

If most investors were risk neutral, however, an open interest differential could not last long. By shifting massively into British bonds, investors would drive up the prices of those bonds, reducing the British interest rate, and drive down the prices of U. S. bonds, raising the U.S. rate. With a flexible exchange rate, moreover, the pound would appreciate immediately in response to the demand for pounds reflecting the demand for British bonds. This would reduce $\hat{\pi}$ (unless the expected exchange rate, π^e, kept pace with the current rate, π). The movements in r^*, r, and $\hat{\pi}$ would not cease until the open interest differential fell to zero.

When the differential is zero, equation (1a) asserts that

$$\hat{\pi} = r - r^*. \tag{3}$$

This condition is called *open interest parity*. It says that the expected change in the exchange rate is exactly equal to the interest-rate difference, and it has two implications. First, it repeats in slightly different form a statement made before about monetary policy. If investors are risk neutral and thus treat domestic and foreign bonds as perfect substitutes, the central bank cannot control the domestic interest rate unless it can influence exchange-rate expectations. If r^* and $\hat{\pi}$ are given, r is also given. Second, the condition provides a way to measure market views about the future exchange rate. If the U.S. interest rate is 8 percent and the British interest rate is 6 percent, the numbers used before, the typical investor-speculator must expect the dollar to depreciate by 2 percent.

Risk Aversion and Portfolio Selection

If investors are *risk averse* rather than risk neutral, an open interest differential can persist indefinitely. It will still induce a shift from one bond to the other, but the size of the shift will be limited by exchange-rate risk and by the degree of risk aversion. This proposition is illustrated in Figure 16-1.

The vertical axis of the figure shows the expected return on a portfolio containing domestic and foreign bonds. When the whole portfolio is invested in the domestic bond, the expected return is $(1 + r)$. Let it be the distance OD. When the whole portfolio is invested in the foreign bond, the expected return is $(1 + r^*)(1 + \hat{\pi})$. Let it be the distance OF. Note that

$$u \approx OF - OD = FD.$$

When a fraction n of the whole portfolio is invested in the foreign bond, the expected return is a weighted average of the returns on the two bonds:

$$v = n(OF) + (1 - n)OD = OD + n(OF - OD) = OD + n(FD).$$

Let v be the distance OV in the diagram, so that $n(FD) = OV - OD = VD$, and $n = VD/FD$. When $n = 0.5$, for example, V lies halfway between D and F.

The horizontal axis of Figure 16-1 measures the riskiness of the portfolio for an investor whose wealth is denominated in domestic currency. Riskiness depends on the dispersion of the possibilities that underlie investors' expectations and on their exposure to that dispersion. In technical terms, it can be measured by the *standard deviation* of the return on the portfolio, a term defined precisely in Note 16-1. When the whole portfolio is invested in the domestic bond, there is no exchange-rate risk because there is no exposure; the standard deviation is zero. When the whole portfolio is invested in the foreign bond, exchange-rate risk is maximized because exposure is maximized; the standard deviation is $O\bar{S}$ and can get no larger.[3] What happens when a fraction of the total portfolio is invested in the foreign bond? Note 16-1 shows that the standard deviation rises at a constant rate with the fraction n invested in the foreign bond. Therefore, the standard deviation is $OS = nO\bar{S}$. When n is 0.5, for example, S lies halfway between O and $\bar{S}$. Thus, the straight line DI represents the simple relationship between expected return and riskiness.

The indifference curves in Figure 16-1 show how a risk-averse investor looks at opportunities involving uncertainty about the future exchange rate. Clearly, the investor is better off with a high return and low standard deviation. Therefore, points on the indifference curve U' are better than points on U. Furthermore, a risk-averse investor will want the expected return OV to rise at a growing rate to offset successive increases in risk. Therefore, the indifference curves get steeper as OS increases. The curves are drawn, however, to reflect one more assumption. The investor's willingness to sacrifice return for safety, a lower standard deviation, does not vary with OV. Therefore, the indifference curves are "stacked up" vertically; the slope of U' at Q'' is the same as the slope of U at Q.

Faced with the tradeoff between return and risk represented by the line DI, a risk-averse investor will go to Q, because U is the highest attainable indifference curve. Given the open interest differential FD and the way that risk rises with n, the investor will choose the value of n at which the expected return on the investor's portfolio is OV and the standard deviation is OS.

How will the investor respond to an increase in u resulting from an increase in the foreign interest rate? Note 16-1 shows that an increase in r^* does not change the standard deviation. In Figure 16-1, then, the increase in u from DF to DF' shifts DI to DI', and the investor goes to Q' on the higher indifference curve U'. Q' must lie to the northeast of Q, because the indifference curves are stacked up vertically. Therefore, v rises to OV', and the standard deviation rises to OS'. But the

---

[3]This last statement is not strictly true. An investor can borrow at home in order to invest abroad. When that happens, the fraction n will exceed 1, and the standard deviation will exceed $O\bar{S}$. To keep matters simple, however, we say no more about this possibility. (Note that a domestic investor will hold no foreign bonds when OD is larger than OF. The safest portfolio will be the most profitable. In that same circumstance, however, a foreign investor will hold some domestic bonds. We should therefore work with two diagrams, one for the domestic investor whose wealth is denominated in domestic currency and another for the foreign investor whose wealth is denominated in foreign currency. When the open interest differential is positive, as in Figure 16-1, the domestic investor will take a risky position and the foreign investor will take a safe position. When the differential is negative, the domestic investor will take a safe position and the foreign investor will take a risky position.)

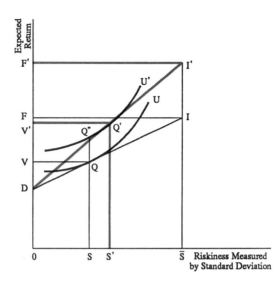

FIGURE 16-1
Portfolio Selection by a Risk-Averse Investor
The curve *DI* shows how the expected return and riskiness of a portfolio change with its composition. When the whole portfolio is invested in the domestic bond, the return is *OD* and the standard deviation is zero; when it is invested in the foreign bond, the return is *OF* and the standard deviation is $O\bar{S}$; when it is divided between the two bonds, the return is *OV* and the standard deviation is *OS*. The indifference curves show that an investor's welfare rises with an increase in the return and falls with an increase in the standard deviation; *U′* represents a higher level of welfare than *U*. Facing the set of returns and risks given by the line *DI*, the investor goes to *Q*, as *U* is the highest attainable indifference curve. An increase in the foreign interest rate raises the open interest differential from *DF* to *DF′* and shifts *DI* to *DI′*. The investor goes to *Q′*, as *U′* is the highest attainable indifference curve. The return rises from *OV* to *OV′*, and the standard deviation rises from *OS* to *OS′*. As the latter cannot rise without an increase in the fraction of the portfolio invested in the foreign bond, that fraction must be higher at *Q′* than at *Q*.

standard deviation cannot rise unless there is an increase in exposure to exchange-rate risk, which means that there has been an increase in the fraction *n* invested in the foreign bond. An increase in the foreign interest rate induces a risk-averse investor to substitute foreign bonds for domestic bonds but not to shift completely out of domestic bonds.

EXPECTATIONS AND EXCHANGE-RATE BEHAVIOR

Investors' expectations about future exchange rates strongly affect the current exchange rate. Some economists even argue that short-term fluctuations in the actual exchange rate are due mainly to revisions in investors' expectations, reflecting the arrival of new information about forces that will influence future exchange rates. But the effects of changes in expectations depend importantly on attitudes toward risk.

Note 16-1
Measuring the Riskiness of a Portfolio

Suppose an investor believes that there is a probability p_1 that the domestic currency will depreciate by $\hat{\pi}_1$ percent and a probability p_2 that it will depreciate by $\hat{\pi}_2$ percent, where $p_1 + p_2 = 1$. The expected depreciation is

$$\hat{\pi} = p_1\hat{\pi}_1 + p_2\hat{\pi}_2.$$

The definition of the expected return follows directly:

$$\begin{aligned} v &= n[p_1(1 + r^*)(1 + \hat{\pi}_1) + p_2(1 + r^*)(1 + \hat{\pi}_2)] + (1 - n)(1 + r) \\ &= n(1 + r^*)[1 + (p_1\hat{\pi}_1 + p_2\hat{\pi}_2)] + (1 - n)(1 + r) \\ &= n(1 + r^*)(1 + \hat{\pi}) + (1 - n)(1 + r) = (1 + r) + nu, \end{aligned}$$

where n is the fraction of the investor's portfolio invested in the foreign bond. Note that an increase in r^* raises u, which raises v when $n > 0$.

If the domestic currency does indeed depreciate by $\hat{\pi}_i$ $(i = 1, 2)$, the actual return on the portfolio will differ from the expected return by

$$\begin{aligned} e_i &= [n(1 + \hat{\pi}_i)(1 + r^*) + (1 - n)(1 + r)] - [n(1 + \hat{\pi})(1 + r^*) + (1 - n)(1 + r)] \\ &= n(1 + r^*)(\hat{\pi}_i - \hat{\pi}) \approx n(\hat{\pi}_i - \hat{\pi}). \end{aligned}$$

This is why the portfolio is risky when $n > 0$. Its riskiness can be measured by its standard deviation, which is defined by

$$\sigma_v = \sqrt{p_1 e_1^2 + p_2 e_2^2} \approx n\sqrt{(p_1 p_2)(\hat{\pi}_1 - \hat{\pi}_2)^2} = n\bar{\sigma}_v,$$

where $\bar{\sigma}_v$ is the value of σ_v when the whole portfolio is invested in the foreign bond (and thus equals $O\bar{S}$ in Figure 16-1). Note that $\bar{\sigma}_v$ depends on the forecasts $\hat{\pi}_1$ and $\hat{\pi}_2$ and their probabilities, that σ_v rises as n rises, given $\bar{\sigma}_v$, and that an increase in r^* does not affect σ_v (because it does not affect $\bar{\sigma}_v$).

Another Look at the Foreign-Exchange Market

The statements made above are illustrated in the next two diagrams, which give us a new way to look at the foreign-exchange market. In Figure 16-2, the exchange rate is measured on the vertical axis; purchases and sales of foreign currency are measured on the horizontal axis. The *ED* curve describes the *excess demand* for foreign currency coming from investor-speculators. The *ES* curve describes the *excess supply* coming from all other market participants.

The *ES* curve can be derived from the ordinary supply and demand curves introduced in Chapter 12. At some exchange rate, *OP*, the total supply of foreign

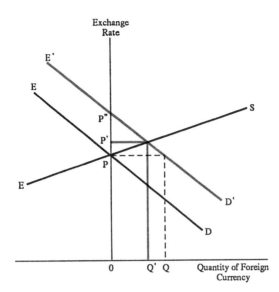

FIGURE 16-2
An Increase in the Foreign Interest Rate
The *ED* curve shows the excess demand for foreign currency coming from investor-speculators. When foreign and domestic interest rates are equal and the actual and expected exchange rates are both equal to *OP*, the *ED* curve will cross the vertical axis at *P*. The open interest differential will be zero, and excess demand will be zero. If the actual exchange rate falls below *OP* without affecting the expected rate, the open interest differential will be positive, and investors will demand more foreign currency with which to buy foreign bonds. The *ES* curve shows the excess supply of foreign currency coming from all other market participants. At the exchange rate *OP*, the total supply of foreign currency coming from foreign buyers of domestic goods and services equals the total demand for foreign currency coming from domestic buyers of foreign goods and services. If the actual exchange rate rises above *OP*, total supply will increase, total demand will decrease, and excess supply will be positive. When the actual exchange rate is *OP*, excess demand equals excess supply, because both are zero. Therefore, *OP* is the market-clearing rate. If the foreign interest rate rises without affecting the expected exchange rate, the demand curve will shift from *ED* to *E'D'*. The open interest differential will be positive, and investors will demand *OQ* foreign currency at the initial exchange rate. Excess demand will exceed excess supply, and the actual exchange rate will go to *OP'* to clear the foreign-exchange market.

currency coming from foreign buyers of domestic goods and services will equal the total demand coming from domestic buyers of foreign goods and services. Excess supply will be zero. Suppose that the domestic currency depreciates. The supply of foreign currency will rise as foreign buyers of domestic goods and services increase their purchases, and the demand for foreign currency will fall as domestic buyers of foreign goods and services decrease their purchases. Excess supply will be positive. Accordingly, the *ES* curve slopes upward. (The slope of the *ES* curve depends on the Marshall–Lerner–Robinson condition. Whenever it is satisfied, a depreciation of the domestic currency improves the current-account balance and thus raises the excess supply of foreign currency.)

The position of the *ED* curve depends on interest rates and expectations. When the open interest differential is zero, investors will not want to buy foreign bonds. Therefore, they will not want to buy foreign currency. Excess demand will be zero. A simple case is shown in Figure 16-2. Let foreign and domestic interest rates be equal. The open interest differential will be zero if investors expect the exchange rate to be constant—if OP equals π, the actual exchange rate, and also equals π^e, the expected future rate, so that $\hat{\pi}$ is zero. The slope of the ED curve depends on the riskiness of foreign investment and on the degree of risk aversion. Suppose that the domestic currency appreciates without affecting the expected exchange rate—that π falls but π^e remains at OP. Because $\hat{\pi}$ becomes positive, the open interest differential becomes positive, too. Investors will expect the domestic currency to depreciate and will buy foreign currency in order to buy foreign bonds, so excess demand will be positive. When investors are risk averse, however, they will not switch completely into foreign bonds, and their demand for foreign currency will be limited. Accordingly, the ED curve slopes downward. The greater the uncertainty about the expected rate and the higher the degree of risk aversion, the steeper is the ED curve.

Effects of a Change in the Foreign Interest Rate

Before showing how a revision of investors' expectations affects the actual exchange rate, let us see how an increase in the foreign interest rate affects the situation. Start with the simple case in Figure 16-2. Interest rates are equal initially, and the expected exchange rate is OP. If the actual exchange rate also equals OP, excess demand will be zero and excess supply will be zero, too. Therefore, the actual exchange rate must be OP. It is the market-clearing rate.

An increase in the foreign interest rate leads investors to buy foreign bonds and thus buy foreign currency. It shifts the demand curve to $E'D'$. Investors will demand OQ foreign currency at the initial exchange rate OP.[4] The domestic currency must depreciate to OP' to reduce excess demand and raise excess supply until both of them equal OQ'. The excess supply OQ' represents the current-account surplus produced by the depreciation. The excess demand OQ' represents the capital outflow produced by the increase in the foreign interest rate.

The two situations in Figure 16-2 can be compared by examining the open interest differential. Open interest parity prevailed in the initial situation; foreign and domestic interest rates were equal and $\hat{\pi}$ was zero. It does not prevail in the new situation. If the actual exchange rate were to go to OP'', it would reduce excess demand to zero. Open interest parity would prevail, because $\hat{\pi}$ would be large enough to offset the increase in the foreign interest rate. But the actual exchange rate goes only to OP', which does not eliminate excess demand. By implication, there must be an open interest differential favoring foreign investment.

---

[4]There are two ways to look at this shift: (1) It can be treated as a rightward shift, showing the amount of foreign currency investors will demand at the initial exchange rate. (2) It can be treated as an upward shift, showing the change in the actual exchange rate required to eliminate the open interest differential and reduce excess demand to zero.

Effects of a Change in Expectations

Figure 16-3 illustrates the impact of a change in investors' expectations. It starts with the same special case used in Figure 16-2. Interest rates are equal, and the actual and expected exchange rates are both equal to OP. Suppose that investors come to anticipate a change in fundamental economic conditions that will increase the domestic demand for imports. This amounts to predicting a *future* shift in the supply curve to E^*S^*. The expected exchange rate must go at once to OP^*, because that is the rate which investors associate with the E^*S^* curve. Therefore, the investors' demand curve must shift immediately to E^*D^* to reflect the change in expectations. As OP^* exceeds OP, investors must expect the domestic currency to depreciate, and $\hat{\pi}$ becomes positive, producing an open interest differential that favors foreign investment. The actual exchange rate must go at once to OP', the rate that clears the foreign-exchange market when the demand curve is E^*D^* and the supply curve is still ES. The domestic currency must depreciate immediately when it is expected to depreciate eventually. The immediate depreciation is caused by the capital outflow produced by the open interest differential. The outflow is matched by the current-account surplus induced by the depreciation, as in Figure 16-2.

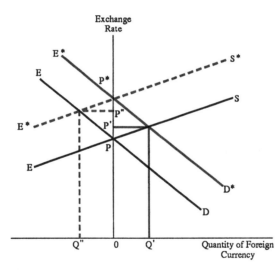

FIGURE 16-3
A Change in Expectations
Foreign and domestic interest rates are equal initially and the actual and expected exchange rates are OP. When investors anticipate a future shift in the supply curve from ES to E^*S^*, the expected exchange rate goes to OP^*, which is the rate associated with the supply curve E^*S^*. Therefore, the investors' demand curve goes at once to E^*D^*, driving the actual exchange rate to OP', which is the market-clearing rate when the demand curve is E^*D^* and the supply curve is still ES. If investors are right, and the supply curve does shift to E^*S^*, the exchange rate will go to OP^* eventually. If investors are wrong, and the supply curve remains at ES, investors will have to revise their expectations; the demand curve will return to ED, and the exchange rate will return to OP. When investors fail to anticipate a future shift in the supply curve, the exchange rate remains at OP until the shift takes place. At that time, the rate goes to OP'', which is the market-clearing rate when the demand curve is still ED and the supply curve is E^*S^*. But investors have then to revise their expectations, taking the demand curve to E^*D^* and driving the exchange rate to OP^* eventually.

If investors are right about the supply curve and it does shift to E^*S^* eventually, the market-clearing exchange rate will go to OP^*. At that point, actual and expected exchange rates will be equal once again, the open interest differential will be zero, and the capital outflow will cease. If investors are wrong about the supply curve and it does not shift at all, they will revise their expectations. (The persistence of the current-account surplus OQ' will tell them to do so.) The investors' demand curve will shift back to ED eventually, and the exchange rate will return to OP.

Figure 16-3 is drawn on three suppositions: that the shift in the supply curve is fully anticipated, that investors are risk averse, and that the current account responds immediately to a change in the exchange rate. What happens when the shift is not anticipated, when investors are risk neutral, and when there are lags in the adjustment process?

Speculation, Stability, and Profitability

When investors anticipate a change in the exchange rate and they are correct, their behavior is stabilizing, and they make profits. Their behavior is stabilizing because it drives the exchange rate to OP' immediately and thus in the direction of OP^*, the rate that must prevail in the long run. Investors make profits because they buy foreign currency at the price OP' and sell it thereafter at the higher price OP^*. When investors anticipate a shift in the supply curve and turn out to be wrong, their behavior is destabilizing and they take losses. Their behavior is destabilizing because it drives the exchange rate to OP' when the rate should stay at OP. Investors take losses because they buy foreign currency at the price OP' and sell it later at the lower price OP.

When investors fail to anticipate a shift in the supply curve, their demand curve does not shift, and the exchange rate does not change until the shift in the supply curve takes place. At that point, the domestic currency depreciates to OP'', the rate that clears the foreign-exchange market when the demand curve is still ED and the supply curve has shifted to E^*S^*. The depreciation is produced by the current-account deficit resulting from the shift in the supply curve. It induces a matching capital inflow OQ'' because investors expect the exchange rate to return to OP and thus sell foreign currency. If the shift in the supply curve is permanent, however, investors will revise their expectations eventually (helped this time by the current-account deficit OQ''). The demand curve will move to E^*D^*, driving the exchange rate to OP^*. Once again, investors behave in a destabilizing way and they take losses. Their behavior is destabilizing because it delays the necessary change in the exchange rate. Investors take losses because they sell foreign currency at the price OP'' and buy it later at the higher price OP^*.

There would thus appear to be a systematic link between the profitability of speculation and its contribution to exchange-rate stability. Milton Friedman put it this way:[5]

---

[5] Milton Friedman, "The Case for Flexible Exchange Rates," in *Essays in Positive Economics* (Chicago: University of Chicago Press, 1953), p. 175.

> People who argue that speculation is generally destabilizing seldom realize that this is largely equivalent to saying that speculators lose money, since speculation can be destabilizing in general only if speculators on the average sell when the currency is low in price and buy when it is high.

But be careful about the conclusion you draw from this quotation. Some economists have taken it to mean that speculation will *always* be stabilizing: as destabilizing speculators will take losses, they will be driven out of business and will thus leave the market to the stabilizing speculators, those who make profits and prosper in the long run. Friedman saw the flaw in this interpretation; he warned that "professional speculators might on average make money while a changing body of amateurs regularly lost larger sums."[6]

In recent years, economists have advanced another reason for believing that speculation will be stabilizing. It is the *rational expectations hypothesis*, which says that all decision makers, including speculators, forecast the future using an accurate model of the whole economy. They may make mistakes from time to time, because they do not have enough information or cannot distinguish information from mere rumor. But they will be right, on average, because they use an accurate model. Hence, speculation will tend to be stabilizing.[7]

This hypothesis is attractive analytically and appealing intellectually. If we could not believe that economic decisions are based on rational calculations, we would have grave doubts about the optimality of resource allocation in a market economy. But watch out for a leap in logic. Advocates of the rational expectations hypothesis identify rightness with rationality and thus identify wrongness with *ir*rationality. This is an invalid inference. It is vital to distinguish between ways in which decision makers form their expectations about rapidly changing market prices, such as stock prices and exchange rates, and ways in which they make infrequent but major decisions about building a factory, entering a new market, and so on. When making the first type of decision, it may be necessary to use rules of thumb for processing information; when making the second type of decision, there is time to collect and process information carefully. Those who use rules of thumb are not behaving irrationally, and we would expect them to learn from experience and improve their rules. But rules of thumb may be wrong in a particular instance, and speculation in the foreign-exchange market can be destabilizing, not because market participants are irrational but because they must act quickly.

---

[6]Ibid., pp. 175–176. Friedman went on to argue, however, that the presumption favors stabilizing speculation. If private speculation were destabilizing, he said, governments could engage in stabilizing speculation and make large sums of money. But this is equivalent to supposing "that government officials risking funds that they do not themselves own are better judges of the likely movements in foreign-exchange markets than private individuals risking their own funds."

[7]The rational expectations hypothesis does not rule out instability completely. In fact, it typically gives rise to a multiplicity of paths for the economy, and investors may be unable to choose the stable path. If they choose an unstable path, they will produce a "speculative bubble" that must burst eventually but is destabilizing in the short run. It drives the economy away from long-run equilibrium.

Risk Neutrality Once Again

Suppose that investors are risk neutral rather than risk averse. The tiniest open interest differential will lead them to demand huge quantities of foreign currency, because they will try to switch completely to the foreign bond. The excess demand curve will become horizontal, as in Figure 16-4. When investors expect the supply curve to shift in the future to E^*S^*, the demand curve will shift immediately to E^*D^*, and the market-clearing exchange rate will go at once to OP^*. The capital outflow will be OQ'. There will thus be no further change in the exchange rate when the supply curve actually shifts to E^*S^*.

When investors are risk neutral, then, expectations about the future exchange rate determine the actual rate completely. In Figure 16-4, the change in the expected rate drives the actual rate directly to OP^*. The responses of other market participants affect the size of the resulting capital flow but not the exchange-rate change itself. When investors are risk averse, by contrast, expectations influence the actual exchange rate but do not determine it by themselves. In Figure 16-3, the change in the expected rate to OP^* drove the actual rate to OP'. The change in the actual rate depended in part on the change in the expected rate, but also on the way that other participants responded to events in the foreign-exchange market—on the slope of the ES curve.

The same point can be put differently. When investors are risk neutral, expectations are completely *self-fulfilling*. The actual exchange rate goes immediately to OP^* in Figure 16-4 and does not change again when the supply curve shifts. When investors are risk averse, expectations are partly but not completely self-fulfilling.

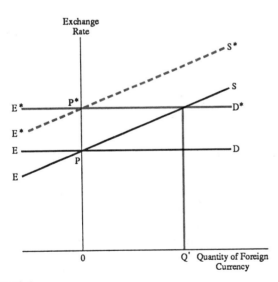

FIGURE 16-4
A Change in Expectations with Risk-Neutral Investors
When investors are risk neutral, the *ED* curve becomes horizontal. If investors anticipate a future shift in the supply curve from *ES* to *E*S**, their demand curve goes at once to *E*D**, because the expected exchange rate goes to *OP**. The actual exchange rate goes at once to *OP**, which is the market-clearing rate when the demand curve is *E*D** and the supply curve is still *ES*. The rate remains at *OP** even after the supply curve has shifted to *E*S**.

The exchange rate went immediately to *OP′* in Figure 16-3. It did not go to *OP**
until the supply curve shifted.

Lagged Adjustment and Exchange-Rate Overshooting

In all of the cases considered thus far, a change in the exchange rate
produced an immediate change in the trade balance. When the actual exchange rate
moved from *OP* to *OP′* in Figure 16-3, for example, the trade balance improved
immediately, and the supply of foreign currency coming from traders increased by
OQ′. In earlier chapters, however, we noted that exports and imports may not
respond immediately to a change in the exchange rate. The *ES* and *ED* curves can
be used to illustrate the consequences. The exchange rate may "overshoot" its
long-run equilibrium level in order to produce the capital flows required to clear the
foreign-exchange market.

Figure 16-5 shows what happens when there is a permanent increase in imports,

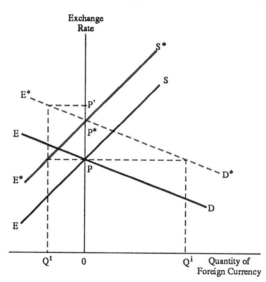

FIGURE 16-5
Lagged Adjustment and Exchange-Rate Overshooting
An increase of imports shifts the *ES* curve to *E*S**. Traders will demand an additional
OQ^t of foreign currency at the initial exchange rate *OP*. As investors are assumed to
identify correctly the reason for the increase in the traders' demand, they will revise
their expectations. The expected exchange rate will move from *OP* to *OP**, the new
market-clearing rate in the long run, and the *ED* curve will shift to *E*D**. Investors
will demand an additional *OQ^i* of foreign currency, hoping to sell it later at the higher
price *OP**. The excess demand for foreign currency causes the domestic currency to
depreciate. If the trade balance were to respond immediately to the depreciation, the
exchange rate would move directly to *OP**, eliminating both parts of the excess
demand. If the trade balance responds with a lag, the traders' excess demand can
remain at *OQ^t* temporarily, which means that the domestic currency must depreciate
to *OP′* and thus overshoot the long-run rate *OP**. When the actual rate is *OP′*,
investors will supply *OQ^t* foreign currency, hoping to buy it later at the lower price
OP*. The investors' excess supply will match the traders' excess demand. With the
passage of time, the trade balance will respond to the depreciation of the domestic
currency, and the exchange rate will move eventually to *OP**.

which raises the traders' demand for foreign currency at the initial exchange rate OP. Let the additional demand be OQ^t, which shifts the ES curve to E^*S^*. The domestic currency must depreciate eventually to OP^* to eliminate the current-account deficit resulting from the increase in imports. Assume that investors realize this promptly and revise their expectations. The expected exchange rate will move to OP^*, shifting the ED curve to E^*D^* and raising the investors' demand for foreign currency to OQ^i. Investors will want to buy foreign currency at the initial price OP in the hope of selling it later at the higher price OP^*. With excess demand coming from both traders and investors, the domestic currency will depreciate.

If the trade balance were to adjust immediately to the change in the exchange rate, the actual rate would go directly to OP^*, eliminating both components of the excess demand. If the trade balance adjusts slowly, however, the traders' excess demand will not fall immediately as the domestic currency depreciates, and the exchange rate will be driven beyond OP^*. It may go all the way to OP'. When the actual rate is OP' and the expected rate is OP^*, investors will supply OQ^t foreign currency. They will want to sell it at the price OP' in the hope of buying it later at the lower price OP^*. The investors' excess supply will thus match the traders' excess demand, clearing the foreign-exchange market.[8] With the passage of time, of course, the trade balance will respond to the depreciation of the domestic currency, and the exchange rate will move eventually to OP^*, validating the investors' expectations.

This sort of overshooting was identified formally by Rudiger Dornbusch of MIT, using a model more elaborate than the one implicit in Figure 16-5. Another form of overshooting will be illustrated in Chapter 18, where it will play a different role. The various forms of overshooting are often cited to account for the short-run volatility of flexible exchange rates, a phenomenon illustrated vividly by Figure 12-1 in Chapter 12. But that volatility may be due to something else. Investors must assimilate large amounts of information and must update their exchange-rate forecasts frequently. In other words, the ED curve moves up and down incessantly as investors revise their expectations about future exchange rates.

THE FORWARD FOREIGN-EXCHANGE MARKET

In the discussion just concluded, investors were exposed to exchange-rate risk. Therefore, the demand curve ED reflected their attitudes toward risk as well as their forecasts about future exchange rates. Other participants in the foreign-exchange market were not exposed to risk because they did not take *positions* in foreign currency. Domestic buyers of foreign goods and services paid for them immediately and bought foreign currency when they needed it. Foreign buyers of

---

[8]The case shown in Figure 16-5, where the trade balance stays at OQ^t temporarily, despite the depreciation of the domestic currency, is one where the sum of the short-run elasticities of demand for the country's exports and imports equals 1 exactly (i.e., the MLR condition is just on the edge of being fulfilled). If the sum were smaller than 1, a depreciation of the domestic currency would worsen the trade balance and there would be a J-curve. The exchange rate would have then to move beyond OP' to raise the quantity of foreign currency supplied by investors and clear the foreign-exchange market.

domestic goods and services behaved in the same way. Therefore, the supply curve *ES* did not reflect attitudes toward risk or expectations; it reflected the influence of the actual exchange rate on demands for goods and services.

In many cases, however, goods and services are delivered long after they are ordered, and payments are not made until deliveries take place. Accordingly, someone is exposed to risk. An American firm that agrees to pay for British goods in pounds faces the risk that the pound will appreciate against the dollar between the day when goods are ordered and the day when payment must be made. A British firm that agrees to be paid in dollars faces the same risk. But firms that acquire trade claims or obligations can *hedge* against exchange-rate risk. An American firm that agrees to pay for British goods in pounds can buy pounds right away and hold them until it needs them. Alternatively, it can buy pounds for delivery weeks or months from now by using the forward foreign-exchange market.

Transactions in the Forward Market

A transaction in the forward foreign-exchange market involves an exchange of promises. One party promises to provide a stated quantity of dollars on an agreed date and to take up a stated quantity of pounds. The other party promises to take up the dollars and provide the pounds. Money does not change hands when the contract is made. An exchange rate is set now, however, at which dollars and pounds will change hands later. If you undertake to provide $175,000 in 90 days and to take up £100,000 in exchange, you have set the forward exchange rate at $1.75 per pound.

Clearly, your willingness to make this contract will depend on your forecast of the spot exchange rate 90 days from now, as that is the rate you will have to pay if you delay your purchase. If you expect the spot rate to be $1.80, you have an incentive to buy pounds forward at $1.75 per pound. Your willingness to do so, however, will also depend on interest rates in Britain and the United States, because they determine the cost of hedging by purchasing pounds now and holding them for 90 days, which is the alternative to a forward purchase. To purchase pounds now, you must give up (or borrow) dollars now. The cost of hedging will therefore depend on the interest rate you can earn on pounds compared to the interest rate you can earn on dollars (or must pay to borrow them). Finally, your willingness to make a forward contract will depend on your attitude toward risk.

An example will help us look more carefully at these ways to hedge against exchange-rate risk. The spot exchange rate is $1.75 per pound today. An American firm buys British goods and agrees to pay £200,000 when they are delivered 90 days from now. It incurs a £200,000 obligation to its supplier.

Suppose that the firm borrows $350,000 from its bank, uses the dollars to buy pounds, and invests the pounds for 90 days. The £200,000 obligation remains but is offset by a £200,000 claim, the pounds bought with the borrowed dollars. The firm has hedged its foreign-currency position. It has replaced a net liability in pounds with a net liability in dollars, the $350,000 it owes to its bank.

Suppose that the firm goes to the forward market instead and that the forward rate is $1.75 per pound. The firm undertakes to provide $350,000 in 90 days in exchange for the £200,000 it will need. The £200,000 obligation is offset by the other party's promise to deliver pounds, and the firm has hedged its foreign-currency position. Once again, it has replaced a net liability in pounds with a net liability in dollars, represented by its promise to deliver dollars.

Investors use the forward market just as traders do. Let the British interest rate be higher than the U.S. rate. An investor wants to take advantage of the higher British rate but does not want exposure to exchange-rate risk. Suppose that the investor starts out with $700,000, that the spot exchange rate is $1.75 now, and that the British interest rate is 6 percent. The investor can acquire £400,000 now and can therefore expect to have £424,000 a year from now. The investor can avoid exchange-rate risk by selling the £424,000 for dollars on the forward market.

Finally, speculators use the forward market. Let the forward exchange rate be $1.75 per pound. A speculator believes that the spot exchange rate will be $1.80 per pound 90 days from now. The speculator will buy pounds forward at $1.75 in the hope of selling them 90 days from now at $1.80 and thus making a five-cent profit on each pound. Note that this form of speculation does not tie up cash. Transfers take place only after 90 days have passed, when the speculator turns over dollars in exchange for pounds and sells the pounds for dollars at the then-current spot rate.

Forward Rates and Interest Rates

When we looked at the behavior of an investor-speculator choosing between foreign and domestic bonds, we worked through a comparison that defined the open interest differential and open parity condition. An investor who chooses between those bonds but plans to avoid exchange-rate risk by going to the forward market must work through a similar comparison.

The investor can buy $1/\pi$ foreign-currency units of the foreign bond with one unit of domestic currency and can thus expect to have $(1/\pi)(1 + r^*)$ units of foreign currency when the bonds mature. To avoid exchange-rate risk, the investor can sell foreign currency now at the forward foreign-exchange rate, π^f. Therefore, an investment in the foreign bond is worth $(1/\pi)(1 + r^*)\pi^f$ units of domestic currency. Alternatively, the investor can buy the domestic bond and can thus earn $1 + r$ of domestic currency. Use c to define the difference between these two returns:

$$c = \frac{1}{\pi}(1 + r^*)\pi^f - (1 + r). \tag{4}$$

This is the *covered interest differential*. When c is positive, an investor will buy foreign currency at the current spot rate π in order to buy foreign bonds, but will also sell foreign currency at the forward rate π^f to hedge against exchange-rate risk. In the language of the forward market, the investor will engage in *covered interest arbitrage*.[9]

---

[9]A similar calculation will govern a firm's choice between two ways of hedging a commercial obligation. Suppose that the firm can borrow dollars at the interest rate r, buy pounds immediately at the spot rate π, and invest the pounds at the interest rate r^*. For every pound needed in the future, the firm must buy $1/(1 + r^*)$ pounds now and spend $\pi[1/(1 + r^*)]$ dollars. But it will incur $(1 + r)$ dollars of debt, including interest, for every dollar borrowed to buy pounds. Therefore, the dollar cost of hedging in this way is $\pi[1/(1 + r^*)](1 + r)$ dollars per

Footnote 9 continued on next page.

We can simplify equation (4). Use δ *to* define the *forward premium* on the foreign currency, the difference between its forward and spot prices measured in relation to its spot price:

$$\delta = \frac{\pi^f - \pi}{\pi}. \tag{5}$$

As $\pi^f = (1 + \delta)\pi$, by definition, equation (4) becomes

$$c = \frac{1}{\pi}(1 + r^*)(1 + \delta)\pi - (1 + r) = (r^* - r) + (1 + r^*)\delta$$

$$\approx (r^* - r) + \delta, \tag{4a}$$

because $(1 + r^*)\delta$ is approximately equal to δ.

There are two ways to look at the covered interest differential, just as there were two ways to look at the open differential. Investors concerned mainly with earning income on their bonds will read equation (4a) to say that an additional gain or loss can come from buying the foreign bond. There is an additional gain when δ is positive—when the foreign currency is selling at a premium on the forward market. There is a loss when δ is negative—when the foreign currency is selling at a discount. Traders in the foreign-exchange market will read equation (4a) to say that profits made from *swaps* between spot and forward markets must be adjusted for the interest-rate difference. When δ is positive, a foreign-exchange trader will be tempted to buy foreign currency spot and sell it forward. The profit from this swap will be larger than δ when r^* is higher than r, because the trader will be holding foreign currency rather than domestic currency while waiting to deliver the foreign currency. The profit will be smaller than δ and can turn into a loss when r^* is lower than r.

When the open interest differential was positive, risk-neutral investors shifted completely into the foreign bond. In the process, however, they drove that differential to zero. When the covered differential is positive, risk-averse investors will want to shift completely, too, and strong market forces will keep c close to zero. When those forces are strong enough to keep c at zero, equation (4a) asserts that

$$\delta = r - r^*. \tag{6}$$

---

pound needed in the future. The dollar cost of hedging in the forward market is, of course, the forward rate, π^f, because it is the dollar cost of purchasing a pound for future delivery. Define the difference between the two dollar costs:

$$c^* = \pi^f - \pi[1/(1 + r^*)](1 + r).$$

If c^* is positive, it is cheaper to buy pounds with borrowed dollars. If c^* is negative, it is cheaper to use the forward market. But the expression for c^* can be rewritten. Multiply both sides by $1 + r^*$ and divide by π:

$$(1/\pi)(1 + r^*)c^* = (1/\pi)(1 + r^*)\pi^f - (1 + r) = c.$$

Thus, the firm will buy pounds forward whenever the covered differential is negative. (When the covered differential is zero, the firm will have no reason to prefer one way of hedging over the other. Under assumptions made later, moreover, the differential *will* be close to zero. Therefore, we will not go far wrong by assuming that firms rely completely on the forward market to hedge their positions.)

This condition is called *covered interest parity*. It says that the forward premium on the foreign currency is exactly equal to the interest-rate difference, and no profits can be made from arbitrage. (The process may not go that far, however, because covered arbitrage is not totally risk free. By selling foreign currency forward, an investor avoids exchange-rate risk but incurs another risk. The other party to the forward contract may not honor its commitment. Default risk replaces exchange-rate risk.)

The open and covered interest differentials look much alike, and both are used to show how capital movements respond to interest rates. The two are very different in character, however, because $\hat{\pi}$ and δ are different. The term $\hat{\pi}$ involves a comparison between the actual spot exchange rate today and the expected future rate. It is surrounded by uncertainty. The term δ involves a comparison between the spot and forward rates today. It is not surrounded by uncertainty, because both rates are known now.

DETERMINANTS OF THE FORWARD RATE

A realistic model of the forward market would be inhabited by firms that hedge commercial claims and obligations, investors who engage in covered interest arbitrage, and speculators who bet on expectations about future exchange rates. It would not include all firms, because some of them do not hedge (or do so by borrowing and other methods rather than using the forward market). It would not include all investors, because some do not cover their positions; they are investor-speculators of the sort encountered earlier in this chapter. And it would not include all speculators, because some have other ways to place their bets. But the essential features of the forward market can be captured by a very simple model:

(1) All firms engaged in foreign trade hedge in the forward market. Trade is balanced, however, so the demand for forward contracts coming from one country's firms always equals the supply of forward contracts coming from the other's firms. Therefore, commercial hedging drops out of the model.

(2) All investors cover their foreign-currency positions. Therefore, capital movements depend on the covered interest differential. Interest rates are equal initially, however, so that the investors' demand for forward contracts depends exclusively on δ, the forward premium on the foreign currency. When δ is positive, investors sell foreign currrency forward; when δ is negative, they buy it.

(3) All speculators operate in the forward market. When their forecast of $\hat{\pi}$ is larger than the market value of δ, they buy foreign currency forward. If they are right about $\hat{\pi}$, they make profits; foreign currency bought forward now can be sold at a higher spot rate later. When their forecast of $\hat{\pi}$ is smaller than the market value of δ, they sell foreign currency forward.

(4) The spot exchange rate is pegged, and the balance of payments is in equilibrium initially. Therefore, events in the forward market that also impinge on the spot market affect official reserves rather than the spot exchange rate. When investors demand foreign currency spot in order to buy foreign bonds, the foreign central bank intervenes to prevent its country's currency from appreciating, and its

reserves rise. In ordinary circumstances, moreover, $\hat{\pi}$ will zero. It can differ from zero only when speculators come to expect that the central bank will devalue or revalue its currency—change the peg at which it intervenes in the spot market.[10]

This model is set out in Figure 16-6. The forward premium on the foreign currency, δ, is measured on the vertical axis. Forward purchases and sales of foreign currency are measured on the horizontal axis.

The *FD* curve shows the forward demand for foreign currency coming from speculators. It is drawn on two suppositions, that $\hat{\pi}$ is zero initially and that speculators are risk averse. When $\hat{\pi}$ is zero, speculators' purchases depend entirely on the forward premium. They buy foreign currency forward when it goes to a discount (δ is negative); they sell foreign currency forward when it goes to a premium (δ is positive). When speculators are risk averse, their behavior depends on the riskiness of speculation as well as the expected profit. Hence, *FD* is downward sloping. (If speculators were risk neutral, their positions would not be limited by riskiness, and *FD* would be horizontal.)

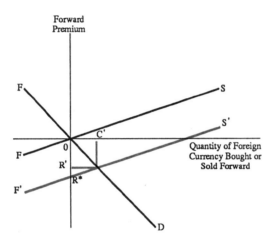

FIGURE 16-6
Response of the Forward Rate to an Increase in the Foreign Interest Rate
The *FS* curve shows the quantity of foreign currency that investors sell forward to engage in covered interest arbitrage. When foreign and domestic interest rates are equal, investors sell foreign currency forward whenever it goes to a premium. The *FD* curve shows the quantity of foreign currency that speculators buy forward. When $\hat{\pi}$ is zero, speculators buy foreign currency forward whenever it goes to a discount. When interest rates are equal and $\hat{\pi}$ is zero, the *FS* and *FD* curve intersect at zero, and the forward premium is zero. An increase in the foreign interest rate lowers the investors' supply curve from *FS* to *F'S'*; investors will buy foreign bonds and will cover their positions by selling foreign currency forward. The foreign currency will go to a discount, *OR'*, at which investors want to sell *OC'* foreign currency forward and speculators want to buy it forward.

[10]If the spot rate were flexible, we would have to analyze simultaneously the behavior of the spot and forward rates. This is not hard conceptually but difficult diagrammatically. Any change in π that is not accompanied by a change in π^e produces a change in $\hat{\pi}$, affecting the position of the *FD* curve in Figure 16-6. Therefore, it affects the equilibrium in the forward market.

The *FS* curve shows the forward supply of foreign currency coming from investors. When interest rates are equal initially, investors' sales of foreign currency depend on the forward premium. They sell foreign currency forward when it goes to a premium and buy foreign currency forward when it goes to a discount.[11]

Effects of a Change in the Foreign Interest Rate

When interest rates are equal and $\hat{\pi}$ is zero, the *FS* and *FD* curves intersect at zero, and the forward premium must be zero. That is the initial situation in Figure 16-6. What happens when the foreign interest rate rises? The covered interest differential turns positive when δ starts at zero, and the investors' supply curve shifts to $F'S'$. Investors want to buy foreign bonds and want therefore to sell foreign currency forward. The market-clearing value of δ goes to OR'. This discount on the foreign currency, however, is not large enough to eliminate the covered interest differential. The discount that would do so is OR^*, because it would restore covered interest parity and reduce investors' sales to zero. Therefore, investors buy some foreign bonds and sell OC' foreign currency forward. Speculators buy OC' forward because they expect to gain by selling it later. (In this particular example, where $\hat{\pi}$ is zero, they expect to sell at a constant spot rate the foreign currency they buy forward at the discount OR'.)

The transactions shown in Figure 16-6 are listed in Table 16-1, along with others that go with them. When investors buy foreign bonds, they must buy foreign currency in the spot market. But speculators do not enter the spot market, not yet. Therefore, the increase in the foreign interest rate produces excess demand in the spot market, and the foreign central bank gains reserves. When investments and forward contracts mature, investors need not enter the spot market; their forward contracts allow them to switch back to domestic currency. But speculators must sell foreign currency in the spot market; they must acquire the domestic currency they promised to deliver when they made their forward contracts. Excess demand in the spot market gives way at this point to excess supply, and the foreign central bank loses the reserves it gained earlier.

The story told in Table 16-1 can be carried further. Suppose that the foreign interest rate continues to exceed the domestic rate at the end of the cycle shown in the table. A new cycle will begin immediately. Investors will buy foreign currency spot and sell it forward, keeping the forward discount at OR' in Figure 16-6. Speculators will buy foreign currency forward. There will be excess demand in the spot market at the start of the new cycle. (It will indeed offset the excess supply that

---

[11]When investors engage in covered interest arbitrage, they avoid exchange-rate risk completely. We noted earlier, however, that investors face another risk. Someone may default on a forward contract. Accordingly, the *FS* curve is fairly flat but not completely horizontal. Investors are risk averse and do not shift completely to the foreign bond when δ is positive. If covered interest arbitrage were riskless in all respects, the *FS* curve would be horizontal. (Figure 16-6 differs importantly from earlier diagrams that dealt with the spot market. In Figure 16-6, distances along the vertical axis measure δ and $\hat{\pi}$, the forward premium and the expected rate of change in the spot exchange rate. In earlier diagrams, by contrast, vertical distances measured π and π^e, the *levels* of the actual and expected spot rates. Figure 16-6 could be drawn in terms of π, π^f, and π^e, the levels of the spot rate, forward rate, and expected spot rate, but would get rather cluttered.)

Table 16-1. Transactions in Spot and Forward Markets Resulting from an Increase in the Foreign Interest Rate

Time	Spot Market	Forward Market
When the foreign interest rate rises	Investors buy foreign currency to buy foreign bonds Speculators do not enter spot market	Investors sell foreign currency to cover their positions Speculators buy foreign currency to open their positions
When investments and forward contracts mature	Investors do not enter spot market Speculators sell foreign currency for the domestic currency they owe under their contracts	Investors deliver the foreign currency they sold forward for domestic currency Speculators deliver the domestic currency they bought spot for the foreign currency they bought forward

emerged at the close of the old cycle.) At the end of the new cycle, investors will move back into domestic currency, having sold foreign currency forward, and speculators must buy domestic currency to honor their forward contracts. Suppose instead that the foreign interest rate drops back to equality with the domestic rate at the end of the first cycle. The cycle will not be repeated. The supply curve in Figure 16-6 will shift back from $F'S'$ to FS, and the forward discount will return to zero.

Effects of a Change in Expectations

What happens when expectations change? Suppose that speculators begin to believe that the foreign currency will be revalued. As $\hat{\pi}$ becomes positive, the speculators' demand curve shifts to $F'D'$ in Figure 16-7. The new value of $\hat{\pi}$ is given by OR^*, which is the forward premium at which speculators cannot make a profit and will not buy or sell foreign currency forward. The market-clearing value of δ goes to OR', which is smaller than OR^*, so speculators can expect to make a profit. Accordingly, they buy OC' foreign currency forward and investors sell it, because there is a covered interest differential that leads investors to buy foreign bonds. (Interest rates are equal, and δ is positive.)

Although the forward rate goes to a premium here and went to a discount in the previous diagram, the two cases lead to a similar sequence of transactions. Returning to Table 16-1, the increase in $\hat{\pi}$ leads to forward purchases by speculators, drives the foreign currency to a forward premium, and induces investors to buy foreign bonds. Therefore, investors buy foreign currency spot and sell it forward. Later, investors

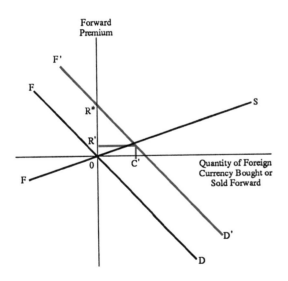

FIGURE 16-7
Response of the Forward Rate to a Change in Expectations
When interest rates are equal initially and $\hat{\pi}$ is zero, the *FS* and *FD* curves intersect at zero. When speculators start to believe that the foreign currency will appreciate, they begin to buy it forward; when $\hat{\pi}$ rises from zero to OR^*, the speculators' demand curve shifts from *FD* to *F'D'*. The foreign currency goes to a premium on the forward market, and the premium creates a covered interest differential favoring investment in the foreign bond. The market-clearing premium is OR', at which speculators want to buy OC' foreign currency forward and investors want to sell it forward.

use their forward contracts to switch back to domestic currency, but speculators must buy domestic currency in the spot market to honor their forward contracts. If the spot exchange rate is not revalued, the foreign central bank gains reserves at the start of the process and loses them at the end.

Using the Forward Rate to Predict the Spot Rate

If speculators were risk neutral, the FD curve would be horizontal in Figures 16-6 and 16-7, and the market value of δ could not differ from $\hat{\pi}$, the expected change in the spot rate. Therefore, δ could be used to represent $\hat{\pi}$ in research on a number of important issues, including the formation of expectations.

This approach cannot be tested directly unless we have an independent measure of $\hat{\pi}$. But we can construct and test a *joint* hypothesis about the behavior of speculators. Suppose that speculators are risk neutral *and* that they do not make systematic errors when forecasting future exchange rates (i.e., they conform to the rational expectations hypothesis). On the first supposition, δ will represent the market's view about $\hat{\pi}$. On the second supposition, $\hat{\pi}$ will not differ systematically from $\dot{\pi}$, the actual percentage change in the spot rate. Therefore, the joint hypothesis can be tested by estimating this equation:

$$\dot{\pi}_{t+1} = a + b\delta_t,$$

where $\dot{\pi}_{t+1}$ is the actual percentage change in the spot rate between time t and time $t + 1$, and δ_t is the forward premium at time t. If $a = 0$ and $b = 1$, the joint hypothesis stands up. If those two conditions are not met, it must be rejected (but we cannot know whether to reject the first or second supposition, or both of them together).

Many economists have estimated this sort of equation. Some have obtained values for a and b that satisfy the test of the joint hypothesis, but most have obtained values

Table 16-2. Forecasting Equations for U.S. Dollar Exchange Rates

Currency	a	b
Pound sterling	0.0086	−0.2881
Deutsche mark	0.0214	−0.7815
Swiss franc	0.0481	−2.2145
Canadian dollar	−0.0076	0.8285
Japanese yen	0.0311	−2.8316

Source: Adapted from Robert E. Cumby and Maurice Obstfeld, "International Interest Rate and Price Level Linkages Under Flexible Exchange Rates," in J. F. O. Bilson and R. C. Marston, eds., *Exchange Rate Theory and Practice* (Chicago: University of Chicago Press, 1984), Table 3.4. The calculations are based on weekly data from 1976 to 1981.

for a that differ significantly from zero and values for b that differ significantly from 1. That is what happens in Table 16-2, where four values of a are close to zero but four values of b have the wrong sign (and the Canadian equation, which has the right sign for b, has a negative value of a). In most studies, moreover, δ_t proves to be a poor predictor of $\dot{\pi}_{t+1}$. The equation does not "explain" much of the variation in the actual exchange rate.

More research must be done on attitudes toward risk and on the formation of expectations before we know why. Recent work with survey data on exchange-rate expectations suggests that forecasts made by foreign-exchange traders differ systematically from the forward exchange rates. This finding raises doubts about the rational expectations hypothesis. But it may also mean that foreign-exchange traders are risk averse, rather than risk neutral. We have no simple way of choosing between these interpretations. (We cannot be sure, moreover, that the exchange-rate forecasts gathered by such surveys are the forecasts that drive the traders' own behavior.)

SUMMARY

Investors must take account of future changes in exchange rates when comparing returns on foreign assets with returns on domestic assets. They must look at the *open interest differential*, which adjusts the ordinary interest-rate difference for the expected change in the exchange rate. If investors believe that the foreign currency will appreciate, the open interest differential can favor investment in the foreign bond even when the foreign interest rate is lower than the domestic rate.

If investors are *risk neutral*, they will tend to treat foreign and domestic bonds as perfect substitutes. An open interest differential favoring the foreign bond will induce investors to shift to that bond completely, producing a capital outflow. As they do so, however, they will reduce the foreign interest rate and raise the domestic rate, so the capital outflow will maintain *open interest parity*. The difference in interest rates will equal the expected rate of change in the exchange rate.

If investors are *risk averse*, they will tend to treat foreign and domestic bonds as imperfect substitutes. An open interest differential favoring the foreign bond will induce investors to buy that bond but not shift into it completely. They will hold diversified portfolios. An increase in the foreign interest rate will still produce a capital outflow, but its size will be limited by the intensity of risk aversion, and it cannot restore open interest parity.

As expectations influence capital movements, they must also influence the behavior of a flexible exchange rate. An increase in the foreign interest rate will cause the foreign currency to appreciate. A change in expectations can do so, too. If investors begin to believe that other participants in the foreign-exchange market will increase their demand for the foreign currency, the open interest differential will favor foreign investment and investors will demand more foreign currency. The foreign currency will appreciate immediately when it is expected to appreciate later.

When expectations are borne out by events, speculators will make money and speculation itself will be stabilizing. When expectations are contradicted, speculators will lose money and speculation will be destabilizing. But stabilizing speculation will not necessarily dominate foreign-exchange markets, even when stabilizing speculators prosper.

When there are lags in the adjustment of trade flows to exchange-rate changes, capital flows may be needed to clear the foreign-exchange market. In such cases, the exchange rate has to overshoot its long-term equilibrium level to produce the necessary capital flows. To induce a capital inflow, for example, the domestic currency must depreciate by more in the short run than it is expected to depreciate in the long run.

The forward foreign-exchange market is used by traders and investors to hedge against exchange-rate risk. A forward contract is a promise to exchange one currency for another at an agreed future date. The forward exchange rate is built into the contract. The forward rate can be at a premium or discount, compared with the spot rate, depending on supply and demand conditions in the forward market. The premium is used to compute the *covered interest differential*, which adjusts the ordinary interest-rate difference for the cost of hedging in the forward market.

When the covered interest differential is positive, investors buy foreign bonds and sell the foreign-currency proceeds forward. This is covered interest arbitrage, which tends to maintain *covered interest parity*. Speculators use the forward market to place bets on their forecasts of future exchange rates. When they expect a currency to appreciate by an amount larger than the forward premium, they buy it forward.

An increase in the foreign interest rate leads investors to buy foreign currency spot and sell it forward. The currency will appreciate immediately and go to a discount on the forward market. Speculators will buy it forward to take advantage of the discount. When forward contracts mature, investors will deliver foreign currency to speculators in exchange for domestic currency. But speculators must then sell foreign currency spot to obtain the domestic currency they must deliver, causing the foreign currency to depreciate. A change in expectations can have similar effects. This time, however, speculators take the lead, and the foreign currency goes to a premium rather than a discount.

If speculators were risk neutral, the forward rate would be an efficient predictor of the future spot rate. This hypothesis can be tested jointly with another, that speculators form rational expectations and do not make systematic forecasting errors. The evidence tends to reject the joint hypothesis.

RECOMMENDED READINGS

For a thorough treatment of hedging, investing, and speculating under exchange-rate uncertainty, with well-chosen examples, see Ronald I. McKinnon, *Money in International Exchange* (New York: Oxford University Press, 1979), chs. 4, 5, and 7. The same subjects are examined more rigorously, with attention to stability, profitability, and related issues, in Egon Sohmen, *Flexible Exchange Rates* (Chicago: University of Chicago Press, 1969), chs. iii–iv.

The analysis of the forward market in this chapter is based on a celebrated paper by S. C. Tsiang, "The Theory of Forward Exchange and Effects of Government Intervention on the Forward Exchange Market," *International Monetary Fund Staff Papers*, 7 (April 1959), See also J. Marcus Fleming and Robert A. Mundell, "Official Intervention on the Forward Market," *International Monetary Fund Staff Papers*, 11 (March 1964); reprinted in J. M.

Fleming, *Essays in International Economics* (Cambridge, Mass.: Harvard University Press, 1971), ch. 10.

On overshooting in the foreign-exchange market, see Rudiger Dornbusch, "Expectations and Exchange Rate Dynamics," *Journal of Political Economy*, 84 (August 1976). Many other papers deal with the influence of expectations, but most of them used methods more advanced than those adopted in this book. Two papers illustrate the general approach using rather simple models: Rudiger Dornbusch, "Monetary Policy Under Exchange-Rate Flexibility," in J. R. Artus et al., *Managed Exchange-Rate Flexibility* (Boston: Federal Reserve Bank of Boston, 1978), and Maurice Obstfeld, "Capital Mobility and Devaluation in an Optimizing Model with Rational Expectations," *American Economic Review*, 71 (May 1981).

For the influence of information on expectations and the effects on the exchange rate, see Jacob A. Frenkel, "Flexible Exchange Rates, Prices and the Role of 'News': Lessons from the 1970s," *Journal of Political Economy*, 89 (June 1981).

The assertion that destabilizing speculators are bound to suffer losses has been used to appraise the effects of official intervention in the foreign-exchange market; see Helmut Mayer and H. Taguchi, *Official Intervention in the Exchange Markets: Stabilizing or Destabilizing?* (Basle: Bank for International Settlements, 1983).

On the use of the forward rate to forecast the spot rate and the "efficiency" of foreign-exchange markets, see Richard M. Levich, "Empirical Studies of Exchange Rates: Price Behavior, Rate Determination and Market Efficiency," in R. W. Jones and P. B. Kenen, eds., *Handbook of International Economics* (Amsterdam: North-Holland, 1985), ch. 19.

For the use of survey data to investigate the rationality of expectations, see Jeffrey Frankel and Kenneth Froot, "Using Survey Data to Test Some Standard Propositions Regarding Exchange Rate Expectations," *American Economic Review*, 77 (March 1987). On the use of rules of thumb to make exchange-rate forecasts and the profitability of speculation based on those rules, see Helen Allen and Mark P. Taylor, "Charts, Noise and Fundamentals in the London Foreign Exchange Market," *Economic Journal*, 100 (Supplement 1990).

QUESTIONS AND PROBLEMS

(1) The U.S. interest rate is 4.5 percent, the British interest rate is 8.5 percent, and the spot exchange rate is $1.75 per pound. What exchange rate must be expected to prevail one year from now for open interest parity to hold?

(2) Adapt Figure 16-1 to show how a fall in the domestic interest rate affects the behavior of a risk-averse investor. What can you say about the share of the foreign (risky) asset in the investor's portfolio?

(3) Adapt Figure 16-2 to show the effects of an increase in the domestic interest rate. Is there a capital inflow or outflow? A current-account surplus or deficit? Explain.

(4) Modify your answer to (3) to illustrate the case in which investors are risk neutral. What are the main consequences?

(5) Adapt Figure 16-3 to show what happens when investors forecast a future increase in the excess supply of foreign currency coming from traders in goods and services. Deal first with the case in which the forecast is correct and show that speculators make profits. Deal next with the case in which the forecast is wrong and show that speculators make losses.

(6) Consult Figure 1-2, which shows exchange rates for January 15, 1993. On that same date, the interest rate on 3-month (90-day) U.S. Treasury bills was 3 percent and the interest rate on 3-month British Treasury bills was 6.5 percent. Compute the covered interest differential. Does it favor investment in the United States or Britain? (Note: The interest rates quoted above are annual rates, so you must convert them to their 3-month equivalents. Dividing them by 4 will give you a close approximation.)

(7) Adapt Figure 16-7 to show what happens when speculators come to believe that the foreign currency will depreciate. Produce the counterpart of Table 16-1 to show what happens in the spot and forward markets. Suppose that the speculators are right—that the foreign currency does depreciate—and show that they make profits. Then suppose that they are wrong and show that they make losses.

17

Stocks, Flows, and Monetary Equilibrium

TWO VIEWS OF THE BALANCE OF PAYMENTS

In Chapter 12, we went through the balance-of-payments accounts from the top down. We started with trade in goods and services and investment-income flows, paused to calculate the current-account balance, and went on to the capital account. The surplus or deficit in the balance of payments appeared at the end as the change in official reserves. It reflected official purchases or sales of foreign currency designed to keep the exchange rate from changing.

Therefore, we came to think of surpluses and deficits as measures of disequilibrium in the flow market for foreign exchange. More important, we saw them as reflections of events in many other markets—foreign and domestic markets for goods, services, and assets. In subsequent chapters, we looked at ways of dealing with surpluses and deficits by policies affecting those events and markets. In Chapters 13 and 14, we studied ways of altering demands for goods and services—policies affecting interest rates and exchange-rate expectations.

There is another way to look at the balance of payments. It is very old but has been revived and modernized. Instead of focusing on flows in the foreign-exchange market and the flows that lie behind them in markets for goods, services, and assets, it focuses directly on their monetary counterparts, the change in the stock of domestic money resulting from a balance-of-payments surplus or deficit.

This is the *monetary approach* to balance-of-payments theory, which provides a monetary approach to exchange-rate theory as well. The monetary approach is built on a simple proposition:

A surplus in the balance of payments necessarily testifies to an excess demand for money at home and to an excess supply abroad. A deficit testifies to an excess supply of money at home and to an excess demand abroad.

Accordingly, the monetary approach stresses forces affecting the demand for money, rather than forces affecting the demands for goods, services, and assets. It also puts particular emphasis on monetary policy, the main force affecting the supply of money.

ORIGINS AND ISSUES

It is easy to prove the basic proposition of the monetary approach. We will do that shortly. It is less easy to accept the strong conclusions often drawn from it. Advocates of the monetary approach have made assumptions about prices, incomes, and other variables that allow them to construct very simple models in which money is the *only* thing that matters for balance-of-payments behavior. We will build a monetary model to show how this conclusion is obtained. Thereafter, we will show how the balance-of-payments model can be converted into an exchange-rate model.

Because the monetary model depends on restrictive assumptions, its predictions are not always borne out by experience. That is why it is hard to accept the strong policy recommendations drawn from it. Nevertheless, there are three reasons for looking at the model carefully. First, it is the direct descendant of the oldest balance-of-payments model, a model even older than the Ricardian model of comparative advantage. Second, it has inspired a large body of research on the implications of monetary policy for the behavior of a flexible exchange rate, and some economists still regard it as the best framework for policy analysis. Finally, the simplicity of the monetary model allows us to see clearly how stocks and flows of assets interact to influence the dynamics of adjustment in an open economy. One such interaction cropped up in Chapter 15, where *IS* and *LM* curves were used to show how the stock of money is affected by balance-of-payments flows. Others will crop up in Chapter 18, which develops a model with several stocks and flows.

David Hume and the Specie-Flow Doctrine

The monetary approach to the balance of payments can be traced back to the middle of the eighteenth century. Writing in 1752, David Hume used the quantity theory of money, connecting the price level to the money supply, to produce a clear statement of the *specie-flow doctrine*, the earliest version of the monetary approach. He began with examples remarkably similar to those used in the modern literature, but his language was more elegant:[1]

> Suppose four-fifths of all the money in Great Britain to be annihilated in one night, and the nation reduced to the same condition with regard to specie [money], as in the reigns of the Harrys and Edwards, what would be the consequence? Must not the price of all labour and commodities sink in proportion, and everything be sold as cheap as they were in those ages? What nation could then dispute with us in any foreign market, or pretend to

---

[1] David Hume, "Of the Balance of Trade," in *Essays, Moral, Political and Literary*, 1752 (1777 edition).

navigate or to sell manufactures at the same price, which to us would afford sufficient profit? In how little time, therefore, must this bring back the money which we had lost, and raise us to the level of all the neighbouring nations? Where, after we have arrived, we immediately lose the advantage of the cheapness of labour and commodities; and the farther flowing in of money is stopped by our fulness and repletion.

Again, suppose that all the money in Great Britain were multiplied fivefold in a night, must not the contrary effect follow? Must not all labour and commodities rise to such an exorbitant height, that no neighbouring nations could afford to buy from us; while their commodities, on the other hand, became comparatively so cheap, that, in spite of all the laws which could be formed, they would run in upon us, and our money flow out; till we fall to a level with foreigners, and lose that great superiority of riches [money] which had laid us under such disadvantages?

In a manner typical of classical economists. Hume went on to invoke natural law to prove that there must be a unique distribution of money among countries. It cannot be altered by mercantilist policies—by limiting imports and promoting exports to bring about a surplus in the balance of payments:

Now, it is evident, that the same causes, which would correct these exorbitant inequalities, were they to happen miraculously, must prevent their happening in the common course of nature, and must for ever, in all neighbouring nations, preserve money nearly proportionable to the arts and industry [income] of each nation. All water, wherever it communicates, remains always at a level. Ask naturalists the reason; they tell you, that, were it to be raised in any one place, the superior gravity of that part... must depress it, till it meets a counterpoise....

Can one imagine, that it had ever been possible, by any laws, or even by any art or industry, to have kept all the money in Spain, which the galleons have brought from the Indies? Or that all commodities could be sold in France for a tenth of the price which they would yield on the other side of the Pyrenees, without finding their way thither [to Spain], and draining from that immense treasure? What other reason, indeed, is there, why all nations, at present, gain in their trade with Spain and Portugal; but because it is impossible to heap up money, more than any fluid, beyond its proper level.

Price effects play an important role in Hume's analysis. It can, indeed, be shown that his argument breaks down when the Marshall–Lerner–Robinson condition is not satisfied. An increase in the quantity of money, whether it is "miraculous" or comes in galleons, raises the price level. Higher prices, in turn, induce a switch in expenditure from home to foreign goods, causing a trade deficit, an outflow of money, and a return to monetary equilibrium. In some modern versions of the argument, by contrast, the increase in the quantity of money leads directly to an increase in imports, because it raises expenditure (absorption); the trade deficit develops immediately, without any observable increase in the price level.

An Echo of the Specie-Flow Doctrine

The main point made by Hume, that monetary equilibrium is preserved automatically by market forces, can be demonstrated without adopting the monetary approach to the balance of payments or invoking the quantity theory of money. The point was made in Chapter 15, when examining the effects of monetary policy under a pegged exchange rate.

Look back at Figure 15-4, which used *IS* and *LM* curves to trace the effects of an increase in the money supply produced by an open-market purchase of domestic bonds. In the absence of capital mobility, the increase in the money supply reduced the domestic interest rate and raised domestic expenditure, causing an increase in imports and a balance-of-payments deficit. With the passage of time, however, the deficit reduced the stock of reserves, which reduced the money supply. Eventually, the economy returned to its initial situation. The introduction of capital mobility speeded up the process. With perfect capital mobility, indeed, the whole increase in the money supply spilled out of the economy immediately. The open-market purchase of domestic bonds was offset completely by a capital outflow, as investors bought foreign bonds to replace the domestic bonds sold to the central bank. The central bank lost reserves equal in amount to the increase in its bond holdings, and the money supply did not change, even temporarily. Monetary policy had no influence whatsoever on the domestic economy.

These conclusions were reached by looking at events in the goods and bond markets rather than events in the money market. Furthermore, they held in a modern economy, where money is created by open-market operations, not brought in by galleons. In what follows, we adopt the monetary approach and look at the money market.

There is, of course, no "market" for money in a closed economy, and money does not have a price of its own. In an open economy, however, the foreign-exchange market can be viewed as the market for money and the exchange rate as its price. A difference between supply and demand will show up in the foreign-exchange market, affecting the exchange rate (the price of money) or reserves (the quantity of money).

DERIVING THE BASIC PROPOSITION

Although David Hume used a monetary model in the eighteenth century, proof of the basic proposition that justifies its use was not worked out until the nineteenth century. It is a special case of a general law named after Léon Walras, the French economist who built the first formal model of general equilibrium, in which all markets are interdependent.

An algebraic demonstration of Walras' law is given in Section 3 of Appendix B. This is what it says:

An economy cannot have excess demands in all its markets simultaneously. If there are excess demands in some markets, there must be excess supplies in other markets.

In an economy with markets for goods, markets for securities, and a market for money, Walras' law asserts that

> Excess demand for goods + excess demand for securities + excess demand for money = 0.

If there are positive excess demands for goods and securities, there must be a negative excess demand for money, and a negative excess demand is an excess supply.

To turn Walras' law into the basic proposition of the monetary approach, consider the economy just described, with markets for goods, securities, and money. When it has a deficit on current account, the economy is importing more goods than it is exporting, and we can say that it is meeting an excess demand for goods by drawing them from other countries. When it has a deficit on capital account, it is importing more securities than it is exporting, and we can say that it is meeting an excess demand for securities by drawing them from other countries. But when it has a deficit in its balance of payments, it has excess demands for goods and securities taken together. Therefore, it must have an excess supply of money. Rewriting the previous equation,

> Excess demand for goods + excess demand for securities = excess supply of money.

Accordingly, the loss of reserves resulting from a balance-of-payments deficit can be viewed as the way in which the economy "exports" money to remove excess supply from its money market. The causes and cure of a balance-of-payments deficit can be studied by examining events in the goods and securities markets, or by examining events in the money market.

A SIMPLE MONETARY MODEL

A simple model of the money market can be used to illustrate the monetary approach and its implications. We begin with factors affecting the demand for money, turn next to factors affecting the supply, and then introduce the three assumptions that lead to the strong conclusions drawn from the monetary model.

The Demand for Money

The demand for money may be taken to depend on the price level, real income, and the interest rate,

$$\frac{L^d}{P} = L(r, y), \tag{1}$$

where L^d is the quantity of money demanded, P is a price index, r is the domestic interest rate, and y is real income (output).[2] Multiplying both sides of the equation by the price level,

$$L^d = L(r, y)P. \tag{1a}$$

The demand for money rises with an increase in the price level and in real income, because households and firms need larger cash balances to handle larger flows of payments. The demand for money falls with an increase in the interest rate because bonds and other interest-bearing assets become more attractive when interest rates are high. Holders of money try to get along with smaller cash balances to build up their bond holdings.

The Supply of Money

The supply of money consists of currency and bank deposits. Currency is supplied by the government, represented by the central bank. Its balance sheet looks like this:

CENTRAL BANK

Assets	Liabilities
Government securities	Currency outstanding
Foreign-exchange reserves	Cash reserves of commercial banks

Banks deposits appear on the balance sheets of commercial banks, which look like this:

COMMERCIAL BANKS

Assets	Liabilities
Cash reserves at central bank	Deposits
Government securities	
Loans to public, etc.	

When these balance sheets are consolidated, cash reserves drop out, and the balance sheet for the whole banking system is:

BANKING SYSTEM

Assets	Liabilities
Domestic credit:	Money supply:
Government securities	Currency outstanding
Loans to public, etc.	Deposits
Foreign-exchange reserves	

---

[2]A different formulation is used in Chapter 18, where the demand for money is made to depend on wealth, not income, and is affected by the foreign interest rate as well as the domestic rate.

Writing this balance sheet as an equation,

Money supply = domestic credit + foreign-exchange reserves.

Using L^s for the money supply, H for domestic credit, and R for foreign-exchange reserves,

$$L^s = H + \pi R. \qquad (2)$$

As foreign-exchange reserves are measured in foreign currency, they are multiplied by the exchange rate, π, to convert them into domestic currency. (An increase in π, however, does not automatically raise L^s, although this equation seems to say so. The central bank obtains a capital gain on its foreign-exchange reserves but does not issue money to balance its books. It tucks the gain away in its capital account, an item omitted from the central bank's balance sheet shown above and from the corresponding equation.)

Three Assumptions

Three assumptions are used to draw strong conclusions from the simple monetary model we are building:

(1) There are no rigidities in domestic factor markets. The money wage rate is flexible enough to keep the real wage at its full-employment level. Therefore, real output stays at its full-employment level, and so does real income.[3]

(2) There are no barriers to capital movements, and asset holders are risk neutral. Therefore, open interest parity obtains. From equation (3) in Chapter 16,

$$r = r^* + \hat{\pi}, \qquad (3)$$

where r is the domestic interest rate, r^* is the foreign interest rate, and $\hat{\pi}$ is the expected rate of change of the spot exchange rate. Hereafter, however, we assume that asset holders have *stationary expectations* ($\hat{\pi} = 0$), so that $r = r^*$.

(3) The prices of domestic and foreign goods are linked by a strict relationship known as *purchasing-power parity* (PPP). It can be expressed algebraically by adapting the definition of the real exchange rate given in Chapter 14:

$$\bar{v}p = \pi p^*, \qquad (4)$$

---

[3]To see how flexible factor prices maintain full employment, return to Figure 9-10. The demand for labor in the cloth industry is given by the E_C curve, and the demand in the wine industry is given by the E'_W curve. Let the prices of cloth and wine be fixed by world markets (the third assumption made below). If the money wage is rigid and too high, there will be unemployment. Suppose that it is set at a level that puts the real wage at $O\bar{V}$ in terms of cloth, given the fixed price of cloth. The wine industry will demand OL'_1 labor, the cloth industry will demand $\bar{L}L_1$, and $L_1L'_1$ labor will be unemployed. If the money wage is flexible, by contrast, it will fall as soon as unemployment appears. When it reaches a level that reduces the real wage to OV^*, the wine industry will demand OL^*_1 labor and the cloth industry will demand $\bar{L}L^*_1$. There will be no unemployment.

where $\bar{v}$ is the (constant) real exchange rate, p is the price of the domestic good in domestic currency, and p^* is the price of the foreign good in foreign currency.

The third assumption plays an important role in many balance-of-payments and exchange-rate models, and we study it closely later in this chapter, examining conditions under which $\bar{v}$ is likely to be constant and considering evidence concerning its stability. Here we merely need to note what the assumption says about the prices p and p^* that enter the price index P affecting the demand for money. Let that index be a weighted average of p and πp^*, the prices of domestic and foreign goods measured in domestic currency:

$$P = \alpha p + (1 - \alpha)\pi p^*, \tag{5}$$

where α is the weight assigned to the domestic good and $1 - \alpha$ is the weight assigned to the foreign good. Using equation (4) to replace p in equation (5),

$$P = \alpha(\pi p^*/\bar{v}) + (1 - \alpha)\pi p^* = [1 + \alpha(1 - \bar{v})/\bar{v}]\pi p^* = k \cdot \pi p^*, \tag{5a}$$

where $k = 1 + \alpha(1 - \bar{v})/\bar{v}$, so k is a constant because α and $\bar{v}$ are constants. Furthermore, π is constant when the exchange rate is pegged. Therefore, the price index P depends entirely on p^*, the foreign-currency price of the foreign good. It is not affected by anything that happens in the domestic economy.

When we make all three assumptions, assume in addition that r^* and p^* are constant, and peg the exchange rate, we fix y, r, and P. Therefore, we fix the demand for money.

The Money Market and Balance of Payments

There are two ways to link money-market conditions with the balance of payments—by looking at the requirements of long-run equilibrium in the money market or by looking at the short-run effects of disequilibrium in that market. We start with the requirements of long-run equilibrium.

In long-run equilibrium, the demand for money must equal the supply. When the demand is constant, the supply must be constant. Accordingly, any increase in the money supply must reverse itself eventually, and this is accomplished by a balance-of-payments deficit. In long-run equilibrium,

$$L^d = L^s = H + \pi R. \tag{6}$$

Set the (pegged) exchange rate equal to 1 for convenience, use $\bar{L}^d$ to denote the constant demand for money that obtains when r, y, and P are constant, and rearrange equation (6):

$$R = \bar{L}^d - H. \tag{6a}$$

This relationship is shown by the line LL in Figure 17-1. The demand for money is OL initially, and it equals the supply. If the quantity of domestic credit is OH

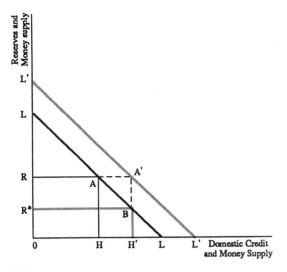

FIGURE 17-1
Long-Run Equilibrium in the Money Market
The demand for money is constant at *OL*. The supply is equal initially to the demand.
The quantity of domestic credit is *OH*, and the stock of reserves is *OR* (which equals
HL). When the quantity of domestic credit rises to *OH'*, the supply of money rises to
OL' (the increase is *LL'*, which equals *HH'*). Therefore, the economy moves first from
A to *A'*. But the supply of money exceeds the demand by *LL'*, and the economy has
thus to run a balance-of-payments deficit. It will reduce the money supply by reducing
reserves. When reserves have fallen to *OR**, the supply of money returns to *OL*, and
the economy moves to *B*. The money market is back in long-run equilibrium.

initially, the stock of reserves is given by *A* and must be *OR*. Suppose that the
banking system creates *HH'* domestic credit. If reserves do not adjust instantaneously, the economy must move temporarily to *A'* on the new line *L'L'*. The
money supply increases to *OL'*. The economy cannot stay at *A'*, however, because
there is an excess supply of money; the demand for money is still *OL*. Therefore, the
economy must move eventually to *B*, which implies that the stock of reserves must
fall to *OR**. The economy must run a balance-of-payments deficit until it has
expelled the excess supply of money.

Under the assumptions adopted here regarding income, the interest rate, and the
price level, domestic credit creation produces a balance-of-payments deficit. It is
indeed the only event that can do so. Similarly, credit contraction is the only event
that can eliminate a balance-of-payments deficit and halt a loss of reserves. The
balance of payments is a monetary phenomenon.

With perfect capital mobility, the assumption that gave us equation (3), the stock
of reserves can change instantaneously. Therefore, reserves can fall as soon as credit
creation occurs, and the economy can move directly from *A* to *B* in Figure 17-1.
Under any other circumstance, the stock of reserves changes gradually, and the
economy must go from *A* to *B* by way of *A'*. To examine this process more closely,
we investigate the short-run effects of monetary disequilibrium.

Consider a simple economy in which money is the only asset, there is no capital
formation, and the government's budget is always balanced. From equation (6) of

Chapter 12,

$$X - M = S - I + T - G = S, \tag{7}$$

because $I = 0$ when there is no capital formation and $T = G$ when the budget is balanced. When money is the only asset, moreover, there can be no bonds, and we can make two more statements.

First, there can be no capital movements, and a current-account surplus has to produce a balance-of-payments surplus,

$$\pi\dot{R} = X - M, \tag{8}$$

where $\dot{R}$ is the rate of increase in reserves and thus measures the surplus.

Second, households will not save unless they want to hold more money,

$$S = \lambda(\bar{L}^d - L^s), \tag{9}$$

where λ represents the speed of adjustment, the rate at which households save in order to close the gap between the stock of money they want to hold (the demand for money) and the stock they actually hold (the supply of money).

Putting these three equations together and setting the exchange rate at 1 for convenience,

$$\dot{R} = S = \lambda(\bar{L}^d - L^s). \tag{9a}$$

When there is an excess demand for money ($\bar{L}^d > L^s$), households save by reducing expenditure (absorption), and the current account moves into surplus; an inflow of reserves raises the quantity of money and gradually eliminates the excess demand. When there is an excess supply of money ($\bar{L}^d < L^s$), households *dis*save by raising expenditure, and the current account moves into deficit; an outflow of reserves reduces the quantity of money and gradually eliminates the excess supply.

This adjustment process is illustrated in Figure 17-2. The upper panel reproduces Figure 17-1. The money market begins in long-run equilibrium. The demand for money is constant at OL and equal initially to the supply. When the quantity of credit rises to OH', the quantity of money rises to OL' and there is excess supply. The line SS in the lower panel represents the relationship defined by equation (9a), showing how saving depends on the state of the money market. When there is no excess demand or supply in that market, there is no saving, and reserves are constant. That is the case initially. When credit creation raises the quantity of money to OL', there is LL' excess supply. Households begin to dissave at the rate OT', and reserves fall at that same rate, because dissaving is fully reflected in a balance-of-payments deficit. Therefore, the money supply declines. When reserves have fallen to OR', for example, the money supply has declined to OL'', reducing the excess supply of money to LL''. Dissaving slows down to OT'', which diminishes the rate at which reserves are falling. But the adjustment process cannot stop until the reduction of reserves has cut the money supply to OL and eliminated the excess supply completely.

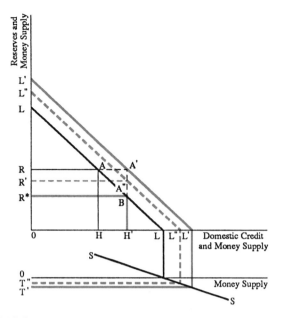

FIGURE 17-2
Adjustment in the Money Market
The demand for money is *OL* and is constant. The supply of money is equal initially to the demand but rises to *OL'* when the quantity of credit is increased from *OH* to *OH'*. The line *SS* describes the role of saving in the adjustment process. When the supply of money is *OL* and thus equal to the demand for money, saving is zero. When the supply is *OL'*, exceeding the demand by *LL'*, there is dissaving at the rate *OT'*, and reserves fall at that same rate, because dissaving is fully reflected in a balance-of-payments deficit. When the balance-of-payments deficit has reduced the stock of reserves to *OR'*, the excess supply of money is reduced to *LL"*, and dissaving falls to *OT"*, which slows down the adjustment process. But the process cannot end until reserves fall to *OR**, taking the money supply back to *OL* and taking dissaving to zero.

Stocks, Flows, and Dynamics in the Monetary Model

The adjustment process can be summarized by a simple diagram connecting the stock and flow of reserves. Using equation (2) to rewrite equation (9a),

$$\dot{R} = \lambda[\bar{L}^d - (H + R)] = \lambda(\bar{L}^d - H) - \lambda R. \tag{9b}$$

This relationship defines the *DD* curve in Figure 17-3. Its position is given by the first term of the equation, which depends on the difference between the demand for money and the quantity of domestic credit. An increase in the demand for money shifts it up; an increase in the quantity of domestic credit shifts it down. The slope of the curve is given by the second term of the equation; it says that there is an *inverse* relationship between R and $\dot{R}$, the stock of reserves and flow of reserves (the balance of payments).

The *DD* curve in Figure 17-3 is drawn to reflect the initial situation shown by Figure 17-2. When the demand for money was *OL,* the quantity of credit was *OH*, and the stock of reserves was *OR*; furthermore, there was no saving or dissaving, and

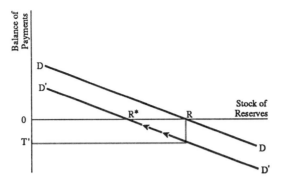

FIGURE 17-3
Credit Creation, the Balance of Payments, and Reserves
The *DD* curve describes the relationship between the stock of reserves and the balance of payments, given the demand for money and the quantity of domestic credit. In the initial situation shown before by Figure 17-2, the demand for money was *OL*, the quantity of credit was *OH*, the stock of reserves was *OR*, and there was no saving or dissaving. That situation is represented here by the *DD* curve. When reserves are *OR*, there is no balance-of-payments surplus or deficit, and reserves stay at *OR*. The increase in the quantity of credit to *OH'* shown in Figure 17-2 is represented here by shifting the stock-flow relationship downward to *D'D'*. When reserves are *OR*, the increase in the quantity of credit causes a deficit *OT'* in the balance of payments, and reserves start to fall. The economy travels along *D'D'*, following the arrows, until reserves have dropped to *OR**. The deficit is eliminated, and reserves stay at *OR**.

reserves were constant. In Figure 17-3, there is no surplus or deficit in the balance of payments when the stock of reserves is *OR*. This means that the stock will stay at *OR*. When the quantity of credit rose to *OH'* in Figure 17-2, there was dissaving, and reserves began to fall. In Figure 17-3, the *DD* curve shifts downward to *D'D'*, producing a deficit *OT'* in the balance of payments. Thereafter, the economy moves along *D'D'*, following the arrows, and the balance-of-payments deficit declines. It is not eliminated, however, until the stock of reserves falls to *OR**.

Dynamics of Devaluation

The *DD* curve in Figure 17-3 can be used to show how an exchange-rate change affects the balance of payments in the monetary model. Return to equation (1a), defining the demand for money, and use equation (5a) to replace the price index:

$$L^d = L(r, y)P = [L(r, y)k \cdot p^*]\pi. \tag{1b}$$

A devaluation of the domestic currency, raising π, also raises the price level. Therefore, it increases the demand for money. In Figure 17-4, the *DD* curve shifts upward to *D'D'*, producing a balance-of-payments surplus and inflow of reserves. But the surplus does not last forever. By raising the stock of reserves, it drives the economy along the *D'D'* curve. The surplus gets smaller and disappears completely when the stock of reserves reaches *OR**. The inflow of reserves produced by the devaluation raises the money supply, reducing the excess demand for money

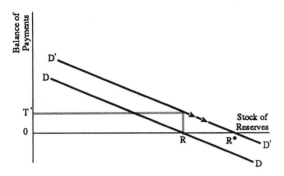

FIGURE 17-4
Devaluation in the Monetary Model
A devaluation raises the price level, increasing the demand for money. Therefore, it shifts the *DD* curve upward to *D'D'*, producing a surplus *OT'* in the balance of payments. But the surplus raises the stock of reserves, increasing the money supply, and the economy follows the arrows along *D'D'*. The surplus gets smaller as reserves get larger, and it vanishes completely when the stock of reserves reaches *OR**.

produced by the higher price level. The effects of a devaluation are temporary, although they may last a long time.

What has happened to the MLR condition? It does not seem to play a role in Figure 17-4, and some proponents of the monetary approach say it is irrelevant. They are wrong. The PPP assumption used to derive the monetary model is, in fact, a statement about the MLR condition. It amounts to saying that the real exchange rate is not affected by the volume of trade, so a country can increase its exports without reducing their relative price. In other words, the foreign demand for the country's exports is infinitely elastic, and the MLR condition is satisfied. When households save to build up their holdings of money, the goods they do not consume are sold to foreigners; the excess supply of domestic goods turns automatically into a trade surplus, and households are able to satisfy their demand for money.

A MONETARY MODEL OF EXCHANGE-RATE BEHAVIOR

The exchange rate is the price of one money in terms of another. That is a definition. But it becomes a strong prediction under the assumptions of the monetary model. The behavior of a flexible exchange rate can be explained by movements in money supplies. Those movements, moreover, depend primarily on national monetary policies, because there are no reserve movements to neutralize those policies.

Money Stocks and the Exchange Rate

When the exchange rate is pegged, an economy can satisfy an excess demand for money by running a balance-of-payments surplus; it can export excess supplies of goods and bonds to import additional money. Conversely, it can expel an excess supply of money by running a balance-of-payments deficit.

When the exchange rate is flexible, an economy cannot adjust its money supply by running a surplus or deficit. Excess supply or demand in the money market must be eliminated by adjusting the demand for money rather than the supply. Under the assumptions of the monetary model, moreover, there is just one way to adjust the demand for money, by raising or reducing the price level. And there is just one way to alter the price level, by raising or reducing the exchange rate. In the monetary model, then, the exchange rate is the price that clears the money market.

This point can be illustrated by reinterpreting the Fleming-Mundell model developed in Chapter 15. As the monetary model assumes perfect capital mobility, the domestic interest rate must always equal the foreign interest rate when, as in this chapter, exchange-rate expectations are stationary. Therefore, the domestic interest rate is fixed at Or^* in Figure 17-5. As the monetary model assumes that wages are flexible, real income stays at its full-employment level. Therefore, income is fixed at OY_0. Accordingly, the economy must stay at E_0. This means, in turn, that the LM

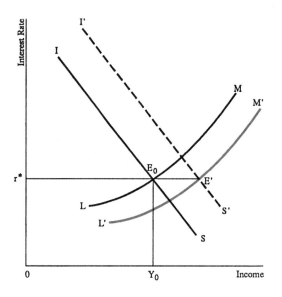

FIGURE 17-5
Comparing the Monetary and Fleming-Mundell Models
Under the assumptions of the monetary model, the domestic interest rate is fixed at Or^*, where it equals the foreign rate, and real income is fixed at OY_0. The economy cannot depart from equilibrium at E_0, even temporarily. Under a pegged exchange rate, the effects of a change in the money supply are much the same in the monetary model as in the Fleming–Mundell model. An open-market purchase shifts the LM curve to $L'M'$, but perfect capital mobility keeps it from staying there. A large capital outflow reduces reserves, offsets the effect of the open-market purchase, and snaps the LM curve back to its initial position. Under a flexible exchange rate, the two models behave differently. There is, again, a capital outflow, which causes the domestic currency to depreciate. In the Fleming–Mundell model, the real exchange rate depreciates too, shifting the IS curve to $I'S'$ and establishing a new equilibrium at E', where income is higher than it was initially. In the monetary model, PPP prevents the real exchange rate from changing. Instead, the depreciation of the domestic currency raises the price level, which raises the demand for money and snaps the LM curve back to its initial position.

curve cannot shift or, more precisely, that it must "snap back" immediately to its initial position whenever it is shifted by monetary policy.

When the exchange rate is pegged, the story told by Figure 17-5 resembles the one told by the Fleming–Mundell model. An open-market purchase of domestic bonds shifts the LM curve to $L'M'$, putting downward pressure on the domestic interest rate. This induces a large capital outflow, reduces the stock of reserves, and thus offsets the effect of the open-market purchae. It is therefore the loss of reserves that causes the LM curve to snap back to its initial position.

When the exchange rate is flexible, the story told by Figure 17-5 is quite different from the one told by the Fleming–Mundell model. It starts as before, with downward pressure on the domestic interest rate and a large capital outflow. With a flexible exchange rate, however, reserves cannot change, and the domestic currency must depreciate. In the Fleming–Mundell model, the real exchange rate moved in tandem with the nominal exchange rate, and this shifted the IS curve to $I'S'$. The new equilibrium was established at E', and the increase in the money supply raised real income. In the monetary model, PPP prevents the real exchange rate from changing when the domestic currency depreciates, and the IS curve cannot shift. There is instead an immediate increase in the price level, proportional to the depreciation, which serves two purposes. First, it keeps the real exchange rate constant. Second, it raises the demand for money by an amount equal to the increase in the supply of money provided by the open-market purchase.[4] It is therefore the increase in the domestic price level resulting from the depreciation that causes the LM curve to snap back to its initial position.

The same point can be made more generally by using a simple two-country model to show how the exchange rate responds to a change in the relative scarcity of one country's money. Note 17-1 rearranges the equations of the monetary model to make a simple statement:

$$\pi = \theta\left(\frac{L^s}{L^{*s}}\right), \tag{10}$$

where L^s is the domestic money supply, L^{*s} is the foreign money supply, and θ is a constant. The size of θ depends on domestic and foreign interest rates, r and r^*, on domestic and foreign incomes, y and y^*, and on the domestic and foreign constants k and k^* defined by equation (5a), which depend in turn on the constants α and α^* and on $\bar{v}$, the constant real exchange rate.

This equation is the fundamental statement of the monetary approach to exchange-rate theory. It is illustrated by the line OL in Figure 17-6, which has a slope equal to θ. When the ratio of money supplies is OB, the exchange rate is $O\pi$. An increase in the domestic money supply that raises the ratio to OB' will drive the exchange rate to $O\pi'$. The domestic currency will depreciate whenever domestic money becomes more plentiful relative to foreign money.

---

[4]This result can be rephrased. The increase in the price level reduces the supply of *real* money, L^s/P, until it is equal once again to the demand for *real* money given by equation (1) in the text.

Note 17-1
The Monetary Model of the Exchange Rate

Under a flexible exchange rate, $\dot{R} = 0$, so equation (9a) says that $L^s = L^d$. But equation (1b) can be used to replace L^d, so that

$$L^s = L(r, y)k \cdot \pi p^*.$$

Under the assumptions of the monetary model, however, r, y, and p^* are constant. Therefore, the exchange rate, π, is the only variable that can maintain monetary equilibrium. Represent this conclusion by solving the previous equation for π:

$$\pi = \frac{L^s}{L(r, y)k \cdot p^*}.$$

The exchange rate depends on the money supply, L^s, on r, y, and p^*, and on the constant k (which depends on the constants α and $\bar{v}$). Now write out the foreign counterpart of the first equation:

$$L^{*s} = L^*(r^*, y^*)k^* \cdot p^*,$$

where L^{*s} is the foreign money supply expressed in foreign currency, r^* is the foreign interest rate, y^* is foreign real income, and k^* is the foreign counterpart of k (defined by the weight α^* in the foreign price index and the constant $\bar{v}$ in the PPP equation). Solving this equation for p^* and using the result to replace p^* in the exchange-rate equation,

$$\pi = \left[\frac{L^*(r^*, y^*)k^*}{L(r, y)k}\right]\left(\frac{L^s}{L^{*s}}\right).$$

But the first term of this equation is constant when r, r^*, y, y^*, k, and k^* are constant, and it appears as θ in equation (10) of the text.

Testing the Monetary Model

Attempts have been made to test the hypothesis illustrated by Figure 17-6. It works fairly well for periods in which one country's money supply is rising rapidly compared to those of other countries. It does not work well otherwise. It is based on strong assumptions about incomes and interest rates, as well as the PPP assumption, and those assumptions do not stand up to experience. Real incomes are not constant. Interest rates do not always conform to open interest parity, the condition imposed by equation (3). Therefore, most tests of the monetary approach to exchange-rate theory are based on less restrictive assumptions about incomes and interest rates.

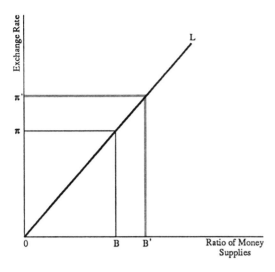

FIGURE 17-6
Exchange Rates and Money Supplies
The *OL* curve makes the fundamental statement of the monetary approach to exchange-rate theory. The value of the domestic currency depends on the supply of domestic money compared with the supply of foreign money. When the ratio of domestic to foreign money is *OB*, the exchange rate is *Oπ*. When the supply of domestic money rises, raising the ratio to *OB'*, the exchange rate rises to *Oπ'*. The domestic currency depreciates.

One such formulation is derived in Note 17-2. It can be written as

$$N(\pi) = N(L^s) - N(L^{*s}) + n[N(y^*) - N(y)] + b\delta \tag{11}$$

where $N(\pi)$ is the *logarithm* of the exchange rate, $N(L^s)$ and $N(L^{*s})$ are the logarithms of the countries' money supplies, $N(y^*)$ and $N(y)$ are the logarithms of their real incomes, b is a constant, and δ is the forward premium on the foreign currency defined in Chapter 16.

What does this equation say? It starts by saying the same thing as equation (10). The domestic currency will depreciate when the domestic money supply rises more rapidly than the foreign money supply. But it makes three more statements. The domestic currency will appreciate when domestic income rises, because an increase in y raises the demand for domestic money. The domestic currency will depreciate when foreign income rises, because an increase in y^* raises the demand for foreign money. Finally, the domestic currency will depreciate whenever investors expect it to depreciate. That is the meaning of the last term, which uses the forward premium to represent investors' expectations. (Remember that a forward premium on the foreign currency is equivalent to a forward discount on the domestic currency. When δ is positive, investors expect the domestic currency to depreciate, and they start to sell it. Their sales cause it to depreciate immediately.)

Equations like the one above have been estimated for many periods and currencies. Here is an estimate pertaining to the exchange rate between the Deutsche mark

---

Note 17-2
A Testable Version of the Monetary Model

Let the domestic demand function for money take the special form

$$L(r, y) = Ay^n e^{-br},$$

where A, n, and b are constants and e is the base of the system of natural logarithms. Let the foreign demand function be identical. Finally, let domestic and foreign consumers have identical tastes, so that $\alpha = \alpha^*$, and $k = k^*$. Under these assumptions, θ in equation (10) becomes

$$\theta = \frac{Ay^{*n}e^{-br^*}}{Ay^n e^{-br}} = \left(\frac{y^*}{y}\right)^n e^{b(r-r^*)}.$$

According to equation (3), however, the interest-rate difference must equal $\hat{\pi}$, the expected rate of change of the exchange rate. Furthermore, $\hat{\pi}$ must equal δ, the forward premium on the foreign currency, when investors are risk neutral, as in the monetary model. Therefore,

$$\theta = \left(\frac{y^*}{y}\right)^n e^{b\delta}.$$

Substituting this expression into equation (10) and taking logarithms, we obtain equation (11). Its assumptions about demand functions are more restrictive than those of equation (10). Its assumptions about real incomes and interest rates are less restrictive.

---

and pound sterling:[5]

$$N(\pi) = 4.454 + 0.418\,N(L^s) - 0.915\,N(L^{*s}) - 0.171\,N(y^*) - 0.208\,N(y) + 0.0015\,\delta.$$

This test is not very successful. The coefficients for the two money supplies have the expected signs; an increase in the German money supply, L^s, causes the Deutsche mark to depreciate vis-à-vis the pound; an increase in the British money supply, L^{*s}, causes the Deutsche mark to appreciate. But the coefficient for the German money supply is much smaller than 1, the value predicted by equation (11); in fact, it is not significantly different from zero. The coefficient for British income, y^*, is negative, whereas equation (11) says that it should be positive. And, although the coefficient for δ has the expected positive sign, it is very small. The author of this particular study concludes that his equation does not validate the monetary model represented by equation (11). Other authors come to similar conclusions.

---

[5]John F. O. Bilson, "Rational Expectations and the Exchange Rate," in J. A. Frenkel and H. G. Johnson, eds., *The Economics of Exchange Rates* (Reading, Mass.: Addison-Wesley, 1978), p. 88.

PURCHASING-POWER PARITY

Although equation (11) relaxes one assumption adopted earlier in this chapter, allowing y and y^* to change, it relies on two other assumptions. The use of the forward premium, δ, to represent investors' expectations is based on the assumption that investors are risk neutral. Furthermore, the derivation of equation (11) depends strongly on the assumption that domestic and foreign prices are tightly linked by purchasing-power parity.

The PPP doctrine is quite old. Its modern version is ascribed to a Swedish economist, Gustav Cassel, who was trying to define equilibrium exchange rates after World War I. According to Cassel, the exchange rate between two currencies is in equilibrium only when those currencies can buy the same bundles of goods and services:[6]

> The purchasing power parities represent the true equilibrium of the exchanges, and it is of great practical value to know those parities. It is in fact to them we have to refer when we wish to get an idea of the real value of currencies whose exchanges are subject to arbitrary and sometimes wild fluctuations.

Note that Cassel was concerned with the use of PPP to choose or appraise exchange rates. Other economists treat it differently. They use it to predict exchange-rate behavior.

In this chapter, for example, PPP was introduced by equation (4). It was used to restrict the behavior of the price index P, which was used in turn to determine the demand for money. Therefore, PPP was used implicitly to explain the behavior of the supply of money under a pegged exchange rate and thus the behavior of the balance of payments; furthermore, it was used implicitly to explain the behavior of the demand for money under a floating exchange rate and thus the behavior of the exchange rate itself.

The monetary approach depends on the validity of the PPP doctrine, but the doctrine does not depend on the validity of the monetary approach. In fact, it is invoked by many economists who have reservations about the monetary approach, which is another reason for looking at it carefully.

Two propositions are employed to justify the expectation that exchange rates will conform to PPP. The first is the *law of one price*. The second has to do with the *neutrality of money*.

The Law of One Price and PPP

When used by itself, the law of one price is a statement about markets for a single product. It says that the price of the product must be the same in all its markets, after allowing for transport costs and tariffs. This assertion is sensible enough, and we have been using it all along.

---

[6]Gustav Cassel, *The World's Monetary Problems* (London: Constable, 1921), p. 28; quoted in Jacob A. Frenkel, "Purchasing Power Parity: Doctrinal Perspective and Evidence from the 1920s," *Journal of International Economics*, 8 (May 1978), p. 171.

Table 17-1. Changes in German and U.S. Prices for Selected Product Groups, 1968 to 1975

Product Group	Percentage Change in Ratio of German to U.S. Price
Apparel	64.3
Industrial chemicals	7.2
Agricultural chemicals	16.1
Plastic materials	13.4
Paper products	19.8
Metalworking machinery	69.2
Electrical industrial equipment	59.7
Home electronic equipment	77.5
Glass products	27.5

Source: Adapted from Peter Isard, "How Far Can We Push the 'Law of One Price'?" *American Economic Review,* 67 (December 1977), Table 1. German prices are converted into dollars for comparison with U.S. prices.

When used to support the PPP doctrine, however, the law of one price is extended *across* products. It is made to say that the price *level* in one country will always equal the price level in another. This extension is not strictly valid. There are two objections to it.

First, the products whose prices define the price level may not be identical from country to country. Even products that seem similar are frequently different, which means that their prices will be different too. This point is illustrated by Table 17-1, which shows price movements for similar products in Germany and the United States. If the law of one price held within each product group, the two countries' prices would move together. In fact, they move quite differently, which says that the products in each group may not be identical in the two countries.

Second, the products that define price levels may be weighted differently from country to country, and differences in weights can drive a wedge between price levels even when the law of one price holds for each product individually. This point is illustrated by Note 17-3, which shows that a change in relative prices can change the relationship between price levels when national price indexes use different weights.

In brief, the law of one price properly applied does not validate PPP. The law breaks when it is stretched.

The Neutrality of Money and PPP

What do we mean by the neutrality of money, and what does it do for the PPP doctrine?

Suppose that the quantity of money doubles overnight but all prices and incomes double, too, along with all assets and debts. No one will be better or worse off. No one will have more purchasing power. Therefore, there will be no changes in behavior and no change in any *real* magnitude. That is what is meant by the

---

Note 17-3
Consumer Preferences and Purchasing-Power Parity

The domestic price index, P, was defined by equation (5a). It can be rewritten as

$$P = \left(\frac{1}{\bar{v}}\right)[\bar{v} + \alpha(1 - \bar{v})]\pi p^*.$$

The foreign price index, P^*, can be defined in the same way:

$$P^* = \left(\frac{1}{\bar{v}}\right)[\bar{v} + \alpha^*(1 - \bar{v})]p^*.$$

Multiplying P^* by π to convert it into its domestic-currency equivalent and dividing it into P,

$$\left(\frac{P}{\pi P^*}\right) = \frac{\bar{v} + \alpha(1 - \bar{v})}{\bar{v} + \alpha^*(1 - \bar{v})}.$$

If the weights α and α^* are the same, a change in the real exchange rate, $\bar{v}$, cannot change the ratio of price indexes. (This would be the case if P and P^* were indexes of consumer prices and the countries' consumers purchased identical baskets of goods.) If the weights are different, however, a change in $\bar{v}$ will drive a wedge between the price indexes.

---

neutrality of money. It says that economic actors cannot be fooled by a purely numerical exercise.

Now transfer this example to an open economy. Let nominal (money) magnitudes double in one country but stay the same in the rest of the world. If the exchange rate does not change, domestic purchasing power will double in terms of foreign goods, even though it does not change in terms of domestic goods. If the exchange rate also doubles, however, domestic purchasing power will not change in terms of foreign or domestic goods. When money is neutral, PPP holds.

This illustration shows clearly the limited applicability of PPP. When a doubling of all prices is associated with a doubling of all other nominal magnitudes, a doubling of the exchange rate will neutralize it. If all other nominal magnitudes do not change, however, a doubling of prices will have real effects on the domestic economy, and a doubling of the exchange rate will not neutralize it. There is another problem. The doubling of money and prices must take place without lags and must be accompanied by an immediate doubling of all assets and debts. These things do not happen. Therefore, a careful economist will say that money is neutral in the long run, which means that PPP can hold only in the long run. In other words, PPP can be used to define the long-run response of the exchange rate to a purely monetary shock but not to describe actual exchange-rate behavior.

Table 17-2. PPP Equations for U.S. Dollar
Exchange Rates in the 1920s and 1970s

Currency	a	b
1921–1925		
French franc	−1.183	1.091
Pound sterling	−1.118	0.897
1973–1979		
French franc	−1.521	0.184
Pound sterling	0.712	0.165
Deutsche mark	−0.900	1.786

Source: Adapted from Jacob A. Frenkel, "The Collapse
of Purchasing Power Parities during the 1970s," *European Economic Review*, 16 (May 1981), Tables 1 and 2.
The equations use wholesale prices for the United States
and the other country involved in each comparison.

Some Evidence

Most economists are careful, but many look for short cuts. Therefore, PPP
is frequently used as a rule of thumb, even by those who know that it has serious
limitations. Recent evidence, however, calls this practice into question. It says that
PPP can mislead us badly.

Let us solve equation (4) for the exchange rate and put the solution into
logarithmic form:

$$N(\pi) = N(\bar{v}) + [N(p) - N(p^*)]. \tag{3a}$$

The validity of the PPP doctrine can therefore be tested by making statistical
estimates of the equation

$$N(\pi) = a + b[N(p) - N(p^*)]$$

where *a* represents $N(\bar{v})$ and *b* should be approximately equal to 1 when the PPP
doctrine holds.

Five such estimates are shown in Table 17-2, two for the 1920s and three for the
1970s. The estimates of *b* for the 1920s conform rather well to the PPP doctrine.
Those for the 1970s do not; two are quite low and the third is quite high. The author
of these estimates used to assume PPP in most of his own theoretical work. He built
models similar to those in this chapter. His empirical research, however, has led him
to conclude that purchasing-power parity collapsed in the 1970s.

SUMMARY

The monetary approach to the balance of payments can be traced back to
David Hume, who argued that surpluses and deficits are self-correcting, because of

their effects on the money supply. The modern version is an application of Walras' law, which says that excess demands and supplies must sum to zero. Applied to an open economy, it says that a country with a balance-of-payments deficit can be regarded as having excess demands in its goods and bond markets taken together, and must therefore have excess supply in its money market. It "exports" the excess supply of money to satisfy the excess demands for goods and bonds.

Monetary models of the balance of payments are usually based on three assumptions. (1) There are no rigidities in factor markets, so output (income) stays at its full-employment level. (2) There is perfect capital mobility, so the domestic interest rate is tied tightly to the foreign rate. (3) Domestic and foreign prices are held together by purchasing-power parity, so the domestic price level is fixed when the exchange rate is pegged.

Under these assumptions, the demand for money is constant, and changes in the supply of money are reflected directly in the balance of payments. An increase in the quantity of domestic credit spills out as a balance-of-payments deficit. But a deficit reduces the money supply and is therefore self-correcting. Some monetary models focus on the requirements of long-run equilibrium in the money market. They show that there must be an inverse relationship between the quantity of domestic credit and the stock of reserves. Other models focus on adjustment to short-run disequilibria. They show that an increase in the quantity of credit stimulates expenditure, producing excess demand in the goods market, a current-account deficit, and a loss of reserves.

Monetary models of the balance of payments have been adapted to explain the behavior of a flexible exchange rate. When there is no intervention in the foreign-exchange market, reserves cannot change, and the supply of money is determined by the quantity of domestic credit. The demand for money depends on the exchange rate, however, because it affects the price level. An increase in the quantity of credit adds to the money supply, causes the domestic currency to depreciate, and thus raises the price level. The resulting increase in the demand for money restores equilibrium in the money market.

Monetary models depend too heavily on restrictive assumptions. The purchasing-power parity doctrine plays a central role in those models, and there are strong reasons for doubting its validity. The PPP doctrine cannot be derived from the law of one price, which holds only across markets for a single good. It can be derived from the supposition that money is neutral, but this means that it can hold only to the long run and only with regard to monetary shocks. PPP should not be used to predict actual exchange-rate behavior, even as a crude rule of thumb.

RECOMMENDED READINGS

The best brief introduction to the monetary approach is provided in Jacob A. Frenkel and Harry G. Johnson, "The Monetary Approach to the Balance of Payments: Essential Concepts and Historical Origins," in J. A. Frenkel and H. G. Johnson, eds., *The Monetary Approach to the Balance of Payments* (Toronto: University of Toronto Press, 1976), ch. 1. The simple monetary model used in this chapter is adapted from Rudiger Dornbusch, "Devaluation, Hoarding, and Relative Prices," *Journal of Political Economy*, 81 (July 1973).

For a comparison of the monetary approach with others, see Harry G. Johnson, "Elasticity, Absorption, Keynesian Multiplier, Keynesian Policy, and Monetary Approaches to Devaluation Theory: A Simple Geometric Exposition," *American Economic Review*, 66 (June 1976).

On the monetary approach to exchange-rate theory, see Rudiger Dornbusch, "The Theory of Flexible Exchange Rate Regimes and Macroeconomic Policy," and John F. O. Bilson, "Rational Expectations and the Exchange Rate," in J. A. Frenkel and H. G. Johnson, eds., *The Economics of Exchange Rates* (Reading, Mass.: Addison-Wesley, 1978), chs. 2 and 5. For a critical review of the literature, see James M. Boughton, *The Monetary Approach to Exchange Rates: What Now Remains?*, Essays in International Finance 171 (Princeton, N.J.: International Finance Section, Princeton University, 1988).

The evolution of thinking about PPP can be traced by comparing two papers by Jacob A. Frenkel; look first at "Purchasing Power Parity: Doctrinal Perspective and Evidence from the 1920s," *Journal of International Economics*, 8 (May 1978), and then at "The Collapse of Purchasing Power Parities During the 1970s," *European Economic Review*, 16 (May 1981).

Most economists have strong doubts about the validity of PPP, but some continue to follow Cassel and use it to define equilibrium exchange rates; see Ronald I. McKinnon, "Monetary and Exchange Rate Policies for International Financial Stability, *Journal of Economic Perspectives*, 1 (Winter 1988).

QUESTIONS AND PROBLEMS

(1) Using a monetary model of a small economy with a pegged exchange rate, show how a reduction in the quantity of domestic credit affects the balance of payments in the short run and the stock of reserves in the long run. Is there any change in the domestic price level?

(2) How would your answer to (1) be affected if the same economy had a flexible exchange rate?

(3) How would your answer to (1) be affected if the economy were large enough to affect the outside world? Do not try to solve the problem formally, but ask what would happen to the money supply in the outside world and to price levels at home and in the outside world. Would the long-run change in reserves be larger or smaller than in the small-country case, relative to the size of the economy?

(4) Using a monetary model of a small economy with a pegged exchange rate, show how a revaluation of the domestic currency affects the balance of payments and the stock of reserves. Describe the adjustment process that leads to these results. Is there any change in the domestic price level?

(5) Use your answer to (4) to explain why a devaluation or revaluation of the domestic currency cannot affect the positions of the *IS* and *LM* curves under the assumptions of the monetary model.

(6) Note 17-2 assumed that the domestic and foreign demand functions for money were identical. Suppose that the foreign demand function takes the form

$$L^*(r^*, y^*) = A^* y^{*n^*} e^{-br^*},$$

where the constants A^* and n^* are different from their domestic counterparts. How would you rewrite equation (11) in the text?

18

Asset Markets, Exchange Rates, and Economic Policy

INTRODUCTION

The monetary model in Chapter 17 drew attention to important propositions. It reminded us that markets are interdependent, that an excess demand for goods and bonds must be matched by an excess supply of money. It stressed the role of the exchange-rate regime in determining how an open economy maintains monetary equilibrium. It showed why we must distinguish between the short- and long-run effects of policy changes. We saw that a devaluation led at once to a balance-of-payments surplus, but that it did not last; by raising reserves and the money supply, it raised absorption and reduced the balance-of-payments surplus.

But the framework of the monetary model is too restrictive. Factor prices are perfectly flexible, leaving output constant at its full-employment level, and this assumption keeps real income constant. Domestic and foreign prices are tied together by purchasing-power parity. Investors are risk neutral, so open interest parity obtains when there are no obstacles to capital movements. To focus our attention on the money market, the monetary model drastically simplifies behavior in the labor, product, and bond markets.

This chapter presents a model richer than the monetary model. Output does not always stay at its full-employment level; the price level does not depend exclusively on the exchange rate; the domestic interest rate is not tightly tied to the foreign rate.

A PORTFOLIO-BALANCE MODEL

The new model synthesizes much of our earlier work. It borrows its treatment of wage rates, employment, and output from the simple Ricardian model in Chapter 3. It borrows its treatment of income and price effects from Chapters 13 and 14. It borrows its treatment of capital flows from Chapter 16, where risk-averse investors held domestic and foreign bonds, and it takes its name from this characteristic. Because investors hold diversified portfolios, the model itself is described as a *portfolio-balance model*.

The new model follows the monetary model in distinguishing sharply between the short run and long run. The short run is defined as a period too short for flows to have any influence on stocks. The long run is defined as a period long enough for the economy to reach a *stationary state*, where all *stocks* are constant because the flows affecting them have ceased. The same definitions were used implicitly in Chapter 17. In Figure 17-4, for example, the short run was a period too short for the balance-of-payments surplus to drive reserves away from OR, their initial level. The long run was a period long enough for the balance-of-payments surplus to raise reserves to OR^*, at which they were stationary because the balance-of-payments surplus had disappeared.

But this chapter stresses a different stock-flow relationship. It is the link between the stock of wealth and the flow of saving. The economy reaches a stationary state when wealth becomes constant. This happens when there is no more saving or dissaving.

Although the model synthesizes much of our earlier work, it is still too simple to be realistic. There is no capital formation (investment). The government balances its budget at all times. Interest payments are ignored in the definitions of income, government budget, and current-account balance. The demand for money depends on interest rates and wealth but not on income. Expectations are stationary. And the economy under study is too small to influence incomes, prices, and interest rates in the outside world.

Prices and Production

The economy specializes completely in a single good and has Ricardian characteristics. Labor requirements are fixed, so that employment, N, depends on output, Q:

$$N = a \cdot Q, \tag{1}$$

where a is the fixed labor requirement per unit of output. The price of the domestic good depends on the labor requirement and wage rate:

$$p_1 = a \cdot w, \tag{2}$$

where p_1 is the price of the good and w is the wage rate. In a one-product economy, moreover, national income is the value of that product:

$$Y = p_1 \cdot Q, \tag{3}$$

where Y is national income measured in domestic currency.

These equations can be given two interpretations: When the wage rate is fixed, equation (2) fixes the price of the domestic good, and an increase in national income raises output and employment. When employment is fixed, equation (1) fixes output, and an increase in national income raises the price of the domestic good and the wage rate.

These two interpretations are illustrated in Figure 18-1. The curve HH describes the relationship between the wage rate and employment at a particular level of income.[1] If the wage rate is Ow, employment will be ON. Let this be the full-employment level. Next, let national income fall, displacing HH to $H'H'$. If the wage rate is fixed at Ow, employment falls to ON'. If employment is fixed at ON, the wage rate falls to Ow'.

In the rest of this chapter, then, we can concentrate on the behavior of national income measured in domestic currency. Whenever it rises in response to a disturbance or policy change, we can interpret the increase in either of two ways. We can assume that the wage rate is rigid, in which case output rises and the price of the domestic good does not change. Alternatively, we can assume that the wage rate is flexible, in which case the price of the domestic good rises and output does not change. These two possibilities can be combined in a single equation connecting the change in the price of the domestic good with the change in national income:

$$\frac{dp_1}{p_1} = u\left(\frac{dY}{Y}\right). \tag{4}$$

When the wage rate is rigid, $u = 0$ and p_1 does not change. When the wage rate is flexible, $u = 1$, and the change in p_1 is proportional to the change in Y.

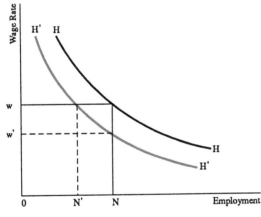

FIGURE 18-1
The Wage Rate and Employment
The HH curve describes the relationship between the wage rate and employment at a particular level of national income. When the wage rate is Ow, employment is ON. The effects of a change in national income depend on the behavior of the wage rate. A fall in income displaces HH to $H'H'$. If the wage rate is fixed, employment falls to ON'. If the wage rate is flexible, employment stays at ON, and the wage falls to Ow'.

---

[1]The HH curve is a *rectangular hyperbola*; all rectangles inscribed beneath it have areas equal to wN, which equals Y. A decrease in national income is represented by an inward shift, such as the shift from HH to $H'H'$. The areas of rectangles beneath $H'H'$ are equal to the new, lower level of national income.

Consumption, Saving, and the Current Account

Labor is the only factor of production in this model, and households supply labor. Therefore, households earn the whole national income. They use it for consumption, tax payments, and saving:

$$Y = C + T + S, \tag{5}$$

where C, T, and S are defined in the usual way and are measured in domestic currency. Households divide their consumption between the domestic good and an imported good:

$$C = p_1 c_1 + p_2 c_2, \tag{6}$$

where p_1 and p_2 are the prices of those goods measured in domestic currency, while c_1 and c_2 are the quantities consumed. The behavior of p_1 was described by equation (4). The behavior of p_2 is described by

$$p_2 = \pi p_2^*, \tag{7}$$

where π is the exchange rate and p_2^* is the price of the foreign good measured in foreign currency. Unless otherwise indicated, p_2^* is fixed because the economy studied here is too small to affect it.

Households are one source of demand for the domestic good. There are two others. Foreigners buy c_1^*, and the government buys c_1^q. The total demand must equal the supply:

$$c_1 + c_1^* + c_1^q = Q. \tag{8}$$

Multiplying both sides of equation (8) by p_1 and using equation (3),

$$p_1 c_1 + p_1 c_1^* + p_1 c_1^q = p_1 Q = Y. \tag{8a}$$

But $p_1 c_1^*$ is X, the value of exports, and $p_1 c_1^q$ is G, the value of government spending (the government does not buy the foreign good). Furthermore, equation (6) says that $p_1 c_1 = C - p_2 c_2$, and $p_2 c_2$ is M, the value of imports. Therefore, equation (8a) becomes

$$C + X + G = Y + M, \tag{8b}$$

which is the familiar national-income equation. (There is no investment in it because there is none in the model.)

Finally, use equation (5) to replace Y in equation (8b), and set $G = T$, because the government balances its budget:

$$X - M = S. \tag{9}$$

This equation is equally familiar. It says that a current-account surplus must be matched by saving and a current-account deficit by dissaving. It is especially important here because of the role played by saving.

Saving and Wealth

In earlier chapters, saving depended on income. Here, it depends on disposable income (the difference between Y and T) and on interest rates and wealth:

$$S = S(Y - T, r, r^*, W), \qquad (10)$$

where r and r^* are the interest rates on domestic and foreign bonds, and W is household wealth in domestic currency.

An increase in disposable income raises saving. Increases in interest rates do so, too, because they strengthen the incentive to save. An increase in wealth reduces saving, because it weakens the incentive to accumulate more wealth, and this gives us the basic dynamic relationship that drives the whole economy.

This basic relationship is illustrated by Figure 18-2, which deals with the simplest case in which disposable income is constant during the adjustment process. (In most cases studied later, disposable income changes, permanently or temporarily, depending on the nature of the disturbance and on the exchange-rate regime.) The SY curve shows what households want to save at each income level; its slope is the marginal propensity to save out of disposable income. The position of the curve depends on interest rates and wealth. Let disposable income be OY so that saving is OS. Equation (9) says that the economy must have a current-account surplus. But saving adds to wealth, making the SY curve shift downward gradually. There is less and less saving at each income level. Eventually, the curve must drop to $S'Y'$, and saving ceases altogether if income remains at OY. At this juncture, moreover, the current account must be balanced.

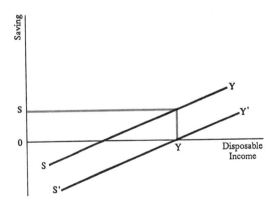

FIGURE 18-2
Saving and Income
The SY curve shows the relationship between saving and disposable income, given the interest rates and wealth. When disposable income is OY, saving is OS. But saving adds to wealth, and an increase in wealth reduces the incentive to save. The SY curve shifts downward gradually. When it falls to $S'Y'$, saving ceases, and wealth remains constant thereafter.

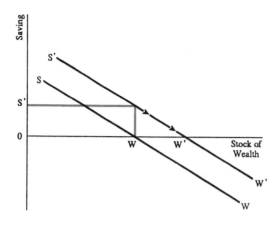

FIGURE 18-3
Saving and Wealth
The curve *SM* shows the relationship between saving and the stock of wealth, given the interest rates and disposable income. When wealth is *OW*, saving is zero. An increase in disposable income shifts the curve to *S'W'*, so saving rises to *OS'* when wealth is *OW*. The economy travels along *S'W'*, following the arrows, until wealth rises to *OW'* and saving goes to zero.

The relationship between saving and wealth resembles the relationship between the balance of payments and stock of reserves in the monetary model, and it can be drawn in a similar manner. In Figure 18-3, the curve *SW* describes the relationship between saving and wealth when interest rates and disposable income are constant. Let wealth be *OW* to start so that there is no saving and the current account is balanced. In other words, the economy begins in a stationary state. Suppose that there is an increase in the domestic interest rate. The curve is displaced to *S'W'*, households start to save, and the current account moves into surplus. As saving adds to wealth, however, the economy travels along *S'W'*, following the arrows, until wealth reaches *OW'*, where saving ceases, the current account is balanced, and wealth is stabilized.

Equilibrium in the Goods Market

All the relationships described thus far can be combined in a single diagram to depict equilibrium in the goods market. In Figure 18-4, income is measured on the vertical axis and the exchange rate is measured on the horizontal axis. The *zz* and *ZZ* curves identify goods-market equilibria.

The *zz* curve pertains to short-run equilibria. It shows how a change in the exchange rate affects national income before wealth has had time to change in response to the saving or dissaving that occurs when the economy departs from its stationary state. By implication, the stock of wealth is the same at all points on the *zz* curve, but saving and the current-account balance vary from point to point. The *zz* curve is upward sloping whenever the MLR condition is satisfied; a devaluation or depreciation of the domestic currency raises national income by switching domestic and foreign demands to the domestic good. When the exchange rate is $O\pi_0$, national income is OY_0. When the exchange rate is $O\pi_1$, national income is OY_1.

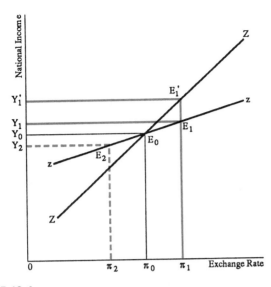

FIGURE 18-4
Equilibrium in the Goods Market
At points on the *zz* curve, the economy is in short-run equilibrium. The stock of wealth is the same at all points on the curve, but saving and the current-account balance vary from point to point. At points on the *ZZ* curve, the economy is in long-run equilibrium. The stock of wealth differs from point to point, but it is constant at each point, because the current account is balanced and saving is zero. The *zz* curve is upward sloping because a devaluation or depreciation of the domestic currency improves the current account and raises income. The *ZZ* curve is upward sloping and steeper than the *zz* curve because it shows the increase in income required to balance the current account at the new exchange rate. When the exchange rate is $O\pi_0$, the economy is at E_0, where *zz* and *ZZ* intersect; income is OY_0, the current account is balanced, and saving is zero. When the exchange rate is $O\pi_1$, the economy is at E_1 in the short run, where income is OY_1, the current account is in surplus, and saving is positive; it must go to E_1' in the long run, however, where income is OY_1', the current account is balanced again, and saving has gone back to zero.

The position of the *zz* curve depends on foreign spending and the foreign-currency price of the foreign good. An increase in either one of them shifts the curve upward by raising demand for the domestic good and thus raising national income at each exchange rate. Its position also depends on interest rates and wealth, because they affect saving. An increase in an interest rate shifts *zz* downward; by enhancing the incentive to save, it reduces absorption (consumption), which reduces income. An increase in wealth shifts *zz* upward; by weakening the incentive to save, it raises absorption, which raises income. All these propositions are proved algebraically in Section 4 of Appendix B.

The *ZZ* curve pertains to long-run equilibria. It shows what must happen to national income, given the exchange rate, to keep the economy in a stationary state, where the current account is balanced, saving is zero, and wealth is constant. By implication, the stock of wealth is constant at each point on the *ZZ* curve but not the same from point to point; it must rise with income to keep saving at zero. Whenever the MLR condition is satisfied, the *ZZ* curve is upward sloping, but we must interpret this statement differently than in the case of the *zz* curve.

Suppose that the economy starts at E_0, where zz and ZZ intersect. Because E_0 lies on ZZ, the current account is balanced, there is no saving, and wealth is constant. Change the exchange rate from $O\pi_0$ to $O\pi_1$, but hold wealth constant temporarily. The economy must move along zz to E_1, the new short-run equilibrium point, and income must rise to OY_1. But part of any increase in income is saved in the short run, which means that the current account is in surplus. The ZZ curve tells us what must happen in the long run when the exchange rate remains at $O\pi_1$. The economy must move to E'_1, the new long-run equilibrium point, where income must rise to OY'_1 in order to raise imports by enough to balance the current account. Wealth must rise with income as the economy moves along ZZ to E'_1, because saving must fall back to zero. If wealth did not rise with income in the long run, the current account would go to zero but saving would increase, and that is impossible. Later we will represent this increase in wealth by shifting the zz curve upward to intersect ZZ at E'_1.)

The position of the ZZ curve depends on some of the same variables that determine the position of the zz curve. We can describe their influence in terms of their effects on the current-account balance and, therefore, the long-run change in income required to bring that balance back to zero. An increase in foreign spending or the foreign-currency price of the foreign good produces a current-account surplus. Therefore, it shifts the ZZ curve upward, showing the increase in income needed to eliminate the surplus. The position of the curve, however, does not depend on interest rates or wealth. The current account is balanced all along the ZZ curve, so saving must be zero. Therefore, the position of the curve cannot be affected by changes in saving induced by changes in interest rates or wealth.

Summing up, the zz curve shows the short-run change in income produced by the expenditure-switching effects of an exchange-rate change. At points such as E_1, below the ZZ curve, there is saving and a current-account surplus. At points such as E_2, above the ZZ curve, there is dissaving and a current-account deficit. The ZZ curve shows the long-run change in income required to balance the current account at each exchange rate, eliminate saving or dissaving, and thus bring the economy back to a stationary state.

Wealth and Demands for Assets

Households hold three assets in this model: money, a domestic bond, and a foreign bond denominated in foreign currency. Formally,

$$W = L^h + B^h + \pi F^h, \tag{11}$$

where L^h is the quantity of money held by households, B^h is the quantity of domestic bonds, and F^h is the quantity of foreign bonds.

The demands for the three assets depend on interest rates and wealth. We can write them this way:

$$L^h = L(r, r^*, W) \tag{12}$$

$$B^h = B(r, r^*, W) \tag{13}$$

$$\pi F^h = F(r, r^*, W) \tag{14}$$

These equations look alike but are very different. An increase in the domestic interest rate raises the demand for the domestic bond but reduces the demands for money and the foreign bond. An increase in the foreign interest rate raises the demand for the foreign bond but reduces the demands for money and the domestic bond. An increase in wealth raises the demand for each asset but need not do so uniformly.

One of the three demand equations is redundant. When we know the level of wealth and the demands for two of the assets, we know the demand for the third. In this chapter, moreover, the foreign interest rate is fixed, which makes it most convenient to omit the demand equation for the foreign bond and to concentrate on the characteristics of the markets for money and the domestic bond.

Households are the only holders of money (there are no firms), and the central bank is the only supplier of money (there are no commercial banks). The supply of money, L, is given by

$$L = B^c + \pi R, \tag{15}$$

where B^c is the quantity of domestic bonds held by the central bank and R is the quantity of foreign-exchange reserves measured in foreign currency. An increase in B^c represents an open-market purchase designed to raise the money supply. An increase in R represents intervention in the foreign-exchange market (a purchase of foreign currency) designed to prevent the domestic currency from appreciating. The demand for money must equal the supply, so

$$L(r, r^*, W) - (B^c + \pi R) = 0. \tag{16}$$

There are two holders of the domestic bond: households and the central bank. The supply of bonds is fixed, because the government balances its budget. Therefore, demand will equal supply in the bond market when

$$B(r, r^*, W) + B^c - B = 0, \tag{17}$$

where B is the fixed supply.

Wealth and the Exchange Rate

We need one more relationship to complete this model. It is the relationship between wealth and the exchange rate. The stock of wealth is affected gradually by saving. It is affected immediately by a change in the exchange rate. Part of wealth is invested in the foreign bond, which is denominated in foreign currency. Therefore, a depreciation or devaluation of the domestic currency raises wealth instantaneously by conferring a capital gain on holders of the foreign bond. It raises the value of that bond in terms of domestic currency.

This relationship can be expressed algebraically, but a picture is more helpful. In Figure 18-5, the economy begins in long-run equilibrium. The stock of wealth is constant at OW_0. At time $t = t_1$, the domestic currency is devalued. Domestic holders of the foreign bond obtain a capital gain, and wealth jumps abruptly. The size of the jump increases with the size of the devaluation and with the fraction of wealth

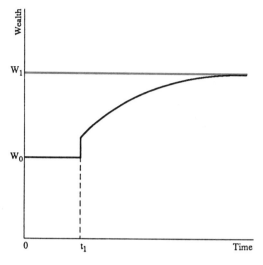

FIGURE 18-5
Wealth and the Exchange Rate
From time $t = 0$ to time $t = t_1$, the economy is in long-run equilibrium. Wealth is constant at OW_0. At time $t = t_1$, the domestic currency is devalued. Holders of the foreign bond obtain a capital gain, so wealth rises immediately. If the devaluation produces a current-account surplus, wealth will rise gradually thereafter, due to the saving that accompanies a current-account surplus. But the subsequent increase in wealth reduces saving, which slows down the increase in wealth. Eventually, wealth becomes constant at OW_1, the new long-run level.

invested in the foreign bond. If the devaluation produces a current-account surplus, wealth will grow gradually thereafter, because of the saving that accompanies a current-account surplus. But the resulting increase in wealth reduces saving, which slows down the growth of wealth itself. Eventually, the economy reaches a long-run equilibrium in which the stock of wealth is OW_1.[2]

Equilibrium in the Asset Markets

A single diagram can depict equilibrium in the money and bond markets. In Figure 18-6, the interest rate is shown on the vertical axis and wealth is shown in the horizontal axis. The LL and BB curves identify asset-market equilibria.

Points on the LL curve are those at which the money market is in equilibrium, given the supply of money. The curve is upward sloping because an increase in wealth raises the demand for money and calls for an increase in the interest rate to reduce demand and clear the money market. (There is excess supply in the money market above LL and excess demand below it.) The position of the curve depends on the supply of money. An increase in supply shifts the curve downward, because the demand for money must rise to absorb the additional supply, so the interest rate must fall at each level of wealth. By implication, the LL curve shifts downward in response to an open-market purchase or an increase in foreign-exchange reserves.

---

[2]This last statement is not quite accurate. Wealth *approaches* OW_1 but does not actually reach it. In mathematical terms, long-run equilibrium is a state to which the economy converges *asymptotically*. It is a never-never land, because it does not exist in finite time.

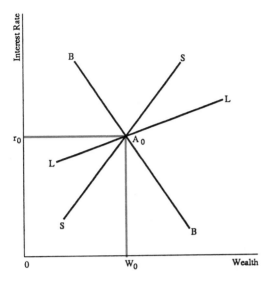

FIGURE 18-6
Equilibrium in the Asset Markets
At points on the *LL* curve, the money market is in equilibrium. The curve is upward sloping because an increase in wealth raises the demand for money and calls for an increase in the interest rate to maintain money-market equilibrium. At points on the *BB* curve, the bond market is in equilibrium. The curve is downward sloping because an increase in wealth raises the demand for domestic bonds and calls for a decrease in the interest rate to maintain bond-market equilibrium. As both markets must be in equilibrium continuously and this can happen only at point A_0, the interest rate must be Or_0 and wealth must be OW_0. At points on the *SS* curve, saving is zero and the economy is in long-run equilibrium. This curve is upward sloping because an increase in wealth would induce dissaving and an increase in the interest rate would be needed to keep saving at zero. The *SS* curve shifts downward with an increase in disposable income; as an increase in disposable income would induce saving, a decrease in the interest rate or increase in wealth would be needed to keep saving at zero. As the *SS* curve passes through A_0, the economy is in long-run equilibrium when the interest rate is Or_0 and wealth is OW_0.

Points on the *BB* curve are those at which the bond market is in equilibrium, given the supply of domestic bonds. The curve is downward sloping because an increase in wealth raises the demand for bonds and calls for a decrease in the interest rate to reduce demand and clear the bond market. (There is excess demand in the bond market above *BB* and excess supply below it.) The position of the curve depends on the supply of bonds available to households. The total supply is constant when, as here, the government balances its budget, but an open-market purchase by the central bank reduces the supply available to households. Accordingly, an open-market purchase shifts the curve downward; the demand for bonds must fall to match the decrease in supply, so the interest rate must fall at each level of wealth.

The properties of the *LL* and *BB* curves are derived algebraically in Section 4 of Appendix B, which also proves some propositions needed later in this chapter.

The money and bond markets must be in equilibrium at all times. Therefore, the interest rate and wealth are given by point A_0, where *LL* intersects *BB*. This is the only point at which both markets can be in equilibrium simultaneously. The ways that the markets reach equilibrium are described in the next section. They depend importantly on the exchange-rate regime.

The SS curve in Figure 18-6 describes a relationship that holds only in long-run equilibrium, where wealth is constant because there is no saving. It is derived from equation (10) by setting $S = 0$. Points on the SS curve show the combinations of the interest rate and wealth that are compatible with long-run equilibrium. The curve is upward sloping because an increase in wealth would induce dissaving and a higher interest rate would be needed to offset it. The position of the SS curve depends on the level of disposable income. An increase in disposable income would induce saving, and a lower interest rate or larger stock of wealth would be needed to offset it. Therefore, a permanent increase in disposable income shifts the SS curve downward, showing the reduction in the interest rate required to keep the economy in long-run equilibrium. The SS curve has been drawn to pass through point A_0 in Figure 18-6. This says that the economy is in long-run equilibrium when the interest rate is Or_0 and wealth is OW_0.

USING THE PORTFOLIO-BALANCE MODEL

We can use the relationships shown in Figures 18-4 and 18-6 to examine the effects of various disturbances and policy changes. In each exercise, the economy will start in long-run equilibrium (at a point such as E_0 in Figure 18-4 and a point such as A_0 in Figure 18-6). The disturbance or policy change will shift one or two curves immediately, driving the economy away from long-run equilibrium. We will look first for the new short-run equilibrium, examine its properties, and ascertain its implications for the subsequent path of the economy. This information will help us to locate the new long-run equilibrium. Each exercise must be conducted twice, however, because the behavior of the economy depends crucially on the exchange-rate regime.

When the exchange rate is pegged, the stock of wealth can change only slowly, in response to saving or dissaving. In Figure 18-4, the exchange rate remains permanently at $O\pi_0$. In Figure 18-6, wealth remains temporarily at OW_0. But inflows and outflows of reserves affect the money supply, so the LL curve can move even when the central bank does not conduct open-market operations.

When the exchange rate is flexible, wealth can change immediately because of capital gains and losses on the foreign bond resulting from exchange-rate changes. In Figure 18-4, the exchange rate need not remain at $O\pi_0$. In Figure 18-6, wealth need not remain at OW_0, even temporarily. But there are no inflows or outflows of reserves, so the LL curve cannot move unless the central bank conducts open-market operations.

AN INCREASE IN FOREIGN EXPENDITURE

Let there be a permanent increase in foreign expenditure (consumption), raising the demand for the domestic good. In Figure 18-7, the zz curve shifts upward

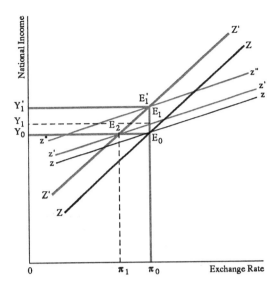

FIGURE 18-7
Effects of an Increase in Foreign Expenditure on Goods Markets
The goods market begins in equilibrium at E_0, with income at OY_0 and the exchange rate at $O\pi_0$. An increase in foreign expenditure shifts the zz curve to $z'z'$ and the ZZ curve to $Z'Z'$. The exchange rate remains at $O\pi_0$ temporarily, even when it is flexible, but equilibrium is displaced immediately to E_1, raising income to OY_1. As E_1 lies below $Z'Z'$, the adjustment process is driven by saving and a current-account surplus. When the exchange rate is pegged at $O\pi_0$, the new long-run equilibrium must lie at E_1', so the short-run curve must move gradually to $z''z''$, and income must rise gradually to OY_1'. The upward movement from $z'z'$ to $z''z''$ is produced by the decrease in the interest rate and increase in wealth shown in Figure 18-8. When the exchange rate is flexible, the new long-run equilibrium must lie at E_2. This is because the interest rate and wealth are constant in Figure 18-8, which means that the short-run curve must stay at $z'z'$. Therefore, income must fall back on OY_0. The domestic currency appreciates gradually from $O\pi_0$ to $O\pi_1$, and the expenditure-switching effect of the appreciation explains the reduction in income from OY_1 to OY_0. A flexible exchange rate insulates the economy from the income-raising effect of the increase in foreign expenditure, but full insulation is not achieved until the economy has returned to long-run equilibrium.

to $z'z'$, and the ZZ curve shifts upward to $Z'Z'$. If the exchange rate does not change, short-run equilibrium is displaced to E_1, and income rises immediately. Furthermore, E_1 lies below $Z'Z'$, which says that households start to save and the current account moves into surplus.[3]

---

[3] Proof that E_1 lies below $Z'Z'$ is given in Section 4 of Appendix B. As N_s is larger than N_L, the upward shift in zz is smaller than the upward shift in ZZ. The same point can be made by showing that E_2 lies horizontally to the left of E_0. Hold Y constant in Figure 18-7 and measure the change in π given by eqs. (4.4) and (4.5) in Appendix B. They are identical, which says that the zz and ZZ curves shift leftward by the same amounts. The effects of an increase in foreign expenditure closely resemble those of an increase in the price of the foreign good. An increase in C^* raises the foreign demand for the domestic good, and an increase in p_2^* switches foreign demand to the domestic good. (It switches domestic demand, too, but this merely reinforces the switch in foreign demand.) Therefore, the discussion in this section applies without much modification to an increase in the price of the foreign good.

Behavior Under a Pegged Exchange Rate

When the exchange rate is pegged, it must remain at $O\pi_0$ in Figure 18-7, which says that E_1 does in fact define the new short-run outcome, and income rises immediately to OY_1. This result is recorded in Table 18-1, which lists all the short-and long-run effects of the increase in foreign spending. But income does not remain at its new short-run level. It rises gradually through time, reflecting the increase in wealth produced by saving, until it reaches OY'_1. The proof is simple. When the long-run curve is $Z'Z'$ and the exchange rate is pegged at $O\pi_0$, the new long-run equilibrium must lie at E'_1. Therefore, the short-run curve must move gradually upward to $z''z''$, to intersect the long-run curve at E'_1, and income must move with it.

The upward movement of the short-run curve is due to the increase in wealth and decrease in the interest rate shown in Figure 18-8. They reduce the incentive to save and thus raise absorption. The economy begins at A_0, and it stays at that point temporarily, because the increase in foreign spending does not have any immediate effect on the positions of the BB and LL curves, which depend on the supplies of bonds and money. With the passage of time, however, asset-market equilibrium is displaced to some such point as A_1, where the interest rate has fallen and wealth has risen. As households save, wealth rises, raising the demands for bonds and money. The increase in demand for bonds is met by a reduction in the interest rate; the economy must move along the BB curve, because the supply of bonds cannot change when the government balances its budget continuously. The increase in demand for money is met by an increase in supply resulting from an increase in reserves. This increase in reserves is due to the balance-of-payments surplus produced by the current-account surplus, and it drives the LL curve downward.[4]

Table 18-1. Effects of an Increase in Foreign Expenditure

Variable	Change in:	
	Short Run	Long Run
Pegged exchange rate		
Income	+	+
Interest rate	0	−
Stock of wealth	0	+
Stock of reserves	0	+
Flexible exchange rate		
Income	+	0
Interest rate	0	0
Stock of wealth	0	0
Exchange rate	0	−

---

[4]The balance-of-payments surplus is smaller than the current-account surplus, because the increase in wealth and decrease in the interest rate raise domestic demand for the foreign bond, producing a capital outflow as the economy moves to long-run equilibrium.

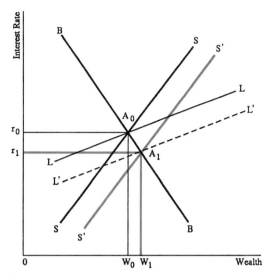

FIGURE 18-8
Effects of an Increase in Foreign Expenditure on Asset Markets
Assets markets begin in equilibrium at A_0, with the interest rate at Or_0 and wealth at
OW_0. An increase in foreign expenditure does not affect the situation in the short run.
Under a pegged exchange rate, however, saving raises wealth gradually and the
interest rate falls. The economy travels along the BB curve to some such point as A_1,
where the interest rate is Or_1 and wealth is OW_1. The corresponding movement of
the LL curve to $L'L'$ testifies to an increase in reserves, which means that the balance
of payments was in surplus during the adjustment process. The movement of the SS
curve to $S'S'$ testifies to a permanent increase in disposable income, which goes with
the increase in national income shown in Figure 18-7. Under a flexible exchange rate,
the LL curve cannot move, and asset-market equilibrium must remain at A_0. There is
a gradual appreciation of the domestic currency during the adjustment process, which
imposes capital losses on holders of the foreign bond. The losses offset saving,
keeping wealth constant at OW_0. As asset-market equilibrium stays at A_0, the SS curve
cannot move, which says that there can be no permanent change in disposable
income. This assertion is matched by the long-run result in Figure 18-7; the appreciation of the domestic currency takes national income back to its initial level.

There is another way to see what is happening here. In Figure 18-7, income must
rise permanently to OY'_1, because the economy must move gradually to E'_1 when the
exchange rate is pegged. Taxes are constant, however, so disposable income must
rise by as much as national income. Accordingly, the SS curve must shift downward
to $S'S'$ in Figure 18-8, which says that asset-market equilibrium must be displaced
eventually to A_1, where $S'S'$ intersects BB. The movement of the money-market
curve can be deduced from this result, because that curve must pass through A_1
when the economy reaches its new long-run equilibrium. The downward movement
of the money-market curve says in turn that there is a balance-of-payments surplus
on the way to the new stationary state; the stock of reserves must rise gradually
during the adjustment process.

Summing up for the pegged-rate case, an increase in foreign expenditure causes an
immediate increase in national income, and the increase gets larger as time passes.
The path of income looks like the path of wealth in Figure 18-5. An increase in
foreign expenditure at time $t = t_1$ raises income abruptly, and income continues to

rise thereafter until it reaches its new long-run level. The adjustment process involves saving, so wealth rises gradually, and the interest rate falls. The current account moves into surplus immediately, taking the balance of payments with it, and the inflow of reserves raises the money supply. When the economy reaches its new long-run equilibrium, saving ceases and the current account moves back into balance, as does the balance of payments.

Behavior Under a Flexible Exchange Rate

When the exchange rate is flexible, it does not have to stay at $O\pi_0$ in Figure 18-7. In this particular instance, however, it does not change immediately. An increase in foreign spending does not alter the positions of the BB and LL curves in Figure 18-8, so asset-market equilibrium remains temporarily at A_0. Therefore, wealth remains at its initial level, which says that the exchange rate does not change right away. The movement of national income to OY_1 in Figure 18-7 describes the short-run outcome with a flexible exchange rate, just as it did with a pegged exchange rate.

When the exchange rate is flexible, however, the short-run goods-market curve must remain at $z'z'$; it cannot rise gradually to $z''z''$, as it did when the rate was pegged. Therefore, the new long-run equilibrium must lie at E_2, where $z'z'$ intersects $Z'Z'$. The domestic currency must appreciate gradually to $O\pi_1$, and income must fall back to OY_0, the level at which it started.

What causes the domestic currency to appreciate? What keeps the short-run goods-market curve from rising? When the exchange rate was pegged, the economy ran a balance-of-payments surplus at E_1. The central bank intervened in the foreign-exchange market to keep the exchange rate from changing. When the exchange rate is flexible, the central bank does not intervene, and the domestic currency must therefore appreciate. When there is no intervention, moreover, the money supply does not change. In Figure 18-8, then, the money-market curve must stay at LL, instead of falling as it did in the pegged-rate case, and asset-market equilibrium must remain at A_0. Wealth and the interest rate must be constant. When they are constant, however, the short-run goods-market curve must stay at $z'z'$ in Figure 18-7, and the new long-run equilibrium must lie at E_2, where income is OY_0. The same result regarding income can be obtained directly from Figure 18-8. When asset-market equilibrium remains at A_0, the SS curve cannot shift. By implication, there can be no permanent change in disposable or national income. The short-run increase to OY_1 in Figure 18-7 must be reversed eventually.

There does appear to be something wrong here. When income is at OY_1 in Figure 18-7, households are saving, and wealth should be rising. How can wealth be constant in Figure 18-8? Two forces are at work, and they offset each other. Saving adds to wealth, just as in the pegged-rate case. But the gradual appreciation of the domestic currency imposes capital losses on holders of the foreign bond. Those capital losses cancel the effects of saving and keep wealth from changing. This may seem to be a very special outcome, but it is fundamental to the logic of the model.

Summing up for the flexible-rate case, the increase in foreign expenditure raises national income immediately by as much as it did in the pegged-rate case, but income falls thereafter. The adjustment process involves saving and a current-account surplus, and the domestic currency appreciates gradually. Wealth and the interest rate remain constant. When the economy has reached long-run equilibrium, income has returned to its initial level.

Insulation Under a Flexible Exchange Rate

In Chapter 13, we saw that a flexible exchange rate can insulate the domestic economy against external shocks. That is what happened here. The increase in foreign expenditure raised national income in the short run, and the increase in income raised imports. But the increase in imports was not large enough to offset completely the increase in exports resulting from the increase in foreign expenditure. The current-account balance moved into surplus, and the domestic currency began to appreciate. The expenditure-switching effects of the appreciation drove the economy back along the $z'z'$ curve in Figure 18-7 until income returned to OY_0.

Insulation can occur in other cases, including a switch in domestic demand between domestic and foreign goods. But the example given here warns us against counting on exchange-rate flexibility for *continuous* insulation. Insulation does not occur instantaneously, because income does not return to its initial level until the economy reaches long-run equilibrium.

AN OPEN-MARKET PURCHASE

In the monetary model of the balance of payments, an increase in the money supply led to a gradual loss of reserves under a pegged exchange rate, and the loss of reserves reduced the money supply until it returned to its initial level. In the model studied here, an increase in the money supply leads to an *instantaneous* loss of reserves and a gradual loss thereafter. In long-run equilibrium, moreover, the money supply may not be back at its initial level. When the exchange rate is flexible, an increase in the money supply leads to an immediate depreciation of the domestic currency, but the exchange rate can go up or down thereafter. It need not depreciate steadily as it did in the monetary model.

An open-market purchase does not directly alter the positions of the zz and ZZ curves. By affecting asset-market variables, however, it affects the position of the zz curve indirectly. Accordingly, we start with the effects on asset markets, shown in Figure 18-9.

An open-market purchase reduces the supply of domestic bonds available to the public, and a lower interest rate is needed to clear the bond market. The BB curve shifts downward to $B'B'$. But an open-market purchase raises the money supply, and a lower interest rate is needed to clear the money market. The LL curve shifts downward to $L'L'$. The two curves intersect at A_1, below and to the right of A_0. (This is proven in Section 4 of Appendix B.)

Behavior Under a Pegged Exchange Rate

When the exchange rate is pegged, wealth cannot change instantaneously, and A_1 cannot be an equilibrium point. Asset-market equilibrium must lie at A'_1 in

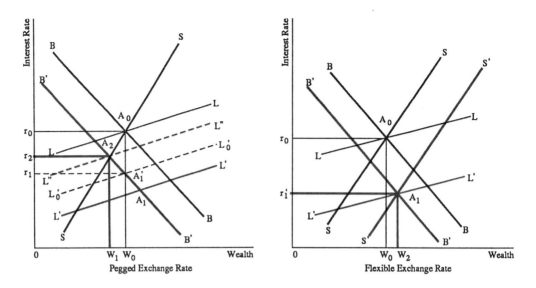

FIGURE 18-9
Effects of an Open-Market Purchase on Asset Markets
The asset markets begin in equilibrium at A_0, with the interest rate at Or_0 and wealth at OW_0. An open-market purchase shifts the BB curve to $B'B'$ and the LL curve to $L'L'$. They intersect at A_1, below and to the right of A_0. Under a pegged exchange rate, however, wealth cannot change immediately, so asset-market equilibrium is displaced to A_1'. The interest rate falls to Or_1 and the money-market curve shifts back, to $L_0'L_0'$, which says that there is an immediate loss of reserves. As an open-market purchase does not shift the ZZ curve in Figure 18-10, there can be no permanent change in national or disposable income, and the SS curve cannot shift. Hence, long-run equilibrium must be established at A_2, where $B'B'$ and SS intersect. Wealth falls gradually to OW_1, and the interest rate rises to Or_2. The money-market curve rises to $L''L''$, which says that there was a balance-of-payments deficit during the adjustment process. Under a flexible exchange rate, the money-market curve must stay at $L'L'$. Hence, asset-market equilibrium is displaced to A_1. The interest rate falls to OR_1', by more than in the pegged-rate case, and wealth rises to OW_2, which means that there is an immediate depreciation of the domestic currency. Accordingly, income rises in Figure 18-10 by more than in the pegged-rate case. As the bond-market and money-market curves cannot shift again, long-run equilibrium must likewise lie at A_1, and the SS curve must thus shift to $S'S'$. There is a permanent increase in disposable income, corresponding to the permanent increase in national income shown in Figure 18-10. If there is dissaving and a current-account deficit during the adjustment process, the domestic currency depreciates gradually to keep wealth constant at OW_2. If there is saving and a current-account surplus, the domestic currency appreciates gradually.

the left panel of the diagram, where wealth remains at OW_0 and the interest rate falls to Or_1.

How does the economy get to this point? When the central bank buys domestic bonds, driving down the interest rate, households want to hold more foreign bonds as well as more money. They keep some of the money created by the open-market purchase and use the rest to buy foreign currency in order to buy foreign bonds. The central bank must intervene in the foreign-exchange market to prevent the domestic currency from depreciating; it must use some of its reserves to meet the households' demand for foreign currency and and thus take back some of the money created by its open-market purchase. The loss of reserves and reduction in the money supply are shown in Figure 18-9 by the shift of the money-market curve from $L'L'$ to $L_0'L_0'$, which intersects the new bond-market curve at A_1'. The bond market is cleared by the reduction in the interest rate. The money market is cleared by the loss of reserves, which cuts back the increase in the money supply produced by the open-market purchase. These effects are listed in Table 18-2, which summarizes the results of an open-market purchase.

The reduction in the interest rate to Or_1 stimulates consumption by weakening the households' incentive to save. Therefore, the zz curve shifts upward to $z'z'$ in the left panel of Figure 18-10, and short-run goods-market equilibrium is displaced to E_1 when the exchange rate is pegged. Income rises immediately to OY_1. But a change in the interest rate cannot shift the ZZ curve, and E_1 lies above it. Accordingly, the subsequent adjustment process is driven by dissaving and a current-account deficit.

As the ZZ curve does not shift and the exchange rate is pegged, the new long-run equilibrium must lie at E_0 in the left panel of Figure 18-10. This is the only point at which dissaving ceases and the current-account deficit disappears. By implication, the short-run goods-market curve must drop back gradually to zz, and income must return to OY_0. This is the same long-run result obtained in Chapter 15. The income-raising effect of an open-market purchase must wear off eventually under a pegged exchange rate.

To see why the short-run goods-market curve must move downward, return to the left panel of Figure 18-9. When national income must return to its initial level, disposable income must do so, too. Therefore, the SS curve cannot shift, and the new long-run equilibrium must lie at A_2. Dissaving must reduce wealth gradually, and

Table 18-2. Effects of an Open-Market Purchase

Variable	Change in:	
	Short Run	Long Run
Pegged exchange rate		
Income	+	0
Interest rate	−	−
Stock of wealth	0	−
Stock of reserves	−	−
Flexible exchange rate		
Income	+	+
Interest rate	−	−
Stock of wealth	+	+
Exchange rate	+	+

Note: These results pertain to the general case in which the domestic and foreign bond are imperfect substitutes. In the limiting case of perfect substitutability (perfect capital mobility), the interest rate does not change, and there is no short-run change in income under a pegged exchange rate.

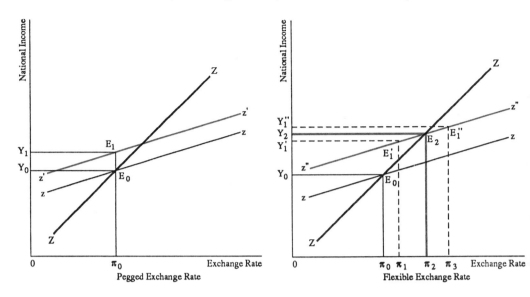

FIGURE 18-10
Effects of an Open-Market Purchase on Goods Markets
The goods market begins in equilibrium at E_0, with national income at OY_0 and the exchange rate at $O\pi_0$. Under a pegged exchange rate, an open-market purchase shifts the zz curve to $z'z'$ because it reduces the interest rate. Equilibrium is displaced to E_1, and income rises to OY_1. There is dissaving and a current-account deficit. But long-run equilibrium must remain at E_0, because the ZZ curve cannot shift. Therefore, the short-run curve must move gradually downward from $z'z'$ to zz. This movement is produced by the increase in the interest rate and decrease in wealth shown in Figure 18-9. Income goes back to its initial level. Under a flexible exchange rate, the open-market purchase shifts the zz curve to $z''z''$, by more than in the pegged-rate case, because the interest rate falls further and wealth rises immediately, reflecting the depreciation of the domestic currency. This larger shift is reinforced by the demand-switching effects of the depreciation. If the exchange rate goes from $O\pi_0$ to $O\pi_1$, equilibrium is displaced to E_1' and income rises to OY_1'. If the exchange rate goes to $O\pi_3$, equilibrium is displaced to E_1'' and income rises all the way to OY_1''. In the first case, there is dissaving and a current-account deficit. In the second, there is saving and a current-account surplus. As the interest rate remains at OR_1' in Figure 18-9 and wealth remains at OW_2, the short-run goods-market curve stays at $z''z''$ and long-run equilibrium must lie at E_2. National income must go to OY_2, and the exchange rate must go to $O\pi_2$. If the exchange rate goes to $O\pi_1$ in the short run, the domestic currency must continue to depreciate during the adjustment process; if it goes to $O\pi_3$ in the short run, the domestic currency must appreciate during the adjustment process.

the interest rate must rise to Or_2 as the decline in wealth reduces the demand for bonds. In the left panel of Figure 18-10, the zz curve is driven back to its initial position because the increase in the interest rate and decrease in wealth combine to reduce absorption.

As the economy moves to A_2 in the left panel of Figure 18-9, the money-market curve must move upward to $L''L''$. Reserves fall during the adjustment process, which says that the current-account deficit is accompanied by a balance-of-payments deficit. The decline in reserves, however, is not large enough to reduce the money supply to its initial level, as it did in the monetary model. Because $L''L''$ lies below LL, the money supply must be larger at A_2 than at A_0. The loss of reserves does not completely offset the open-market purchase.[5]

Summing up for the pegged-rate case, an open-market purchase leads to an immediate increase in income, an immediate fall in the interest rate, and an immediate loss of reserves, because households add to their holdings of the foreign bond. Households start to dissave, the current account moves into deficit, and the balance of payments moves into deficit, too. There is a gradual decline in wealth and an additional loss of reserves. As in other models, monetary policy does not have any permanent effect on income under a pegged exchange rate. The income-raising effect of the open-market purchase wears off gradually as the economy approaches long-run equilibrium.

Behavior Under a Flexible Exchange Rate

When the exchange rate is flexible, reserves cannot change. Therefore, the money-market curve must stay at $L'L'$ after the open-market purchase has shifted it, and A_1 must represent short-run equilibrium in the right panel of Figure 18-9. It *can* represent short-run equilibrium, because wealth can change instantaneously. As households attempt to buy foreign currency in order to buy foreign bonds, the domestic currency depreciates, conferring a capital gain on holders of that bond and raising wealth immediately to OW_2. The interest rate falls immediately to Or'_1, by more than in the pegged-rate case.[6]

Earlier chapters showed that monetary policy is more powerful under a flexible exchange rate, and that is true here, too. Look at the right panel of Figure 18-10. The short-run goods-market curve shifts to $z''z''$, by more than in the pegged-rate case (when it shifted to $z'z'$), because there is a larger reduction in the interest rate and it is reinforced by an increase in wealth. Furthermore, the depreciation of the domestic currency to $O\pi_1$ switches domestic and foreign demands to the domestic good. Short-run equilibrium is displaced to E'_1, and income rises to OY'_1. As in the pegged-rate case, however, the new equilibrium point lies above the ZZ curve; there is dissaving and a current-account deficit during the adjustment process.

---

[5]This difference between the portfolio-balance and monetary models reflects the difference in assumptions about attitudes toward risk. In the monetary model, asset holders are risk neutral, so that foreign and domestic bonds are perfect substitutes, and the domestic interest rate cannot differ from the foreign rate when exchange-rate expectations are stationary. Therefore, an open-market purchase cannot reduce the domestic interest rate. In the portfolio-balance model, asset holders are risk averse, so that foreign and domestic bonds are imperfect substitutes, and the domestic interest rate can differ from the foreign rate. Therefore, an open-market purchase can reduce the domestic interest rate, which raises the quantity of money that households want to hold. Accordingly, the economy does not have to "export" as much money as it did in the monetary model, and the loss of reserves is smaller.

[6]It is easy to show why the capital gain must be just large enough to raise wealth to OW_2. As $B'B'$ and $L'L'$ intersect at A_1, the money and bond markets clear when wealth is OW_2 and the interest rate is Or'_1. There is no excess demand for money or for the domestic bond. In that case, however, there can be no excess domestic demand for the foreign bond and no excess demand for foreign currency. Therefore, the depreciation of the domestic currency that raises wealth to OW_2 is just large enough to clear the foreign-exchange market.

When dealing with an increase in foreign expenditure, we found that income changed permanently under a pegged exchange rate but only temporarily under a flexible rate. Here, the outcomes are reversed. We have already shown that the change in income is temporary under a pegged rate. We will now show that it is permanent under a flexible rate.

When there is no intervention in the foreign-exchange market, the balance-of-payments deficit that emerged in the pegged-rate case is replaced by a gradual depreciation of the domestic currency. In the absence of intervention, moreover, the money-market curve remains at $L'L'$ in the right panel of Figure 18-9, and asset-market equilibrium remains at A_1. Wealth and the interest rate cannot change during the adjustment process. (There is, of course, dissaving, but its effect on wealth is offset by the depreciation of the domestic currency; holders of the foreign bond receive capital gains, and these keep wealth constant at OW_2.)

When wealth and the interest rate are constant, however, the short-run goods-market curve cannot move downward, as it did in the pegged-rate case. It must remain at $z''z''$ in the right panel of Figure 18-10, and the new long-run equilibrium must thus lie at E_2, where $z''z''$ intersects ZZ. The domestic currency must depreciate to $O\pi_2$, and income must rise gradually to OY_2. Note finally that this outcome is fully consistent with the outcome in Figure 18-9. The permanent increase in income implies a permanent increase in disposable income, and that is what shifts the SS curve in Figure 18-9. It must move to $S'S'$ when long-equilibrium remains at A_1.

Summing up for the flexible-rate case, an open-market purchase leads to an immediate increase in income, an immediate depreciation of the domestic currency that raises wealth, and an immediate reduction in the interest rate. The increase in income is larger than in the pegged-rate case. In this particular example, the subsequent adjustment process is driven by dissaving and a current-account deficit. There is an additional depreciation of the domestic currency, which reinforces the income-raising effect of the open-market purchase. (The path of the exchange rate looks like the path of wealth in Figure 18-5. An open-market purchase at time $t = t_1$ causes an immediate depreciation, and there is more depreciation on the way to the new long-run equilibrium.)

Another Outcome

The language used in the previous paragraph hints at another possibility. Under a flexible exchange rate, there can be saving, a current-account surplus, and an appreciation of the domestic currency during the adjustment process.

Suppose that holdings of the foreign bond are very small initially, so that a large depreciation of the domestic currency is needed to raise wealth to OW_2 in the right panel of Figure 18-9. Let the exchange rate go all the way to $O\pi_3$ in the right panel of Figure 18-10, so short-run equilibrium is displaced to E''_1 and income rises to OY''_1. There will be saving and a current-account surplus during the adjustment process, because E''_1 lies below the ZZ curve. Therefore, the domestic currency will appreciate to $O\pi_2$ and income will fall to OY_2.

This is, of course, another case of "overshooting" in the foreign-exchange market. The explanation offered here, the small initial holdings of the foreign bond, may not be the most important reason for overshooting. The reason given in Chapter 16, the slow rate at which trade flows respond to exchange-rate changes, may be more important. The phenomenon itself, however, is very important. Flexible exchange rates have been very volatile, and their volatility may be due to an inherent tendency for exchange rates to overshoot their long-run levels.

Implications of Capital Mobility

Chapter 15 showed that capital mobility has important implications for the effectiveness of monetary policy. When the exchange rate is pegged, high capital mobility increases the speed with which income falls back to its initial level, and perfect capital mobility deprives monetary policy of *any* influence on income. When the exchange rate is flexible, high capital mobility enhances the effectiveness of monetary policy, and perfect capital mobility maximizes its effectiveness. Figure 18-11 shows that the same things happen here.

When there is no capital mobility whatsoever, the bond-market curve is very steep, and an open-market purchase shifts it downward by as much as it shifts the money-market curve. The bond-market curve is $\bar{B}\bar{B}$ in Figure 18-11, steeper than curves in earlier diagrams, and an open-market purchase shifts it downward to $\bar{B}'\bar{B}'$. The money-market curve is LL, and an open-market purchase shifts it downward to $L'L'$. The two curves intersect at A_1^0.

When there is perfect capital mobility, the domestic interest rate is tied firmly to the foreign rate, as in the monetary model. The bond-market curve is B^*B^*, which is horizontal and does not shift at all. The money-market curve shifts downward as it did before, and the intersection point is A_1^*.

Look first at the implications for monetary policy under a pegged exchange rate. As wealth cannot change immediately when the exchange rate is pegged, the short-run equilibrium point must lie on the vertical line $A_0A_1^0$. Without any capital mobility, A_1^0 is the equilibrium point. There is no backward shift of the money-market curve and no immediate loss of reserves. With perfect capital mobility, by contrast A_0 is the equilibrium point. There is no change in the interest rate. The money-market curve must snap back immediately to LL, and the instantaneous loss of reserves is exactly large enough to offset the open-market purchase. The money supply does not change. When the interest rate and wealth are constant, moreover, there can be no change in absorption of the sort shown in Figure 18-10 by the shift in the zz curve. Therefore, there can be no increase in income, even temporarily. Collecting these conclusions, an increase in capital mobility reduces the effectiveness of monetary policy under a pegged exchange rate. The short-run equilibrium points travel upward along $A_0A_1^0$, the immediate loss of reserves gets larger, and the immediate increase in income gets smaller.

Look next at the implications of capital mobility under a flexible exchange rate and concentrate first on the short run.[7] As the money-market curve cannot move after it has shifted initially, the short-run equilibrium point must lie on $L'L'$ between A_1^0 and A_1^*. Without any capital mobility, A_1^0 is the equilibrium point, and wealth is

---

[7]There was no need to distinguish between short and long run in the pegged-rate case, because monetary policy does not have any permanent influence on income, regardless of the degree of capital mobility.

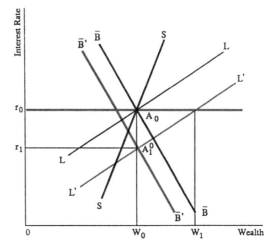

FIGURE 18-11

Capital Mobility and the Effectiveness of Monetary Policy

Without any capital mobility, the bond-market curve is $\bar{B}\bar{B}$, and an open-market purchase shifts it downward to $\bar{B}'\bar{B}'$, by as much as the downward shift of the money-market curve. With perfect capital mobility, the bond-market curve is $B*B*$, and it does not shift at all; the interest rate remains at Or_0. As wealth cannot change immediately under a pegged exchange rate, asset-market equilibria must lie on the line $A_0A_1^0$. Hence, A_1^0 is the equilibrium point without capital mobility, and there is no immediate loss of reserves (no backward shift of $L'L'$). But A_0 is the equilibrium point with perfect mobility, and the loss of reserves offsets the whole open-market purchase ($L'L'$ shifts back to LL). As the money-market curve must remain at $L'L'$ under a flexible exchange rate, asset-market equilibria must lie on the line $A_1^0A_1^*$. Hence, A_1^0 is the equilibrium point without any capital mobility, and there is no immediate change in wealth (no depreciation of the domestic currency). But A_1^* is the equilibrium point with perfect mobility, and there is a large increase in wealth (a large depreciation). Furthermore, long-run equilibrium lies at A_1^0 without capital mobility and at A_1^* with perfect mobility, and SS curves must pass through those points. As the curve passing through A_1^* must lie below the curve passing through A_1^0, the permanent increase in disposable income is larger with perfect capital mobility, and the permanent increase in national income must be larger, too.

unchanged, which means that the exchange rate is unchanged. Furthermore, the change in absorption is no larger than it was in the pegged-rate case, because the change in the interest rate is the same. Therefore, the short-run change in income is the same under flexible and pegged rates. With perfect capital mobility, by contrast, A_1^* is the equilibrium point. The interest rate is constant, but wealth rises to OW_1. The absence of an interest-rate effect reduces the size of the upward shift in the zz curve, but the wealth effect enlarges it, and it can be shown that the wealth effect dominates. Hence, income rises further than it did in the pegged-rate cases.[8]

---

[8] Rewrite the relevant portion of eq. (4.5) in Section 4 of Appendix B:

$$dY = (nY/N_S)e_\pi\dot{\pi} - (1/N_S)(1 - m_2)(s_r dr + s_w dW).$$

The first term is the slope of the zz curve. The second tells us by how much it shifts. Without

Footnote 8 continued on next page

Furthermore, the increase in wealth implies an immediate depreciation of the domestic currency, which adds even more to the increase in income. Collecting these conclusions, an increase in capital mobility enhances the effectiveness of monetary policy in the short run. The short-run equilibrium points travel upward along $A_1^0 A_1^*$, the shift in the zz curve gets bigger in Figure 18-10, and the movement along the zz curve gets bigger too, because the exchange-rate change gets bigger. Therefore, income rises farther.

What about the effect of capital mobility on the size of the permanent change in income? It gets bigger. The larger the upward shift of the zz curve, the larger the increase in income needed to achieve long-run equilibrium. The same point can be made differently. When A_1^0 is the short-run equilibrium point, it is the long-run point, too, and a new SS curve must pass through it. When A_1^* is the equilibrium point, a new SS curve must pass through it instead, and it must lie below the curve passing through A_1^0. Therefore, the permanent increase in disposable income is larger at A_1^*, and so is the permanent increase in national income.

THE ANALYSIS OF DEVALUATION

In the monetary model, a devaluation led to a balance-of-payments surplus and a gradual increase in reserves. But the increase in reserves raised the money supply, which raised absorption and reduced the balance-of-payments surplus. The surplus disappeared eventually. In the portfolio-balance model, a devaluation causes an *immediate* increase in reserves, analogous to the immediate decrease caused by an open-market purchase. But the balance of payments can move into surplus or deficit which means that reserves can rise or fall during the subsequent adjustment process.

In Figure 18-12, a devaluation is represented by a permanent increase in the exchange rate from $O\pi_0$ to $O\pi_1$ in the left panel and an immediate increase in wealth from OW_0 to OW_1 in the right panel; the increase in wealth is due to the capital gain conferred on holders of the foreign bond. Any increase in wealth, however, leads households to demand more money and more domestic bonds. Therefore, they will use some of their capital gain to bid for those two assets; they will try to switch from foreign bonds into money and domestic bonds. When they sell foreign bonds, moreover, they obtain foreign currency and sell it on the foreign-exchange market. Hence, the central bank must intervene to keep the exchange rate pegged. The central bank gains reserves, and the money supply rises, shifting LL downward to

---

any capital mobility, the change in the interest rate is the vertical distance $r_0 r_1$ in Figure 18-11, and there is no change in wealth. The resulting shift in the zz curve can be written as $dY^0 = (1 - m_2)(s_r/N_S)r_0 r_1$. With perfect capital mobility, there is no change in the interest rate, and the change in wealth is the horizontal distance $W_0 W_1$. The resulting shift in the zz curve can be written as $dY^* = (1 - m_2)(-s_w/N_S)W_0 W_1$. But A_1^0 and A_1^* lie on the $L'L'$ curve, and the equation for that curve says that $dW = (-L_r/L_w)dr$. Therefore, $W_0 W_1 = (-L_r/L_w)r_0 r_1$, and $dY^* = (1 - m_2)s_w/N_S)(L_r/L_w)r_0 r_1$. Thus

$$dY^* - dY^0 = (1/N_S)(1 - m_2)[s_w(L_r/L_w) - s_r]r_0 r_1 = (1/L_w N_S)(1 - m_2)(s_w L_r - s_r L_w)r_0 r_1.$$

In Section 4 of Appendix B, however, we assume that $s_w L_r > s_r L_w$. Therefore, $dY^* > dY^0$. The wealth effect dominates the interest-rate effect.

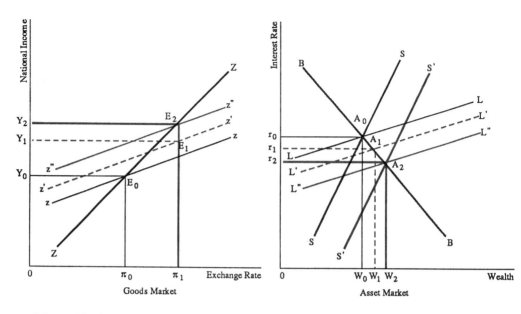

FIGURE 18-12
Devaluation in the Portfolio-Balance Model
The economy begins in long-run equilibrium. The domestic currency is devalued from $O\pi_0$ to $O\pi_1$. Looking first at the long-run effects, goods-market equilibrium must be established eventually at E_2, which means that the zz curve must move to $z''z''$ and raise national income from OY_0 to OY_2. As disposable income must rise with national income, the SS curve moves downward from SS to $S'S'$, and long-run asset-market equilibrium must be established at A_2, where $S'S'$ intersects BB. Therefore, the money-market curve must from LL to $L''L''$, and devaluation raises the stock of reserves. But there are two ways of reaching these long run outcomes. In this example, the devaluation raises wealth immediately from OW_0 to OW_1, reducing the interest rate from Or_0 to Or_1 and shifting the money-market curve to $L'L'$. There is an immediate increase in reserves, but it is smaller than the long-run increase ($L'L'$ lies above $L''L''$). The balance of payments must be in surplus during the adjustment process. Furthermore, the zz curve shifts to $z'z'$ in the short run, displacing goods-market equilibrium to E_1 and raising income to OY_1. As E_1 lies below the ZZ curve, there is saving and a current-account surplus during the adjustment process.

$L'L'$. Asset-market equilibrium is displaced to A_1. The domestic interest rate falls to clear the bond market, and the money supply rises to clear the money market. These effects are listed in Table 18-3, along with other results of a devaluation.

The rise in wealth and fall in the interest rate stimulate absorption, and the zz curve shifts upward to $z'z'$. (The ZZ curve does not shift because there is no change in the level of income required to balance the current account.) Goods-market equilibrium is displaced to E_1, and national income rises to OY_1. The increase in income is the joint result of the increase in absorption denoted by the shift of the zz curve and the demand-switching effect of the devaluation denoted by the movement along the curve. In this particular example, the new goods-market equilibrium lies below the ZZ curve, so households start to save, which means that the current account moves into surplus.

In the long run, goods-market equilibrium must lie at E_2, because the exchange

Table 18-3. Effects of a Devaluation

Variable	Change in:	
	Short Run	Long Run
Income	+	+
Interest rate	−	−
Stock of wealth	+	+
Stock of reserves	+	+

rate is pegged at $O\pi_1$. Therefore, the short-run curve must rise gradually to $z''z''$, and income must rise to OY_2. The shift in the curve is driven by rising wealth and a falling interest rate. Saving raises wealth to OW_2, and the interest rate falls to Or_2. Long-run asset-market equilibrium lies at A_2, below A_1, and the money-market curve must move gradually downward to $L''L''$. The money supply rises during the adjustment process, which tells us that reserves rise. The devaluation generates a balance-of-payments surplus. As in the monetary model, however, the surplus disappears when the economy reaches long-run equilibrium.

There is another possibility. The long-run outcomes are the same as those in Figure 18-12, but the short-run results are different. The long-run outcomes are the same because they are defined completely by the size of the devaluation. Long-run goods-market equilibrium must lie at E_2 when the exchange rate is $O\pi_1$. Income must rise eventually to OY_2, and there must thus be a permanent increase in disposable income. Hence, the SS curve must shift to $S'S'$, which says that long-run asset-market equilibrium must lie at A_2. But the short-run results depend on the size of the increase in wealth produced by the devaluation.

Suppose that wealth rises immediately to a level higher than OW_2, because foreign bonds bulk large in households' portfolios, and households make very large capital gains when the domestic currency is devalued. Asset-market equilibrium is displaced to a point on BB below A_2, reducing the interest rate below Or_2, so the money-market curve must lie below $L''L''$. With a larger increase in wealth and larger decrease in the interest rate, there is a larger shift in the zz curve; it must lie above $z''z''$. Goods-market equilibrium is displaced to a point above E_2, and income rises above OY_2. As the goods-market equilibrium point lies above the ZZ curve, there must be dissaving and a current-account deficit, which throw the adjustment process into reverse; wealth must fall, and the interest rate must rise. Hence, the money-market curve must rise to $L''L''$, which means that reserves must fall, and there must be a balance-of-payments deficit during the adjustment process. Finally, the goods-market curve must move gradually down to reach $z''z''$ and bring income down to its long-run level.

To repeat, the long-run outcomes are the same in the two cases. The devaluation raises income and adds to the stock of reserves. But the paths are different. In the case described by Figure 18-12, income and other variables undershoot their long-run levels. In the other case, they overshoot them.

Summary

The portfolio-balance model synthesizes much of our earlier work on the macroeconomics of an open economy. Supply conditions are Ricardian. Demand conditions reflect the income and price effects examined in Chapters 13 and 14. There are three assets—money, a government bond, and a foreign bond denominated in foreign currency. Investors are risk averse and thus hold all three assets.

The model separates short-run from long-run effects. Short-run effects are those that occur before flows have affected stocks. Long-run effects are those that pertain to the new stationary state, where all stocks are constant because the flows affecting them have ceased. The strategic stock-flow relationship in the model is the double link between saving and wealth. Saving adds to wealth, but an increase in wealth reduces saving. A change in the exchange rate affects wealth, too, because it confers a capital gain or loss on holders of the foreign bond.

An increase in foreign expenditure leads to a permanent increase in income when the exchange rate is pegged. There is a temporary increase when the rate is flexible, but the domestic currency appreciates gradually, reducing absorption and switching demand back to the foreign good. There is thus insulation from foreign disturbances, but it does not take place instantaneously.

An open-market purchase leads to a temporary increase in income when the exchange rate is pegged and to a permanent loss of reserves. With imperfect capital mobility, however, the loss is not large enough to offset completely the open-market purchase, and there is a permanent increase in the money supply. When the exchange rate is flexible, there is a permanent increase in income and a permanent depreciation of the domestic currency. But the permanent depreciation can be larger or smaller than the depreciation that takes place instantaneously; the exchange rate can undershoot or overshoot its long-run level. As in other models, capital mobility diminishes the effectiveness of monetary policy under a pegged exchange rate, reducing the temporary increase in income. It enhances the effectiveness of monetary policy under a flexible rate, raising the increase in income in the short run and the long run.

A devaluation of the domestic currency leads to a permanent increase in income and in the stock of reserves. But there are two ways of getting to this long-run result. When foreign bonds do not bulk large in investors' portfolios, wealth does not rise much on account of the devaluation. Income and reserves rise immediately but by less than they must rise eventually, and the economy runs a balance-of-payments surplus during the adjustment process. When holdings of foreign bonds are large, wealth rises sharply. Income and reserves rise immediately by more than they must rise permanently, and the economy runs a balance-of-payments deficit during the adjustment process.

RECOMMENDED READINGS

The model in this chapter is adapted from the model in Polly R. Allen and Peter B. Kenen, *Asset Markets and Exchange Rates: Modeling an Open Economy* (New York:

Cambridge University Press, 1983). But that model is more elaborate. It deals with changes in the supply of bonds resulting from budget deficits and surpluses, offers a more general treatment of goods markets, and introduces nonstationary expectations.

For a survey of theoretical work on exchange-rate behavior that focuses on differences between monetary and portfolio-balance models, see Rudiger Dornbusch, "Exchange Rate Economics: Where Do We Stand?" *Brookings Papers on Economic Activity*, 1980 (1). For a survey that stresses empirical work, see Maurice Obstfeld, "Floating Exchange Rates: Experience and Prospects," *Brookings Papers on Economic Activity*, 1985 (2).

QUESTIONS AND PROBLEMS

(1) Adapt Figures 18-7 and 18-8 to trace the short-run and long-run effects of a fall in foreign demand for the domestic good under a pegged exchange rate. What happens to income, the interest rate, wealth, and the stock of reserves? Explain how saving, the current-account balance, and the overall balance of payments work to drive the economy from short-run to long-run equilibrium. Repeat your answer for a flexible exchange rate, showing the short-run and long-run effects on income, the interest rate, wealth, and the exchange rate and tracing the path from short-run to long-run equilibrium. What does your answer say about the ability of a flexible exchange rate to insulate the economy from an external disturbance?

(2) Show how your answers to (1) are affected when foreign and domestic bonds are perfect substitutes (i.e., the *BB* curve is horizontal). You should find two differences in the pegged-rate case (a larger change in wealth and a smaller change in reserves) and no difference at all in the flexible rate case. Provide an intuitive explanation for the larger change in wealth.

(3) Trace the short-run and long-run effects of an open-market sale of domestic bonds under a flexible exchange rate.

(4) When a flexible exchange-rate undershoots its long-run level in response to an open-market purchase, the path of the exchange rate looks like the path of wealth in Figure 18-5. Adapt that diagram to show the path of the exchange rate when it overshoots its long-run level.

(5) Adapt Figure 18-12 to describe the case in which devaluation leads to dissaving and a balance-of-payments deficit on the way from short-run to long-run equilibrium.

(6) Suppose that households switch some of their wealth from domestic bonds to foreign bonds. Adapt Figure 18-12 to show the long-run effects on income, the interest rate, wealth, and reserves under a pegged exchange rate. (Represent the switch in the households' portfolio preferences by shifting the *BB* curve.)

(7) Repeat your answer to (6) to show what happens when the central bank undertakes an open-market operation to prevent any change in the money supply (i.e., sterilizes the intervention required to keep the exchange rate pegged). Have you shown an open-market purchase or sale? You should find that there is no permanent change in income, the interest rate, or wealth. Explain this special outcome. What does it say about the appropriateness of sterilized intervention for dealing with shifts in households' portfolio preferences?

(8) Suppose that the government runs a temporary budget deficit and finances it by issuing bonds. Compare the long-run effects of the increase in the supply of bonds under a pegged and a flexible exchange rate. (There is no shift in the *ZZ* curve under either regime, and no shift in the *LL* curve under a flexible exchange rate.)

(9) How would your answer to (8) be affected if domestic and foreign bonds were perfect substitutes?

19

The Evolution of the Monetary System

THE ISSUES

At the end of our survey of trade theory, in Chapters 10 and 11, we reviewed the evolution of trade policy and looked at new policy problems. This chapter and the next play an analogous role. This chapter reviews the hstory of the international monetary system. The next one examines current policy problems and the outlook for the monetary system.

The history of trade policy in Chapter 10 began with the early nineteenth century, when the United States embraced infant-industry protection and Great Britain moved toward free trade. Much can be learned from the monetary history of the nineteenth century, when Great Britain was the key-currency country and gold was important in theory and practice. But modern monetary systems are different from those of the nineteenth century, as is modern montary theory, leaving less to learn from nineteenth-century experience than from close inspection of recent experience.

Accordingly, this chapter concentrates on events since the Bretton Woods Conference of 1944, which designed the monetary system that came into being after World War II. It pays particular attention to the role of the United States, because the U.S. dollar has been the main international currency, and U.S. policies have greatly affected the evolution of the system. The chapter focuses on three issues:

- How interpretations of monetary history have affected the design of the monetary system.

- How the system has adapted to the needs and problems of the major countries, most notably those of the United States.

- How governments have tried to solve the basic nth country problem—that the number of countries is always larger than the number of exchange rates.

The chapters starts by reviewing events in the 1920s and 1930s that influenced the authors of the Bretton Woods agreement, then describes the agreement itself and the monetary system it produced. It goes on to review international monetary relations under the Bretton Woods system, the breakdown of the system in the early 1970s, and the resulting shift from pegged to floating exchange rates. Thereafter, it examines the behavior of exchange rates in the 1970s and 1980s, the effects of the "oil shocks" of 1973 and 1979 and of major changes in natonal policies, and the problems of financing, adjustment, and debt arising from these and other events.

THE BRETTON WOODS SYSTEM

In Chapter 10, we noted that plans for postwar reconstruction were being made long before the end of World War II. American and British officials began to discuss them even before the attack on Pearl Harbor that brought the United States into the war, and they drafted an agrement on monetary matters that was ratified formally in 1944 by the Interational Monetary and Financial Conference held at Bretton Woods, New Hampshire. The conference established the International Monetary Fund and the International Bank for Reconstruction and Development commonly known as the World Bank.[1]

Two aspects of earlier experience affected the design of the Bretton Woods system. Problems inherited from World War I, together with subsequent policy mistakes, contributed to a breakdown of exchange-rate arrangements after the start of the depression in 1929. Furthermore, defects of the monetary system help to explain the worldwide character of the depression and its severity.

Monetary Reconstruction in the 1920s

Some of the problems of the 1920s were mentioned in Chapter 10. International indebtedness grew rapidly during World War I and continued to grow thereafter, due partly to the Versailles Treaty, which imposed large reparation payments on Germany. There were big changes in current-account balances, resulting from changes in competitive positions and from wartime sales of income-producing assets. After the war, moreover, Germany and other Central European countries experienced terrible inflations. The German housewife, it is said, needed a shopping basket to carry her money to market but could use a change purse to carry her groceries home. The inflations led to large exchange-rate changes, which fed back into prices and made the inflations worse, producing long-lasting doubts about the stability of floating exchange rates.

---

[1] In official usage, the term World Bank denotes a *pair* of institutions that make long-term loans to developing countries. The International Bank for Reconstruction and Development obtains its money by borrowing on international capital markets and lends it on market-related terms. The International Development Association (IDA) obtains its money from contributions by developed countries and lends it on concessional terms to the poorest countries. A third institution, the International Finance Corporation (IFC), is affiliated with the World Bank; it provides risk capital directly to private-sector projects in developing countries.

Governments stabilized their currencies eventually by linking the value of each currency to gold. They did so sequentially, however, without much consultation, and they did not pay enough attention to the exchange-rate pattern that their decisions were producing. In 1925, for example, Great Britain reinstated the prewar link between the pound and gold, thus reinstating automatically the prewar exchange rate between the pound and dollar. This rate was unrealistic, because British prices were higher, compared to American prices, than before the war. France then chose a new, low gold price for the franc, making the franc too cheap in terms of pounds and dollars. (The purchasing-power-parity doctrine discussed in Chapter 17 was developed by its author, Gustav Cassel, to deal with these situations. Although it has serious defects, adherence to the PPP doctrine might have led to more sensible exchange rates.)

This disorganized way of returning to pegged exchange rates is frequently blamed for the subsequent collapse of the monetary system. The attempt to restore the gold standard, however, was probably doomed from the start. Governments did not fully understand how it had worked before the war and could not therefore understand why it would not work in the postwar world.

The gold standard that came into being in the 1870s and lasted until World War I was different from the system described in the textbooks of the day. Currencies were less closely linked to gold. In the United States, banks could issue paper money that was backed by government bonds instead of gold. In Britain, the Bank of England conducted open-market operations to ease or tighten credit. Governments did not obey the "rules of the game," which called on them to reinforce the money-supply effects of gold flows rather than offset (sterilize) those flows.

Furthermore, the process of balance-of-payments adjustment was more complicated than the specie-flow mechanism described by David Hume. Gold outflows did not cause prices to fall promptly. They led to higher short-term interest rates and to capital inflows. These could halt gold losses but could not correct deep-seated imbalances. When gold outflows did depress demand, moreover, they tended to cut incomes rather than prices; they brought into play the foreign-trade multiplier rather than the price effects featured in textbook descriptions of the system.

The burden of adjustment was not always shared between surplus and deficit countries. It was often borne by countries at the fringes of the monetary system, including the United States, because they were doubly dependent on credit flows from London. They depended directly on long-term flows to finance their current-account deficits, and these flows fell sharply whenever the Bank of England tightened credit to combat gold losses. They depended indirectly on short-term flows that were used to finance world trade in grain, cotton, wool, and other commodities. When credit conditions tightened in London, commodity dealers had to sell off inventories; their sales depressed prices and reduced the export earnings of the commodity-producing countries. Great Britain's trade balance improved, halting its gold losses, but some of the improvement was achieved by shifting the terms of trade in favor of Britain rather than changing the volume of trade.

If governments had understood the differences between prewar theory and practive, they might have been more sensitive to differences between old and new realities. But they did not fully grasp the extent to which World War I has altered those realities.

The international economy had become less flexible. We have already mentioned the piling up of debt, the building of new tariff walls, and the growing use of quotas. National economies had also lost some of their flexibility. Wage rates had become more rigid, due partly to the spread of unionization. Furthermore, many more governments could insulate their monetary systems from credit and gold flows, because they had established their own central banks, including the Federal Reserve System in the United States, and could thus flout the "rules of the game" by sterilizing gold flows.

There was weakness at the center of the system. Great Britain's competitive position has started to deteriorate long before World War I, but wartime inflation weakened it some more, and the restoration of the old gold parity in 1925 made it even harder for British industry to compete in world markets. Furthermore, New York and Paris had become important financial centers, so London could not dominate credit conditions as it had before the war.

Finally, there were changes in the role of gold itself. Governments and central banks had started to hold pounds and dollars as reserves, instead of gold, and some of them held most of their reserves in London. Even the Bank of France, a pillar of monetary orthodoxy, built up large holdings of pounds in the early 1920s.

Money Disintegration in the 1930s

The substitution of currencies for gold was seen at the time as a way to reduce the dependence of the monetary system on new gold supplies, but it proved to be a major flaw in the system. Great Britain had become a banker to foreign governments but was in a weak competitive position and had only small reserves of its own with which to "back" its obligations. Like any ordinary bank, Britain was exposed to a "run" by its depositors; unlike an ordinary bank, it did not have a "lender of last resort" to which it could turn for cash. The run finally came in 1931, ending the attempt to restore the gold standard.

During most of the 1920s, countries such as Germany ran current-account deficits and had to make large payments on their foreign debts. They were able to meet their obligations only by borrowing more money in New York and other financial centers and thus going further into debt. Great Britain borrowed, too, but less directly; other countries built up their short-term claims on London. In 1928, however, the stock market boom in New York drained funds away from the bond market, reducing the capital outflow from the United States, and the outflow ended completely in 1929, with the start of the depression. Germany and other countries halted payments on their debts, because they could not borrow more, and dealt a sharp blow to confidence in the monetary system. Furthermore, the Bank of France started to convert pounds into gold, depleting Britain's gold reserves. In 1931, Britain was forced to leave the gold standard, when a panic that began with the collapse of the Credit Anstalt, a major Austrian bank, spread across Europe to London and threatened to strip away the rest of Britain's reserves.

The system unraveled rapidly thereafter, as the depression deepened. Some small countries had left the gold standard in 1929 and 1930; other countries followed in 1931 and 1932. They let their exchange rates float, and many put direct controls on trade and payments in a further effort to insulate themselves from the spread of the depression. The United States devalued the dollar in 1934. It had left the gold standard voluntarily in 1933 but chose a new gold price in 1934; the difference between the old price ($20.67 per ounce) and the new one ($35.00 per ounce) amounted to a 70 percent devaluation of the dollar in terms of the currencies that were still linked to gold.

Countries that continued to peg their currencies to gold, such as France and Italy, tried to defend their exchange rates by erecting trade controls to reduce their imports, but they had also to pursue deflationary policies to keep from losing gold. They abandoned the effort in 1936, and their currencies depreciated. Thereafter, exchange rates settled down, and despite the large changes that had taken place, the new rates were not very different from those that had prevailed in 1930, before Britain left the gold standard. But the stabilization of exchange rates was not accompanied by any significant relaxation of controls on trade and payments.

Lessons Drawn from the Interwar Period

What lessons were learned from this sad history? A study written for the League of Nations in 1944, *International Currency Experience*, put them in terms that were widely accepted.

The setting of exchange rates, it concluded, must not be left to market forces, because floating exchange rates tend to be too volatile:[2]

> The twenty years between the wars have furnished ample evidence concerning the question of fluctuating *versus* stable exchanges. A system of completely free and flexible exchange rates is conceivable and may have certain attractions in theory.... Yet nothing would be more at variance with the lessons of the past.
>
> Freely fluctuating exchanges involve three serious disadvantages. In the first place, they create an element of risk, which tends to discourage international trade. The risk may be covered by "hedging" operations where a forward exchange market exists; but such insurance, if obtainable at all, is obtainable only at a price and therefore generally adds to the cost of trading....
>
> Secondly, as a means of adjusting the balance of payments, exchange fluctuations involve constant shifts of labour and other resources between production for the home market and production for export. Such shifts may be costly and disturbing; they tend to create frictional unemployment, and are obviously wasteful if the exchange-market conditions that call for them are temporary....
>
> Thirdly, experience has shown that fluctuating exchange rates cannot always be relied upon to promote adjustment. Any considerable or continuous movement of the exchange rate is liable to generate anticipations of a further movement in the same direction, thus giving rise to speculative capital transfers of a disequilibrating kind....

---

[2]League of Nations, *International Currency Experience*, 1944, p. 210. The principal author was Ragnar Nurkse.

But the setting of exchange rates, the study said, must not be left entirely to individual governments:[3]

> An exchange rate by definition concerns more currencies than one. Yet exchange stabilization was carried out as an act of national sovereignty in one country after another with little or no regard for the resulting interrelationship of currency values in comparison with cost and price levels. This was so even where help was received from financial centers abroad. Stabilization of a currency was conceived in terms of gold rather than of other currencies.... From the very start, therefore, the system was subject to stresses and strains.

Looking to the future, the study argued that exchange-rate decisions should be carefully coordinated.

Turning to experience in the 1930s, the study concluded that governments cannot be expected to sacrifice domestic economic stability merely to maintain exchange-rate stability:[4]

> Experience has shown that stability of exchange rates can no longer be achieved by domestic income adjustments if these involve depression and unemployment. Nor can it be achieved if such income adjustments involve a general inflation of prices which the country concerned is not prepared to endure. It is therefore only as a consequence of internal stability, above all in the major countries, that there can be any hope of securing a satisfactory degree of exchange stability as well.

To achieve internal stability, moreover, major countries must harmonize their policies, expecially their monetary policies.

Even in the best of worlds, however, governments should not be expected to achieve complete stability and must therefore expect to experience balance-of-payments problems stemming from economic fluctuations at home and abroad. Furthermore, they should not have to count on short-term borrowing to finance balance-of-payments deficits. Flows of private capital can be perverse, the study argued, and can dry up completely just when they are needed. Therefore, official reserves should be large enough to meet normal needs and should be backed up by reliable supplies of reserve credit. These views were to influence strongly the design of the Bretton Woods system.

The Bretton Woods Agreement

One troublesome problem in the inter-war period, the piling up of debt, was avoided in the 1940s. The United States gave outright aid to its allies during World War II; they did not have to borrow to pay for war materiel. Furthermore, wartime planners tried to distinguish carefully between the short-run needs of postwar reconstruction and long-run needs of monetary management. To help with recon-

---

[3]Ibid., pp. 116–117.

[4]Ibid., p. 229.

1944	Bretton Woods Conference agrees to establish International Monetary Fund (IMF) and World Bank
1945	United States terminates wartime aid to allies
1946	IMF comes into existence United States makes large loans to Britain and France
1947	President Truman proposes aid for Greece and Turkey France is first country to draw on IMF Britain restores and then suspends convertibility of pound
1948	Marshall Plan begins IMF decides that Marshall Plan recipients should not normally draw on IMF
1949	Britain and many other countries devalue their currencies
1950	European Payments Union (EPU) established Canada allows its currency to float
1956	Britain and France draw on IMF during Suez crisis
1958	European Economic Community (EEC) established Ten European countries restore currency convertibility and dissolve EPU United States begins to run large balance-of-payments deficits
1959	First increase in IMF quotas approved
1960	Gold price rises in London, and major governments stabilize it by selling gold President Eisenhower takes measures to reduce U.S. balance-of-payments deficit
1961	Germany and the Netherlands revalue their currencies United States starts to intervene on foreign-exchange markets and to build credit network
1962	IMF resources supplemented by General Arrangements to Borrow (GAB) Canada restores pegged exchange rate
1963	President Kennedy proposes interest equalization tax on purchases of foreign securities Major governments begin first study of international monetary system
1964	Britain decides against devaluation, draws on IMF, and obtains credits from other governments and Bank for International Settlements (BIS)
1965	President Johnson imposes "voluntary" restraints on foreign lending by American banks and corporations Britain draws again on IMF and obtains additional credits
1967	Announcement of German agreement not to buy gold from the United States IMF adopts plan for creating Special Drawing Rights (SDRs) Britain devalues pound
1968	United States moves from voluntary to mandatory capital controls Management of gold price abandoned in favor of two-tiered market France and Germany fail to agree on exchange-rate realignment
1969	First Amendment to IMF Articles of Agreement comes into effect, authorizing SDR creation France devalues franc and Germany allows mark to float upward before pegging it
1970	First three-year allocation of SDRs begins Canadian dollar allowed to float again United States runs very large balance-of-payments deficit
1971	Germans propose joint float of European currencies; French propose devaluation of dollar Austria and Switzerland revalue their currencies, and Germany and the Netherlands allow their currencies to float

President Nixon imposes wage-price freeze and 10 percent import tax and
suspends convertibility between dollar and gold
Japan allows yen to float
At Smithsonian Institution in Washington, governments agree to realign and
peg exchange rates, devaluing dollar against most major currencies

1972   European and Japanese governments intervene heavily to support dollar
IMF establishes Committee of Twenty on reform of the monetary system
Britain allows pound to float

FIGURE 19-1
Monetary Chronology under the Bretton Woods System
Source: Adapted from Robert Solomon, *The International Monetary System*
1945–1981 (New York: Harper & Row, 1982), pp. 383–398.

struction, the United States made a large loan to Britain and smaller loans to
France, and it subscribed to the capital of the World Bank. When reconstruction
proved to be more costly than anticipated, the United States started its own
foreign-aid program. These and other highlights of monetary history under the
Bretton Woods system are listed in Figure 19-1.

At the Bretton Woods Conference, governments tried to make sure that exchange
rates would be chosen sensibly and altered only with good reason, that trade
controls would not be used for balance-of-payments purposes, and that governments
would be able to finance temporary balance-of-payments deficits and thus be able
to avoid changing their exchange rates frequently.

Under the Articles of Agreement of the International Monetary Fund, adopted at
Bretton Woods, member governments were required to peg their currencies to gold
or to the U.S. dollar (which was, in turn, pegged to gold at $35 per ounce). The IMF
had to approve those initial exchange rates and most changes made thereafter. To
justify a change in its exchange rate, a government had to demonstrate to the IMF
that it faced a "fundamental disequilibrium" in its balance of payments.

The Articles of Agreement required governments to make their currencies *convertible* as soon as possible. They could continue to regulate capital movements; recall
the view expressed in the League of Nations study that capital flows had been
destabilizing during the interwar period. But they could not interfere with currency
dealings required to conduct current-account transactions. If a resident of Belgium
acquired pounds by selling goods or services to Britain or from an investment-
income payment, the Belgian was entitled to use them for another current-account
transaction, sell them to someone else who wanted to do so, or sell them to the
Belgian central bank, which could then require the Bank of England to convert them
into Belgian francs.

Britain made its currency fully convertible in 1947, but it had to retreat very
quickly; countries that had built up balances in London during the war rushed to
cash them in for dollars and drained away much of the U.S. loan to Britain.
Chastened by this experience, most governments moved slowly toward convertibility; European countries did not reach it until 1958, and many developing countries
have never done so. (Czechoslovakia, Hungary, and Poland moved rapidly toward
convertibility after they abandoned central planning in 1989; they saw it as a way to

"import" world prices and link their economies to world markets. But Russia and the other republics of the former Soviet Union have made much less progress.

Finally, the Articles of Agreement of the IMF attempted to provide a reliable source of reserve credit. Under an early British plan drafted by John Maynard Keynes, the IMF would have functioned as a global central bank. It would have issued its own money, to be known as *bancor*. When a country ran a balance-of-payments deficit too large to be financed by drawing down reserves, it would have borrowed bancor from the IMF and paid the bancor to the countries with balance-of-payments surpluses. But this plan was too radical for the United States, which feared that it would wind up holding all the bancor. It proposed a different plan, adopted eventually at Bretton Woods. Rather than issue a new currency, the IMF would hold a pool of national currencies, and these would be available to deficit countries. Each member's contribution to the currency pool would be governed by a *quota*, which would also regulate its access to the pool and its voting power in the IMF.

These arrangements are illustrated by Figure 19-2, which shows what happens when two countries, Nord and Sud, join the IMF and make the payments necessary to obtain their quotas. Each country must pay a quarter of its quota in an international reserve asset and the balance in its national currency.[5] As Nord's quota is equivalent to $400 million and Sud's is equivalent to $200 million, the two countries' payments give the IMF $150 million of reserve assets, $300 million of Nordian francs, and $150 million of Sudian pesos. These amounts appear at the top of Figure 19-2, along with the *positions* of Nord and Sud, which depend on the Fund's holdings of their national currencies expressed as percentages of their quotas.

When the IMF's holdings of a member's currency are smaller than the member's quota, the member is said to have a *reserve position* equal to the difference. Thus, Nord starts with a reserve position equivalent to $100 million and Sud starts with a position equivalent to $50 million, corresponding to the reserve-asset payments they made to obtain their quotas.

When the IMF's holdings of a member's currency are larger than the member's quota, the member is said to be using *Fund credit*. Under the rules normally applied, the IMF's holdings of a member's currency must not exceed 200 percent of the member's quota; therefore, the use of Fund credit is usually limited to 100 percent of a member's quota.[6] This cumulative ceiling is divided into four *credit tranches*, each equal to a quarter of a member's quota. Drawings in the first tranche are approved routinely; drawings in the higher tranches are not approved unless the member adopts policies designed to improve its balance of payments. This practice is known as *conditionality*.

To draw on IMF resources, a member purchases reserve assets and other countries' currencies in exchange for the member's own national currency. The IMF

---

[5] In the early years of the IMF, reserve-asset payments were made in gold. These days, they are usually made in Special Drawing Rights (SDRs), which are defined and discussed in the next section of this chapter. (Furthermore, the IMF keeps its accounts in SDRs rather than in the dollar equivalents used in this example.)

[6] In recent years, however, the IMF has created a number of special credit facilities that members can use at the same time that they draw on its general resources. Therefore, a member's access to Fund credit can often exceed 100 percent of quota.

Quotas and Subscriptions

Nord's IMF quota is equivalent to $400 million, and Sud's is equivalent to $200 million. The IMF will hold these assets after Nord and Sud have made their subscriptions:

Asset	Millions of Dollars	Percentage of Member's Quota
Reserve assets	150	—
Nordian francs	300	75
Sudian pesos	150	75

Nord's *reserve position* is 25 percent of quota, equivalent to $100 million, and Sud's is 25 percent of quota, equivalent to $50 million.

A Purchase by Sud

Sud uses Sudian pesos to purchase the equivalent of $150 million from the IMF, obtaining $50 million of reserve assets and $100 million of Nordian francs. The IMF will then hold these assets:

Asset	Millions of Dollars	Percentage of Member's Quota
Reserve assets	100	—
Nordian francs	200	50
Sudian pesos	300	150

Nord's *reserve position* has risen to 50 percent of quota, or $200 million. Sud has used up its *reserve position* and also used $100 million of *Fund credit*; the IMF's holdings of pesos amount to 150 percent of Sud's quota, so the purchase has taken Sud through its second *credit tranche*.

A Repurchase by Sud

To repay Fund credit, Sud uses Nordian francs to buy back pesos worth $100 million. The IMF will then hold these assets:

Asset	Millions of Dollars	Percentage of Member's Quota
Reserve assets	100	—
Nordian francs	300	75
Sudian pesos	200	100

Nord's *reserve position* has fallen back to 25 percent of quota, or $100 million. Sud has not rebuilt its *reserve position* (the IMF's holdings of pesos are equal to Sud's quota) but has repaid the *Fund credit* it used earlier.

FIGURE 19-2
Transactions with the International Monetary Fund

decides what assets and currencies to provide. Suppose that Sud runs a balance-of-payments deficit and is allowed to purchase the equivalent of $150 million. The IMF provides $50 million of reserve assets and $100 million of Nordian francs. The effects appear in the middle of Figure 19-2. As the IMF's holdings of Sudian pesos rise to 150 percent of Sud's quota, Sud has used up its reserve position and has also used Fund credit. As the IMF's holdings of Nordian francs fall to 50 percent of Nord's quota, Nord's reserve position has risen to 50 percent of its quota.

In the normal course of events, Sud must repay Fund credit by repurchasing some of its currency. Suppose that it uses $100 million of Nordian francs to buy back Sudian pesos. The effects appear at the bottom of Figure 19-2. Sud has not rebuilt its reserve position; the IMF's holdings of Sudian pesos are exactly equal to Sud's quota. But Nord's reserve position has fallen back to 25 percent of quota.

There is another route to this same result. Suppose that Nord's balance of payments moves into deficit as Sud's balance of payments improves, and Nord makes a $100 million purchase to finance its deficit. If the IMF chooses to provide Sudian pesos in exchange for Nordian francs, the outcomes for Nord, Sud, and the IMF will be the same as those in Figure 19-2. Nord's purchase of pesos will repay Sud's use of Fund credit. This is how the IMF was expected to work. It was to be a revolving pool of currencies and reserve assets, whose composition would reflect temporary fluctuations in its member's balance-of-payments positions.

There have been several increases in IMF quotas. At the end of 1992, after the most recent increase, quotas totaled about $209 billion and the U.S. quota was about $38 billion, amounting to 18.2 percent of the global total. (U.S. voting power was thus large enough to veto certain classes of decisions, including decisions to amend the Articles of Agreement.)

MONETARY RELATIONS UNDER THE BRETTON WOODS SYSTEM

When looking back at monetary history since World War II, it is tempting to contrast the instability of the 1970s and 1980s with the apparent stability of the 1950s and 1960s, the years of the Bretton Woods system. Inflation and unemployment were high in the 1970s and the early 1980s, world trade grew slowly, and there were very large exchange-rate fluctuations. Inflation and unemployment were lower in most countries in the 1950s and 1960s, world trade grew rapidly, and exchange rates were quite stable. But we tend to forget the balance-of-payments problems and exchange-rate crises of the 1950s and 1960s and the widespread criticism of the Bretton Woods system.

An Overview

The United States and the U.S. dollar played important roles in the Bretton Woods system, but their roles changed sharply between 1945, when the system came into being, and 1971, when it started to disintegrate.

The United States dominated the world economy during the first postwar decade, and debates about the monetary situation focused on the so-called *dollar shortage*. The other industrial countries had suffered serious damage during the war and looked to the United States for the capital goods they needed to repair that damage, as well as for essential consumer goods they could not produce until the damage was repaired. Furthermore, the American economy was less open than it is today, and the

United States could afford to be passive in international monetary matters. It served as the nth country in the system, whose balance of payments and exchange rate reflected the policies of all other countries. When American officials paid any attention to the international monetary situation, they viewed it in terms of other countries' problems.

In 1949, for example, Great Britain and many other countries devalued their currencies, making their economies more competitive relative to the American economy, but U.S. officials did not object. In fact, the British government was reluctant to devalue the pound, but American officials advocated the devaluation because they were concerned about the outlook for Britain's balance of payments.

During that same decade, foreign governments and central banks started to accumulate dollars, just as they had accumulated pounds after World War I. The dollar began to serve as the main reserve currency. Like many other developments after Bretton Woods, this had not been planned. Washington did not deliberately seek a reserve-currency role for the dollar and did not give it much attention until the 1960s.

The situation changed when postwar reconstruction was completed. Although the American economy was still comparatively closed, it began to experience competition in domestic and foreign markets. Furthermore, American firms began to invest in Europe, causing a large capital outflow from the United States. The U.S. balance of payments moved into deficit, and there was talk about a *dollar glut* instead of a dollar shortage. The United States continued to act as the nth country but became increasingly uncomfortable about its role. It did not try to pursue an independent exchange-rate policy, but its views about other countries' problems began to reflect it concerns about the dollar.

In 1968, for example, France ran into a balance-of-payments problem that called for a devaluation of the French franc in terms of the Deutsche mark, but Paris and Bonn disagreed about the best way to achieve it. Each wanted the other to act. Paris wanted the mark revalued in terms of the dollar; Bonn wanted the franc devalued in terms of the dollar. Washington supported Paris, because a revaluation of the mark would strengthen the competitive position of the United States relative to Germany, whereas a devaluation of the franc would worsen it relative to France.

The United States abandoned its nth-country role in 1971, when its balance-of-payments deficit became very large. It set out to achieve a general realignment of exchange rates aimed at a significant devaluation of the dollar. The weakness of the U.S. balance of payments, however, did not reduce the dollar's role as a reserve currency. On the contrary, foreign official holdings of dollars grew faster. But most governments were dissatisfied with the situation and called for reform of the Bretton Woods system.

The Dollar Shortage

When Congress was asked to approve U.S. membership in the IMF and World Bank, it was promised that the American subscriptions to those institutions would be the last large contribution it would have to make to postwar reconstruction. This forecast proved to be too optimistic. As relations with the Soviet Union deteriorated, the economic problems of Western Europe were compounded by political problems culminating in the Berlin blockade of 1948 and formation of the North Atlantic Treaty Organization (NATO) in 1949. Europe was obliged to divert scarce resources from reconstruction to rearmament, and it was thus clear that the United States would have to make another contribution.

In a speech at Harvard, Secretary of State George Marshall proposed a new approach, which came to bear his name. If European governments would help each other, the United States would assist them:

> The role of this country should consist of friendly aid in the drafting of a European program and in later support of such a program as far as it may be practical for us to do so. The program should be a joint one, agreed to by a number, if not all, European nations.

The Soviet Union was invited to participate, to avoid a permanent division of Europe. But Moscow opposed joint economic planning, because it would weaken Soviet control over Eastern Europe, and the governments of Western Europe went ahead on their own. They drafted a joint program and set up an organization to monitor it, and Congress approved the first U.S. contribution in 1948. During the first three years of the Marshall Plan, that contribution totaled almost $11 billion, equivalent to more than $100 billion today.

The Marshall Plan made three vital contributions to European reconstruction. First, it allowed the Europeans to purchase capital goods and raw materials, which they needed to start up their industries again. In other words, it relieved the dollar shortage directly. Second, it allowed them to dismantle the controls on trade and payments they had kept in place to conserve scarce dollars. They started by establishing the European Payments Union (EPU), a credit network that helped them to trade among themselves without using dollars to settle all imbalances. In consequence, they liberalized intra-European trade faster than trade with the United States. As they began to export more to the United States, however, they relaxed their restrictions on the use of dollar earnings. Third, the Marshall Plan helped European countries to acquire reserves—to buy a significant quantity of gold from the United States and to accumulate dollar balances. At the beginning of 1958, when the European Economic Community came into being, European governments were ready to make their currencies convertible, and they abolished the EPU.

Nothing has been said thus far about the IMF, because its role was small at first. In fact, the IMF decided that countries covered by the Marshall Plan should not purchase dollars from the IMF, a decision consistent with earlier attempts to distinguish clearly between the special needs of reconstruction and the ordinary need for balance-of-payments financing. But something worrisome was also happening. Governments had started to alter exchange rates without consulting the IMF. In 1949, the IMF learned officially about the impending devaluation of the pound just before it was announced—and it was told that it would happen, not asked if it should happen. In 1950, Canada violated the Bretton Woods agreement by allowing the Canadian dollar to float, but it did not suffer any significant penalty.

The IMF became more active in 1956, not in overseeing exchange-rate policies but as a source of credit. War between Israel and Egypt, in which Britain and France were also involved, closed the Suez Canal. Trade in oil was disrupted, damaging the British and French economies, and foreign-exchange markets began to expect devaluations of the pound and franc. The British and French authorities had to intervene to keep their currencies from depreciating, and both countries drew heavily on the IMF (as did Israel and Egypt).

These drawings were important for the precedents they set, as well as for their size. France had to commit itself to deflationary policies, because its problems were due largely to domestic inflation, not the Suez crisis, and the IMF was involved in the discussions that led to the subsequent devaluation of the franc. Furthermore, the drawings were made under *stand-by arrangements* that have since become standard practice. France was given the right to draw a large sum from the IMF, more than it needed immediately, if it carried out the policies to which it was committed. Stand-by arrangements can combat speculation against a currency by showing that a government can mobilize enough reserves to intervene massively on the foreign-exchange market.

The Dollar Glut

In the early 1950s, some economists believed that the dollar shortage could be permanent. Other countries might not "catch up" with the United States, even after repairing war damage, because the American economy was more innovative. (Their argument was similar to one we hear today, that the United States and Europe will not catch up with Japan unless they imitate Japanese methods.) In 1958, however, the U.S. balance of payments deteriorated sharply. The dollar shortage gave way to a dollar glut.

Most economists welcomed this development at first, as proof that Europe and Japan had recovered from World War II. They predicted that the U.S. balance of payments would improve after American firms had adapted to foreign competition. The payments deficit did not go away, however, and made a sizable dent in the U.S. gold stock. Hence, some economists began to believe that the dollar had become *overvalued* in terms of other currencies, partly because many of those currencies had been devalued during the previous decade and partly because of inflation in the United States.

Just before the U.S. election of 1960, speculation flared up in the London gold market, where most private gold trading takes place. It was fueled by rumors that the next American administration would raise the price of gold in order to devalue the dollar in terms of other currencies. The United States sold gold in London in collaboration with other governments, and the price of gold declined. Even before his election, however, John Kennedy felt compelled to promise that he would not devalue the dollar.

The long-term outlook for the dollar was hard to evaluate. On the one hand, American goods were becoming more competitive. Recessions in 1957–1958 and 1960–1961 had reduced inflation in the United States, and exports were rising faster than imports. The balance-of-payments statistics in Table 19-1 and Figure 19-3 show this clearly; there were current-account surpluses in the early 1960s, and they were fairly large by the standards of the time. On the other hand, American firms were investing heavily in Europe, and other capital outflows were also growing. Believing that the current-account surplus would continue to grow and that capital outflows would taper off after American firms had built up their facilities in Europe,

Table 19-1. The U.S. Balance of Payments, 1960–1991 (annual averages in billions of dollars)

Item	60–64	65–69	70–74	75–79	80–82	83–85	86–88	89–91
Exports of goods and services	34.2	50.7	96.9	204.6	362.3	374.4	464.7	671.8
Merchandise	21.7	31.3	61.0	133.8	224.2	212.5	264.6	388.8
Services	6.9	10.8	18.2	32.2	56.3	69.4	98.4	146.5
Investment income	5.6	8.7	17.7	38.6	81.8	92.4	101.7	136.5
Imports of goods and services	−25.8	−43.1	−88.4	−200.0	−351.3	−442.0	−586.6	−720.0
Merchandise	−16.3	−28.5	−63.1	−152.5	−254.2	−313.1	−408.5	−488.1
Services	−8.1	−11.4	−17.4	−28.6	−46.2	−65.1	−89.4	−112.1
Investment income	−1.4	−3.1	−7.9	−18.9	−50.9	−63.7	−88.7	−119.8
Unilateral transfers	−4.2	−5.2	−7.7	−6.1	−12.4	−20.4	−24.0	−16.8
Balance on current account	4.3	2.4	0.8	−1.5	−1.4	−88.1	−145.9	−65.1
Increase (−) in U.S. assets abroad, net[a]	−7.1	−9.0	−19.5	−49.8	−101.7	−38.0	−83.9	−70.6
U.S. government	−1.3	−2.0	−1.5	−4.0	−5.5	−4.4	0.7	2.3
Direct investment	−3.1	−5.3	−8.7	−15.9	−9.3	−9.7	−19.9	−29.6
Foreign securities	−0.8	−1.2	−1.1	−5.8	−5.8	−6.3	−5.8	−32.0
Other	−1.8	−0.5	−8.3	−24.1	−81.2	−17.5	−58.9	−11.4
Increase (+) in foreign assets in U.S., net[a]	1.3	6.7	8.5	24.9	69.8	102.8	184.0	106.4
Direct investment	0.3	0.7	2.1	6.1	18.2	18.4	50.4	41.5
U.S. gov't securities	−0.1	−0.1	0.1	2.6	4.2	17.4	5.5	14.4
Other U.S. securities	0.2	1.8	2.7	2.0	6.1	23.9	46.5	25.1
Other	0.9	4.3	3.7	14.3	41.3	43.2	81.6	25.4

SDR Allocations[b]	0.0	0.0	0.5	0.2	0.7	0.0	0.0	0.0
Balance on official settlements[c]	2.4	0.1	12.9	15.5	1.9	−0.1	42.1	13.0
Increase (−) in U.S. reserve assets	1.0	0.0	0.7	−0.8	−6.1	−2.7	1.8	−7.2
Increase (+) in U.S. reserve liabilities[d]	1.4	0.2	12.2	16.3	8.0	2.6	40.3	20.3
Errors and omissions	−0.9	−0.2	−3.2	10.6	30.6	23.3	3.7	16.2

Source: U.S. Department of Commerce, *Survey of Current Business*, various issues. Detail may not add to total because of rounding.

[a] Except reserve assets, shown below.

[b] An accounting entry to offset the increase (−) of U.S. reserve assets resulting from new allocations of special drawing rights by the IMF.

[c] A positive entry denotes a balance-of-payments deficit.

[d] Foreign reserve assets held in the United States.

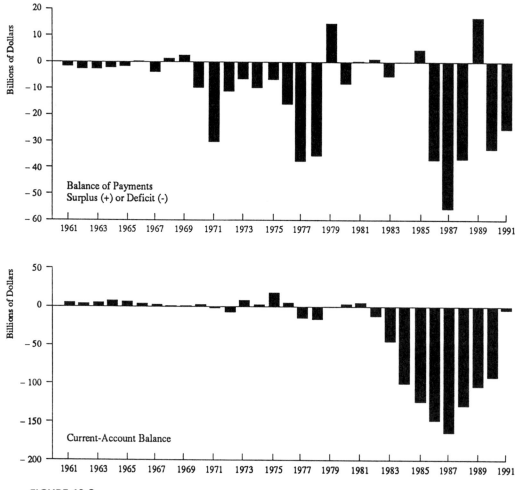

FIGURE 19-3
The U.S. Balance of Payments and Current Account, 1961–1991
Source: U.S. Department of Commerce, *Survey of Current Business* (various issues).
Current-account balance includes official transfers.

the Kennedy administration declined to take drastic action. It tried to reduce the dollar costs of stationing American troops in Europe, and it "tied" U.S. foreign aid to purchases of U.S. goods. But it did not tighten monetary or fiscal policy to restrict domestic demand, because it had promised to reduce unemployment.

Taking an optimistic view about the long-term outlook, the Kennedy administration emphasized financing rather than adjustment and tried in particular to keep down gold losses. It sought to persuade foreign governments to hold dollar balances rather than gold; it built up reciprocal credit lines with foreign central banks; and it made small drawings on the IMF. To make sure that the IMF would have the currencies to handle a larger U.S. drawing, nine major countries joined with the United States in the General Arrangements to Borrow (GAB), promising to lend their currencies to the IMF if it needed them for a large drawing by one of the participants. The participants came to be known as the Group of Ten (G-10). In

1983, the GAB was enlarged and made more flexible; the participants will lend their currencies to the IMF if it needs them for a large drawing by *any* member.

Under the Bretton Woods system, the United States did not intervene regularly on foreign-exchange markets to stabilize the value of the dollar. That task was left to foreign central banks, which bought dollars with their own national currencies whenever the dollar began to depreciate. They had the right to buy gold with those dollars, but most of them declined to exercise that right during the 1960s. France was the only important exception, because the French president, Charles de Gaulle, believed that the reserve-currency role of the dollar conferred an "exorbitant privilege" on the United States—the ability to run a balance-of-payments deficit without losing reserves. He also sought to reduce American influence in Europe by attacking the dominant role of the dollar.

When capital outflows did not taper off, the Kennedy administration imposed an "interest equalization tax" on American purchases of foreign securities, and the Johnson administration carried matters further. In 1965, it asked American banks to limit their lending to foreigners voluntarily and asked American companies to limit their direct investments. In 1968, it shifted from voluntary to mandatory controls. By that time, however, the current account had weakened because of military outlays for the war in Vietnam and the effects of the war on the U.S. economy. The Johnson administration had tried to finance the war without raising taxes, allowing inflationary pressures to build up. The outlook for the dollar was getting worse.

Other countries' problems were also putting strains on the international monetary system, first those of Britain, then those of France.

Britain began to run balance-of-payments deficits in the early 1960s, and some members of the British government favored a devaluation. Washington objected, however, believing that devaluation of the pound would touch off speculation against the dollar—another occasion on which U.S. views about other countries' policies reflected concerns about the impact on the dollar. For this and other reasons, Britain continued to defend the existing exchange rate. It borrowed heavily from other governments and made three large drawings on the IMF. But Britain ran out of credit in 1967, and the pound was finally devalued.

In the spring of 1968, demonstrations and strikes by French students and workers led to capital flight from France. To end the strikes, moreover, the government raised wages, which damaged the competitive positive of French industry. When France and Germany could not agree on an exchange-rate realignment, France postponed action. In 1969, however, after the resignation of President de Gaulle, France devalued the franc without consulting anyone, not even its partners in the EC.

There *was* speculation against the dollar after the devaluation of the pound. It showed up in the gold market, as in 1960, and governments sold gold to keep its price from rising. But they could not calm the market, and sales were suspended in early 1968. Thereafter, there were two gold markets. Governments continued to deal with each other at $35 per ounce, the official price, but would not sell gold on the London market, where the price would be determined by supply and demand.

After the devaluation of the franc, there was more speculation, this time based on rumors that the mark would be revalued. The German authorities tried at first to keep the mark from appreciating by buying dollars in the foreign-exchange market, but they had to buy huge quantities. Therefore, they allowed the exchange rate to float. This was the first major break in the pegged-rate system since 1950, when the Canadian dollar had been allowed to float. It was likewise the first of several occasions on which the German authorities faced the choice between allowing the mark to appreciate and raising the German money supply by intervening hugely on the foreign-exchange market, and they have often opted for appreciation. On this particular occasion, they allowed the mark to appreciate by 10 percent in four weeks, after which they began again to intervene, converting the appreciation into a revaluation by pegging the mark-dollar rate close to the new market level.

First Steps Toward Reform of the Monetary System

Economists began to criticize the Bretton Woods system in the 1950s. Some believed that exchange rates should float. Others did not go that far, but they warned that the political dynamics of the system were making rates too rigid. When a country's balance of payments moved into deficit, rumors of an impending devaluation began to circulate in the foreign-exchange market. If the government did not deny them, capital outflows built up, reserves fell, and the rumors became self-fulfilling; the government had to devalue. Once it had denied the rumors, however, it could not devalue voluntarily without tarnishing its credibility by admitting that its policies had failed.

These political dynamics made it hard for governments to talk about exchange-rate changes, even in the abstract. One official study listed the policy instruments that governments should use to deal with balance-of-payments problems. It did not even mention the exchange rate! Furthermore, most such studies emphasized financing rather than adjustment and devoted much attention to reserve arrangements. Gold was the only reserve asset mentioned in the Bretton Woods agreement, and a change in its price was the only method mentioned for adjusting the supply of international reserves.[7] In the 15 years following World War II, however, gold stocks rose by little more than one percent per year, and the growth of dollar balances accounted for most of the increase in official reserves.

In 1931, shifts in reserves from pounds to gold had precipitated the crisis that forced Britain to leave the gold standard. Robert Triffin of Yale warned that the same thing could happen again. In *Gold and the Dollar Crisis*, published in 1960, shortly before the first flurry of speculation in the London gold market, he posed what is now known as the Triffin dilemma. To supply reserves to the rest of the world, the United States had to run balance-of-payments deficits. As it did so, however, its own reserve position would deteriorate, undermining international confidence in the dollar. The quantity of reserves could be increased only at the risk of reducing their quality.

---

[7]Most governments opposed an increase in the price of gold, however, for a variety of reasons. First, it would confer large benefits on the Soviet Union and South Africa, the largest gold producers. Second, it would have complex effects on gold stocks and flows: it would raise the dollar value of existing gold stocks and the dollar value of gold output, but it would also increase the profitability of gold mining and thus raise the volume of output. No one could be sure that this would be the right combination of effects. Finally, an increase in the price of gold would favor countries holding large amounts of gold, compared to those holding large amounts of dollars. The United States was especially sensitive to this effect, because it was trying to persuade foreign governments to hold dollars rather than gold.

Triffin recommended a new version of the proposal made by Britain during the discussions that led to Bretton Woods. The IMF would issue its own currency when giving credit to its members but would also issue it in two other ways. Governments could buy it from the IMF in exchange for dollars and other reserve assets, and the IMF could conduct open-market operations, buying and selling securities, including World Bank bonds, to raise or reduce official reserves. The IMF would begin to function as a global central bank.

This plan was too radical for most governments, however, and some had very strong reasons to oppose it. The United States wanted other governments to hold dollars and resisted the creation of any new asset that might compete with the dollar. France favored a larger role for gold and was reluctant to sacrifice any sovereignty to an international institution. In 1965, however, the U.S. balance of payments seemed to be on the mend, and Washington changed sides, urging the creation of a new reserve asset. Governments turned from contemplation to negotiation, and they reached agreement in 1967. The IMF would be authorized to create Special Drawing Rights "to meet the long-term global need, as and when it arises, to supplement existing reserve assets."[8]

When SDRs are distributed, each government receives a quantity proportional to its quota in the IMF. Thereafter, it may use its SDRs to buy other members' currencies or for transactions with the IMF itself. Members frequently receive SDRs when they draw on the Fund, and when there is an increase in IMF quotas, a quarter of the requisite subscription is normally paid in SDRs. The SDR was initially defined in terms of gold. It is defined today in terms of a "basket" of five currencies—dollars, pounds, marks, yen, and French francs.[9] The first distribution of SDRs began in 1970, and a second began in 1979, but there have been no further distributions.

The System in Crisis

When Triffin published *Gold and the Dollar Crisis*, the United States still had a strong reserve position. Its gold holdings were larger than its liabilities to foreign official institutions. But the balance-of-payments deficits of the 1960s reduced its gold holdings, raised its liabilities, and weakened its reserve position. It had turned

---

[8]Articles of Agreement of the International Monetary Fund, Article XVIII, Section 1 (a).

[9]The composition of the basket can be changed from time to time. This is how it was defined on June 30, 1992:

Currency	Number of Units	Dollar Value per Unit	Total Dollar Value
U.S. dollar	0.452	$1.0000	$0.452
Deutsche mark	0.527	0.6549	0.345
French franc	1.020	0.1948	0.198
Japanese yen	33.400	0.0080	0.267
U.K. pound	0.089	1.8980	0.169
Total	—	—	$1.431

Thus, 1 SDR was worth a little more than $1.43 in U.S. dollars.

negative by 1970, when the balance-of-payments deficit widened suddenly. (see Figure 19-3).

In the first three months of 1971, foreign governments and central banks had to buy more than $5 billion in the foreign-exchange market to prevent the dollar from depreciating. There were new rumors that the Deutsche mark would be revalued, and speculation focused on the mark-dollar exchange rate. On a single day in May, the German central bank had to buy more than $1 billion. The next day, it had to buy another $1 billion during the first hour of trading. Therefore, it suspended intervention, allowing the mark to float upward for the second time in two years.

In Chapter 13, we saw that a country with high unemployment and a balance-of-payments deficit should adopt an expenditure-switching policy. It should devalue rather than reduce absorption. That was the situation confronting the United States in 1971. In April, the trade balance slipped into deficit for the first time in this century, and the unemployment rate was close to 6 percent, a high level for those days. American officials asked themselves how they could persuade other governments to revalue their currencies vis-à-vis the dollar. They did not want to devalue the dollar directly by raising the official price of gold, the only option open to them, because they did not want to break faith with the foreign governments that were holding dollars, and because they were not sure that the technique would work. A higher dollar price for gold would not bring about a devaluation of the dollar if other governments continued to peg their currencies to the dollar.

Although the balance-of-payments deficit was huge in the first half of 1971, gold losses were small. Early in August, however, France bought some gold in order to repurchase francs from the IMF, and there were rumors of a large gold order by the Bank of England. The rumors were inaccurate but influential. On August 15, President Richard Nixon announced a dramatic policy change. To improve the domestic situation, he froze wages and prices temporarily and asked Congress to enact an investment tax credit to stimulate output and employment. To improve the international situation, he imposed an additional 10 percent tariff on imports and instructed the secretary of the Treasury to close the gold window—to suspend purchases and sales of gold. These measures were designed to bring about an exchange-rate realignment. They imposed two penalties on any foreign government that refused to revalue its currency. Its exports would be penalized by the tariff, and it could no longer count on buying gold with the dollars purchased in the foreign-exchange market to keep its own currency from appreciating. The Nixon administration was widely criticized for adopting these "shock" tactics, and the secretary of the Treasury, John Connally, was accused of being aggressively nationalistic. His blunt rhetoric, however, was partly designed for domestic consumption—to combat protectionist pressures in Congress.

In the days following the president's speech, several governments joined Germany, letting their currencies float. That was what Washington wanted in the short run, but it wanted something different in the long run. It was not trying to substitute floating for pegged rates; it was merely trying to eliminate the U.S. balance-of-payments deficit by forcing large changes in exchange rates before they were pegged again. After months of hard bargaining, a meeting at the Smithsonian Institution in Washington agreed on an exchange-rate realignment. Several governments revalued their currencies in terms of the dollar, and the United States devalued the dollar in terms of gold (the price of gold was raised from $35 to $38 per ounce). The United States, however, did not reopen the gold window. In other words, the new official gold price was the one at which the United States would *not* buy or sell.

The governments also agreed to undertake a thorough review of the monetary system, aimed at achieving "a suitable degree" of exchange-rate flexibility, and to liberalize trade policies. The commitment to review the monetary system led to the creation of the Committee of Twenty, whose work is discussed later in this chapter. The commitment to liberalize trade policies led to the Tokyo Round of trade negotiations.

When examining the effects of a devaluation in Chapter 14, we noted that short-run price elasticities may be too low to satisfy the Marshall–Lerner–Robinson condition. In that case, the current account will trace out a J-shaped curve in response to a devaluation, getting worse before getting better. That is what happened after the Smithsonian realignment, and the problem was compounded by domestic policies; the U.S. economy was expanding too fast. But many observers interpreted the situation differently, saying that the realignment had been too small and recommending another devaluation. In the middle of 1972, moreover, Britain ran into balance-of-payments problems, and the pound was allowed to float, triggering another bout of speculation—capital flight from the dollar into the mark and yen. The Smithsonian Agreement was crumbling and taking the Bretton Woods system with it. The end came early in 1973, with the events listed at the top of Figure 19-4. The U.S. government decided to devalue the dollar again. One by one, however, other industrial countries let their currencies float. Switzerland had done so two weeks before the American decision, because of a huge capital inflow; Japan followed right after the decision; and six members of the EC, including France and Germany, did so jointly four weeks later.

MONETARY RELATIONS UNDER FLOATING EXCHANGE RATES

Some central bankers have said that they favored floating exchange rates before 1973 but could not convince governments to adopt them. In 1973, however, most of them were saying that the float should be temporary. In fact, the Committee of Twenty was instructed to design a system of "stable but adjustable" exchange rates, something like the Bretton Woods regime but with more flexibility in the pegs, in order to improve balance-of-payments adjustment. But exchange rates never seemed quite ripe for pegging, and the temporary float continued. Eventually, the IMF Articles of Agreement were revised to "legalize" the float.

Trying to Put Humpty-Dumpty Together

The Committee of Twenty represented the whole membership of the IMF and, therefore, a wide range of interests and concerns. Nevertheless, its work was dominated by differences in view between the European and American participants. Both sides wanted to construct a more "symmetrical" system but used that term to stand for very different objectives.

1973	Switzerland allows franc to float
	United States announces 10 percent devaluation of dollar
	Japan allows yen to float, and six European countries follow, allowing their currencies to float jointly
	Committee of Twenty issues outline for reform of monetary system
	Oil "embargo" imposed with outbreak of Arab–Israeli war, and oil prices rise, triggering first large increase in OPEC oil prices
1974	France drops out of joint European float (snake)
	United States ends controls on capital outflows and Germany relaxes controls on inflows
	IMF establishes first oil facility
	Committee of Twenty ends its work by proposing "evolutionary" reform
	IMF shifts valuation of SDR from gold to "basket" of currencies
1975	France rejoins European snake
	At Rambouillet summit, major countries agree to "legalize" floating
1976	At Kingston, Jamaica, IMF Interim Committee approves Second Amendment to IMF Articles of Agreement, based on Rambouillet agreement
	France drops out of European snake again
1977	Britain draws on IMF and obtains new credits from other governments to phase out reserve-currency role of pound
	Michael Blumenthal, U.S. secretary of the Treasury, suggests that mark and yen might appreciate against dollar
1978	Second Amendment to IMF Articles of Agreement takes effect, "legalizing" the float and reducing the monetary role of gold
	EEC countries agree to establish European Monetary System (EMS)
	At Bonn summit, Germany and Japan agree to stimulate their economies, and United States agrees to deregulate oil prices
	United States draws on IMF and intervenes in defense of dollar, and Federal Reserve tightens monetary policy
	Unrest in Iran raises oil prices, triggering second increase in OPEC prices
1979	IMF liberalizes access to resources
	EMS comes into being
	United States intervenes heavily to resist depreciation of dollar
	Paul Volcker, Federal Reserve chairman, announces sharp tightening of U.S. monetary policy and introduction of money-supply targets
1980	Germany and Japan borrow from OPEC countries to finance current-account deficits
	United States intervenes to resist appreciation of dollar
1981	IMF adopts "enlarged access" policy, affirming 1979 liberalization, and borrows from Saudi Arabia to augment resources
	United States announces that it will no longer intervene
	Poland begins to experience severe debt problems
1982	Mexico asks commercial banks to reschedule its debts, gets "bridge loans" from United States and BIS, and applies for IMF drawing; Brazil follows Mexico
1983	Debt problems spread as more than 25 countries seek to reschedule debts to banks exceeding $65 billion
	IMF quotas raised to nearly $100 billion, and GAB liberalized
	OPEC countries attempt to impose output quotas as oil prices fall
1984	IMF begins to curtail "enlarged access" to resources
	Mexico and commercial banks agree on multiyear rescheduling of debt amounting to almost $50 billion

1985   United States runs record budget and trade deficits and dollars appreciates sharply

1985   Dollar starts to depreciate, and United States resumes intervention

In Plaza agreement, G-5 governments endorse and pledge to promote further depreciation of dollar

James Baker, U.S. secretary of the Treasury, calls for "adjustment with growth" by debtor countries and more lending by World Bank and commercial banks

1986   At Tokyo summit, industrial countries agree to "multilateral surveillance" of macroeconomic policies

Central banks begin to buy dollars to resist further depreciation

1987   Brazil suspends interest payments on debt

In Louvre agreement, G-5 countries endorse and pledge to stabilize existing exchange rates, and central banks intervene massively to support dollar

Prices fall sharply on world stock markets and dollar starts to depreciate again

1988   Mexico and United States announce plan for banks to reduce Mexican debt and receive guarantees of remaining principal

Central banks intervene to prevent depreciation of dollar, then to prevent appreciation

1989   Nicholas Brady, U.S. secretary of the Treasury, proposes debt reduction backed by IMF and World Bank lending to guarantee debt-service payments

Mexico and other countries begin to negotiate debt-reduction agreements under Brady Plan

Delors Committee publishes report on Economic and Monetary Union (EMU) in Europe

Fall of Berlin Wall and start of transition to market economies in Central Europe

1990   Poland adopts stabilization program, pegging currency to U.S. dollar to combat inflation, and draws on IMF

IMF quotas raised to about $180 billion, and quotas of industrial countries redistributed in favor of Japan and Germany

Political and economic reunification of Germany

Britain joins exchange-rate mechanism of EMS

1991   Russia and other independent states emerge from collapse of Soviet Union and start transition to market economies

EC countries sign Maastricht Treaty committing them to EMU by 1999

1992   Russia and other states of former Soviet Union join IMF and plan stabilization programs to qualify for IMF drawings

Dollar depreciates against mark as Federal Reserve cuts American interest rates to combat recession and Bundesbank raises German rates to combat inflationary pressures due to reunification

Danish referendum rejects Maastricht Treaty

French referendum approves Maastricht Treaty but doubts about outcome trigger European exchange-rate crisis

Britain and Italy leave exchange-rate mechanism of the EMS and allow currencies to float

FIGURE 19-4
Monetary Chronology under Floating Exchange Rates
Source: Adapted from Solomon, *The International Monetary System,* pp. 391–398, and International Monetary Fund, *IMF Survey* (various issues).

The Americans wanted a more symmetrical adjustment process, in which surplus countries as well as deficit countries would work to eliminate imbalances. They also wanted to make sure that the United States would be able to alter its exchange rate without having to disrupt the monetary system, as in 1971. They suggested that an "objective indicator" be used to signal the need for balance-of-payments adjustment. When a country's reserves were lower than some critical level, it would be expected to tighten its domestic policies or devalue its currency. When its reserves were higher than some critical level, it would be expected to ease its domestic policies or revalue its currency.

The Europeans wanted a more symmetrical system of settlements, to prevent the United States from financing a balance-of-payments deficit by piling up dollar debt and thus postponing action to eliminate its deficit. Countries should run down reserves when they have payments deficits, and no country should accumulate another's currency as a reserve asset. They also asked the United States to redeem the existing dollar balances; those balances would be handed over to the IMF in exchange for SDRs, and the United States would redeem them from the IMF at a rate dependent on its balance-of-payments situation.

The Committee of Twenty might perhaps have reached agreement if the Americans and Europeans had put their plans together. The United States might have agreed to reserve-asset settlement if the Europeans had agreed to use an objective indicator and thus participate more fully in correcting future balance-of-payments problems. But each side had strong reservations about the other's plans. The Americans insisted that the dollar's role as a reserve currency had been a burden on the United States, not a privilege, but they did not want to phase it out completely. They were especially reluctant to promise that the United States would redeem other countries' dollar holdings, which were about six times as large as U.S. gold reserves. The Europeans did not trust an objective indicator to trigger policy changes, because it might give false signals.

The work of the committee, however, was overtaken by events—the "oil shock" of 1973 and the problems it produced—and governments concluded that floating rates were here to stay. In November 1975, when the major industrial countries held their first economic summit meeting at Rambouillet, near Paris, they agreed to legitimize floating rates by amending the Articles of Agreement of the IMF. The Interim Committee of the IMF, its senior policymaking body, worked out the details in Kingston, Jamaica, and the Second Amendment to the Articles of Agreement took effect in 1978. It gave governments wide latitude in choosing their exchange-rate arrangements but instructed the IMF to exercise "firm surveillance" over its members' exchange-rate policies. Figure 19-5 reproduces key clauses from Article IV, which defines the obligations of governments and the responsibilities of the IMF.[10]

To carry out those responsibilities, the IMF adopted guidelines for exchange-rate management. Governments should intervene in foreign-exchange markets to counter "disorderly" conditions but should not attempt to maintain unrealistic rates. To spot such situations, the IMF would watch for sustained one-way movements in a

---

[10]The reference there to "cooperative arrangements" was meant to cover the joint float of European currencies, which evolved into the European Monetary System, described later in this chapter.

Article IV
Obligations Regarding Exchange Arrangements
Section 1. *General obligations of members*

Recognizing that the essential purpose of the international monetary system is to provide a framework that facilitates the exchange of goods, services, and capital among countries, and that sustains sound economic growth, and that a principal objective is the continuing development of the orderly underlying conditons that are necessary for financial and economic stability, each member undertakes to collaborate with the Fund to assure orderly exchange arrangements and to promote a stable system of exchange rates...

Section 2. *General exchange arrangements*

   (a) Each member shall notify the Fund ... of the exchange arrangements it intends to apply in fulfillment of its obligations under Section 1 of this Article, and shall notify the Fund promptly of any changes in its exchange arrangements.

   (b) Under an international monetary system of the kind prevailing on January 1, 1976, exchange arrangements may include (i) the maintenance by a member of a value for its currency in terms of the special drawing right or another denominator, other than gold, selected by the member, or (ii) cooperative arrangements by which members maintain the value of their currencies in relation to the value of the currency or currencies of other members, or (iii) other exchange arrangements of a member's choice...

Section 3. *Surveillance over exchange arrangements*

   (a) The Fund shall oversee the international monetary system in order to ensure its effective operation, and shall oversee the compliance of each member with its obligations under Section 1 of this Article.

   (b) In order to fulfill its functions under (a) above, the Fund shall exercise firm surveillance over the exchange rate policies of members, and shall adopt specific principles for the guidance of all members with respect to those policies. Each member shall provide the Fund with the information necessary for such surveillance, and, when requested by the Fund, shall consult with it on the member's exchange rate policies...

FIGURE 19-5
Extract from the Second Amendment to the IMF Articles of Agreement

country's reserves, large amounts of official borrowing or lending for balance-of-payments purposes, the introduction or tightening of controls on trade or capital movements, and the behavior of the exchange rate itself. But the IMF has no power to penalize governments that violate the guidelines, and it has not been able to exercise much influence over the policies of the major countries.

The First Oil Shock

If a single event can take credit or blame for the decision to accept floating exchange rates, it must be the sharp increase in the price of oil that followed the outbreak of war between Egypt and Israel in October 1973. Arab oil producers, such as Saudi Arabia, announced an "embargo" on sales to the Netherlands and the United States, which maintained close relations with Israel. Prices rose sharply as oil companies bid for available supplies to serve their Dutch and American markets and to build up inventories. In December, the Organization of Petroleum Exporting

Countries (OPEC), whose membership included Indonesia, Iran, Nigeria, and Venezuela, as well as Arab countries, looked at the high market prices and decided that the world could afford to pay them. They raised their contract prices—those at which they sell to the large oil companies—from less than $3 per barrel to more than $9 per barrel.

The increase in oil prices had three large effects on the international economy. They show up clearly in Figure 19-6 and Table 19-2, which describe developments in the seven "summit" countries (Canada, France, Germany, Italy, Japan, the United Kingdom, and the United States), and in Figure 19-7, which describes the evolution of current-account balances.

First, it raised the prices of the many goods that are made from oil, from gasoline

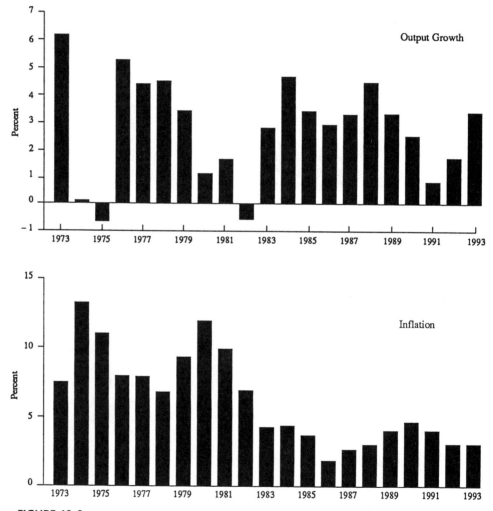

FIGURE 19-6
Output Growth and Inflation in the Seven Summit Countries, 1973–1993
Source: International Monetary Fund, *World Economic Outlook* (various issues). Output measured by gross domestic product; inflation measured by consumer prices; German data through 1989 are for West Germany alone. Entries for 1992 and 1993 are estimates.

Table 19-2. Economic Indicators for the Seven Summit Countries, 1962–1993 (averages of annual percentages)

Indicator	Average 62–73	74–75	76–77	78–79	80–81	82–83	84–85	86–87	88–89	90–91	92–93[a]
Change in output (GDP)											
Seven summit countries	4.8	−0.3	4.9	4.0	1.4	1.1	4.1	3.1	3.9	1.7	2.6
United States	4.2	−0.9	5.5	3.8	0.9	0.6	4.7	3.0	3.2	0.2	2.6
Germany	4.5	−0.6	4.2	3.7	0.8	0.4	2.5	1.9	3.8	2.9	2.5
Japan	10.3	0.6	5.3	5.2	4.1	3.2	4.8	3.5	5.5	4.9	3.1
Inflation rate (CPI)											
Seven summit countries	4.0	12.1	7.9	8.1	11.0	5.7	4.2	2.4	3.7	4.5	3.1
United States	3.6	10.1	6.2	9.5	12.0	4.7	4.0	2.8	4.5	4.8	3.1
Germany	3.5	6.5	4.0	3.4	5.9	4.3	2.3	0.1	2.1	3.1	3.8
Japan	6.2	18.1	8.7	3.8	6.3	2.3	2.1	0.4	1.5	3.2	2.3
Unemployment rate											
Seven summit countries	3.2	4.7	5.4	5.1	6.1	8.1	7.4	7.1	6.1	6.2	6.7
United States	4.7	7.1	7.4	6.0	7.4	9.7	7.4	6.6	5.4	6.2	6.5
Germany	0.9	3.2	4.0	4.6	4.2	7.5	8.0	7.6	7.2	6.4	7.6
Japan	1.2	1.7	2.0	2.2	2.1	2.6	2.7	2.8	2.4	2.1	2.2

Source: International Monetary Fund, *World Economic Outlook* (various issues). Data for seven summit countries are averages weighted by each country's gross domestic product (except for unemployment rates which are weighted by each country's labor force). German data through 1989 are for West Germany alone.

[a]Estimated.

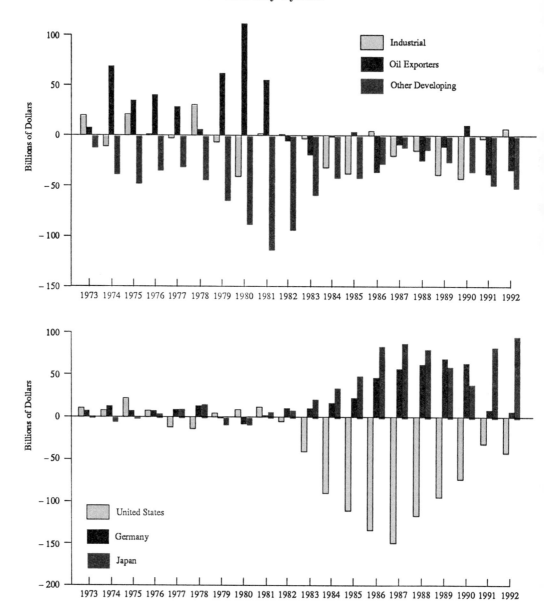

FIGURE 19-7
Current-Account Balances for Main Country Groups and Major Industrial Countries,
1973–1992
Source: International Monetary Fund, *World Economic Outlook* (various issues).
Balances exclude official transfers; German data through 1989 are for West Germany
alone. Entries for 1992 are estimates.

to plastics, and the price increase spread quickly to other goods and services as wage
rates rose to compensate for higher costs of living. Inflation rates were already high,
and the increase in oil prices made them even higher.

Second, it reduced economic activity in the oil-importing industrial countries,
because it acted much like an increase in taxes. Some of the oil-exporting countries,
such as Saudi Arabia, could not spend their huge revenues immediately. As a result,

they ran large trade surpluses which reduced aggregate demand in the oil-importing countries. Furthermore, some industrial countries adopted restrictive economic policies to combat the increase in prices and wages resulting from higher oil prices. For both reasons, their economies slipped into a deep recession.

Third, it drove the oil-importing countries into current-account deficits (which were, of course, the counterparts of the exporters' surpluses). In 1973, the industrial countries had run current-account surpluses totaling $20 billion. In 1974, they ran deficits totaling almost $11 billion. The developing countries were hit even harder. They usually run current-account deficits and cover them by borrowing and aid, but those deficits grew hugely in 1974 and widened again in 1975, when the recession in the industrial countries reduced the demand for the exports of developing countries.

Countries that confront current-account deficits are usually expected to deflate or devalue. But that was not done. Deliberate cuts in aggregate demand would have reduced oil imports and, to that extent, reduced the current-account surpluses of the OPEC countries. For the most part, however, they would have cut back imports of other goods and services, enlarging the deficits of other oil-importing countries. This sort of redistribution occurred in 1975, when the recession in the industrial countries eliminated their current-account deficits but increased those of the developing countries. There was a strong case for financing rather than adjustment, and that is what was done.

Some of the financing took place through the IMF. Many countries made large drawings in the ordinary way, but they also drew on special oil facilities established by the IMF with money borrowed from OPEC countries and a small number of industrial countries. Most of the financing, however, took place through a different channel. Unable to spend their large revenues quickly, OPEC countries deposited huge sums with commercial banks. The banks "recycled" the deposits by making large loans to governments and public-sector companies. At first, they lent mainly to developed countries such as Great Britain and Italy (whch also drew on the IMF), but they soon started lending to developing countries. Table 19-3 shows how rapidly

Table 19-3. Debts of Developing Countries, 1973–1991 (billions of dollars)

Category	1973	1976	1979	1982	1985	1988	1991
Total outstanding	130.1	228.0	504.7	780.9	953.8	1,161.8	1,284.2
By maturity:							
Short-term	18.4[a]	33.2[a]	88.1[a]	146.1	137.7	156.8	164.0
Long-term	111.8	194.9	416.6	634.7	816.1	1,004.8	1,120.1
By type of creditor:							
Official agencies	51.0	82.4	163.5	239.7	342.4	485.5	590.9
Commercial banks	31.1	73.9	208.5	390.1	452.5	484.2	473.6
Others	48.1	71.8	132.7	151.1	158.9	192.1	219.6

Source: International Monetary Fund, *World Economic Outlook* (various issues). Data for 1973 and 1976 cover all developing countries except certain oil exporters; subsequent data cover all developing countries that are net debtors.

[a]Allocation by type of creditor approximated.

their lending grew. At the end of 1973, on the eve of the first oil shock, the debts of developing countries totaled $130 billion, and their debts to banks were about $30 billion. Three years later, their debts totaled $228 billion, and their debts to banks were about $74 billion.

The Years of Dollar Weakness

In the first few months of floating, the dollar depreciated against most major currencies. Look at Figure 19-8, which shows the dollar-mark rate.The Smithsonian Agreement had pegged it at $0.31 per mark, where it stayed until the float began. By the middle of 1973, however, the mark was worth $0.41, and it remained in that neighborhood until the first oil shock, when the dollar began to appreciate against the mark and yen. (Although the United States was the prime target of the Arab "embargo," it was believed to be less vulnerable to the increase in oil prices than countries such as Germany and Japan, which have no oil of their own, and the appreciation of the dollar reflected that belief.) Rates wobbled up and down thereafter, showing sharper short-term fluctuations than had been anticipated. In 1977, however, the dollar began to weaken.

The U.S. economy had recovered rather slowly from the recession of 1974–1975 but more rapidly than the German and Japanese economies. Most governments were fearful of inflation and reluctant to ease fiscal and monetary policies sufficiently to foster rapid recovery. In fact, Washington called on Bonn and Tokyo to join with it in speeding up recovery. The three countries, it said, were the "locomotives" that

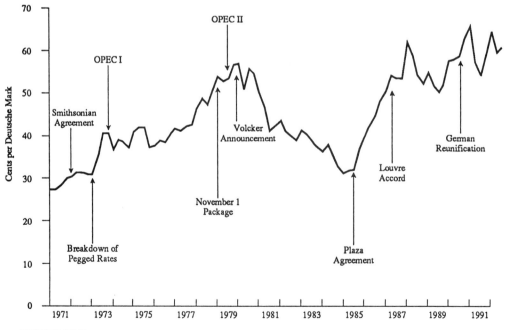

FIGURE 19-8
Exchange Rate Between the U.S. Dollar and Deutsche Mark, 1971–1992 (increase denotes depreciation of the dollar)
Source: International Monetary Fund, *International Financial Statistics* (various issues).

could pull the world economy back to prosperity. The United States could not do it alone. But Germany and Japan were slow to respond.

The more rapid recovery of the U.S. economy was raising imports faster than exports, and price effects were working in the same direction. The previous appreciation of the dollar had weakened the competitive position of the United States, and American prices were rising faster than German or Japanese prices. Therefore, the United States began to run a current-account deficit in 1977. But the dollar did not start to depreciate sharply until the second half of the year, when capital inflows fell as foreign-exchange markets came to believe that U.S. officials *wanted* the dollar to depreciate against the mark and yen.

The dollar continued to weaken early in 1978, despite intervention by the American, German, and Japanese authorities and a modest tightening of U.S. monetary policy. In July, at the Bonn economic summit, the United States agreed to decontrol domestic oil prices and take stronger measures against inflation in return for promises by Germany and Japan to be better "locomotives" and stimulate their own economies. But financial markets did not have much faith in the economic policies of the Carter administration, and the measures it took to combat inflation did not restore confidence. The depreciation of the dollar was not arrested until November, when the Federal Reserve tightened monetary policy more severely and the United States mobilized $30 billion of reserves by drawing on bilateral credit lines and the IMF and by selling bonds denominated in Deutsche marks and Swiss francs. The U.S. authorities used those reserves to intervene on a large scale, and the dollar rose sharply.

The improvement was brief, however, as bad news kept on coming in. Inflation continued to accelerate in the United States, and political unrest in Iran was raising oil prices. (By this time, moreover, higher oil prices were seen as harmful to the United States, because it had raised its energy prices more slowly than most other countries.) The new weakness of the dollar was not ended until a dramatic tightening of monetary policy in October 1979. The chairman of the Federal Reserve Board, Paul Volcker, flew back from an IMF meeting in Belgrade to announce an increase in the discount rate to 12 percent and a major modification in monetary policy. It would no longer focus on interest-rate levels but would instead be guided by money-supply targets. American interest rates rose rapidly, and the dollar began to appreciate.

Two More Attempts at Reform

The weakness of the dollar in the late 1970s inspired two new attempts to improve the international monetary system. One failed. The other succeeded.

When Robert Triffin proposed the conversion of the IMF into a global central bank, he suggested that governments should sell their dollar balances to the IMF in exchange for a new currency. A similar suggestion was made during discussions in the Committee of Twenty—that dollar balances be converted into SDRs. In 1978, the managing director of the IMF revived the idea, hoping to give the SDR a more important role, and the United States was interested for reasons of its own.

Soon after exchange rates started to float, governments and central banks began to diversify their currency reserves. They sold dollars to acquire marks, yen, and other currencies. The German and Japanese governments did not want their currencies to become reserve currencies and tried to discourage diversification. (Britain had already tried to liquidate the reserve role of sterling.) But they could not halt the process. If a foreign government could not deposit marks with German banks, it could go to banks in London, Paris, or Zurich, which were glad to take them. The United States was also worried about diversification, believing that it was helping to weaken the dollar. It began to support the creation of a *substitution account* under IMF management, in which governments could deposit unwanted dollars in exchange for claims denominated in SDRs. Because the SDR is defined in terms of a basket of currencies, it is by itself diversified. Hence, the availability of a substitution account might halt dollar sales by official holders.

Governments agreed in principle that the benefits and costs of any such account should be shared between the United States and the countries depositing the dollars. When it came to deciding how that should be done, however, the agreement broke down. Potential depositors asked the United States to guarantee the SDR value of the dollars. The United States declined, favoring instead the use of gold held by the IMF. By that time, moreover, the dollar was getting stronger, and governments were losing interest in the whole idea; they wanted to keep their dollars, not turn them in for SDRs. The plan was dropped.

The successful innovation was the creation of the European Monetary System (EMS) in 1979. For many years, Europeans had talked about forming a monetary union to complement their customs union. Six countries had taken a major step in 1973, when they let their currencies float jointly after the breakdown of the Bretton Woods system. The joint float was called the "snake" because it looked like one. The girth of the snake was determined by the narrow band in which European exchange rates could fluctuate; the wiggling of the snake was produced by the joint float against the dollar. Britain and Italy did not participate in the joint float, and France participated intermittently.

France and Germany proposed a more formal arrangement in 1978, designed to create a "zone of monetary stability" in Europe. It took effect in 1979. Although modeled on the Bretton Woods system, it has its own currency unit, the European Currency Unit (ECU), and it has more elastic credit facilities than the IMF. The ECU is defined in terms of a basket of currencies, much like the SDR, but includes only EC currencies; the dollar and yen are left out. The credit arrangements permit each member country to borrow unlimited quantities of the other members' currencies when it has to intervene on the foreign-exchange market. These credits have to be repaid in a matter of months, however, so governments have not misused them to postpone balance-of-payments adjustment.

Each member of the EMS agrees to fix the value of its currency in terms of the ECU, producing a system of pegged exchange rates among the members' currencies. The pegged rates can be realigned by mutual agreement, and there were frequent realignments in the early years of the EMS, some involving several currencies at once. The EMS thus appeared to be more flexible than the Bretton Woods system, and it was meant to be more symmetrical as well. When the exchange rate between two EMS currencies reaches the edge of its band, both of the countries involved are supposed to intervene; the task is not left entirely to the country having the weak currency. (Both countries are also expected to adjust their monetary policies, but that task has usually fallen in practice to the country having the weak currency.)

In the 1980s, however, the EMS became more rigid and less symmetical. To combat inflation more effectively, France, Italy, and some smaller EC countries committed themselves to maintain fixed exchange rates between their currencies and the Deutsche mark, and Great Britain adopted that same strategy when it joined the EMS in 1990. In effect, these countries tried to "borrow credibility" from the Bundesbank, which is firmly committed to price stability. By renouncing exchange-rate realignments and thus tying their monetary policies to those of the Bundesbank, they sought to warn trade unions and employers that higher wages could not be translated into higher prices without reducing sales, output, and employment.

The strategy seemed to be working in the late 1980s. There were no more realignments, and inflation rates fell sharply in several European countries. The strategy was painful for the countries adopting it, but the costs were not unacceptably high, because Germany itself was able to combine a low inflation rate with a low interest rate. The costs rose sharply in the 1990s, however, when the German situation changed, with results we will encounter later in this chapter.

The Second Oil Shock and the Onset of Debt Problems

The second oil shock started like the first, with political turmoil in the Middle East, and had similar effects on the world economy. Its long-run consequences, however, turned out to be more serious.

The price of oil started to rise at the end of 1978, when the Iranian revolution disrupted that country's oil exports. Oil companies began again to scramble for supplies, and contract prices followed market prices, just as before. The average OPEC price rose from about $13 per barrel in mid-1978 to almost $32 per barrel in mid-1980. The OPEC countries ran a huge current-account surplus, which reached $111 billion in 1980, and other countries ran huge current-account deficits. Inflation rates rose, but not as sharply as they did in the wake of the first oil shock, partly because many governments adopted sterner policies. The tightening of U.S. monetary policy in 1979 was the most dramatic instance. Those stern policies, however, produced another deep recession.

It took about five years for the OPEC surplus to disappear after the first oil shock. It disappeared more rapidly after the second shock. In fact, the OPEC countries moved into current-account deficit in 1982, because of a sharp fall in their oil revenues. The worldwide recession had reduced the demand for OPEC oil and so had the high price of oil itself. Two price effects were working to reduce it. First, high prices were encouraging conservation. Second, they were encouraging production by countries outside OPEC, such as Mexico. But the developing countries continued to run large current-account deficits, and a new problem emerged.

Bank lending to the developing countries did not drop when the effects of the first oil shock wore off. Look back at Table 19-3, which shows that bank loans outstanding were more than twice as large at the end of 1979 than at the end of 1976. Some of the borrowing was used for capital formation, especially by public-sector companies; some was used to subsidize consumption. Looking at the matter from a balance-of-payments standpoint, some was used to cover current-account deficits and some to build up reserves. Lending got even larger in subsequent years, when current-account deficits were widened by higher oil prices. By the end of 1982, the total debts of developing countries, excluding those of OPEC countries, amounted to more than $780 billion.

The sheer size of the debt was not the main reason for concern, because no one expected it to be paid off quickly. (The United States was a large borrower in the nineteenth century and did not repay its debts completely until World War I.) Concerns arose because the debts were getting more burdensome.

Look at Table 19-4. When large borrowing began in 1973, the debts of developing countries, taken together, were not much bigger than their exports and amounted to about 20 percent of their gross domestic products. Furthermore, debt-service payments, including amortization payments, amounted to only 16 percent of the countries' current-account earnings. There were, of course, large differences among countries, with the figures for the countries of the Western Hemisphere exceeding those for others. From 1973 through 1979, most of the numbers got bigger, but not very rapidly. The borrowers' economies were growing along with their debts, and their export earnings were rising almost as rapidly as their debt-service payments. From 1979 to 1982, however, the debt-service burden grew faster, partly because of the further increase in debt, but largely because of a change in international financial conditions.

Table 19-4. Perspectives on the Debts of Developing Countries, 1973–1991

Category	1973[a]	1979	1982	1985	1988	1991
Debt as percentage of exports:						
Africa	71.5	107.1	153.8	189.0	262.1	236.7
Asia	92.9	75.7	188.4	104.8	78.4	65.7
Western Hemisphere	176.2	197.7	273.8	293.8	295.0	263.4
Debt as percentage of gross domestic product:						
Africa	19.4	30.6	37.5	46.6	65.1	61.0
Asia	19.7	16.7	22.1	24.9	24.7	24.6
Western Hemisphere	23.0	32.2	42.9	53.7	50.4	42.9
Debt service payments as percentage of exports:						
Africa	8.8	15.3	22.1	27.6	25.8	26.7
Asia	9.6	9.4	11.9	14.3	10.9	7.9
Western Hemisphere	29.3	39.6	51.0	42.2	43.9	31.5
All developing countries[b]	15.9	14.1	19.5	20.9	18.8	14.2
Interest component	6.1	6.0	11.4	12.0	9.3	7.1
Amortization component[c]	9.8	8.1	8.1	8.9	9.5	7.1

Source: International Monetary Fund, *World Economic Outlook* (various issues).
[a]Excludes certain oil exporters.
[b]Includes countries in Europe and the Middle East not shown separately.
[c]Long-term debt only.

Interest rates rose to very high levels in international capital markets, because of a big increase in U.S. interest rates. Furthermore, the debtors' export earnings were reduced by the worldwide recession. By 1982, debt-service payments were about 20 percent of exports, thanks mainly to the increase in the interest component, and the figure for the Western Hemisphere was far higher. In fact, some countries had to pay more in interest on their old loans than they could raise by floating new loans, and that is an unsustainable situation.

The first major debt crisis took place in 1981, when Poland could not meet its obligations and asked its creditors to *reschedule* maturing debts—to turn them into longer-term obligations. The second crisis took place in 1982, when Mexico had to make a similar request, followed months later by Brazil, Argentina, and several other countries. The problems of Poland led to deep concerns in Europe, because European banks held most of the claims on Poland. The problems of Mexico and Brazil led to deep concerns in the United States, because American banks were heavily involved. The claims of the major American banks on the largest debtor countries were twice as big as the banks' own capital, and the banks would have been insolvent if they had been compelled to write off their claims. In fact, they would have been in very serious trouble if either one of the two largest debtors had walked away from its obligations.

The Mexican crisis broke out in August 1982. The Mexican government suspended payments due to banks in 1983, pending an agreement to reschedule those payments, and it started discussions with the IMF about the policies that Mexico would have to follow to qualify for a large drawing. These announcements halted all new lending to Mexico and threatened to undermine confidence in banks that had large claims on Mexico. Therefore, the U.S. government and the Bank for International Settlements (BIS) moved promptly to provide the Mexican government with short-term credit. In November, moreover, the managing director of the IMF asked the banks to make new loans to Mexico. On many previous occasions, IMF assistance had set a "seal of approval" on a country's policies and thus unlocked new lending by private institutions. This time, the IMF was asking banks to act in tandem with it.

The subsequent negotiations were complicated, because hundreds of banks were involved and Mexico was in the midst of changing governments. In December, the IMF approved the "letter of intent" in which Mexico set forth the policies it would follow to bring down inflation and reduce its balance-of-payments deficit. The IMF authorized a large three-year drawing. Several months later, the banks agreed to lend Mexico about $5 billion of new money, so that it could make its interest payments, and to stretch out the repayment of old debt due in 1983. By that time, however, many other countries had run into problems, including Brazil, Argentina, and some OPEC countries such as Nigeria, and they had to go through a similar process.

It was widely thought at first that the debt crisis would end quickly. Interest rates would fall, and the world economy would recover from the global recession, raising the debtors' exports and their export prices. They would be able to meet their obligations without having to extract "involuntary" lending from the banks. By following domestic policies approved by the IMF, moreover, the debtors would stabilize their own economies, restore their creditworthiness, and attract voluntary lending. It made sense, then, for the debtors to go more deeply into debt, by drawing on the IMF and borrowing more from the banks, to deal with the temporary crisis.

Most of the debtors *were* able to reduce their current-account deficits. (They had little choice, because they could not finance them.) But the domestic costs were very high. Growth rates and standards of living fell sharply, and unemployment rose. Furthermore, the largest debtors were unsuccessful in their efforts to control inflation. Their governments could no longer borrow freely from foreign banks and had to cover their budget deficits by printing money. Time after time, the IMF was compelled to declare that the debtors had failed to meet the policy targets in their agreements with the Fund, and new policy packages had to be negotiated. In the process, the debtors grew increasingly hostile to the IMF, and some refused to have further dealings with it. This meant, in turn, that they could not negotiate with the commercial banks, which insisted that a government's policies have IMF approval before they would reschedule its debts or give it additional credit. To make matters worse, the world economy was growing rather slowly, and the debtors' export earnings were not rising as rapidly as previously expected.

Although events were challenging the economic forecasts on which the debt strategy was based, creditors and debtors were equally reluctant to abandon that strategy. Special efforts were made to help the poorest debtors, especially in Africa, and the banks cut interest rates and lengthened maturities when making new agreements with middle-income debtors. In 1985, moreover, the U.S. secretary of the Treasury, James Baker, proposed a shift of emphasis in the debtors' policies. They should go on working closely with the IMF to achieve economic stability but should also undertake structural reforms aimed at achieving "adjustment with growth" over the long run. Commercial banks should support those reforms by joining with the World Bank in making more loans to the debtors; they should indeed adopt specific targets for lending to the heavily indebted countries. The banks fell short of those targets, however, and some debtor countries began to adopt radical tactics. In 1986, Peru limited its interest payments to 10 percent of its export earnings. In 1987, Brazil stopped making any interest payments whatsover. The debts of many developing countries were selling at deep discounts in the open market.

These discounts, however, gave rise to a new approach. In 1988, Mexico offered to buy back some of its debt at a 30 percent discount in exchange for new long-term bonds. Mexico would guarantee repayment of the bonds by using some of its reserves to buy zero-coupon bonds from the U.S. Treasury and setting them aside as backing for the Mexican bonds. Sales of the Mexican bonds were smaller than expected, because the interest payments were not guaranteed, but the scheme produced a basic change in the debt strategy. Late in 1988, the IMF endorsed the use of "voluntary market-based techniques" to reduce the stock of debt. In March 1989, the new U.S. secretary of the Treasury, Nicholas Brady, urged commercial banks "to accelerate sharply the pace of debt reduction and pass the benefits directly to the debtor nations." He called on the IMF and World Bank to support the process by lending debtor countries some of the money they would need to buy back debt for cash, collateralize debt-for-bond swaps of the Mexican type, and, most importantly, guarantee the interest payments on their newly issued bonds.

Events moved rapidly thereafter. The IMF extended new credits to Mexico, Costa Rica, and the Philippines to finance debt-reduction schemes, and those countries, among others, began negotiating with their creditors. In a matter of months, Mexico announced an agreement that offered each bank three options: (1) swapping Mexican debt for a new long-term bond at a 35 percent discount; (2) switching from old debt paying a 10 percent interest rate to a new bond paying $6\frac{1}{4}$ percent without cutting the face value of the debt; (3) granting neither debt reduction nor interest-rate reduction but making additional loans to Mexico. Repayment of the new Mexican bonds would be guaranteed by Mexican investments in zero-coupon U.S. government bonds. Interest payments on the bonds would be covered by an 18-month guarantee, backed by funds deposited by Mexico in a special account with the IMF. Once the banks had made their choices, the package as a whole reduced Mexico's debt burden by close to 25 percent. But the agreement had important indirect effects as well. By helping Mexico to manage its financial affairs more easily, it led to a sharp fall in Mexican interest rates and a large capital inflow, which tripled Mexico's reserves in the next two years.

Several other debtor countries reached similar agreements in 1990 and 1991, and the effects show up in Figure 19-4, which records a large decline in debt-service burdens between 1988 and 1991, especially for countries in the Western Hemisphere.

The Years of Dollar Strength

The sharp increase in American interest rates, which was partly responsible for the debt crisis, also ushered in the years of the strong dollar. Look back at Figure 19-8, which shows that the dollar appreciated sharply in 1980 and continued to appreciate until 1985. But fiscal policy took over from monetary policy as the principal cause of the appreciation.

During his campaign for the presidency in 1980, Ronald Reagan promised to raise defense spending, reduce taxes, and balance the budget. He kept the first two promises but could not keep the third, and we may never know how he expected to keep it.

Some of his advisers subscribed to an extravagant version of "supply-side economics," which said that tax cuts would transform economic behavior; firms would invest more, labor would work harder, and economic activity would rise rapidly enough to bring in more tax revenue. Other advisers subscribed to the more orthodox views that the prospect of large budget deficits would force Congress to cut nondefense spending and thus achieve one of their long-run objectives—reducing the size of government. But both were wrong. The economy did grow strongly but not strongly enough to offset the large tax cuts (and its growth can be explained by conventional economics—the workings of the national-income multiplier). Congress did reduce nondefense spending but it could not cut it far enough to balance the budget. The budget deficit grew from $16 billion in 1979, the last year of the Carter administration, to a peak of $201 billion in 1986.[11]

The Fleming–Mundell model in Chapter 15 helps to explain what the budget deficit did to the dollar. As the government borrowed to cover its deficit, it put upward pressure on domestic interest rates, attracting the very large capital inflows shown in Table 19-1. The resulting increase in the demand for dollars raised the price

---

[11]These are calendar-year figures, not fiscal-year figures, and are based on the definitions used in the national-income accounts, not those used in budget documents.

of the dollar, and the expenditure-switching effects of this appreciation, combined with the increase in imports produced by faster economic growth, drove the current account into deficit.

To understand the process fully, however, we must amend the Fleming–Mundell model to allow for the sluggish behavior of the current account; it did not start to deteriorate as soon as the dollar began to appreciate in 1980, and it did not start to improve as soon as the dollar began to depreciate in 1985. Therefore, market forces had to adjust the size of the actual capital inflow to match the slowly moving current-account balance. What market forces were at work?

Recall a point made in Chapter 16. Capital movements are governed by the open interest differential, which allows for the influence of expectations as well as the difference between national interest rates. A capital inflow too large to match the current-account balance can thus be limited by an expectation that the dollar will depreciate. It will reduce the open interest differential. To generate that expectation, however, the dollar must appreciate sharply in the short run, by more than it can be expected to appreciate in the long run, to foster the belief that it will begin to depreciate. The dollar has to overshoot, and that is what happened.

The Reagan administration welcomed the strong dollar at first, as a vote of confidence in U.S. policies. With the passage of time, however, the current account moved into deficit, averaging about $88 billion from 1983 to 1985 and rising to about $146 billion from 1986 to 1988, a number more than half as large as the total value of U.S. merchandise exports. Large sectors of the American economy experienced unprecedented foreign competition at home and abroad, with the usual result. Industry and labor demanded an aggressive trade policy—more protection from import competition and retaliation against "unfair" practices pursued by other countries. Washington began to view the strong dollar as a liability.

Managing the Float

In the early 1980s, governments and central banks were heavily influenced by the monetary interpretation of exchange-rate behavior. Exchange rates were determined by monetary policies and expectations about future monetary policies, and intervention could not have any lasting impact, apart from its effect on the money supply. In 1985, however, those same governments began to manage exchange rates intensively. They sought first to bring the dollar down, then to prop it up. It is hard to assess their success, however, because the dollar began to depreciate before they tried to bring it down, and it continued to depreciate after they started to prop it up.

The attempt to bring the dollar down was organized by the United States. Like the earlier effort in 1971, it was meant in part to blunt protectionist pressures. In September 1985, the finance ministers of the G-5 (France, Germany, Japan, the United Kingdom, and the United States) issued a communique known as the Plaza Agreement, named after the New York hotel at which they met. They said that foreign-exchange markets had not fully reflected recent shifts in "economic fundamentals" and policy objectives, including the commitment of the United States to reduce its budget deficit. In light of those shifts, they said, "some further orderly appreciation of the main non-dollar currencies against the dollar is desirable." Then came the key sentence. "They stand ready to cooperate more closely to encourage this when to do so would be helpful." To make their meaning perfectly clear, they started immediately to intervene, selling dollars for marks and yen.

The dollar continued to depreciate in 1986, and governments themselves began to disagree about the fundamentals. The appreciation of the yen was cutting into profits and production in Japan. Tokyo wanted to stabilize exchange rates. But the corresponding depreciation of the dollar had not halted the growth of the U.S. current-account deficit, and Washington wanted the dollar to fall further. In October 1986, however, the two governments agreed that the yen-dollar rate should be stabilized for the time being, and in February 1987, the G-5 met in Paris to issue another communique, known as the Louvre Accord. A portion of the text is reproduced in Figure 19-9, but other important parts of the agreement cannot be reproduced because they were not written down. It is therefore difficult to know who "broke" the Louvre Accord eight months later, when everyone was looking for someone to blame for the sharp drop in stock markets and the further fall in the value of the dollar.

The Louvre Accord

The Ministers and Governors were of the view that further progress had been made... in their efforts to achieve sustainable, non-inflationary expansion. Their national economies are now in the fifth year of expansion,... although the level of unemployment remains unacceptably high in some countries. A high degree of price stability has been attained, and there have been substantial reductions in interest rates. Exchange rate adjustments have occurred which will contribute importantly in the period ahead to the restoration of a more sustainable pattern of current accounts.

Progress is being made in reducing budget deficits in deficit countries, and... important structural reforms are also being carried forward, including deregulation of business to increase efficiency and privatization of government enterprises to strengthen reliance on... market forces.

These positive developments notwithstanding, the Ministers and Governors recognized that the large trade and current account imbalances posed serious economic and political risks. They agreed that the reduction of the large unsustainable trade imbalances was a matter of high priority, and that the achievement of more balanced growth should play a central role in bringing about such a reduction....

[They] agreed to intensify their economic policy coordination efforts in order to promote more balanced global growth and to reduce external imbalances. Surplus countries committed themselves to following policies designed to strengthen domestic demand and to reducing their external surpluses while maintaining price stability. Deficit countries committed themselves to following policies designed to encourage steady, low-inflation growth while reducing their domestic imbalances and external deficits....

The Ministers and Governors agreed that the substantial exchange rate changes since the Plaza Agreement will increasingly contribute to reducing external imbalances and have now brought their currencies within ranges broadly consistent with underlying economic fundamentals, given the policy commitments summarized in this statement. Further substantial exchange rate shifts among their currencies could damage growth and adjustment prospects in their countries. In current circumstances, therefore, they agreed to cooperate closely to foster stability of exchange rates around current levels.

FIGURE 19-9
Extract from the 1987 Louvre Accord

Some say that the rest of the Louvre Accord was rather vague; the governments agreed in principle on unspecified measures to keep exchange rates within an unspecified range for an unspecified time. Others say that it was tighter, involving a firm commitment to stabilize exchange rates within narrow bands, and this interpretation became increasingly popular because of the subsequent behavior of governments and markets.

Exchange rates were stable for several months following the Louvre Accord, despite frequent warnings by many economists that the dollar had not fallen far enough to correct the U.S. current-account deficit. But this stability was due in part to massive intervention. Official purchases of dollars were far larger than at any other time since the collapse of the Bretton Woods system. Furthermore, central banks were working together to keep U.S. interest rates higher than German and Japanese rates.

These arrangements started to unravel, however, in the autumn of 1987. The U.S. current-account deficit was not shrinking, expectations of inflation were reviving, and markets began to believe that central banks would have to raise interest rates. Furthermore, stock markets appeared to be faltering after rising steeply in the first half of the year. Matters came to a head in mid-October, when a small increase in one key German interest rate was criticized by Washington as a violation of the Louvre Accord (because it would require higher U.S. interest rates to maintain existing differentials). Prices fell on Wall Street at the end of that week, and the pessimism was contagious. When trading resumed on the following Monday, stock prices tumbled all over the world, wiping out a whole year's profits.

Central banks responded boldly to the stock market crash by reducing interest rates and by making credit available to prevent a further fall in prices. But the dollar began to depreciate again, despite official intervention, as governments continued to quarrel publicly. The very large depreciation of the dollar after the Plaza Agreement had been expected to reduce the current-account deficit of the United States and the corresponding surpluses of Germany and Japan, but that had not happened. In fact, the imbalances were still growing (see Figure 19-7). Hence, Germany and Japan refused to promise further support for the dollar unless the United States acted promptly to reduce the U.S. budget deficit. Washington resisted this pressure at first, fearing that the stock-market crash could by itself produce a recession in the United States and that a tighter fiscal policy would make matters worse. At the end of the year, however, Congress and the White House agreed on modest budget cuts, and the depreciation of the dollar was ended abruptly in early 1988. Central banks intervened forcefully enough to raise the value of the dollar and impose large losses on foreign-exchange dealers—those who had sold dollars forward and had therefore to buy them spot to meet their obligations. Furthermore, the U.S. trade balance began to respond to the previous depreciation, and the current-account deficit started to shrink.

Attention Turns to Europe

Central banks undertook huge amounts of intervention before and after the Louvre Accord. Foreign official purchases of dollars averaged $40 billion yearly from 1986 to 1988 (see Table 19-1), and the U.S. balance-of-payments deficits during that three-year period exceeded those from 1970 to 1972, the last years of the Bretton Woods system (see Figure 19-3). But much more intervention took place in September 1992, when European central banks tried to defend EMS exchange rates against massive speculation. The Bundesbank had to acquire more than $60 billion worth of other EC currencies in fewer than three weeks, and Britain, France, and Italy had to draw heavily on their foreign-currency reserves.

To explain the 1992 crisis, we must go back to 1989 and two unrelated events—the fall of the Berlin Wall, which opened the way for German unification in 1990, and the report of the Delors Committee on Economic and Monetary Union (EMU) in the EC.

East Germany was thought to have the most efficient economy in Eastern Europe, yet productivity and real wages were far below those in West Germany. Therefore, unification posed a painful dilemma. If Eastern wages were held down, Eastern industry could perhaps compete successfully in West German and world markets. But many East Germans could be expected to seek higher wages by moving to West Germany, where they would then need jobs, housing, and health care, and East Germany would probably lose many of its skilled workers. If Eastern wages were allowed to rise, there might be less migration and fewer problems in West Germany, but Eastern industry would be unable to compete successfully. West Germany would have to subsidize Eastern industry or pay unemployment compensation to large numbers of Eastern workers.

It proved impossible, however, to keep East German wages down; market forces and trade union pressures raised them rapidly, helped along by the decision of the German government to replace the old East German currency with Deutsche marks on a one-for-one basis. But the costs of propping up Eastern industry, along with the other costs of unification, were much higher than expected and lasted longer. The German budget moved into deficit, prices and wages rose, and the Bundesbank, committed to price stability, started to raise interest rates. The German policy mix came to resemble the American policy mix of the early Reagan years; monetary and fiscal policies were working at cross purposes, and the Deutsche mark began to appreciate, just like the dollar in the early 1980s.

A realignment of EMS exchange rates would have helped. By raising the value of the Deutsche mark in terms of other EMS currencies, it would have reduced prices in Germany, limiting the need for the Bundesbank to raise German interest rates. But France would not agree to a realignment, because of its decision, described earlier, to enhance the credibility of French economic policy by tying the franc firmly to the Deutsche mark. Hence, interest rates rose sharply across Europe, even in Britain, which was experiencing a deep recession. At the same time, a U.S. recession prompted the Federal Reserve to cut American interest rates, which widened the interest-rate difference between Deutsche mark and dollar assets.

These developments might have led eventually to a crisis in the EMS, but the timing and nature of the actual crisis cannot be explained without listing the events that followed the report of the Delors Committee.

European monetary union was not a new idea, but support for it began to grow in the 1980s. Some saw monetary union as the logical counterpart of the move to the single European market, begun in 1985 and discussed in Chapter 11. In fact, the move to the single market was seen to require a move to monetary union by ruling out the use of capital controls. Without such controls, it was argued, the EMS countries would have to adopt a common monetary policy in order to defend their exchange rates against speculative capital movements. But this policy should be a European policy, formulated by an EC institution and aimed at European policy objectives, not one formulated by the Bundesbank and aimed exclusively at German policy objectives.

The growing interest in monetary union led the EC governments to appoint a committee chaired by Jacques Delors, president of the EC Commission, to study ways of reaching monetary union. Its report, published in 1989, proposed a gradual move to monetary union. The report was vague about the schedule but very clear about the ultimate outcome—an "irrevocable locking" of EC exchange rates and the joining of the national central banks into a European System of Central Banks (ESCB), which would pursue a single monetary policy and, perhaps, issue a single EC currency in place of the national currencies.

At the end of 1989, the EC countries agreed to start the first stage of this process and decided to convene a conference to work on the remaining stages. Soon thereafter, they agreed to convene a second conference on closer political union. Just before those conferences began, moreover, they endorsed the basic recommendations of the Delors Committee, to create an ESCB and move eventually to a single currency, but said that these steps should not be taken until the EC countries had achieved much more economic convergence.[12]

In December 1991, the two conferences produced an extensive revision of the Treaty of Rome, the constitution of the EC. The revision was adopted by the EC governments at a meeting in the Dutch town of Maastricht and is thus known as the Maastricht Treaty. Under the new treaty, discussed at length in Chapter 20, a full-fledged monetary union is scheduled for 1999 and could start even earlier. To join that union, however, each EC country must meet a number of "convergence criteria" having to do with inflation rates, exchange rates, interest rates, and budget deficits. Some EC countries cannot hope to meet these criteria unless they start immediately to modify their policies.

These decisions, taken together, helped to produce the EMS crisis. France had scheduled a national referendum on ratification of the Maastricht Treaty, to take place on September 20, 1992, and the vote was expected to be very close.[13] Shortly before the referendum, moreover, the Italian government announced a set of fiscal reforms to meet the convergence criteria in the treaty. As the French referendum approached, investors began to question the ability of the Italian government to force through its reforms if France were to reject the treaty and thus remove the discipline imposed by the convergence criteria. In that case, it was said, Italy's budget deficit would rise, not fall, raising the Italian inflation rate and forcing Italy to devalue the lira. So investors began to sell lire.

As pressures built up in the foreign-exchange market, some central banks began

---

[12]Britain refused to endorse the move to monetary union proposed by the Delors Committee and suggested a different approach. Later, it reserved its right to "opt out" of monetary union.

[13]Denmark had conducted a referendum in June, and voters had rejected the treaty by a narrow margin, but this result was not seen as a fatal blow. The Danish government supported the treaty and was seeking ways to meet the voters' objections.

to believe that it would be wise to realign exchange rates immediately, even before the French referendum. The Bundesbank, in particular, had familiar reasons for favoring a realignment. A revaluation of the mark would reduce inflationary pressures in Germany and allow the Bundesbank to cut German interest rates. Without a realignment, moreover, speculative pressures would force the Bundesbank to intervene in the foreign-exchange market, and large-scale intervention would raise the German money supply.

A deal was struck between Germany and Italy. The lira would be devalued, and the Bundesbank would reduce German interest rates. But both changes were too small to convince investors that exchange rates would not change again if French voters said "non" to the Maastricht Treaty. Furthermore, it was rumored that Helmut Schlesinger, president of the Bundesbank, favored a devaluation of the pound, and investors began to sell sterling. The Bank of England raised interest rates, but not by enough to halt the capital outflow. Hence, Britain withdrew from the EMS two days after the Italian devaluation, allowing the pound to float, and Italy had to follow. Ironically, the Bundesbank got what it wanted, an appreciation of the mark, but it did not prevent what it wanted to avoid, the need for massive intervention. To add to the irony, French voters approved the Maastricht Treaty by a narrow margin, but there was a run on the franc after the referendum. This time, the central banks involved—the Bundesbank and Banque de France—were determined to defend the existing exchange rate, and they succeeded for a time. But speculative pressures built up again in July 1993, when investors became convinced that France could not afford high interest rates at a time when unemployment was high and rising and that the Bundesbank would not cut German interest rates until it was firmly convinced that inflation was under control in Germany

The French government suggested that Germany withdraw temporarily from the EMS and allow the Deutsche mark to appreciate, much as it had done in 1969 and 1973. But the German government refused, and the EMS countries decided instead to widen the EMS exchange-rate bands from $2\frac{1}{4}$ percent to 15 percent. This made it more risky to speculate against the franc and reduced the need for the Banque de France to emulate the Bundesbank's strict monetary policy. Hence, speculative pressures subsided quickly, but the move from tightly pegged exchange rates to more nearly floating rates was widely seen as a damaging blow to the plan for monetary union contained in the Maastricht Treaty

SUMMARY

The number of independent exchange rates is always smaller by one than the number of national currencies. Therefore, it is impossible in principle for all governments to pursue independent exchange-rate policies. The history recorded in this chapter can be summarized by looking at ways in which governments have dealt with that problem.

At the end of World War I, the problem was ignored, not solved. Governments chose gold values for their currencies, and the resulting exchange rates led to large imbalances. Monetary arrangements broke down soon after the start of the depression, contributing to the economic damage done by the depression itself. The Bretton Woods Conference of 1944 tried to develop more orderly exchange-rate arrangements by establishing the International Monetary Fund to oversee exchange-rate policies and give balance-of-payments credit to governments that maintained pegged exchange rates in the face of temporary deficits. The IMF would deal with the nth-country problem by supervising national exchange-rate policies.

Matters worked out differently. The IMF could not control exchange-rate policies, although it came to be an important source of balance-of-payments credit. The nth-country problem was resolved by the willingness of the United States to let other countries adjust their exchange rates vis-à-vis the dollar. This solution worked well in the years of the dollar shortage. With the completion of postwar recovery, however, the United States began to run a balance-of-payments deficit, and the dollar shortage turned into a dollar glut. Believing that the deficit was temporary, the U.S. government opted mainly for financing rather than adjustment. It was able to postpone adjustment because of the reserve role of the dollar; the surplus countries built up dollar balances instead of buying gold.

But the U.S. balance of payments worsened in the late 1960s, when inflationary pressures intensified in the United States. In 1971, the United States tried to initiate a general exchange-rate realignment—a political solution to the nth-country problem. The realignment was achieved by the Smithsonian Agreement, but it fell apart in 1973, when the United States tried to devalue the dollar unilaterally. One by one, other governments let their currencies float.

At first, the float was expected to be temporary, and an attempt was made to design a new monetary system in which exchange rates would be pegged but more readily adjustable than under the Bretton Woods system. The nth-country problem would be solved by using "objective indicators" to signal the need for balance-of-payments adjustment. But the effort failed in the wake of the first oil shock, and the Articles of Agreement of the IMF were amended to "legalize" floating.

If governments allowed exchange rates to float freely, the regime would represent a market solution to the nth-country problem. There would be no need to reconcile national exchange-rate targets if governments did not pursue them. But governments have not allowed exchange rates to float freely, because exchange-rate fluctuations affect their economies in larger and different ways than predicted by the early advocates of floating rates. In 1978, the members of the European Community established the European Monetary System to peg the exchange rates connecting their own currencies. The United States intervened heavily in 1978 to halt a depreciation of the dollar and tightened its monetary policy sharply in 1979 when the dollar began to depreciate again. Under the Plaza Agreement and Louvre Accord, moreover, it joined with other major countries in an effort to reverse an appreciation of the dollar, then to halt the subsequent depreciation.

There is another way to look at the evolution of the monetary system. Pegged exchange rates have worked well when one large country has dominated the monetary system and has followed policies acceptable to the other major countries. This was true before World War I, when Great Britain led the system; the gold standard was in large degree a sterling standard. It was also true in the decades after World War II, when the United States led the system; the Bretton Woods system was in fact a dollar standard. The European Monetary System likewise functioned as a pegged-rate system when other EC countries followed German leadership. When the center country runs into trouble, however, and ceases to provide an economic environment agreeable to its partners, pegged-rate regimes break down. That happened at the end of the 1970s, when the United States ran into trouble, and in 1992, when Germany ran into trouble. By implication, it is hard to establish or maintain a pegged-rate regime when there is no single leader. That was true between the two World Wars, when Britain could no longer exercise leadership and the United States was not ready to do so. It is also true today, in a world dominated by three great economic powers—the United States, Japan, and the European Community. They can cooperate closely from time to time, as in 1985, under the Plaza Agreement, and in the late 1980s, under the Louvre Accord, but these arrangements tend to be fragile. We will return to this problem at the end of the next chapter.

RECOMMENDED READINGS

The best history of the monetary system, on which this chapter draws heavily, is in Robert Solomon, *The International Monetary System, 1945–1981*(New York: Harper & Row, 1982); for a personal account by two key participants, see Paul A. Volcker and Toyoo Gyohten, *Changing Fortunes* (New York: Times Books, 1992).

On the attempt by the Committee of Twenty to rebuild the system, see John Williamson, "The Failure of World Monetary Reform: A Reassessment," in R. N. Cooper, et al., eds., *The International Monetary System Under Flexible Exchange Rates* (Cambridge, Mass.: Ballinger, 1982). The economics and politics of recent attempts at exchange-rate management are explored in Yoichi Funabashi, *Managing the Dollar: From the Plaza to the Louvre* (Washington, D.C.: Institute for International Economics, 1989).

The role of the IMF is described in Margaret Garritsen de Vries, *Balance of Payments Adjustment, 1945 to 1986: The IMF Experience* (Washington, D.C.: International Monetary Fund, 1987). Its policies and future are examined by Jacques J. Polak, Peter B. Kenen, and Jeffrey D. Sachs in C. Gwin and R. E. Feinberg, eds., *The International Monetary Fund in a Multipolar World: Pulling Together* (Washington, D.C.: Overseas Development Council, 1989).

An early and influential analysis of the problems posed by the U.S. budget and trade deficits was provided by Stephen Marris, *Deficits and the Dollar: The World Economy at Risk*, Policy Analysis in International Economics 14 (Washington, D.C.: Institute for International Economics, 1987); the issues are set out clearly in Paul R. Krugman, *Currencies and Crisis* (Cambridge, Mass.: MIT Press, 1992), chs. 1–2. The same issues are examined in C. Fred Bergsten, ed., *International Adjustment and Financing* (Washington, D.C.: Institute for International Economics, 1991); see especially the papers by Paul R. Krugman, William R. Cline, Stephen Marris, and Peter B. Kenen.

The origins and nature of the debt problem are analyzed in Jeffrey Sachs, ed., *Developing Country Debt and Economic Performance* (Chicago: University of Chicago Press, 1989), chs. 1, 6, 8, and 9. On the case for debt reduction, see Paul R. Krugman, *Currencies and Crisis* (Cambridge, Mass.: MIT Press, 1992), chs. 7–8, and Kenneth Rogoff et al., "Symposium on New Institutions for Developing Country Debt," *Journal of Economic Perspectives*, 4 (Winter 1990).

For a history and evaluation of the EMS, see Daniel Gros and Niels Thygesen, *European Monetary Integration* (New York: St. Martins Press, 1992), chs. 3–5.

More readings on some of these subjects are listed at the end of Chapter 20.

QUESTIONS AND PROBLEMS

(1) The Bretton Woods system aimed at avoiding a repetition of policy mistakes made in the 1920s and 1930s. Focusing on the experience of the 1950s and 1960s, indicate ways in which it succeeded and ways in which it failed.

(2) When the United States began to run large current-account deficits in the 1980s, it was fortunate in being able to attract large capital inflows. Criticize this statement.

(3) When the United States closed the gold window in 1971, the secretary of the Treasury told other governments that "the dollar is our currency but your problem." In the 1980s, another U.S. official answered foreign critics of U.S. policy by saying that "we'll take care of our exchange rate; you take care of your exchange rate." Comment.

(4) An appreciation of the Deutsche mark would have reduced inflationary pressures produced by German unification, but there was another reason for wanting an appreciation— the increase in the German budget deficit. Explain.

(5) The dollar began to depreciate in 1985, but the U.S. current account did not improve until 1988. Explain the lag.

(6) When the center country in a pegged-rate system seeks to change its exchange rate, it may have to break the rules of the system. Use the cases of the United States in 1971 and Germany in 1992 to illustrate this statement. How were their situations similar? How were they different? What rules, if any, did they break?

(7) "The Brady plan for debt reduction was a mistake. By imposing losses on the banks, it will make it harder for countries to borrow again. By using IMF and World Bank credit to finance debt-reduction agreements, it shifted the risk of lending from the banks to taxpayers in the developed countries. And it was morally wrong. Borrowers should pay their debts." Explain and comment.

20

The Future of the Monetary System

INTRODUCTION

The history of the monetary system, outlined in Chapter 19, is the story of sharp shifts in exchange-rate arrangements. The present system, moreover, spans a wide variety of exchange-rate arrangements.

Recall British monetary history. Great Britain returned to the gold standard in 1925, fixing the value of the pound in terms of gold. It abandoned the gold standard in 1931, however, and the pound was allowed to float. Britain joined the International Monetary Fund in 1945, and the pound was pegged to the dollar, although it was devalued twice, in 1949 and 1967. When the United States closed the gold window in 1971, the pound was allowed to float, but it was pegged a few months later under the Smithsonian Agreement. It was allowed to float again in 1972, however, six months before the final breakdown of the Bretton Woods system, and it continued to float until 1990, when Britain joined the exchange-rate mechanism of the EMS, only to depart in 1992.

Under the Articles of Agreement of the IMF, member countries may adopt "exchange arrangements of their choice" but must notify the IMF of any change in those arrangements. Table 20-1 summarizes the arrangements reported by 140 countries that have been members of the IMF since 1982. Note, first, the wide variety of exchange-rate arrangements used in 1991, when 87 countries had pegged rates of one sort or another, 26 countries had floating rates, and 27 countries had intermediate arrangements. Note, next, the large differences among types of countries. Only 2 small developing countries had floating rates in 1991, and a majority had rates pegged to a single foreign currency, whereas 19 large developing countries had floating rates, and only 22 had rates pegged to a single foreign currency. In that same year, moreover, none of the industrial countries pegged its currency to a single foreign currency. (It should also be remembered that the 10 members of the EMS, with pegged rates among themselves, had floating rates vis-à-vis other currencies,

Table 20-1. Exchange-Rate Arrangements at End of Year, 1982 and 1991

| | Industrial Countries | | Developing Countries | | | |
| | | | Small | | Large | |
Arangement	1982	1991	1982	1991	1982	1991
Pegged-rate arrangements:						
To single foreign currency[a]	—	—	24	21	39	22
To "basket" of currencies[b]	4	5	12	10	20	19
Members of EMS	8	10	—	—	—	—
Intermediate arrangements:						
Adjusted by indicators	1	—	—	—	4	4
Other managed arrangements	5	2	1	4	14	17
Independently floating	4	5	—	2	4	19
Total	22	22	37	37	81	81

Source: Adapted from International Monetary Fund, *International Financial Statistics*, various issues. Developing countries include those that were members of the IMF at the end of 1982 (but exclude Cambodia, Hungary, Laos, Romania, and Vietnam); small countries are those with populations no larger than 2 million persons.
[a]Includes countries with exchange rates limited in terms of a single foreign currency.
[b]Includes countries with exchange rates pegged to the SDR.

including the dollar and yen.) Note, finally, the migration to exchange-rate flexibility by the large developing countries; 19 had floating rates in 1991, compared with only 4 in 1982.

A number of questions arise. What do countries gain from pegging? What do they gain from floating? Why might the answers differ between groups of countries? Why have countries changed their exchange-rate arrangements?

Previous chapters of this book offered partial answers. We saw, for example, that a change in the real exchange rate is the optimal response to an expenditure-switching disturbance. We also saw that exchange-rate arrangements affect the functioning of domestic policies and a country's freedom to pursue an independent monetary policy. In Chapter 19, moreover, we saw that changes in the exchange-rate regime may reflect errors in domestic policies. The collapse of the Bretton Woods system in the early 1970s resulted from the weakening of the American competitive position in the late 1960s, which resulted in turn from policy mistakes made in dealing with the economic impact of the Vietnam war. The EMS crisis of September 1992 was due to the tightening of German monetary policy provoked by inflation in Germany, which resulted in turn from policy mistakes made in dealing with the impact of German unification.

These explanations, however, may not go far enough. Critics of the Bretton Wood system, for example, say that it was undermined by the basic defects of the system itself. They recall the point made by Robert Triffin, that the system allowed the United States to finance its balance-of-payments deficits by accumulating dollar liabilities to other countries and that the growth of those liabilities undermined confidence in the dollar. Other critics say that the United States might not have made the mistakes that led to the collapse of the Bretton Woods system if the system had not allowed it to exploit the reserve-currency role of the dollar; if it had been made to pay out reserves when running a balance-of-payments deficit, the United States might have acted faster and more decisively to eliminate its deficit.

One clear lesson does emerge from monetary history. Whenever governments have souhgt to improve or reform the international monetary system, they have tried to move to pegged exchange rates. They reinstated the gold standard at the end of World War I. They set up the Bretton Woods system at the end of World War II. And when that regime broke down in the 1970s, the Committee of Twenty tried to devise a new system of "stable but adjustable" rates.

For many economists, floating exchange rates represent the best way to regulate relations among sovereign states, and a move to floating rates is thus seen as progress toward a better monetary system. For governments, by contrast, a move to floating rates has represented a retreat to an inferior system—the best that can be had, perhaps, but one with which they are not satisfied. Few officials in Washington, Tokyo, and Bonn would favor an early move to pegged exchange rates between the dollar, mark, and yen. When asked about the EC currencies, however, most European officials would praise the pegged exchange rates of the EMS as being far superior to floating rates, and they would view the widening of the EMS bands in 1993 as a tactical retreat, to be reversed as soon as possible

THE ISSUES

Where do these observations lead us? What can we say about the future of the monetary system? Let us focus on four issues:

- The benefits and costs of fixed and floating exchange rates.
- The case for coordinating national policies among the major industrial countries.
- The logic and limits of the case for full-fledged monetary union.
- The methods and problems of exchange-rate management.

The logic of this sequence will become quite clear as we go along.

THE BENEFITS AND COSTS OF FIXED AND FLOATING EXCHANGE RATES

When comparing the merits of fixed and floating exchange rates, it is best to start with a small economy, too small to affect its partners' economies and, by implication, too small for its choice between fixed and floating rates to have much impact on the overall behavior of its partners' exchange rates.[1]

---

[1]The developing countries listed as "large" in Table 20-1 are not large in this economic sense.

If the Greek drachma is allowed to float, changes in drachma exchange rates will not cause large changes in the effective (average) exchange rates for the Deutsche mark, French franc, or Italian lira. But the converse is not true. The effective exchange rate for the drachma will be affected by other countries' exchange-rate arrangements. If the lira is pegged to the mark, then pegging the drachma to the mark will peg it to the lira, too; if, instead, the lira floats against the mark, then pegging the drachma to the mark will cause it to float against the lira. (That is why many of the countries covered by Table 20-1 peg their currencies to "baskets" of foreign currencies rather than to a single foreign currency.)

When we turn to the case of a large economy, we will have to deal with two complications. First, a large country cannot peg or float its currency without affecting its partners' exchange-rate arrangements. Second, events within a large economy will, by definition, affect other economies, and this structural interdependence leads to policy interdependence. Therefore, we will have to consider the problem of policy coordination among the major industrial countries and the case for a full-fledged monetary union like the one defined by the Maastricht Treaty.

Finally, bear in mind that comparisons between truly fixed and freely floating rates, while useful in highlighting benefits and costs, do not really represent the choices faced by governments. Few countries have maintained fully fixed rates for more than a decade or so. Britain and France devalued their currencies twice under the Bretton Woods system, and Germany revalued twice. Japan was the only major country that kept its exchange rate fixed from the end of World War II until the Bretton Woods system broke down in 1971. In the floating-rate era that followed, moreover, the major industrial countries wandered between freely floating rates and more or less intensive exchange-rate management. They were not always satisfied with the judgments made by markets. That is why we will conclude by examining proposals to make exchange-rate management more effective.

The Small-Country Case

Chapter 17 presented a monetary model in which prices and wages were perfectly flexible. In that sort of world, it is hard to choose between fixed and floating exchange rates, because the nominal exchange rate cannot affect the real rate. A small country that is capable of exercising firm control over its domestic money supply and can thus maintain stable prices should probably prefer a floating rate. If other countries fail to achieve as much price stability, the floating rate will insulate it from their failures. If it expects to make mistakes in monetary policy, however, it should probably prefer a pegged exchange rate. It can then count on changes in reserves to offset fluctuations in its money supply.

When wages and prices are sticky, by contrast, a change in the nominal exchange rate may be the fastest and least costly way to change the real exchange rate. This conclusion argues for some sort of exchange-rate flexibility; it makes more sense to change a single price—the price of foreign currency—than to wait for market forces to change all other prices.

A freely floating rate, however, may impart too much flexibility to the nominal exchange rate and thus to the real rate. The foreign-exchange market cannot know or care about the nature of the underlying shock to which the market is responding—whether it is a switch in expenditure, which can be offset by changing the real exchange rate, or a change in expenditure, which can be aggravated by changing the real rate. With a freely floating rate, moreover, disturbances arising in asset markets are transmitted directly to goods markets. An appreciation of the domestic currency resulting from a capital inflow switches expenditure from domestic to foreign goods, reducing output and employment in sectors producing traded goods. That is what happened to the United States in the early 1980s, when the dollar appreciated sharply and provoked an surge of protectionist pressures. We have also encountered several reasons for believing that a floating rate will tend to overshoot its long-run equilibrium level.

These are valid objections to a floating exchange rate, but they are not decisive. Governments may be more fallible than markets. They may allow too little exchange-rate flexilility by doggedly defending pegged exchange rates. The dynamics of the game in the foreign-exchange market often lead to this result. When governments believe that exchange rates should not change, they are tempted to make strong commitments. "We will not devalue!" It is then hard to change the rate without losing credibility, even when there are good reasons for changing it.[2] The resulting risk of excessive rigidity is compounded by using an exchange-rate commitment to raise the credibility of domestic monetary policy, a practice discussed later in this chapter.

Three more considerations bear on the choice between fixed and floating rates. They pertain to the nature of price and wage stickiness, the shocks affecting a particular economy, and the quality of domestic policies.

Two Types of Price Stickiness

When prices and wages are sticky in nominal terms, changes in the nominal exchange rate will change the real exchange rate; they are, indeed, the fastest way to change it. Even in this case, however, the real rate may not change as rapidly as the nominal rate. Recall a point made in Chapter 14 about "pricing to market" by foreign firms with large U.S. markets. Whereas the pricing policies of American firms depend primarily on conditions in the firms' home markets, the pricing policies of Japanese and other foreign firms depend on conditions in the firms' export markets and on expectations about future conditions. Therefore, a depreciation of the dollar reduces the foreign-currency prices of U.S. exports but may be slow to raise the dollar prices of U.S. imports; foreign firms may reduce the home-currency prices of their exports in order hold down their dollar prices and defend their market shares, expecially when they expect the depreciation to be reversed. Hence, changes in the real exchange rate for the dollar will tend to lag behind changes in the nominal rate.

When prices and wages are sticky in real terms, by contrast, a change in the nominal exchange rate cannot affect the real rate. Because it raises the home-currency price of imports, a depreciation of the nominal rate raises the cost of living. The increase in the cost of living tends to raise the nominal wage rate, as workers

---

[2]These difficulties could be reduced if governments could make *contingent* commitments, promising not to devalue unless certain events were to occur. But that would not be easy. It is hard to state precisely the circumstances under which the exchange rate would be changed or to anticipate all of those contingencies.

try to keep their real wage from falling, and the higher wage rate pushes up producers' prices. The real exchange rate does not change. These processes are very strong in countries where nominal wage rates are tied tightly to the cost of living. They are also strong in very open economies, where changes in the nominal exchange rate have large effects on the cost of living. That is why many small developing countries peg their exchange rates rigidly, foreswearing the use of exchange-rate changes for balance-of-payments adjustment. But the practice is not confined to those countries. Some of the smaller European countries have pegged their currencies to the Deutsche mark and thus tied their monetary policies to German policy. Belgium and the Netherlands have done this within the EMS; Austria has done it outside the EMS.

Two Types of Shocks

Floating exchange rates would be attractive if expenditure-switching shocks were large and frequent, compared to expenditure-changing shocks. We would not need to worry about the ability of the foreign-exchange market to change exchange rates when that would be optimal and to stabilize exchange rates when they should not change. We might still worry about overshooting, however, and the ability of the market to distinguish between permanent and transitory shocks. When a shock is permanent, labor and capital must be reallocated, and a prompt change in the real exchange rate will accelerate the process. When a shock is transitory, there is no need to redeploy resources and thus no need to change the real rate.

Floating rates would likewise be attractive if governments were able to distinguish among types of shocks and could deal with expenditure-changing shocks by adjusting their macroeconomic policies. In the language of Chapter 14, the governments would maintain internal balance, and the foreign-exchange market would maintain external balance by adjusting the exchange rate to offset expenditure-switching shocks.[3] Unfortunately, this division of labor does not work very well. Internal balance is not easy to define unambiguously, because it has several dimensions; policies to stabilize output and employment can ignite inflation, and policies to fight inflation can be costly in terms of output and employment. Furthermore, few countries can adjust their fiscal policies quickly, and monetary policies, although more flexible, may be less effective at combatting unemployment than inflation. Finally, many economists would argue that the largest fluctuations in expenditure reflect mistakes in fiscal and monetary policies, not autonomous changes

---

[3] If *all* governments were able to maintain internal balance, however, it might not be necessary to change exchange rates often in order to maintain external balance. From the standpoint of a single, small economy, fluctuations in foreign demand represent expenditure-switching shocks even though they are really departures from internal balance in the outside world, and exchange-rate changes are needed to offset them. If foreign governments were able to eliminate those fluctuations, the small country would have only to face pure expenditure-switching shocks, reflecting changes in tastes or technology. Such shocks may be fairly rare and may develop gradually enough to be offset by changing the prices of the relevant goods rather than changing exchange rates. In large, diversified economies, moreover, the shocks impinging on individual goods markets may average out across those markets and thus have little impact on the current-account balance, reducing the need for exchange-rate changes. Accordingly, well-diversified economies with well-behaved governments might favor pegged exchange rates.

in private-sector spending, and that the largest movements in floating exchange rates have been due to these mistakes. Hence, participants in the foreign-exchange market have to spend much time forecasting policy changes (or, at one remove, forecasting other participants' forecasts), rather than forecasting truly autonomous shocks.

Exchange-Rate Arrangements and the Quality of Policies

It is impossible to keep exchange rates fixed when governments fail to control inflation, and that has been the case in many developing countries. Accordingly, several of those countries have moved from pegged exchange rates to more flexible arrangements. This was the big change shown in Table 20-1, and Table 20-2 suggests that there is indeed a close link between a country's ability to maintain price stability and its ability to fix its exchange rate. The countries that changed their exchange-rate arrangements were those that had the highest inflation rates at both ends of the period covered by the table, and most of them moved from pegged to flexible exchange rates.

A few high-inflation countries went the other way, however, in an effort to "import" price stability by pegging their exchange rates. Israel, Poland, and Argentina belong to this group. Some of these countries failed to achieve price stability and have returned to more flexible arrangements. Nevertheless, their strategy deserves attention. First, it resembles the strategy adopted by France and Italy in the 1980s, a strategy that turned the EMS into a rigid exchange-rate regime. Second, it reflects a basic change in the way we think about exchange-rate arrangements.

Most books dealing with the monetary system, including this one, stress the ways in which the exchange-rate regime affects the transmission of shocks and policies from country to country. In other words, they seek to understand the effects of the

Table 20-2. Exchange-Rate Arrangements and Inflation in Selected Developing Countries, 1982–1991.

Country Group (and number of countries)	Inflation Rate	
	1981–1983	1988–1990
Stayed with pegged-rate arrangement (24)	10.2	9.3
Stayed with flexible-rate arrangement (14)[a]	30.5	143.3
Changed exchange-rate arrangement (25)[b]	40.5	283.5

Source: Peter B. Kenen, "Financial Opening and the Exchange Rate Regime," in H. Reisen and B. Fischer, eds., *Financial Opening* (Paris: OECD Development Centre, 1993). The 63 countries covered are the "large" developing countries in Table 20-1 for which it is possible to calculate inflation rates in the relevant years; the first group includes those countries that switched between various pegged-rate arrangements, and the second includes those countries that switched between various flexible-rate arrangements.

[a]When Brazil is deleted, because of its very high inflation rate, the averages fall to 24.0 percent in the first period and 28.5 percent in the second.

[b]When Argentina and Peru are deleted, because of their very high inflation rates, the averages fall to 31.5 percent in the first period and 57.7 percent in the second.

exchange-rate regime on economic interdependence. In the last few years, however, economists and governments have begun to ask how the exchange-rate regime may affect the quality of national policies, most notably the quality of monetary policies. This approach has produced three arguments for fixed exchange rates.

The first argument looks to a combination of exchange-rate pegging and asset-market arbitrage to minimize the impact of policy mistakes. Recall a point made frequently in earlier chapters. Under a pegged exchange rate, high capital mobility limits the influence of monetary policy on the domestic economy, and perfect capital mobility deprives it of any influence whatsoever. Those who believe that central banks can conduct sensible monetary policies regard this result as a cost of exchange-rate pegging; those who believe that central banks are likely to make policy mistakes regard this result as a benefit of exchange-rate pegging. But the argument assumes implicitly that capital flows are rather passive, responding in the main to interest-rate changes resulting from central-bank policies, so that they serve to stabilize the money supply. When economic or political uncertainties affect investors' expectations, capital flows can be very volatile, causing movements in reserves that are hard to sterilize, and they can thus destabilize the money supply. This has happened in Latin America, where improvements in economic and political conditions have attracted large capital inflows, forcing governments to choose between higher inflation, *via* the growth in the money supply produced by rising reserves, and appreciation of the nominal exchange rate.[4]

The second argument looks to a combination of exchange-rate pegging and goods-market arbitrage to combat inflation by tying down the prices of traded goods. It has been advanced in two quite different contexts. In Latin America, advocates of "heterodox" stabilization have argued that inflation can be ended abruptly by freezing wages and prices temporarily and pegging the exchange rate to link domestic and foreign prices. These measures cannot stop inflation permanently but can perhaps alter expectations temporarily and thus buy time for "orthodox" monetary and fiscal policies to banish inflation permanently. In Central and Eastern Europe, exchange-rate pegging and trade liberalization have been seen as an efficient way to "import" sensible prices into countries where prices were badly distorted by central planing. This strategy was adopted by Poland in 1990, and it cut inflation sharply. Unfortunately, pegged exchange rates and trade liberalization cannot stabilize the whole price level or hold down the wage rate. They can keep the prices of traded goods from rising, but not the prices of nontraded goods, and higher prices for those goods can drive up wages, making domestic producers less competitive. The trade balance tends to deteriorate, impairing confidence in the sustainability of

---

[4]In both cases, of course, the real exchange rate must appreciate and drive the current account into deficit. This result is not worrisome when a country can count on a continuing capital inflow, but that is not a safe bet in Latin America. It may thus be better to let the nominal exchange appreciate than to allow an increase in domestic prices, which is harder to reverse. In the case of Argentina, mentioned earlier, the capital inflow has been particularly trouble-some, because the pegging of the Argentine peso was accompanied by a fundamental monetary reform. The central bank has to hold foreign-currency assets as backing for the peso; it cannot buy or sell domestic assets to sterilize an increase in reserves. Therefore, the recent capital inflow has led to a large increase in the price level, which threatens the sustainability of the pegged exchange rate.

the pegged exchange rate. For this and other reasons, Poland shifted to a more flexible exchange rate in 1991.

The third argument would use exchange-rate pegging to make monetary policy more credible. It has been the main theme of the literature on the EMS, discussed in Chapter 19. Participation in the EMS was seen as a way to promise that a country's monetary policy will not differ greatly from German policy and thus as a way to "borrow" the Bundesbank's commitment to price stability. The argument, however, implies that a commitment to exchange-rate stability will be more credible than a straightforward commitment to price stability. Why should this be true? Clearly, a commitment to exchange-rate stability is more transparent and easier to monitor. But these features bear mainly on accountability, not on credibility. A commitment to exchange-rate stability will not be more credible than a commitment to price stability unless it is more *costly* to abandon a pegged rate than to abandon the effort to eliminate inflation. That was probably true under the Bretton Woods system, when a decision to devalue reduced the political life expectancy of a finance minister.[5] It may not be equally true today, because governments have more freedom to choose, change, and customize their exchange-rate arrangements.

Furthermore, the use of a pegged exchange rate to buy credibility is a high-risk strategy. When a government pegs the exchange rate, it deprives itself of the policy instrument most useful in offsetting the effects of previous inflation and of the additional inflation that typically occurs before the price level can be stabilized. It can be argued, moreover, that the recent literature has misrepresented the workings of the EMS. France has been the country most strongly committed to a fixed exchange rate in the EMS. But France did not achieve price stability by fixing the franc-mark exchange rate and then using domestic policies to defend that rate. It used domestic policies to achieve price stability, which imparted credibility to the franc-mark rate. Use of a pegged exchange rate to "anchor" expectations about future monetary policy may be effective when a country has already achieved price stability. It is less effective and more risky as a way of reaching price stability. A colleague with long experience of nautical matters put the point nicely: No sensible sailor throws out an anchor until the boat has stopped.

Note, finally, that these arguments for exchange-rate pegging break down when applied to all countries together. No country can import price stability unless another country can produce and export it. You can see this clearly by thinking about a world comprising one big country and many small ones. The small ones cannot import price stability unless the big one produces it. And matters are worse in a world with many large countries, because they are interdependent.

The Large-Country Case

Recall the complications posed by the large-country case: (1) A large country cannot peg or float its exchange rate without affecting its partners' exchange-rate arrangements. This is the familiar nth country problem; large countries must choose their exchange-rate arrangements jointly or, at least, consistently.

---

[5]See Richard N. Cooper, *Currency Devaluation in Developing Countries*, Essays in International Finance 86 (Princeton, N.J.: International Finance Section, Princeton University, 1971).

(2) A large country cannot alter its policies without affecting its partners' economies and therefore provoking policy responses that may keep it from achieving its own objectives. The exchange-rate regime affects the form taken by policy interdependence but cannot greatly affect the extent of policy interdependence.

In Chapter 19, we saw that the major industrial countries have tried many ways of solving the nth country problem. Under the Bretton Woods system, governments were not supposed to change their exchange rates without the consent of the International Monetary Fund, but this rule was not enforced. The nth country problem was resolved in practice by the passivity of the United States, which did not have an active exchange-rate policy of its own. This asymmetrical solution broke down, however, when the United States could no longer afford to be passive but could not devalue the dollar on its own. It had to change the whole institutional framework—a process that began in August 1971 with the closing of the gold window and ended in December 1971 with the Smithsonian Agreement, which represented a political solution to the nth country problem.

The history of the EMS has not been very different. It is supposed to function symmetrically; no country can change its exchange rate without the consent of the rest. But it has operated asymmetrically; EMS members have been able to adjust their exchange rates vis-à-vis the Deutsche mark because the Bundesbank has attached less importance to the maintenance of a fixed exchange rate than to the maintenance of domestic price stability. And the analogy can be carried further. When Germany tried to achieve a general exchange-rate realignment in September 1992 and ran into opposition, it had to adopt tactics that damaged the framework of the EMS itself.

If exchange rates were allowed to float freely, without any intervention, the task of solving the nth country problem would be shifted to the foreign-exchange market. There would be no need to negotiate exchange-rate realignments and no need for the IMF to review the exchange-rate policies of governments, because they would have none. Why, then, have governments been so strongly averse to freely floating rates? Why have they tried to establish pegged-rate regimes or, at least, to manage exchange rates rather than allow them to float freely?

A political scientist might answer that the costs of trying to organize the monetary system are fairly low, compared to the costs of organizing and maintaining other international arrangements. Less political capital has to be invested in an arrangement such as the EMS than an arrangement such as the EC itself. But a rational government will not invest *any* political capital in an exchange-rate regime unless it expects to derive some benefit from it. We have therefore to ask what benefits governments expect to derive from fixing or managing exchange rates.

If freely floating exchange rates were to follow purchasing-power parity, it would be hard to justify any interference with them. Nominal rates would change smoothly and gradually, in response to differences in national inflation rates, and real exchange rates would be stable. In a world of high capital mobility, however, changes in nominal exchange rates reflect events and expectations in asset markets, and these expectations can be very volatile. In the words of Michael Mussa, an advocate of floating rates:[6]

---

[6]Michael L. Mussa, *Exchange Rates in Theory and in Reality*, Essays in International Finance 179 (Princeton, N.J.: International Finance Section, Princeton University, 1990) p. 7.

> I have long been sympathetic to the view that the behavior of asset prices, including exchange rates, is afflicted by some degree of craziness. Many aspects of human behavior impress me as being not entirely sane, and I see no reason why the behavior of asset prices should be a virtually unique exception.

As goods prices are sticky, moreover, real and nominal exchange rates move together, so that the volatility of expectations affects the behavior of the real economy. Three consequences are cited frequently. First, the uncertainty produced by exchange-rate fluctuations acts as a tax on trade, reducing the volume of trade itself and, more importantly, discouraging investment in the production of traded goods. Second, movements in real exchange rates affect output and employment in export and import-competing industries. Labor and capital must be reallocated, which is costly in itself, and the reallocations must then be reversed when the exchange-rate movement has been reversed. The output and employment effects of exchange-rate swings also lead to political pressures for changes in trade policies— for subsidies and other export-promoting measures and for tariffs and other import-reducing measures.

Research on the effects of exchange-rate uncertainty has not adduced convincing evidence that it reduces the volume of trade or level of investment in the production of traded goods. Some studies have found trade-reducing effects, but they are not large. It is even harder to adduce quantitative evidence on the link between exchange-rate fluctuations and the ebb and flow of protectionist pressures. Studies of U.S. exchange-rate policy, however, suggest that the most prominent attempts to reduce the value of the dollar—the 1971 Smithsonian Agreement and the 1985 Plaza Agreement—reflected fears that Congress would impose trade barriers in response to political pressures produced by previous appreciations—by the gradual appreciation of the late 1960s and the more dramatic appreciation of the early 1980s. More generally, governments appear to regard exchange-rate stability as a *public good*, because it helps them stabilize trade-policy arrangements.

In the years immediately after the collapse of the Bretton Woods system, the major industrial countries favored an early return to pegged exchange rates, and the Committee of Twenty sought to design a viable, symmetrical successor to the Bretton Woods system. Its failure and the reasons were discussed in Chapter 19, and there has been no comparable effort since. In fact, the major countries have even backed away from the limited form of exchange-rate management embodied in the 1987 Louvre Accord. They have found it hard to coordinate their national policies closely enough to manage exchange rates effectively, let alone to peg them firmly.

THE PROBLEM OF POLICY COORDINATION

Governments engage in many forms of economic cooperation and in many policy domains. They engage in *consultation* when they exchange information about their economies and policies without making firm commitments to modify those policies. International institutions such as the IMF and the Organization for

Economic Co-operation and Development play major roles in this process. Governments engage in *collaboration* when they adopt specific measures aimed at achieving agreed objectives but do not undertake to modify their domestic policies. This form of cooperation is best illustrated by programs providing economic assistance to developing countries, including the programs of the World Bank. Governments engage in *coordination*, strictly defined, when they make specific, mutual commitments to modify their domestic policies. Coordination involves a "package" of policy changes that would not take place otherwise.

The case for coordination derives from the proposition that small-group behavior can produce suboptimal policy outcomes when the members of the group conduct their affairs independently. The governments of the major industrial countries can be viewed as a small group of economic actors and are subject to this risk.

Two Versions of the Case for Coordination

How can policy coordination avoid the risk arising from small-group behavior? There are two views of coordination, which give two answers to this question. The first is the *policy-optimizing* approach, which argues that coordination can help each country reach its own national objectives. The second is the *regime-preserving* or *public-goods* approach, which argues that coordination can help countries reach their common objectives. The policy-optimizing approach dominates the academic literature, but the public-goods approach may come closer to describing the way in which governments themselves appraise the benefits and costs of policy coordination.

The Policy-Optimizing Approach

The policy-optimizing approach can be illustrated easily by supposing that there has been a worldwide recession. No single country may be able to recover on its own by expanding its money supply or by taking other measures to stimulate demand. It runs the risk of getting ahead of the rest and thus facing a balance-of-payments deficit or having its currency depreciate if it has a floating exchange rate. An increase in domestic demand will raise its imports, and it can experience a capital outflow, too, if it uses monetary policy to stimulate demand. The United States encountered these problems in 1977–1978, when it stimulated demand more actively than did Europe and Japan. The dollar depreciated, the inflation rate rose, and monetary policy had to be tightened in 1979. Incomplete recovery gave way to another recession.

In situations of this sort, each government has an incentive to hang back and wait for other governments to act. Each may count on others' imports to raise its exports and produce an export-led recovery. The temptation is particularly strong under floating exchange rates, because a government that hangs back can hope to experience an appreciation of its currency. This will slow the growth of the country's exports stemming from recovery elsewhere in the world, weakening its own export-led recovery, but it will reduce the home-currency prices of the country's imports and offset some of the inflationary pressure that often accompanies an economic recovery. In other words, laggards can hope for a better short-run trade-off between expansion and inflation than if they tried to generate a homemade recovery.

When governments fail to coordinate their policies, each may act too timidly and thus disappoint the others' expectations. When they act jointly, by contrast, they can avoid these disappointments. When each government agrees to generate *some* homemade recovery, using the appropriate policy instruments, each can hope to benefit from the others' efforts and all can count more firmly on complete recovery.

One phrase in the previous sentence deserves extra emphasis—the one about appropriate policy instruments. The case for policy coordination stems partly from the need for each country to use an appropriate combination of fiscal and monetary policies. In the late 1970s, the United States relied mainly on monetary policy to promote recovery, and the dollar depreciated. In the early 1980s, it relied mainly on fiscal policy, and Chapter 19 described the results. The budget deficit induced a capital inflow, and the dollar appreciated hugely. To complicate matters, other governments were cutting their budget deficits. Hence, the policy mix was skewed one way in the United States and skewed the other way elsewhere.

Modeling Policy Optimization

Policy coordination can be viewed as a way of giving every government partial control over its partners' policy instruments and thus raising the number of instruments it has at its disposal to achieve its own objectives. This can be demonstrated by using a two-country version of the portfolio-balance model presented in Chapter 18 but making one modification. Instead of assuming that prices are permanently rigid or perfectly flexible, assume that prices are sticky. They are rigid in the short run, so that an easier monetary policy raises output temporarily; they are flexible in the long run, so that an easier monetary policy raises prices permanently, and output falls back to its long-run equilibrium level. Let us also assume that governments desire economic stability and will therefore try to prevent any short-run change in output or long-run change in the price level.

These assumptions are embodied in Figure 20-1, where the horizontal axis measures the temporary change in U.S. output caused by a change in the U.S. money supply or some other shock, and the vertical axis measures the permanent change in the U.S. price level. Hence, the origin represents the initial long-run equilibrium, where output and prices are constant. Assume that the U.S. economy starts at the origin and that the government wants to stay there. The origin is therefore described as the U.S. government's *bliss point* (i.e., the first-best outcome from its standpoint), and all other points are inferior to it. Thus, each point on the ellipse surrounding the origin is welfare-inferior to the origin (but all of them are equally inferior from the U.S. government's standpoint). The line BB and the arrows on it show how an open-market operation by the U.S. central bank affects the U.S. economy when it begins at the origin. An open-market purchase, raising the U.S. money supply, involves an upward movement along *BB*. It raises output temporarily and raises the price level permanently. The line *FF* and the arrows on it show how an open-market operation by the Japanese central bank affects the U.S. economy when the yen-dollar exchange rate is pegged. An open-market purchase has the same price-raising effect

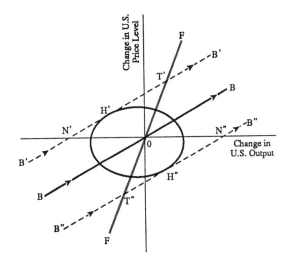

FIGURE 20-1

Policy Preferences and Monetary Policies under a Pegged Exchange Rate

The U.S. economy begins at the origin, which represents long-run equilibrium and the U.S. government's bliss point. The line *BB* says that an open-market purchase by the U.S. central bank raises output temporarily and raises the price level permanently. The line *FF* says that an open-market purchase by the Japanese central bank has similar effects on the U.S. economy, but the output effect is weaker. Points on the ellipse represent outcomes inferior to the one at the origin (but all outcomes on it are equally inferior); outcomes outside the ellipse are inferior to those on it. When a Japanese open-market purchase takes the U.S. economy to *T'*, the policy options of the U.S. government are given by the line *B'B'* passing through *T'*, and the best option is at *H'*, where *B'B'* is tangent to the ellipse. All other outcomes on *B'B'* are outside the ellipse. To go from *T'* to *H'*, the U.S. central bank must make an open-market sale, reducing output and the price level. Nevertheless, the price level remains above the one at the origin, which says that the U.S. open-market sale is smaller than the Japanese purchase. (This result is reflected in Figure 20-2, where the U.S. reaction curve is steeper absolutely than a 45° line.) The point *N'* represents a shock that reduces U.S. output temporarily without affecting the U.S. price level. This shock could be offset by a U.S. open-market purchase to take the U.S. economy from *N'* to *T'* and a Japanese sale to take the U.S. economy from *T'* to the origin. Hence, the bliss point on the new U.S. reaction curve is P_1 in Figure 20-2, where the U.S. central bank holds more bonds than at *P* and the Japanese central bank holds fewer bonds. If the same shock took the Japanese economy to *N"* in the Japanese counterpart of this figure, it could be offset by a Japanese open-market sale to take the Japanese economy from *N"* to *T"* and a U.S. purchase to take it from *T"* to the origin. Hence, the new Japanese bliss point is P_2 in Figure 20-2, where the Japanese central bank holds fewer bonds than at *P* and the U.S. central bank holds more bonds (but the sizes of the changes in bond holdings are different than in the U.S. case).

as an identical U.S. open-market purchase but the output effect is smaller. Hence, *FF* is steeper than *BB*.[7]

---

[7]The difference in output effects reflects an assumption often used in two-country models: Each country's spending is biased toward its own home good. Under a floating exchange rate, and increase in the Japanese money supply causes the dollar to appreciate, reducing U.S. output and the U.S. price level. Hence, the arrows on the *FF* curve point downward under a floating rate (and *FF* can be flatter or steeper than *BB*). The reaction curves will thus be upward sloping in the floating-rate version of Figure 20-2, but the case for coordination will still hold.

Figure 20-1 can be used to derive a reaction curve for the U.S. central bank, showing how it will respond to a change in Japanese monetary policy, and the Japanese counterpart of Figure 20-1 can be used to derive a reaction curve for the Japanese central bank. (These reaction curves will resemble those in Chapter 7, which showed how countries' trade policies respond to changes in their partner's trade policy.) A Japanese open-market purchase takes the U.S. economy to a point such as T' in Figure 20-1, raising U.S. output in the short run and the U.S. price level in the long run. The options open to the U.S. central bank are shown by drawing a new line, $B'B'$, passing through T', and the best of these options is given by the point H', where $B'B'$ is tangent to the ellipse describing U.S. policy preferences. (All other points on $B'B'$ lie outside that ellipse. Hence, they are further from the origin and welfare-inferior to any point on the ellipse.) To move from T' to H', the U.S. central bank must make an open-market sale. But the U.S. price level is higher at H' than at the origin, which says that the U.S. open-market sale is smaller than the Japanese open-market purchase. (The global money supply has risen, raising both countries' price levels.)

These results are reproduced in Figure 20-2, where the horizontal axis measures the bond holdings of the U.S. central bank, and the vertical axis measures the bond holdings of the Japanese central bank. Let P be the initial U.S. bliss point (and the Japanese bliss point too, because its economy also starts in long-run equilibrium, and its government wants to stay there). The line I_1 is the U.S. reaction curve, showing how the U.S. central bank responds to an open-market purchase or sale by the Japanese central bank. The reaction curve is downward sloping, because the U.S. central bank makes an open-market sale, reducing its bond holdings, when the Japanese central bank makes an open-market purchase. It is steeper absolutely than a 45° line, because the U.S. sale is smaller than the corresponding Japanese purchase. The line I_2 is the Japanese reaction curve, derived from the Japanese version of Figure 20-1.

As both governments' bliss points coincide at P, they will not leave it until some shock affects the situation. Return to Figure 20-1 and consider a shock that drives the U.S. economy to the point N'. It reduces U.S. output temporarily but does not affect the price level. The U.S. central bank can go again to H', accepting a higher price level to reduce the fall in output. But it could do better if it had complete control of Japanese open-market operations. Suppose it were to make an open-market purchase that moved the U.S. economy along $B'B'$ from N' to T' and then told the Japanese central bank to make an open-market sale that moved the U.S. economy along FF from T' to the origin. The shock would be neutralized completely. This ideal outcome is shown in Figure 20-2 by shifting the U.S. bliss point to P_1, where the U.S. central bank holds more bonds and the Japanese central bank holds fewer bonds, and then shifting the U.S. reaction curve to I'_1, making it pass through the new bliss point.

Suppose that the same shock drives the Japanese economy to N'' in the Japanese version of Figure 20-1, raising Japanese output but not affecting the Japanese price level. The effects could be neutralized completely if the Japanese central bank were to make an open-market sale that moved the Japanese economy from N'' to T'' and then told the U.S. central bank to make a purchase that moved the Japanese

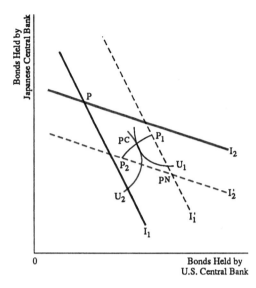

FIGURE 20-2
Reaction Curves and Policy Coordination
As the U.S. and Japanese economies begin in long-run equilibrium, and both governments want to stay there, they have the same initial bliss point, P. The U.S. reaction curve is I_1, and the Japanese curve is I_2. When one country's central bank makes an open-market purchase, raising its bond holdings, the other central bank will make an open-market sale, reducing its bond holdings, but the sale will be smaller than the purchase. Consider a shock that reduces U.S. output and raises Japanese output but has no permanent effect on the countries' price levels. Its impact on the U.S. economy could be offset if the U.S. central bank were to make an open-market purchase and the Japanese central bank were to make a smaller open-market sale. Hence, the shock shifts the U.S. bliss point from P to P_1 and the U.S. reaction curve from I_1 to I_1'. Its impact on the Japanese economy could be offset if the Japanese central bank were to make an open-market sale and the U.S. central bank were to make a smaller open-market purchase. Hence, the shock shifts the Japanese bliss point from P to P_2 and the Japanese reaction curve from I_2 to I_2'. If the two central banks do not coordinate their policies, they will go to P^N. If they do coordinate their policies, they can go to a point such as P^C, which is better for both countries. Bliss points such as P_1 and P_2 are surrounded by indifference curves like U_1 for the United States and U_2 for Japan. As U_1 cuts I_1' between P^N and P_1, all points on U_1, including P^C, are superior to P^N from the U.S. standpoint. As U_2 cuts I_2' between P^N and P_2, all points on U_2, including P^C, are superior to P^N from the Japanese standpoint. Therefore, the coordinated outcome at P^C is better for both countries than the noncoordinated outcome at P^N.

economy from T'' to the origin. In Figure 20-2, then, the Japanese bliss point shifts to P_2, and the new Japanese reaction curve is I_2'.

As the two countries' bliss points no longer coincide, the central banks cannot expect to reach them. The Japanese central bank will not follow the instructions of the U.S. central bank, because it wants to make the open-market sale required to reach P_2, which is larger than the sale required for the U.S. central bank to reach P_1. The U.S. central bank will not follow the instructions of the Japanese central bank, because it wants to make the open-market purchase required to reach P_1, which is larger than the purchase required for the Japanese central bank to reach P_2.

What will they do instead? If each central bank acts independently, without taking account of the other's decisions, they will go to P^N.[8] If they coordinate their policies, however, they can reach a point such as P^C, lying on the curve connecting their bliss points, and the outcome at this point will be better than the outcome at P^N from each country's standpoint. Bliss points such as P_1 and P_2 are surrounded by indifference curves, and two of these are drawn in Figure 20-2. They are the curves whose tangency locates the point P^C. But the U.S. indifference curve, U_1, cuts the U.S. reaction curve between P^N and the new U.S. bliss point, so the U.S. welfare loss is smaller at P^C than it would be at P^N. And the Japanese indifference curve, U_2, cuts the Japanese reaction curve between P^N and the new Japanese bliss point, making an analogous statement for Japan.

Clearly, policy coordination cannot neutralize completely the output effects of the shock. Those effects can be neutralized completely only when a government can reach its bliss point, and P^C lies between the bliss points. But the coordinated outcome at P^C is better than the outcome at P^N. It reduces the welfare loss resulting from the shock.

Exceptions, Qualifications, and Anomalies

Other macroeconomic models can be used to show that coordination fosters policy optimization, but there are exceptions and qualifications.

My Princeton colleague, Kenneth Rogoff, has called attention to one such exception. Return to the example at the start of this section, where the balance-of-payments effects of acting individually kept governments from dealing with a global recession. Coordination led them to do the right thing by relaxing the balance-of-payments constraint. In many macroeconomic models, however, governments tend to pursue inflationary policies unless they are constrained by the balance-of-payments effects of acting individually. In those cases, coordination leads them to do the wrong thing.

Two other economists, Jeffrey Frankel and Katharine Rockett, have drawn attention to an important qualification. If governments do not know how the world economy works, they can make welfare-worsening policy bargains. Frankel and Rockett use ten multicountry econometric models to represent two governments' views about the world economy. By ascribing those views, one by one, to each government, they can produce 100 policy bargains between the two governments. They can then examine the welfare effects of the policy bargains when each model is taken to be the "true" model of the world economy. Both governments gain from coordination when they happen to use the true model, and they can even gain when they use the wrong model, but they can also suffer losses. In fact, they suffer losses in more than a third of the possible cases.[9]

Furthermore, the policy-optimizing approach has two implications that impair its usefulness as a way to represent policy coordination. First, it implies that coordina-

---

[8]To prove this, start at P and assume that the Japanese central bank moves first. It will make an open-market sale to move vertically from P to a point on I_2'. The U.S. central bank will then make an open-market purchase to move horizontally to a point on I_1'. The Japanese central bank will respond by making another sale to return to its reaction curve, and the process will continue until both central banks reach P^N.

tion should take place continuously, not episodically. Yet there have been very few policy bargains of the type illustrated in Figure 20-2. The bargain made at the 1978 Bonn summit is often cited as an example, but it was not confined to macroeconomic policies; Germany and Japan agreed to modify their fiscal policies, but they did so in exchange for a commitment by the United States to modify its energy policies. Second, the policy-optimizing approach implies that it should be easy to make policy bargains. Governments can be expected to haggle about the distribution of the welfare gains (the precise location of the point P^c on the curve connecting P_1 and P_2 in Figure 20-2). But there should be no reason for them to haggle about the "burden" of coordination, as there should be no net burden. Under the policy-optimizing approach, moreover, disagreements about policy preferences should not prevent coordination; in fact, they may even raise the benefits from coordination. Yet governments frequently fail to coordinate their policies because they disagree about priorities and preferences and about sharing the costs of coordination. The public-goods approach helps us to explain why that can happen.

The Public-Goods Approach

Under the policy-optimizing approach, governments gain from coordination because it helps them to achieve their own national objectives. Under the public-goods approach, governments gain because coordination helps them to achieve certain global objectives, as well as their own national objectives. These global objectives are public goods, because it is hard to prevent any country from "consuming" them even when it does not contribute to producing them. To produce them in adequate amounts, however, governments may have to adopt policies that interfere with the pursuit of their national objectives.

The public-goods approach can therefore explain why disagreements about policy objectives interfere with coordination and why coordination is seen to be costly. It also explains why coordination has been sporadic. Coordination is most likely to occur when governments face a clear and serious threat to the international economic system—an increase in the price of oil like that of the early 1970s, which led to the policy bargain at the 1978 Bonn summit, or a large exchange-rate misalignment like that of the early 1980s, which led to the 1985 Plaza Agreement. When the threat is less obvious or serious, the costs of coordination seem too high, and governments place their national objectives ahead of their global objectives.

Critics of policy coordination seem sometimes to argue that governments should pay more attention to their national objectives. One well-known critic, Martin

---

[9]In many of these cases, however, a government knowingly makes a bargain harmful to its partner on its own view of the world or one harmful to itself on its partner's view. A government acting in good faith might not want to make a bargain harmful to its partner; and a prudent government might not want to make a bargain that would be harmful to itself if its partner's view turned out to be true. These restrictions rule out about 60 percent of the bargains, including some that would be mutually beneficial. But most of those they rule out are welfare-reducing bargains; these fall from a third to a quarter of the total number. See Gerald Holtham and Andrew Hughes Hallett, "International Macroeconomic Policy Coordination When Policymakers Do Not Agree on the True Model: Comment," and Jeffrey Frenkel, Scott Erwin, and Katharine Rockett, "Reply," *American Economic Review*, 82 (September 1992).

Feldstein of Harvard, wrote these paragraphs shortly after the 1987 stock-market crash:[10]

> Washington's explicit recognition of its responsibility for America's economic future would... reassure financial markets that have become unnecessarily frightened by the prospect that international economic coordination will collapse. Unfortunately, ever since the 1985 Plaza meeting, the administration and the governments of other industrial nations have emphatically asserted that international economic coordination is crucial to a healthy international economy in general and to continued U.S. growth in particular. Since such assertions are not justified by the actual interdependence of the industrial economies, Americans have been inappropriately worried...
>
> The U.S. should now in a clear but friendly way end the international economic coordination of macroeconomic policy. We should continue to cooperate with other governments by exchanging information about current and future policy decisions, but we should recognize explicitly that Japan and Germany have the right to pursue the monetary and fiscal policies that they believe are in their own best interests.
>
> It is frightening to the American public and upsetting to our financial markets to believe that the fate of our economy depends on the decisions made in Bonn and Tokyo. Portfolio investors, business managers and the public in general need to be reassured that we are not hostages to foreign economic policies, that the U.S. is the master of its own economic destiny, and that our government can and will do what is needed to maintain healthy economic growth.

These objections would perhaps be valid if governments were truly committed to intensive policy-optimizing coordination instead of sporadic regime-preserving coordination. In fact, the governments' aims are rather modest. Furthermore, critics of coordination seem to assume that governments are comfortable with freely floating exchange rates, and that assumption is unrealistic. Monetary history strongly suggests that governments regard exchange-rate stability as a public good and will try to achieve it or, at least, to limit exchange-rate fluctuations. We will return to the problem of exchange-rate management at the end of this chapter, after examining the benefits and costs of a full-fledged monetary union—the most ambitious form of policy coordination.

THE BENEFITS AND COSTS OF MONETARY UNIONS

Chapter 11 noted that political considerations have motivated decisions to form customs unions, like the European Community. Political considerations also help to explain why the EC has sought to form a monetary union. A country's

---

[10]Martin Feldstein, "The End of Policy Coordination," *The Wall Street Journal* (November 9, 1987).

currency, like its flag, is a conspicuous symbol of national identity. The nature and timing of the effort, however, reflect economic concerns as well.

Monetary Integration in Western Europe

Monetary cooperation in Western Europe began before the creation of the common market in 1958 but was intensified thereafter. In 1971, the EC agreed to move gradually toward economic and monetary union (EMU) during the next decade and took steps in that direction. Fluctuations in exchange rates between EC currencies were reduced by keeping the rates within bands narrower than those imposed by the Bretton Woods system, and a European Monetary Cooperation Fund (EMCF) was established to give reserve credit to EC countries with balance-of-payments problems. The process stalled, however, when oil prices rose abruptly in the early 1970s. The EC countries had agreed to achieve a high degree of economic convergence before they moved to monetary union, but the increase in the price of oil led to economic divergence, not convergence, as individual EC countries adapted to it differently.

A few EC countries continued to peg their bilateral exchange rates after the collapse of the Bretton Woods system, so their currencies floated jointly against other currencies. In 1979, however, the EC countries agreed to create the European Monetary System to peg their exchange rates comprehensively. They revived the narrow exchange-rate bands to which they had agreed in 1971 and enlarged the EMCF to help them defend their exchange rates. Chapter 19 traced the history of the EMS. It was meant to be a more flexible and symmetrical version of the Bretton Woods system, but it became more rigid and less symmetrical in the late 1980s.

As governments began to view the EMS as a truly fixed-rate system, the case for going further became more appealing, and the case was reinforced by the signing of the Single European Act—the decision described in Chapter 11 to transform the EC into a single internal market by the end of 1992.

First, the decision to form the single market reinforced the view long held in Europe that closely integrated national economies have more to gain from exchange-rate stability than from occasional realignments. It was argued, indeed, that the gains from forming the single European market would not be fully achieved without eliminating the exchange-rate uncertainties and conversion costs arising from the use of separate national currencies. This view is debatable, but it was influential.

Second, the formation of the single market called for the abolition of capital controls. Once they were abolished, however, doubts about the fixity of EMS exchange rates might generate speculative capital flows large enough to force exchange-rate realignments or, at least, to interfere with the normal conduct of monetary policies. This point was put vividly by Tommaso Padoa-Schioppa, an official of the Banca d'Italia, who warned against trying to meet an "inconsistent quartet" of policy objectives—free trade, full capital mobility, fixed exchange rates, and independent monetary policies. "In the long run," he said, "the only solution to the inconsistency is to complement the internal market with a monetary union."[11]

---

[11]Tommaso Padoa-Schioppa, "The European Monetary System: A Long-Term View," in F. Giavazzi et al., eds., *The European Monetary System* (Cambridge: Cambridge University Press, 1988), p. 376.

These two points were summed up by the argument made in the previous chapter. To keep exchange rates fixed in the EMS, the EC countries must adopt a common monetary policy, but it must be a European policy fashioned by a European institution, not a German policy fashioned by the Bundesbank. This argument was made when Germany was still a low-inflation country with low interest rates, but it became more persuasive after German unification, when the German inflation rate rose and the Bundesbank raised interest rates.

This argument is sometimes taken to mean that a European central bank would have different policy preferences than the Bundesbank and would not pursue price stability at the expense of other economic objectives. But that would not be the case under the Maastricht Treaty, discussed in the next section. The treaty would establish a European Central Bank (ECB), which would be required to pursue price stability as its primary objective. The argument, however, has another, more subtle interpretation. The Bundesbank pursues price stability in Germany. A European central bank would pursue price stability in the EC as a whole, just as the Federal Reserve System in the United States defines its policy stance with reference to conditions in the whole American economy, not any single Federal Reserve District. Hence, monetary union would change the *domain* of the institution making European monetary policy.

The next steps were described in Chapter 19. In 1989, the Delors Report recommended the creation of a single central-banking system for the EC and the substitution of a single currency for the separate national currencies:[12]

> A new monetary institution would be needed because a single monetary policy cannot result from independent decisions and actions by different central banks.... [The] domestic and international monetary policy-making of the Community should be organized in a federal form, in what might be called a *European System of Central Banks* (ESCB)... [It] could consist of a central institution (with its own balance sheet) and the national central banks....
>
> The adoption of a *single currency*, while not strictly necessary for the creation of a monetary union, might be seen—for economic as well as psychological and political reasons—as a natural and desirable further development of the monetary union. A single currency would clearly demonstrate the irreversibility of the... monetary union, considerably facilitate the monetary management of the Community and avoid the transactions costs of converting currencies.

The Delors Report outlined a three-stage process for reaching economic and monetary union. The first stage would see completion of the single market, the abolition of all capital controls, and the introduction of a comprehensive framework for policy coordination. All of the EC currencies would enter the exchange-rate mechanism of the EMS, but realignments would still be permitted. The second stage would see the creation of the ESCB, which would begin by coordinating the

---

[12] *Report of the Committee for the Study of Economic and Monetary Union*, (Luxembourg: Office for Official Publications of the European Communities, 1989), paragraphs 32 and 23 (italics in original).

monetary policies of the individual EC countries but would soon start to formulate a single EC policy. Realignments of exchange rates would still be possible, but only in exceptional circumstances. The second stage would also see the introduction of strict limits on national budget deficits—a controversial matter to which we will return. The third stage would begin with the irrevocable locking of exchange rates; the ESCB would take charge of monetary policy; and a single currency would be issued eventually to replace the national currencies.

Soon after the Delors Report was published, the EC governments agreed to begin the first stage in 1990 and to start negotiations on the second and third stages. Nevertheless, they declined to endorse any gradual transfer of monetary sovereignty during the second stage. In fact, they decided that the ESCB should not begin to function until the the third stage. Another institution, the European Monetary Institute (EMI), would coordinate national policies during the second stage.

While these decisions were being taken, however, the EC was starting to ask how it would be affected by the disintegration of the Soviet empire, by German unification, and by the collapse of the Soviet Union itself. Would a larger, more powerful Germany dominate Europe and pursue a more independent foreign policy? Would the EC continue to function efficiently after admitting more members? Two groups of countries seek to join the EC—those in Western Europe, such as Sweden and Finland, which did not join earlier to avoid "taking sides" in the superpower conflict, and those in Central Europe, such as Hungary and Poland, which see membership as vital to their future prosperity and domestic political stability. The new political situation led the EC countries to adopt a broader agenda—to revise the decision-making processes of the EC itself and find ways of following a common foreign policy and cooperating closely in matters of defense. All of these matters were covered by the Maastricht Treaty signed in December 1991.

The Maastricht Treaty

The Maastricht Treaty may be modified, formally or otherwise, before it is implemented. The EMS crises of 1992 and 1993 drew attention to problems that were not seen clearly by the authors of the treaty. Nevertheless, the treaty deserves close attention, because it illustrates the problems and requirements of a monetary union. We will start at the end of the process—the plan for full-fledged monetary union—look next at the fiscal provisions, and then study the transition.

On the first day of the third stage, the countries participating in the monetary union will lock their exchange rates permanently , and the ESCB will take charge of monetary policy. The ESCB will consist of a European Central Bank (ECB) and the national central banks of the participating countries. (It is necessary to speak of "participating countries" rather than "EC countries" because some EC countries may not participate.) At the same time, "the ECU will become a currency in its own right," instead of being a basket of national currencies. It will eventually replace the national currencies.[13]

The ECB will have an Executive Board, with a president and five other members;

---

[13]Quotations in this and subsequent paragraphs come from the Maastricht Treaty or Statute of the ECB and ESCB, which is part of the Treaty.

they will be chosen by the national governments, acting jointly. It will have a Governing Council, comprising the Board members and the governors of the national central banks. The Council will formulate monetary policy, and the Board will execute it. Whenever "possible and appropriate," however, the Board must use the national central banks to conduct its monetary operations. (These arrangements resemble those in the United States, where the Board of Governors of the Federal Reserve System has a role much like that of the ECB Board, and the Open Market Committee has a role much like that of the Council. In the United States, however, the Federal Reserve Bank of New York operates on behalf of the entire Federal Reserve System, whereas the ECB will have to use all of the national central banks—a requirement bound to produce inefficiencies.)

When participating in the work of the Council, the national central bank governors are expected to act as individuals, not representatives of their countries, and the treaty contains several provisions designed to protect the independence of the ECB. The ECB will pursue price stability as its "primary objective," but it must also pay attention to growth, employment, and other economic goals insofar as it can do so without jeopardizing price stability.

Who will determine exchange-rate policy vis-à-vis the outside world? The answer in the treaty reflects an awkard compromise. Finance ministers wanted to control exchange-rate policy. Central bankers wanted to be sure that the ECB would not be kept from pursuing price stability by the need to intervene on foreign-exchange markets. Hence, Article 109 of the treaty, reproduced in Figure 20-3, gives the Council of Ministers the power to decide whether the EC will make international agreements to peg exchange rates for the ECU. In the absence of these agreements, however, the finance ministers can only issue "general orientations" for exchange-rate policy, which must be consistent with price stability. Read Article 109 carefully and ask yourself who will decide whether the EC should make an *informal* agreement with the United States and Japan, like the 1985 Plaza Agreement or 1987 Louvre Accord, to influence exchange rates or limit fluctuations.

Fiscal Policy and Monetary Union

In Chapter 14, we looked at the shocks experienced by EC countries and the problems they would face in a monetary union. The shocks have been smaller but less symmetrical than those experienced by states or regions in the United States. How can individual EC countries deal with such shocks after exchange rates have been locked and monetary policy has been transferred to the ECB? The completion of the single market will make adjustment easier by raising the mobility of capital and labor, but that will not happen quickly.

Chapter 14 drew attention to another possibility. When countries belong to a fiscal union as well as a monetary union, the need for adjustment can be reduced and the costs can be redistributed. When a state or region in the United States suffers an output-reducing shock, its citizens' tax payments to the federal government fall automatically, reducing the income effects of the shock. According to a study cited in Chapter 14, the automatic workings of the U.S. fiscal system offset about a third of any short-run output loss. But this will not happen in the EC, where, in the words of the Delors Report, "the centrally managed Community budget is likely to remain

---

Conducting Exchange-Rate Policy under the Maastricht Treaty

1. [The Council of Ministers] may, acting unanimously on a recommendation from the ECB or from the [EC] Commission, and after consulting the ECB in an endeavor to reach a consensus consistent with the objective of price stability, after consulting the European Parliament, in accordance with procedure in paragraph 3..., conclude formal agreements on an exchange-rate system for the ECU in relation to non-Community currencies. The Council may, acting by a qualified majority on a recommendation from the ECB or from the Commission, and after consulting the ECB... adopt, adjust, or abandon the central rates of the ECU within the exchange rate system.

2. In the absence of an exchange rate system in relation to one or more non-Community currencies as referred to in paragraph 1, the Council may, acting by a qualified majority either on a recommendation from the Commission and after consulting the ECB, or on a recommendation from the ECB, formulate general orientations for exchange rate policy... These general orientations shall be without prejudice to the general objective of the ESCB to maintain price stability...

3. [Where] agreements concerning monetary or foreign exchange regime matters need to be negotiated by the Community with one or more states or international organizations, the Council... shall decide the arrangements for the negotiations and for the conclusion of such agreements. These arrangements shall ensure that the Community expresses a single position. The Commission shall be fully associated in the negotiations.

Agreements concluded in accordance with this paragraph shall be binding on the institutions of the Community, on the ECB and on Member States.

FIGURE 20-3
Extracts from Article 109 of the Maastricht Treaty.

---

a very small part of total public-sector spending and... much of this budget will not be available for cyclical adjustments."[14]

There will indeed be *two* fiscal-policy problems when the EC countries move to monetary union. On the one hand, individual governments will want to use their national fiscal policies to maintain domestic stability in the face of country-specific shocks, as they will not have their own monetary policies. On the other hand, they will have to coordinate their fiscal policies in order to achieve an appropriate policy mix for the EC as a whole, as the EC budget is not sufficiently large or flexible for that purpose. The Maastricht Treaty, however, does not meet these needs. Its fiscal provisions were drafted to deal with the so-called solvency problem, not the policy-mix or stabilization problem.

A government is solvent if its debts do not exceed the present value of the future revenues available to service them. Solvency is not a problem for most large EC countries but may be a problem for Italy and some smaller EC countries, including Belgium, Greece, and Ireland. There are two ways in which the solvency problem of an individual country might interfere with the conduct of monetary policy in a monetary union. The first is the possibility of political pressure coming from a

---

[14]*Report of the Committee for the Study of Economic and Monetary Union*, (Luxembourg: Office for Official Publications of the European Communities, 1989), paragraph 30.

heavily indebted government that wants the ECB to help it by buying some of its debt. The second is the possibility of market pressure coming from the threat to financial stability posed by a prospective or actual default.

Economists are fond of putting the first possibility in Machiavellian terms. Heavily indebted governments, they say, will want the ECB to inflate away their debts by sacrificing price stability. This view is simplistic and is rejected by recent research. Pressure from a government is more likely to develop when investors realize that the government faces a solvency problem and refuse to buy its debt without a big increase in interest rates. The government may want the ECB to keep interest rates from rising.

Market pressures would arise in this same situation. When a government is expected to default, the prices of its bonds will fall. Holders of those bonds, including banks, will suffer large capital losses, posing a threat to *their* solvency. The ECB need not buy up the debt of the government itself, but it may be obliged to make other open-market purchases to stave off a crisis of confidence in the banking system.

The Maastricht Treaty tries to deal with these risks by imposing strict limits on national budget deficits. Each EC government must avoid "excessive budget deficits," and the EC Commission will monitor the fiscal situation, using the criteria listed in Figure 20-4. If it finds that a government has an excessive deficit, and the Council of Ministers agrees, the Council will make recommendations to the government concerned, and it can go further if the government does not respond. It can instruct the government to reduce its deficit by a specified amount and can impose certain penalties if the government does not comply.

The "reference values" listed in Figure 20-4 are very strict. At the end of 1991, when the treaty was signed, seven EC countries had debts larger than 60 percent of GDP, and eight had budget deficits larger than 3 percent of GDP. The reference values, however, will not be applied mechanically; each of them is followed by qualifying phrases, and there is no way to know how these will be interpreted.

The Transition to Monetary Union

The fiscal criteria just discussed are doubly important, as a country with an excessive deficit cannot join the monetary union at the start of the third stage. Each country will have to meet four "convergence criteria" before it can join. They are listed in Figure 20-5.

During the transition to monetary union, which began formally in January 1994, with the start of the second stage, the EMI will manage the EMS, coordinate national monetary policies, and plan for the creation of the ESCB. It must decide how the ESCB will conduct its monetary operations and how it will operate in foreign-exchange markets. Three years later, the EMI and EC Commission will report to the Council of Ministers on the readiness of each EC country to move to the third stage, using the four convergence criteria listed in Figure 20-5. The Council must then decide whether a majority of EC countries is ready to join the monetary union and whether it would be "appropriate" to start the third stage. If so, it will set a date. If not, the whole procedure will be repeated periodically—but not indefinitely. If no date is set before the end of 1997, the third stage will start automatically at

---

Defining an Excessive Deficit under the Maastricht Treaty

The [EC] Commission shall monitor the development of the budgetary situation and of the stock of government debt in the Member States with a view to identifying gross errors. In particular it shall examine compliance with budgetary discipline on the basis of the following two criteria:

(a) whether the ratio of the planned or actual government deficit to gross domestic product exceeds a reference value [3 percent of GDP], unless

— either the ratio has declined substantially and continuously and has reached a level that comes close to the reference value;

— or, alternatively, the excess over the reference value is only exceptional and temporary and the deficit remains close to the reference value;

(b) whether the ratio of government debt to gross domestic product exceeds a reference value [60 percent of GDP], unless the ratio is sufficiently diminishing and approaching the reference value at a satisfactory pace...

If a Member State does not fulfil the requirements under one or both of these criteria, the Commission shall prepare a report. The report...shall also take into account whether the government deficit exceeds government investment expenditure and...other relevant factors, including the medium term economic and budgetary position of the Member State.

FIGURE 20-4
Extract from Article 104c of the Maastricht Treaty.

the beginning of 1999, and every eligible country will join the monetary union.[15]

These arrangements have been widely criticized. Many Germans object to the notion of automaticity. They are reluctant to trade the Bundesbank for the ECB and the Deutsche mark for the ECU, and they want the German parliament to decide whether Germany should join the monetary union. Other critics take the opposite view. They favor automaticity and object to the convergence criteria. Why must a country prove that it can adhere to the rules of the EMS in order to join a monetary union in which it will have no exchange rate of its own? Why must it reduce its inflation rate before it can join, when the monetary policy of the ECB will impose the same inflation rate on every EC country? The EMS crises of 1992 and 1993 point to another problem. A long transition to monetary union is bound to be accident prone. If doubts about the outcome of the French referendum could cause massive speculation against the pound and lira, how will the foreign-exchange market behave just before the EMI and EC Commission must report on the readiness of each EC country to join the monetary union?

Concerns of this sort have inspired proposals for a two-speed approach to monetary union. Countries that are ready now should move ahead promptly. The rest should move when they are ready. A two-speed strategy is, of course, implicit in

---

[15]Denmark and Britain will not have to do so; the treaty gives them the right to "opt out" of the third stage.

The Convergence Criteria of the Maastricht Treaty

1. *Achieving a high degree of price stability*, which is taken to mean

   ...an average rate of inflation, observed over a period of one year before the examination, that does not exceed by more than $1\frac{1}{2}$ percentage points that of, at most, the three best performing Member States in terms of price stability.

2. *Achieving a sustainable financial position*, which is taken to mean that

   ...at the time of the examination the Member State is not the subject of a Council decision ... that an excessive deficit exists.

3. *Maintaining the country's exchange rate within the normal EMS band*, which is taken to mean that

   ...the Member State has respected the normal [$2\frac{1}{4}$ percent] fluctuation margins ... without severe tensions for at least the last two years before the examination. In particular, the Member State shall not have devalued its currency's bilateral central rate against any other Member State's currency on its own initiative for the same period.

4. *Achieving a long-term interest rate indicative of durable convergence and of the country's participation in the EMS*, which is taken to mean that

   ...over a period of one year before the examination a Member State has an average nominal long-term interest rate that does not exceed by more than 2 percentage points that of, at most, the three best performing Member States in terms of price stability...

FIGURE 20-5
Extracts from the Protocol on the Convergence Criteria Attached to the Maastricht Treaty.

the treaty. No one truly believes that every EC country will be ready for monetary union, even in 1999. Under the treaty, however, all 12 EC countries will start out together, participate in the work of the EMI, and submit to the fiscal-policy rules of the treaty. The separation of fast and slow countries will occur on the eve of the third stage, and the subsequent admission of the slow countries will be decided by EC bodies, not by the fast countries acting on their own. Those who favor a two-speed strategy outside the framework of the treaty contemplate a rapid move to monetary union by a self-selected group of strong-currency countries, which would then decide whether to admit additional countries. The fast and slow countries would be separated right away. Because it would scuttle the Maastricht Treaty, this strategy raises a number of problems. How would a German government justify its decision to join a monetary union without the steps toward closer political union that have been Germany's price for giving up the Deutsche mark? Would the slow-speed countries take their revenge by blocking vital decisions, such as decisions about admitting new members to the EC itself?

THE PROBLEM OF EXCHANGE-RATE MANAGEMENT

In a world with global capital markets, there may be no safe half-way house between freely floating exchange rates and permanently fixed rates. Floating rates have been extremely volatile, however, because they are so sensitive to expectations, and the volatility of nominal rates has affected real rates. Once thought to be the best defense against imperfect policies, they have instead transmitted policy mistakes from asset markets to goods markets. Yet fixed rates cannot be maintained unless governments adopt a common monetary policy—which raises the same question posed in Europe. Who will make that policy? There are three answers.

The first is the hegemonic answer, which says that the common monetary policy will be imposed by the largest, most powerful country. That was the answer given by the Bretton Woods system, where the United States became the hegemonic country, and by the EMS, where Germany became the hegemonic country. It is a poor answer, however, because it assumes that the leading country will follow a monetary policy appropriate to its partners' needs—which does not always happen.

The second is the answer given by the Maastricht Treaty—move from fixed exchange rates to a monetary union. It is also given by Richard Cooper of Harvard, who argues that the major industrial countries, including the United States, should move eventually to a common currency managed by a single central bank. But the complexity and defects of the Maastricht Treaty illustrate the obstacles. The treaty has been described as an awkward attempt to reconcile Germany's insistence on price stability with its partners' insistence on a voice in making EC monetary policy. Compromise was possible only because the EC countries attach great importance to their economic and political cohesion. It would be very much harder to agree on a monetary union spanning the EC, Japan, and the United States.

The third answer would tie national monetary policies to some sort of rule compatible with keeping exchange rates from changing, and a number of economists favor this solution. A few want to reinstate a full-fledged gold standard. Others want to use gold-standard rules without giving gold a role. Central banks would be expected to engage in nonsterilized intervention and thus subordinate their monetary policies to the maintenance of fixed exchange rates. Under one such plan, proposed by Ronald McKinnon of Stanford, central banks would choose the most appropriate growth rate for the global money stock, and each bank would then follow a monetary policy designed to achieve that growth rate. But each bank would also engage in nonsterilized intervention to fix its exchange rate. Therefore, its national money stock would grow faster than the global money stock when its currency was strong and more slowly than the global stock when its currency was weak. The system would be symmetrical, however, so that changes in the growth rates of the national money stocks would not affect the growth rate of the global money stock.

These rule-based plans are rather unrealistic. They are meant to impose more discipline on governments, but those very governments would have to accept them. Rules by themselves, moreover, may not be obeyed. Britain left the gold standard in 1931. The United States did fatal damage to the Bretton Woods system in 1971, when it tried to realign exchange rates for the dollar. Germany did damage to the fixed-rate version of the EMS in 1992, when it tried to realign exchange rates in Europe. Discipline cannot be imposed merely by telling governments to maintain fixed exchange rates—not without establishing an international institution strong enough to hold them to their obligations when it does not suit them to do that on their own, and we are very far from that sort of world.

The same point can be put more generally. It is wrong to compare the existing exchange-rate regime, laboring under imperfect policies, with an idealized version of some other regime, where governments are well informed and well behaved. This is done too often, especially by those who have not studied monetary history and do not know how various regimes have worked in practice. Such comparisons are bound to be misleading, by favoring reforms that cannot turn out well.

We noted earlier, moreover, that the choice in practice does not lie between freely floating rates and firmly fixed rates. The governments of the major industrial countries no longer favor freely floating rates, which led to the large movements in real rates seen in the 1980s. Yet they doubt their ability to defend pegged rates in a world of high capital mobility. Rumors of a realignment can touch off waves of speculation, causing huge amounts of money to flee one currency for another, and the rumors can become self-fulfilling prophesies when central banks must intervene and thus run down their reserves.

Many proposals have been made for managing exchange rates among the key currencies. Some of them are adaptations of the EMS. Others would use looser *target zones* to limit exchange-rate fluctuations and to trigger the policy changes required to maintain exchange-rate stability.

An EMS Approach to Exchange-Rate Management

The early EMS was a pegged-rate system, and it is seen as a success by many who believed initially that it was bound to fail. Its principal features were described in Chapter 19 and need not be repeated here. It should be recalled, however, that several realignments took place in the early years, which gave the EMS some flexibility but did not provoke speculative flows large enough to overwhelm the system itself. The success of the EMS has led some economists to ask whether a similar system might be used to stabilize exchange rates among the key currencies, including the dollar and the yen, without inviting governments to make mistakes of the sort that wrecked the earlier Bretton Woods system. Yet certain special features of the EMS should warn us against using it as a model for a global exchange-rate regime.

First, the EMS is a creature of the EC, which has fostered political cohesion among its members and a sense of collective responsibility for the survival of the system. No country had withdrawn before 1992, even temporarily, although France had been tempted to leave in the early 1980s, when France was trying to stimulate domestic demand more vigorously than other EMS countries.

Second, the EMS countries were able to agree speedily on realignments, and the realignments were fairly small, partly because it was possible to make them frequently. Small changes of this sort are not likely to provoke huge amounts of speculation. Prospective profits are necessarily small when the realignments are small and unpredictable. With small realignments, moreover, the actual exchange-rate changes are unpredictable, even when the realignments are quite predictable.

The new and old exchange-rate bands can overlap, and the actual exchange rate may not change at all.[16]

Third, some of the EMS countries used exchange controls. These limited capital flows and, more importantly, helped central banks to insulate domestic interest rates from the large changes in foreign interest rates that often accompany exchange-rate speculation. Look back at Figure 15-5 in Chapter 15 to see how large the gaps could be, and recall the point made by Padoa-Schioppa, that the abolition of capital controls might undermine the stability of the EMS in the absence of a common monetary policy. There is some tendency, however, to exaggerate the contribution of capital controls to the stability of the EMS. Two other features of the system have been quite important.

On the one hand, the EMS had unusual credit arrangements that prevented individual central banks from running out of reserves when they intervened to combat speculation. Each central bank could borrow unlimited amounts of its partners' currencies when it had to intervene. These elastic credit arrangements minimized the risk that rumors of a realignment would be self-fulfilling.

On the other hand, the Deutsche mark was the only world-class currency in the EMS and the strongest European currency, and these features limited speculative pressures. In the 1987 edition of this book, written before Britain entered the EMS and long before the 1992 crisis, I put this point hypothetically:

> Supppse that the foreign-exchange market comes to expect a revaluation of the Deutsche mark against the French franc. Frenchmen will sell francs for marks. But they are the only large holders of francs. Anyone else wanting to speculate against the franc must borrow francs to sell them. This limits the volume of speculation and tends to reverse it quickly (because Frenchmen will need their francs for domestic purposes, and others will want to pay back their debts). Now let us imagine that Britain joins the EMS, bringing in the pound, another world-class currency. Suppose that the foreign-exchange market comes to expect a revaluation of the mark against the pound. As there are many more footloose holders of sterling than francs, more money could move from London to Frankfurt than currently moves from Paris to Frankfurt. Furthermore, this would not be borrowed money, though that could move too, and it might not return to London quickly.

These examples do not fully explain why Britain was forced to leave the EMS in September 1992 and France was not. The franc was stronger fundamentally, and the Bundesbank supported the franc but expressed misgivings about the pound. Nevertheless, they shed light on the difference between the two outcomes and warn against basing an exchange-rate regime for the three most important world-class currencies,

---

[16]Advocates of using the EMS as a model for more general exchange-rate arrangements usually favor bands wider than those normally used in the EMS. They do so for the reason mentioned in the text, and because a wide band raises the size of the loss a speculator can experience when betting wrongly on a realignment. Someone who sells francs when the franc is at the edge of its band is apt to make a profit if the franc is devalued but can suffer a loss otherwise, because the actual exchange rate can move to the opposite edge of its band. But the size of the loss is limited by the width of the band. Therefore, a wide band reduces the expected profit from currency speculation.(That is why the EMS widened its own bands during the 1993 crisis.)

the dollar, mark, and yen, on an adaptation of the early EMS. It would be very hard, moreover, to negotiate open-ended credit arrangements among a group of countries that included the United States, which was criticized in the 1960s for exploiting the role of the dollar to finance its balance-of-payments deficits and was criticized again in the 1980s for a similar offense.

Arrangements for the management of the key currencies are thus likely to be looser than those of the EMS, even in its early form. But those arrangements should be more structured and durable than the Louvre Accord. They might therefore be modeled on one of the several target-zone proposals made in recent years.

A Target-Zone Approach to Exchange-Rate Management

The various target-zone proposals differ in the methods used to choose the *central rates*, which provide the reference points for the target zones, and the ways in which the central rates would be realigned. They also differ in the sizes of the zones surrounding the central rates, the hardness of the boundaries surrounding the zones, and the methods used to keep actual exchange rates from leaving the zones. Finally, they differ in the extent to which the plans themselves would be made public or be known only to the governments involved, as in the case of the Louvre Accord.

The best-known target-zone proposal was developed by John Williamson. It is reproduced in Figure 20-6. Under this proposal, the central rates would be defined by the equilibrium values of the countries' real effective exchange rates—those that would preserve internal and external balance over the long run. By implication, the central rates would be adjusted whenever econometric calculations showed that a country could not maintain internal and external balance at its existing central rate. The zones around the central rates would be quite wide, and the boundaries would be soft, so larger deviations could take place temporarily. Central banks would intervene whenever movements in nominal exchange rates threatened to drive real effective rates outside their target zones, and they would coordinate their interest-rate policies to back up their interventions. The plan itself would be made public, to stabilize the market's expectations about future exchange rates and thus discourage speculation.

Experience under the Louvre Accord suggests that Williamson is right about the need for publicity. Governments run two risks when they are vague or secretive. First, they may find that they disagree among themselves about their obligations. Second, market participants will try to guess what the governments have agreed to do and will base their conduct on *their* versions of the governments' obligations. They will then charge the governments with weakness or bad faith if they fail to live up to the market's expectations. Both of these things happened in October 1987, when the Louvre Accord broke down. Governments may lose more credibility by refusing to commit themselves than by falling short of well-publicized commitments.

Other features of Williamson's proposal may be less satisfactory. An attempt to set and realign exchange rates by computing long-run equilibrium rates may put excessive faith in econometric methods and fail to achieve Williamson's purpose—to keep politics out of the process. If governments dislike the central rates produced by the computations, they will find other econometricians to criticize them. Finally, Williamson's wide, soft bands may fail to stabilize exchange-rate expectations. His

---

The Blueprint

The participating countries [the Group of Seven] agree that they will conduct their macroeconomic policies with a view to pursuing the following two intermediate targets:

(1) A rate of growth of domestic demand in each country calculated according to a formula designed to promote the fastest growth of output consistent with a gradual reduction of inflation to an acceptable level and agreed adjustment of the current account of the balance of payments.

(2) A real effective exchange rate that will not deviate by more than [10] percent from an internationally agreed estimate of the "fundamental equilibrium exchange rate," the rate estimated to be consistent with simultaneous internal and external balance in the medium term.

To that end, the participants agree that they will modify their monetary and fiscal policies according to the following principles:

(A) The *average level* of world (real) short-term interest rates should be revised up (down) if aggregate growth of national income is threatening to exceed (fall short of) the sum of the target growth of nominal demand for the participating countries.

(B) *Differences* in short-term interest rates among countries should be revised when necessary to supplement intervention in the exchange markets to prevent the deviation of currencies from their target ranges.

(C) National *fiscal policies* should be revised with a view to achieving national target rates of growth of domestic demand.

The rules (A) to (C) should be constrained by the medium-term objective of maintaining the real interest rate in its historically normal range and of avoiding an increasing or excessive ratio of public debt to GNP.

FIGURE 20-6

The Williamson Target-Zone Proposal

Source: John Williamson and Marcus H. Miller, *Targets and Indicators: A Blueprint for the International Coordination of Economic Policy,* Policy Analysis in International Economics 22 (Washington, D.C.: Institute for International Economics, 1987).

plan has the obvious merit, however, of embedding rules for exchange-rate management in a framework for policy coordination.

The governments of the major industrial countries are not likely to undertake a major reform of exchange-rate arrangements in the near future. Other economic problems demand immediate attention. Yet efforts might be made to build a sturdier framework for policy coordination and exchange-rate management. Paul Volcker, former chairman of the Federal Reserve Board, has described the essential ingredients:[17]

> The kind of coordination I foresee would not require an elaborate institutional structure. Indeed, the strength of the G-5 or G-7, to my mind, rests on its informality and flexibility. I am not... convinced that elaborate schemes of statistical indicators are practical or that a special secretariat

---

[17]Paul A. Volcker and Toyoo Gyohten, *Changing Fortunes* (New York: Times Books, 1992), p. 300.

would be particularly useful. Nor would I wish to impair the independence and authority of central banks, undermining the usefulness of the most flexible tool of economic policy. Indeed, without some method of insulating central banks from partisan political pressures and focussing attention on price stability, efforts to stabilize exchange rates are likely to fail.

What seems to me possible within that framework is the development of some reasoned and broad judgments about what range of exchange rate fluctuation among the regions is reasonable and tolerable, and what is not. I am thinking of ranges significantly broader than the plus or minus 5 percent that was meant to trigger consultation in the Louvre agreement. At the same time,... governments should stand ready to support a broad and agreed range by more than just intervention in currency markets. They would have to be prepared to support their agreements in the short term with changes in monetary policy, and in the medium and longer term by a willingness to alter the basic orientation of their fiscal policies...

For the whole idea to have any meaning, governments would have to accept that strong pressures on exchange rates would be prime indicator of the need for policy action. The agreed ranges would also have to be publicly known. The official statement of a target zone would influence market expectations, helping to stabilize trading activity.... But that result will be achieved only if the target zone for any country or region is in fact taken seriously in the conduct of monetary policy and in developing general economic policies.

SUMMARY

Economic differences help to explain why countries choose different exchange-rate arrangements and why they should do so. Small open economies and those with sticky real wages tend to peg their exchange rates, because they have little to gain from exchange-rate flexibility. Larger economies and those with sticky nominal wages are likely to have more flexible exchange-rate arrangements, but few countries allow their exchange rates to float freely.

In recent years, moreover, several countries have used exchange-rate pegging to combat inflation by stabilizing the prices of traded goods, anchoring expectations, and conferring credibility on domestic policies. But this is a high-risk strategy. A government that ties down the exchange rate deprives itself of the policy instrument it will have to use if the strategy fails. Exchange-rate pegging can help to maintain price stability but may be a risky and costly way to achieve price stability.

Large industrial countries must choose their exchange-rate arrangements collectively, because of the nth country problem and because their economies and policies are interdependent. They have, indeed, to coordinate their policies to achieve their individual and common objectives. There are two ways to demonstrate this proposition. The policy-optimizing approach shows that policy coordination can be beneficial to each country individually by giving each government partial control over its partners' policy instruments. The public-goods approach shows that policy coordination can be beneficial by combatting the tendency for individual governments to underinvest in the production of international "public goods" such as exchange-rate stability and the preservation of an open trading system. There are serious obstacles to coordination, however, including disagreements about the "true model" of the world economy and, in the public-goods framework, disagreements about the ranking of policy objectives.

A full-fledged monetary union represents the most ambitious form of policy coordination, and the complexities of the Maastricht Treaty illustrate the difficulties. As Germany attached great importance of price stability, it insisted on strict convergence criteria as conditions for eligibility. Because most countries will need time to meet those criteria, there will be a long transition period, which may be perilous. The treaty also reflects the concerns of the national central banks, which insisted on participating in the operations of the European Central Bank, and the concerns of the national finance ministries, which insisted on participating in the formulation of exchange-rate policy.

The EC countries may find it impossible to implement the Maastricht Treaty, and it would be far harder to form a monetary union among the major industrial countries, including Japan and the United States. Nevertheless, there may be ways of improving the present exchange-rate regime. Some economists favor a return to pegged but adjustable exchange rates—a system resembling the early version of the EMS. Others believe that any such system would be very vulnerable to speculative pressures and to policy disagreements among the governments themselves. They advocate looser target-zone arrangements designed to promote exchange-rate stability and policy coordination. But progress in these matters is likely to be slow, as governments have other, more urgent concerns.

RECOMMENDED READINGS

This chapter draws heavily on three of my books: *Exchange Rates and Policy Coordination* (Manchester: Manchester University Press, 1989), which develops the distinction between policy-optimizing and regime-preserving coordination and presents the model used in the text to show why coordination is mutually beneficial; *EMU After Maastricht* (Washington, D.C.: Group of Thirty, 1992), which examines the Maastricht Treaty in detail; and *Managing Exchange Rates* (London: Royal Institute of International Affairs, 1988), which compares various plans for limiting exchange-rate fluctuations.

Two other works deal briefly with the broad themes in this chapter: Paul R. Krugman, *Exchange Rate Instability* (Cambridge, Mass.: MIT Press, 1988), and Morris Goldstein et al., *Policy Issues in the Evolving International Monetary System* (Washington, D.C.: International Monetary Fund, 1992).

On the contribution of exchange-rate pegging to economic stabilization, see Miguel A. Kiguel and Nissan Liviatan, "Do Heterodox Stabilization Policies Work?," *World Bank Research Observer*, 7, 1992. On the trade-reducing effects of exchange-rate volatility, see Peter B. Kenen and Dani Rodrik, "Measuring and Analyzing the Effects of Short-Term Volatility in Real Exchange Rates," *Review of Economics and Statistics*, 68 (May 1986), and Paul De Grauwe, "Exchange Rate Variability and the Slowdown in Growth of International Trade," *International Monetary Fund Staff Papers*, 35 (March 1988).

For simple but elegant models of speculation, crises, and exchange-rate behavior under pegged-rate regimes, see Paul R. Krugman, *Currencies and Crises* (Cambridge, Mass.:

MIT Press, 1992), chs. 4–5. For a survey of recent research on exchange-rate behavior under pegged rates, see Lars E. O. Svennson, "An Interpretation of Recent Research on Exchange Rate Target Zones," *Journal of Economic Perspectives*, 6 (Fall 1992).

The vast literature on policy coordination is surveyed critically by Stanley Fischer, "International Macroeconomic Policy Coordination," in M. Feldstein, ed., *International Economic Cooperation* (Chicago: University of Chicago Press, 1988); for the views and proposals of a participant, see Wendy Dobson, *Economic Policy Coordination: Requiem or Prologue?*, Policy Analysis in International Economics 30 (Washington, D.C.: Institute for International Economics, 1991).

The origins and defects of the Maastricht Treaty are examined by Daniel Gros and Niels Thygesen, *European Monetary Integration* (New York: St. Martins Press, 1992), chs. 7–14. For a more critical assessment, see Barry Eichengreen, *Should the Maastricht Treaty Be Saved?* Princeton Studies in International Finance 74 (Princeton, N.J.: International Finance Section, Princeton University, 1992).

On the monetary and exchange-rate problems of Central and Eastern Europe, not discussed in the text, see John Williamson, ed., *Convertibility in Eastern Europe* (Washington, D.C.: Institute for International Economics, 1991, Parts 3–4; Stanley Fischer, "Stabilization and Economic Reform in Russia," *Brookings Papers on Economic Activity*, 1992 (2); Michael Bruno, "Stabilization and Reform in Eastern Europe," *International Monetary Fund Staff Papers*, 39 (December 1992); and John Williamson, *Trade and Payments After Soviet Disintegration*, Policy Analysis in International Economics 37 (Washington, D.C.: Institute for International Economics, 1992).

The proposals by Cooper, McKinnon, and Williamson for reforming the monetary system will be found in Richard N. Cooper, "A Monetary System for the Future," *Foreign Affairs*, 63 (Fall 1984); Ronald I. McKinnon, *An International Standard for Monetary Stabilization*, Policy Analysis in International Economics 8 (Washington, D.C.: Institute for International Economics, 1984); and John Williamson "Target Zones and the Management of the Dollar," *Brookings Papers on Economic Activity*, 1986 (1). For critical assessments, see Jacob A. Frenkel and Morris Goldstein, "A Guide to Target Zones," *International Monetary Fund Staff Papers*, 33 (December 1986), and Richard N. Cooper, "What Future for the International Monetary System?," in J. A. Frenkel and M. Goldstein, eds., *International Financial Policy: Essays in Honor of Jacques J. Polak* (Washington, D.C.: International Monetary Fund, 1991).

QUESTIONS AND PROBLEMS

(1) You are asked to advise two countries concerning their exchange-rate arrangements. These are their main characteristics:

Item	Markland	Francland
Gross domestic product ($ billions)	100	30
Exports ($ billions)	20	20
Budget deficit ($ billions)	10	2
Inflation rate (percent)	40	15
Length (in months) of typical wage contract	36	12

Would you advise them to choose different exchange-rate arrangements? Would you want more information about them? Explain.

(2) When locating the shift in the U.S. bliss point in Figure 20-2, we asked what the U.S. central bank would tell the Japanese central bank if it had full control over the Japanese central bank. How does the move from the noncooperative equilibrium, P^N, to the cooperative equilibrium, P^C, resemble a situation in which each central bank has partial control over the other's operations?

(3) Suppose that a disturbance reduces U.S. and Japanese outputs by the same amounts but does not affect price levels. Use Figure 20-1 to determine how the governments' reaction curves will shift. Then draw the curves and show the new noncooperative equilibrium.

(4) The text asked you to examine Article 109 of the Maastricht Treaty, reproduced as Figure 20-3, to determine who will decide whether the EC should make an *informal* agreement with the United States and Japan to limit exchange-rate fluctuations. Do it.

(5) Draft a memorandum for the French finance minister explaining why France should favor an immediate move to monetary union with Germany and other strong-currency countries, outside the framework of the Maastricht Treaty. Anticipate and answer possible objections.

(6) McKinnon's proposal for a "gold standard without gold" makes no mention of coordinating or restricting national fiscal policies. Is that a serious shortcoming?

(7) Canada, Mexico, and the United States are forming a free trade area. Should they also form a monetary union?

(8) Should target zones use "hard" boundaries, requiring enough official intervention to keep exchange rates from crossing them, or should they use "soft" boundaries, permitting intervention and interest-rate adjustments but not requiring them?

(9) Contrast the Williamson target-zone proposal with Paul Volcker's suggestions for improving the monetary system.

APPENDIX A

Mathematical Notes on Trade Theory and Policy

Section 1. Maximizing Output and Clearing Markets

Let the economy produce x_1 cameras at price p_1 and x_2 grain at price p_2. The value of national output, y, is

$$y = p_1 x_1 + p_2 x_2. \tag{1.1}$$

Keeping prices constant, let firms move along the transformation curve, changing camera output to x_1' and grain output to x_2'. The value of output will change to

$$y' = p_1 x_1' + p_2 x_2'.$$

Subtracting y from y',

$$y' - y = p_1(x_1' - x_1) + p_2(x_2' - x_2).$$

Let d denote a change in any variable, so $dy = (y' - y)$, and so on. Therefore,

$$dy = p_1 dx_1 + p_2 dx_2. \tag{1.2}$$

Competitive firms that maximize profits will increase camera output ($dx_1 > 0$) and decrease grain output ($dx_2 < 0$) whenever this raises the value of national output ($dy > 0$). But they cannot do so indefinitely, because the transformation curve is *convex*. Each increase in camera output causes a larger decrease in grain output, reducing the net addition to the value of output. Eventually, the changes in camera and grain outputs will neutralize each other so that $dy = 0$, and

$$p_1 dx_1 = -p_2 dx_2,$$

or

$$\frac{p_1}{p_2} = -\frac{dx_2}{dx_1}.$$ (1.3)

The left side of eq. (1.3) is the relative price of a camera. It measures the amount of grain that must be paid to buy a camera. The right side is the slope of the transformation curve at the point that maximizes the value of national output; it measures the amount of grain that must be sacrificed to produce an additional camera. This result is used to locate the output point on the transformation curve.

In simple economic models, national output must equal national income. In a closed economy, moreover, national income must equal total spending (consumption) on cameras and grain. Therefore,

$$y = p_1 c_1 + p_2 c_2,$$ (1.4)

where c_1 and c_2 are the quantities of grain and camera demanded by consumers. Combining eqs. (1.1) and (1.3),

$$p_1 c_1 + p_2 c_2 = p_1 x_1 + p_2 x_2.$$

Rearranging terms,

$$p_1(c_1 - x_1) = p_2(x_2 - c_2).$$ (1.5)

If there is an *excess demand* for cameras ($c_1 > x_1$), there must be an *excess supply* of grain ($x_2 > c_2$). If the camera market clears ($x_1 = c_1$), the grain market must also clear ($x_2 = c_2$). In an open economy, an excess demand for cameras shows up as a demand for camera imports, and the corresponding excess supply of grain shows up as a supply of grain exports. Therefore, a country's demand for imports will equal its supply of exports at each set of prices. This result is used to construct *trade triangles* and *offer curves*.

When world markets clear, the global supply of a product must equal the global demand for it. Therefore,

$$x_1 + x_1^* = c_1 + c_1^*,$$

where x_1^* and c_1^* are foreign production and consumption. Rearranging terms,

$$x_1^* - c_1^* = c_1 - x_1.$$ (1.6)

The foreign supply of camera exports must equal the domestic demand for camera imports. This result is used to show why two countries' trade triangles must be identical in equilibrium.

Section 2. Labor Requirements, Outputs, and Prices in the Ricardian Model

There are $\bar{L}$ workers in Britain and all are employed in cloth or wine production:

$$\bar{L} = L_1 + L_2, \tag{2.1}$$

where L_1 is employment in cloth production and L_2 is employment in wine production. A fixed number of workers, a_1, is required to produce a yard of cloth and another fixed number, a_2, to produce a gallon of wine. Therefore,

$$L_1 = a_1 x_1, \quad \text{and} \quad L_2 = a_2 x_2,$$

where x_1 is cloth output and x_2 is wine output.

Substituting into the labor equation,

$$\bar{L} = a_1 x_1 + a_2 x_2.$$

Solving for x_2,

$$x_2 = \frac{\bar{L}}{a_2} - \left(\frac{a_1}{a_2}\right) x_1. \tag{2.2}$$

That is the equation for the British transformation curve. Its vertical intercept is $\bar{L}/a_2$, measuring wine output when there is no cloth output. Its slope, the marginal rate of transformation, is a_1/a_2, the ratio of labor requirements, and it is constant.

When labor is the only factor of production, wages are the only costs. When labor requirements are constant, moreover, average and marginal costs are equal. As prices equal marginal costs under competitive conditions,

$$p_1 = w a_1, \quad \text{and} \quad p_2 = w a_2, \tag{2.3}$$

where p_1 is the price of cloth, p_2 is the price of wine, and w is the wage rate. Therefore,

$$\frac{p_1}{p_2} = \frac{w a_1}{w a_2} = \frac{a_1}{a_2}. \tag{2.4}$$

The relative price of cloth, p_1/p_2, equals the ratio of labor requirements and thus equals the slope of the transformation curve.

When Britain specializes completely in cloth, the world price of cloth is given by

$$p_1 = w a_1. \tag{2.5}$$

When Portugal specializes completely in wine the world price of wine is given by

$$p_2 = w^* a_2^*, \tag{2.6}$$

where w^* is the Portuguese wage rate, expressed in the same currency as the British wage rate, and a_2^* is the labor requirement in Portuguese wine production.

Under complete specialization, then, the relative price of cloth is

$$\frac{p_1}{p_2} = \left(\frac{w}{w^*}\right)\left(\frac{a_1}{a_2^*}\right). \tag{2.7}$$

When this price must be changed to reach equilibrium in world markets, the change must be brought about by altering the wage-rate ratio w/w^*, because a_1 and a_2^* are constants.

Eq. (2.5) can be used to obtain the real wage in Britain measured in cloth:

$$\frac{w}{p_1} = \frac{1}{a_1}.$$

The higher the labor requirement in cloth production, the lower the real wage measured in cloth.

The real wage in Britain measured in wine can then be defined by

$$\frac{w}{p_2} = \left(\frac{w}{p_1}\right)\left(\frac{p_1}{p_2}\right) = \left(\frac{1}{a_1}\right)\left(\frac{p_1}{p_2}\right).$$

The higher the relative price of cloth, the higher the real wage measured in wine, given the labor requirement in cloth production. By implication, the real wage measured in the import good rises as Britain's terms of trade improve.

Section 3. Factors Supplies, Outputs, and Prices in the Factor-Endowments Model

In the x_1 industry, one unit of output requires a_1 labor and b_1 capital, so the amounts employed are

$$L_1 = a_1 x_1, \quad \text{and} \quad K_1 = b_1 x_1. \tag{3.1}$$

In the x_2 industry, one unit of output requires a_2 labor and b_2 capital, so the amounts employed are

$$L_2 = a_2 x_2, \quad \text{and} \quad K_2 = b_2 x_2. \tag{3.2}$$

When a country has fixed supplies of labor and capital, $\bar{L}$ and $\bar{K}$, and they are fully employed,

$$\bar{L} = L_1 + L_2 = a_1 x_1 + a_2 x_2,$$

$$\bar{K} = K_1 + K_2 = b_1 x_1 + b_2 x_2. \tag{3.3}$$

Solving eqs. (3.3) for x_2 in terms of x_1, we obtain the labor and capital constraints:

$$x_2 = \frac{\bar{L}}{a_2} - \left(\frac{a_1}{a_2}\right)x_1, \quad \text{and} \quad x_2 = \frac{\bar{K}}{b_2} - \left(\frac{b_1}{b_2}\right)x_1.$$

When $(a_1/a_2) > (b_1/b_2)$, the labor constraint is steeper (as in Figure 4-1). But this condition can be written as $(b_2/a_2) > (b_1/a_1)$. Furthermore, (b_2/a_2) is the ratio of capital to labor required to produce a unit of x_2 and is known as the capital-labor ratio, k_2, in the x_2 industry. Similarly, (b_1/a_1) is the capital-labor ratio, k_1, in the x_1 industry. When the labor constraint is steeper, then, it is because $k_2 > k_1$ (the x_2 industry is more capital intensive than the x_1 industry).

Solving eqs. (3.3) simultaneously for x_1 and x_2, the full-employment outputs,

$$x_1 = \frac{b_2\bar{L} - a_2\bar{K}}{a_1b_2 - a_2b_1}, \quad \text{and} \quad x_2 = \frac{a_1\bar{K} - b_1\bar{L}}{a_1b_2 - a_2b_1}. \tag{3.4}$$

But $(a_1b_2) > (a_2b_1)$ when $(b_2/a_2) > (b_1/a_1)$, so the denominator is positive. Call it D hereafter. Therefore, an increase in $\bar{K}$ raises x_2 output and reduces x_1 output. This proves the Rybczynski theorem.

In long-run competitive equilibrium, prices equal total unit costs, which are equal in turn to factor payments per unit of output. Therefore,

$$p_1 = wa_1 + rb_1, \quad \text{and} \quad p_2 = wa_2 + rb_2, \tag{3.5}$$

where p_1 and p_2 are the prices of x_1 and x_2, w is the wage rate, and r is the return to capital. Solving eqs. (3.5) simultaneously,

$$w = \frac{b_2p_1 - b_1p_2}{D}, \quad \text{and} \quad r = \frac{a_1p_2 - a_2p_1}{D},$$

where D is positive, as before. Furthermore, the numerators are positive at the full-employment point. Rewriting these equations,

$$w = \frac{b_2p_2}{D}\left(\frac{p_1}{p_2} - \frac{b_1}{b_2}\right), \tag{3.6}$$

$$r = \frac{a_2p_2}{D}\left(\frac{a_1}{a_2} - \frac{p_1}{p_2}\right). \tag{3.7}$$

We know that $(p_1/p_2) > (b_1/b_2)$; otherwise, the economy would be on its capital constraint. Therefore, w is positive. We also know that $(p_1/p_2) < (a_1/a_2)$; otherwise, the economy would be on its labor constraint. Therefore, r is positive.

To derive the general relationship between relative factor prices and relative commodity prices, divide eq. (3.6) by eq. (3.7):

$$\frac{w}{r} = \frac{b_2}{a_2}\left[\frac{(p_1/p_2) - (b_1/b_2)}{(a_1/a_2) - (p_1/p_2)}\right].$$

Therefore, an increase in (p_1/p_2) raises (w/r); it increases the numerator and decreases the denominator.

Eqs (3.6) and (3.7) can be used to show how a change in relative prices affects the real wage and real return to capital. Beginning with the real wage and the real return measured in x_2, divide both sides of both equations by p_2:

$$\frac{w}{p_2} = \frac{b_2}{D}\left(\frac{p_1}{p_2} - \frac{b_1}{b_2}\right), \quad \text{and} \quad \frac{r}{p_2} = \frac{a_2}{D}\left(\frac{a_1}{a_2} - \frac{p_1}{p_2}\right).$$

Therefore, an increase in (p_1/p_2), the relative price of the labor-intensive good, raises the real wage and reduces the real return to capital when they are measured in x_2. Turning to the real wage and real return measured in x_1, divide both sides of both equations by p_1:

$$\frac{w}{p_1} = \left(\frac{b_2}{D}\right)\left(\frac{p_2}{p_1}\right)\left(\frac{p_1}{p_2} - \frac{b_1}{b_2}\right)$$

$$= \frac{b_2}{D}\left[1 - \left(\frac{b_1}{b_2}\right)\left(\frac{p_2}{p_1}\right)\right],$$

$$\frac{r}{p_1} = \left(\frac{a_2}{D}\right)\left(\frac{p_2}{p_1}\right)\left(\frac{a_1}{a_2} - \frac{p_1}{p_2}\right)$$

$$= \frac{a_2}{D}\left[\left(\frac{a_1}{a_2}\right)\left(\frac{p_2}{p_1}\right) - 1\right].$$

But (p_2/p_1) falls when (p_1/p_2) rises, raising the numerator of the first equation and reducing the numerator of the second. Therefore, an increase in the relative price of the labor-intensive good also raises the real wage and reduces the real return to capital when they are measured in x_1.

Notice, finally, the implications for the factor-price-equalization theorem. When (p_1/p_2) is the same in both countries, real wage rates and real returns to capital are the same in both countries.

Section 4. Factor Substitution, Marginal Products, and Isoquants

The production function of a firm in industry i is given by

$$x_i = f^i(L_i, K_i),$$

which says that output, x_i, depends on the amounts of labor, L_i, and capital, K_i, used by the firm. Hence, the change in x_i is

$$dx_i = f_L^i dL_i + f_K^i dK_i, \tag{4.1}$$

where f_L^i is the marginal product of labor and f_K^i is the marginal product of capital. Note that an increase in L_i reduces f_L^i and raises f_K^i, while an increase in K_i has the opposite effects. The firm's profits, q_i, are the difference between its revenue and cost,

$$q_i = p_i x_i - (wL_i + rK_i),$$

and the change in q_i is

$$dq_i = p_i dx_i - (wdL_i + rdK_i). \tag{4.2}$$

Changes in p_i, w, and r will also change q_i, but these effects are omitted, because a competitive firm does not control p_i, w, or r. Using eq. (4.1) to replace dx_i,

$$dq_i = p_i(f_L^i dL_i + f_K^i dK_i) - (wdL_i + rdK_i)$$

$$= (p_i f_L^i - w)dL_i + (p_i f_K^i - r)dK_i.$$

When $p_i f_L^i > w$, an increase in L_i raises profit (it raises revenue by more than cost). But f_L^i will fall and f_K^i will rise, affecting the profitability of additional changes in L_i and K_i. To maximize profit, the firm must choose levels of L_i and K_i at which $p_i f_L^i - w = 0$ and $p_i f_K^i - r = 0$, as these are the levels at which $dq_i = 0$ (those at which changes in L_i and K_i cease to be profitable). These conditions give

$$f_L^i = \frac{w}{p_i}, \quad \text{and} \quad f_K^i = \frac{r}{p_i}. \tag{4.3}$$

The marginal product of labor must equal the real wage expressed in x_i, and the marginal product of capital must equal the real return to capital.

When there is a fixed factor in an industry, the change in output is given by the change in the use of the variable factor (labor) and the marginal product of that factor:

$$dx_i = f_L^i dL_i.$$

When labor is transferred between industries, then

$$\frac{dx_2}{dx_1} = \frac{f_L^2 dL_2}{f_L^1 dL_1} = -\frac{f_L^2}{f_L^1}, \tag{4.4}$$

because $dL_2 = -dL_1$ when the total labor supply is fixed. As (dx_2/dx_1) is the slope of the transformation curve (the rate at which x_2 output falls as x_1 output rises), that slope is equal absolutely to the ratio of marginal products. But f_L^1 falls as labor is transferred to the x_1 industry, and f_L^2 rises as labor is transferred from the x_2 industry. Therefore, the slope of the transformation curve increases as x_1 output rises.

Combining eq. (4.4) with eq. (4.3),

$$\frac{dx_2}{dx_1} = -\frac{w/p_2}{w/p_1} = -\frac{p_1}{p_2}.$$

The slope of the transformation curve is equal absolutely to the relative price of x_1.

As output is constant along any isoquant, the change in output is zero. From eq. (4.1), then,

$$dx_i = f_L^i \, dL_i + f_K^i dK_i = 0.$$

Therefore,

$$f_K^i dK_i = -f_L^i \, dL_i,$$

or

$$\frac{dK_i}{dL_i} = -\frac{f_L^i}{f_K^i}. \tag{4.5}$$

The slope of the isoquant is equal (absolutely) to the ratio of marginal products. When a firm maximizes profits, moreover, it equates the marginal product of labor to the real wage and the marginal product of capital to the real return. From eqs. (4.3) and (4.5), then,

$$\frac{dK_i}{dL_i} = -\frac{w/p_i}{r/p_i} = -\frac{w}{r}.$$

The firm chooses the point on its isoquant where the slope is equal (absolutely) to the relative price of labor.

The notation of this section can be used for one more purpose. The value of national product can be written as the sum of payments to labor and capital:

$$y = wL + rK = r\left(\frac{w}{r} + \frac{K}{L}\right)L \, .$$

Dividing by N, the number of persons (consumers), to obtain income per capita,

$$y_c = \frac{y}{N} = r\left(\frac{w}{r} + \frac{K}{L}\right)\left(\frac{L}{N}\right).$$

Dividing by p_i, the price of the ith commodity, to obtain real income per capita,

$$\frac{y_c}{p_i} = \frac{r}{p_i}\left(\frac{w}{r} + \frac{K}{L}\right)\left(\frac{L}{N}\right). \tag{4.6}$$

But (r/p_i) is the real return to capital measured in the ith commodity and eq. (4.3) says it must equal the marginal product of capital in the ith industry. It cannot change without a change in the factor intensity of that industry resulting from a change in relative prices. Furthermore, (w/r) cannot change without a change in commodity prices. Finally, the ratio of workers to persons, (L/N), is a measure of labor-force participation, and we can assume that it is constant in the long run. When relative prices are constant, then, real income per capita depends only on (K/L), capital per worker in the whole economy. An increase in the supply of labor reduces (K/L) and thus reduces real income per capita. Increases in labor and capital at the same rates keep (K/L) constant, and real income per capita does not change.

Eq. (4.6) can be used to refute a famous fallacy. Critics of the Heckscher–Ohlin model say that the factor-price-equalization theorem must be false, because incomes per capita are different across countries. But factor-price equalization does not imply the equalization of incomes per capita. The (w/r) and (r/p_i) are equalized across countries, but not (L/N) or (K/L). In fact, differences in (K/L) are the basis for trade in the Heckscher–Ohlin model.

Section 5. Trade under Oligopoly

The American and Japanese demand curves for robots are

$$p_1 = a_1 - b_1(x_1 + x_1^*), \quad \text{and} \quad p_2 = a_2 - b_2(x_2 + x_2^*), \tag{5.1}$$

where p_1 and p_2 are the prices of robots in the American and Japanese markets, respectively, expressed in a common currency, x_1 and x_2 are the quantities sold by the American firm (Acme), and x_1^* and x_2^* are the quantities sold by the Japanese firm (Edo). Therefore, Acme's total revenues from the two markets are

$$R_1 = p_1 x_1 = [a_1 - b_1(x_1 + x_1^*)]x_1, \quad \text{and} \quad R_2 = p_2 x_2 = [a_2 - b_2(x_2 + x_2^*)]x_2,$$

and Acme's marginal revenues are

$$MR_1 = a_1 - b_1(2x_1 + x_1^*), \quad \text{and} \quad MR_2 = a_2 - b_2(2x_2 + x_2^*).$$

Similarly, Edo's marginal revenues are

$$MR_1^* = a_1 - b_1(x_1 + 2x_1^*), \quad \text{and} \quad MR_2^* = a_2 - b_2(x_2 + 2x_2^*).$$

The firms' marginal costs are constant and independent of the market in which output is sold (there are no transport costs). Therefore,

$$MC = c, \quad \text{and} \quad MC^* = c^*,$$

for Acme and Edo, respectively. Finally, the two firms' profits are

$$N = R_1 + R_2 - c(x_1 + x_2) - k, \quad \text{and} \quad N^* = R_1^* + R_2^* - c^*(x_1^* + x_2^*) - k^*, \tag{5.2}$$

where k and k^* are their fixed costs.

Before trade is opened, $x_1^* = x_2 = 0$. Setting each firm's marginal cost equal to its marginal revenue in its home market and solving for its sales,

$$\hat{x}_1 = (1/2b_1)(a_1 - c), \quad \text{and} \quad \hat{x}_2^* = (1/2b_2)(a_2 - c^*).$$

Substituting into eqs. (5.1),

$$\hat{p}_1 = (1/2)(a_1 + c), \quad \text{and} \quad \hat{p}_2 = (1/2)(a_2 + c^*),$$

When $a_1 = a_2$, $b_1 = b_2$, and $c = c^*$, as in the text, $\hat{x}_1 = \hat{x}_2^*$ and $\hat{p}_1 = \hat{p}_2$. Substituting into eqs. (5.2),

$$\hat{N}_1 = (1/4b_1)(a_1 - c)^2 - k, \quad \text{and} \quad \hat{N}_2 = (1/4b_2)(a_2 - c^*)^2 - k^*.$$

When trade is opened, each firm invades the other's market. We focus on outcomes in the American market. (Those in the Japanese market will be identical when demand and cost conditions are identical.) Setting each firm's marginal cost equal to its marginal revenue in the American market and solving for its sales,

$$x_1 = (1/2b_1)(a_1 - c) - (1/2)x_1^*, \quad \text{and} \quad x_1^* = (1/2b_1)(a_1 - c^*) - (1/2)x_1,$$

which are the firms' reaction curves in the American market. Solving them simultaneously for actual sales,

$$x_1 = (1/3b_1)(a_1 - 2c + c^*), \quad \text{and} \quad x_1^* = (1/3b_1)(a_1 - 2c^* + c).$$

So $x_1 - x_1^* = (1/b_1)(c^* - c)$. Acme's sales will be larger when Edo's costs are higher. Replacing x_1 and x_1^* in eq. (5.1),

$$p_1 = (1/3)(a_1 + c + c^*).$$

Therefore,

$$p_1 - \hat{p}_1 = -(1/6)(a_1 - 2c^* + c).$$

But $(a_1 - 2c^* + c) > 0$ whenever $x_1^* > 0$ (whenever Edo exports to the American market). Hence, trade reduces the price of robots.

These results can be combined with those for Edo's market to calculate the two firm's profits. With identical demand and cost conditions, $x_1 = x_1^* = x_2 = x_2^* = (1/3b)(a - c)$. Each firm has half of each national market. Furthermore, $p_1 = p_2 = (1/3)(a + 2c)$. Substituting into eqs. (5.2),

$$N_1 = N_2 = (2/9b)(a - c)^2 - k.$$

Therefore,

$$N_1 - \hat{N}_1 = N_2 - \hat{N}_2 = -(1/9b)(a - c)^2 < 0.$$

Trade reduces both firms' profits.

Suppose that Acme and Edo do not sell robots in America or Japan but sell them in Brazil, where the demand curve is

$$p = a - b(x + x^*). \tag{5.3}$$

The two firms' total and marginal revenues are obtained as before, and their (constant) marginal costs are set equal to their marginal revenues to obtain their sales:

$$x = (1/3b)(a - 2c + c^*), \quad \text{and} \quad x^* = (1/3b)(a - 2c^* + c).$$

Therefore,

$$p = (1/3)(a + c + c^*).$$

The firms' profits are

$$N = (1/9b)(a - 2c + c^*)^2 - k, \quad \text{and} \quad N^* = (1/9b)(a - 2c^* + c)^2 - k^*. \quad (5.4)$$

Suppose that their marginal costs are equal, apart from the subsidies, s and s^*, given by their governments. Then

$$x = (1/3b)(a - c + 2s - s^*), \quad \text{and} \quad x^* = (1/3b)(a - c + 2s^* - s). \quad (5.5)$$

Therefore,

$$p = (1/3)(a + 2c - s - s^*),$$

and

$$N = (1/9b)(a - c + 2s - s^*)^2 - k, \quad \text{and} \quad N^* = (1/9b)(a - c + 2s^* - s)^2 - k^*. \quad (5.6)$$

Each country's subsidy raises its own firm's sales and profits, but the other country's subsidy reduces them. Both subsidies reduce the price of robots in Brazil. But each country's subsidy is meant to raise its national income. Hence, it must raise the profits of its country's firm by more than the amount of the subsidy. This gain is measured by

$$U = N - \tilde{N} - sx, \quad \text{and} \quad U^* = N^* - \tilde{N}^* - s^*x^*, \quad (5.7)$$

where $\tilde{N}$ and $\tilde{N}^*$ are the firms' profits when $s = s^* = 0$. Using eqs. (5.5) and (5.6) to rewrite these definitions,

$$U = (1/9b)[(a - c)(s - 2s^*) - (2s - s^*)(s + s^*)], \quad (5.8)$$

$$U^* = (1/9b)[(a - c)(s^* - 2s) - (2s^* - s)(s + s^*)]. \quad (5.9)$$

The American government chooses the value of s that maximizes U, given the Japanese subsidy s^*, and the Japanese government behaves symmetrically. To replicate their behavior, we differentiate eq. (5.8) with respect to s and eq. (5.9) with respect to s^*, set the derivatives equal to zero, and solve for the subsidies:

$$s = (1/4)(a - c - s^*), \quad \text{and} \quad s^* = (1/4)(a - c - s). \quad (5.10)$$

These are the government's policy reaction curves.

Suppose that Acme gets a subsidy and Edo does not. Then $s^* = 0$ and $s = (1/4)(a - c)$, so

$$U = (1/9b)(1/8)(a - c)^2 > 0, \quad \text{and} \quad U^* = -(1/9b)(7/16)(a - c)^2 < 0.$$

The subsidy to Acme raises American income and reduces Japanese income (by more than it raises American). A subsidy to Edo has symmetrical effects.

Suppose both countries subsidize their firms. Solving eqs. (5.10) simultaneously,

$$s = s^* = (1/5)(a - c).$$

The American subsidy is slightly smaller than when there was no Japanese subsidy. Furthermore,

$$U = U^* = -(1/9b)(3/25)(a - c)^2 < 0.$$

The subsidies reduce both countries' national incomes. (They serve merely to reduce the price of robots in Brazil and raise both countries' exports to the benefit of Brazil and the detriment of America and Japan.)

APPENDIX B

Mathematical Notes on Monetary Theory and Policy

Section 1. Economic Interdependence and Optimal Policies

Using eq. (11) in Chapter 13, write the change in U.S. income as

$$dY_1 = \left(\frac{1}{s_1 + m_1}\right) m_2 dY_2 + \left(\frac{1}{s_1 + m_1}\right)(dA_1^a + dA_1^q + dN_1^a), \qquad (1.1)$$

where s_1 and m_1 are the marginal propensities to save and import for the United States, m_2 is the marginal propensity to import for Japan, dY_2 is the change in Japanese income, dA_1^a and dA_1^q are autonomous and policy-induced changes in U.S. expenditure, and dN_1^a is the autonomous change in U.S. net exports. This last term, however, can be written as

$$dN_1^a = dX_1^a - dM_1^a = dX_1^a - dX_2^a,$$

where dX_1^a is an autonomous increase in U.S. exports reflecting a switch in Japanese demand from Japanese to U.S. goods, and dX_2^a is an autonomous increase in Japanese exports reflecting a switch in U.S. demand from U.S. to Japanese goods. Therefore, $dN_2^a = -dN_1^a$, and this result can be used when writing the change in Japanese income,

$$dY_2 = \left(\frac{1}{s_2 + m_2}\right) m_1 dY_1 + \left(\frac{1}{s_2 + m_2}\right)(dA_2^a + dA_2^q - dN_1^a), \qquad (1.2)$$

where s_2 is the marginal propensity to save for Japan, and dA_2^a and dA_2^q are autonomous and policy-induced changes in Japanese expenditure.

Eqs. (1.1) and (1.2) can be solved simultaneously,

$$dY_1 = \frac{1}{H}[(s_2 + m_2)(dA_1^a + dA_1^q) + m_2(dA_2^a + dA_2^q) + s_2 dN_1^a], \qquad (1.3)$$

$$dY_2 = \frac{1}{H}[(s_1 + m_1)(dA_2^a + dA_2^g) + m_1(dA_1^a + dA_1^g) - s_1 dN_1^a), \qquad (1.4)$$

where $H = s_1 m_2 + s_2 m_1 + s_1 s_2$. An increase in U.S. expenditure ($dA_1^a > 0$ or $dA_1^g > 0$) raises both countries' incomes; so does an increase in Japanese expenditure. A switch in demand ($dN_1^a \gtrless 0$) raises income in one country and lowers it in the other.

Using eq. (13a) in Chapter 13, write the change in the U.S. current-account balance:

$$dN_1 = (dX_1^a + m_2 dY_2) - (dX_2^a + m_1 dY_1) = dN_1^a + m_2 dY_2 - m_1 dY_1.$$

Inserting the solutions for dY_1 and dY_2 given by eqs. (1.3) and (1.4),

$$dN_1 = \frac{1}{H}[s_1 m_2(dA_2^a + dA_2^g) - s_2 m_1(dA_1^a + dA_1^g) + s_1 s_2 dN_1^a]. \qquad (1.5)$$

An increase in Japanese expenditure improves the U.S. current-account balance; it raises incomes in both countries but raises Japanese imports by more than U.S. imports. An increase in U.S. expenditure has the opposite effect. A switch in demand to U.S. goods improves the U.S. current-account balance, even though it raises U.S. income and reduces Japanese income.

Let there be an autonomous increase in U.S. expenditure ($dA_1^a > 0$). The effects on U.S. and Japanese incomes are given by eqs. (1.3) and (1.4), and the effect on the current-account balance by eq. (1.5). The optimal response from a global standpoint is a policy-induced reduction in U.S. expenditure ($dA_1^g = -dA_1^a$). It can restore internal balance in both countries and external balance, too ($dY_1 = dY_2 = dN_1 = 0$).

If the United States fails to adopt that policy, Japan has three options:

(1) An expenditure-changing policy for internal balance defined by setting $dY_2 = 0$ and solving eq. (1.4) for the requisite change in Japanese expenditure:

$$dA_2^g = -[m_1/(s_1 + m_1)]dA_1^a.$$

This policy reduces U.S. income, but not by enough to restore internal balance in the United States. Substituting the solution for dA_2^g into eq. (1.3),

$$dY_1 = \frac{1}{H}\left[(s_2 + m_2)dA_1^a - m_2\left(\frac{m_1}{s_1 + m_1}\right)dA_1^a\right] = \frac{1}{s_1 + m_1}dA_1^a.$$

This is the same change in U.S. income that was given for a small economy by eq. (11a) in Chapter 13, because Japanese income has not been allowed to change. Furthermore, the policy worsens the external imbalance, because Japanese imports cannot rise when Japanese income does not change. The resulting change in the current-account balance is the same as the change for a small economy given by eq. (13c) in Chapter 13. This policy is not globally optimal and not nationally optimal even for Japan, which is driven further from external balance.

(2) An expenditure-changing policy for external balance defined by setting

$dN_1 = 0$ and solving eq. (1.5) for the requisite change in Japanese expenditure:

$$dA_2^q = (s_2 m_1 / s_1 m_2) dA_1^q.$$

As this change has the same sign as the autonomous change in U.S. expenditure, it amplifies the changes in both countries' incomes, driving them further from internal balance.

(3) An expenditure-switching policy for internal balance defined by setting $dY_2 = 0$ and solving eq. (1.4) for the requisite switch in expenditure:

$$dN_1^a = (m_1 / s_1) dA_1^a.$$

The same result is obtained by setting $dN_1 = 0$ and solving eq. (1.5). By implication, the expenditure-switching policy that restores internal balance also restores external balance. Therefore, this policy is nationally optimal for Japan. It is not globally optimal, however, because it amplifies the change in U.S. income.

Let there be an autonomous switch in U.S. expenditure ($dN_1^a \gtrless 0$). The optimal response from a global standpoint is a U.S. or Japanese policy to switch expenditure back again. Expenditure-changing policies are not globally or nationally optimal. Consider the options open to the United States. (Those open to Japan have symmetrical effects.)

(1) An expenditure-changing policy for internal balance defined by setting $dY_1 = 0$:

$$dA_1^q = -[s_2 / (s_2 + m_2)] dN_1^a.$$

This policy increases the external imbalance (because dA_1^q and dN_1^a have opposite signs and appear with opposite signs in the current-account equation). It also increases the change in Japanese income (the reason is the same).

(2) An expenditure-changing policy for external balance defined by setting $dN_1 = 0$:

$$dA_1^q = (s_1 / m_1) dN_1^a.$$

This policy is not nationally optimal for the United States. It increases the change in U.S. income (because dA_1^q and dN_1^a have the same signs and appear with the same signs in the U.S. income equation). But:

$$dY_2 = \frac{1}{H}(m_1 dA_1^q - s_1 dN_1^a) = \frac{1}{H}\left[\left(\frac{s_1}{m_1}\right)m_1 dN_1^a - s_1 dN_1^a\right] = 0.$$

When used to deal with an autonomous switch in expenditure, an expenditure-changing policy for external balance is nationally optimal in an *altruistic* sense. It restores internal balance in the *foreign* country.

Section 2. Devaluation and the Current Account

To derive the MLR condition, define the trade balance as

$$N = p_1 c_1^* - \pi p_2^* c_2. \tag{2.1}$$

Here, p_1 is the home-currency price of the home (export) good, and c_1^* is the quantity demanded by foreign consumers; p_2^* is the foreign-currency price of the foreign (import) good, and c_2 is the quantity demanded by domestic consumers; and π is the exchange rate in units of home currency per unit of foreign currency. But the change in any product, ab, can be written as $ab(\dot{a} + \dot{b})$, where $\dot{a}$ is (da/a), the proportionate change in a. Therefore, the change in N is

$$dN = p_1 c_1^*(\dot{p}_1 + \dot{c}_1^*) - \pi p_2^* c_2(\dot{\pi} + \dot{p}_2^* + \dot{c}_2). \tag{2.2}$$

The foreign demand for the home good depends on the prices of home and foreign goods and on foreign income, all expressed in foreign currency; the domestic demand for the foreign good depends on those same prices and on domestic income, all expressed in home currency. Formally,

$$c_1^* = g^*(p_1^*, p_2^*, Y^*), \tag{2.3}$$

$$c_2 = g(p_1, p_2, Y), \tag{2.4}$$

where $p_1^* = (p_1/\pi)$ and $p_2 = \pi p_2^*$, while Y^* and Y are foreign and home incomes.
  The change in c_1^* can therefore be written as

$$dc_1^* = g_1^* dp_1^* + g_2^* dp_2^* + g_Y^* dY^*, \tag{2.5}$$

where g_1^* is the change in c_1^* induced by a small change in p_1^*, and so on. (As quantity demanded normally falls when the price of a good rises but rises when incomes rise, $g_1^* < 0$, and $g_Y^* > 0$. The sign of g_2^* is uncertain.) Let e_1^* be the *own*-price elasticity of the foreign demand for the home good, let e_2^* be its *cross*-price elasticity, and let e_Y^* be its income elasticity, so that

$$e_1^* = -g_1^*(p_1^*/c_1^*) > 0,$$
$$e_2^* = g_2^*(p_2^*/c_1^*) \gtrless 0,$$
$$e_Y^* = g_Y^*(Y^*/c_1^*) > 0.$$

Eq. (2.5) can then be rewritten as

$$\dot{c}_1^* = -e_1^* \dot{p}_1^* + e_2^* \dot{p}_2^* + e_Y^* \dot{Y}^*, \tag{2.5a}$$

where $\dot{c}_1^*$ is the proportionate change in the foreign demand for the home good. Similarly, the change in c_2 can be written as

$$\dot{c}_2 = e_1 \dot{p}_1 - e_2 \dot{p}_2 + e_Y \dot{Y}, \tag{2.6}$$

where e_1 is the *cross*-price elasticity of the domestic demand for the foreign good, e_2 is its *own*-price elasticity, and e_Y is its income elasticity. But the change-in-product rule says that $\dot{p}_1^* = \dot{p}_1 - \dot{\pi}$, and $\dot{p}_2 = \dot{p}_2^* + \dot{\pi}$. Substituting these expressions for $\dot{p}_1^*$ and $\dot{p}_2$ into eqs. (2.5a) and (2.6) and using those equations to replace $\dot{c}_1^*$ and $\dot{c}_2$ in eq. (2.2), defining the change in N,

$$dN = p_1 c_1^*[\dot{p}_1 - e_1^*(\dot{p}_1 - \dot{\pi}) + e_2^* \dot{p}_2^* + e_Y^* \dot{Y}^*]$$

$$- p_2^* c_2[\dot{\pi} + \dot{p}_2^* + e_1 \dot{p}_1 - e_2(\dot{p}_2^* + \dot{\pi}) + e_Y \dot{Y}]. \tag{2.2a}$$

In the text, however, the MLR condition is stated under three restrictions: Trade is balanced initially ($p_1 c_1^* = \pi p_2^* c_2$); home and foreign prices are constant ($\dot{p}_1 = \dot{p}_2^* = 0$); and incomes are constant ($\dot{Y}^* = \dot{Y} = 0$). Imposing these restrictions on eq. (2.2a),

$$dN = p_1 c_1^*(e_1^* \dot{\pi} - \dot{\pi} + e_2 \dot{\pi}) = p_1 c_1^*(e_1^* + e_2 - 1)\dot{\pi}. \tag{2.7}$$

As e_1^* is the price elasticity of the foreign demand for imports and e_2 is the price elasticity of the domestic demand for imports, eq. (2.7) embodies the MLR condition. A devaluation or depreciation of the domestic currency ($\dot{\pi} > 0$) improves the current-account balance ($dN > 0$) when the sum of the elasticities of demand is larger than unity. Hereafter, we write $e_\pi = e_1^* + e_2 - 1$, so that $e_\pi > 0$ satisfies the MLR condition.

To show that the current-account balance depends on the real exchange rate, not the nominal rate, return to eq. (2.3), defining the foreign demand for imports. Because quantities demanded depend fundamentally on relative prices and real incomes, uniform changes in p_1^*, p_2^* and Y^* should not affect c_1^*, because they do not affect relative prices or foreign real income. Algebraically,

$$c_1^* = g^*(\lambda p_1^*, \lambda p_2^*, \lambda Y^*), \tag{2.8}$$

which says that the uniform change, λ, in all nominal variables does not alter c_1^*. When a demand function takes this form, however, we can show that

$$p_1^* g_1^* + p_2^* g_2^* + Y^* g_Y^* = 0, \tag{2.9}$$

which can be used in turn to show that $e_2^* = e_1^* - e_Y^*$. Working with eq. (2.4), we can likewise show that $e_1 = e_2 - e_Y$.

Substituting these expressions into eq. (2.2a),

$$dN = p_1 c_1^*[\dot{p}_1 - e_1^*(\dot{p}_1 - \dot{\pi}) + (e_1^* - e_Y^*)\dot{p}_2^* + e_Y^* \dot{Y}^*] - \pi p_2^* c_2[\dot{\pi} + \dot{p}_2^*$$

$$+ (e_2 - e_Y)\dot{p}_1 - e_2(\dot{p}_2^* + \dot{\pi}) + e_Y \dot{Y}]. \tag{2.2b}$$

Setting $p_1 c_1^* = \pi p_2^* c_2$ (as trade is balanced initially) and grouping terms,

$$dN = p_1 c_1^*[(e_1^* + e_2 - 1)(\dot{\pi} + \dot{p}_2^* - \dot{p}_1) + e_Y^*(\dot{Y}^* - \dot{p}_2^*) - e_Y(\dot{Y} - \dot{p}_1)]. \tag{2.2c}$$

The real exchange rate, however, is $v = \pi p_2^*/p_1$, so $\dot{v} = \dot{\pi} + \dot{p}_2^* - \dot{p}_1$. Furthermore, foreign real income is $y^* = Y^*/p_2^*$, so $\dot{y}^* = \dot{Y}^* - \dot{p}_2^*$, and domestic real income is $y = Y/p_1$, so $\dot{y} = \dot{Y} - \dot{p}_1$. Substituting $\dot{v}$, $\dot{y}^*$, and $\dot{y}$ into eq. (2.2c),

$$dN = p_1 c_1^* [(e_1^* + e_2 - 1)\dot{v} + e_Y^* \dot{y}^* - e_Y \dot{y}]. \tag{2.10}$$

Hence, devaluation or depreciation improves the current-account balance when the MLR condition is satisfied, the devaluation or depreciation is not offset by changes in domestic and foreign prices that prevent the real exchange rate from changing, and real incomes are constant.

Section 3. Walras' Law

Consider an economy that has households, firms, banks, and a government. Households hold money, bonds, and claims on firms (shares) and have debts to banks. This is their balance sheet:

$$W^h = L^h + B^h + \pi F^h + E^h - H^h, \tag{3.1}$$

where W^h is household wealth (net worth); L^h, B^h, and F^h are households' holdings of money, government bonds, and foreign bonds; E^h is the value of their claims on firms; and H^h is their debt to banks. (As foreign bonds are denominated in foreign currency, they are multiplied by the exchange rate, π.)

Firms hold money, bonds, and capital (factories, etc.) and have debts to banks:

$$W^f = L^f + B^f + \pi F^f + K - H^f, \tag{3.2}$$

where W^f is their net worth; L^f, B^f, and F^f are their holdings of money and bonds; K is their capital stock; and H^f is their debt to banks.

Banks hold cash reserves with the central bank, government and foreign bonds, and claims on households and firms:

$$L = L^c + B^b + \pi F^b + H^h + H^f, \tag{3.3}$$

where L is the money supply (bank deposits), L^c is cash held with the central bank, and B^b and F^b are banks' bond holdings. The central bank holds government bonds and foreign-exchange reserves:

$$L^c = B^c + \pi R. \tag{3.4}$$

Changes in B^c (bond holdings) reflect open-market operations. Changes in R (reserves) reflect intervention in the foreign-exchange market.

Assume that foreigners do not hold domestic money, bonds, or claims on firms, while domestic households, firms, and banks hold no claims on foreigners other than foreign bonds. Households will then own all firms ($E^h = W^f$), households and firms will be the only holders of money, and so on. Adding up the four balance-sheet equations, canceling common terms, and rearranging,

$$K + \pi R + \pi F^d - W^h + B^d + L^d - L = 0, \tag{3.5}$$

where L^d is the total demand for money ($L^d = L^h + L^f$), while B^d and F^d are the total demands for bonds ($B^d = B^h + B^f + B^b + B^c$, and $F^d = F^h + F^f + F^b$).

Let B represent the supply of government bonds. Adding and subtracting it from the left side of eq. (3.5),

$$(K + B + \pi R + \pi F^d - W^h) + (B^d - B) + (L^d - L) = 0. \tag{3.6}$$

Finally, take rates of change through time but fix the exchange rate:

$$(\dot{K} + \dot{B} + \pi \dot{R} + \pi \dot{F}^d - \dot{W}^h) + (\dot{B}^d - \dot{B}) + (\dot{L}^d - \dot{L}) = 0, \tag{3.7}$$

where $\dot{K}$ is the rate of change of the capital stock, and so on.

But the change in the capital stock is investment ($\dot{K} = I$), and the change in the supply of government bonds is the government's budget deficit ($\dot{B} = G - T$). Furthermore, the definition of the balance of payments says that

$$\pi \dot{R} = (X - M) - \pi \dot{F}^d, \tag{3.8}$$

because a country gains reserves when the current-account surplus exceeds the capital outflow (the increase in holding of foreign bonds). Finally, the change in wealth is saving, which is defined in the familiar way ($\dot{W}^h = S = Y - C - T$). Therefore,

$$\dot{K} + \dot{B} + \pi \dot{R} + \pi \dot{F}^d - \dot{W}^h = (C + I + G + X) - (Y + M).$$

But $C + I + G + X$ is aggregate demand in the goods market, and $Y + M$ is aggregate supply, so the excess demand for goods is defined by

$$D(Y) = (C + I + G + X) - (Y + M).$$

Similarly, the excess flow demands for bonds and money are defined by

$$D(B) = \dot{B}^d - \dot{B} \quad \text{and} \quad D(L) = \dot{L}^d - \dot{L}.$$

Therefore, eq. (3.7) can be rewritten as

$$D(Y) + D(B) + D(L) = 0. \tag{3.9}$$

This is Walras' law. It says that the sum of excess demands must be zero. If some are positive, others must be negative (i.e., excess supplies).

Section 4. The Portfolio-Balance Model

To derive the zz and ZZ curves in Figure 18-4, we begin by rewriting equation (9) in Chapter 18 and defining demand functions for exports and imports:

$$S = p_1 c_1^* - p_2 c_2,$$

$$c_1^* = f^*(p_1^*, p_2^*, C^*), \quad \text{and} \quad c_2 = f(p_1, p_2, C),$$

where p_1^* is the foreign-currency price of the domestic good (so $p_1 = \pi p_1^*$), and C^* is foreign consumption in foreign currency. (All of the other variables are defined in Chapter 18). Using the product rule given in Section 2, above, we can write

$$dS = p_1 c_1^*(\dot{p}_1 + \dot{c}_1^*) - p_2 c_2(\dot{p}_2 + \dot{c}_2), \tag{4.1}$$

where a dotted variable denotes a proportionate rate of change. But the economy begins in long-run equilibrium, so $S = 0$ initially, and $p_1 c_1^* = p_2 c_2$. Furthermore, $\dot{p}_1^* = \dot{p}_1 - \dot{\pi}$, and $\dot{p}_2 = \dot{p}_2^* + \dot{\pi}$. Therefore,

$$dS = p_1 c_1^*[\dot{p}_1 + \dot{c}_1^* - (\dot{p}_2^* + \dot{\pi}) - \dot{c}_2]. \tag{4.1a}$$

The changes in quantities, $\dot{c}_1^*$ and $\dot{c}_2$, can be written as

$$\dot{c}_1^* = -e_1^* \dot{p}_1^* + e_2^* \dot{p}_2^* + \left(\frac{1}{p_1^* c_1^*}\right) m_1^* dC^* = -e_1^*(\dot{p}_1 - \dot{\pi}) + e_2^* \dot{p}_2^*$$

$$+ \left(\frac{\pi}{p_1 c_1^*}\right) m_1^* dC^*,$$

$$\dot{c}_2 = -e_2 \dot{p}_2 + e_1 \dot{p}_1 + \left(\frac{1}{p_2 c_2}\right) m_2 dC = -e_2(\dot{p}_2^* + \dot{\pi}) + e_1 \dot{p}_1$$

$$+ \left(\frac{1}{p_1 c_1^*}\right) m_2 dC. \tag{4.2}$$

Here, e_1^* is the own-price elasticity of foreign demand for the domestic good, e_2^* is the cross-price elasticity, and m_1^* is the fraction of any increase in foreign consumption that is spent on the domestic good. Similarly, e_2 is the own-price elasticity of domestic demand for the foreign good, e_1 is the cross-price elasticity, and m_2 is the fraction of any increase in domestic consumption that is spent on the foreign good. Substituting the expressions for $\dot{c}_1^*$ and $\dot{c}_2$ into eq. (4.1a) and rearranging terms,

$$dS = p_1 c_1^*(e_\pi \dot{\pi} - e_{1t} \dot{p}_1 + e_{2t} \dot{p}_2^*) + \pi m_1^* dC^* - m_2 dC, \tag{4.16}$$

where $e_\pi = e_1^* + e_2 - 1$, the MLR condition, while $e_{1t} = e_1^* + e_1 - 1$, and $e_{2t} = e_2^* + e_2 - 1$.

Three assumptions simplify this statement: (1) Uniform changes in nominal variables do not affect quantities; this assumption was introduced in Section 2, above, and it says that $e_2^* = e_1^* - e_c^*$, and $e_1 = e_2 - e_c$, where e_c^* and e_c are the consumption elasticities of foreign and domestic demands. (2) A change in total consumption induces an equiproportional change in the demand for each good; this assumption says that $e_c^* = e_c = 1$. (3) Goods are gross substitutes, meaning that an increase in the price of one good raises demand for the other; this assumption says that $e_2^* > 0$ and $e_1 > 0$. Under these three assumptions, $e_{1t} = e_{2t} = e_t = e_2^* + e_1 > 0$. Furthermore, $e_\pi = 1 + e_t$, which says that the ML R condition is satisfied.

Finally, equation (4) in Chapter 18 says that $\dot{p}_1 = u(dY/Y)$, and equation (5) says that $dC = dY - dS$ when, as here, T and G are fixed. Using these expressions to replace $\dot{p}_1$ and dC in eq. (4.16) we obtain the basic goods-market equation:

$$(1 - m_2)dS = nYe_t\dot{\pi} - (m_2 + nue_t)dY + \pi m_1^* dC^* + nYe_t\dot{p}_2^*, \qquad (4.3)$$

where $n = (p_1 c_1^*/Y)$, the share of exports in national income.

At all points on the ZZ curve, the current account is balanced, so saving is zero. Therefore, $dS = 0$ on the ZZ curve, and we can solve eq. (4.3) for the change in Y which satisfies that condition:

$$dY = \left(\frac{nY}{N_L}\right)e_\pi\dot{\pi} + \left(\frac{1}{N_L}\right)(\pi m_1^* dC^* + nYe_t\dot{p}_2^*), \qquad (4.4)$$

where $N_L = m_2 + nue_t$. This is the relationship given by the ZZ curve. The curve is upward sloping because $(nY/N_L)e_\pi > 0$ when the ML R condition is satisfied. It shifts upward with increases in C^* and p_2^*.

Saving is not always zero on the zz curve. When T and r^* are constant, however, equation (10) in Chapter 18 says that

$$dS = s_Y dY + s_r dr + s_W dW.$$

Remember that an increase in wealth reduces saving ($s_W < 0$). Substituting this expression into eq. (4.3) and solving for the change in Y,

$$dY = \left(\frac{nY}{N_S}\right)e_\pi\dot{\pi} + \left(\frac{1}{N_S}\right)(\pi m_1^* dC^* + nYe_t\dot{p}_2^*) - \left(\frac{1}{N_S}\right)(1 - m_2)(s_r dr + s_W dW), \quad (4.5)$$

where $N_S = s_Y + m_2(1 - s_Y) + nue_t$. This is the relationship given by the zz curve. The curve is upward sloping because $(nY/N_S)e_\pi > 0$ when the ML R condition is satisfied. But it is flatter than the ZZ curve, because $N_S - N_L = (1 - m_2)s_Y > 0$, so $N_S > N_L$. The zz curve shifts upward with increases in C^* and p_2^*; it shifts downward with an increase in r, which reduces consumption by encouraging saving; it shifts upward with an increase in W, which raises consumption by discouraging saving.

When the wage rate is rigid ($u = 0$), $N_S = s_Y + m_2(1 - s_Y)$, which corresponds to the expression $s + m$ in Chapter 13, because s_Y is the marginal propensity to save and $m_2(1 - s_Y)$ is the marginal propensity to import, each defined with respect to an increase in income.

To derive the LL curve in Figure 18-6, use equation (16) in Chapter 18 to write

$$L_r dr + L_W dW - dB^c - \pi dR = 0. \qquad (4.6)$$

The effect of a change in r^* is omitted, as before, because r^* is constant in Chapter 18. (The effect of a change in π is also omitted because capital gains and losses on foreign-currency reserves are absorbed by the central bank and do not affect the money supply.) Solving for the change in r,

$$dr = -\left(\frac{L_W}{L_r}\right)dW + \left(\frac{1}{L_r}\right)(dB^c + \pi dR). \tag{4.6a}$$

This is the relationship given by the LL curve. Remember that $L_r < 0$, because an increase in r reduces the demand for money. Therefore, the LL curve is upward sloping and shifts downward with increases in B^c and R.

To derive the BB curve, use equation (17) in Chapter 18 to write

$$B_r dr + B_W dW + dB^c = 0. \tag{4.7}$$

The effect of a change in B is omitted, because B is constant when the government balances its budget. Solving for the change in r,

$$dr = -\left(\frac{B_W}{B_r}\right)dW - \left(\frac{1}{B_r}\right)dB^c. \tag{4.7a}$$

This is the relationship given by the BB curve. Remember that $B_r > 0$, because an increase in r raises the demand for the domestic bond. Therefore, the BB curve is downward sloping and shifts downward with an increase in B^c.

To derive the SS curve, set $S = 0$, hold T constant, and use equation (10) in Chapter 18 to write

$$s_Y dY + s_r dr + s_W dW = 0. \tag{4.8}$$

Solving for the change in r,

$$dr = -\left(\frac{s_W}{s_r}\right)dW - \left(\frac{s_Y}{s_r}\right)dY. \tag{4.8a}$$

This is the relationship given by the SS curve. Remember that $s_W < 0$, because an increase in wealth reduces saving. Therefore, the SS curve is upward sloping, and an increase in disposable income shifts the curve downward.

In Figure 18-6, the SS curve is steeper than the LL curve. This is true when $(-s_W/s_r) > (-L_W/L_r)$ or $s_W L_r > s_r L_W$, which says that saving (absorption) is comparatively sensitive to changes in wealth, whereas the demand for money is comparatively sensitive to changes in the interest rate. (This assumption is made in many macroeconomic models; when it is violated, a budget deficit reduces output because it "crowds out" private spending by raising interest rates.)

The equations for the LL and BB curves can be solved for the short-run changes in W and R produced by an open-market purchase. Multiply both sides of eqs. (4.6) and (4.7) by $B_r L_r$ and put them together:

$$B_r L_W dW - B_r(dB^c + \pi dR) = L_r B_W dW + L_r dB^c.$$

Therefore,

$$(B_r L_W - L_r B_W)dW - B_r \pi dR = (B_r + L_r)dB^c. \tag{4.9}$$

But $B_r L_W - L_r B_W > 0$ (because $L_r < 0$), and equations (11) through (14) in Chapter 18 tell us that $B_r + L_r + F_r = 0$, so $B_r + L_r = -F_r > 0$ (as an increase in r reduces the demand for the foreign bond). Under a flexible exchange rate, R is constant, so an increase in B^c must raise W instantaneously; by implication, the domestic currency must depreciate to confer a capital gain on holders of the foreign bond. Under a pegged exchange rate, W cannot change right away, so an increase in B^c must reduce R instantaneously. (These results prove that the point A_1 in Figure 18-9 must lie below and to the right of the point A_0.)

Finally, use the relationship among B_r, F_r, and L_r to rewrite eq. (4.7a):

$$dr = \left(\frac{B_W}{L_r + F_r}\right)dW + \left(\frac{1}{L_r + F_r}\right)dB^c. \tag{4.76}$$

Without any capital mobility, $F_r = 0$. The slope of the BB curve becomes B_W/L_r, and an open-market purchase shifts BB downward by as much as it shifts LL downward. With some capital mobility, $F_r < 0$. The BB curve gets flatter and shifts down less sharply. With perfect capital mobility, $F_r \to -\infty$. Foreign and domestic bonds become perfect substitutes, and r cannot change unless r^* changes, so the BB curve becomes horizontal and does not shift at all.

APPENDIX C

Outlines of Answers to Selected Problems

This appendix outlines answers to the even-numbered problems posed at the ends of various chapters. Because these are *outlines*, not complete answers, make sure that your own answers respond fully to the corresponding questions.

Chapter 2

(2) Draw a new world supply curve, S'_W, intersecting the vertical axis at a point P'' below P'. Use N' and N'' to label the points at which S'_W intersects S_H and D_H (i.e., the counterparts of E' and E''). You can now show that the quantity of imports increases (because domestic production falls and domestic consumption rises). You can also show that producer surplus falls by $P''N'E'P'$, that consumer surplus rises by $P''N''E''P'$, and that the increase in consumer surplus exceeds the decrease in producer surplus, raising economic welfare.

(4) Redraw Figure 2-7 to show the initial situation of the country exporting cameras:

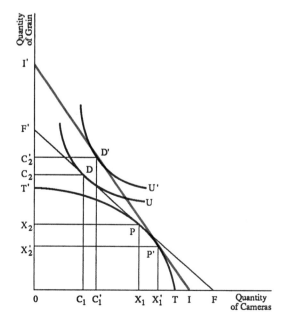

Initially, the relative price of a camera is given by the slope of FF', so the country produces at P and consumes at D. The increase in the relative price of a camera is shown by replacing FF' with II', so that production moves to P' and consumption moves to D'. Camera production rises from OX_1 to OX'_1, and camera consumption rises from OC_1 to OC'_1. In this particular instance, then, camera exports rise from C_1X_1 to $C'_1X'_1$ (but ask yourself whether they could fall). Go on by yourself to identify the changes in the country's production, consumption, and imports of grain (but ask yourself whether they could move in the opposite direction). Show that economic welfare rises.

(6) An import tariff is added to the world price of the imported good. An export tariff is added to the domestic price of the export good. From Note 2-2, then, $p_2^* = (1 + t')p_2$, where t' is the tariff on grain. When there is no import tariff, moreover, $p_1 = p_1^*$ so

$$p_1/p_2(1 + t') = p_1^*/p_2^* = p^*$$

Hence, $p = p_1/p_2 = (1 + t')p^*$. An export tariff t' equal in size to an import tariff t drives the same-sized wedge between p and p^*. But Note 2-2 also showed that t equals $W'Z'/Z'V'$ in Figure 2-12, and you should be able to show that t' equals $V''V'/OV'$. To complete the proof, you must now show that $V''V'/OV'$ equals $W'Z'/Z'V'$. But the triangles $OV'Z'$ and $OV''Z''$ are similar, so $OV''/OV' = Z''V''/Z'V'$. Furthermore, $OV'' = OV' + V'V''$, and $Z''V'' = W'Z' + Z'V'$. The rest is easy.

Chapter 3

(2) The quotation is wrong in one way and right in another. It is wrong because it confuses the wage in terms of the import good with the wage in the industry facing import competition. Workers can move freely between sectors in the Ricardian model, so all workers must earn the same wage, wherever they work. Hence, the opening of trade raises *every* worker's wage in terms of the import good. In that case, however, every worker should favor trade, so the quotation is right to say that something must be wrong with the Ricardian model. Workers in industries facing import competition *do* tend to oppose trade and thus favor protection. (The flaw in the model is the assumption that workers can move freely between sectors. If workers cannot leave the import-competing sector, trade will reduce their real wage in terms of the export good without raising it in terms of the import good, and those workers will favor protection. This matter is examined in later chapters.)

(4) The relative price of steel is 10/6 or 1.667 pairs of shoes per ton in Germany; the real wage in terms of steel is 1/10 or 0.10 ton; and the real wage in terms of shoes is 1/6 or 0.167 pair. The relative price of steel is 20/1 or 20 shoes per ton in Italy; the real wage in steel is 1/20 or 0.05 ton; and the real wage in shoes is 1/1 or 1 pair. If the relative price of steel is 4 pairs of shoes per ton after trade is opened, Germany will specialize in steel and Italy will specialize in shoes. The real wage in Germany will not change in terms of steel but will rise in terms of shoes to 0.4 pair. (It must equal the real wage in terms of steel *times* the relative price of shoes, or 0.10 ton $\times$ 4 pairs per ton.) The real wage in Italy will not change in terms of shoes but will rise

in terms of steel to 0.25 ton. (It must equal the real wage in terms of shoes *times* the relative price of steel, or 1 pair × 1/4 ton per pair.)

(6) The ratios of German to Italian labor requirements, listed from lowest to highest, are 10/20 or 0.5 for steel, 4/5 or 0.8 for grain, and 6/1 or 6 for shoes. The ratio of German to Italian wages cannot be higher than 1/0.5 or 2.0; at higher ratios, it would be cheaper to produce all three goods in Italy. When the wage ratio equals 2.0, Germany produces steel, and Italy produces grain and shoes (and may produce some steel); Germany exports steel to import grain and shoes. Similarly, the ratio cannot be lower than 1/6 or 0.167; at lower ratios, it would be cheaper to produce all three goods in Germany. When the ratio equals 0.167, Italy produces shoes, and Germany produces steel and grain (and may produce some shoes); Italy exports shoes to import steel and grain. When the ratio equals 1.25, Germany produces steel and grain, and Italy produces grain and shoes; Germany exports steel, Italy exports shoes, and the grain trade can go either way.

Chapter 4

(2) A country's labor and capital constraints must both hold exactly at the full-employment output point. In this case, the constraints are:

$$\text{Workers} = 4 \text{ Ball bearings} + 6 \text{ Shoes}$$

$$\text{Machines} = 10 \text{ Ball bearings} + 5 \text{ Shoes}$$

Solving for Sweden, with 400 workers and 600 machines, we get 40 ball bearings and 40 shoes. Solving for Italy, with 400 workers and 400 machines, we get 10 ball bearings and 60 shoes. As Italy makes more shoes and fewer ball bearings it will export shoes. To draw the transformation curves, solve for ball-bearing output:

$$\text{Ball bearings} = (1/4) \text{ Workers} - (3/2) \text{ Shoes}$$

$$\text{Ball bearings} = (1/10) \text{ Machines} - (1/2) \text{ Shoes}$$

Your diagram should look like this:

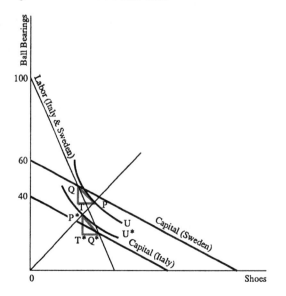

Sweden's full-employment output point is Q, and Italy's is Q^*. Sweden exports QT ball bearings, imports TP shoes, and reaches U. Italy exports Q^*T^* ($= TP$) shoes, imports T^*P^* ($= QT$) ball bearings, and reaches U^*.

(4) Demand reversals occur when differences in demand conditions more than offset differences in factor endowments. Hence, Swedish consumers must have tastes strongly biased toward ball bearings and Italian consumers must have tastes strongly biased toward shoes, so that Sweden will import ball bearings and Italy will import shoes. Your diagram should look like this:

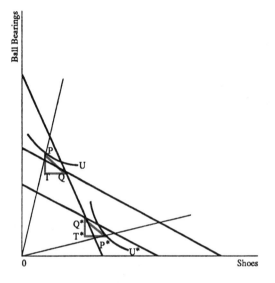

Sweden exports QT shoes, imports TP ball bearings, and reaches U. Italy exports Q^*T^* ($= TP$) ball bearings, imports T^*P^* ($= QT$) shoes, and reaches U^*.

(6) You can invoke three propositions: (1) Under free trade, prices must be the same in both countries. (2) When a country produces at a point on its labor or capital constraint, rather than its full-employment point, relative prices in that country must equal the slope of the relevant constraint. (3) When a country produces on its labor or capital constraint, it cannot gain from trade (its situation resembles that of a Ricardian economy that does not specialize completely). Propositions (1) and (2) rule out one possibility—that one country produces on its labor constraint and the other produces on its capital constraint. In that case, proposition (2) says that the two countries' prices are different (because the slopes of the labor and capital constraints are different when relative factor requirements differ), and this contradicts proposition (1). Proposition (3) rules out the other possibility—that both countries produce on the same constraint. In that case, neither country could gain from trade.

(8) When labor and capital are the only factors of production, the value of output must equal total payments to labor *plus* total payments to capital. Working in millions of dollars:

$1.0 Exports = 10 Workers × Wage + $2.5 Capital × Rate of return

$1.0 Imports = 8 Workers × Wage + $3.0 Capital × Rate of return

Solve these equations simultaneously to show that the annual wage is $50,000 and the rate of return to capital is 20 percent.

Chapter 5

(2) Represent the increase in the Dutch labor force by lengthening the horizontal axis of the labor-market diagram and redrawing one demand curve:

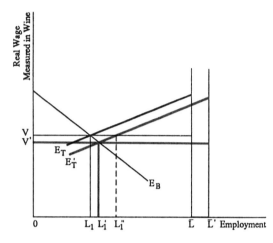

The increase in the labor force is $\overline{L}L'$. The real wage in terms of tulips falls from OV to OV', raising employment in the bicycle industry from OL_1 to OL'_1 and raising employment in the tulip industry from $L_1\overline{L}$ to $L'_1\overline{L}'$. (How can you be sure that employment rises in the tulip industry—that $L_1L'_1$ does not exceed the whole increase in the labor force? Hint: The new demand curve for labor in the tulip industry, E'_T, is identical in all respects to the original demand curve, E_T, so $L_1L''_1$ must equal $\overline{L}L'$.) As both industries use more labor than before but use unchanged quantities of land and capital, the marginal products of land and capital must rise. Hence, the real rental rate for land must rise in terms of tulips, and the real return to capital must rise in terms of bicycles. When the terms of trade are constant, however, an increase in real earnings measured in one good implies an increase measured in the other good. Therefore, the real wage falls in terms of both goods, while the real rental rate and real return to capital rise in terms of both goods.

(4) The demand curve for labor by the bicycle industry will shift up with the increase in the marginal product of labor. When you draw a diagram to show this, you will see that the real wage rises in terms of bicycles, while employment rises in the bicycle industry and falls in the tulip industry. Lower employment in the tulip industry raises the land-labor ratio in that industry, reducing the marginal product of land, so the real rental rate for land must fall in terms of tulips. Higher employment in the bicycle industry reduces the capital-labor ratio in that industry, raising the marginal product of capital and reinforcing the increase resulting from the invention itself, so the real return to capital must rise in terms of bicycles. As in question (4), moreover, real earnings in terms of tulips and bicycle move together.

(6) Your answer to (5) should predict an increase in the relative price of tulips. (Dutch tulip output falls with the fall in employment in the tulip industry, and the

Dutch demand for tulips rises with the increase in real income resulting from the invention. Therefore, the Dutch supply of tulip exports must fall, raising the relative price of tulips on the world market.) The Haberler theorem provides the rest of the answer. The real rental rate for land must rise in the country importing tulips, whether measured in tulips or bicycles, and the real return to capital must fall. The real wage must fall in terms of tulips and rise in terms of bicycles. Therefore, owners of capital might favor a tariff on Dutch tulips (along with those workers who buy many tulips and few bicycles).

Chapter 6

(2) For both countries to specialize completely, trade must take each country to an end of the line segment defining its production possibilities. This can be made to happen by enlarging the difference between the countries' factor endowments until the two line segment cease to overlap:

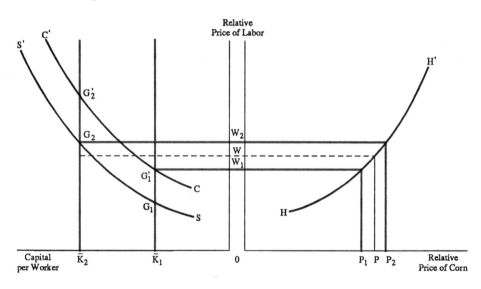

When Manymen has $O\bar{K}_1$ capital per worker, its production possibilities lie on $G_1 G_1'$. When Fewmen has $O\bar{K}_2$ capital per worker, its production possibilities lie on $G_2 G_2'$. It is therefore impossible to draw a single horizontal line that intersects both countries' segments. Under free trade, then, Manymen produces at G_1', specializing completely in corn, the labor-intensive good, while Fewmen produces at G_2, specializing completely in steel, the capital-intensive good. The relative price of labor is OW_1 in Manymen and OW_2 in Fewmen. (Labor is scarcer in Fewmen than Manymen, because free trade cannot equalize the countries' factor prices.) The relative price of corn is OP, between OP_1 and OP_2. As in the simple Ricardian model, free-trade prices depend on demand conditions when both countries specialize completely.

(4) Your diagram should look like Figure 8-4 in Chapter 8. The CC' and SS' curves intersect at Y. Steel is more capital intensive than corn when the relative price of labor is below OW but less capital intensive than corn when the relative price of labor is above OW. The HH' curve bends backward when the relative price of labor

exceeds OW. (An increase in the relative price of labor raises the relative price of the labor-intensive good, and steel is more labor intensive than corn when the relative price of labor exceeds OW. But an increase in the relative price of steel is a decrease in the relative price of corn.) Let the relative price of corn be OP with free trade. The relative price of labor is OW_1 in Manymen, which produces at M; the capital intensity of corn is W_1U_1, and the capital intensity of steel is W_1V_1 (steel is more capital intensive than corn in Manymen). The relative price of labor is OW_2 in Fewmen, which produces at F; the capital intensity of corn is W_2U_2, and the capital intensity of steel is W_2V_2 (corn is more capital intensive than steel in Fewmen). But *both* industries are more capital intensive in Fewmen than in Manymen (W_2V_2, the capital intensity of the *labor*-intensive good in Fewmen, exceeds W_1V_1, the capital intensity of the *capital*-intensive good in Manymen.) Hence, the marginal product of labor is higher in Fewmen, so the real wage is higher, too. The factor reversal prevents factor-price equalization.

(6) Your diagram should resemble Figure 5-6 in Chapter 5, with steel replacing cloth on the horizontal axis and corn replacing wine on the vertical axis. But there should then be two important differences: (1) The increase of efficiency in the corn industry should shift the transformation curve *upward* rather than *rightward*; the curve should be "anchored" at Z_1 rather than Z_2. (2) The point E' on the new transformation curve having the same slope as the point E on the old transformation curve should lie to the northwest of E rather than the southeast. At constant prices, then, Fewmen produces more corn and less steel, reducing its demand for corn imports and improving its terms of trade. Economic welfare rises in Fewmen (which enjoys the income-raising increase of efficiency and an improvement in its terms of trade), and welfare falls in Manymen (which suffers a corresponding deterioration in its terms of trade).

Chapter 7

(2) Your adaptation of Figure 7-3 should look like this:

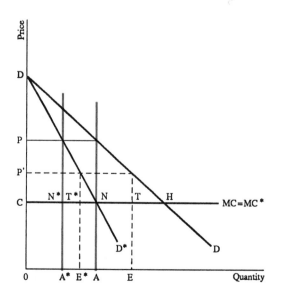

The American demand curve is DD, as before. Hence, Acme will sell OA robots at the price OP before trade is opened ($OA = CN = \frac{1}{2}CH$). With the opening of trade, Edo will start to sell AE robots in the American market ($AE = NT = \frac{1}{2}NH$); the price will fall to OP'. The Japanese demand curve is DD^* (quantity demanded at each price is half that in America). Hence, Edo will sell OA^* robots at the price OP before trade is opened ($OA^* = CN^* = \frac{1}{2}CN$); the price is the same in both markets, but Edo's home sales are half as large as Acme's home sales. With the opening of trade, Acme will start to sell A^*E^* robots in the Japanese market ($A^*E^* = N^*T^* = \frac{1}{2}N^*N$); the price will fall to OP', just as it did in the American market. These results tell you how to adapt Figure 7-4:

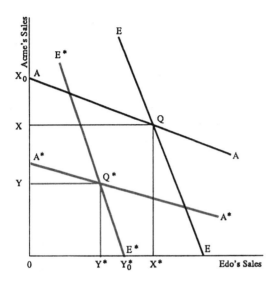

The reaction curves for Acme and Edo in the American market are drawn as before. Acme sells OX_0 in the American market before trade, and the two firms move eventually to Q after trade is opened, so that Edo's exports to America are OX^*. The reaction curves for Edo and Acme in the Japanese market are labeled E^*E^* and A^*A^*, respectively. As the Japanese market is half as large as the American market, Edo sells OY_0^* in the Japanese market before trade ($OY_0^* = \frac{1}{2}OX_0$), and the two firms move eventually to Q^* after trade is opened, so that Acme's exports to Japan are OY (half as large as Edo's exports to the American market). Can you prove that prices will be the same at Q^* and Q?

(4) When the two governments do not subsidize their firms, each one can expect the Brazilian robot market to contribute $1 billion to its national income ($10 billion *times* 0.4 *times* 0.5 *less* $1 billion). When both of them subsidize their firms by $1 billion each government can expect the Brazilian market to contribute $2 billion to its national income ($10 billion *times* 0.8 *times* 0.5 *less* $2 billion). Therefore, it pays both governments to subsidize.

Chapter 8

(2) When the marginal products of capital are equalized in Britain and Portugal, their cloth industries must have the same capital-to-labor ratio, and the

marginal products of labor must also be equalized in Britain and Portugal, whether measured in cloth or wine. This means, in turn, that the marginal products of land must be equalized and that the two countries' wine industries must have the same land-to-labor ratio. Now, invoke the initial conditions—that Portugal has more land and both countries have the same amounts of labor. If Portugal has more land and both countries' wine industries have the same land-to-labor ratio, Portugal must use more labor in its wine industry and must thus use less labor in its cloth industry (because both countries have the same amounts of labor). But both countries' cloth industries have the same capital-to-labor ratio, so Portugal must use less capital in cloth production. Hence, Britain must have more capital than Portugal and must produce more cloth.

(4) Your diagram should be based on the one in the answer for Question (2) in Chapter 6, where Manymen starts with $O\bar{K}_1$ capital per worker and Fewmen starts with $O\bar{K}_2$ capital per worker. When the relative price of corn is OP, Manymen produces at G'_1 specializing completely in corn, while Fewmen produces at G'_2, specializing completely in steel. The relative price of labor is OW_1 in Manymen and OW_2 in Fewmen. Hence, capital will move from Fewmen to Manymen. The capital transfer will narrow the gap between the two countries' endowments until they cease to specialize completely and free trade can equalize factor prices. (To illustrate this outcome, let the relative price of labor be OW with factor-price equalization. Move left along the horizontal line from W to the point where it crosses the CC' curve; this point tells us how much capital per worker Manymen must have to produce any steel. Continue to move left along the horizontal line to the point where it crosses the SS' curve; this point tells us how much capital per worker Fewmen must have to produce any cloth. Use these two points to measure the size of the capital transfer required before trade can equalize factor prices.)

(6) Income after tax on investing in A is $21 ($30 *less* 0.3 *times* $30 in tax paid to A). Income after tax on investing in B depends on tax treatment in A. If A gives a credit for tax paid in B, income after tax on investing in B is:

Income before tax..	$40.0
Tax paid to B (0.2 *times* $40)...............................	8.0
Gross tax due to A (0.3 *times* $40).........................	12.0
Less credit for tax paid to B...............................	8.0
Net tax paid to A ($12 *less* $8)............................	4.0
Income after tax...	28.0

Therefore, the citizen of A will invest in B. If A gives a deduction for tax paid in B, income after tax on investing in B is:

Tax paid to B (as before).....................................	8.0
Tax due to A (0.3 *times* ($40 *less* $8))......................	9.6
Income after tax..	22.4

Therefore, the citizen of A will still invest in B.

When the tax rate in B is 40 percent, investing in B is less profitable. If A gives a tax credit:

Income before tax..	$40.0
Tax paid to B (0.4 *times* $40)..............................	16.0
Gross tax due to A (0.3 *times* $40).........................	12.0
Less credit for tax paid to B.................................	12.0
Net tax paid to A ($12 *less* $12)............................	0.0
Income after tax...	24.0

The credit is $12, not $16, as it cannot exceed the gross tax due to A (the investor cannot get a cash refund). Even so, the citizen of A will invest in B. If A gives a deduction instead:

Tax paid to B (as before)......................................	16.0
Tax due to A (0.3 *times* ($40 *less* $16)).....................	7.2
Income after tax...	16.8

The larger deduction does not completely offset the higher tax rate in B, so the citizen of A will invest in A.

Chapter 9

(2) You have merely to reverse the labels P_F and P_H, as shown below, and add the line UU' passing through the point W':

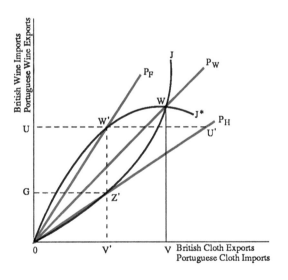

The relative price of cloth is given in Portugal by the slope of the line OP_F and is given in Britain by the slope of the flatter line OP_H. The tariff protects Britain's wine industry by reducing the relative price of cloth in Britain (raising the relative price of wine); it improves Britain's terms of trade by raising the relative price of cloth in Portugal. As British consumers use cloth to pay for wine imports, the tariff rate must be measured in cloth and is given by $U'W'/W'U$, the difference between relative prices in Britain and Portugal. In the new equilibrium, Britain collects OW' cloth in tariff revenue but uses it to buy $W'Z'$ wine. Therefore, the cloth and wine markets clear. (Britain supplies OV' cloth exports, its consumers demand $V'Z'$ wine imports, and its government demands $Z'W'$ wine imports. But $V'Z'$ and $Z'W'$ sum to $V'W'$, Portugal's offer of wine exports.) To compare the two countries' tariff rates, draw the line GZ' to form the similar triangles OUU' and OGZ', so that $OU/OG = UU'/GZ'$. But $OU/OG = V'W'/V'Z' = 1 + W'Z'/Z'V'$, and $W'Z'/Z'V'$ is the Portuguese tariff rate. Furthermore, $UU'/GZ' = UU'/UW' = 1 + U'W'/W'U$, and $U'W'/W'U$ is the British tariff rate. Therefore, the rates are equal.

(4) As in your answer to (2), switch the labels on the price lines OP_F and OP_H and assume that Britain spends the tariff revenue on wine. In your answer to (2), you showed that $W'Z'/Z'V'$ measures the British tariff on wine imports as well as the Portuguese tariff on cloth imports when the government collecting the tariff spends it entirely on wine. Your result is perverse in that the tariff worsens Britain's terms of trade. It protects the British wine industry by raising the relative price of wine in Britain (reducing the relative price of cloth) but reduces the relative price of cloth in Portugal.

(6) The tariff-inclusive domestic price of a widget is $\$20.00(1 + 0.3) = \$26.00$. The tariff-inclusive prices of the parts are $\$4.00(1 + 0.5) = \$6.00$, and $\$3.00(1 + 0.25) = \$3.75$. Therefore, domestic value added is $\$26.00 - \$9.75 = \$16.25$, and the profit per widget is $\$16.25 - \$6.00 = \$10.25$. With free trade, domestic value added would be $\$20.00 - (\$4.00 + \$3.00) = \$13.00$. The effective rate is $(\$16.25 - \$13.00)/\$13.00 = 25$ per cent.

(8) Redraw the diagram to reduce the vertical distance between Q and Q', so that the price line EE', passing through Q', is tangent to an indifference curve higher than U_0. There is an output loss and unemployment, but the resulting welfare loss is smaller than the welfare gain resulting directly from the opening of trade. A rigid real wage is one that can rise but cannot fall. Accordingly, the opening of trade does not cause unemployment when the real wage is rigid in terms of the import-competing good. That is because trade reduces the domestic price of the import-competing good, raising the real wage in terms of that good rather than reducing it. More generally, the opening of trade can cause unemployment only when expanding export industries are prevented from absorbing the labor released by shrinking import-competing industries. This can happen only when the real wage is kept from falling in terms of the goods produced by the expanding export industries.

Chapter 10

(2) A clear answer should note immediately that this statement tries to distinguish between protecting or promoting production in the United States and protecting or promoting the interests of American firms wherever they produce. If American trade policy is concerned with production in the United States, it should not try to open Japanese markets to products made in Taiwan, even when they are made by American firms. But it should try to open European markets to Japanese cars made in the United States, even though they will compete with cars made in Europe by American firms. If American policy is concerned instead with the interests of American firms, it should take the opposite stance in each case. A good answer

would also point out that the "territorial" view is labor oriented and the "national" view capital oriented. It would also point out that American multinationals are not owned only by Americans but have foreign stockholders, and foreign multinationals have American stockholders, which makes it even harder to decide how such cases should be treated. A good answer, however, would criticize the statement for assuming uncritically that protection and promotion are justified when one can identify the appropriate beneficiary. It neglects the basic objection to protection, which reduces welfare by injuring consumers.

(4) Recall the formula itself:

$$\Delta W = -\tfrac{1}{2} \times \Delta M \times p_w \times t$$

where ΔW is the change in welfare, ΔM is the change in import volume, p_w is the world price, and t is the tariff rate. The formula has to be adapted because the domestic industry is protected by an import quota (or a method very similar to it). Hence, you must use something other than t, and you must allow for the possibility that the foreign exporter captures some of the profit that is the quota counterpart of tariff revenue. (The formula above was based on the assumption that the tariff revenue collected by the government is returned to consumers by reducing other taxes.) Therefore, you need to know:

(a) The increase in the domestic price resulting from the quota; you can approximate it by $(p_D - p_W)$, where p_D is the domestic price after the quota is imposed; this new term replaces $p_W \times t$.

(b) The quota profit captured by the foreign exporter; approximate it by $\alpha(p_D - p_W)M$, where p_D and p_W are defined as before, M is the volume of imports allowed by the quota, and α is the foreign exporter's share of the quota profit.

(c) The change in the volume of imports, ΔM, resulting from the quota; approximate it by the difference between the levels of imports before and after the imposition of the quota.

When you have replaced $p_W \times t$ and allowed for the foreigner's part of the quota profit, your formula will be:

$$\Delta W = -\tfrac{1}{2} \times \Delta M \times (p_D - p_W) - \alpha(p_D - p_W)M = -(p_D - p_W)(\tfrac{1}{2}\Delta M + \alpha M)$$

The hardest part is guessing at α, the foreigner's share of the quota profit.

(6) You have merely to re-label the left panel as the export market and re-label the middle panel as the home market.

Chapter 11

(2) Your answer should use a diagram like this:

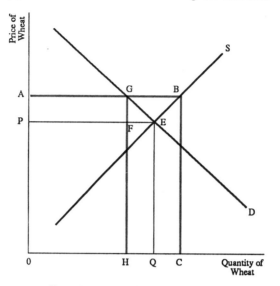

Without any policy, the price of wheat would be *OP*, production and consumption would be *OQ*, and farmers would receive *OPEQ*. To raise their receipts to, say, *OABC* by supporting the price of wheat, the government would have to raise it to *OA*. Production would rise to *OC*, but consumption would fall to *OH*, and the government would have to spend *HGBC* to buy the surplus (and more money to store it). The total cost would be the tax cost *HGBC* *plus* the extra consumer cost *PAGF*. If the government were to raise farmers' receipts to *OABC* by deficiency payments, it would leave the wheat price at *OP* but pay farmers the difference between *OABC* and *OPEQ*, which is *HFEQ* smaller than the total cost of supporting farm prices. (A precise answer would note that *QEBC* is the resource cost of growing *QC* more wheat, not an increase in the farmers' incomes. Therefore, this amount should be excluded from the deficiency payments, raising the amount that would be saved by switching to deficiency payments.)

(4) No. Britain's gain from eliminating the tariff on cloth can exceed its loss from eliminating the tariff on wine, so Britain can gain from the customs union. In that case, however, Portugal must lose from the union. There is a net loss to the union as a whole from the elimination of each tariff. Hence, Portugal's loss on cloth must exceed its gain on wine if Britain's gain on cloth exceeds its loss on wine.

(6) Your diagram should show that domestic production falls and that consumption does not change. Therefore, imports have to rise by the amount of the fall in production. The effluent tax is successful in reducing domestic pollution because it reduces domestic production. (But it may raise pollution in the country supplying the imports.) If an import tax is used to prevent a fall in domestic production, there must be a fall in consumption and thus a fall in imports compared to the level obtaining before the imposition of the effluent tax. The tariff prevents the effluent tax from reducing domestic pollution, because it keeps domestic production from falling. (But it may lower pollution in the country supplying the imports.) If it is right to impose the effluent tax, it must therefore be wrong to impose the tariff.

(8) If the policy is aimed at raising high-technology output in the United States for the benefit of the whole U.S. economy (i.e., to enjoy the spillover effects allegedly provided by high-technology industries), it makes sense to include the American affiliates of foreign firms. The benefits derive from producing high-technology goods *in* the United States, not from production by U.S. firms alone. This argument is reinforced by the possibility that the American affiliates of foreign firms can furnish spillover effects different from those of American firms. The argument is weakened, however, by the possibility that the American affiliates of foreign firms will pass the benefits of U.S. policies back to their parent companies, helping them to compete more effectively with U.S. firms in American markets. You must also consider the ways in which foreign governments are likely to respond. If the United States excludes U.S. affiliates of foreign firms from the coverage of U.S. policies, other countries will exclude foreign affiliates of U.S. firms from the coverage of their policies. The gains that might be passed back to foreign firms having American affiliates and benefiting from U.S. policies must be weighed against the gains that might be passed back to American firms having foreign affiliates and benefiting from other governments' policies.

Chapter 12

(2) The Japanese capital account should look like this:

Item	Credit	Debit
Increase (+) in foreign claims on Japan:		
Claims of foreign banks on Japanese banks (a, c)	50	200
Claims of foreign banks on Japanese banks (i)		50
Increase (−) in Japanese claims on foreigners:		
Foreign securities (b)		150
Claims of Japanese banks on foreign banks (b)	150	
Claims on foreign official institutions (i)	50	

There is no change in the balance on capital account. But Japan runs a deficit in its balance of payments, because its official reserves fall by 50.

The balance sheet of Japanese commercial banks should look like this:

Assets		Liabilities	
Balances with:		Deposit liabilities to:	
NY bank (b)	− 150	Chip maker (a)	+ 200
Bank of Japan (i)	− 50	French bank (a)	− 200
		Insurance company (b)	− 150
		Subsidiary (c)	− 50
		German bank (c, i)	0

The banks' cash reserves fall by 50.

(4) The balance-of-payments table in your answer to (3) should show a current-account surplus of 20 (140 of exports *less* 110 of imports *plus* 15 of foreign tourism *less* 15 of interest payments to foreigners). Therefore, the definition of national income gives:

$$Y = C + I + G + X - M = 400 + 75 + 150 + 20 = 645$$

There are two ways to calculate the government budget:

(a) As $(X - M) = (S - I) + (T - G)$, it follows that

$$(T - G) = (X - M) - (S - I) = 20 - (80 - 75) = 15$$

(b) As $Y = C + S + T$, it follows that

$$T = Y - C - S = 645 - 400 - 80 = 165,$$

and

$$(T - G) = 165 - 150 = 15$$

The budget is thus in surplus by 15.

Chapter 13

(2) As the marginal propensities to save and import add up to 0.25, the national-income multiplier is 4, and a $2 billion decrease in the foreign demand for the country's exports will reduce its income by $8 billion. From equation (13c), the change in the current-account balance is $4 \times 0.15 \times (-\$2) = -\$1.2$.

(4) Suppose that the United States wants to raise its income from OY_1 to OY_1^* and Japan wants to raise its income from OY_2 to OY_2^*:

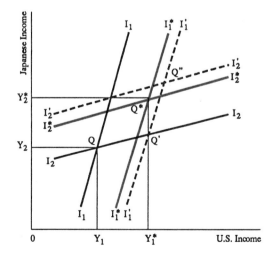

If the United States allows for the interdependence of incomes but ignores the change in Japanese policy, it will adopt an expenditure policy that shifts its income curve to

$I'_1 I'_1$. If Japanese policy does not change, the new equilibrium will be established at Q', and U.S. income will rise to OY^*_1, as desired. If Japan follows the same strategy, however, its expenditure policy will shift its income curve to $I'_2 I'_2$, and equilibrium will be established at Q'', where both countries' incomes will be higher than desired. For both countries to reach their income targets precisely, both must follow expenditure policies that shift their income curves to $I^*_1 I^*_1$ and $I^*_2 I^*_2$, so that they intersect at Q^*. Hence, each must stimulate expenditure by less than it would if the other country's policy did not change.

(6) An expenditure-changing policy to raise Japanese income can be represented by shifting the Japanese income curve from $I_2 I_2$ to $I'_2 I'_2$:

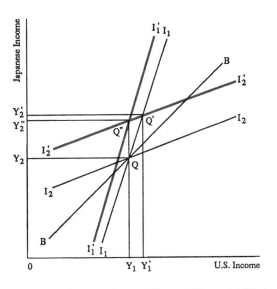

It raises Japanese income from OY_2 to OY'_2 and U.S. income from OY_1 to OY'_1, and it drives the U.S. current-account balance into surplus (because Q' lies above BB). The expenditure-changing response by the United States can be represented by shifting the U.S. income curve to $I'_1 I'_1$, which reduces U.S. income to its initial level, cuts the increase in Japanese income to OY''_2, and enlarges the current-account surplus (because the vertical distance from Q'' to BB is larger than the distance from Q' to BB).

Chapter 14

(2) When the price elasticity of domestic demand is 1, devaluation does not change the domestic-currency value of imports ($OE'F'G' = OEFG$). When the price elasticity of foreign demand exceeds zero, however, devaluation raises the quantity of exports ($OC' > OC$) and thus raises the domestic-currency value of exports ($OAB'C' > OABC$). Therefore, devaluation improves the trade balance measured in domestic currency. When the price elasticity of domestic demand is 1, devaluation reduces the quantity of imports by an amount proportional to the devaluation ($GG'/OG = EE'/OE$); hence, it reduces the foreign-currency value of imports by an amount proportional to the devaluation ($g'f'fg/Oefg = EE'/OE$). It may raise or reduce the foreign-currency value of exports ($Oa'b'c'$ may be larger or smaller than

Oabc), but it raises the quantity of exports (*cc'* > 0) whenever the foreign elasticity of demand is greater than zero. Hence, the reduction, if any, in the foreign-currency value of exports must be less than proportional to the devaluation and thus smaller than the reduction in the foreign-currency value of imports. Therefore, devaluation improves the trade balance measured in foreign currency.

(4) The *FF* curve shifts up, because a tightening of expenditure policy would be needed to maintain external balance if there were no change in the exchange rate. The *YY* curve shifts down, because an easing of expenditure policy would be needed to maintain internal balance if there were no change in the exchange rate. But the two curves intersect at a point on an extension of the line *AP*. There is no need to change expenditure policy if the domestic currency is devalued to offset the switch in expenditure to foreign goods.

(6) When the *FF* curve is flatter than the *YY* curve, your diagram should show that the sequence of policy changes takes the economy farther and farther from *P*. The policy assignment is unstable. It can be stabilized, however, by assigning expenditure policy to external balance and assigning the exchange rate to internal balance:

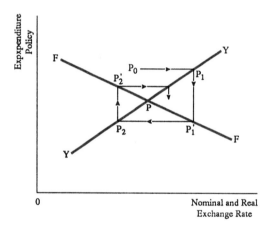

When the economy starts at P_0, the manager of the exchange rate will revalue the domestic currency to achieve internal balance, taking the economy to P_1. But there must then be an easing of expenditure policy to achieve external balance, taking the economy to P'_1. The next exchange-rate change takes the economy to P_2, and so on.

Chapter 15

(2) Shift the *LM* curve to the left, not to the right, so the counterpart of point E_1 lies above E_0, not below it. Income falls in the short run, and the interest rate rises. The fall in income reduces imports, producing a current-account surplus, and the rise in the interest rate induces a capital inflow. Both results contribute to a balance-of-payments surplus, which raises reserves and the money supply under a pegged exchange rate. Therefore, the *LM* curve drifts rightward. Income and imports rise; the interest rate and capital inflow fall. Hence, the balance-of-payments surplus is reduced gradually, reducing the growth rates of reserves and the money supply. These do not cease to rise, however, until the *LM* curve returns to its initial position,

where income and the interest rate return to their initial levels. Hence, the open-market sale has no long-run effect, apart from changing the composition of the central bank's assets. With perfect capital mobility, any upward pressure on the domestic interest rate induces a very large capital inflow and increase in reserves and the corresponding increase in the money supply offsets the open-market sale immediately. Income and the interest rate do not change at all

(4) The government should cut taxes, shifting the *IS* curve to the right. Income and the interest rate will rise. The increase in income will raise imports; the increase in the interest rate will induce a capital inflow. With high capital mobility, the capital inflow will exceed the increase in imports, and the domestic currency will tend to appreciate. To prevent an appreciation, the central bank should make an open-market purchase, shifting the *LM* curve to the right and reducing the interest rate. But it must not cut the interest rate back to its initial level; that would eliminate the capital inflow, and the increase in imports would then cause the currency to depreciate. Thus, your diagram should look like this:

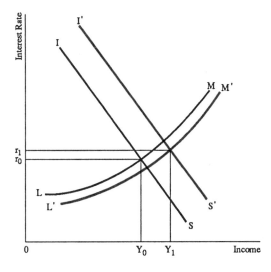

In Figure 15-3, the government sought to raise income and employment because of an increase in the labor force. It cut taxes to increase income and raised the interest rate to attract a capital inflow and defend the pegged exchange rate. In Figure 15-3, the tax rate and interest rate were treated as policy instruments; therefore, we said that taxes should be cut and the interest rate should be raised. In the *IS-LM* model, the tax rate and money supply are treated as policy instruments; therefore, we must say that the government should cut taxes and the central bank should make an open-market purchase to keep the interest rate from rising excessively. (If there were low capital mobility, however, the increase in the interest rate resulting from the shift of the *IS* curve would produce a capital inflow too small to cover the increase in imports. Therefore, the central bank would have to make an open-market sale to raise the interest rate further.)

(6) With perfect capital mobility, the domestic interest rate cannot differ from the foreign interest rate. Therefore, an increase in the foreign rate raises the domestic rate. In the process, however, it causes a large capital outflow, which reduces reserves

and the money supply. Hence, the *LM* curve shifts leftward until it intersects the *IS* curve at the new foreign interest rate. Your diagram should look just like the one drawn to answer (4), although it has a different economic interpretation.

Chapter 16

(2) Place a new point D' below D, so that the return on the domestic asset is OD'. Draw a new line $D'I$ to represent the new combinations of risk and return on the whole portfolio. As the indifference curves are stacked up vertically, $D'I$ should be tangent to an indifference curve lower than U at a new point Q' below and to the right of Q. The total return on the portfolio has fallen and the standard deviation has risen. The higher standard deviation says that the share of the foreign (risky) asset has risen.

(4) In your answer to (3), you should have drawn a new curve $E'D'$ below the old curve ED and located a new point, P', beneath P but above P'' (where $E'D'$ intersected the vertical axis). You should therefore have shown that the domestic currency appreciates but not by enough to restore open interest parity. Finally, you should have shown that $E'D'$ intersects ES to the left of the vertical axis, so there is an excess supply of foreign currency coming from investors, who have switched from foreign to domestic bonds (i.e., there is a capital inflow). When investors are risk neutral, the DE and $D'E'$ curves become horizontal. (The former coincides with the horizontal axis.) Therefore, the domestic currency appreciates all the way to OP'', restoring open interest parity, and there is a larger excess supply of foreign currency coming from investors (i.e., a larger capital inflow).

(6) The spot rate was $1.5300 and the 3-month forward rate was $1.5162, so the pound was at a forward discount equal to $(1.5162 - 1.5300)/1.5300$ or 0.9 percent. Therefore,

$$c = (6.5/4 - 0.9) - 3.0/4 = -0.25$$

This favors investment in the United States.

Chapter 17

(2) As reserves cannot change when the exchange rate is flexible, a reduction in the stock of domestic credit would produce a permanent reduction in the supply of money and, therefore, an excess demand for money. Households would try to increase their money holdings by saving more and spending less. They would therefore spend less on imports, causing the domestic currency to appreciate. Under *PPP*, the appreciation would reduce the domestic price level, which would reduce the demand for money and thus eliminate the excess demand. Under a pegged exchange rate, changes in reserves clear the money market by changing the supply of money; under a flexible rate, exchange-rate changes clear the market by changing the price level and demand for money.

(4) The revaluation reduces the domestic price level, which reduces the demand for money. There will thus be an excess supply of money, and households will start to dissave. They will therefore increase their demand for imports, producing a balance-

of-payments deficit, a gradual loss of reserves, and a gradual reduction in the money supply. You can adapt Figure 17-4 to illustrate your answer. Shift the *DD* curve downward, not upward, and identify the resulting balance-of-payments deficit and the long-run reduction in the stock of reserves.

(6) Equation (11) will look like this:

$$N(\pi) = N(A^*) - N(A) + N(L^s) - N(L^{*s}) + n^*N(y^*) - nN(y) + b\delta$$

There will be a constant term, $N(A^*) - N(A)$, and the income terms will have separate coefficients, n^* and n, but the roles of the money stocks, L^s and L^{*s}, will not be altered.

Chapter 18

(2) The degree of substitutability between bonds cannot influence any short-run response to the fall in foreign demand. That fall does not affect asset markets immediately, so there is no short-run change in the interest rate or wealth. Accordingly, the degree of substitutability cannot affect any short-run goods-market outcome (the size of the shift in the *zz* curve, the resulting fall in income, and the initial amount of dissaving). In your answer to (1), moreover, you should have shown that the long-run goods-market outcomes are determined uniquely by the size of the shift in the *ZZ* curve, which does not depend on asset-market outcomes. Under a pegged exchange rate, the long-run income change is measured by the (downward) shift of the *ZZ* curve; under a flexible rate, income goes back to its initial level, and the long-run exchange-rate change is measured by the (rightward) shift of the *ZZ* curve. Furthermore, you should have shown that there is no change in any asset-market variable under a flexible exchange rate; the *LL* curve cannot shift without an open-market purchase or sale, and the *SS* curve cannot shift without a permanent change in income. Under a pegged exchange rate, however, the *SS* curve shifts upward because of the permanent fall in income, and this calls for an upward shift in the *LL* curve. Therefore, your answer should look like this:

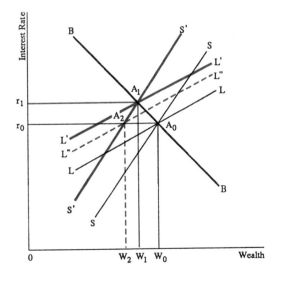

When foreign and domestic bonds are imperfect substitutes, the *BB* curve is downward sloping, and the shift in the *SS* curve to *S'S'* takes asset-market equilibrium from A_0 to A_1, raising the domestic interest rate from Or_0 to Or_1 and reducing wealth from OW_0 to OW_1. The *LL* curve shifts upward from *LL* to *L'L'*, which says that there is a fall in the money supply due to a loss of reserves (a balance-of-payments deficit during the adjustment process). When the two bonds are perfect substitutes, the *BB* curve is horizontal, and the domestic interest rate must remain at Or_0. Hence, the shift in the *SS* curve to *S'S'* takes asset-market equilibrium to A_2, reducing wealth all the way to OW_2. The *LL* curve shifts upward from *LL* to *L"L"*, which says that there is a smaller fall in the money supply and thus a smaller loss of reserves. The larger fall in wealth must reflect a larger amount of dissaving during the adjustment process. As the degree of substitutability cannot affect the initial amount of dissaving, the larger amount of dissaving thereafter must reflect a slower reduction in dissaving, which means that the *zz* curve must fall more slowly on its way to its long-run equilibrium position. And that is what happens. When foreign and domestic bonds are imperfect substitutes, the *zz* curve is driven downward by two forces—the gradual fall in wealth and the gradual increase in the domestic interest rate. When the two bonds are perfect substitutes, preventing any change in the domestic interest rate, there is only one force driving the *zz* curve downward, so it moves more slowly.

(4) Your diagram should look like this:

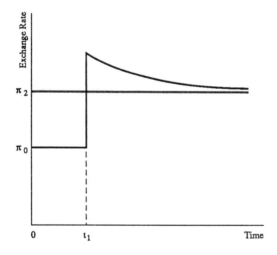

The economy is in long-run equilibrium from time $t = 0$ to time $t = t_1$, and the exchange rate is constant at $O\pi_0$. The central bank makes an open-market purchase at time $t = t_1$, and the domestic currency depreciates by enough to overshoot its new long-run level, $O\pi_2$, and it must appreciate thereafter to reach that long-run level.

(6) A reduced demand for domestic bonds shifts the *BB* curve upward, as a higher domestic interest rate is needed to clear the bond market. But the *ZZ* curve is unaffected. Under a pegged exchange rate, then, there can be no permanent change in income, so the *SS* curve cannot shift. Therefore, the *LL* curve must shift gradually upward to intersect the new *BB* curve where the *BB* curve intersects the initial *SS* curve. The interest rate rises, and wealth rises too (because of the saving that occurs as the economy moves to its new stationary state). The money supply falls, which

says that there is a reserve loss (a balance-of-payments deficit during the adjustment process.)

(8) The long-run effects under a pegged exchange rate are identical to those obtained at (6), as a higher domestic interest rate is needed to clear the bond market after an increase in the supply of bonds. But the long-run effects are different under a flexible rate. As the LL curve cannot shift, the SS curve must shift downward to intersect the BB curve where it intersects the initial LL curve. This shift in the SS curve implies a permanent increase in income. In the goods-market diagram, then, long-run equilibrium must lie at a point on the ZZ curve where income is higher and the domestic currency has depreciated.

Chapter 19

(2) The United States did attract large capital inflows in the 1980s (see Table 19-1), which did indeed finance its current-account deficits. But the statement is wrong analytically in suggesting that the current-account deficits happened independently of the capital inflows. The current-account deficits resulted partly from the appreciation of the dollar, which was the *result* of the capital inflows.

(4) Recall the basic national-income relationship:

$$(X - M) = (S - I) + (T - G)$$

The budget deficit resulting from unification (an increase in G relative to T) had to be matched by shifting the private-sector balance (a fall in I relative to S) or shifting the current-account balance (a fall in X relative to M). But a real appreciation of the Deutsche mark was needed to shift the current-account balance. (Go on to explain why a shift in the current-account balance would be better in the long run than a fall in investment relative to saving.)

(6) A good answer should cite two similarities: (1) Both countries were constrained by the rules of the systems to which they belonged. The United States could change the price of gold but could not change exchange rates for the dollar, which were chosen and defended by other governments. Germany could not change exchange rates for the mark without the consent of other EMS countries. (2) Both countries broke the rules of the systems to which they belonged. The United States closed the gold window and raised its tariffs. The Bundesbank let markets know that it thought the pound should be devalued, encouraging capital flight from Britain. But you should also cite some major differences. The United States was moved to act because it was threatened by gold losses; Germany was moved to act because it might otherwise be obliged to buy other EMS currencies in the foreign-exchange market, which would raise the German money supply. The United States was reluctant to tighten its monetary policy and sought to reduce the value of the dollar; Germany was reluctant to relax its monetary policy and sought to raise the value of the mark.

Chapter 20

(2) If the U.S. central bank had full control over both central banks' open-market operations, it would make an open-market purchase and instruct the

Japanese central bank to make an open-market sale. The two operations would take the U.S. economy from P to P_1 in Figure 20-2 (i.e., from the old bliss point to the new one). When they cannot control their partner's operations, they will move to P^N in Figure 20-2. The U.S. central bank will make an open-market purchase larger than it would make if it could issue instructions to the Japanese central bank; the Japanese central bank will make an open-market sale larger than it would make if it could issue instructions to the U.S. central bank. In effect, each central bank must offset part of its partner's open-market operation. When the two central banks cooperate, however, they can move to P^C. The U.S. central bank makes a smaller open-market purchase than the one made to reach P^N, and the Japanese central bank makes a smaller open-market sale. Each central bank can induce the other to scale down its open-market operation. (Note, however, that each bank's open-market operation is smaller than it would conduct if it had complete control over its partner's operations and could thus reach its own bliss point.)

(4) You cannot answer this question clearly. Paragraph (3) tells the Council of Ministers to decide who will negotiate with non-Community countries and international organizations, but that paragraph may not apply to informal agreements. Note that paragraph (1) refers explicitly to paragraph (3), but paragraph (2) does not. Furthermore, paragraph (3) cannot possibly apply to informal arrangements, because it says that agreements negotiated under it will be binding on the *ECB*. Yet paragraph (2) says that, in the absence of a formal agreement, the exchange-rate policies of the EC cannot conflict with the objective of price stability, which means that they cannot be binding on the *ECB*. (Presumably, the Council of Ministers will conduct or supervise the negotiation of informal agreements and then formulate "general orientations" to implement them.) If you are confused, take comfort in the fact that two European central bankers, when asked this same question, said that Article 109 is quite clear, but then answered the question differently.

(6) It is a serious shortcoming. Recall the events of the early 1980s, when the United States was running large budget deficits and experienced large capital inflows that caused the dollar to appreciate. If it had been obliged to keep the dollar from appreciating by engaging in nonsterilized intervention, the U.S. money supply would have increased rapidly, interfering with the Federal Reserve's attempt to combat inflation. The Bundesbank would have faced the same problem in 1991–1992, when Germany ran large budget deficits and the Deutsche mark began to appreciate. (McKinnon argues, however, that the *world* money supply is the chief determinant of inflation under pegged exchange rates, and his plan would have required Japan and Germany to intervene jointly with the United States in the early 1980s, which would have reduced their money supplies, offsetting the increase in the U.S. money supply and stabilizing the world money supply.)

(8) The answer to this question turns largely on the credibility of the governments' commitment to prevent exchange rates from crossing the edges of their bands and to refrain from realignments. If the commitment is credible, market participants will engage in stabilizing speculation; they will buy a weak currency as it approaches the edge of its band. Therefore, governments may not have to engage in any intervention to keep exchange rates within their bands. If the commitment is not credible, governments may have to intervene heavily. A weak-currency country will then lose reserves, which may generate expectations of a devaluation and thus intensify the

need for intervention, producing a balance-of-payments crisis and forcing the devaluation. When governments cannot commit themselves credibly to the defense of hard bands, it may be safer to use soft bands. For more on these issues, see the chapters in Krugman's *Currencies and Crises* and the article by Svennson listed in the recommended readings for this chapter.

List of Abbreviations

BCCI	Bank for Credit and Commerce International
BIS	Bank for International Settlements
CAP	Common Agricultural Policy (European Community)
CCC	Commodity Credit Corporation (United States)
CMEA	Council for Mutual Econmic Assistance
EC	European Community
ECB	European Central Bank
ECU	European Currency Unit
EEC	European Economic Community
EIB	Export–Import Bank
EMCF	European Monetary Cooperation Fund
EMI	European Monetary Institute
EMS	European Monetary System
EMU	Economic and Monetary Union (Europe)
EPU	European Payments Union
ESCB	European System of Central Banks
GAB	General Arrangements to Borrow
GATT	General Agreement on Tariffs and Trade
GDP	Gross Domestic Product
GNP	Gross National Product
GSP	Generalized System of Preferences
G-5	Group of Five (France, Germany, Japan, the United Kingdom, and the Unite States)
G-7	Group of Seven (G-5 *plus* Canada and Italy)
G-10	Group of Ten (G-7 *plus* Belgium, the Netherlands, and Sweden)
IBF	International Banking Facility

IBRD	International Bank for Reconstruction and Development
IDA	International Development Association
IFC	International Finance Corporation
IMF	International Monetary Fund
ITC	International Trade Commission (United States)
ITO	International Trade Organization
MFA	Multifibre Agreement
MITI	Ministry of International Trade and Industry (Japan)
MLR	Marshall-Lerner-Robinson (condition)
MTO	Multilateral Trade Organization
NAFTA	North American Free Trade Agreement
NATO	North Atlantic Treaty Organization
OECD	Organization for Economic Co-operation and Development
OPEC	Organization of Petroleum Exporting Countries
PPP	Purchasing: power parity
SDR	Special Drawing Right
SII	Structural Impediments Initiative
TAA	Trade adjustment assistance (program)
UI	Unemployment Insurance
VER	Voluntary Export Restraint

Index